CRIMINAL LAW AND PROCEDURE FOR THE PARALEGAL

2nd Edition

Neal R. Bevans

CENGAGE
Learning·

Australia • Brazil • Japan • Korea • Mexico • Singapore • Spain • United Kingdom • United States

CENGAGE
Learning®

Criminal Law and Procedure for the Paralegal, 2nd Edition

Neal R. Bevans

Senior Vice President,General Manager for Skills and Global Product Management: Dawn Gerrain

Product Manager: Paul Lamond

Senior Director, Development/Global Product Management Skills: Marah Bellegarde

Senior Product Development Manager: Larry Main

Content Developer: Diane Chrysler

Marketing Manager: Scott Chrysler

Senior Production Director: Wendy Troeger

Production Manager: Mark Bernard

Senior Content Project Manager: Betty L. Dickson

Art Director: Heather Marshall, PMG

Senior Technology Project Manager: Joe Pliss

Media Editor: Deborah Bordeaux

Cover image(s):

First Row:
1. ©EmiliaUngur/Shutterstock.com
2. ©Frances Twitty/istockphoto.com
3. ©Sponner/Shutterstock.com

Second Row:
4. ©FernandoAH/istockphoto.com
5. ©vilcha/Shutterstock.com
6. ©Rob Marmion/Shutterstock.com

Background texture/image of leather:
©Piotr Neffe/Shutterstock.com

For product information and technology assistance, contact us at **Cengage Learning Customer & Sales Support, 1-800-354-9706**

For permission to use material from this text or product, submit all requests online at **www.cengage.com/permissions.** Further permissions questions can be e-mailed to **permissionrequest@cengage.com**

Library of Congress Control Number: 2013957915

ISBN-13: 978-1-133-69358-1

ISBN-10: 1-133-69358-X

Cengage Learning
200 First Stamford Place, 4th Floor
Stamford, CT 06902
USA

Cengage Learning is a leading provider of customized learning solutions with office locations around the globe, including Singapore, the United Kingdom, Australia, Mexico, Brazil, and Japan. Locate your local office at: **www.cengage.com/global**

Cengage Learning products are represented in Canada by Nelson Education, Ltd.

To learn more about Cengage Learning, visit **www.cengage.com**

Purchase any of our products at your local college store or at our preferred online store **www.cengagebrain.com**

Notice to the Reader

Publisher does not warrant or guarantee any of the products described herein or perform any independent analysis in connection with any of the product information contained herein. Publisher does not assume, and expressly disclaims, any obligation to obtain and include information other than that provided to it by the manufacturer. The reader is expressly warned to consider and adopt all safety precautions that might be indicated by the activities described herein and to avoid all potential hazards. By following the instructions contained herein, the reader willingly assumes all risks in connection with such instructions. The reader is notified that this text is an educational tool, not a practice book. Since the law is in constant change, no rule or statement of law in this book should be relied upon for any service to the client. The reader should always refer to standard legal sources for the current rule or law. If legal advice or other expert assistance is required, the services of the appropriate professional should be sought. The publisher makes no representations or warranties of any kind, including but not limited to, the warranties of fitness for particular purpose or merchantability, nor are any such representations implied with respect to the material set forth herein, and the publisher takes no responsibility with respect to such material. The publisher shall not be liable for any special, consequential, or exemplary damages resulting, in whole or part, from the readers' use of, or reliance upon, this material.

Printed in the United States of America
1 2 3 4 5 6 7 18 17 16 15 14

Dedication:
For my wife, Nilsa Bevans

TABLE OF CONTENTS

CHAPTER **2**

Arrest, Search, and Seizure   32

CHAPTER 7

Principals, Accessories, and Attempt   164

CHAPTER 10

Crimes Against Property   245

CHAPTER 11

Crimes Against Public Order, Morality, and Health 271

PREFACE

Introduction to the Second Edition

There have been many changes in the law since the first edition of this book, but the subject remains as fascinating as ever. Like the first edition, this text strives to present an in-depth and thorough presentation of criminal law as it applies to the paralegal. Throughout the text, there are references to other professions as well, including probation officers, corrections officers, law enforcement officials, and government workers, but every chapter refers to the various functions of the paralegal at every stage of a criminal proceeding.

There have also been some revisions. All chapters have updated case law references and have been edited and rewritten with recent changes in regard to the law. New exhibits have been added to encourage the more visually oriented learner. The author has also included bullet points in each chapter that condense the relevant material for quick reference. All lists of web sites have been updated.

Features of the Text

The text contains several unique features designed to assist students. The features include Insider's Viewpoint, definitions, The Role of the Paralegal, and Paralegal to-do List, among others.

Insider's Viewpoint

Each chapter contains several Insider's Viewpoint features. These are excerpted interviews with criminal law professionals—from paralegals to police officers, detectives to defense attorneys. Students hear about various aspects of the criminal law system in the voices of people who work in it every day. This is a refreshing feature not found in other texts. It allows students to make a closer connection to paralegals and others in the field and see what their day-to-day experiences are like.

The author uses his extensive contacts in the legal community to obtain quotes from the following:

- Detectives and police officers
- Judges
- Paralegals
- Crime scene technicians
- Fingerprint experts
- DNA specialists
- Prosecutors
- Sexual assault nurse examiners
- Private detectives
- Defense attorneys
- Probation officers
- Rape counselors
- Crime victims

Definitions of Key Terms

The first time a key word or legal term is mentioned in the text, its definition appears in the margin. This helps students grasp the meaning of the term without breaking the flow of the reading by having to turn to the glossary.

The Role of the Paralegal

Each chapter contains explanations and amplifications on what paralegals do. In addition to checklists, the author discusses the day-to-day activities of paralegals, from meeting with clients to preparing appellate brief banks.

Sidebars

Each chapter also contains numerous sidebars. These explore aspects of the text in greater detail, explaining how homicide detectives review a crime scene, for instance, or detailing significant crime statistics.

Internet Sites

At the end of each chapter is an extensive list of web resources focusing on the issues raised in the chapter. Students are provided links to various government and other web sites that expand the discussion in the text and allow students to delve deeper on issues.

Case Excerpts

In addition to the detailed examination of substantive and procedural law, important U.S. Supreme Court cases are cited, and detailed analysis is provided of the impact of these decisions on the everyday practice of criminal law.

Bullet Points

This feature condenses relevant information to a quick and handy reference for students.

End-of-Chapter Exercises

At the end of each chapter, students are presented with review questions to help them focus on the material, as well as questions that go to the very core of criminal law. These questions are designed to make students ponder the principles behind the rules. In addition, many of the end-of-chapter exercises are based on the sample cases mentioned in the text and more fully set out in the Appendix.

Sample Cases

Provided in the Appendices are three sample cases that include the details of cases about which students have been reading throughout the text. These are not hypothetical cases. They are based on real crimes, from murder to stalking and kidnapping. The names have been changed to protect the identities of the people involved, but the statements of the witnesses and the crimes they describe are true to life.

Pedagogy

The text is designed with the student in mind. The author uses creativity and enthusiasm for the subject to create questions and assignments that take advantage of many different learning styles. From bulleted lists to sidebars, the text is designed to help students master the material and stay engaged. The text is filled with real-world examples.

Organization of the Text

The text is organized as an overview of the criminal justice system before it proceeds to a discussion of the more in-depth developments of a criminal case from both the defense and prosecution viewpoints. Arrest and investigation are examined. Other topics covered include search and seizure; confessions and *Miranda*; arraignment; specific kinds of crimes, including crimes against the person, crimes against property, and crimes against public morality and health.

Ancillary Materials

Instructor Companion Site

Instructor's Manual Written by the author of the text, the Instructor's Manual contains the following:

- Chapter Outlines
- Notes About Specific Issues in Chapter Outlines
- Review Questions with Answers
- Answers to "Questions for Reflection" that appear in the text
- Practical Applications
- Test Banks Available for each chapter, containing the following:
- Multiple-Choice Questions
- True/False Questions
- Customizable PowerPoint® Presentations focus on key points for each chapter. (PowerPoint® is a registered trademark of the Microsoft Corporation.)

You can access these materials online at login.cengage.com, using your SSO (single sign on) login. Additional materials can also be accessed via SSO.

Student Companion Site

The text has a corresponding Student Companion Site that, among other things, has a section for each chapter that includes the following:

- Weblinks
- Review Questions
- Insider's Viewpoints
- Appendices

To access these materials, visit www.cengagebrain.com and search for the title or ISBN (9781133693581) of this book.

Supplements at a Glance

Supplement:	What it is:	What's in it:
Online Instructor's Companion Site	Resources for the instructor accessible via Cengage Single Sign On	■ Instructor's Manual with answers to text questions and test bank and answer key ■ Computerized Testbank in Cognero, with many questions and styles to choose from to create customized assessments for your students ■ PowerPoint® presentations
Online Student Companion Site	Resources for students available via cengagebrain.com	■ Weblinks ■ Review Questions ■ Insider's Viewpoints ■ Appendices

> Please note the Internet resources are of a time-sensitive nature and that URL addresses often change or are deleted.

Acknowledgments

The author would like to thank the following people for their assistance in preparing this book:

Jack Burnette, Steve Weaver, Tom Garmon, Kathy Singleton, Keith Miles, B.J. Bernstein, Debra Holbrook, Linda McCurry, Eric Shehan, Ben Smith, Carl Raphael, David Cheek, George Hutchinson, Richard Hinson, Susan Keller, Rosanna Hartley, Ann Marie Radiskiewicz, Robert Riffe, Brenda Parker, Cherie Eddy, Paula Barnes, Michael Burgamy, Jacqueline Landis, Diane Chrysler, Shelley Esposito, and Raghavi Khullar.

The author would like to extend his appreciation to the following reviewers for providing valuable feedback throughout the review process:

Scott Silvis
Southern Crescent Technical College

Jennifer Allen
Davidson County Community College

David Movsesian
Kaplan Higher Education

Patricia Gustin
Freelance Instructor

Gerald Rogers
Front Range Community College

Chapter 1

AN INTRODUCTION TO CRIMINAL LAW

Chapter Objectives

At the completion of this chapter, you should be able to:

- Outline the important steps necessary to bring a defendant to trial for a crime
- Describe the differences between criminal law and civil law
- Explain the differences and the similarities between the federal government and the various state governments
- Define the three branches of government on both the state and federal level and the role each plays
- Explain what common law is and why it remains important in many states
- Define the roles of the various participants in the criminal justice system, including judges, prosecutors, police, and defense attorneys

I. Introduction: The Drama of a Criminal Trial

A hush falls over the courtroom as the jury returns. Filing in one by one, the twelve members of the jury do not look at anyone. As they sit down, the judge addresses the group. "Mr. Foreperson, have you reached a **verdict**?"

"Yes, Your Honor," the man says, "we have."

You have seen it countless times in movies: the dramatic moment when the verdict is announced. The tension mounts as the judge glances at the verdict form, glances around the room, and then announces the

verdict
The jury's finding in a trial.

verdict. If the verdict is "guilty," the defendant's life will never be quite the same. If the verdict is "not guilty," the defendant will go free.

A trial is like a novel or a movie. It has a beginning, a middle, and an end. It has characters (witnesses) that are both good and bad and a great many in between. Like any good story, there is conflict between the characters in the story and the trial works to resolve those differences. Like a good mystery, the trial is the search for the truth. The details come out through the people, their relationships, their actions, their thoughts and motives, and their desires and shortcomings. All of the people appearing in the trial have very specific roles to play.

We are all affected by crime in one way or another. Some of us have been victims of crimes, and we all know someone who has suffered some kind of criminal victimization. See Exhibit 1-1. What is often surprising is to learn that over the last few decades, violent crime has tended downward, except for a period in 2006. See Exhibit 1-2.

Exhibit 1-1

Number of criminal victimizations and percent change, by type of crime, 2001, 2009, and 2010

Type of crime	Number of victimizations			Percent change, 2001–2010[a]	Percent change, 2009–2010[a]	Average annual change, 2001–2009
	2001	2009	2010			
All crime	24,215,700	20,057,180	18,725,710	−22.7%[†]	−6.6%[†]	−2.1%
Violent crime[b]	5,743,820	4,343,450	3,817,380	−33.5%[†]	−12.1%[†]	−3.1%
Serious violent crime[c]	2,101,100	1,483,050	1,394,310	−33.6[†]	−6.0	−3.9
Rape/sexual assault[d]	248,250	125,920	188,380	−24.1	49.6[‡]	−7.5
Robbery	630,690	533,790	480,750	−23.8[†]	−9.9	−1.9
Assault	4,864,890	3,683,750	3,148,250	−35.3[†]	−14.5[†]	−3.1
Aggravated	1,222,160	823,340	725,180	−40.7[†]	−11.9	−4.4
Simple	3,642,720	2,860,410	2,423,060	−33.5[†]	−15.3[†]	−2.7
Personal theft[e]	188,370	133,210	138,340	−26.6%	3.9%	−3.9%
Property crime	18,283,510	15,580,520	14,769,990	−19.2%[†]	−5.2%[‡]	−1.8%
Household burglary	3,139,700	3,134,930	2,923,430	−6.9[†]	−6.7	—
Motor vehicle theft	1,008,730	735,770	606,990	−39.8[†]	−17.5[‡]	−3.5
Theft	14,135,090	11,709,830	11,239,560	−20.5[†]	−4.0	−2.1

Note: Detail may not sum to total due to rounding. Total population age 12 or older was 229,215,290 in 2001, 254,105,610 in 2009, and 255,961,940 in 2010. Total number of households was 109,568,450 in 2001, 122,327,660 in 2009, and 122,885,160 in 2010. See Appendix table 2 for standard errors.
[†]Significant at 95%.
[‡]Significant at 90%.
—Less than 0.5.
[a]Percent change calculated based on unrounded estimates.
[b]Excludes homicide because the NCVS is based on interviews with victims and therefore cannot measure murder.
[c]Includes rape or sexual assault, robbery, and aggravated assault.
[d]Care should be taken in interpreting the increase in the number of rape or sexual assault (49.6%) between 2009 and 2010, because the estimates are based on a small number of cases reported in the survey. See *Methodology* for details on the measurement of rape/sexual assault in the NCVS.
[e]Includes pocket picking, completed purse snatching, and attempted purse snatching.

Source: Criminal Victimization in the U.S., 2010, Bureau of Justice Statistics, U.S. Department of Justice.

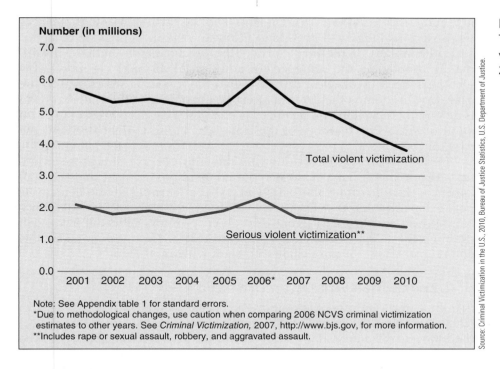

Number (in millions)

Total violent victimization

Serious violent victimization**

Note: See Appendix table 1 for standard errors.
*Due to methodological changes, use caution when comparing 2006 NCVS criminal victimization estimates to other years. See *Criminal Victimization*, 2007, http://www.bjs.gov, for more information.
**Includes rape or sexual assault, robbery, and aggravated assault.

Source: Criminal Victimization in the U.S., 2010, Bureau of Justice Statistics, U.S. Department of Justice.

Exhibit 1-2
Total violent and serious violent victimizations, 2001–2010

II. An Overview of a Criminal Case

The trial is actually a culmination of a long series of very different procedural steps beginning with the arrest of the defendant and continuing through the trial and afterwards. Following the defendant's arrest, there are proceedings in magistrate court, bond hearings, grand jury presentments, and an indictment issued. At each phase of the prosecution, the defendant is protected by the United States Constitution.

A. The Various Participants in the Criminal Justice System

Many people are involved in a criminal case. Police officers respond to a call from a victim. Detectives investigate the case. A magistrate or another judge may sign a warrant for the defendant's arrest or authorize a search of the defendant's home. In addition to law enforcement, others will also be involved. Members of the community will appear throughout the various stages, either as witnesses, grand jurors, or trial jurors. At the defendant's trial, a superior court judge will be seated behind a bench and will make decisions on a wide variety of issues that will certainly arise during the trial. The defendant will have an attorney to represent him. Another attorney, the prosecutor, will be assigned to prove the defendant guilty.

Specific procedural steps also occur in a criminal prosecution. There will often be an initial appearance hearing, a preliminary hearing, a grand jury indictment, and an arraignment. The trial will come at the end of these steps. A judge will preside at the trial, making rulings on evidence and other issues. If the jury convicts the defendant, the judge will ultimately pronounce the sentence. In addition to all of those individuals who have been involved in this case, two more people are crucial to the case. One of them is the defense attorney, a member of the state bar, who is defending the defendant against the charges. There is a prosecutor, also an attorney, also a member of the state bar, whose job is to present the case for the state.

In this book, we will be following the entire course of a prosecution, from the moment that a crime is reported up to the moment that the final appeal is heard. Along the way, you will be learning about detectives, police departments, District Attorneys' offices, and the role of the defense bar, as well as learning a great deal about criminal procedure. We will examine these issues from the perspective of prosecution, defense, law enforcement, and the paralegals who work with all of them.

B. Criminal Trials Are Often Dramatic

Criminal trials hold people's attention because unlike what they see on television, this story is real. The names have not been changed to protect the innocent. The defendant is present in the courtroom, right where the jury can see her. The witnesses are real people, with all the prejudices and weaknesses of real people. That is the fascination. These days, viewers watch "reality shows" to see the fascinating and bizarre aspects of other people's lives. In a trial, these lives are laid bare for all to see. That is what a trial is all about. In this book, we will unfold the story of a criminal trial, beginning with the crime and examining the various aspects of the defendant's arrest, the procedural rights of the criminal defendant, and ultimately the trial.

Before we begin to discuss the details of criminal law, let us first answer the question "What is criminal law?"

III. What Is Criminal Law and How Is It Different from Civil Law?

Criminal law is a field of law that is as specialized in its own way as tax law or divorce law. One of the problems in dealing with criminal law, however, is that there are many misconceptions about what criminal law is. One way of demonstrating the differences between civil and criminal cases is to profile a prominent criminal case, such as Ted Bundy.

A. Ted Bundy

Ted Bundy was smart, on the fast track to a career in both law and politics. Charming and good-looking, he attracted women, which made it easy for him to become one of the most prolific serial killers in United States history.

Born in Burlington, Vermont, to an unmarried mother in 1946, Bundy believed until adulthood that his mother was his sister and his grandparents were his true parents. The identity of his father remains a mystery, but many family members suspected that his grandfather, a violent, abusive bully, might have fathered Bundy. His mother eventually moved with her son to Tacoma, Washington, where she married Johnnie Bundy, who adopted young Ted.

Ted Bundy attended both the University of Puget Sound and the University of Washington (UW), but he was not an accomplished student. After a painful breakup with a girlfriend, he dropped out in 1968, getting by on a succession of minimum wage jobs. It was around this time that he learned of his true parentage and plunged into depression. Before long, however, Bundy met a new girl and, feeling reenergized, returned to UW, from which he graduated in 1972. After college, he joined Governor Daniel Evans's reelection campaign and applied to law school in Utah. He also became the assistant to the chairman of the Washington State Republican Party. At the same time, young women began disappearing in the Pacific Northwest.

It is unknown who Bundy's first victim was or how many women he murdered, but he confessed to 30 homicides in seven states between 1974 and 1978. It is widely suspected that he began murdering as a teenager. But by the time he commenced his rampage in 1974, he had perfected his ability to leave few clues at the scene of the murder. His method for luring women was simple: He would wear a fake cast or feign some other disability and ask for help. His sham helplessness, combined with his good looks, made women trust him and eagerly offer assistance. Once Bundy had them isolated, he overpowered and killed them, usually with blunt force to the head. Twelve of his victims were decapitated. All of the women were young, white, and attractive and had long hair parted in the middle.

Bundy frequently revisited the sites of his murder, performing sex acts on the corpses, combing their hair, and applying makeup until they had decomposed to the point it was no longer possible. In addition, he kept some of the severed heads in his apartment as mementos. In the fall of 1974, Bundy moved to Utah to attend law school. The series of murders in the Pacific Northwest abruptly ceased, and women then began disappearing in Utah.

While in Salt Lake City, Bundy's modus operandi expanded from feigning injury. He picked up hitchhikers; he even posed as a police officer, using assumed authority to convince young women to leave with him. His girlfriend back in Washington became suspicious when the Pacific Northwest homicides seemed to shift to Utah, appearing to follow Bundy. She alerted police, who added Bundy's name to a list of suspects. But they had no solid evidence to link him to the crimes in either state.

Bundy was first arrested outside Salt Lake City by a Utah Highway Patrol officer. The officer tried to pull him over for a routine traffic violation, but Bundy sped away. When the officer caught up with him, he saw that the front passenger seat was missing. Upon searching the car, he found a pantyhose mask with cutouts for eye holes, a crowbar, handcuffs, and other questionable items. Following further investigation, police thought they had enough evidence, including strands of hair, to charge him with kidnapping Carol DaRonch, one of his victims who managed to escape. DaRonch identified Bundy in a lineup, and he was convicted and sentenced to 15 years.

With Bundy safely in prison, investigators pieced together enough evidence to link him to the murders in Colorado. He was extradited to Colorado, but during his trial in December 1977, he managed to escape from custody, using a smuggled hacksaw to cut a hole in the ceiling of his cell. He fled first to Chicago and then to Atlanta, before finally boarding a bus to Tallahassee, Florida, on January 8, 1978. During the next month, Bundy continued his murderous ways, killing two women at a Florida State University (FSU) sorority house, seriously injuring two other sorority members and another FSU student, and killing a 12-year-old junior high school girl in Lake City, Florida.

Running out of money and fearing that authorities were closing in, Bundy stole a car and drove west across the Florida panhandle. On February 15, a Pensacola police officer stopped and arrested him when a warrants check showed that the car was stolen. As the officer transported Bundy to jail, Bundy said, "I wish you had killed me."

In two separate trials, one in 1979 and one in 1980, Bundy was convicted of the sorority house murders and the murder of the 12-year-old girl. He was sentenced to death in Florida's electric chair. After his string of appeals had been exhausted, Bundy was due to be put to death on January 24, 1989. Before his execution, he gave the details of at least 30 murders, but many believe he could have been responsible for as many as 100. Bundy was electrocuted on schedule, and those who had gathered outside the prison cheered his death.

B. The Differences between Civil and Criminal Cases

As the Bundy case demonstrates, criminal and civil cases are remarkably different. Bundy was executed for his crimes. This is an outcome that will never occur at the conclusion of a civil trial. See Exhibit 1-3 for an example of various types of civil and criminal cases. In this section, we will address the differences between civil and criminal cases, beginning with the outcome of each type of case.

1. Outcomes in Civil and Criminal Cases

You could argue that the most critical difference between criminal cases and civil cases is the outcome. The government has very stringent restrictions

Civil Case Examples	Criminal Case Examples
■ Defamation	■ Theft
■ Contract law cases	■ Assault
■ Car wreck cases (also known as personal injury cases)	■ Battery
■ Medical and legal malpractice	■ Aggravated Assault
	■ Forgery
	■ Kidnapping
	■ Murder
	■ Rape
	■ Arson
	■ Armed robbery
	■ Cruelty to animals

Exhibit 1-3
Examples of civil and criminal cases

on how it can try a case. For instance, in a criminal trial, the government is not permitted to call the defendant to the stand to ask him any questions or to make any negative inference from the defendant's failure to take the stand. But in civil cases, the evidence that can be presented against a defendant has less stringent rules. The reason for this is simple: It is, and should be, harder to put someone in jail than it is to make her pay money to the other side. Putting someone in jail, making that person a prisoner, depriving that person of some civil rights, and branding that person a convicted felon should not be an easy thing to do.

2. Burden of Proof Is Different

The standard that a prosecutor must meet in order to convict someone is much higher than what a plaintiff in a civil suit is called upon to prove in order show that the defendant was **liable**. In a criminal case, a defendant may be found **guilty** or not guilty. This is called the **burden of proof**, and it refers to the level of difficulty involved in presenting a case. In a criminal case, the burden of proof is beyond a **reasonable doubt**. Although difficult to quantify, a reasonable doubt refers to a juror's doubt about the evidence or the guilt of the defendant. This doubt must be based on common sense and not mere fancy. Proving that someone has committed a crime beyond a reasonable doubt is quite a high standard. The reason that the burden is so high is that in our country, the accused is presumed innocent until proven guilty. When a defendant has been found not guilty, he will be set free (assuming that there are no other cases pending against the defendant). A not guilty verdict has specific legal and constitutional implications. For example, a defendant who has been found not guilty cannot be retried for

liable
A finding in a civil action that one party must pay money or take some other action in favor of the opposing side.

guilty
A finding by a criminal court that a defendant is guilty beyond a reasonable doubt.

burden of proof
The burden that a party must meet in order to establish the minimum facts of a case.

reasonable doubt
The standard of proof that the prosecution must meet in order to prove that a defendant committed a crime.

■ **BULLET POINT**
In civil cases, a defendant may be found liable to the plaintiff. In a criminal case, the defendant may be found guilty or not guilty.

INSIDER'S VIEWPOINT

The life of a criminal defense paralegal

Paralegals often play an essential role in the defense or prosecution of a criminal case. A paralegal who works with a criminal defense attorney is often called upon to do several things, all at one time. "A lot of times there's a lot of interaction with the client. We try to make sure that the client knows which court to go to, how to dress appropriately, things like that. In a small office, you have to wear lots of different hats. There's not enough of me to go around. I don't get bored. I don't have time for it."

—Debra Holbrook, Criminal defense paralegal.

---

preponderance (of the evidence)
A showing by one side in a suit that its version of the facts is more likely to be true than not.

plaintiff
The common name for the party who brings a civil suit against another; also known as a petitioner

damages
Money that a court orders to be paid to a person who has suffered damages by the person who caused the injury.

style
The title or heading listing the parties to the case; caption.

the same offense. The Fifth Amendment to the United States Constitution specifically prohibits this practice under its double jeopardy clause.

Proof beyond a reasonable doubt is not the same standard used in other countries. It is also not the standard used to prove civil cases in the United States. In civil cases, the burden of proof in a civil case is **preponderance (of the evidence).** This simply means "more likely than not." If the plaintiff proves that the defendant more likely than not was liable for certain acts that resulted in the plaintiff being physically or legally injured, then the plaintiff is entitled to win. But the burden of proof is not the only important difference between civil and criminal cases.

3. Parties Are Different

A criminal prosecution is brought by federal or state governments in the name of their citizens. A private individual, referred to as a **plaintiff** (or by other names in some jurisdictions) brings a civil lawsuit. A crime is a violation of law and infringes on everyone's rights when it occurs. Although there may be a specific victim, it is, in the final analysis, a wrong committed against all of society. A civil action, on the other hand, is generally personal to the parties involved in the lawsuit. It is a private wrong and therefore a private lawsuit.

In a civil trial, the jury can award monetary payments from one party to another. For instance, a jury can award compensatory **damages**—money payments from the defendant designed to compensate the plaintiffs for their losses. A civil jury can also award punitive damages against a defendant. Simply put, punitive damages are monetary assessments designed to punish the defendant and send a message to the community that such behavior will not be tolerated.

One way to understand the difference between civil cases and criminal cases is to examine the main charging documents in each case. As you can see in Exhibits 1-2 and 1-3, the **style** or caption of the pleadings themselves reveal just how different a civil case is from a criminal case.

	Civil Law	Criminal Law
Initiating the Action	A private party files a civil complaint on the defendant, demanding monetary damages or an injunction.	The state brings a citation or indictment after a defendant has been arrested.
Parties	Private parties bring actions against other private parties for legal wrongs to one another.	The state investigates the charges, makes the arrest, and prosecutes the defendant for the violation of public law.
Burden of Proof	A private plaintiff must prove the defendant committed a legal wrong against him or her. The standard the plaintiff must meet is preponderance of the evidence.	The defendant is presumed to be innocent, and the prosecutor must prove that the defendant is guilty beyond a reasonable doubt.
Disposition	The losing side may have to pay money to the winning side.	If a defendant is found guilty he or she may be sent to prison and/or fined.

Exhibit 1-4
Summarizing the important differences between civil and criminal law

IN THE SUPERIOR COURT OF FULTON COUNTY
STATE OF PLACID

EUGENE WARTON, JR.,
Plaintiff,
v.
DR. MICHAEL WORTHY,
Defendant.

Civil Action No. 99CV-861

Exhibit 1-5
Caption of a civil case

IN THE SUPERIOR COURT OF FULTON COUNTY
STATE OF PLACID

STATE OF PLACID,
v.
JAMES LITTLE,
Defendant.

Indictment No. 98-861

Exhibit 1-6
Caption of a criminal case

pleadings
In a civil case, the pleadings set out the wrong suffered by the parties against one another.

complaint
In a criminal case, the pleadings are often referred to as indictments (in felony cases) and accusations/information (in misdemeanor cases) where the state sets out an infraction by the defendant who violates the law.

answer
The defendant's written response to the complaint, usually containing denials of the defendant's responsibility for the plaintiff's injuries.

indictment
A document that charges a defendant with a felony.

■ **BULLET POINT**
In civil cases, the parties file their factual allegations and request damages in Complaints and Answers; in criminal cases, the government files charges against a defendant through an indictment or a similar charging document.

felony
A crime with a sentence of one year or more to be served in prison or on probation; often includes mandatory minimum fines.

misdemeanor
A criminal offense that is punishable by 12 months or less in custody or on probation.

Pleadings refer to the legal documents that describe the nature of the claim against the parties. In a civil lawsuit, most states refer to the plaintiff's pleading as a **complaint** (also known as a petition). This document sets out the plaintiff's factual allegations against the defendant and requests the jury to award monetary damages to the plaintiff as a result of the defendant's actions. The defendant, on the other hand, responds with an **answer**, also known as a reply. In the answer, the defendant denies the plaintiff's factual allegations and denies any responsibility for the plaintiff's injuries. In civil pleadings, the defendant may also request damages against the plaintiff.

In criminal cases, the state files charges against a defendant through various means. Although the defendant may have initially been arrested on a warrant or given a citation by a police officer, the prosecutor is allowed to alter the charges against the defendant, as long as they are supported by the evidence. In most states, prosecutors charge defendants with felonies through indictments. An **indictment** lists the known facts of the offense, including date, time, and location, as well as the name of the crime and the statute that the defendant is alleged to have violated. Should a prosecutor decide to charge the defendant with a lesser count, the prosecutor might use a different charging document. We will discuss charging decisions and charging documents in Chapter 3.

C. Classes of Crimes: Felonies vs. Misdemeanors

Crimes are broken down into two general divisions: felonies and misdemeanors. A **felony** is a crime punishable by more than one year in custody. These crimes include all major crimes such as murder, rape, arson, and robbery. Felonies may also be punishable by life in custody or by a sentence of death. In contrast, a **misdemeanor** is a less serious crime, punishable by less than a year in custody. In many states, misdemeanors also have a maximum limit of a $1,000 to $5,000 fine that may be imposed. Misdemeanors include crimes such as shoplifting, driving under the influence of alcohol, and other minor offenses. See Exhibit 1-7.

Other important differences between felonies and misdemeanors focus on the process of charging a defendant. In a later chapter, we will examine how defendants charged with a felony are often indicted by a grand jury, whereas defendants charged with a misdemeanor do not have to be indicted.

D. The Government's Power to Bring Criminal Actions

Simply put, the United States Constitution grants power to the states and the federal government to create laws criminalizing certain behaviors. As you will see in later chapters, most prosecutions are actually violations of state statutes, not federal statutes. In creating our government, the writers of the Constitution designated certain powers to be held in the federal government and vested the remaining powers in the states. Among these powers was the power to create laws listing certain activities as illegal.

Felony

Sentence: prison term exceeding one year
Examples: murder, rape, arson, armed robbery, aggravated assault

Misdemeanor

Sentence: twelve months or less, often served at the local jail
Examples: shoplifting, simple battery, driving under the influence or driving while intoxicated

Copyright © 2015 Cengage Learning®

Exhibit 1-7
Felonies v. misdemeanors

Exhibit 1-8
Felony defendants, by most serious arrest charge, 2006

| Most serious arrest charge | Felony defendants in the 75 largest counties | | | |
| | Number | Percent | 95% Confidence interval | |
			Lower bound	Upper bound
All offenses	58,100	100.0%		
Violent offenses	13,295	22.9%	21.6%	24.2%
Murder	370	0.6	0.5	0.8
Rape	669	1.2	1.0	1.4
Robbery	3,451	5.9	5.2	6.8
Assault	6,386	11.0	10.1	12.0
Other violent	2,419	4.2	3.5	4.9
Property offenses	16,948	29.2%	27.7%	30.7%
Burglary	4,495	7.7	7.0	8.5
Larceny/theft	5,268	9.1	8.1	10.1
Motor vehicle theft	1,661	2.9	2.5	3.3
Forgery	1,416	2.4	2.1	2.9
Fraud	2,128	3.7	3.0	4.4
Other property	1,980	3.4	2.9	4.0
Drug offenses	21,232	36.5%	34.8%	38.3%
Trafficking	8,487	14.6	13.0	16.4
Other drug	12,745	21.9	19.9	24.1
Public-order offenses	6,624	11.4%	10.4%	12.5%
Weapons	1,958	3.4	2.9	3.9
Driving-related	1,837	3.2	2.5	3.9
Other public-order	2,830	4.9	4.3	5.6

Note: Data for the specific arrest charge were available for all cases. Detail may not add to total because of rounding.

Source: Felony Defendants in Large Urban Counties, 2006, Bureau of Justice Statistics, U.S. Department of Justice.

E. The Organization of the Federal Government

The organization of the federal government is a topic that justifies its own textbook. However, it is important to understand the inter-relationship of the various branches of government in bringing a criminal charge.

1. Separation of Powers among the Branches

The organization of the federal government is actually a model of efficiency and balance. Recognizing the dangers of vesting too much power

BULLET POINT
Felonies are considered to be far more serious than misdemeanors. That's why the sentences for felonies are much worse.

in any one individual or institution, the framers of the Constitution opted to divide up the powers and responsibilities of government. This division of power, called *separation of powers*, forms the very core of the organization of the federal government. The United States Constitution divided up the functions of government into three separate branches: the Judicial, Executive, and Legislative.

a. The Judicial Branch This branch oversees the courts and is responsible for the fair administration of justice. The highest level of the judicial branch on the federal level is the United States Supreme Court. This court is responsible for interpreting the United States Constitution and is the highest court in the nation.

b. The Executive Branch This branch is responsible for running the day-to-day business of government and for enforcing the laws. The President of the United States holds the top executive position in the United States. Through the various agencies controlled by the president and his cabinet, he exercises considerable control over many aspects of law enforcement and other areas.

c. The Legislative Branch This branch creates laws. The United States Congress is responsible for enacting legislation. Divided into two houses, the House of Representatives and the United States Senate, these two bodies create legislation.

F. The Three Branches of State Government

On the state level, the same division into three branches of government also exists. There is a judicial branch, an executive branch (headed by the state governor), and a legislative branch (the state legislature). Laws are created in much the same way they are on the federal level and are passed

■ **BULLET POINT**
Federal and state governments are divided into three branches, each with some power to oversee the other in a system called "checks and balances."

Exhibit 1-9
Legislative–executive–judicial (federal examples)

Legislative	Executive	Judicial
Makes law	Enforces law	Interprets law
Example:	*Example:*	*Example:*
United States Congress	President of the United State	United States supreme court

Copyright © 2015 Cengage Learning®

Exhibit 1-10
Legislative–executive–judicial (state examples)

Legislative	Executive	Judicial
Makes law	Enforces law	Interprets law
Example:	*Example:*	*Example:*
States legislature	State governor	State supreme court

on to the governor for signature. The governor also has veto power over a law, meaning that the governor can negate, or vote against, the law passed by the legislature. If the law is enacted, the state supreme court has the power to invalidate it by ruling that it violates either the United States Constitution or the state constitution. This system that permits one branch some control over the other branches is referred to as the *checks and balances* system.

1. State Constitutions

All states have a state constitution. Most of them are similar to the United States Constitution. All state constitutions divide the functions of the state government in much the same way that the federal government does: three branches of government, each with some power over the other branch in a checks and balances scheme.

a. The Variation among the States It is tempting to assume that all states follow a similar pattern in arresting, charging, and prosecuting defendants. However, this assumption is wrong. Because states have the power to enact their own laws, they also have the power to enact their own procedural rules. We will discuss the various procedural steps involved in charging a suspect with a crime in later chapters. However, it is important to note that no two states follow exactly the same procedures or even use the same terms for the various stages of a prosecution. A prosecutor skilled in Georgia law, for instance, would be completely out of his depth in a New York or California courtroom. The same would hold true for a New York attorney in Nevada. A criminal suspect enjoys fundamental rights in all states and in the federal system, but how and when these rights are exercised can be vastly different from state to state. Because there is no way that any textbook could adequately address the variations among all the states and the federal court system, the best remedy is to learn the general principles that apply to all and then concentrate on the specifics of the particular jurisdiction.

2. Criminal Statutes

Once a bill has been enacted, it is referred to as a **statute**. Not all statutes involve criminal activity. Many statutes created every year, on both the federal and state levels, have nothing to do with criminal law. The statutes that deal with crime are usually grouped together in the state **code** for ease of reference. Most crimes are violations of state laws, not federal statutes. There are comparatively few federal crimes, but there are fifty states and each state has its own criminal statutes.

3. Ordinances

Statutes are laws passed by a state or federal government, but there are other laws that are equally binding on individuals that do not go through this process. Some laws passed by local governments, such as municipalities and towns, regulate behavior at a local level. These are not referred to

■ **BULLET POINT**
Although there is only one federal government, there are fifty state governments and each has its own set of criminal statutes.

statute
A law that is voted on by the Legislature branch of and enacted by the Executive branch.

code
A collection of laws.

ordinance
A law passed by a local government, such as a town council or city government, that often regulates matters dealing with peace, noise levels, or nuisances such as trash burning.

as statutes. Instead, they are called **ordinances**. An ordinance has limited application. It has a strict geographic limit, such as the town limits or the county boundary. Ordinances cannot conflict with statutes. If they do, the ordinance is ruled unconstitutional and the statute takes precedence. Examples of ordinances include excessively loud automobiles, illegal parking, and failure to leash a dog.

People who are charged with ordinance violations are usually given citations and told to report to a local court, where they may face a small fine. Generally, there is no right to a jury trial for an ordinance violation.

IV. The Federal and State Court Systems

The organization of the federal and state court systems may, at first glance, seem extremely confusing. In the federal system, there is the top court, called the United States **Supreme Court**, which has final authority over all federal courts. Below the U.S. Supreme Court are the various federal circuit courts of appeal. These courts hear appeals from federal district courts, where federal trials occur. On the state level, there is also a top court, which is often called the state supreme court. Below that court, there is a state court of appeals, and below that court are the individual state trial courts. However, the United States Supreme Court has authority over state courts, as well. In fact, the United States Supreme Court is the final appellate court for both the state and the federal system. To better understand these systems and how they interconnect, we will start with the basic organizational scheme of a court system.

Supreme Court
The name for the highest court of the United States courts and the the name used by the highest court of most, but not all, of the states. In some states, the highest state court is referred to by another name. In New York, for example, this court is called the superior court.

A. The Hierarchy of Courts

Whether on the federal or the state level, all court systems are designed as a hierarchy. At the top of the court system is a court that is often, but not always, referred to as the "Supreme Court." This court is responsible for making final decisions on appeals in cases. It interprets both state and federal constitutions and applies these principles to individual cases on appeal.

At the top of the federal system is the United States Supreme Court. Below this court are a number of United States courts of appeal. These are intermediate appellate courts. See Exhibit 1-11.

There are thirteen circuit courts of appeal on the federal level. These circuits comprise several states and hear appeals from all district courts located in any of those states.

In the example provided in Exhibit 1-12, appeals from any of the district courts located in a state would go directly to the circuit court of appeals.

jurisdiction
The persons about whom and the subject matters about which a court has the right and power to make decisions that are legally binding.

The federal courts are courts of limited **jurisdiction**, meaning that they can hear only certain kinds of cases.

Exhibit 1-11

United states federal court svstem

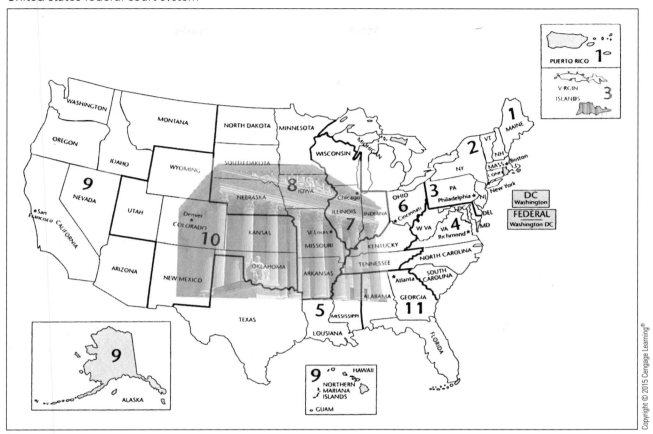

Exhibit 1-12

U.S. courts of appeal (thirteen circuits in all)

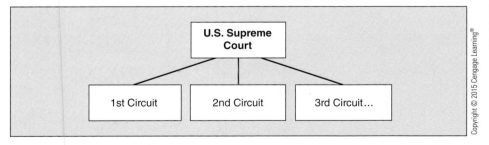

1. The State Court Appellate System

State courts mirror the federal model in many ways. Cases are heard in a trial court, which may be called a variety of names, such as "superior court" and "district court." When a party loses in the trial court, she must first

Exhibit 1-13
U.S. district courts: 94 districts scattered over all fifty states

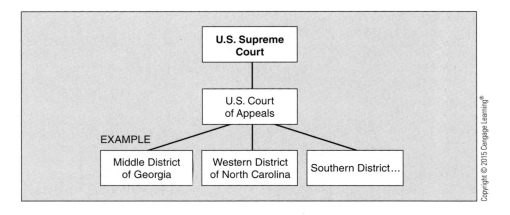

appeal to the intermediate court of appeals. Similar to the United States Circuit Court of Appeals, this court is usually called the state court of appeals. Almost all appeals are heard in this court before being allowed to proceed to the highest court in the state, which may be called the state supreme court. In Chapter 15, we examine in much greater detail the entire appeal of a criminal case.

2. The Criminal Court System

Appeals from verdicts in criminal trials often follow the procedure set out above. But as previously noted, each state has its own system. In some states, an appeal from the trial court goes directly to a court of appeals, whereas in other states, this case would go first to another trial court. At this point, we will speak only in general terms about appeals. Once a verdict is reached in the trial court, it may then be appealed to the state court of appeals. The party losing the appeal at this level may be permitted to appeal to the state supreme court.

Exhibit 1-14
State court appellate system

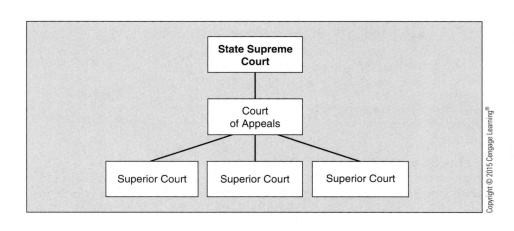

B. State Prosecutions vs. Federal Prosecutions

In this text, we focus a great deal of attention on prosecution at the state level for the simple reason that that is where most prosecutions occur. There are far more state-based prosecutions than there are federal prosecutions. After all, there is only one federal government, whereas there are fifty states.

There are times when a crime comes under both state and federal jurisdiction. This means that either the federal or state government could prosecute. In such a situation, a conflict often arises as to which government takes priority. Fortunately, the **Supremacy Clause** exists to clear up any problems in a comparison of state to federal law. This constitutional provision dictates that when there is a conflict between federal and state law, federal law takes priority. In such a situation, the federal authorities would have the right to try the defendant first. They may decide to waive their priority and turn the defendant over to the state government. In addition to jurisdictional questions about federal and state law, there is an additional element to consider in many states: common law.

V. Common Law

To further complicate the issue, one more important source of law has a huge impact in the area of criminal law in several states. It is the **common law**. The development of the common law in the United States has a very interesting history.

In 1776, when the fledgling colonies of the Americas broke away from Great Britain and decided to form their own country, they were faced with several immediate organizational problems. For instance, how would the courts function? What law would control? There were no state-created laws because there were no state legislatures. Rather than create an entire body of law overnight, the colonists did what anyone in that situation would do: They borrowed someone else's. In this example, they borrowed Great Britain's system because they were already familiar with it. Almost immediately, American jurists began making changes to the English system, but in its foundations, American law is closely patterned on the legal system of Great Britain. Borrowing the English legal system solved several important problems and provided several enormous benefits. For one thing, Britain has a long history of common law.

England has had many centuries to develop its court system. In the past, judges in England literally "rode their circuits" on horseback. As they went from town to town, they dispensed justice according to the cases that were brought before them. Many times, judges were faced with unique situations that no written law had been created to address. In the absence of a written law, a judge would decide the case for himself. These decisions carried as much weight as a written law created by parliament. Judges from various jurisdictions would meet and discuss their decisions

Supremacy Clause
The provision in Article VI of the United States Constitution that the Constitution, laws, and treaties take precedence over conflicting state constitutions or laws.

■ **BULLET POINT**
Under the Supremacy Clause, whenever there is a dispute between federal and state authorities concerning who has jurisdiction, the federal authorities get preference. However, they can waive it and allow the states to proceed first.

common law
Either (1) all case law or the case law that is made by judges in the absence of relevant statutes or (2) The legal system that originated in England and is composed of case law and statutes that grow and change.

in their cases. Early on, judges saw the benefit of creating a uniform system of decisions. In order to show that the legal system was fair, judges agreed that each judge would be bound by decisions of other judges on specific issues. This is common law.

A. "Possession Is Nine-Tenths of the Law"

For instance, suppose a judge was presented with a case in which a farm animal had wandered away from his farm and had then been captured by another farmer. Neither farmer could produce any proof of who originally owned the animal. The judge would be asked to decide who should be allowed to keep the animal. In such a situation, a judge would refer to a previous decision handed down by another judge who had been faced with a similar problem. The previous judge may have stated the rule that "possession is nine-tenths of the law." This ruling meant that when doubt exists about ownership, preference would be given to the person who had possession.

These decisions were written down and embodied in casebooks (called reporters) so that others could have the benefit of the judge's reasoning on a particular case. This body of judge-made law became quite extensive over the centuries. Because these decisions were the laws governing issues among the common people, this body of law came to be known as *common law*. These decisions were not statutes created by some governing body, but rules and legal traditions created by judges who sat hearing cases across the English countryside. The common law became an important element of the law of England, expanding on written laws and creating a rich tradition of judicial interpretations. This is the system that our country adopted shortly after its creation. See Exhibit 1-15 for other examples of common law.

B. The Importance of Common Law

Common law was adopted to create a body of law that the early colonial court systems could use as a ready-made legal framework. The common

Exhibit 1-15
Additional examples
of common laws

Year and a day rule – Holds that when a defendant beats a victim but it takes the victim more than a year and a day to die, the defendant cannot be charged with murder (repealed in most common law states).

Common law marriage – Holds that a man and a woman who announce to others that they are married are considered to be legally married (not valid in all common law states).

Rule of thumb – A husband could not beat his wife with a switch or another implement that was thicker than his own thumb (no longer recognized as valid).

law found a valued place in situations where no other law was applicable. Once states were formed, however, many state legislatures began enacting *statutes*. In an ideal situation, these statutes would have replaced common law. With a written statute in place, there would seem to be no need for common law. In fact, many new states kept their common law in place only long enough to create a body of statutes to replace it. They then abolished common law in favor of the statutes. However, not all states followed this course. Several states, such as Virginia and North Carolina, never abolished their common law. Their state legislatures create statutes, but these statutes exist side by side with the much older common law.

Some states abolished only part of the common law and kept other parts. What this means is that for people in common law states, it is possible to have two different kinds of criminal violations. In North Carolina, for example, a suspect can be charged with statutory burglary or common law burglary. In Virginia, a criminal defendant can be charged with statutory arson or common law arson. The only way to find out if your state is a common law state is to research the criminal statutes and cases.

C. Common Law Crimes vs. Statutory Crimes

In states where common law exists side by side with statutory law, a defendant can be charged with either violation. Often, she will be charged with both (but be convicted of only one because there was only one crime). There are important differences between common law crimes and statutory offenses.

Proving someone guilty of a common law offense involves different evidence than would be required to prove someone guilty of a statutory offense. In Exhibit 1-16, we see the different elements of the crime of burglary as it is set out in common law and as a statutory violation. In order

> **■ BULLET POINT**
> Common law is followed in only a small number of states, including North Carolina and Virginia.

Common-Law Burglary	Statutory Burglary
(1) The breaking; (2) the entering; (3) that the breaking and entry be into a mansion house; (4) that the breaking and entering were in the nighttime and that the breaking and entering were with the intent to commit a felony	The crime of burglary in the first degree is complete when an occupied dwelling is broken and entered in the nighttime with the intent to commit larceny therein whether or not anything was actually stolen from the house.

Copyright © 2015 Cengage Learning®

Exhibit 1-16
Elements of common law offense compared with statutory offenses

Exhibit 1-17

> - Guidance on sentencing when the statute does not provide one.
> - Assistance when the court is confronted with a novel legal issue.
> - Statutes have developed in conjunction with the common law.
> - The state has an entire body of case law developed around common law.

to prove someone guilty of common law burglary, it is necessary to show that the burglary occurred at night, among other things. No such proof is required for statutory burglary. If the prosecution fails to prove that the burglary occurred at night, then the common law charge of burglary against the defendant may be dismissed. As you can see, the common law offenses have elements that many would consider outdated. Most modern statutes, for example, no longer require that the burglary occur at night. In fact, most residential burglaries occur during the day when people are at work.

Although a defendant can be charged with either the common law offense or the statutory offense, he can be sentenced for only one crime. Even if the jury convicted him of both offenses, common law and statutory, a judge may impose only one sentence because the defendant committed only one crime.

D. The Uses of Common Law

Although it would seem that there is no further need for common law, the states that retain the common law have no intention of doing away with it. These states claim that the common law still serves several important functions.

1. Sentencing

Legislatures often enact a new crime without specifying what the punishment will be. Faced with this situation, common law states are allowed to rely on the punishment set out for a similar common law crime.

2. Novel Legal Issues

Common law has a long history, stretching back over several hundred years. In that time, most legal issues have been considered. The old saying that there is nothing new under the sun is especially true when dealing with law. Judges presented with a novel legal argument may consider the decisions of prior judges. These judges can rely on each other's wisdom and experience going back for decades in order to help them decide what is best to do in the current situation.

VI. The Participants in the Criminal Justice System

Numerous participants are involved at all levels of a criminal prosecution. They range from police to prosecutors to jurors. However, the entire process would be incomplete without the main component: the defendant.

A. Defendants

Any discussion of the various individuals involved in the criminal justice system would be meaningless without first addressing the pivotal position: the **defendant**. The terms *defendant* and *suspect* are not interchangeable. A **suspect** is a person whom the police believe may be involved in a crime. A defendant is the person officially charged with committing a crime. Without a suspect, there would be no need for police, prosecutors, judges, or probation officers. When the suspect becomes a defendant, many of her constitutional rights are triggered. Throughout this text, the role of the defendant will be discussed. The defendant enters the criminal justice arena protected by a wide variety of constitutional and other legal protections. He also has a long history of judicial decisions guaranteeing his rights. However, no system is perfect. Our system was founded on the belief that in protecting the rights of a criminal defendant, the law protects us all. By ensuring that a person charged with a crime is provided with basic legal protections, no one could use the law to gain complete power over the citizenry, as has been done in many other countries.

As we explore the various safeguards established to protect a suspect, some attention will be given to famous errors. The history of our country has been highlighted by both great legal battles and tremendous miscarriages of justice. Later, we will discuss the famous *Gideon* case, where the United States Supreme Court ruled that a suspect charged with a felony must be provided with competent counsel. In other chapters, we will discuss the more infamous cases of the "Scottsboro boys" and others that illustrate how a system can wrong. Throughout our system, the defendant keeps it going. The entire edifice would crumble overnight without a suspect to pursue. This causes an interdependence of police, criminal defense attorneys, prosecutors, and defendants. In the everyday world of prosecution, it is not unusual to see this relationship in action. Most people would be surprised at the often cordial dealings between prosecutors, police, defense attorneys, and defendants.

B. Police

Police officers serve the obviously important role of arresting suspects. They gather evidence, confer with witnesses, and initiate almost all criminal prosecutions. In a later chapter, we will spend more time discussing the role of law enforcement. Most police officers earn minimal salaries.

defendant
The person charged with the commission of a crime.

suspect
A person who has been implicated in a crime but has yet to be charged with a crime.

■ **BULLET POINT**
Defendants are people charged with a crime; suspects are people implicated in a crime, but have not, and may never be, charged with a crime.

police officer
A law enforcement officer who is empowered to make arrests within a specific jurisdiction.

Exhibit 1-18

Percent of full-time federal officers with arrest and firearm authority

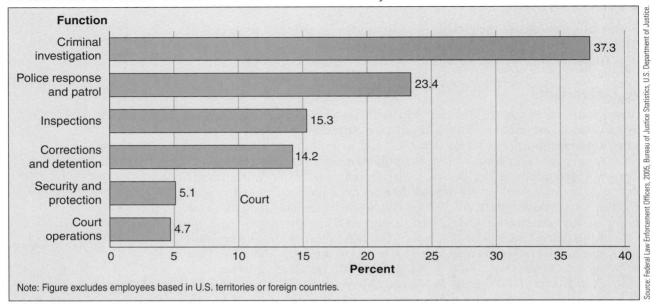

Source: Federal Law Enforcement Officers, 2005, Bureau of Justice Statistics, U.S. Department of Justice.

Note: Figure excludes employees based in U.S. territories or foreign countries.

They work long shifts at odd hours. Their lives consist of long, boring hours punctuated every so often with heart-pounding excitement. A professional basketball player makes more in a week than the average police officer makes in a year. When someone is breaking into your home, you cannot call on the professional athlete. Instead, you phone the police, confident that one of them will appear and try to protect you. It is a grueling job that takes a tremendous toll on police officers, in terms of their personal lives and often their health. Some of them are arrogant and some brutal, but most of them are professionals who enjoy their jobs and have a deep commitment to their communities. See Exhibit 1-18 for an overview of federal officers with arrest powers.

C. Judges

judge
The legal authority in the courtroom; a person empowered to make and enforce rulings and to keep the peace during court proceedings.

Judges preside at trials and make rulings on evidence and control the course of the trial. The **judge**, in many situations, will also be the person who imposes sentence on the defendant (although some states permit the jury to sentence the defendant—Chapter 15). Judges are required to be neutral during the trial. A judge is in a very powerful position. Most judges strive to be fair, work hard at not being swayed by either side in a trial (a very difficult thing to do), and devote themselves to what they believe is in the best interest of the community.

Judges are often well paid and enjoy great esteem in the community. This respect and salary encourage many attorneys to seek appointment or election as a judge. In some states, judges are elected. In others, the judges are appointed to their positions.

Judges are bound by their own code of ethics, and a special panel hears complaints made against judges. In most situations, judges are not allowed to meet with one party in a conflict without the other side also being present. In trial, the judge rules on all evidentiary issues and ensures that the proceedings are dignified. A judge has the power of contempt (discussed in a later chapter) to enforce this stability in the courtroom. Contempt powers give the judge the right to put an unruly person in jail for a short period and/or fine the person.

D. Prosecutors

A **prosecutor** is the representative of the government. She must be a member of the state bar, meaning that the prosecutor is a fully licensed attorney. Like all lawyers, prosecutors attend three years of law school. Young attorneys enter a prosecutor's office knowing full well that the pay will never be as high as what the attorneys in private practice earn. What attracts them? Why do so many seek such employment? Primarily, they are drawn to it out of a sense of adventure or a desire to become a trial attorney or by a genuine wish to serve their communities. They often put the lie to the statement that all attorneys want to get rich. No one ever gets rich working as a prosecutor. Some see the job simply as a stepping-stone to a much better paying job at a private firm. They see their tenure as a prosecutor as a way of improving their trial skills, thus making themselves more marketable for a job in a private firm. Some see the life of a prosecutor as a step toward becoming a judge. Oddly enough, most prosecutors do what they do because they love it. They enjoy the excitement and thrill of trying cases, pitting themselves against other attorneys. They enjoy the challenge of having to think on their feet and the mental gymnastics that a trial attorney must master.

Besides acting as the representative of the government in all prosecutions, prosecutors often act as legal advisers to the police. In many states, the prosecutor may spearhead a grand jury investigation or conduct preliminary hearings, both of which are discussed in detail in later chapters. Prosecutors usually draft the indictments relied upon by the grand jury in their deliberations and present the evidence at trial to prove a defendant is guilty.

E. Defense Attorneys

Criminal **defense attorneys** represent the people charged with criminal violations. They are the flip side of the coin from prosecutors. They are often drawn to the life for the same reasons that prosecutors are drawn to it. Despite the fact that Hollywood often portrays them in a negative light,

prosecutor
A representative of the local, state, or federal government whose duty is to bring charges against defendants and to prove those charges at trial beyond a reasonable doubt.

defense attorney
A member of the bar who represents individuals who have been charged with or are suspected of committing a crime.

> ### INSIDER'S VIEWPOINT
>
> #### *How defense attorneys deal with the press*
> "First of all, you've got to remember that they can cut and paste your statement anyway that they feel like. You need to mean what you say and say what you mean. You probably should speak with the reporters that you've come to trust somewhat. I speak with reporters because generally by the time I've gotten the case the police or the DA has made a statement and I'm just trying to do my damage control."
>
> —W. Keith Davidson, Criminal Defense Attorney

■ **BULLET POINT**
Both prosecutors and defense attorneys are attorneys and must have passed the state bar exam and be members of the state bar.

most defense attorneys are ethical, honest, and trustworthy people. They work very hard for clients who frequently do not appreciate them—and even more often do not pay them. They pit their meager resources against the investigative power of the state. They fulfill a crucial role in our legal system: safeguarding the rights of the accused. For their efforts, they are often castigated in the press and asked, "How can you defend those people?" Their answer is frequently that if they did not, who would?

F. Paralegals

paralegal
A legal assistant who provides services and support to an attorney.

Paralegals are found in every phase of criminal prosecution. They work for criminal defense attorneys and for prosecutors. A paralegal who works in a criminal defense firm is often called upon to interview clients, obtain police reports, draft motions and other criminal discovery pleadings, and attend court to help the attorney during the trial. Paralegals are found less frequently in prosecution offices, but that situation is slowly changing. Prosecution paralegals often draft charging documents such as indictments and accusations, coordinate witness appearances with victim-witness programs, and work closely with the prosecutor and police when further investigation of a case is called for. Just as in private practice, many government offices are beginning to see the advantages of having someone who is trained in the law to assist attorneys with cases.

■ **BULLET POINT**
Paralegals play larger and larger roles in criminal law cases, both for the prosecution and the defense.

G. Clerk of Court

clerk (of court)
A court official who maintains records of dispositions in both civil and criminal cases.

Clerks are responsible for storing and maintaining all records of court proceedings. Clerks' offices are open to the public. Clerks and deputy clerks keep track of each case and store documents relating to all cases. Their role is crucial to the orderly administration of justice because they keep track of the payment of fines, the assessment of sentences, and the organization of the mountain of paperwork generated by even the most routine criminal cases. Deputy clerks are often found in the courtroom during calendar calls and sentencing hearings because they are charged with the duty of keeping a record of the disposition of every case.

H. Probation Officers

When a defendant is sentenced to a term of probation or parole, a **probation (parole) officer** monitors the defendant. Probation officers are usually poorly paid and overworked. They are despised by the defendants who are serving their sentences, not the least because the defendant pays his court fines to the probation officer. The probation officer ensures that the defendant is gainfully employed and that the defendant obeys the terms of his sentence. If a defendant is sentenced to community service, for instance, the probation officer coordinates the defendant's service and keeps a record of his compliance. Probation officers may bring a petition to revoke a defendant's probation when the defendant commits a new crime or fails to abide by the terms of his probation. At this point, the defendant will be referred to as a probationer and the hearing is referred to as a probation revocation hearing. If the judge agrees with the probation officer, the judge can order the defendant to serve the remainder of his sentence in prison.

probation (parole) officer
The official who is responsible for supervising a convicted defendants while they serve their sentence on probation or parole; they are responsible for ensuring that the defendant complies with all terms of his or her sentence, including paying fines, making restitution and completely community service.

I. Other Personnel

This list is by no means exhaustive. Throughout this text, we will also encounter federal agents, prison counselors, federal and state correction agencies, federal and state law enforcement agencies, and many others.

THE ROLE OF THE PARALEGAL:

Many times a client has no firm idea of what the various participants in the criminal justice system actually do. Paralegals who have worked in the field for a long time must remember that not everyone understands the system. The paralegal should be prepared to give the client an overview of what is going to happen, who the participants are, and what function each plays.

ETHICAL CONSIDERATION: PARALEGALS AND ETHICS

Although lawyers have had support staff since law as a profession first emerged, the arrival of a professional class of paralegals did not begin until the 1960s. The American Bar Association recognized the role of paralegals in 1967. As paralegals have grown in numbers, their role has expanded. Today, they are given broad responsibilities, but their training in the complex ethics of the legal field has often lagged behind the increased duties. With the founding of national organizations for paralegals and the creation of paralegal codes of ethics, the profession's increasing attention to the ethical duties of a paralegal has begun to receive the attention it deserves. Throughout this text, the ethical duties of the paralegal will be explored in as much detail as is given to the practical duties.

At the conclusion of each chapter, the complicated role of the paralegal will be dissected and the ethical duty pinpointed. Paralegals in the criminal field are presented with ethical challenges that are distinct from those facing paralegals in other branches of the law. The criminal law paralegal must be prepared to deal with these complex issues.

✓ Paralegal To Do List

At the initial meeting it is important to build a picture of the client. Speak with the client and get the following information:

- Name
- Home address
- Telephone numbers, including work, cell, and beeper
- Marital status
- Spouse's name (if applicable)
- Does spouse work? If so, what is his or her job?
- Children? How many? Names, ages?
- Work address
- Name of Employer
- Description of Job
- Starting pay; Current pay
- If unemployed, since what date?
- Prior employment, dates, description, etc.
- Would employer make a good character witness? Why or why not?
- Reason for leaving prior jobs?
- Any prior problems with the law? Prior convictions?

Case Excerpt. When Is It "Night Time" for Purposes of Common Law Burglary?

STATE V. BROWN L 2282549, 1-5 (N.C.APP., 2012) STEELMAN, JUDGE.

The trial court did not err in denying defendant's motion to dismiss the charges of first-degree burglary and felony larceny. The trial court did not commit error, much less plain error, in its jury instructions.

I. Factual and Procedural Background

On 20 July 2010, Octavis White (White) and his wife went to bed in their home in Mebane after dark. After showering the next morning, White noticed that his wallet and money clip that he had left on his bedroom dresser were missing. He subsequently discovered that several laptop computers were missing.

Marcus Lee Brown (defendant) left his girlfriend's apartment in Durham after 10:00 P.M. on 20 July 2010. He returned about 6:00 A.M. the next morning, carrying several bags. One contained a laptop computer that his girlfriend turned on. The name "Octavis White" appeared on the screen. The police were called. They discovered a number of items that had been stolen from the Whites.

Defendant was indicted for first-degree burglary and felony larceny. On 30 March 2011, defendant was found guilty of both charges. Defendant was sentenced as a Level III offender to consecutive active terms of imprisonment of 84–110 months for the first-degree burglary conviction and 10–12 months for the felony larceny conviction.

Defendant appeals.

II. Motion to Dismiss

In his first argument, defendant contends that the trial court erred in denying his motion to dismiss the charge of first-degree burglary because the State failed to produce evidence that the offense occurred at nighttime and that defendant was the perpetrator. Defendant also argues that the State failed to produce evidence that defendant was the perpetrator of the larceny.

B. Nighttime Requirement for First-Degree Burglary

"The elements of first-degree burglary are: (i) the breaking (ii) and entering (iii) in the nighttime (iv) into the dwelling house or sleeping apartment (v) of another (vi) which is actually occupied at the time of the offense (vii) with the intent to commit a felony therein." *State v. Singletary*, 344 N.C. 95, 101, 472 S.E.2d 895, 899 (1996). See also N.C. Gen.Stat. § 14–51 (2011).

North Carolina has no statutory definition of nighttime. *State v. McKeithan*, 140 N.C.App. 422, 432, 537 S.E.2d 526, 533 (2000). "However, our courts adhere to the common law definition of nighttime as that time after sunset and before sunrise when it is so dark that a man's face cannot be identified except by artificial light or moonlight." Id.

White testified that it was dark when he went to bed on the night of 20 July 2010. Defendant requests that we take judicial notice that civil twilight began in Mebane, North Carolina on 21 July 2010 at 5:47 A.M. As our Supreme Court did in *State v. Garrison*, 294 N.C. 270, 280, 240 S.E.2d 377, 383 (1978), we take judicial notice that in Mebane, on 21 July 2010, civil twilight began at 5:47 A.M., as computed by the Astronomical Applications Department of the United States Naval Observatory in "Sun and Moon Data for One Day."

Defendant left his girlfriend's apartment in Durham after 10:00 P.M. on 20 July 2010. He returned about 6:00 A.M. the next morning, carrying several bags.

[Prosecutor]: Okay. And [defendant] left the house Tuesday night sometime after 10:00; is that correct?

[Defendant's Girlfriend]: Yes.

Q. Okay. And when did you see him next?
A. The next morning.

Q. That would be Wednesday morning?
A. Yeah.

Q. About what time?
A. About 6:00.

Q. Was it light outside or dark or what?
A. It was getting light.

White showered between 6:30 and 7:00 A.M. After showering, White noticed that his wallet and money clip that he had left on his bedroom dresser were missing. He subsequently discovered that several laptop computers were missing. White woke his wife to ask about his missing belongings about 7:30 A.M.

Defendant argues that this evidence was insufficient to establish that the break-in occurred during the nighttime.

"A judicially noticed fact must be one not subject to reasonable dispute in that it is either (1) generally known within the territorial jurisdiction of the trial court or (2) capable of accurate and ready determination by resort to sources whose accuracy cannot reasonably be questioned." N.C.R. Evid. 201(b) (2011). "Judicial notice may be taken at any stage of the proceeding." N.C.R. Evid. 201(f) (2011).

As we have taken judicial notice of the time of the commencement of civil twilight on 21 July 2010, we also take judicial notice of the driving distance between White's residence and defendant's girlfriend's apartment as being in excess of 27 miles.

In *State v. Saunders*, 245 N.C. 338, 342, 95 S.E.2d 876, 879 (1957), our Supreme Court held that it was appropriate for the trial court to take judicial notice of the distance in miles between cities in Virginia and North Carolina. "It is generally held that the courts will take judicial notice of the placing of the important towns within their jurisdiction ..." Id..

A much stronger case for taking such notice can be made out today when almost every town in the country is connected by a ribbon of concrete or asphalt over which a constant stream of traffic flows.... In fact, so complete and so general is the common knowledge of places and distances that the court may be presumed to know the distances between important cities and towns in this State and likewise in adjoining states. *Saunders*, 245 N.C. at 343, 95 S.E.2d at 879.

In the event that defendant committed the break-in after 5:47 A.M., he would not have been able to steal the items from the White residence, place them in an automobile, and traverse the distance between Mebane and Durham by 6:00 A.M., even if he drove directly to his girlfriend's apartment.

Viewing the evidence in the light most favorable to the State, the State presented sufficient evidence that the offense occurred in the nighttime. The trial court properly denied defendant's motion to dismiss, but, out of an abundance of caution, submitted felonious breaking and entering as a lesser-included offense. The trial court properly left the determination of whether the offense occurred in the nighttime to the jury.

C. Identification of Defendant as Perpetrator of Crimes and Doctrine of Recent Possession

The doctrine of recent possession is "a rule of law that, upon an indictment for larceny, possession of recently stolen property raises a presumption of the possessor's guilt of the larceny of such property." *State v. Maines*, 301 N.C. 669, 673, 273 S.E.2d 289, 293 (1981). When "there is sufficient evidence that a building has been broken into and entered and thereby the property in question has been stolen, the possession of such stolen property recently after the larceny raises presumptions that the possessor is guilty of the larceny and also of the breaking and entering." *Maines*, 301 N.C. at 674, 273 S.E.2d at 293. "When the doctrine of recent possession applies in a particular case, it suffices to repel a motion for non-suit and defendant's guilt or innocence becomes a jury question." Id.

"The possession must be so recent after the breaking or entering and larceny as to show that the possessor could not have reasonably come by it, except by stealing it himself or by his concurrence." *State v. Hamlet*, 316 N.C. 41, 43, 340 S.E.2d 418, 420 (1986). In Hamlet, "approximately thirty days" passed before the items were discovered in the defendant's possession.

Defendant argues that there was no testimony about when the items discovered in defendant's possession were last known to be secure. However, the evidence presented at trial was that the time period between when the items were missing and when defendant was discovered with the items was a matter of hours. Based upon the doctrine of recent possession, the State presented sufficient evidence of defendant's identity as the perpetrator of both first-degree burglary and felony larceny.

The trial court did not err in denying defendant's motion to dismiss.

NO ERROR.

Judges ELMORE and STROUD concur.

CASE QUESTIONS

1. What are the basic facts of this case?
2. What was the basis of the defendant's motion to dismiss?
3. Does North Carolina have a statutory definition of nighttime?
4. What is a "judicially noticed fact?"
5. How did judicial notice of the time of day affect the defendant's appeal?

Chapter Summary

In any criminal prosecution, numerous steps must occur before a defendant is brought to trial. In the following chapters, we will be exploring these various steps as well as focusing on the laws that govern the process and the people who are involved in the day-to-day business of criminal justice. A trial occurs at the end of a long sequence of events that began with the arrest and proceeded through other stages before defendants face the jury who will hear the charges against them. The government is given the right to prosecute a defendant by the United States Constitution. Each state also has its own constitution, closely modeled on the federal constitution. Both state and federal constitutions provide that government be divided into three branches: Executive, Legislative, and Judicial. Because federal laws govern the entire nation, whereas state law only governs the citizens of a particular state, the United States is a system of two tiers of government: federal and state. Where federal law and state laws conflict on any issue, the Supremacy Clause of the United States Constitution provides that federal law will prevail.

State law is built not only on legislatively enacted law, but also on a long history of common law. Although many states have abolished this so-called "judge made" law, several states retain both common law and statutory law. These common law states maintain these two systems side by side, resulting in the unusual situation of being able to bring a common law crime or a statutory crime against a defendant. The common law is generally less sophisticated than statutory law. Even in states that have long since abandoned common law, it still remains important as a guide for future judicial decisions.

WEB SITES

Alabama State Court System
www.judicial.alabama.gov

California Court System
www.courts.ca.gov

Cengage Learning
www.cengage.com

Federal Bureau of Investigations (FBI)
www.fbi.gov

Florida Supreme Court:
www.floridasupremecourt.org

Locating specific U.S. Supreme Court cases
www.findlaw.com

Rules of the U.S. Supreme Court
www.law.cornell.edu

The Federal Judiciary Home Page
www.uscourts.gov

The United States Supreme Court home page
www.supremecourt.gov

U.S. Department of Justice
www.justice.gov

Wyoming State Court System
www.courts.state.wy.us

REVIEW QUESTIONS

1. List the various participants in the criminal justice system and explain the function of each.
2. What is the Supremacy Clause?
3. What is the common law? Is the common law still in use in the United States? Does the common law still serve a useful purpose? Explain.
4. List and explain the important differences between criminal law and civil law.
5. What are the three branches of government? Give a brief summary of the role each branch plays.

6. Compare and contrast the various roles of the participants in the criminal justice system.

QUESTIONS FOR REFLECTION

1. What are two arguments for revising the organization of the federal and state governments? What are two arguments against such a proposal?

2. Are the safeguards in the Constitution actually necessary? Do these prohibitions on the various branches of government serve to unnecessarily limit the effectiveness of government? Why or why not?

KEYWORDS AND PHRASES

Burden of proof
Felony
Misdemeanor
Supremacy Clause
Statute
Common law
Defendants
Police
Judges
Prosecutors
Defense attorneys
Clerk of court
Probation officers
Paralegal
Suspect
Jurisdiction

Supreme Court
Ordinance
Code
Indictment
Answer
Complaint
Pleadings
Style
Damages
Plaintiff
Preponderance of evidence
Verdict
Liable
Guilty
Reasonable doubt

PRACTICAL APPLICATIONS

1. Review the Kline, Marbles, and Fortner case overviews in the Appendix. These cases will provide the basis of questions and problems through the text.

2. Contact your local superior Court clerk's office and find out if any court hearings are scheduled. The clerk publishes a calendar of such cases, and because most trials (except juvenile cases) are open to the public, you may visit the courthouse and see the criminal justice system in action.

Chapter 2

ARREST, SEARCH, AND SEIZURE

Chapter Objectives

At the completion of this chapter, you should be able to:

- Define *arrest*
- Explain what probable cause is and how it is important to both arrests and searches
- Explain the importance of the Fourth Amendment and its relationship to police arrests, searches, and seizures
- Explain what a Terry stop is
- Explain how and under what circumstances a search warrant may be issued
- Explain the circumstances under which a search warrant is not required

probable cause
The first court proceeding on a criminal charge in federal courts and many state courts by a magistrate or a judge to decide whether there is enough evidence for the government to continue with the case and to require the defendant to post bail or be held for trial.

I. Introduction

To arrest someone is to detain a person suspected of committing a crime. When a person is under arrest, he is not free to go about his business. He is often restrained by being handcuffed or detained in some way. However, a person can be "arrested" without the use of force. The United States Constitution places strict limits on the arrest powers of police officers. The Fourth Amendment requires that when a warrant issues for a person's arrest—or when a search warrant issues to seize property—probable cause must exist. **Probable cause**, in its simplest form, refers to the objective evidence that a crime has been or is about to be committed.

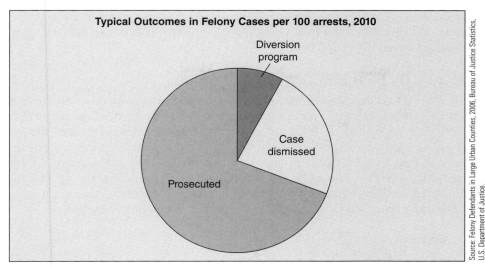

Typical Outcomes in Felony Cases per 100 arrests, 2010

Source: Felony Defendants in Large Urban Counties, 2006, Bureau of Justice Statistics, U.S. Department of Justice.

Exhibit 2-1
Typical outcomes in felony cases per 100 arrests, 2010

Arrest refers to the detention of a person. Warrants may also be issued for the seizure of property, such as the evidence of a crime. These warrants are often referred to under the slightly misleading term of *search warrants*. They should be called "search and seizure" warrants because when police have such a warrant, they can search and remove specific items. We will examine the law of arrest and of search warrants later in this chapter. See Exhibit 2-1 for an overview of felony arrests.

II. Arrest

In the United States, hundreds of individuals are arrested on a daily basis. Law enforcement officers make arrests under all types of situations. Some are inherently dangerous, such as serving an arrest warrant on a person who is armed and dangerous. Arrests may occur without warrants, such as when officers have reason to believe that a person has committed a crime. No matter what the situation, the Fourth Amendment of the United States Constitution requires that each arrest must be supported by probable cause.

A. What Is Arrest?

To arrest someone is to prevent him from going about his business. An arrested person no longer has the freedom of movement; he or she is under the control of someone else—usually a police officer. Normally, an arrest is made under the authority of an arrest warrant (see later). However, a police officer is legally authorized to arrest a person without a warrant if the officer has probable cause to believe that a crime has

arrest
The official taking of a person to answer criminal charges. This involves at least temporarily depriving the person of liberty and may involve the use of force.

**Amendment IV.
Search and Seizure**

"The right of the people to be secure in their persons, houses, papers, and effects, against unreasonable searches and seizures, shall not be violated, and no Warrants shall issue, but upon probable cause, supported by Oath or affirmation, and particularly describing the place to be searched, and the persons or things to be seized."

been committed. We will examine probable cause in much greater detail later in this chapter. First, we will explore who can make arrests, then how an arrest is carried out.

B. Arrests by Police Officers and Others

In most situations, law enforcement officers are the only people who can make arrests. They are specifically empowered by the local, state, or federal government to do so. Law enforcement officers are trained how to make a legal arrest and are certified by the government to carry out an arrest. Police officers can make an arrest when they are on duty or off duty. They may make an arrest when they are in uniform or out of uniform. However, no matter what the situation at the time of the arrest, officers must have probable cause for the arrest to be constitutional.

1. Citizen's Arrest

In some situations, non-police civilians may arrest suspects, referred to as a **citizen's arrest**. Many states allow citizens to make arrests when a crime has been committed in the citizen's presence or within his immediate knowledge. Some states even go so far as to say that private citizens have as much power to arrest a felon—in an emergency situation—as does a police officer. Private citizens can make a citizen's arrest (in most states) for a felony occurring in their presence. They may also have the right to arrest someone to prevent a felony from occurring. When the crime is a misdemeanor, usually the citizen can arrest a person only if the citizen actually saw the person commit the crime. Generally, there is

---

BULLET POINT

The test to determine when a person is under arrest is when a reasonable person, reviewing the facts, would believe that the suspect is not free to leave.

---

citizen's arrest

An arrest by a private person, rather than by a police or other law enforcement officer. A person usually may arrest another for any crime committed in his or her presence or for a felony committed elsewhere.

INSIDER'S VIEWPOINT

Becoming a police officer

Once a police officer attends a police or other academy, they often receive additional training at the hands of older, more experienced police officers. One such officer is Detective Jack Burnette, former Chief of Homicide. "Once recruits finish their 18 to 20 weeks training they go into what is called a 'ride-a-long' program. Generally what we will do is rotate them for several weeks between each watch. In other words, they'll start out assigned to a training officer on the morning watch and they will ride with them for several weeks. Then they will be assigned to an officer on the evening watch and they'll ride with him. Then they'll ride with one on the day watch for several weeks. Each one of these training officers will evaluate the recruit.

"They evaluate him on how he handles situations dealing with the public, various calls, how he responds to the calls. What they are doing is trying to get a feel for him before they cut him loose by himself."

—Jack Burnette, Homicide Detective

no right of citizen's arrest to *prevent* a misdemeanor. Many states have dramatically curtailed the right of citizen's arrest, preferring to leave it in the hands of the people who have been specifically trained to carry it out, namely, police officers. This doctrine has more importance in the area of civil law, where it protects the citizen from being sued for battery in restraining the individual and holding him or her until the police arrive to effectuate a real arrest.[1]

C. How an Arrest Is Carried Out

In some countries, a police officer must actually touch the person before he or she is considered to be under arrest. That is not the case in the United States. A police officer can make a legal arrest simply by giving a verbal command to a suspect. In most cases, of course, the officer does touch the person, usually restraining him and putting handcuffs on his wrist. However, force is not a requirement of an arrest. A person can be arrested simply by the verbal command of a police officer. If the person voluntarily submits to an arrest or agrees to limit his movement, then he is considered legally arrested. However, in many situations, a defendant is arrested for a violent felony. See Exhibit 2-2.

D. Why Is the Question of When the Suspect Was Under Arrest So Important?

If a person is arrested without probable cause, then the arrest is unconstitutional. There is often no direct penalty against the officer for making an unconstitutional arrest, so why is the issue of arrest so important? The United States Supreme Court has held on many occasions that unconstitutional arrests are subject to the Exclusionary Rule. This rule, explored in greater detail in Chapter 4, requires that any evidence discovered after an unconstitutional arrest or search must be disregarded. If a suspect has been arrested without probable cause, then any evidence obtained may be inadmissible at the trial. The suspect will often be released, and any evidence discovered after the unconstitutional arrest will be inadmissible in court. As a result, police are normally very careful about when they put a person under arrest. Defendants, on the other hand, are eager to build a case that establishes that the arrest was unconstitutional because it will result in the evidence being invalidated.

1. Objective Test Used in Arrests

The question of *when* a person is under arrest is often of vital importance. This question goes to the very heart of the police-suspect interaction. Because the result of an unconstitutional arrest is so drastic for the state, police officers and suspects often have very different impressions of when an arrest occurred. Fortunately, the United States Supreme Court does not rely on the subjective impressions of either to make the determination. In its many cases on this issue, the Court has stated that an objective test

■ BULLET POINT
Perhaps the most important thing to remember about citizen's arrest is that it is not actually an arrest. Citizens are not empowered to arrest anyone. The phrase should, more correctly, be called *citizen's detention.*

Exhibit 2-2

Rate of violent victimization and percent change, by type of violent crime, 2002, 2010, and 2011

Type of violent crime	Victimization rates[a] 2002	2010	2011	Percent change, 2002–2011[b]	Percent change, 2010–2011[b]	Average annual change, 2002–2010[b]
Violent crime[c]	32.1	19.3	22.5	−30%[†]	17%[†]	−6%
Rape/sexual assault	1.5	1.0	0.9	−37[†]	−10	−4
Robbery	2.7	2.2	2.2	−20[‡]	−3	−2
Assault	27.9	16.0	19.4	−30[†]	21[†]	−6
Aggravated assault	5.8	3.4	4.1	−29[†]	22[‡]	−6
Simple assault	22.1	12.7	15.3	−31[†]	21[†]	−6
Domestic violence[d]	5.6	4.4	5.3	−7	19	−3
Intimate partner violence[e]	4.0	3.0	3.3	−18[‡]	9	−3
Violent crime involving injury	8.2	5.0	5.6	−31[†]	12	−5
Serious violent crime[f]	10.0	6.6	7.2	−28%[†]	9%	−5%
Serious domestic violence[d]	1.9	1.5	1.4	−26[‡]	−4	−3
Serious intimate partner violence[e]	1.3	1.1	1.0	−21	−3	−2
Serious violent crime involving weapons	6.9	4.2	4.6	−33[†]	11	−6
Serious violent crime involving injury	3.3	2.6	2.7	−19	3	−3

Note: Total population age 12 or older was 231,589,260 in 2002; 255,961,940 in 2010; and 257,542,240 in 2011.
[†]Significant at 95%.
[‡]Significant at 90%.
[a]Per 1,000 persons age 12 or older.
[b]Calculated based on unrounded estimates.
[c]Excludes homicide. The NCVS is based on interviews with victims and therefore cannot measure murder.
[d]Includes victimization committed by intimate partners (current of former spouses, boyfriends, or girlfriends) and family members.
[e]Includes victimization committed by current or former spouses, boyfriends, or girlfriends.
[f]Includes rape or sexual assault, robbery, and aggravated assault.

Source: Criminal Victimization in the U.S., 2010, Bureau of Justice Statistics, U.S. Department of Justice.

is used, not a subjective test. The objective test is whether under the circumstances at the time, a reasonable person would believe that he or she was under arrest. The subjective beliefs of the police officer and the suspect are ignored. For instance, a police officer may testify that the suspect was definitely not under arrest, but the objective facts may suggest otherwise. Most people would agree that it certainly looks like an arrest when someone is handcuffed, placed in the back of a police car, and taken to the police station. The officer's statement is not the final determination. For instance, a police officer could claim that the suspect was not under arrest at the time he was handcuffed and taken to jail, but most courts would probably rule that he was. Similarly, a suspect might state that when the police officer asked him his name and told him to stand still for a moment, he *felt* that he was under arrest. The suspect's beliefs are not relevant either. What is relevant is what happened, not how the people involved felt. If the objective facts suggest that an arrest has occurred, then it must be supported by probable cause. See Exhibit 2-3.

- Threatening presence of several officers
- A tone of voice, or certain types of language that would indicate that an individual must obey an officer's request
- Suspect detained longer than a "reasonable time"
- Suspect told he is not "free to leave"
- Placing suspect in police car and taking him to police station or other law enforcement area for questioning

Exhibit 2-3
Situations where the court has decreed an arrest has occurred

E. Arrests and Probable Cause

The term *probable cause* has already been mentioned in several contexts in this discussion of arrest. The United States Constitution requires probable cause before the issuance of warrants, but this begs the question: What exactly is probable cause?

III. Probable Cause

At its simplest, probable cause refers to the reasonable suspicion that a particular set of facts is true. These facts may be that the suspect has committed a crime or that certain evidence will be found in a particular location. In either event, the Fourth Amendment requires that probable cause exists before arrest or search warrants are issued. The existence of probable cause to arrest is based on objective standards and is determined from the viewpoint of what a prudent person would believe when presented with the same facts and circumstances as the officer. These courts describe probable cause as a factor of the "totality of the circumstance," including the location, time of day, and suspect's demeanor, all viewed through the eyes of a reasonable, prudent police officer.[2]

Determining probable cause is often not a simple matter. "In dealing with probable cause...as the very name implies, we deal with probabilities. These probabilities are technical; they are the essentially factual and practical considerations of everyday life on which reasonable and prudent men, not legal technicians, act."[3] Probable cause at the time of arrest means that at the moment the arrest was made, the officers had reasonable belief that a crime had been (or was about to be) committed. Put another way, probable cause exists if at the time of the arrest the officers had knowledge and reasonably trustworthy information about facts and circumstances sufficient to warrant a prudent man in believing that the defendant had committed the offense. See Exhibit 2-4.

The Fourth Amendment provides that "The right of the people to be secure in their persons...against unreasonable searches and seizures, shall not be violated."

BULLET POINT
All arrests must be supported by probable cause.

Exhibit 2-4
Probable cause

A police officer has probable cause when
- She has a reasonable belief that a crime has been committed
- She has a reasonable belief that a crime is about to be committed

This reasonable belief can be based on:
- Suspect's statements and actions
- Training and experience
- Reports by other officers
- Statements by witnesses

An arrest is constitutionally valid "if, at the moment the arrest is made, the facts and circumstances within the knowledge of the arresting officers and of which they had reasonably trustworthy information were sufficient to warrant a prudent man in believing that the accused had committed or was committing an offense."[4] A person is under arrest when a third party, viewing the facts and circumstances, would believe that the suspect was not free to leave.[5] This classification of not being free to leave is the linchpin of the definition of arrest, and it this definition that defines precisely when a suspect's numerous post-arrest rights are triggered. See Exhibit 2-5 for a summary of arrests for various crimes. Compare the

Exhibit 2-5
Summary of Arrests

HIGHLIGHTS

- The rate of violent victimization increased 17%, from 19.3 victimizations per 1,000 persons age 12 or older in 2010 to 22.5 in 2011.

- There was no statistically significant change in the rate of serious violent victimization from 2010 to 2011.

- A 22% increase in the number of assaults accounted for all of the increase in violent crime.

- No measurable change was detected in the rate of intimate partner violence from 2010 to 2011.

- Increases in the rates of violent victimizations for whites, Hispanics, younger persons, and males accounted for the majority of the increase in violent crime.

- Residents in urban areas continued to experience the highest rates of total and serious violence.

- The rate of property crime increased 11%, from 125.4 per 1,000 households in 2010 to 138.7 in 2011.

- From 2010 to 2011, household burglary increased 14% from 25.8 to 29.4 per 1,000 households

Source: Arrest in the U.S. 1990-2010, Bureau of Justice Statistics, U.S. Department of Justice.

- Rumor
- Speculation
- "Gut feelings"
- Stereotypes

Exhibit 2-6
Probable cause cannot be
based on . . .

definition of what probable cause is with Exhibit 2-6 which shows what probable cause cannot be based upon.

A. Degree of Proof Not as High as Proving the Defendant Guilty

The degree of proof needed to establish probable cause is not as high as the standard that will later be used to prove the defendant is guilty of the crime. Probable cause does not mean proof beyond a reasonable doubt (the standard used at trial). The proof needed for probable cause is lower. The standard is whether the facts available to the officers at the moment of arrest would "warrant a man of reasonable caution in the belief that an offense had been committed."[6] Probable cause must be based on something more substantial than mere rumor or speculation.[7] This means that police officers must often independently verify facts related to them before they will have sufficient probable cause to make an arrest. Probable cause is a middle ground between proof beyond a reasonable doubt and mere suspicion that an action may be a criminal act.

1. Different Types of Interaction Between Police and Civilians

Not all contacts between police and citizens involve arrests or seizures. Obviously, there is some dividing line between a voluntary conversation with a police officer and a full-blown constitutionally protected arrest. Generally, there are three distinct types of interaction, each with its own legal standard.

When a person engages in a voluntary discussion with a police officer, there is no constitutionally mandated legal standard for the officer. People approach officers with questions every day; officers ask people questions. There would be nothing gained, and a great deal lost, if the police were required to have a legal basis for asking a simple question such as "What's your name?" However, if the officer wants to detain the person briefly, there is a legal requirement: reasonable suspicion. An officer is justified in briefly detaining a person to ask questions or conduct further investigation. This brief detention does not have to meet the level of probable cause. If the officer's suspicions become justified, then probable cause will be established and the officer can make an arrest. If the officer's suspicions prove to be groundless, then the officer must allow the person to leave. See Exhibit 2-7.

BULLET POINT
Police do not have to prove that a defendant is guilty beyond a reasonable doubt in order to arrest him or her.

Voluntary Interactions with Police

The Fourth Amendment does not prohibit voluntary interaction between citizens and the police.[8]

Exhibit 2-7

Different levels of interactions between police and civilians

Type of contact	Legal standard required:
Voluntary interaction	None
Brief detention	Reasonable suspicion
Arrest	Probable cause

2. Reasonable Suspicion (Not Probable Cause) Required in Brief Detentions
A police officer may briefly detain a person to ask questions and conduct a short investigation. This detention is not an arrest; therefore, probable cause is not required. These brief stops are called "Terry stops" in reference to a famous United States Supreme Court case that first dealt with this issue. Under *Terry v. Ohio*,[9] a police officer who lacks probable cause may momentarily detain a suspicious individual to determine his identity or to gather more information.

United States Supreme Court's Definition of Seizure

"Not all personal interactions between police officers and citizens involve seizures of persons. Only when the officer, by means of physical force or show of authority, has in some way restrained the liberty of a citizen have the Courts concluded that a seizure has occurred."[10]

a. How Brief Is "Brief"? In Terry stops, the question often becomes when did the brief detention become an arrest? For example, a suspect may be detained in the backseat of a police car for 10 to 15 minutes as part of a Terry stop without being considered under arrest. The U. S. Supreme Court has consistently stayed away from any predetermined time frame that will automatically no longer be considered "brief." Generally, the facts of the case and the kind of investigation required will determine how reasonable the officer was. In some cases, it will take only a few minutes to verify information. Holding the person longer than that would be considered an arrest. However, in other cases, it may take an hour or longer to verify certain information. Whatever the situation, under *Terry*, a detention is no longer "brief" when a police officer requests that the suspect accompany him to the police station—or does anything else that a reasonable person would consider to be an arrest. At that point, the suspect is under arrest and the arrest must be supported by probable cause to be constitutional.[11]

■ BULLET POINT

Reasonable suspicion, not probable cause, is required for brief detentions.

b. Stop and Frisk In some situations, a police officer is authorized to pat down the outer clothing of an individual he has briefly detained. Patting down, or frisking, a suspect for weapons is permitted under various U.S. Supreme decisions, especially *Terry v. Ohio*. However, *Terry* only authorizes such a frisk when it is supported by a reasonable belief that the suspect is armed and dangerous.[12] Suppose, for example, that a police officer approaches a suspect and asks if he or she is carrying a weapon. The suspect says, "No." However, when the officer conducts a frisk, the officer discovers a concealed weapon. This, by itself, would justify the officer in arresting the suspect for carrying a concealed weapon because the circumstances, including the suspect's statement and the officer's recovery of the weapon, are enough to establish probable cause.[13]

c. The Officer's Right to Protection *Terry v. Ohio* does not limit a police officer, under all circumstances, to a simple pat down. "A *Terry* investigation…involves a police investigation at close range, when the officer remains particularly vulnerable in part because a full custodial arrest has not been effected, and the officer must make a quick decision as to how to protect himself and others from possible danger."[17]

In such potentially dangerous circumstances, the Supreme Court has never required that officers place themselves in jeopardy simply to avoid the intrusion involved in a *Terry* encounter.

Whether a given contact between the police and citizens constitutes a seizure within the meaning of the Fourth Amendment is determined by "balancing the government interest involved against the nature of the intrusion on the individual."[18]

3. Probable Cause Required in Full Detention

The U.S. Supreme Court has held that the full impact of the Fourth Amendment comes into play only when the officer, by means of physical force or show of authority, has in some way restrained the liberty of a citizen.[19] Such a seizure must be supported by probable cause; otherwise, the arrest is unconstitutional. See Exhibit 2-8 for the consequences of an unconstitutional search or arrest. The effect of an unconstitutional arrest often has a profound impact on the state's case.

B. Probable Cause and Warrants

Later in this chapter, we will discuss how warrants are issued and the requirement of probable cause for both arrest and search warrants.

C. Probable Cause and Consent

Where the defendant **consents** to a search and seizure of potential evidence, the need for either a warrant or a showing of probable cause is eliminated.[20] Police officers who pull over motorists whom they believe to be acting suspiciously often ask for consent to search the automobile. If the driver consents, the police officer no longer needs probable cause. The suspect's consent has overridden the constitutional requirements. What is often so surprising is how many people who are transporting large amounts of illegal drugs often consent to a search of their vehicles.

> ### Pat Downs in Terry Stops
> "*Terry v. Ohio*,[14] has held that even though a police pat-down of a potentially dangerous individual may constitute a seizure within the meaning of the Fourth Amendment, it can be based on a showing of 'reasonable suspicion' to believe that criminal activity is afoot rather than the more rigorous standard of 'probable cause' to believe that a particular crime has been committed."[15]
>
> The officer is permitted to pat down and then "intrude beneath the surface only if he confirms his reasonable belief or suspicion by coming upon something which feels like a weapon."[16]

consent
Voluntary and active agreement.

- Evidence seized is ruled inadmissible.
- Suspect will often be released.
- Suspect may have civil remedy against officer.

Exhibit 2-8
Consequence of unconstitutional arrest or seizure

■ **BULLET POINT**
When a person gives valid consent to a search, he or she waives any objections to the evidence recovered.

INSIDER'S VIEWPOINT

Meeting with the client

Occasionally, a paralegal is called on to meet with the client to help prepare him or her for trial, or just to get some basic information about the warrant. "If the attorney gets tied up in court and he has an appointment with someone and can't see them then I could conduct the initial interview. I take the warrant, or citation or indictment that's been served against them and get some general information about what they've been charged with and any witnesses that they might have that we could communicate with. I make arrangements to get a copy of their criminal history."

—Linda McCurry, Criminal Defense Paralegal

fresh pursuit doctrine
A court-created doctrine that allows police officers to arrest suspects without warrants and to cross territorial boundaries while they are still pursuing the suspect.

Example of Probable Cause

In *Chambers v. Maroney*,[22] the arresting officers had a description of an alleged robber's clothing and car. The officers stopped a car matching the description, containing people who matched the description. The officers arrested them after discovering corroborating evidence in the car. The Supreme Court stated that the officers had sufficient probable cause to make the arrests, saying that a prudent officer would have believed that the defendants had committed a crime.

D. Specific Acts That Give Rise to Probable Cause

The U.S. Supreme Court has made rulings on very specific fact patterns in its interpretation of when probable cause does and does not exist.

1. Description Over the Radio

The Court has stated that an arresting officer does not need personal or direct knowledge of the facts that support probable cause. For instance, an officer may arrest a person simply because he matches a description relayed to the officer over the police radio.[21]

2. Suspicious or Unusual Behavior

When a police officer observes a suspect acting in a strange or unusual way, that behavior, coupled with other information about a crime having occurred, will often be enough to satisfy probable cause.[23]

3. Fresh Pursuit Doctrine

In addition to descriptions over the radio and suspicious behavior, an officer who is engaged in high-speed pursuit (otherwise known as "fresh pursuit") already has probable cause to detain because the suspect is actively fleeing the police. Under the **fresh pursuit doctrine**, if a police officer is pursuing a suspect who has committed a felony, then the officer can chase that person across county or state lines and arrest him even though the officer has no lawful authority to arrest in that jurisdiction. Of course, the fresh pursuit doctrine has its limitations, including rulings on just how "fresh" the pursuit must be. It is obviously not fresh pursuit if the officer arrests the suspect hours or even days after the pursuit has ended. In court rulings, fresh pursuit means just what it suggests—an ongoing, immediate pursuit that happens to cross some boundary.

4. Information Provided by Others: Confidential Informants

In *Illinois v. Gates*,[24] the United States Supreme Court held that probable cause may be based on an informant's tip. However, probable cause will exist only if, "under the totality of the circumstances, including the veracity and basis of knowledge of the informant, there is a fair probability that contraband or evidence of a crime will be found in a particular place."[25] In another case, a tip was received from a confidential informant who previously had provided reliable information to the police. This tip was corroborated on several essential elements. The Supreme Court held that "it is not unreasonable to conclude in this case that the independent corroboration by the police of significant aspects of the informer's predictions imparted some degree of reliability (to the other information provided by the informant)."[26]

Corroboration of the informant's tip can come from the officer's previous knowledge of the defendant's criminal activities.[27] When another police officer is the informant, the reliability of the information and of the informant is presumed as a matter of law.[28]

5. Anonymous Phone Calls

When police receive an anonymous phone call stating that a specific individual has committed a crime, that fact coupled with the officer's independent investigation or corroboration can provide sufficient probable cause. However, anonymous phone calls by themselves cannot establish probable cause. Courts give them a much higher degree of scrutiny. In a recent case, the U.S. Supreme Court ruled an arrest unconstitutional when police officers responded to a location after receiving an anonymous phone call and immediately arrested the suspect. Their failure to corroborate the details, according to the court, meant that they lacked probable cause.

Even when the anonymous phone caller gives detailed descriptions, probable cause may not be established. Something more is needed. For instance, did the anonymous phone caller predict the suspect's future actions? Such a prediction would demonstrate that the caller has some "inside information."[29]

Case Excerpt. Fresh Pursuit Doctrine

BOST V. STATE, 406 MD. 341, 958 A.2D 356 (2008) RAKER, J.

The question presented in this case is whether the Circuit Court for Prince George's County erred in denying the motion to suppress evidence seized by District of Columbia police officers after they entered Prince George's County, Maryland. Appellant challenges the validity of the officers' actions as violating the Maryland Uniform Act on Fresh Pursuit. Maryland Uniform Act on Fresh Pursuit, Md.Code (2001, 2006 Cum.Supp.), § 2–304 to–309 of the Criminal Procedure Article ("the Act"). We shall hold that the Act was not violated because the officers reasonably suspected that Bost had committed a felony when they crossed into Maryland and they had probable cause to arrest Bost at the time of his arrest.

The relevant provisions of Uniform Act on Fresh Pursuit in the case sub judice include § § 2–304 and 2–305. Section 2–305 of the Uniform Act on Fresh Pursuit reads in its entirety as follows:

(a) A member of a state, county, or municipal law enforcement unit of another state who enters this State in fresh pursuit and continues within this State in fresh pursuit of a person to arrest the person on the ground that the person is believed to have committed a felony in the other state has the same authority to arrest and hold the person in custody as has a member of a duly organized State, county, or municipal corporation law enforcement unit of this State to arrest and hold a person in custody on the ground that the person is believed to have committed a felony in this State.

(b) This section does not make unlawful an arrest in this State that would otherwise be lawful."

Section 2–304(b) sets forth the definition of "fresh pursuit" as follows:

(b) 'Fresh pursuit' includes:

   (1) fresh pursuit as defined by the common law; and
   (2) pursuit without unreasonable delay, but not necessarily instant pursuit, of a person who:

      (i) has committed or is reasonably suspected of having committed a felony; or
      (ii) is suspected of having committed a felony, although a felony has not been committed, if there is reasonable ground for believing that a felony has been committed."

I.

Appellant, Robert Bost, was indicted by the Grand Jury for Prince George's County on charges of possession with intent to distribute cocaine, possession of cocaine, wearing a dangerous weapon concealed on or about the person, and use of a machine gun for an aggressive purpose, which the State later amended to carrying a handgun on or about his person. Bost filed a motion to suppress the evidence seized by the police incident to his arrest, arguing that the out-of-state District of Columbia Metropolitan police, in arresting appellant in Maryland, acted in violation of the Maryland Uniform Act on Fresh Pursuit.

The Circuit Court held an evidentiary hearing on the motion to suppress the evidence. Various officers from the District of Columbia Metropolitan Police Department testified that, on November 29, 2005, sixteen Metropolitan police officers in four unmarked cars were patrolling the 800 block of Southern Avenue, SE, in Washington, D.C., as part of a Focus Mission Unit targeting street level narcotics and firearm recovery in high crime areas. The block divides the District of Columbia and Maryland. At approximately 6:00 P.M., three officers, wearing jackets with "Police" written across them, left their vehicle and walked towards about a dozen people who were drinking alcohol on the sidewalk in a no-loitering area. Officer Phillip testified that he "conducted a 'contact'," at which time, one of the people, later identified as Robert Bost, immediately left, walking away "in a briskful manner" while clutching his right waistband with his right elbow.

Officer Phillip said that Bost started picked up his pace, and "immediately took flight on foot crossing the street onto the Prince George's County side." Officer Phillip testified that he had reasonable, articulable suspicion that Bost was concealing something and that based upon his experience, he believed that Bost was "trying to conceal a weapon" and because Bost was "holding...his waistband, continuously looking back."

Bost ran into a wooded area, falling several times, each time clutching at his right side. The officers followed in pursuit, eventually crossing into Prince George's County, Maryland. Once in Maryland, the officers caught up to Bost and physically restrained him on the ground. As one officer attempted to grab Bost's elbows to turn him onto his side, the officer felt a metal object and indicated to the other officers "gun, gun." The officer unzipped Bost's jacket and discovered a black nine millimeter semiautomatic pistol with 21 rounds of ammunition. The gun was tied around Bost's neck to his body. Bost was arrested, and a further search incident to arrest revealed two large, white, rock-like substances and $140 from the pocket of Bost's pants. The Metropolitan Police immediately contacted Prince George's County officials, who responded and took custody of Bost.

The trial court denied Bost's motion to suppress the evidence. The trial court reasoned as follows:

> "This is one of those difficult cases where you have to balance a person's right to run I suppose versus the police department and law enforcement in general's right to inquire based on the circumstances of this case.
>
> "The facts are fairly clear, the defendant is in a drug trafficking area known to the police department in the District of Columbia. A group of people that number between 12 and 15 I believe. When the police arrive the defendant took flight clutching at his waistband. Certainly the police department and the police officers involved in this instance based on their training, experience, had cause to believe that crime was afoot here.
>
> "In chasing the defendant, after ordering him to stop several times, he continued to clutch at his side as if he had a weapon or something else illegal. Of course, they couldn't tell at the time. The question is do they have a right to inquire? I think they do.
>
> "I will deny the motion to suppress for those reasons. I think they had a right to inquire. I appreciate the argument of counsel, it is certainly to his credit. I will deny the motion to suppress."

Following the court's ruling, the case proceeded to trial before the court on a not guilty plea, agreed statement of facts, to the possession with intent to distribute cocaine and carrying a handgun on or about his person. The trial court found Bost guilty and sentenced him to three years incarceration, with all but one year suspended.

Bost noted a timely appeal to the Court of Special Appeals. This Court, on its own initiative, issued a writ of certiorari before the intermediate court decided the appeal to consider the ruling of the Circuit Court on appellant's motion to suppress.

II.

Appellant presents a single argument to this Court. He argues that the Circuit Court erred in denying appellant's motion to suppress, because the Metropolitan police officers violated the Uniform Act on Fresh Pursuit. In particular, appellant maintains that the Metropolitan officers lacked the authority to cross the state line into Maryland under § 2–305 of the Act, which grants the authority for an out-of-state officer "who enters this State in fresh pursuit and continues within this State in fresh pursuit of a person to arrest the person on the ground that the person is believed to have committed a felony in the other state." Appellant contends that the Metropolitan Police Officers did not have reasonable grounds to believe that Bost had committed a felony in the District of Columbia at the time the officers crossed into Maryland. He maintains that the fact that appellant was observed clutching his waistband did not give rise to a reasonable belief that a felony had been committed.

The State presents three arguments to support the search and seizure. First, the State contends that the Metropolitan police officers were authorized under the Act to enter into Maryland in fresh pursuit because they in fact had reasonable suspicion to believe that appellant had committed a felony. The State argues that the Act requires only reasonable suspicion at the time officers cross the border into Maryland, and not probable cause. Under this analysis, the State argues that the totality of the circumstances involved—including factors such as the high crime area in which Bost was located, Bost's unprovoked flight from police, and the police officer's experience and training in recognizing behavior such as Bost's clutching at his waistband as consistent with possession of a concealed weapon— meets the standard of reasonable suspicion. Second, the State argues that the arrest was lawful because one of the District of Columbia police officers had been deputized by the United States Marshal Service and therefore, while on duty, he is authorized to go anywhere to investigate cases and to arrest outside of the District of Columbia. Finally, the State argues that even if the statute was violated, the evidence should not be suppressed because the Act does not contain an exclusionary rule.

III.

In reviewing the ruling on a motion to suppress evidence, we consider only the evidence contained in the record of the suppression hearing. We extend great deference to the hearing judge's findings of fact and those findings will not be disturbed unless clearly erroneous. We review the evidence and the inferences that may be reasonably drawn in the light most favorable to the prevailing party. We make our own independent appraisal as to whether a constitutional right has been violated by reviewing the law and applying it to the facts of the case.

IV.
A.

Appellant does not contend that the police officers lacked probable cause to arrest him. Nor does he contend that his arrest violated the Fourth Amendment to the United States Constitution or Article 26 of the Maryland Declaration of Rights. His argument on appeal rests solely on an interpretation of the Uniform Act found at § 2–305 of the Criminal Law Article. Appellant claims that the Metropolitan police officers lacked the authority under the statute to cross the border into Maryland at the time they did so, and that the statute would be ineffective unless read broadly to include an exclusionary rule. In order to determine whether the Act was violated, we look to the canons of statutory interpretation.

The cardinal rule of statutory interpretation is to ascertain and effectuate the intent of the Legislature. In construing a statute, we look first to the plain language of the statute, and if that language is clear and unambiguous, we look no further than the text of the statute. A plain reading of the statute assumes none of its language is superfluous or nugatory. "We neither add nor delete words to a clear and unambiguous statute to give it a meaning not reflected by the words the Legislature used or engage in forced or subtle interpretation in an attempt to extend or limit the statute's meaning." We have often stated that if the language of the statute is not ambiguous, either inherently or by reference to other relevant laws or circumstances, our inquiry as to legislative intent ends. If the meaning of the plain language is ambiguous or unclear, to discern legislative intent, we look to the legislative history, prior case law, the purposes upon which the statutory framework was based, and the statute as a whole.

The Uniform Act on Fresh Pursuit, including Maryland's version of the model act, "consists of a grant of authority from the enacting state to officers from other states, permitting those officers to enter the enacting state." The Maryland Uniform Act on Fresh Pursuit reads, in relevant part, as follows:

(a) "A member of a state, county, or municipal law enforcement unit of another state who enters this State in fresh pursuit and continues within this State in fresh pursuit of a person to arrest the person on the ground that the person is believed to have committed a felony in the other state has the same authority to arrest and hold the person in custody as has a member of a duly organized State, county, or municipal corporation law enforcement unit of this State to arrest and hold a person in custody on the ground that the person is believed to have committed a felony in this State."

Based on a plain reading, the statute authorizes a state, county, or municipal law enforcement officer of another state to enter Maryland if in "fresh pursuit." Both Maryland and the District of Columbia expressly permit officers from the other jurisdiction to enter their respective state territories for the purpose of pursuing persons (in hot pursuit) who reasonably are believed to have committed a felony. A valid arrest requires probable cause. In keeping with the law of arrest, the Act requires that the officer have probable cause at the time of the arrest. In order to determine whether the officer has authority to enter into Maryland, however, it is necessary to examine the concept of "fresh pursuit" and its statutory definition.

The Act, in § 2–304(b), defines fresh pursuit as follows:

(b) "'Fresh pursuit' includes:

   (1) fresh pursuit as defined by the common law
   "Two exceptions have developed under the common law rule, whereby an officer acting outside his jurisdiction may arrest an individual: (1) if the officer is engaging in fresh pursuit of a suspected felon; or (2) if the officer is acting with the authority of a private citizen to make an arrest."
   Therefore, under the common law, police officers may effect an extra-territorial arrest outside their jurisdiction if they are in "fresh pursuit" of a person that has committed a felony.

   (2) pursuit without unreasonable delay, but not necessarily instant pursuit, of a person who:

      (i) has committed or is reasonably suspected of having committed a felony; or

(ii) is suspected of having committed a felony, although a felony has not been committed, if there is reasonable ground for believing that a felony has been committed."

We focus on the language of § 2–304(b)(2)(i), which includes pursuit of one who "is reasonably suspected of having committed a felony."

Under the Act, an out-of-state officer is authorized to enter Maryland to arrest and hold a person in custody if that officer has reasonable suspicion that a person has committed a felony. "Reasonable suspicion" is a less demanding standard than probable cause. As the Supreme Court stated in Sokolow, reasonable suspicion is more than an "inchoate and unparticularized suspicion or 'hunch,'" but is "considerably less than proof of wrongdoing by a preponderance of the evidence" and less than probable cause, which is "'a fair probability that contraband or evidence of a crime will be found.'" While less than probable cause is required under the Act, nonetheless, "reasonable suspicion" requires that the officer articulate more than an "inchoate and unparticularized suspicion or 'hunch'" of criminal activity.

Our reading of the statute conforms with the purpose of the Uniform Act on Fresh Pursuit, which is to extend authority to officers from other jurisdictions to cross state lines to arrest criminals who might otherwise use state lines to escape apprehension. The Council of State Governments, The Handbook on Interstate Crime Control 119 (Rev. ed.1966), states as follows:

> "The purpose of the Uniform Act on Interstate Fresh Pursuit is to prevent criminals from utilizing state lines to handicap our police in their apprehension. At the present time our most desperate criminals head straight across state lines after the commission of a crime, knowing that there is comparative safety beyond the border. For in the foreign state the pursuing officer from the state wherein the crime was committed is, in general, no longer an officer. This abnormality, so contrary to all justice and reason, is remedied in a simple manner by the Fresh Pursuit Act. Thereunder, the moment an officer in fresh pursuit of a criminal crosses a state line, the state he enters will authorize him to catch and arrest such criminal within its bounds. The statute grants this right only when the officer is in fresh pursuit of a criminal, that is, pursuit without unreasonable delay, by a member of a duly organized peace unit, and only in cases of felonies or supposed felonies occurring outside the boundaries of the state adopting the act. It is thus based upon the little-known common-law doctrine of fresh pursuit, from which the statute has derived its name."

The Court of Special Appeals reached the same conclusion when considering the Uniform Act on Fresh Pursuit in *Hutchinson v. State*, 38 Md.App. 160, 380 A.2d 232 (1977). In Hutchinson, a Montgomery County police officer entered into the District of Columbia and arrested Hutchinson in relation to a homicide. Hutchinson was convicted and sentenced for felony murder and use of a handgun in the Circuit Court for Montgomery County. Hutchinson appealed, arguing that, among other things, the arrest by a Montgomery County officer in the District of Columbia was unlawful. It was clear that the officer had probable cause at the time of Hutchinson's arrest, but not at the point at which the officer crossed the border into the District of Columbia, following Hutchinson's car. Interpreting the District of Columbia statute, which mirrors essentially the Maryland statute, the Court of Special Appeals stated as follows:

"Was the statute intended to blind the eye and stop the ear of an officer who entered the District under its authority? We think not.

"The circumstances in *State v. Tillman*, 208 Kan. 954, 494 P.2d 1178 (1972), closely parallel the subject case. Both Kansas and Missouri had enacted the Uniform Law on Fresh Pursuit. In Tillman, as here, the arresting officers entered the foreign State without probable cause to arrest. In Tillman, as here, a missing factor essential to probable cause was supplied by knowledge gained in the foreign State. The Supreme Court of Kansas, sustaining the validity of the arrest, said at 1182:

"In the case at bar the robbers fled from the scene of the robbery in Kansas City, Kansas, to Kansas City, Missouri, where they were apprehended 90 minutes later. The pursuit was continuous, uninterrupted and without unreasonable delay. It was a "fresh pursuit"; hence the arrest of the appellants by the Kansas police officers in Missouri was a valid arrest since the police had actual knowledge that the robbery had been committed and since the appellants were identified in Missouri as the robbers by Craig (Moon) Davis prior to their arrest at Southtown Motors." The court then reasoned as follows:

> "The Uniform Act on Fresh Pursuit should not be so narrowly construed as to alter the firmly fixed rule of law that the existence of probable cause at the time of an arrest should be the measure of its validity. We think that the statute intended no such alteration."

"Accordingly, we hold that the statute was intended to permit any member of an organized peace unit of any State to enter in fresh pursuit; to continue in fresh pursuit within the District; and to arrest the person pursued, whom he has probable cause to believe, at the time of arrest, committed a felony in the place of the officer's jurisdiction." Implicit in the court's holding was that probable cause was not required when the officer crossed into the District of Columbia in fresh pursuit.

Our holding comports with the standard adopted by several states that have examined the issue. In *State v. Ferrell*, 218 Neb. 463, 356 N.W.2d 868 (1984), the Supreme Court of Nebraska held that requiring probable cause at the time of crossing the state line into Iowa "is too strict an interpretation of the statute which authorizes pursuit of a person 'who is reasonably suspected of having committed a felony.' This is sufficient to authorize an investigatory stop." One commentator notes as follows:

"In some states, fresh pursuit statutes have been interpreted to authorize not only pursuit in order to arrest, but also pursuit for the purpose of conducting a Terry stop The justification generally given is that police need not have probable cause to arrest at the time they cross their jurisdictional limits, but only at the time they make the arrest. One court has noted also its belief that a close pursuit stop is within the 'spirit' of the state fresh pursuit statute.

B.

We turn to the facts of the instant case. Reviewing whether reasonable suspicion exists, we have stated as follows:

> "While there is no litmus test to define the 'reasonable suspicion' standard, it has been defined as nothing more than 'a particularized and objective basis for suspecting the particular person stopped of criminal activity,' and as a common sense, nontechnical conception that considers factual and practical aspects of daily life and how reasonable and prudent people act...Moreover,

'when evaluating the validity of a detention, we must examine the totality of the circumstances the whole picture.'"

The test is "the totality of the circumstances," viewed through the eyes of a reasonable, prudent, police officer. In *Ferris v. State*, 355 Md. 356, 391–92, 735 A.2d 491, 510 (1999), we explained as follows:

"A police officer, 'by reason of training and experience, may be able to explain the special significance of...observed facts.' Thus, conduct that appears innocuous to the average layperson may in fact be suspicious when observed by a trained law enforcement official. The Fourth Amendment, however, does not allow the law enforcement official to simply assert that apparently innocent conduct was suspicious to him or her; rather the officer must offer 'the factual basis upon which he or she bases the conclusion.'"

In *Alabama v. White*, 496 U.S. 325, 110 S.Ct. 2412, 110 L.Ed.2d 301 (1990), the Supreme Court elaborated on the concept of reasonable suspicion, stating as follows:

"Reasonable suspicion is a less demanding standard than probable cause not only in the sense that reasonable suspicion can be established with information that is different in quantity or content than that required to establish probable cause, but also in the sense that reasonable suspicion can arise from information that is less reliable than that required to show probable cause...An unverified tip from a known informant might not have been reliable enough to establish probable cause, but nevertheless found it sufficiently reliable to justify a Terry stop. Reasonable suspicion, like probable cause, is dependent upon both the content of information possessed by police and its degree of reliability. Both factors—quantity and quality—are considered in the 'totality of the circumstances—the whole picture,' that must be taken into account when evaluating whether there is reasonable suspicion."

In *United States v. Cortez*, 449 U.S. 411, 418, 101 S.Ct. 690, 695, 66 L.Ed.2d 621 (1981), former Chief Justice Burger discussed the appropriate test, the totality of the circumstances test, pointing out that it contains two interdependent analytical techniques:

"The idea that an assessment of the whole picture must yield a particularized suspicion contains two elements, each of which must be present before a stop is permissible. First, the assessment must be based upon all of the circumstances. The analysis proceeds with various objective observations, information from police reports, if such are available, and consideration of the modes or patterns of operation of certain kinds of lawbreakers. From these data, a trained officer draws inferences and makes deductions—inferences and deductions that might well elude an untrained person."

The United States Supreme Court has made clear that unprovoked flight is enough to support reasonable suspicion that a crime has been committed. The Court explained as follows:

"In this case, moreover, it was not merely respondent's presence in an area of heavy narcotics trafficking that aroused the officers' suspicion, but his unprovoked flight upon noticing the police. Our cases have also recognized that nervous, evasive behavior is a pertinent factor in determining reasonable suspicion. Headlong flight—wherever it occurs—is the consummate act of evasion: it is not necessarily indicative of wrongdoing, but it is certainly suggestive of such. In reviewing the propriety of an officer's conduct, courts do not have available empirical studies dealing with inferences drawn from suspicious behavior, and we cannot reasonably demand scientific certainty from judges or law enforcement officers where none exists. Thus, the determination of reasonable suspicion must be based on commonsense judgments and inferences about human behavior. We conclude Officer Nolan was justified in suspecting that Wardlow was involved in criminal activity, and, therefore, in investigating further."

The Circuit Court, in its ruling, pointed out that the police saw appellant in a drug trafficking area, and that when the police approached, he fled, clutching his waistband. The court found also that after ordering appellant to stop several times, appellant continued to clutch at his side as if he had a weapon or something else illegal. The court's finding that "they had a right to inquire" was in effect a finding that the officer's had reasonable suspicion to stop appellant for further investigation.

We hold that the Metropolitan police officers had reasonable suspicion to believe that appellant had committed a felony and therefore, they were authorized under the Act to pursue appellant into the State of Maryland. Under the law of the District of Columbia, it is a felony to carry a pistol without a license. We take judicial notice of the law of the District of Columbia pursuant to Md.Code (1974, 2006 Repl.Vol.), § 10–501 of the Courts & Judicial Proceedings Article, which states that "every court of this State shall take judicial notice of the common law and statutes of every state, territory, and other jurisdiction of the United States, and of every other jurisdiction having a system of law based on the common law of England."

Appellant was seen by the police in a high crime, drug trafficking area. Appellant fled from the police and the flight was unprovoked. The nature of the area is a factor in assessing reasonable suspicion. The officers testified that they believed that appellant was clutching and concealing a weapon at his right side and that, based on their experience with other suspects, the clutching conduct was consistent with possession of a concealed weapon. Guns often accompany drugs, and many courts have found an "indisputable nexus between drugs and guns."

The Metropolitan police officers were authorized under the Uniform Act on Fresh Pursuit to enter into Maryland in fresh pursuit of appellant. The Circuit Court did not err in denying appellant's motion to suppress the evidence seized from him.

JUDGMENT OF THE CIRCUIT COURT FOR PRINCE GEORGE'S COUNTY AFFIRMED. COSTS TO BE PAID BY APPELLANT.

CASE QUESTIONS

1. What is the primary question in this appeal?
2. What crime did the original officer believe that Bost was committing?
3. What reason did the trial judge give for denying the motion to suppress?
4. Were the officers justified in crossing into Maryland to apprehend Bost? Why or why not?
5. Does the Maryland statute apply to out-of-state officers? Explain.

6. Stops at Sobriety, or Roadside, Check Points

Police often set up roadblocks for the purpose of checking vehicles for compliance with state automobile regulations. These roadblocks are generally established on secondary streets, and all cars going in both directions are briefly stopped and the drivers questioned. If while speaking with a driver the officer suspects that some crime had occurred or is occurring (such as driving under the influence), the officer is justified in detaining the driver. The Supreme Court has specifically stated that roadblocks are not a constitutional violation as long as certain safeguards are in place. For instance, all cars must be stopped. Police are not allowed to single out cars for "special treatment" unless they have some suspicion of foul play. Officers cannot stop cars driven only by African Americans, for instance, because this would violate the U.S. Constitution.

The rationale for roadside checkpoints is to prevent drunk driving. "No one can seriously dispute the magnitude of the drunken driving problem or the States' interest in eradicating it. Conversely, the weight bearing on the other scale—the measure of the intrusion on motorists stopped briefly at sobriety checkpoints—is slight."[30]

Several factors will determine whether a roadblock is reasonable and constitutional. One factor is whether the roadblock was established "as a legitimate law enforcement technique to subject all drivers along the road...to a brief stop so as to detect signs of intoxication." Another factor to be considered is whether the defendant was singled out by officers (unconstitutional) or whether all drivers were stopped (constitutional).[31]

7. Stopping for Unrelated Offenses—Pretextual Stops

A police officer's decision to stop a suspect for the commission of a traffic violation is not unlawful merely because the officer had reason to believe that the suspect was implicated in committing other crimes. What is necessary is that when the officer pulls over a suspect, he has a valid reason for doing so, independent of the officer's suspicion regarding the other crimes. These are referred to as **pretextual stops** and are constitutional as long as the stop is based on a real violation.[32] Even if the officer had a strong suspicion that the defendant was involved in some other crime, if the officer detains the suspect for a minor traffic violation merely as a means of trying to gather more information on the other suspected crime, it is not a violation of the Constitution.

8. Flight

One question that often comes up is what happens when the police encounter a person on the street and when they begin to question him or her, the suspect flees? Courts have ruled that **flight** gives the officers probable cause to arrest.[33] Flight, by itself, may give rise to probable cause to arrest.

9. Presence at a Crime Scene

Mere presence at a scene where a crime has occurred does not, without something more, give rise to probable cause to detain all persons present.

pretextual stop
The detention or arrest of a person for a minor offense, usually a traffic violation, when the officer suspects that the defendant has committed a more serious crime.

flight
When a suspect flees the police after being told to stop.

■ **BULLET POINT**
An officer can stop a motorist for a traffic violation even though the officer suspects the driver of committing an unrelated crime.

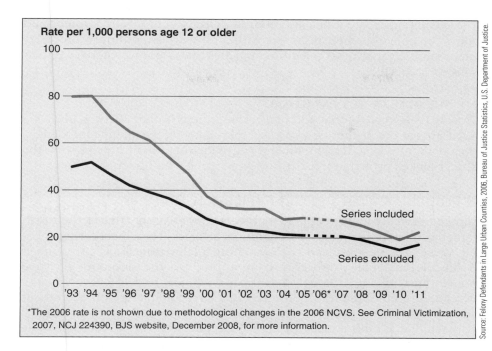

Rate per 1,000 persons age 12 or older

Series included

Series excluded

*The 2006 rate is not shown due to methodological changes in the 2006 NCVS. See Criminal Victimization, 2007, NCJ 224390, BJS website, December 2008, for more information.

Exhibit 2-9
Violent victimization with series included and excluded, 1993–2011

Source: Felony Defendants in Large Urban Counties, 2006, Bureau of Justice Statistics, U.S. Department of Justice.

A person must take some action that gives the officer probable cause to arrest a specific person, not just simply arrest everyone at the scene where evidence of a crime has been found, especially when the evidence is found on the person of a single individual and not on the others present.[34]

Interestingly enough, although the overall perception in society is that there are many crime scenes and that violent crime in general has increased, the reality is quite different. See Exhibit 2-9.

THE ROLE OF THE PARALEGAL:

Case law in the area of probable cause is constantly changing. Always stay on top of the most recent decisions by the U.S.Supreme Court and state supreme courts in this area. One way to do this is to review Advance Sheets from these courts. Another way is to subscribe to the various web sites that now routinely post these decisions. (See "Web Sites" at the end of this chapter.)

E. Probable Cause and Exigent Circumstances

Although warrants are generally preferred, there are times when the police cannot procure one. For instance, where police have reason to believe that vital evidence is about to be destroyed or that by failing to act some crime will be committed, police are authorized to seize evidence and make arrests without a warrant. When a person's life is in danger, for example, the police may enter the premises or conduct a search without a warrant.

exigent circumstances
Circumstances that permit law enforcement officers to conduct a search or arrest a person without a warrant, but only when there is a legitimate threat to persons or evidence.

These emergency situations are referred to as **exigent circumstances** and allow the police to enter premises without a warrant, but only after they can show that there was a legitimate belief that there was danger to persons or property.

THE ROLE OF THE PARALEGAL:
Closely reviewing the file and questioning the criminal client is always a good idea at the beginning of a case. For instance, the client can be questioned about any statements the officer made that might indicate that the officer lacked probable cause, or was operating on a hunch.

F. Probable Cause and Gut-Feelings or Hunches

Unlike television cops, real police officers cannot simply follow their own hunches in stopping a car or detaining a suspect. They must have probable cause. The next time you are watching a television show, ask yourself if the fictional police are even coming close to the standard that real police must follow. Although an officer does not need to prove that the defendant committed an offense beyond a reasonable doubt, the officer cannot base probable cause on mere suspicion, gut feelings, or hunches.[35] In a real-life situation, activities are fluid, and what began as reasonable suspicion for a stop and frisk can, in just a few seconds, move to probable cause to arrest.[36]

■ **BULLET POINT**
Probable cause cannot be based on feelings, gut feelings, or emotional factors.

G. Probable Cause and the Drug Courier Profile

In recent years, the use of the "drug courier profile" has fallen into disuse, primarily because of challenges to the use of the profile as a means to assist law enforcement to stop suspected drug couriers. In reality, profiling resulted in a disproportionate number of cases involving minorities. The idea behind the drug courier profile was that individuals who transported narcotics frequently followed similar patterns. These days, law enforcement uses other methods to identify suspected drug couriers and dealers, relying more on individual and specific facts than on whether the person fits a set of predetermined characteristics in a profile.

IV. Arrest and Search Warrants

warrant
Written permission given by a judge to a police officer to arrest a person, conduct a search, seize an item, etc.

At law, **warrants** are preferable over arrests without warrants. There are times, however, when it is impossible for a police officer to obtain a warrant—for instance, when he seeks to arrest a fleeing suspect. When dealing with seizures of evidence, the warrant preference is even greater. Courts take a dim view of evidence seizures carried out without warrants, except in certain situations.

The fourth amendment states "no Warrants shall issue, but upon probable cause, supported by Oath or affirmation, and particularly describing the place to be searched, and the persons or things to be seized." This provision sets the ground rules for all warrants and search warrants in particular.

Although probable cause to arrest and probable cause to search have generally been considered to amount to the same standard, in practice they are applied differently. Probable cause to arrest really goes to the ultimate issue of the guilt of the defendant. Probable cause to search boils down to the likelihood of finding evidence in a particular place. In many cases, it appears that probable cause to arrest is actually a higher standard than the probable cause necessary to justify a search warrant. Certainly, the consequences to the defendant are different. In one, he loses his liberty; in another, his property.

A **search warrant** is a warrant issued by a judge that authorizes the police to search a private residence or another area and seize particular kinds of property. As such, a search warrant should more properly be called a *search and seizure warrant*. One of the most important issues that a magistrate must determine before issuing a warrant is the level of **expectation of privacy** in the area to be searched. There are instances, for example, where a person's expectation of privacy is very low, such as activities carried out in public, where a warrant may not be required. On the other hand, a person has his or her highest level of expectation of privacy in the home. In such a case, a search warrant would almost always be required to search a home. Expectation of privacy involves an analysis of the level of protections that the Constitution offers to individuals. Police are authorized to enter the private residence of a person, conduct a search, and take away items described in the warrant. When presented with a fully authorized search warrant, the property owner cannot legally interfere with the police. When in doubt, the courts usually require a warrant. "In a doubtful or marginal case a search under a warrant may be sustainable where without one it would fail."[38]

A. Warrants Required Only for "Government" Conduct

It is important to note at the outset that the search warrant requirement applies only to the government, or more specifically, law enforcement. Private individuals are not required to seek search warrants unless they are acting under the direction of law enforcement.

B. Applying for a Search Warrant

When police officers want to obtain a search warrant, they usually go to a local judge and fill out an **affidavit** for a search warrant. Remember that the actual procedure can vary considerably from jurisdiction to jurisdiction. In this application, police officers list all of the relevant facts to support their request, including the nature of the suspected crime, the facts lending support to their contention that evidence of a crime will be found in a certain place, and the items they want to seize at that place. At this point,

---

Probable Cause

"Whether or not a warrant has been issued, all arrests and search warrants must be based on probable cause."[37]

search warrant
A warrant that authorizes the police to enter and conduct a search and to seize items that are evidence of a crime.

expectation of privacy
A constitutional standard that a court must determine before issuing a search warrant. In situations where a suspect has a high expectation of privacy, such as in the suspect's home, a warrant will be required; if low or nonexistent, no warrant is required.

■ **BULLET POINT**
A search warrant allows law enforcement to search and to seize evidence of a crime.

affidavit
A written statement in which a person swears an oath that the facts contained are true.

the judge reviews the affidavit and then has the police officer take an oath that the material contained in it is true.

The reason that the U.S. Constitution calls for a warrant is that the process of applying for a search warrant necessarily involves a disinterested, neutral third party: the judge. The judge is usually the only person who is authorized to issue a warrant. A police officer must convince the judge (or magistrate) that probable cause exists to search and seize evidence. To do this, police officers must present the basic case to the judge. This acts as a safeguard against police overreaction. The judge is required by law to act in a neutral manner. If the judge does not believe that there is sufficient probable cause to issue the warrant, the judge has the responsibility of refusing to do so. On the other hand, if a judge does believe that probable cause exists, this has the effect of insulating the police officer from claims of exceeding his or her authority.

A police officer can establish this evidence through live testimony or, in the case of a search warrant, through a signed affidavit. The affidavit does not have to establish the suspect's guilt. It only has to establish that it is more likely than not that the suspect committed the crime or that evidence tending to prove a crime will be found in a particular place.

Whatever the source of the information, the judge must make a commonsense evaluation of the evidence and then decide if there is a fair probability that evidence of a crime is likely to be found at a specific place. When the search warrant is later challenged at trial as unconstitutional, reviewing courts will only require that the judge had a "substantial basis" for reaching this conclusion. See Exhibit 2-12 for the requirements for the issuance of a warrant. If the judge did not, then the search will be ruled unconstitutional and the evidence obtained will be inadmissible. Because appellate courts will make this ruling only when the judge is

> "Affidavits are normally drafted by non-lawyers in the midst and haste of a criminal investigation. Technical requirements of elaborate specificity once exacted under common law pleadings have no proper place in this area."[39]

Exhibit 2-10

Probable cause for a search warrant can be based on

1. Physical observations by the police officer or;
2. Hearsay evidence provided to the officer by another source or informant

Exhibit 2-11

Law enforcement can obtain information for a search warrant

- Police officers
- Government agents
- Citizens
- Paid informants
- Eye witnesses
- Victims

- Sworn testimony and/or affidavit by a police officer
- Describing with particularity the place to be searched and the items sought to be seized
- Basis for the belief that evidence will be found at this location
- Signature by judge authorizing the search and seizure of specific items

Exhibit 2-12
Format requirements for issuance of a search warrant

"clearly wrong," the chances of overturning a search warrant on appeal are usually slim.

Numerous court decisions have established that warrants should be read in a commonsense fashion. The U.S. Supreme Court does not impose highly technical rules on search warrants. Common misspellings, for instance, will not invalidate a search warrant. Although television and movie producers commonly complain about mass murderers being released on a "technicality," in the real world, warrants are given some latitude. The U.S. Supreme Court has approved of this more lenient treatment of affidavits and search warrants, reasoning that a highly technical requirement would only discourage police officers from applying for search warrants in the first place.

C. Exceptions to the Search Warrant Requirement

Although there is a preference for searches and seizures to be carried out with a warrant, that does not mean that a search is automatically invalid without one. The U.S. Supreme Court has created several categories of searches that may be conducted without a warrant. Almost all of these exceptions, however, involve unusual situations or time constraints on law enforcement. The general rule remains: Unless the search falls within one of the exceptions, a warrant must be obtained. The exceptions include the following:

- "Plain view"
- "Open fields"
- Dropped evidence or "dropsy cases"
- Garbage
- Contraband
- Stop and frisk
- U.S. Border searches
- Use of specially trained dogs
- Consent
- Good faith

BULLET POINT
There are numerous exceptions to the general rule that a search must be conducted with a warrant.

plain view doctrine
A court doctrine that allows police to search without a warrant when they see evidence of a crime in an unconcealed manner.

open fields doctrine
A court principle that allows police to search without a warrant when the evidence is located in a public setting such as farmland or beside a road.

1. "Plain View"

Courts developed the **plain view doctrine** in response to a common dilemma. When police officers execute a search warrant looking for specific items but come across other items that are clearly illegal, are they permitted to seize them? Under the plain view doctrine, the answer is yes. As the U.S. Supreme Court said in *Harris v. U.S.*,[40] "It has long been settled that objects falling in the plain view of an officer who has a right to be in the position to have that view are subject to seizure and may be introduced into evidence." However, the plain view doctrine does not permit police officers to seize any evidence at any time. The officers must have a legitimate reason to be in position to see the object. For instance, an officer who stops a motorist for speeding and while questioning the motorist sees an automatic weapon lying on the front seat would be justified in seizing the item without a warrant.

2. "Open Fields"

Another exception to the search warrant requirement involves items in open fields or farmland. The Fourth Amendment was specifically designed to protect people in their homes and businesses. Courts have been reluctant to apply this same level of protection to open fields. "An individual may not legitimately demand privacy for activities conducted out of doors in fields, except in the area immediately surrounding the home."[41]

Some states have not extended the **open fields doctrine** as far as the U.S. Supreme Court has indicated. You should study to what extent the open fields doctrine applies in your state.

3. Dropped Evidence or "Dropsy Cases"

When police officers are chasing a fleeing suspect and the suspect drops or throws away some evidence, police do not have to obtain a search warrant to seize it. Many courts refer to these cases as "dropsy" cases because many suspects drop incriminating evidence when confronted by the police. The inherent problem with these cases is making the connection between the recovered evidence and the suspect. For instance, police chase a suspected drug dealer, they see him fling out an arm, and then they retrieve a bag containing three rocks of crack cocaine. How can the police be sure that this bag belongs to this suspect? Generally, a police officer will testify about the circumstances of the arrest, the area in which the item was thrown, and the condition of the item when it was recovered. For example, if it was a rainy night but the bag was still relatively dry when it was recovered, that would indicate that the bag was not lying on the ground for a long period of time.

4. Garbage

In *California v. Greenwood*,[42] the U.S. Supreme Court held that there is no privacy expectation in garbage. When police want to search trashcans that have been placed on the street for collection, they do not have to obtain a warrant to do so. The U.S. Supreme Court has ruled that there is no reasonable expectation of privacy for discarded garbage.[43]

5. Contraband

The Fourth Amendment does not protect items that are illegal to possess. **Contraband**, such as illegal weapons or narcotics, can be seized by law enforcement without a warrant whenever they are discovered. Under the Fourth Amendment, there is no reasonable expectation of privacy in items that are illegal to possess in the first place.

contraband
Things that are illegal to import, export, transport, or possess.

6. Stop and Frisk

Police officers have the right to pat down a suspect during a brief detention and to remove any weapons without a search warrant. This provision is designed primarily to protect the safety of the officers, but when a weapon is discovered during a pat down, it can be admitted into evidence at trial even though the officers seized it without a warrant.

7. U.S. Border Searches

U.S. Customs and Border Patrol officers, among others, are authorized to search luggage and other belongings at border crossings into the United States. These searches can be carried out without a search warrant, but they do not give the officers involved complete freedom to search anyone and everything. As a general rule, these officers can perform a cursory search. Any additional or intrusive searches would likely require a search warrant.

8. Use of Specially Trained Dogs

The U.S. Supreme Court has stated that the use of specially trained dogs to detect narcotics, explosives, or other items does not fall under the protection of the Fourth Amendment. Therefore, no search warrant is required to use a "drug dog" to sniff the exterior of luggage or automobiles.[44]

9. Consent

When a person gives law enforcement officers consent to search, the requirement of a search warrant is waived. Once valid and knowing consent has been given, police are permitted to conduct a thorough search and do not have to apply for a search warrant. In cases where police testify that a suspect gave them consent to search, the issue is often whether the consent was given knowingly and intelligently. Consent that is obtained by force or threats is not consent at all, and any evidence obtained may be suppressed by application of the Exclusionary Rule. (See Chapter 4.)

10. Good Faith

Several cases have upheld technically faulty warrants when the police officers were obviously acting in good faith. When a police officer has no reason to suspect that a warrant is technically flawed, the courts may not employ the Exclusionary Rule (see later) to keep the seized evidence from being admitted at trial. However, good faith will only go so far. Before applying the good faith exception, courts must also look to other features of the case.[45] A police officer must have an objective, reasonable ground to believe that the warrant was validly issued. Where a warrant is so obviously defective that no trained police officer could reasonably believe that the warrant was correct, the **good faith exception** does not apply.[46]

D. Limitations on Search Warrants

Search warrants must be executed within a reasonable time period after they are issued. If not, they become **stale**. A stale warrant is no longer valid. A warrant becomes stale when the circumstances originally involved in issuing it have changed substantially. For instance, a magistrate judge issues a warrant authorizing the search of a vessel believed to be storing a large quantity of drugs. By the time the warrant is executed, the ship has been unloaded and has already set out to sea. The warrant is now stale. If the police now want to search the trucks on which the drugs were loaded, they most likely must apply for a new warrant.

Staleness is an issue that is very much dependent on the facts and the items to be searched. Two days between issuance and execution of a search warrant for drugs might be too long, but in one case, a court held that a seven-month wait between the issuance and execution of a search warrant for child pornography did not make the warrant stale.[47]

To avoid this problem, a warrant may have to be executed quickly. Narcotics, for example, are produced for the express purpose of being consumed.[48] Staleness may not be such an issue when the goods are more permanent in nature (illegal automatic weapons, for instance). In some cases, law enforcement may apply for an **anticipatory warrant** (i.e., a warrant authorizing a search and seizure of illegal items at some future time).

A warrant must state with "specificity" the places to be searched and the items to be seized. If a warrant fails to meet this standard, the subsequent search may be ruled unconstitutional because it is too **vague**. A warrant must state with specificity the place to be searched and the items to be seized. A warrant authorizing the seizure of "all suspected items" would be vague to the point of absurdity. Such a warrant would give the police the power to seize anything and everything they chose to take. Such a warrant would be considered too vague to be enforceable.

E. Penalty for an Unconstitutional Search: the Exclusionary Rule

When a court finds that a search was unconstitutional, what penalty does it impose? The simple answer is that whatever evidence has been seized cannot be used at trial. This is the so-called Exclusionary Rule. By refusing to permit law enforcement to use illegally obtained evidence, the courts force police and prosecution to follow the constitutional requirements. (For a detailed discussion of the Exclusionary Rule, see Chapter 4.)

---

good faith exception
An exception to the rule that a valid search warrant must be issued; under this doctrine, if the officer has a reasonable belief that a search warrant is properly executed, any evidence seized, even though the warrant is defective, will not be excluded.

stale
When too much time has passed between the application and issuance of a warrant and the search that it authorizes.

anticipatory warrant
A warrant issued for contraband or evidence that has not yet arrived at its final destination.

vague
A warrant that fails to meet the specificity requirements of the Fourth Amendment.

ETHICAL CONSIDERATION: SPECIAL ISSUES FOR THE PROSECUTION PARALEGAL

Prosecutors have an ethical duty to seek justice, not get convictions. A paralegal who works with prosecutors must keep this duty foremost in mind. Occasionally, a prosecution paralegal will come across evidence that is beneficial to the defense or shows that the defendant is innocent of the crime. This material must be brought to the attention of the prosecutor immediately. In most cases, this evidence will result in the dismissal of the case or other action. Prosecutors take this duty very seriously, and correspondingly, paralegals who work with them must have a high standard of honesty and fair dealing. A lax attitude toward ethics for a prosecution office can result in a black mark against the entire criminal justice system.

Having said this, however, there are specific issues that often develop early in the case that a defense is not entitled to know. One of them involves confidential informants. A confidential informant is someone who provides information to the police. These people are often placed in a dangerous position: If their identity were to become known early in the prosecution, the person arrested might take drastic action in retaliation. As a result, prosecutors often zealously guard the identity of confidential informants during the early phases of a case. Later, as the case comes to trial, the confidential informant's identity will often be known to the defendant, but a prosecution paralegal should be on guard not to reveal this information until given the go-ahead by the prosecutor.

✓ Paralegal To Do List

Information about the client's arrest that could prove to be important later:

- Was the client warned?
- That he had a right to remain silent?
- That anything could be used against him?
- That he had a right to a lawyer before making a statement?
- That if he could not afford a lawyer, that one would be appointed for him?
- What did client say to these warning?
- Was he searched? If yes, where? When? Who else was present? Was anything seized?
- Did the client give permission for the search?
- Did the officer explain why the search was being done?
- Was anything found?
- To whom did it belong?
- What did the police do with the item?

Chapter Summary

Both arrests and search warrants must be justified by probable cause. The probable cause requirement is set out in the Fourth Amendment. Police officers are prohibited from simply arresting someone on a hunch. They must have an explainable, rational basis for arresting a suspect. However, not all detentions result in arrests. Police officers are authorized to detain a person briefly without the requirement of probable cause. In these brief encounters, police may ask questions of a person and even pat down the person for weapons. However, to go any further than that, police must have probable cause. Search warrants also have a probable cause requirement. Before police are authorized to search, they must demonstrate this probable cause to a judge or magistrate. If the magistrate agrees, he or she will issue a search warrant. A search warrant allows police to enter premises, conduct a thorough search, and seize evidence of a crime. If police seize items without a warrant and without any other justification, the Exclusionary Rule may be employed against them. This means that the evidence seized illegally cannot be used at trial.

WEB SITES

Immigration & Customs Enforcement (ICE)
www.ice.gov

Legal Information Institute – Search Warrants
http://www.law.cornell.edu/wex/search_warrant

Maine State Court System
http://www.courts.state.me.us/

New York Court System
www.courts.state.ny.us/litigants/courtguides/index.shtml

Overview of Search Warrants
www.law.cornell.edu/wex/search_warrant

Texas Court System
www.courts.state.tx.us

Washington State Court System
http://www.courts.wa.gov/

Wisconsin State Court System
http://www.wicourts.gov/

REVIEW QUESTIONS

1. Is probable cause for an arrest the same standard required for a search warrant? Explain.

2. Can drug search dogs be used to help establish probable cause to search?

3. Why would a person consent do away with any constitutional concerns about search and seizure?

QUESTIONS FOR REFLECTION

1. Does the drug courier profile promote racism, or is it a reasonable law enforcement tool? Explain your answer.
2. Do Terry stops provide an excuse for police to pull over innocent citizens, or are they are necessary tool for law enforcement? Explain your answer.
3. Why would the Founding Fathers of our country devote so much attention to arrest and seizure in drafting the U.S. Constitution?

KEYWORDS AND PHRASES

Arrest	Check points
Fourth Amendment	Hunches
Search and seizure	Drug courier profile
Citizen's arrest	Good faith exception
Probable cause	Open fields doctrine
Terry stop	Plain view doctrine
Stop and frisk	Staleness
Warrant	Consent
Suspicious or unusual behavior	fresh pursuit doctrine
Confidential informants	contraband

PRACTICAL APPLICATIONS

1. Two friends are driving across the country. Ted, the driver, is exceeding the speed limit when the car is pulled over by a state trooper. Ted's friend, Carl, has brought along a half pound of marijuana. When Carl sees that the police are pulling over the car, he panics and throws the marijuana out the window. The state trooper sees the bag fly out of the window and retrieves it. He recognizes the green, leafy substance inside the bag. Does he have sufficient probable cause to arrest both Ted and Carl? If yes, why? If not, what additional information would he need before he could make an arrest?
2. In the *Fortner* case (Appendix), once the police are informed that the suspect may work at the strip mall, they go there and stop every man with light brown hair and a mustache. One of the people they stop is the defendant, Mark Fortner. Based on your readings of the U.S. Supreme Court's interpretation of the Fourth Amendment, is this a valid stop? Do the police need something more? If so, what? (For a complete overview of the *Fortner* case, see the Appendix.)

NOTES

1. *State v. Garcia*, 146 Wash. App. 821, 193 P.3d 181 (Div. 3 2008).

2. *Bost v. State*, 406 Md. 341, 958 A.2d 356 (2008).

3. *Brinegar v. United States*, 338 U.S. 160, 69 S.Ct. 1302, 93 LE 1879 (1948).

4. *Beck v. Ohio*, 379 U.S. 89, 85 S.Ct.223, 13 L.Ed2d 142 (1964).

5. *U.S. v. Hastamorir*, 881 F.2d 1551, 1556 (11th Cir.1989); *United States v. Hammock*, 860 F.2d 390, 393 (11th Cir.1988).

6. *Carroll v. United States*, 267 U.S. 132, 45 S.Ct.280, 69 LE 543 (1925).

7. *Clark v. State*, 189 Ga. App 124, 375 SE2d 230 (1988).

8. *Coolidge v New Hampshire*, 403 U.S. 443, 91 S.Ct.2022, 29 L.Ed2d 564 (1971).

9. 392 U.S. 1, 88 S.Ct.1868, 20 L.Ed2d 889 (1968).

10. *Michigan v. Long*, 463 U.S. 1032, 103 S.Ct.3469, 77 L.Ed2d 1201 (1983).

11. *U.S. v. Leon*, 468 U.S. 897 (1984).

12. *Lo-Ji Sales, Inc. v. New York*, 442 U.S. 319 1979.

13. *Terry v. Ohio*, 392 U.S. 1, 88 S.Ct.1868, 20 L.Ed2d 889 (1968).

14. *United States v. Hill*, 626 F2d 429 (5th Cir 1980).

15. *Adams v. Williams*, 407 U.S. 143; *Terry v. Ohio*, 392 U.S. 1, 88 S.Ct. 1868, 20 L.Ed2d 889 (1968).

16. *U.S. v. Pontoo*, 666 F.3d 20 (1st Cir. 2011).

17. 392 U.S. 1, 88 S.Ct.1868, 20 L.Ed2d 889 (1968).

18. *Adams v. Williams*, 407 U.S. 143, 92 S.Ct.1921, 32 L.Ed2d 612 (1972).

19. *Hayes v State*, 202 Ga. App 204, 414 SE2d 321 (1991).

20. *United States v. Berry*, 670 F2d 583 (5th Cir 1982); *United States v. Brignoni-Ponce*, 422 U.S. 873, 95 S.Ct.2574, 45 L.Ed2d 607 (1975); *Terry v. Ohio*, 392 U.S. 1, 88 S.Ct.1868, 20 L.Ed2d 889 (1968).

21. *Terry v. Ohio*, 392 U.S. 1, 88 S.Ct.1868, 20 L.Ed2d 889 (1968).

22. *Dean v. State*, 250 Ga. 77, 295 SE2d 306 (1982).

23. *Whiteley v. Warden*, 401 U.S. 560, 91 S.Ct.1031, 28 L.Ed2d 306 (1971).

24. 399 U.S. 42, 90 S.Ct.1975, 26 L.Ed2d 419 (1970).

25. *Brinegar v. United States*, 338 U.S. 160, 69 S.Ct.1302, 93 LE 1879 (1949).

26. 462 U.S. 273, 103 S.Ct.2317, 76 L.Ed2d 527 (1983).

27. 462 U.S. 273, 103 S.Ct.2317, 76 L.Ed2d 527 (1983).

28. *Alabama v. White*, 496 U.S. 325, 110 S.Ct.2412, 110 L.Ed2d 301 (1990).

29. *Brinegar v. United States,* 338 U.S. 160, 69 S.Ct.1302, 93 LE 1879 (1948).

30. *Quinn v. State,* 132 Ga. App 395, 208 SE2d 263 (1974).

31. *Alabama v. White,* 496 U.S. 325, 110 S.Ct.2412, 110 L.Ed2d 301 (1990).

32. *Michigan Dept. of State Police v Sitz,* 496 U.S. 444, 110 S.Ct.2481, 110 L.Ed2d 412 (1990).

33. *Mims v. State,* 201 Ga. App 277, 410 SE2d 824 (1991).

34. *U.S. v. Randolph,* 628 F.3d 1022 (8th Cir. 2011).

35. *U.S. v. Laville,* 480 F.3d 187 (3d Cir. 2007).

36. *U.S. v. Castro-Gaxiola,* 479 F.3d 579 (8th Cir. 2007).

37. *U.S. v. Lopez,* 482 F.3d 1067 (9th Cir. 2007).

38. *People v. Flow,* 37 A.D.3d 303, 831 N.Y.S.2d 129 (1st Dep't 2007).

39. *Draper v. U.S.,* 358 U.S. 307 (1959).

40. *U.S. v. Ventresca,* 380 U.S. 102 (1965).

41 *U.S. v. Ventresca,* 380 U.S. 102, 108 (1965).

42. *390 U.S. 234 (1968).*

43. *Oliver v. U.S.,* 466 U.S. 170 (1984).

44. 486 U.S. 35 (1988).

45. *California v. Greenwood,* 486 U.S. 35 (1988).

46. *U.S. v. Place,* 462 U.S. 696 (1983).

47. *U.S. v. Seiver,* 692 F.3d 774, 775 (C.A.7 (Ill.), 2012).

48. *U.S. v. Beltempo,* 675 F. 2d 472 (2d Cir. 1982), cert. denied 457 U.S. 1135 (1982).

Chapter 3

POST ARREST AND GRAND JURY

Chapter Objectives

At the completion of this chapter, you should be able to:

- Explain the procedures after arrest
- Explain how bail or bond works
- Explain the importance of the initial appearance
- Discuss the role of the defense attorney and the prosecutor
- Explain the purpose and function of preliminary hearings
- Describe the members of the prosecutor's staff
- Explain the function and importance of the grand jury
- Differentiate between indictment and accusation

I. Introduction: After the Arrest

prosecutor
A public official who presents the government's case against a person accused of a crime and who asks the court to convict that person.

In almost all situations, police officers make the arrest and bring the initial charges, but the case is only beginning at this point. Now the prosecutor and the defense attorney enter the picture. The **prosecutor** is supported by an entire infrastructure with the one goal: bringing the case to a successful conclusion. The defense attorney's role is to ensure that the state follows the rules in prosecuting his/her client.

Bringing a defendant to trial is a team effort, involving not only the police, but also the prosecutor's office. However, before the prosecutor's

Doug Clark's Ex-wife Indicted by Grand Jury for his Murder

Among the grand jury indictments returned today was one charging Christine Kline with the murder of her ex-husband, Doug Clark. Ms. Kline is accused of smothering him to death by wrapping his head with duct tape while her husband was restrained by at least two other men and handcuffed to the steering wheel of his car. She is currently in the Gannett Jail. No bond has been set in her case. The body of Doug Clark was recovered earlier this year in a wooded area just off the interstate. The body was badly decomposed and had been partially eaten by animals. Coroner Joe Brown eventually identified the remains as Doug Clark, reported missing nearly three months earlier. No trial date has been set.

For a complete overview of this case, see the Appendix.

Exhibit 3-1
Doug Clark's wife indicted

office becomes involved, there are several steps that must occur. The first of these is the initial appearance hearing.

II. Initial Appearance

In some jurisdictions, the **initial appearance** is also called the preliminary examination. This hearing, by whatever name, is usually held within a short period after the defendant's arrest. The purpose of the hearing is to ensure that the accused has not been illegally detained by the police and has been informed of his or her constitutional rights.

A. Right to Counsel at the Initial Appearance (Preliminary Examination)

In many states and at the federal level, the defendant has the right to have an attorney represent him. If an attorney represents the defendant, the attorney will do most of the talking and will often instruct his or her client to remain silent. If an attorney does represent the defendant, the attorney will continue in this capacity from this point forward, representing the defendant at all subsequent hearings.

B. The Purpose of the Initial Appearance

At the initial appearance, the accused is usually informed of the following:

- The seriousness of the charge against him
- The consequences of the hearing and future hearings
- The right to the assistance of counsel

■ **BULLET POINT**
Prosecutors work for the executive branch of government.

initial appearance
A court proceeding held shortly after the suspect's arrest in which he or she is apprised of specific constitutional rights.

The initial appearance hearing is specifically designed to ensure that the defendant is aware of his or her constitutional rights as early in the legal process as possible. The person who informs the defendant of his rights is often a magistrate judge. The judge may appoint an attorney to represent the defendant if the defendant cannot afford to hire his own.

C. Appointment of a Defense Attorney

A defense attorney may enter the picture at any point in the post-arrest process. A defense attorney may be appointed to represent a defendant shortly after his arrest or during his initial Appearance hearing. The defendant or a family member may retain an attorney to represent the defendant. If a defendant cannot afford an attorney and he meets the financial criteria set by the court, he may have an attorney appointed to represent him. This attorney will be paid by the state. In some jurisdictions, public defenders are available to defend the case. The manner in which attorneys are appointed varies considerably from jurisdiction to jurisdiction. When an attorney enters the scene, the first order of business is often attempting to get the defendant out of jail on **bail or bond**.

bail or bond
A written statement of debt that is put up by an arrested person or others who back it. It promises that the arrested person will show up in court or risk losing the amount of the bond.

D. Bail Bond

The initial phases of a criminal prosecution vary dramatically from state to state and on the federal level. Being released from jail on bail or bond prior to trial is one of those areas where there is considerable difference between jurisdictions. For simplicity, we will use the terms *bail* and *bond* interchangeably. Bail may often be set at the initial appearance hearing, but this issue usually comes up more often at preliminary hearings (see below). In many jurisdictions, a judge has wide latitude in deciding on bail. The accused is entitled to a hearing where evidence will be presented to determine the amount of bail required. Usually, there is no set monetary amount for each case. The nature of the charge will determine the monetary amount of bail. The arresting officer has no authority to set the amount of bail. A judge will often consider the officer's recommendation, but is not bound to follow it. The whole reason bail is required is to ensure the defendant's appearance at trial or another proceeding. See Exhibit 3-2

1. Judge-Only Bail Bonds
Some bail bonds can be considered only by the trial judge. Statutes exist that limit the power of a lower court to set bond in serious cases. In murder cases, for example, a common provision is that only a higher court judge may set bond on such a case. See Exhibit 3-3. In that event, the defendant must wait until his case is transferred to that court before a bail hearing can be held.

Detention-release outcome	State court felony defendants in the 75 largest counties	
	Number	Percent
Total	424,252	100
Released before case disposition	264,604	62
Financial conditions	125,650	30
Surety bond	86,107	20
Deposit bond	23,168	6
Full cash bond	12,348	3
Property bond	4,027	1
Non-financial conditions	136,153	32
Personal recognizance	85,330	20
Conditional release	32,882	8
Unsecured bond	17,941	4
Emergency release	2,801	1
Detained until case disposition	159,647	38
Held on bail	132,572	32
Denied bail	27,075	6

Note: Counts based on weighted data representing 8 months (the month of May from each even-numbered year). Detail may not add to total because of rounding.

Source: Felony Defendants in Large Urban Counties, 2006, Bureau of Justice Statistics, U.S. Department of Justice.

Exhibit 3-2
Type of pretrial release or detention for state court felony defendants in the 75 largest counties, 1990–2004

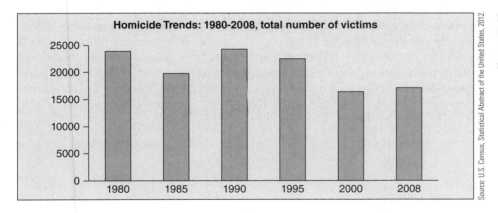

Homicide Trends: 1980-2008, total number of victims

Source: U.S. Census, Statistical Abstract of the United States, 2012.

Exhibit 3-3
Homicide trends: 1980–2008, total number of victims

THE ROLE OF THE PARALEGAL:

A paralegal should know which charges carry provisions prohibiting magistrate court judges from setting bail. This often means that a defendant will remain in jail longer while waiting for a bond hearing.

2. The Purpose of Bail Bond

The purpose of bail bond is to deter the defendant from fleeing the jurisdiction. By being out on bond, a defendant can help to prepare his or her

Exhibit 3-4
Circumstances where a defendant's bond will be revoked

- Defendant fails to appear for arraignment
- Defendant fails to appear for trial

defense. A judge cannot use a bond as a way to punish the defendant, for instance, by setting an astronomically high bond, knowing that the defendant does not have the resources to post such a bond.

3. Forfeiture of Bond

When the defendant fails to appear for court, the judge is authorized to forfeit or seize the bond. Bond forfeiture refers to the procedure where the defendant surrenders all or part of the bond amount. Although the judge is not required to forfeit the bond when the defendant fails to appear, in many cases, she will. A judge will often inquire to make sure that the defendant received sufficient notice of the proceeding before ordering the defendant's bond forfeited.

4. Bonding Companies

A bonding company is in the business of posting bail bonds for people charged with crimes. Generally, a bonding company will charge a 10% nonrefundable fee to the defendant for this purpose. For example, a judge in one case sets a bond at $10,000. The defendant or a family member approaches a local bonding company and pays 10% of that amount, or $1000, to the bonding company. The bonding company posts $10,000 with the court on the understanding that if the defendant fails to appear, the bonding company's money will be forfeited. The bonding company therefore has a stake in making sure that the defendant appears for court.

a. States That Do Not Use Bonding Companies In some states, the use of bonding companies has been eliminated. Instead, the defendant posts 10% of the bond amount in cash with a court clerk. Later, this money may be applied toward payment of a fine or restitution.

III. Preliminary Hearings

A **preliminary** (or probable cause) **hearing** is held shortly after the defendant's arrest. In some jurisdictions, a preliminary hearing must be held within a specified period of time. Because the terminology varies so much from state to state, for the sake of clarity, we will refer to such hearings as preliminary hearings.

A. The Purpose of a Preliminary Hearing

A preliminary hearing is designed for one purpose: to establish that there is sufficient **probable cause** to detain the suspect. As we saw in Chapter 2,

probable cause
The U.S. constitutional requirement that law enforcement officers present sufficient facts to convince a judge to issue a search warrant or an arrest warrant and the requirement that no warrant should be issued unless it more likely than not that a crime has been committed by the person.

the government is required to present evidence to establish probable cause for the defendant's arrest. Usually, a preliminary hearing is held before a magistrate judge. The judge has the responsibility of deciding whether the prosecution has met the burden of showing probable cause.

The procedures involved in preliminary hearings depend on the jurisdiction where it is being held. There are even specialized courts that devote themselves exclusively to specific types of cases, such as drug possession or domestic violence. See Exhibit 3-5. How a preliminary hearing is conducted even varies from county to county within a state. Because there is so much variety, we will focus on the general procedures involved.

B. Procedure at the Preliminary Hearing

Because the purpose of a preliminary hearing is to establish that it is probable that the defendant committed the crime with which he is charged, the state must present some evidence to meet its burden. This normally comes in the form of a police witness who testifies about the basic facts of the case. In some jurisdictions, civilian witnesses and victims are also called to the stand to testify. These witnesses are questioned about the defendant's actions. The standard of probable cause is certainly not as high as the standard the state must meet at trial. At trial, the prosecution must prove that the defendant is guilty beyond a reasonable doubt. At a preliminary hearing, the state simply must show by a **preponderance of evidence** that the defendant committed the crime. Put another way, the state must show that it is more likely than not that the defendant perpetrated the crime.

C. Evidentiary Rules at the Preliminary Hearing

The rules of evidence at a preliminary hearing are more relaxed than those used at the trial. For instance, hearsay testimony, which is inadmissible at trial, can be used in a preliminary hearing. There is more latitude in what can be presented because the purpose of this proceeding is not to establish the defendant's guilt. The end result is a determination of probable cause only.

■ **BULLET POINT**
Preliminary hearings are designed to determine if there is probable cause to arrest the defendant.

preponderance of evidence
The greater weight of evidence not as to quantity, but as to quality.

Exhibit 3-5
Use of specialized jurisdiction courts expanded

Specialty jurisdiction or problem-solving courts, such as drug, family, mental health, and domestic violence courts, became more common over the 18-year period. States developed and expanded the use of these courts to address the large populations of specific types of offenders revolving through the courts and correctional institutions. These specialty courts were designed to couple case-specific treatment services with the administration of justice.

Source: State Court Organization 1987–2004, Bureau of Justice Statistics, U.S. Department of Justice.

A preliminary hearing begins with the state calling a witness to the stand to testify about the facts surrounding the defendant's arrest. Usually, the person who testifies is a police officer, but it also may be the crime victim. Once the state's witness has finished testifying, the defense attorney has the right to cross-examine. This cross-examination is supposed to be limited to the issue of probable cause, but many defense attorneys see this as an opportunity to learn more about the case. They often ask questions outside the scope of the hearing to learn these facts.

THE ROLE OF THE PARALEGAL: ARRANGING THE COURT REPORTER

Contact the court and ask about the recording system it uses. If the court does not normally provide court reporters, then it is up to the defense team to arrange for one to appear. The court reporter is essential in recording the testimony of all of the witnesses. This testimony can make or break the government's case at a later time. A government witness may contradict her earlier testimony, and the transcript of the preliminary hearing will be the only way to show this inconsistency.

Defendants are permitted to testify at a preliminary hearing, but they are normally counseled to remain silent. A defense attorney usually advises her client not to say anything, realizing that because establishing probable cause is an easy thing to do, the chances are extremely high that the court will rule that probable cause exists. Putting the defendant on the stand would only open the defendant to cross-examination by the state.

D. Preliminary Hearing Calendars or Dockets

A preliminary hearing **calendar** or **docket** often contains dozens of cases scheduled for any particular day. The actual hearings are often hectic and seem chaotic to the unprepared. Dozens of witnesses may be standing around. Attorneys are often talking with clients or states' witnesses or the prosecutor. In some jurisdictions, no prosecutor is present and the judge conducts the hearing. People who are not used to it find this babble of voices and closely packed courtrooms to be quite intimidating. Some defense attorneys make a habit of taking paralegals with them to preliminary hearings. A paralegal, trained to observe and document inconsistencies in testimony, can be a tremendous help to an attorney whose attention is often focused on a legal argument and not on the witness.

E. The decision at the preliminary hearing

If the judge reaches the conclusion that the state has established probable cause, the judge normally issues an order often referred to as "binding" or transferring the case to another court. In some states, the case is transferred to superior court. In others, the court would be called a district or state court. If the judge concludes that the government has failed to establish probable cause, the judge will dismiss the charges against the

---

■ **BULLET POINT**
The rules of evidence are more liberal in preliminary hearings than in other court proceedings.

Because preliminary hearings are not difficult to present, this is often the first assignment for a prosecutor fresh out of law school. They are a good training ground for trial attorneys, and because a terrible blunder here can be fixed later, they present few worries to the young attorney's supervisors. Many times law school students, operating under the authority of a third-year clinic program in law school, will handle such hearings under the direct supervision of a fully licensed attorney.

calendar
The day-by-day schedule of trials in a given court.

docket
A list of cases, usually with file numbers, scheduled for trial in a court.

INSIDER'S VIEWPOINT

A defense attorney's approach to preliminary hearings

"I like preliminary hearings. The government stops working on its case once it gets there. They're not going to do anything for a while; so it's your chance to catch up. It helps with your case, too.

(1) You can use it to subpoena evidence, if you need it.
(2) You get people nailed down on their story.
(3) Sometimes it's just to get a feel for how bad the situation is. Whenever you can, you want one."

—B.J. Bernstein, Criminal Defense Attorney

defendant. Assuming that no other charges are pending against the defendant, he will be released. For an overview of typical dispositions in criminal cases, see Exhibit 3-6.

F. Negotiations at the Preliminary Hearing

On any given day, dozens of cases could be pending on the preliminary hearing calendar. However, this does not mean that all of the cases will actually have a hearing. A defendant could waive the hearing (i.e., admit that probable cause exists). Why would a defendant waive this hearing? The answer is quite simple: The defendant or his attorney has negotiated

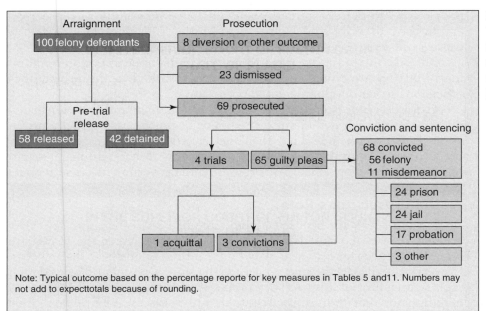

Exhibit 3-6
Typical outcome of 100 felony defendants arraigned in state courts in the 75 largest counties, May 2006

Note: Typical outcome based on the percentage reporte for key measures in Tables 5 and11. Numbers may not add to expecttotals because of rounding.

Source: Felony Defendants in Large Urban Counties, 2006, Bureau of Justice Statistics, U.S. Department of Justice.

with the prosecutor and received something in return for waiving the hearing. The prosecutor may ask the defendant (through the defendant's attorney) to waive the hearing—and agree that probable cause exists—in exchange for a lower bond recommendation by the prosecution. Generally, the judge follows the state's bond recommendation at the preliminary hearing. The magistrate judge knows that the case will soon be transferred to another court where the prosecutor will have control, so there is little reason to oppose the prosecutor's bond recommendation. By negotiating such an outcome, the prosecutor avoids a hearing and shortens by one case what could be a very long day of preliminary hearings. Prosecutors and defense attorneys spend a great deal of time negotiating. They negotiate at preliminary hearings, bond hearings, and motion hearings, and they negotiate plea bargains. In negotiating reduced bonds or other concessions to the defense, prosecutors often rely on information provided to them by the other members of their office.

IV. The Prosecutor's Office

All states have prosecutors. They go by various titles: District Attorney, People's Attorney, State's Attorney, Commonwealth Attorney or Public Prosecutor. For the sake of clarity, we will refer to prosecutors as District Attorneys. The role of the District Attorney is to serve justice, not to get convictions. Prosecutors are expected to exercise good faith and fairness in their decisions. Unfortunately, they don't always live up to those expectations. In general, prosecutors, like defense attorneys, are very ethical people who work very hard at their jobs. The prosecutor is the person empowered to bring the charge against the defendant and to follow through once the case has been brought by the police.

Once the arrest has been made and the initial appearance and preliminary hearing are completed, the case is forwarded to the prosecutor's office for further development and prosecution.

The prosecutor is the person vested with the final authority for bringing charges against defendants. The police begin the case, but the prosecutor's office concludes it. The district attorney is responsible for preparing the charging documents (indictments or accusations), preparing witnesses and evidence, and presenting the government's case at trial.

A. The Prosecutor's Role

District attorneys are licensed by the state like any other attorney. They are members of the state bar, and as such, each has taken the same oath that all attorneys take: to zealously represent the interests of their clients. However, the district attorney's client is the state. District attorneys do not represent victims of crimes. They represent the interests of all citizens by making sure that the criminal statutes are enforced. Victims are often confused by the district attorney's role. Having seen a lot of television

■ **BULLET POINT**
A prosecutor will often negotiate a lower bond recommendation in exchange for a defendant's waiver of a preliminary hearing.

"A prosecutor by any other name . . ."

In some states, the prosecutor is called a solicitor; in others, the state's attorney. In some states and some large cities the duties are divided between two different offices. The solicitor prosecutes all misdemeanors, whereas the district attorney prosecutes all felonies. This division of labor makes sense when there is a large caseload. In many other states, the local prosecutor handles all cases, both misdemeanors and felonies.

shows where an attorney is representing both sides in a civil suit, many victims naturally assume that the district attorneys represent them. They do not. Prosecutors often try to take a victim's feelings and interests into account as they make decisions in a case, but the person with the final say about whom to prosecute and when and how to prosecute a defendant is the district attorney.

District attorneys—and all assistant district attorneys—take an additional oath when they are sworn in as prosecutors. That oath is to seek justice. Their sworn duty is to enforce justice, not seek convictions. This sometimes means that the district attorney will dismiss a case if he or she thinks that justice will be served by doing so. This decision is final. A judge cannot force the district attorney to prosecute a case.

Whether the case involves a felony or misdemeanor, a prosecutor reviews the case file and makes the determination of what charges should be brought. The prosecutor can modify the original charge, add additional charges, or dismiss the charges—all of this is at his or her discretion. Obviously, the district attorney seeks input from police officers and victims about the case, but the final decision to prosecute and what to prosecute for are the prosecutor's alone. The judge has no say in which cases are prosecuted, what charges are brought, or any other control over the prosecutor except to the extent of granting or denying motions brought by the prosecutor or defense attorney. (See Chapter 13.) District attorneys are often elected officials. They are often politicians as much as they are prosecutors. District attorneys hire assistant district attorneys and other staff members to carry out the day-to-day business of prosecution.

B. The District Attorney's Staff

The prosecutor's office is staffed with people who support the state's effort to bring cases to a conclusion. They include the following:

- Assistant district attorneys
- Paralegals
- Secretaries
- Investigators
- Interns

1. Assistant District Attorneys

In almost all jurisdictions, there are too many cases for a single prosecutor to handle. The district attorney therefore hires assistant district attorneys to handle the day-to-day work of prosecuting criminals. Occasionally, the district attorney will handle a case, but in most situations, the district attorney is occupied with the administrative details in keeping the office running and does not have the time it takes to prosecute cases.

An assistant district attorney is the district attorney's representative in the courtroom. Although the title sounds impressive, in reality, an assistant district attorney does not have the kind of sweeping powers or influence commonly portrayed in television and movies.

The Assistant District Attorney's Salary

An assistant district attorney generally makes a great deal less money than his counterpart in private practice. Even criminal defense attorneys, usually the lowest paid of any private attorneys, make more money than assistant district attorneys. Entry-level assistant district attorneys earn anywhere from $20,000 to $40,000 a year. This may surprise many people who assume that all lawyers make a substantial living.

a. Duties of the Assistant District Attorney The assistant district attorney is the person who carries out the normal duties of the prosecutor. The assistant district attorney will decide what charges to bring against a particular defendant. He or she may modify the charge originally brought by the police, as well as add other charges the facts may suggest. The assistant district attorney will create a charging document (called an indictment or accusation, depending on the nature of the charge). An assistant district attorney may present the case to the grand jury (see below) and will conduct the preliminary hearings. The assistant district attorney may also work in conjunction with the investigators in the district attorney's office to follow up on certain matters or even seek more evidence. The assistant district attorney also conducts the trial against the accused. In addition to these duties, in some states, the he or she also handles the appeal of the conviction and represents the state in probation revocation hearings. In many states, an assistant district attorney is authorized to carry a badge and is issued a handgun for protection, but he or she is usually not permitted to make arrests.

2. Paralegals

Many prosecutors' offices are now adding paralegals to the staff. Paralegals are often used to assist in drafting charging documents, to investigate cases in conjunction with detectives, and generally act as assistants to the attorneys. Nationwide, the use of paralegals is not catching on as quickly in prosecutors' offices as they are in private practice. In private firms, the sheer economic pressure makes paralegals almost a necessity. A paralegal can be hired at a rate lower than what the firm would pay a new attorney, and the paralegal can do almost all the same work. However, in prosecutors' offices, the economic pressure is not as great. Assistant district attorneys are not paid well to begin with, so there is less economic reason to replace an attorney with a paralegal. In addition, in place of an attorney in the district attorney's office, a paralegal can perform fewer duties. For instance, only a licensed attorney can conduct preliminary hearings, trials, probation revocations, and presentments to the grand jury. This tends to limit the role of the paralegal in the prosecutor's office. However, that situation is slowly changing.

3. Investigators

The district attorney's office usually has its own investigators, independent of the detectives and police officers that work for the police department. These investigators do not answer to the chief of police; they answer to the district attorney. Many of them are former police officers and detectives, and they often maintain their state certification to arrest individuals like any other police officer. They are often authorized to carry badges and handguns, and in many ways, they are indistinguishable from police officers. Their responsibilities, however, are to investigate a case on behalf of the district attorney and to gather whatever additional evidence may be needed to bring the case to a conclusion. Their focus is slightly different than that of a police officer. A police officer usually gathers only sufficient information to bring a charge. A district attorney investigator must work with the prosecutor to gather enough evidence to convict the defendant.

4. Secretaries

In addition to assistant district attorneys and investigators, no office could function without well-trained and efficient secretaries. The secretaries handle all of the clerical duties, including generating the indictments and/or accusations, setting up and organizing files, maintaining trial calendars, and generally helping assistant district attorneys and investigators. An important distinction should be drawn here between secretarial staff and the attorneys and investigators. When new district attorneys are elected, they generally bring in their own investigators and assistant district attorneys. This often means that the current staff is let go, except for the secretaries and paralegals. In most jurisdictions, this staff is protected from this wholesale house cleaning by local and state merit laws. Because they know office procedures better than anyone else, it makes a great deal of sense for the new district attorney to keep them in their positions.

5. Interns

In addition to the salaried positions in the prosecutor's office, there are normally people who work there for free. The prosecutor's office routinely uses interns—college or law school students—to carry out basic clerical and other work. These interns serve in the district attorney's office to gain experience. Even though the pay is not lucrative, these positions are highly coveted by attorneys and others. Working with the district attorney, even as an intern, can often be exciting. Volunteering at the district attorney's office can also be a smart move for a new attorney. When a position becomes vacant, the district attorney's office is more likely to hire a former or current volunteer than a stranger without a proven work record.

C. Specialized Prosecution Teams

Many district attorneys' offices have created specialized prosecution teams that focus exclusively on certain types of crimes. They include the following:

- Child molestation
- Narcotics
- Domestic violence

- White-collar crime
- Child support (some states)

In addition to these specialized teams, many prosecutors' offices are internally divided between charging or indictment teams and trial teams. The indictment team handles all phases of investigation and presentment to the grand jury. Once a case moves through the indictment phase, it becomes the responsibility of the trial team to conduct the jury trial.

D. Victim-Witness Offices

Many prosecutors' offices have created specialized units to help with victims and witnesses. In some cases, these offices were created by federal grants. These offices coordinate the appearance of witnesses at trial and provide support and counseling for witnesses who have been traumatized by crime. They serve an extremely important role in assisting victims who might otherwise be overwhelmed by the complexity of the criminal justice system.

E. Investigating a Case— The Prosecutor's Perspective

Additional investigation of the case by the prosecutor often occurs in conjunction with the original police officer or detective. Some cases do not require much additional investigation, whereas others require extensive interviews and evidence gathering. At this point, the prosecutor becomes more of a detective than a lawyer, concentrating on the facts needed to convict the defendant of the crime. In this capacity, the prosecutor may do any or all of the following:

- Interview witnesses
- Obtain additional documents through **subpoenas**
- Visit crime scenes
- Research the applicable law
- Talk to experts about certain aspects of the case
- Request additional testing and evaluation of evidence by the state crime lab

Once all of this additional investigation is completed, the assistant district attorney is ready to officially charge the defendant through indictment or accusation.

V. Indictment

The U.S. Constitution mandates that a person charged with a felony must, in most cases, be indicted by the grand jury. We will discuss the functions of the grand jury below, but before describing an indictment, we will examine the accusation.

■ **BULLET POINT**
Victim-witness coordinators work with victims of crime and witnesses to help prepare them for the trial.

subpoena
A court's order to a person that he or she appear in court to testify (give evidence) in a case.

A. Accusation or Information

There is no constitutional requirement that a person charged with a misdemeanor be indicted by the grand jury. In those situations, the prosecutor merely drafts a charging document called an **accusation**. In some states and on the federal level, this document is called an **information**. It may also be referred to as a **complaint**. Whatever term is used, this document officially charges the defendant with a specified crime.

B. Indictment

An **indictment** is the document charging the defendant with a felony. An indictment has a specific form. It must first state the precise nature of the charges against the defendant. It then must list the facts on which these charges are based. The prosecutor drafts the indictment, but it does not become official until the grand jury issues a "true bill."

VI. The Grand Jury

"No person shall be held to answer for a capital, or otherwise infamous crime, unless on a presentment or indictment of a Grand Jury. . . ."

—Amendment V, U.S. Constitution.

The U.S. Constitution requires a grand jury indictment for a person charged with a capital offense (one punishable by death) or "otherwise infamous crime." This phrase has come to mean any **felony** offense. Later, we will see that some felonies can bypass this phase, but the vast majority do not. However, the U.S. Supreme Court has held that this provision does not apply to the states. In fact, some states do not use grand juries at all. However, because most states do, we will spend time examining the functions and procedures of the grand jury.

A. The Purpose of the Grand Jury

The grand jury was devised to act as a buffer between the state and the defendant. Developed in England and later transplanted to the New World, the original concept of the grand jury has existed for more than 700 years. The grand jury is composed of citizens who sit in secret session and listen to evidence about specific cases.

To justify an indictment, the government must present enough information for a **prima facie** case of guilt. This means that the state must present a basic case to the grand jury showing that the defendant is the person who most likely committed the crime. Before the grand jury will permit the case to continue, it must be satisfied that there is sufficient probable cause to believe that the defendant committed the crime. If the

---

accusation, information, complaint
A formal charge made to a court that a person is guilty of a crime.

indictment
A sworn written accusation of a crime made against a person by a prosecutor to a grand jury. If the grand jury approves it as a true bill, the indictment becomes the document used against the person as a defendant in pretrial and trial proceedings.

■ **BULLET POINT**
Most felony cases are brought by means of an indictment.

felony
1. A serious crime.
2. A crime with a sentence of one year or more.

prima facie
(Latin) At first sight; on the face of it, presumably. Describes something that will be considered to be true unless disproved by contrary evidence.

Exhibit 3-7
A summary of the functions of the grand jury

grand jury is satisfied, the words *True Bill* are written on the indictment. If the grand jury is not satisfied, the jurors write *No Bill* on the indictment and the prosecution ends. The grand jury's decision cannot be appealed.

Grand juries exist on both the state and the federal level. In some states, certain felonies can bypass the grand jury. These relatively minor offenses, such as the driving offense of Habitual Violator, may now be presented through other means instead of indictment. The states that have enacted these provisions have been primarily concerned with making more efficient use of the grand jury's time, especially in the face of growing caseloads.

B. Composition of the Grand Jury

The grand jury is made up of citizens of the county or federal district. They must be selected from a cross section of the community, reflecting the community's percentages of race, sex, occupation, etc.[1] Citizens cannot be excluded from a grand jury on the basis of their race, ethnic origin or their sex.[2] The usual number of jurors is between 16 and 23.

C. Functions of the Grand Jury

The grand jury has several functions. First, it is a required step in almost all felony cases. As such, it is a key element of the criminal justice process. Witnesses appear before the grand jury and are asked questions to establish the basic merits of the case. In many states, an assistant district attorney is permitted to enter the grand jury room long enough to question the witness and establish the legal basis of the claim; in other states, the prosecutor is not permitted to be present and law enforcement presents the case. In all states, however, the grand jury votes in secret, with no one else present.

The grand jury is also empowered to conduct its own investigations into criminal allegations. The grand jury can investigate people or activities to determine if crimes have occurred. To this end, the grand jury can subpoena witnesses and documents and does not have to establish probable cause beforehand. As such, the grand jury has more latitude than do police or prosecutors when investigating a case.

In its role as a supervisory body, the grand jury also oversees many local government offices and procedures. The grand jury is often called upon to make a written report about the condition of the buildings and other facilities found in the county—a duty often imposed on the grand jury by state law.

- Charging
- Investigating
- Supervision

D. Presenting a Case Before the Grand Jury

A presentation before the grand jury is a lopsided affair. The grand jury hears only from the state, not the defendant. The defendant has no right to testify before the grand jury or present any favorable evidence. The defendant's attorney is not permitted to attend or make any statements to the grand jury. In addition, the state is not required to present a balanced account of the case. The U.S. Supreme Court has even held that the prosecution is under no obligation to present evidence that is favorable to the defendant during a grand jury hearing.[3]

E. Testifying Before the Grand Jury

The grand jury can request anyone to appear before it to answer questions, but that does not always mean that the person will answer those questions. A witness does not lose his constitutionally guaranteed rights when he is subpoenaed to appear before the grand jury. Other provisions of law also protect the witness, including evidentiary privileges.

1. Pleading the Fifth

"...[No person] shall be compelled in any criminal case to be a witness against himself...."

—Amendment V, U.S. Constitution

The Fifth Amendment, which is the source of so many other rights for criminal defendants, also provides that persons cannot be compelled to give evidence against themselves. This protection follows defendants into the grand jury room as well. If a defendant or another person is subpoenaed before the grand jury, he does not have to admit to any criminal actions or give any testimony that might tend to incriminate him.

2. Privileges

Certain relationships are protected under law by **privileges**. A privilege is a device that protects a person from being compelled to testify about certain matters. Attorney-client discussions are privileged, which means that any discussion between a client and his attorney are protected from disclosure. A witness cannot be compelled to violate this privilege. For instance, if the defendant's attorney is subpoenaed by the grand jury and is asked about discussions the attorney had with the client, the attorney can invoke the attorney-client privilege and refuse to answer. Other examples of privileged communications include pastor-penitent, husband-wife, doctor-patient, and psychiatrist-patient.

privilege
The right to prevent disclosure, or the duty to refrain from disclosing, information communicated within a specially confidential relationship.

■ **BULLET POINT**
When a person claims a legally recognized privilege, he or she can refuse to answer questions.

F. Contempt Powers of the Grand Jury

If a witness fails to answer questions or present subpoenaed documents—and is not protected by the Constitution or an evidentiary privilege—the grand jury can request that a superior court judge hold the witness in contempt. If the judge agrees, the witness can be held in custody, fined, or both.

G. Granting immunity

Sometimes the only way to get a witness to appear and testify before a grand jury is to grant the witness immunity from prosecution. When a person has been granted immunity, the testimony given before the grand jury cannot be used as the basis to prosecute that person. In some states, the grand jury is empowered to grant immunity to a witness for his or her testimony. In other states, the prosecution must petition the court for a grant of immunity for the witness. A grant of immunity means that the testimony the witness gives before the grand jury cannot be used against the witness at some later date. Grants of immunity are provided so that the grand jury can learn more about a case. The person given immunity is often a codefendant or a co-conspirator in the case.

H. Grand Jury Procedures

In some states, the prosecutor attends the grand jury meeting, questions the witnesses, and presents evidence. In other states, the grand jury conducts its own investigation and questioning. In either situation, grand jury members always have the right to ask questions of any witness.

Unlike other court proceedings, the rules of evidence do not apply to grand jury proceedings. This means that the grand jury can consider illegally obtained evidence and listen to hearsay evidence. However, the grand jury does have some limitations. It is not permitted to take unlimited fishing expeditions through private lives and information trying to find evidence of some crime. The grand jury must focus on a specific investigation or risk having the indictment quashed.

1. Quashing an Indictment

quash
Overthrow, annul, completely do away with.

When the grand jury acts in an improper way to bring a true bill, a court may **quash**, or dismiss, the indictment. A defendant will often file such a motion when he believes or even suspects that such unconstitutional action has occurred. An indictment that is legally defective (e.g., one that fails to state the crime with which the defendant is charged) may also be quashed.

2. True Bill vs. No Bill

When the grand jury decides that there is sufficient probable cause to believe that a crime has occurred, they vote "true bill." A vote of true bill means that the case can continue, and the foreperson of the grand jury signs the indictment indicating this fact. If the grand jury does not believe that sufficient probable cause has been established, the grand jury votes "no bill." Such a vote effectively ends the case against the defendant.

Bill of Indictment

Exhibit 3-8
Bill of indictment

| Grand Jury witnesses:
Detective Able | State of Yuma
Gannett Superior Court
March Adjourned Term

State of Yuma
  versus
Christine   Lynn   Kline
  Offense(s):
Count 1: Murder

[True] Bill

This the ___ day of April, this year
~Seamus Kadirka~
_____
Seamus Kadirka,
Grand Jury Foreperson
========================
Received in open court from the sworn Grand Jury Bailiff and filed in office.

This the ___ day of April, this year
Irma Friendly
_____
Irma Friendly, Deputy Clerk
Gannett Superior Court
========================
Derrick Young, District Attorney
Gannett Judicial Circuit |
| We the jury find the defendant:
_____
_____
_____
_____

Foreperson
This ___ day of _____, _____ | The defendant herein waives a copy of indictment, list of witnesses, formal arraignment and pleads _____ guilty.
This ___ day of _____, _____
_____
Defendant
_____
Attorney for the Defendant
_____
Assistant District Attorney |

(continued)

Bill of Indictment, *continued*

Count 1 of 1

The GRAND JURORS selected, chosen and sworn for the County of Gannett, to wit:

1. Seamus Kadirka, Foreperson
2. Randall Makepeace
3. Mary Manz
4. Jessica Etters
5. Janae Freeman
6. Melodie Sisk
7. Yolanda Price
8. Starla Hoke
9. Debra Holbrook
10. Deborah Bolstridge
11. Sharon Ferguson
12. Lisa Mazzonetto
13. Brenda Timmerman
14. Richard Garrison
15. John Farthing
16. Paul Dellinger
17. Paula Barnes
18. Patsy Dellinger
19. Betsy Bevans
20. Christy Wallace
21. Gayle Hartung
22. Marianne Simpson
23. Star Hinkle

In the name and behalf of the citizens of Yuma, charge and accuse Christine Lynn Kline, with the offense of Murder in that the said accused, in the state of Yuma and County of Gannett, on or about the 19th day of November, last year, did then and there unlawfully and with malice aforethought, kill Douglas Betters by smothering him to death, contrary to the laws of said State, the peace, good order and dignity thereof.

Derrick Young, District Attorney
Gannett Judicial Circuit

If a prosecutor does not want to have a case prosecuted, having it dismissed by the grand jury is often a perfect solution. Because the grand jury is composed of members of the community, the grand jury's decision on a particular case can also help the prosecutor understand how the community feels about the case. Many prosecutors are elected officials and will face the community again at election time.

I. After the Grand Jury Indictment

Once a true bill is returned, the case is assigned to a court for further adjudication. The case will then be ready for arraignment. (See Chapter 6.) However, this does not mean that preparation ends for either the government or the defendant. In fact, the real work for the attorneys is just beginning. Both the government attorney assigned to the case and the defense attorney retained on the case must now prepare for the trial.

J. Defense Preparation

It is important to remember that while the state is building its case against the defendant, the criminal defense attorney will also be working for her client. In almost all cases, the defense usually has fewer resources on hand than the state does. A defense attorney might hire a private investigator, but this takes money, and most defendants do not have the financial resources to afford it.

INSIDER'S VIEWPOINT

"Since no one could be ready to try any of one hundred cases, the prosecutor tries to focus on a few cases on each trial calendar that are most likely to go to trial and ignore the others. The best way to do this is to work out negotiated guilty pleas on the other cases so that you can concentrate on the cases you're sure will go to trial."

—R. Keith Miles, Assistant District Attorney

In most cases, the defense attorney becomes her own investigator, locating witnesses, taking photographs, and preparing exhibits. In contrast with the prosecutor, the defense resources are often meager to nonexistent. However, this is not as one-sided as it might seem. State resources can be immense, but these resources are spread across the 25 to 100 cases that the prosecutor has pending on any given week's trial schedule. This means that the state's resources may be spread thin across a variety of cases.

The defense attorney, although hindered by fewer resources, usually has only one to five cases pending that may actually be tried in the near future. Therefore, she can concentrate more completely and take the extra time required to ferret out information that is helpful to the client.

THE ROLE OF PARALEGAL: PARALEGALS ACTING AS INVESTIGATORS

Normally, a private detective is hired to investigate a case for the defense. A good private detective can uncover a lot of information about anybody, but there is a cost concern. Not every client can afford the added expense of a private investigator. "We do use them in some of our more serious criminal matters," says Linda McCurry, a legal assistant with over twenty years of experience in criminal and civil cases. "I've got several private investigators that we work with." But, she adds, they are used only in those cases that are "terribly serious. In more routine cases, the money just isn't there to hire them." In that case, the paralegal may have to become an amateur sleuth. Good investigative skills can be a real asset for a paralegal.

ETHICAL CONSIDERATION: HOW ETHICAL RULES AFFECT ATTORNEYS AND PARALEGALS

Attorneys are regulated by the state bar and often punished by the state's highest court. Depending on the state, an attorney can be investigated by the state bar and sanctioned by the state's highest court. There are different levels of punishments for attorney violators. The lowest form of punishment—usually reserved for technical infractions of ethical rules— is the private reprimand. An attorney is notified, usually by mail, that he or she has violated an ethical rule and is advised not to do so again. After this, the next level of punishment is the public reprimand. Here, an attorney's name and infraction are published so that everyone can read about the attorney's infraction. Other than causing embarrassment and loss of professional credibility, neither of these sanctions affects the attorney's right to practice law. This is not true for the remaining sanctions. Attorneys who commit more serious infractions, such as a criminal offense, are often suspended. A suspension can last for a relatively short period of time or for several years, depending on the nature of the violation. The most severe punishment an attorney can receive is disbarment. An attorney who has been disbarred cannot practice law. Disbarments are often permanent—essentially stripping the lawyer of the right to practice his or her profession. The most common reason for an attorney to be disbarred is through embezzlement of client funds.

Paralegals are not directly supervised or regulated through the state bar. Although they can be charged with the criminal offense of practicing law without a license, they do not face disbarment or other professional sanction. This does not mean, however, that paralegals should not concern themselves with ethical rules. On the contrary, paralegals should be highly attuned to the ethical rules because their actions could result in sanctions against the attorneys with whom they work.

Case Excerpt. When the Initial Appearance is not Held in Time

TIDWELL V. PAXTON, 282 GA. 641, 651 S.E.2D 714 (2007)
MELTON, JUSTICE.

On February 13, 2007, Jerry Tidwell was arrested without a warrant for possession of methamphetamine with intent to distribute. On February 14, 2007, Tidwell was taken for his first appearance before a magistrate judge who issued an arrest warrant for the crime and set Tidwell's commitment hearing for March 26, 2007. On March 7, 2007, Tidwell filed a pre-trial petition for habeas corpus, arguing that he should be released from custody because he had not received a commitment hearing within 48 hours of his arrest pursuant to OCGA § 17-4-62. The habeas court denied Tidwell's petition in a written order filed on March 21, 2007, and this appeal ensued.

OCGA § 17-4-62 provides:
In every case of an arrest without a warrant, the person arresting shall, without delay, convey the offender before the most convenient judicial officer authorized to receive an affidavit and issue a warrant as provided for in Code Section 17-4-40. No such imprisonment shall be legal beyond a reasonable time allowed for this purpose; and any person who is not brought before such judicial officer within 48 hours of arrest shall be released.

Tidwell's appeal has now become moot. After this appeal was filed, Tidwell was indicted by a grand jury on May 7, 2007. "Once an indictment has been returned against a defendant, the question of whether a commitment hearing should have been held becomes moot." *Ross v. Lemacks*, 264 Ga. 839, 452 S.E.2d 109 (1995). Therefore, this appeal must be dismissed.

Although we do not reach the merits of Tidwell's case, we note that, in making his argument to this Court, Tidwell relied on a parenthetical in a footnote in the analogous case of *Boyd v. St. Lawrence*, 281 Ga. 300, 301, n. 3, 637 S.E.2d 687 (2006), which states, in its entirety:

See *Ross v. Lemacks*, 264 Ga. 839, 452 S.E.2d 109 (1995) (although OCGA § 17-4-26 provides that a defendant must be released from custody if not provided a commitment hearing within 72 hours of his arrest pursuant to a warrant, a defendant's indictment moots question of whether he should have been brought before a judicial officer within 72 hours).

OCGA § 17-4-26 provides:

Every law enforcement officer arresting under a warrant shall exercise reasonable diligence in bringing the person arrested before the judicial officer authorized to examine, commit, or receive bail and in any event to present the person arrested before a committing judicial officer within 72 hours after arrest. The accused shall be notified as to when and where the commitment hearing is to be held. An arrested person who is not notified before the hearing of the time and place of the commitment hearing shall be released.

This parenthetical, however, is not accurate. OCGA § 17-4-26 requires that "the person arrested (be brought) before a committing judicial officer within 72 hours after arrest." It does not require a commitment hearing within that time. In *Dodson v. Grimes*, 220 Ga. 269, 270(1), 138 S.E.2d 311 (1964), we held that OCGA § 17-4-26 does not provide that the committing magistrate shall have a hearing within 72 hours after the arrest. The facts here show that the arresting officers did bring the petitioner before the magistrate within 72 hours after the arrest. The fact that the magistrate set the hearing more than 72 hours after the arrest did not make petitioner's detention illegal.

To the extent that the language in footnote 3 of *Boyd v. St. Lawrence* conflicts with this holding, it is hereby disapproved. See also *Dean v. State*, 250 Ga. 77, 81(2)(b), 295 S.E.2d 306 (1982) (OCGA § 17-4-62 "is satisfied where...police obtain an arrest warrant within 48 hours of a valid warrantless arrest.").

Case dismissed.

All the Justices concur.

CASE QUESTIONS

1. What does Tidwell argue in his appeal?
2. What does the statute require?
3. Why does the court declare that Tidwell's appeal is moot?
4. Had Tidwell's appeal not been moot, does the court give any indication about how it might have ruled? Explain.

✓ Paralegal To Do List

For the defense paralegal:

- Review the charging instrument.
- If it is an indictment, does it appear to be in the proper form?
- If it is a citation, accusation, or other, was it signed?

Check with the client about the following:

- After arrest was he/she questioned by the police?
- Did he/she request an attorney before being questioned?
- Did he/she make any statements to a judge?
- When was his/her initial appearance?
- How long after the arrest was this hearing?
- Was the defendant told what the charges were against him/her?
- Has he/she had a preliminary hearing?

For the prosecution paralegal:

- Review the charging instrument for any obvious errors. The most common errors are:
    - Defendants name is misspelled
    - Date is incorrect
    - Place is incorrect
    - Wrong statute is referenced
    - Portions of the document are left blank

Once you have reviewed the charging document, see if you can obtain any additional information, such as:

- Date, time of preliminary hearing?
- Who conducted it? (This person sometimes has very helpful information.)
- Was the hearing recorded or transcribed?
- Did the defendant make any statements at the hearing?
- Was there any indication of what the defense to the charge will be?

Chapter Summary

Following a defendant's arrest, several important procedural steps occur. Usually within hours of the defendant's arrest, an initial appearance hearing is held where the defendant's rights are explained and other inquiries are made. Following the initial appearance, the preliminary hearing is held. The purpose of the preliminary hearing is to establish probable cause for the defendant's arrest. The preliminary hearing, like many other phases of prosecution, is a team effort involving many people. Once a charge has been made, it is up to the prosecution to continue the case through trial. To do this, the government employs attorneys and other staff. Following the preliminary hearing, a felony case is presented to the grand jury. The grand jury has a centuries-long tradition of acting as a buffer between the government and the accused. The grand jury hears presentations from the government and makes a determination that there is enough evidence to justify the charge against the defendant. Not all cases must be presented to the grand jury, however. Misdemeanors charges, for instance, can be brought through an accusation. The grand jury continues to serve a crucial role in the prosecution of people charged with offenses.

WEB SITES

Arkansas State Court System
www.courts.arkansas.gov/

Criminal Cases in the U.S. Supreme Court
www.libraries.psu.edu/psul/researchguides/socialsciences/lawcases.html

Find Law.com
www.findlaw.com

Findlaw – Preliminary Hearing
www.criminal.findlaw.com/criminal-procedure/preliminary-hearing.html

Georgia State Court System
www.georgiacourts.org/

Initial Appearance – Federal Public Defender
www.wvn.fd.org/tl-initappearance.html

Minnesota State Court System
www.mncourts.gov/default.aspx?pageID=100

National Center for Policy Analysis – Criminal Justice issues
www.ncpa.org

Virginia Legal Forms
www.courts.state.va.us/forms/district/home.html

Illinois Court System
www.state.il.us/court

North Carolina Court System
www.nccourts.org

REVIEW QUESTIONS

1. What is an initial appearance? What purpose does it serve?
2. What is bail bond?
3. How do bonding companies work?
4. What circumstances justify the forfeiture of a defendant's bond?
5. What is the purpose of a preliminary hearing?
6. Explain probable cause.

7. What negotiations occur at the preliminary hearing?

8. Explain the procedures at the grand jury.

9. What is the difference between indictment and accusation?

10. List and explain the various positions in the prosecutor's office.

11. What is the difference between a true bill and a no bill?

QUESTIONS FOR REFLECTION

1. A defendant has an initial appearance hearing, a bond hearing, a preliminary hearing, and an arraignment. Are all of the separate proceedings necessary? Is there a way to shorten this process? Devise a way to speed up this process. On the other hand, create an argument justifying each of the steps.

2. The grand jury was developed in the 1300s in England as a way to interpose the citizenry against the absolute power of the monarch. Is such an institution still needed today? Why or why not?

3. John Doe is subpoenaed to appear before the grand jury. Mr. Doe is being questioned about his alleged involvement in a narcotics smuggling ring. The first question he is asked is "Have you ever trafficked in narcotics?" What are John Doe's options at this point? Does he have to answer? Why or why not?

4. Is it fair that prosecutors' offices have all of the resources of the state at their disposal, whereas a defense attorney has only himself/herself and a limited staff? Does this imbalance contribute to a basic unfairness in the criminal justice system? Why or why not?

KEYWORDS AND PHRASES

Prosecutor	Subpoena
Initial appearance	Indictment
Bail or bond	Accusation
Preliminary hearings	Felony
Probable cause	Prima facie
Preponderance of the evidence	Privilege
Calendars or dockets	Quash

PRACTICAL APPLICATIONS

1. Contact the local prosecutor and ask how preliminary examinations are conducted in your state. Are different procedures followed than those outlined in the chapter? Explain.

2. Review the section "Preliminary Hearing" in the Kline case (Appendix); then answer the following question: Given the nature of the charges against Christine, should she testify at her preliminary hearing? Are the facts in her case so unusual that her attorney should consider going against the general rule of not having a defendant testify at a preliminary hearing? Explain your answer.

NOTES

1. *Campbell v. Louisiana*, 118 S.Ct. 1419 (1998).

2. *Taylor v. Louisiana*, 95 S.Ct. 692 (1975); *Castaneda v. Partida*, 97 S.Ct. 1272 (1977).

3. *U.S. v. Williams*, 112 S.Ct. 1735 (1992).

4. *Branzburg v. Hayes*, 92 S.Ct. 2646 (1972).

Chapter 4

EVIDENTIARY ISSUES IN PROSECUTION

Chapter Objectives

At the completion of this chapter, you should be able to:

- Discuss how evidence is used in criminal prosecutions
- Explain the difference between direct and circumstantial evidence
- Discuss the various kinds of evidence, such as physical, demonstrative, and documentary
- Explain the significance of eyewitness testimony
- Discuss the constitutional limits on lineups and showups
- Explain the sanctions for improper lineups, showups, and other identification procedures
- Explain the importance of DNA, its use, and its significance
- Explain the Exclusionary Rule

I. Introduction

evidence
All types of information (observations, recollections, documents, concrete objects, etc.) presented at trial or another hearing. Statements made by judges and lawyers, however, are not evidence.

The issues surrounding **evidence** can easily take up an entire textbook. Here, we discuss criminal evidence in general terms, how it is developed, how it is used, and ultimately what function it serves in the jury's deliberations. Evidence can be divided into two broad categories: direct and circumstantial. Beyond that division, however, evidence can further be broken down into other subcategories, such as testimonial evidence, documentary evidence, and demonstrative evidence. We begin with a review

---

Partially Decomposed Body Found in Woods

The badly decomposed body of a man was located along the interstate today. There was no identification on the body, except for a distinctive tattoo of a rose. Police report that the man had been handcuffed. The body was in such poor shape that the cause of death could not be immediately determined. Police . . .

For a complete overview of this case, please see the Appendix.

Copyright © 2015 Cengage Learning®

Exhibit 4-1

Sample case excerpt: the kline case

of the classifications of evidence and then proceed to a discussion of specific kinds of evidence and how this evidence is used in a criminal case. But first we must address the question of admissibility.

II. Admissibility

A judge rules on the admissibility of evidence during the trial. If a judge rules that certain evidence is **admissible**, this means that the jury will be allowed to hear it. When the evidence consists of physical objects, such as the murder weapon or any other physical evidence, a ruling of admissibility means that the evidence will go into the jury room with the jurors when they deliberate at the end of the case. They will be permitted to handle the evidence and examine it for themselves. However, a judge might rule that particular evidence is inadmissible, meaning that the jury will not be permitted to hear about it or see it. Evidence can be ruled inadmissible for a variety of reasons. The judge might decide that the evidence is not relevant to the issues in the case or that the evidence is too prejudicial and would result in an unfair trial if the jury were to know about it.

admissible

Proper to be used in reaching a decision; describes evidence that should be "let in" or introduced in court, or evidence that the jury may use.

■ **BULLET POINT**

Before any evidence can be shown to the jury, it must be admitted by the trial judge.

III. Classifying Evidence: Direct and Circumstantial

Evidence refers to anything that tends to prove or disprove any fact in a case. Evidence can be divided into two broad categories: direct and circumstantial. Direct evidence refers to any object or testimony that has an immediate connection with the facts in the case. Eyewitness testimony is direct evidence. When a person testifies that she saw the defendant commit the crime, this evidence goes to the very heart of the important issue in the case: the defendant's guilt. Circumstantial evidence, on the other hand, suggests conclusions and inferences but has no direct connection with the facts of the case.

In any trial, there is often a mixture of both **direct evidence** and **circumstantial evidence**. Circumstantial evidence is considered to be

direct evidence

Proof of a fact without the need for other facts leading up to it. For example, direct evidence that dodos are not extinct would be a live dodo.

circumstantial evidence

Facts that indirectly prove a main fact in question.

Exhibit 4-2
Examples of direct and
circumstantial evidence

Direct Evidence	■ **Circumstantial Evidence**
In the Kline case: ■ Earl's testimony that he saw the defendant wrapping the victim's face with duct tape	■ Testimony that Kline worked part time installing heating ducts (and so had access to the kind of duct tape used to smother the victim)
In the Fortner case: ■ Victim's testimony that the defendant held a knife to her throat and ordered her to disrobe	■ Testimony that Fortner often took a break from work around the same time that the attacks on the women occurred
In the Marbles case: ■ Identification of the .25 caliber automatic recovered from the defendant's car shortly after he wrecked it during a high speed chase	■ Testimony that Marbles had friends with access to small caliber guns

Note: For more information about the Kline, Marbles, and Fortner cases, please see the Appendix.

weaker than direct evidence. However, a conviction may be based on circumstantial evidence alone. Basing an entire prosecution on circumstantial evidence is not something the prosecution would prefer to do, but sometimes there is no choice. Circumstantial evidence may be the only type of evidence available. (See "Testimonial Evidence," later.) The classic example of circumstantial evidence is seeing footprints in the snow outside your window. Although you did not actually see a person make the footprints, you have circumstantial evidence that someone walked by your window. Later, you find a set of boots with snow still caked on them. That also is circumstantial evidence that whoever wore the boots made the footprints.

A. Classifications of Direct Evidence

Direct evidence can be further broken down into subcategories. For instance, direct evidence can consist of physical evidence, documentary evidence, and testimonial evidence.

1. Physical Evidence

Physical evidence refers to objects and things. In the Kline case (see Appendix), the victim's body is physical evidence, as is the handcuff manacle found on his wrist. Because physical evidence is unique, "foundation questions" must be asked to determine the relevance and admissibility of the evidence at trial. (See "Admitting Evidence: Foundation Questions" later.)

2. Documentary Evidence

Documentary evidence refers to writings. Contracts, letters, notes, agreements, etc., are all documentary evidence. The reason a distinction is drawn between documents and other forms of physical evidence is that a **document** can be copied, altered, or forged (often in such a way as to make it impossible to tell which was the original). There are special rules about how and when documentary evidence can be admitted at trial.

THE ROLE OF THE PARALEGAL: KEEPING DOCUMENTS ADMISSIBLE

When dealing with documents, it is important to keep in mind that the original document (the document that was actually signed by the parties) should never be marked on or highlighted in any way. If you want to emphasize something on the document, make a copy of the original, store the original in a safe place (where it will not be marked on accidentally), and use the copy for highlighting purposes. An original document that has had additional marks placed on it since it was executed may make the document inadmissible at trial.

3. Testimonial Evidence

The evidence given by the witnesses in the case is testimonial evidence. This **testimony** can involve directly observed facts (thus making it direct evidence), but it can also concern inferences and assumptions (making it fall into the category of circumstantial evidence as well). When a witness testifies about the facts of the crime and how she personally observed them, this is direct testimony. However, in the same breath, a witness can also embark on circumstantial evidence. For instance, a witness could testify that the defendant left the room and while the defendant was gone, she heard a loud noise. Later, she saw that a window had been broken. This evidence would suggest that the defendant broke the window, but because the witness did not actually see the defendant break the window, it is circumstantial evidence.

4. Demonstrative Evidence

Demonstrative evidence refers to any charts, diagrams, etc., used by the attorneys or witnesses to help illustrate or explain testimony. The parties normally prepare these exhibits, and because they are created for use in the trial to help the parties, they generally do not go with the jury when the jury deliberates. Unlike physical and documentary evidence that was produced through the natural course of events, demonstrative evidence was created specifically to persuade the jury. Therefore, most states do not permit it to be moved to the jury room for fear that the jury might give it more weight or credibility than the other forms of evidence.

documentary evidence
Evidence supported by writings and all other documents.

document
Something with a message on it(e.g., a contract, a map, a photograph, or a message on wood.

testimony
Evidence given by a witness under oath. This evidence is "testimonial" and is different from demonstrative evidence.

demonstrative evidence
Charts, diagrams, or other displays designed to persuade the jury to a particular viewpoint.

INSIDER'S VIEWPOINT

Gathering evidence in a rape case

"We explain to the victims that we need some information from them, so we understand exactly what happened. After we get a brief statement, we don't ask for complete, full details generally at that point, just to kind of confirm that the assault is actually what occurred. We explain to them that we need to get them examined. We make arrangements to take them over to the Sexual Assault Center or to have them taken. A lot of times people will call family or friends to be there with them, even before they call us. They sometimes prefer to ride with them. Our Sexual Assault Center has volunteers that come in to be there for a support system for the person. We'll go ahead and have them examined. After that, we do our more in-depth interview with them to get all the details of exactly what happened. If they know who the suspect is, then, generally, if there aren't any other witnesses to interview, then we'll interview the suspect. If there are other witnesses or other information that needs to be followed up on, we'll do that prior to interviewing the suspect. That way we'll have all of the facts before we confront a person."

—Detective Martina L. Pusbach, Sexual Assault Investigator

B. Evidence Used to Identify the Defendant

Because identification of the defendant is such an important part of the case, courts have given close scrutiny to the various methods used by law enforcement to identify the defendant. There are very stringent rules about how such identifications are carried out. This is especially true in the area of lineups and showups.

A **lineup** is often depicted in television and movies. Several people, all roughly similar in appearance, are lined up in front of a two-way mirror. The victim of the crime is then asked to identify the perpetrator. Because the consequences of this lineup are so serious (i.e., that the person identified will be charged with a crime), the United States Supreme Court has placed numerous limitations on how lineups are conducted. For example, police are not permitted to "suggest" which member of the lineup the victim should identify. In addition, the lineup cannot be unduly suggestive. This means that law enforcement cannot place a suspect with dark hair in a lineup with five or six other individuals with blonde hair, making one person stand out from the others. The height and general body appearance of all members of the lineup should be approximately equal. A lineup that suggests the identity of the perpetrator is a violation of a defendant's due process guarantees under the Constitution.[1] The penalty for a suggestive lineup is that the identification of the suspect will be inadmissible at trial.

Sample Case Excerpt: Fortner case

The men in orange jump suits all filed in and stood holding a stiff card with a black number emblazoned on the front. The victim, a sixteen year old girl who had given a man a ride to a nearby by ballpark and then been attacked by him, stood in behind a two-way mirror. The police officer beside her assured her that none of the men could see her.

"All they see is their own reflections." He whispered.

Without hesitation, she pointed to number 3. "That's him," she whispered. "I'll never forget his face as long as I live."(For a complete overview of this case, see the Appendix.)

1. The Importance of an Eyewitness Identification

Witnesses are often asked to identify the perpetrator from some form of lineup. These days, the most common form of lineup is a photographic lineup (discussed later). At the trial, the witness will again be asked to identify the perpetrator and to point him out to the jury. This has a profound psychological effect on the jury.

a. Just How Accurate is Eyewitness Testimony? One area fraught with difficulty for the prosecution and one that should be closely scrutinized by the defense is the identification of the defendant by the victim or witnesses. Eyewitness testimony is notoriously unreliable; yet there is hardly a more dramatic moment in the trial than when the witness points to the defendant and says, "That's the man."

2. Constitutional Limits on Lineups

One of the most important Supreme Court cases in the area of lineups is *U.S. v. Wade*.[1] Wade was placed in a lineup without his attorney's knowledge and identified as the suspect. Prior to the lineup, however, the witness saw Wade standing in the courtroom. The witness knew that Wade was the person charged with the offense before he identified him in the lineup. The Supreme Court held that the subsequent identification was unduly suggestive and testimony about the identification should not have been allowed.

INSIDER'S VIEWPOINT

Problems with eyewitness testimony

In one case, when the old lady on the stand was asked to identify the man who had robbed her, she looked around the room, stared into the public seating area, ran her eyes over the jury, looked everywhere, in fact, except at the defense table. She finally pointed to some guy who was just sitting there watching the trial and said, "That's him. I'd know that face anywhere!"

—Criminal defense attorney who preferred to remain anonymous

a. Right to Counsel at Lineup The defendant]s attorney should be present for any post-indictment lineups. The attorney has the right to observe how the witness responds and to hear anything that the witness says during the identification process. However, the attorney does not have a right to be present when the lineup occurs prior to a formal charge.

b. Participants in a Lineup The people chosen to stand with the suspect at the lineup are selected on the basis of similarity to the suspect: same approximate age and same race, build, hair and skin coloring, etc. The members of the lineup are allowed to pick where they will stand. Each position has a corresponding number so that no names will be used. Police are not permitted to draw the witness's attention to the suspect in any way, such as dressing him in different clothing or selecting people to serve in the lineup who do not resemble the defendant. The entire procedure in the pre-trial lineup should be reliable. Without some indicia of reliability, the identification is useless.[2]

c. Photographic Lineups In many situations, it is not practical to arrange a live lineup. In those situations, a police officer will go through the mug shot books and arrange a photographic lineup to show the eyewitness. Despite the fact that the lineup is photographic, the same rules apply. Those pictured should look something like the suspect. The pictures are often taped to a file folder and numbered. Like a live lineup, no names are provided. The witness must pick the suspect from the photographs. The defendant's attorney does not have the right to be present during a photographic lineup.[3]

Photographic lineups have several advantages over physical lineups. From a purely administrative viewpoint, it is far easier to obtain photographs of people who have a similar appearance than it is to locate on short notice five or six other people who have similar features. The disadvantage of a photo lineup is that the witness does not get to see the suspect in three dimensions. A flat photograph of a person is not always the best way to identify that person. Think about the photo on your driver's license, for example. However, photographic lineups do not have many of the legal problems that physical lineups do.

In either physical lineups or photographic lineups, there can be nothing especially suggestive about the defendant. An unduly suggestive lineup (one that sets off the suspect from the others in some way) may invalidate the entire identification process.

THE ROLE OF THE PARALEGAL:

Always review the photographic lineup to make sure that the police have included pictures of people who do appear to be similar. A witness's identification may be inadmissible if the defendant was somehow singled out in the photographs. There should be no stray marks near the defendant's photograph. In physical lineups, law enforcement makes a videotape of

- Did the victim/witness have an opportunity to see the suspect during the crime?
- Was the victim/witness paying attention to the suspect at the time of the crime?
- How does her description of the suspect match the actual appearance of the person identified in the lineup?
- How certain is the victim/witness of her identification?
- How much time has elapsed between the crime and the identification?

Exhibit 4-3
Questions to determine reliability in lineups

the entire proceeding. This should also be reviewed. Was the defendant wearing something noticeably different from the other members of the live lineup?

d. Single-Suspect Lineups The United States Supreme Court has stated that one-person lineups are obviously impermissibly suggestive and should not be used.[4]

e. One-Person Showups If physical lineups are a potential legal minefield, one-person showups are even worse. Generally, a one-person **showup** occurs when the police arrest a suspect and present him or her to the witness with the question "Is this the person?" Certainly, these situations could fall into the category of unduly suggestive, and the identifications are often ruled inadmissible. However, this does not mean that such identifications are always unconstitutional; they just receive a greater degree of scrutiny. (See this chapter's Case Excerpt for an example).

f. Sanctions for an Improper Lineup When the defendant's right to have his attorney present at a physical lineup has been violated or the lineup has been unduly suggestive, the punishment imposed on the state is that the testimony about the identification is ruled inadmissible.[5]

g. Self-Incrimination and Identification The Fifth Amendment to the United States Constitution prohibits criminal defendants from being coerced into giving testimony against themselves. Although we discuss the application of this constitutional protection in greater detail in the chapter on interrogation, a word about the Fifth Amendment is important here. Is it a violation of the Fifth Amendment to have the defendant stand up in trial and show the jury the facial scar that the victim described as belonging to her attacker? According to the U.S. Supreme Court, the answer is no. Physical traits, especially those that can be seen by ordinary observation, do not fall under the protection of the Fifth Amendment.[6] Making a defendant demonstrate a physical trait such as a scar or tattoo is not the same as compelling the defendant to admit to a crime.[7]

■ **BULLET POINT**
The most common type of lineup is a photographic lineup.

showup
A pretrial identification procedure in which only one suspect and a witness are brought together.

However, some states do not permit this kind of action because of the potential conflict it will cause with the defendant's constitutional rights.

IV. Other Evidentiary Issues

In the next section, we will address specific types of evidence and the challenges and advantages that each offers. There has been no greater revolution in evidence gathering and presentation than the advent of DNA evidence.

A. DNA

In 1953, in work that would later earn them the Nobel Prize, James Watson and Francis Crick discovered the chemical and structural arrangement of **DNA**.

DNA

Material in living organisms used to compare body tissue samples (such as blood, skin, hair, or semen) to see if the genetic materials match. It is used to identify criminals by comparing their DNA with that found at a crime scene and is used to identify a child's parents.

DNA is composed of two strands of molecules arranged in the now famous double-helix configuration. The double helix is like a spiral staircase, where the handrails are composed of sugars and phosphates and the steps are composed of matching pairs of four (and only four) chemical compounds. These bases are adenine, cytosine, guanine, and thymine. Normally abbreviated A, C, G, and T, respectively, these bases combine only in the sequences A–T and C–G, which are referred to as base pairs. The human genetic code, which contains all of the information required to develop a human being from a single cell, consists of 3 billion base pairs. It is the arrangement or sequence of the base pairs that is so important. Base pair arrangements determine the ultimate shape of the animal: cat, dog, or human being.

1. DNA as an Evidentiary Tool

■ **BULLET POINT**

DNA has revolutionized evidence gathering and the ability to identify specific individuals.

The use of DNA as a forensic tool began in the mid 1980s. Researchers realized that because each person's DNA is different (with the exception of identical twins), there should be a way to harness this feature for identification purposes. Like fingerprints, DNA was seen as a method to link a suspect with a crime scene in a way that could eliminate him or implicate him as a suspect with a relatively simple test.

Whether the DNA comes from a person's skin, hair, or body fluid, it contains the identical DNA. This means that DNA forms the basis of the ultimate fingerprint: Every cell, no matter where it originates in a person's body, has exactly the same DNA. This principle underlies the use of DNA as a means of identifying a person. When the known DNA of a person is compared with an unknown sample (e.g., one found at a crime scene), these two samples can be compared. If they match, it can be said quite conclusively that the suspect was at the scene.

DNA cannot show motive or bent of mind or planning. It can show, however, that the suspect was present or that he left behind incriminating

INSIDER'S VIEWPOINT

How DNA databases help prosecutors

"We're really starting to build up the offender DNA database. We're starting to see the number of DNA cold cases, what they call 'cold hits' those are starting to increase pretty dramatically. You get a victim, you get a genetic sample, you run it in, and it comes up against somebody in the database. The really big thing, what's really done it for us is Virginia, when they first passed their database statute that required that all convicted offenders submit a DNA sample, in addition to the sexual crimes they included burglary. What they discovered was that they were finding most of their cold hit sexual offenders in their burglary database. That told them that some burglars move up from burglary to rape. Most states are going back in and adding burglary to their database. In Georgia, right now, if you're convicted of a sexual crime you have to submit a DNA sample, which is done with a swab in your mouth. It's called a mucal swab and that DNA profile is put into the DNA database."

—Daniel J. Porter, District Attorney

evidence. In rape cases, sperm can be checked against the suspect's DNA type and can tell whether the sperm is his.

Technicians can now obtain useful DNA from a wide variety of sources including hair, saliva, blood, semen, tissue, and even badly decomposed bodies. Researchers have obtained DNA from corpses buried for decades, even centuries. DNA can be obtained from the bloodstained clothing of a victim or from any source where a person has left behind cells from his or her body.

The only people in the world who have the same DNA are identical twins. Even fraternal twins do not have the same DNA. Family members have DNA that is close to one another, but is clearly distinguishable.

a. DNA Databases Many state and federal agencies have begun storing the results of DNA tests in computer databases. Similar to the creation of the FBI fingerprint database, the DNA database permits law enforcement to compare an unknown DNA sample with any of the known samples stored in the nationwide database.

Once a DNA sample is collected, an expert extracts cells from the material. Cells contain genetic material, and a DNA analyst is trained to tease this out. Using another technique, the tiny sample is copied over and over until there is enough of the duplicated on which to carry out tests. The methods to carry out these various procedures vary, but there is no question that DNA evidence has become some of the most compelling evidence available to modern law enforcement. Technology evolves

An expert can test for DNA on a specimen that is less than the size of the period that ends this sentence.

chromosome
The site inside the cell where the genes are located.

every day, and the sources from which law enforcement can retrieve DNA evidence expands constantly.

DNA results are checked for accuracy visually and digitally by computer. Using this method, DNA experts can often testify that the chances that a specimen came from someone other than the defendant are several billion to one.

B. Fingerprinting

Everyone is familiar with fingerprints. As early as 1605, scientists had noted that the patterns of grooves and whorls on a person's fingertips were as individual as faces. It wasn't until the early 1900s, however, that law enforcement began using this fact as a means to identify perpetrators.

Fingerprints can be left behind on a variety of surfaces, including human skin. Specially trained technicians search for fingerprints in likely places: doorknobs, tabletops, or anywhere else a person is likely to have put his or her hand.

The Federal Bureau of Investigation maintains a nationwide database of fingerprints, which can now be computer-matched in a short period of time.

Exhibit 4-4
Photograph of fingerprint (original)

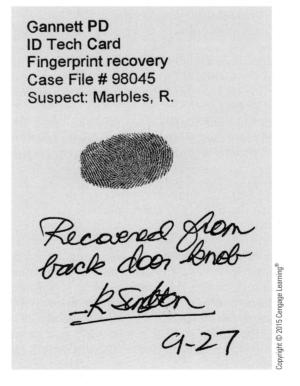

Gannett PD
ID Tech Card
Fingerprint recovery
Case File # 98045
Suspect: Marbles, R.

Recovered from
back door knob
—R Sexton
9-27

INSIDER'S VIEWPOINT

Finding fingerprints

When evidence technicians are called to a crime scene, they must search for fingerprints. How do they know where to look?

"When we go out, we get with the victim and get them to walk us through and we ask them, 'is there anything in here that is not yours?' Or we ask them, 'do you see anything unusual, like something that is out of place, something that was brought from one room to another and left?'"

—Kathy Singleton, Crime Scene Evidence Technician

C. Blood Testing

Blood tests are commonly performed to eliminate rather than implicate a suspect. The reason for this is simple. Blood testing—or typing of the victim's or defendant's blood usually tells the examiner whether the blood is the same type as the unknown specimen found. It does not reveal whether the unknown specimen of blood belongs to any particular person. As such, if the blood found is not the defendant's blood type, the only conclusion that can be reached is that the blood does not belong to him.

D. Polygraph Tests

Polygraph machines, or lie detectors, have been around in one form or another for decades. The basic principle behind any "lie detector" is that when a person tells a lie, it causes him/her physical stress. This stress can be measured, in the form of increased heart rate, minute changes in the skin's resistance to electricity and greater perspiration. However, because of their notorious unreliability, few courts allow them to be used as evidence. Occasionally, defense attorneys will attempt to use them to show that the defendant has been telling the truth, but in almost all cases, polygraph results remain inadmissible in criminal trials.

BULLET POINT
Although identical twins share the same DNA, they have different fingerprints.

BULLET POINT
Polygraph test results are usually not admissible. The only time they are admissible is when a defendant agrees to make the results admissible at trial.

Evidence is examined to:
1. Visually locate bloodstains
2. Identify blood by chemical and/or crystal testing
3. Determine the species (human or animal)
4. Evaluate the evidence and circumstances to determine if DNA evidence is possible
5. Determine blood type when sample size permits this service

Exhibit 4-5
How forensic experts search for blood

E. Voice Testing

A voice stress evaluation test is in some ways similar to a polygraph test. Although the application is different, the theory remains the same: When a person lies, this causes stress and the stress can be measured. A person's voice is recorded and later examined by experts. Like polygraph tests, voice stress tests are normally inadmissible in a criminal trial.[8]

V. Admitting Evidence: Foundation Questions

One important aspect of evidence is the way that is used at the trial. Before the jury is permitted to inspect the evidence in the case, it must first be admitted into evidence. **Admission** refers to the process through which the attorney establishes the relevancy of the evidence and the judge then rules that the jury may view it. An attorney is not permitted to testify about the evidence. Instead, the attorney must ask a witness about the evidence. These questions are called "foundation questions." Establishing how a piece of evidence is relevant is commonly referred to as "laying the foundation." Different types of evidence require different kinds of questions.

A. Chain of Custody Requirements

Whenever evidence is seized, it must be safeguarded. Police agencies have created evidence rooms, where this evidence is stored for later use at trial. Evidence requiring testing by the state crime lab or other agency must also be handled methodically. Before the evidence can be admitted at trial, the state must show that the evidence has not been altered or tampered with in any way. This is called the "**chain of custody**" requirement. All the people who handled the evidence must take the stand and account for what they did with the evidence and where they took it. All of them must testify that they did not tamper with it. The "chain" is established by having the crime scene technician testify to removing the evidence from the crime scene, then placing it in the evidence room. Then the person who removed it from the evidence area testifies, and so on until every person who handled the evidence testifies.

admission
Refers to a decision by a judge to allow evidence to be used by the jury (or if no jury, by the judge).

chain of custody
The chronological list of those in continuous possession of a specific physical object. A person who presents evidence (such as a gun used in a crime) at a trial must account for its possession from time of receipt to time of trial for evidence to be admitted by the judge.

Exhibit 4-6
Sample foundation questions for tape recordings

- Was the tape recorder working properly?
- Was the person operating the machine familiar with its functions?
- Is the tape being offered the original tape taken from the machine?
- Has the tape been altered or tampered with in any way?
- Did the tape remain in the person's custody since the time of the recording?
- Have the people speaking on the tape been identified?

1. Evidence Rooms

The evidence room is a restricted area. The only people permitted in the area are the evidence room technicians. Police, prosecutors, and judges are all barred from entering the evidence room. When police deposit evidence there, they hand it over to technicians who are responsible for storing it. A break in the chain of custody could result in the evidence not being admitted at trial. If this evidence is crucial to the prosecution's case, the entire charge might fail.

B. The Exclusionary Rule

As we saw in previous chapters, the **Exclusionary Rule**, created by the U.S. Supreme Court, dictates the punishment for failing to follow the correct procedures in obtaining evidence. Illegal or unconstitutional evidence cannot be used at trial. By providing such a sanction, the U.S. Supreme court hoped to effectively force all law enforcement agencies to abide by constitutional provisions in seizing evidence. The Exclusionary Rule is the device used in numerous movie and television dramas as the "technicality" that allows an obviously guilty suspect to go free. However, because the court's ruling actually states that the police violated the Constitution in obtaining the evidence, to allow the evidence to be used in one case would invite police to circumvent the Constitution in future cases, too. A ruling that certain evidence was obtained unconstitutionally does not mean that the charges against the defendant are dropped. However, if all evidence against a defendant is ruled illegal, then for all practical purposes, the prosecution has nothing linking the defendant to the crime.

1. "Fruit of the Poisonous Tree"

Occasionally, when evidence has been obtained in violation of the Constitution, this evidence often leads to the discovery of additional evidence. What happens when other evidence is obtained (and obtained constitutionally) but is based on original evidence that was obtained unconstitutionally? The courts have said that the Exclusionary Rule, to have any binding effect, must be applied to this new evidence as well. When new evidence is discovered only through unconstitutionally obtained evidence, this new evidence will be excluded at trial. This is the so-called **fruit of the poisonous tree doctrine**. This doctrine holds that if the original evidence was tainted, any additional evidence obtained from it is also tainted and suffers the same penalty: exclusion at trial.

2. Exceptions to the Exclusionary Rule

The Exclusionary Rule does have certain exceptions. Even though evidence may have been obtained unconstitutionally, provisions such as the following allow it to be used at trial:

- **Inevitable discovery.** Evidence would have been discovered under any circumstances, and the fact that it was obtained unconstitutionally may not necessarily impact its admissibility.

BULLET POINT
To establish the admissibility of certain types of physical evidence, all the people who handled it must testify at trial that they did nothing to tamper, alter, or change the item while it was in their custody.

exclusionary Rule
The Supreme Court ruling that states that illegally obtained evidence may not be used in a criminal trial.

It is extremely rare for all evidence against a defendant to be ruled unconstitutional. Even in cases where some of the evidence was obtained illegally, the prosecution may still continue with the case. The government simply cannot use that evidence and instead will rely on other evidence that was obtained constitutionally.

BULLET POINT
The Exclusionary Rule, created in 1918, prohibits the use of any evidence at trial that was obtained in violation of the U.S. Constitution.

Fruit of the poisonous tree doctrine
The rule that evidence gathered as a result of evidence gained in an illegal search or questioning cannot be used against the person searched or questioned even if later evidence was gathered lawfully.

- **Good faith.** Law enforcement is acting on a good faith belief that the warrant is legally sufficient when, in fact, it is not.
- **Independent source.** The evidence, although obtained unconstitutionally, was also verified by an independent source, and this source is not tainted by any unconstitutional problems.

C. How the Jury Uses Physical Evidence

When evidence has been admitted at trial, the jury will be allowed to view the evidence in the jury room. The murder weapon or the narcotics will go back with the jurors while they deliberate on the case. The jurors are instructed that they have the final say on how much or how little weight to give any particular piece of evidence. Although the jury is not directly informed of this fact, the jury is permitted to disregard evidence entirely and reach a conclusion contrary to what the evidence suggests. The final verdict is always based on the individual jurors' beliefs, not on the quantity or quality of the evidence.

ETHICAL CONSIDERATION: THE ATTORNEY-CLIENT PRIVILEGE

When an attorney advises a client about a legal matter, the substance of that conversation is protected at law by an evidentiary privilege. This privilege protects the client's privacy. An attorney who is called to the stand and asked to testify about a conversation with a client can legally refuse to answer any questions. The attorney cannot be held in contempt or otherwise prosecuted for failure to answer such questions. Is a paralegal protected by a similar privilege? The answer is no. Some jurisdictions have held that the presence of the paralegal during an attorney-client discussion may waive or eliminate the privilege. That being true, a paralegal cannot refuse to answer questions about conversations with a client. As a result, the paralegal should ensure that the attorney-client privilege is not waived under other circumstances. Because the conversations between the attorney and the client are supposed to be private, the paralegal should make sure that they remain so. The best way to do this is not to discuss any client business away from the office. Unless given permission to do so, it is a good idea to refuse to state that a particular person is even represented by the attorney.

Case Excerpt.

PEOPLE V. MOHAMED, 201 CAL.APP.4TH 515, 525, 133 CAL.RPTR.3D 823, 830) (CAL.APP. 4 DIST., 2011) MCCONNELL, P.J.

INTRODUCTION

A jury convicted Abdi Mohamed of robbery (Pen.Code, § 211). The trial court sentenced him to five years in state prison. Mohamed appeals, contending there is insufficient evidence to support the jury's verdict.

BACKGROUND
Prosecution Evidence

Around 12:45 A.M., Breanna Gomez was leaving a café when someone pushed her friend against her. Gomez fell against a wall. She heard someone refer to her and her friend as "b—s." She turned and saw three men wearing sheer, form-fitting masks. She felt an object she thought was a gun in her back and was pushed back against the wall. One man's mask ended up between his nose and lower lip. Gomez could see the man's jaw line and facial structure, including the shape of his chin, cheek, and nose. He was Black, approximately six feet tall and thin. He had a moderate beard defining his jaw line. He wore a black hooded sweatshirt, light colored pants, and a black beanie. He took her cell phone, car keys, and a $20 bill. One of the men also took her purse. Gomez then ran back into the café.

The owner of the café was standing with some customers outside the café when a man walked up. The man asked if the people outside were gang banging, and when he learned they were not, he pulled a mask over his entire face and drew what appeared to be a gun. The man walked over to another group of people that included Gomez and her friend. Meanwhile, the owner went into the café and called 911. During the 911 call, the owner described the man he saw as a six-foot tall Black man around 25 years old. The man had a medium build and wore black pants, a black shirt, and a black and white striped jacket.

Another unidentified person told the 911 operator one of the robbers was Black and wore a black shirt, a black hooded sweatshirt, and gray sweats. The man also wore a black beanie as a mask. The unidentified person said one of the other robbers was wearing a Spiderman backpack.

Froilan Medina was inside the café when the incident occurred. He saw a Black man walk up to the restaurant and pull a black beanie mask down to his mouth area. The man was between five feet ten inches and six feet tall. He had a thin patch of hair on his chin and was wearing dark pants and a red hooded sweater with designs.

Medina went out of the restaurant and saw the man run away with two other Black men following him. One of the followers was around six feet tall and wore a mask, a black and gray hooded sweatshirt, and black baggie sweatpants. The other man wore a black hooded sweatshirt and gray sweatpants. He dropped what appeared to be a gun and went back to pick it up. Police officers found a magazine for a toy pistol in the same area. DNA testing of the magazine was inconclusive as there was not enough DNA for a comparison.

One of the police officers who responded to the incident drove around the neighborhood looking for suspects. Shortly after the robbery, the officer saw Mohamed walking along a street approximately four blocks from the café and holding an umbrella in a manner that partially blocked his face. Mohamed wore gray sweatpants, black hooded sweatshirt, a beanie, and a neck scarf. The officer detained Mohamed, confirmed he fit the description of one of the robbers, and conducted curbside lineups with Gomez and two other witnesses.

Gomez told the officer who brought her to the lineup that she was 80 percent sure Mohamed was one of the men who robbed her because he was wearing the same clothing and had the same facial hair, facial features and build. She could not be 100 percent sure because the men were wearing masks. Gomez later identified Mohamed as one of the robbers at both the preliminary hearing and the trial.

Medina also identified Mohamed as one of the robbers at the curbside lineup. At the time, he said he was "completely sure" about his identification because

Mohamed was wearing the same clothes as one of the robbers. At trial, he said he had "a little bit" of doubt about his identification, but remained confident in it. The owner of the café said Mohamed was not the person he saw.

After Gomez and Medina identified Mohamed as one of the robbers, the officer arrested Mohamed and advised him of his rights under *Miranda v. Arizona* (1966) 384 U.S. 436, 86 S.Ct. 1602, 16 L.Ed.2d 694. The officer searched Mohamed and found a nylon do-rag tucked between his body and his pants.

Mohamed told the officer he was coming from a friend's house where he had been playing video games since 5:00 P.M. The officer went to the friend's house, and the friend's mother told the officer she had not seen her son since about 1:00 P.M. and Mohamed had not been at her house after 5:00 P.M. playing video games. The following day the friend spoke with the officer and confirmed he had not seen Mohamed after 5:00 P.M. the prior evening. At trial, the friend testified he had been with Mohamed until dark, then they split up. He was not with Mohamed after then, and Mohamed was not at his house playing video games until 1:00 A.M.

Defense Evidence

Dr. Scott Fraser, an eyewitness identification expert, testified there are several variables affecting the accuracy of eyewitness identifications. These variables include lighting, distance, and duration of exposure. Generally, the better the lighting, the shorter the distance, and the longer the duration of exposure the more likely an eyewitness identification is to be accurate. In addition, very small obstructions in a witness's view of the perpetrator, such as a partial face mask, can greatly reduce the accuracy of the witness's identification. Likewise, when there is more than one person involved in an incident, the rates of correctly recognizing any single person are significantly reduced. Stress can also affect the accuracy of eyewitness identifications. In very high stress situations, the accuracy of eyewitness identifications drops off rapidly.

Conversely, the existence of distinctive cues, such as tattoos or scars, increases the accuracy of eyewitness identifications. If an eyewitness describes a perpetrator as having a scar in a particular place, the perpetrator will almost certainly have a mark or aberration in that place. If an eyewitness gives a description that omits a distinctive cue, such as the existence of facial hair on the chin, then the perpetrator's chin almost certainly did not have facial hair.

Errors in cross-racial identifications are two to two and a half times higher than same race identifications. Moreover, the errors in cross-racial identifications are almost exclusively false positives, e.g., saying a person is the perpetrator when the person is not the perpetrator.

Of the three recognition tests most commonly used by law enforcement officers—curbside lineups, photo lineups, and live lineups—curbside lineups have the highest error rate and are the least reliable. Like the errors in cross-racial identifications, the errors in curbside lineups are almost exclusively false positives. The error rates are especially high if the person displayed is the same race, size, and gender and is wearing clothing similar to what the perpetrator was seen wearing.

Moreover, once a witness makes an identification, whether through a curbside lineup or other method, the witness is predisposed to identify the same person again. Consequently, any subsequent identification of the same person, such as at a preliminary hearing or a trial, is not an independent assessment. Furthermore, if a witness does not specifically state the person is or is not the perpetrator, but instead makes feature similarity declarations, such as the person has the same kind of clothes or jaw line as the perpetrator, the witness's remarks would more accurately be treated as a rejection than a selection.

DISCUSSION
Sufficiency of the Evidence Claim

Mohamed contends we must reverse his conviction because there was insufficient evidence to show he was one of the robbers. "In reviewing a claim for sufficiency of the evidence, we must determine whether, after viewing the evidence in the light most favorable to the prosecution, any rational trier of fact could have found the essential elements of the crime or special circumstance beyond a reasonable doubt. We review the entire record in the light most favorable to the judgment below to determine whether it discloses sufficient evidence—that is, evidence that is reasonable, credible, and of solid value—supporting the decision, and not whether the evidence proves guilt beyond a reasonable doubt. We neither reweigh the evidence nor reevaluate the credibility of witnesses. We presume in support of the judgment the existence of every fact the jury reasonably could deduce from the evidence. If the circumstances reasonably justify the findings made by the trier of fact, reversal of the judgment is not warranted simply because the circumstances might also reasonably be reconciled with a contrary finding. Apropos the question of identity, to entitle a reviewing court to set aside a jury's finding of guilt the evidence of identity must be so weak as to constitute practically no evidence at all."

In this case, the evidence showed that a short time after the robbery a police officer spotted Mohamed walking along the street four blocks from the crime scene. Mohamed fit the description of one of the robbers. During a curbside lineup, Gomez stated she was 80 percent sure Mohamed was one of the robbers because he was wearing the same clothing, had the same build, and had the same jaw line and chin hair. She also identified Mohamed as one of the robbers at the preliminary hearing and at trial. During a separate curbside lineup, Medina stated he was "completely sure" Mohamed was one of the robbers because Mohamed was wearing the same clothing. After Mohamed's arrest, a police officer found a thin, nylon do-rag on him, which Gomez testified matched the fabric the robbers used to mask their faces. In addition, Mohamed provided the officer with a false alibi, suggesting consciousness of guilt. We conclude this evidence amply supports the jury's verdict in this case.

Gomez's inability to be 100 percent certain of her curbside identification and Medina's expression of "a little bit" of doubt about his curbside identification at trial do not preclude the existence of sufficient support for the jury's verdict. "It is not essential that a witness be free from doubt as to one's identity. He may testify that in his belief, opinion or judgment the accused is the person who perpetrated the crime, and the want of positiveness goes only to the weight of the testimony."

The fact that neither Gomez nor Medina saw the robbers' entire faces also does not preclude the existence of sufficient support for the jury's verdict. "It is not necessary that any of the witnesses called to identify the accused should have seen his face. Identification based on other peculiarities may be reasonably sure. Consequently, the identity of a defendant may be established by proof of any peculiarities of size, appearance, similarity of voice, features or clothing."

Similarly, the discrepancies between Gomez's and Medina's observations and their omission of certain information from their initial descriptions of the robber they identified as Mohamed, including his possession of an umbrella or the presence of a black stripe on the side of his pants, did not necessitate the jury's rejection of their identifications. "The strength or weakness of the identification, the incompatibility of and discrepancies in the testimony, if there were any, the uncertainty of recollection, and the qualification of identity and lack of positiveness in testimony are matters which go to the weight of the evidence and the credibility of the witnesses, and are for the observation and consideration, and directed solely to the attention of the jury in the first instance...."

Moreover, although Dr. Fraser provided the jury with information explaining how certain discrepancies and omissions might indicate an eyewitness identification is inaccurate, the jury was not obliged to accept Dr. Fraser's opinions or find them applicable in this particular case. The jury is not bound to accept the opinion of any expert as conclusive, but should give to it the weight to which they shall find it to be entitled. The jury may, however, disregard any such opinion if it shall be found by them to be unreasonable. Furthermore, given the closeness of Gomez's and Medina's descriptions to Mohamed's physical appearance the night of the robbery, his proximity to the crime scene, his possession of a do-rag with similar characteristics to the masks worn by the robbers, and his false alibi, we are unable to conclude, as Mohamed asserts, that Gomez's and Medinas identifications of him were inherently improbable.

DISPOSITION
The judgment is affirmed.
WE CONCUR: HALLER and IRION, JJ.

CASE QUESTIONS
1. Why does Mohamed claim that his conviction for armed robbery must be reversed?
2. What standard does the appellate court use in determining the sufficiency of eyewitness testimony?
3. Were both witnesses 100% sure of their identifications?
4. Are the witnesses' doubts enough to overturn the conviction? Why or why not?
5. Does the fact that the witnesses never saw the defendant's entire face preclude a finding of guilt? Why or why not?

✓ Paralegal To Do List

For the defense paralegal:

- Was the client given any kind of physical examination?
- Was any blood or other tissue specimen taken?
- Was clients hair taken or combed?
- Was a narcotics or alcohol test performed?
- Was client examined by a doctor or psychiatrist/psychologist?
- Did anyone say anything about the examination? Was it explained?
- Was client told that he/she had a right to refuse?

- Was client asked to stand in a lineup?
- Did the identifying witness say anything? Did the witness hesitate before identifying the client?
- Was the client asked to repeat any words during the lineup?

For the prosecution paralegal:

- Was a search warrant obtained for any evidence seized?
- If not, was the seizure justified by some exception to the warrant requirement?
- Did the defendant consent to the search?
- Did the defendant sign any paperwork showing that he/she consented?
- Has the defendant ever been typed for a DNA match before?
- Is he/she listed in any of the DNA databases for sex offenders? (Sometimes, a "hit" in one of these databases can uncover a person who is committing a different kind of crime.)

Chapter Summary

The use of evidence in criminal cases raises a host of interesting and sometimes complex legal issues. Simply identifying the defendant as the perpetrator of the crime can trigger several constitutional protections. Lineups and showups are fraught with potential problems. Any identification of the defendant that results from unfair or suggestive law enforcement practices could be invalidated, meaning that the jury will never hear that testimony. In addition to eyewitness testimony, which has often been shown to be unreliable, other newly invented technological advances can link a defendant to a crime. DNA has received a great deal of attention in the past few years not only because it can almost conclusively link evidence to a specific person, but also because it can state conclusively that a certain specimen did *not* come from a suspect. Older technologies such as fingerprints also are useful evidentiary tools. However, no one piece of evidence can conclusively decide a defendant's fate. The jury must evaluate all evidence, including their weight and credibility.

WEB SITES

Colorado State Court System
www.courts.state.co.us/Index.cfm

Eyewitness Evidence – A Guide for Law Enforcement
www.ncjrs.gov/pdffiles1/nij/178240.pdf

FBI Handbook on Forensic Evidence
www.fbi.gov/about-us/lab

Federal DNA Database Unit
www.fbi.gov/about-us/lab/biometric-analysis/federal-dna-database

Federal Rules of Evidence
www.law.cornell.edu/rules/fre

Michigan State Court System
www.courts.mi.gov/Pages/default.aspx

National Institute of Justice
http://www.nij.gov/publications/welcome.htm

Pennsylvania Court System
www.pacourts.us

Reference Guide to DNA Evidence – Federal Judiciary Center
www.fjc.gov/public/pdf.nsf/lookup/sciman09.pdf/$file/sciman09.pdf

South Carolina State Court System
www.judicial.state.sc.us/index.cfm

Texas Supreme Court
www.supreme.courts.state.tx.us

Voice Stress Analysis – National Institute of Justice
www.nij.gov/journals/259/voice-stress-analysis.htm

REVIEW QUESTIONS

1. Explain the difference between direct and circumstantial evidence.
2. What limits has the U.S. Supreme Court placed on lineups and showups?
3. When does a defendant have the right to have an attorney present at the lineup?
4. Explain how a photographic lineup is created.
5. What are foundation questions?
6. Is it a constitutional violation to make a defendant stand before the jury and put on evidence linked to the crime (e.g., a bloody glove)? Explain.
7. Explain how DNA evidence is used to identify a suspect.

QUESTIONS FOR REFLECTION

1. This chapter discusses the establishment of nationwide databases containing DNA samples. Do you believe that such a database is vulnerable to misuse by the government? For instance, what if insurance companies asked for access to these records to discover who had inheritable diseases and then refused coverage to those people because they were considered excessive risks? Is such a database a violation of privacy? Explain your answer.

2. Several studies show that eyewitness testimony is unreliable. Why then do prosecutors continue to use it and juries continue to expect it?

3. Do certain kinds of evidence carry greater weight than others? For instance, would you be more likely to believe a person over a photograph? What about a document over a photograph? If a witness testified differently from a videotape of the same incident, would you give the videotape more credibility? Would you trust the witness or your own interpretation of what happened on the videotape? Explain your answer.

4. At various times in the past decades, there have been calls to abolish the Exclusionary Rule. Give two reasons why abolishing this rule would be a good idea.

5. List and explain at least two reasons the Exclusionary Rule is a good idea and should be kept as originally mandated by the U.S. Supreme Court.

KEYWORDS AND PHRASES

Evidence
Circumstantial evidence
Direct evidence
Physical evidence
Documentary evidence
Document
Documentary evidence
Testimonial evidence
Testimony
Demonstrative evidence
Lineup
Showups
Eyewitness Identification
Photographic lineups
Self-incrimination and
    identification

DNA
DNA testing
DNA databases
Fingerprinting
Blood testing
Polygraph tests
Voice testing
Foundation questions
Admission of evidence
Chain of custody
Evidence rooms
Exclusionary Rule
Fruit of the poisonous tree

PRACTICAL APPLICATIONS

1. Locate cases in a local or national newspaper in which DNA evidence was used to secure a conviction or to overturn a conviction. Was DNA the pivotal evidence in the case? Why or why not? Is DNA evidence more reliable than other forms of evidence? Explain.

2. Contact an area police department and ask to speak with an evidence technician. Ask this person how they go about lifting fingerprints from different kinds of surfaces. Ask this person about the FBI

fingerprint database and how it works. Does the local agency have direct computer access to the FBI database or the state database? You may be surprised by the answer.

3. Review the facts in the *Marbles* case (Appendix); then answer this question: During the time that the victim was being held against her will, Richard Marbles forced her to withdraw money from ATM machines around the state. During one of these transactions, the camera in the ATM machine took a picture of Marbles and the victim. The photograph clearly shows that Marbles was pointing a gun at the victim's stomach while she completed her transaction. Is this evidence admissible? Does it matter that the ATM was located outside the county? Who is going to testify that the photograph fairly and accurately depicts the scene (one of the necessary foundation questions for admitting a photograph)?

NOTES

1. *Moore v. Illinois*, 434 U.S. 220, 98 S. Ct. 458, 54 L. Ed. 2d 424 (1977); *Foster v.California*, 394 U.S. 440, 89 S. Ct. 1127, 22 L. Ed. 2d 402 (1969).

2. 388 U.S. 218 (1967).

3. *Manson v. Brathwaite*, 432 U.S. 98, 97 S. Ct. 2243, 53 L. Ed. 2d 140 (1977).

4. *Milholland v. State*, 319 Ark. 604, 893 S.W.2d 327 (1995).

5. *Stovall v. Denno*, 388 U.S. 293, 87 S. Ct. 1967, 18 L. Ed. 2d 1199 (1967) (disapproval on other grounds *Griffith v. Kentucky*, 479 U.S. 314, 107 S.Ct. 708, 93 L.Ed.2d 649 (1987).

6. *Gilbert v California*, 388 US 263, 18 L Ed 2d 1178, 87 S Ct 1951 (1967).

7. *State v. Roy*, 220 La. 1017, 58 So.2d 323 (1952); *State v. Moore*, 308 S.C. 349, 417 S.E.2d 869 (1992).

8. *Holt v. U.S.*, 218 U.S. 245, 31 S. Ct. 2, 54 L. Ed. 1021 (1910).

9. *United States v. Traficant*, 566 F Supp 1046 (ND Ohio); *State v. Thompson*, 381; *Smith v. State*, 355 A2d 527 (1976).

Chapter 5

INTERROGATION, CONFESSIONS, AND *MIRANDA*

Chapter Objectives

At the completion of this chapter, you should be able to:

- Explain the importance of the *Miranda* and subsequent Supreme Court decisions
- Explain how and when Miranda warnings do not have to be read
- Explain how a suspect can waive his/her Miranda rights
- Describe the penalties for violations of *Miranda*
- Describe the basics of a custodial interrogation
- Explain the effect of a request to speak with an attorney on the interrogation
- Explain *Jackson v. Denno* hearings

I. Introduction

When a defendant has been arrested and is being questioned by the police, a host of crucial constitutional rights are triggered that protect the defendant throughout the interrogation. Police interrogations can only proceed once a defendant has been informed of specific rights, and they must end when the defendant no longer wants to speak with law enforcement or when the defendant requests an attorney. The procedural safeguards protecting a defendant are also in evidence later in the proceedings when the government seeks to use the defendant's incriminating statement during the trial. The government must establish that the defendant

Exhibit 5-1
Sample case excerpt: the kline case

"I didn't kill nobody," Christine explained as two police officers hand-cuffed her and removed her from her home. "It was Ellis. He killed Doug! He threatened me, he told me that he done it and that I better keep my mouth shut!"

For a complete overview of this case, see the Appendix.

knowingly and voluntarily gave the statement and did so without coercion, threats, or promises of rewards.

II. Interrogation, Confessions, and *Miranda*

Miranda v. Arizona[1] is one the most famous U.S. Supreme Court cases of the past fifty years. Everyone knows the Miranda rights from hearing them countless times on television. Every night, fictional police officers read suspects their "rights" before placing them under arrest. However, there is a common misconception about Miranda rights. Numerous arrests are made every day where suspects are not read their rights. Miranda applies only when police intend to use the defendant's statement against him at trial. If the police do not intend to question a suspect, there is no reason to read him the rights. However, many police officers do read Miranda rights to suspects on the off chance that they will make an incriminating statement. This is especially true in cases where the police need additional information, such as in murder, robbery, or theft crimes where others may be involved or there may be additional evidence to locate. See Exhibit 5-2.

Before the decision in *Miranda*, the issues surrounding interrogations were confusing. When the Court was considering its decision, numerous police agencies filed briefs requesting that the Court not create a rule that required police officers to advise suspects of their rights. Law enforcement officials argued that because they were not lawyers, they were in the worst position to advise the suspect about his or her rights. However, the Court did fashion the precise rule that law enforcement agencies resisted. The Court's reasoning was based on simple common sense. No matter when, where, or how the interrogation was conducted, the Court must be sure that at least two parties would always be presents: the suspect and the police. Because of this certainty, the U.S. Supreme Court ruled that police officers were responsible for advising suspects of their Miranda rights before they began any post-arrest questioning.

The *Miranda* decision gives very little latitude to police officers. The rights must be read even if the suspect is an attorney, a police officer, or a judge. It does not matter how many times the suspect has been arrested; he or she must be read the rights before being questioned in the present case. The only variation that the Court allows is that as long as the

Exhibit 5-2

Robbery and property crimes by type and average value lost: 1990 to 2009
[639 represents 639,000. For year ending December 31]

Characteristic of offense	Number of offenses (1,000)				Rate per 100,000 population				Average value lost (dol.)			
	1990	2000	2005	2009	1990	2000	2005	2009	1990	2000	2005	2009
Robbery, total[1]	**639**	**408**	**417**	**342**	**256.3**	**144.9**	**140.7**	**125.1**	**631**	**1,127**	**1,239**	**1,246**
Type of crime:												
Street or highway	359	188	184	146	144.2	66.7	62.1	53.5	511	858	1,020	865
Commercial house	73	57	60	46	29.5	20.1	20.1	16.9	945	1,685	1,662	1,774
Gas station	18	12	12	8	7.1	4.1	4.0	3.0	423	679	1,104	862
Convenience store	39	26	24	18	15.6	9.3	8.0	6.7	344	566	677	717
Residence	62	50	59	58	25.1	17.7	20.0	21.1	828	1,243	1,332	1,674
Bank	9	9	9	7	3.8	3.1	3.0	2.7	2,885	4,379	4,113	4,202
Weapon used:												
Firearm	234	161	175	131	94.1	57.0	59.0	55.3	(NA)	(NA)	(NA)	(NA)
Knife or cutting instrument	76	36	37	24	30.7	12.8	12.5	9.9	(NA)	(NA)	(NA)	(NA)
Other weapon	61	53	39	27	24.5	18.9	13.2	11.3	(NA)	(NA)	(NA)	(NA)
Strong-arm	268	159	166	126	107.7	56.4	56.0	53.3	(NA)	(NA)	(NA)	(NA)
Burglary, total	**3,074**	**2,050**	**2,154**	**1,955**	**1,232.2**	**728.4**	**726.7**	**715.7**	**1,014**	**1,458**	**1,771**	**2,087**
Forcible entry[2]	2,150	1,297	1,310	1,224	864.5	460.7	440.0	448.1	(NA)	(NA)	(NA)	(NA)
Unlawful entry[2]	678	615	701	655	272.8	218.7	237.5	239.7	(NA)	(NA)	(NA)	(NA)
Attempted forcible entry[2]	245	138	133	129	98.7	49.0	45.2	47.4	(NA)	(NA)	(NA)	(NA)
Residence	2,033	1,335	1,417	1,127	817.4	474.3	477.9	412.9	1,037	1,378	1,813	2,709
Nonresidence	1,041	715	738	407	418.5	254.1	248.8	148.8	967	1,610	1,687	2,521
Occurred during the night[2]	1,135	699	708	625	456.4	248.3	238.9	229.0	(NA)	(NA)	(NA)	(NA)
Occurred during the day[2]	1,151	836	890	910	462.8	297.2	328.8	332.8	(NA)	(NA)	(NA)	(NA)
Larceny-theft, total	**7,946**	**6,972**	**6,783**	**5,560**	**3,185.1**	**2,477.3**	**2,286.3**	**2,035.1**	**426**	**727**	**857**	**865**
Pocket picking	81	36	29	24	32.4	12.7	9.8	8.8	384	437	346	489
Purse snatching	82	37	42	27	32.8	13.2	14.2	9.8	228	387	404	440
Shoplifting	1,291	959	940	1,002	519.1	340.7	317.0	366.9	104	185	184	178
From motor vehicles	1,744	1,754	1,752	1,520	701.3	623.3	590.6	556.5	461	692	704	737
Motor vehicle accessories	1,185	677	693	501	476.3	240.6	233.6	183.2	297	451	482	528
Bicycles	443	312	249	187	178.2	110.9	83.9	67.6	188	273	267	345
From buildings	1,118	914	852	620	449.4	324.6	287.3	226.8	673	1,184	1,738	1,233
From coin-operated machines	63	46	41	22	25.4	16.2	13.8	8.1	144	272	232	348
Other	1,940	2,232	2,184	1,660	780.0	793.0	736.1	607.5	615	957	1,137	1,439
Motor vehicles, total[3]	**1,636**	**1,160**	**1,236**	**731**	**655.8**	**412.2**	**417.4**	**258.6**	**5,117**	**6,581**	**6,204**	**6,495**
Automobiles	1,304	877	907	527	524.3	311.5	304.5	193.0	(NA)	(NA)	(NA)	(NA)
Trucks and buses	238	209	219	205	95.5	74.1	76.2	74.9	(NA)	(NA)	(NA)	(NA)

NA Not available. [1]Includes other crimes, not shown separately.
[2]Unknown data not included.
[3]Includes other types of motor vehicles, not shown separately.

substance of the rights is conveyed to the suspect, it does not matter in what order they are read.[2]

A. Background on the *Miranda* Case

Ernesto Miranda was arrested for the kidnapping and rape of a young woman. After his arrest, he was questioned for several hours and eventually confessed. The *Miranda* decision came about when Miranda's attorney appealed his conviction on the basis that his confession should not have been used in his trial because he had never been informed of his rights under the law. The U.S. Supreme Court consolidated Miranda's case with several others in which the same issue was raised and then reached its famous decision. The prosecution may not use any statement made by the defendant until the state has demonstrated that all of the constitutional safeguards have been followed. Under the Fifth Amendment, all suspects have the right not to incriminate themselves. The Court determined that before any defendant's statement could be used at trial, the state must show that the defendant was made aware of his or her constitutional rights. Miranda warnings apply to all forms of arrest, even minor infractions, as long as the defendant's statement is going to be used.

Suspects must be warned of their Miranda rights even when they know their rights as well as the officers. For instance, if a person has been arrested many times before, he or she must still be informed of the Miranda rights. The rights must be read to suspects even when these suspects are legal professionals. When the suspect is a police officer, a judge, a lawyer, or another court official, the Miranda rights must still be read to the suspect. This is also true when the defendant has had numerous previous arrests.

Ernesto Miranda was killed
in a bar fight a few years
after this decision.

There are some common misconceptions about the actual interrogation. The most prominent of these is that the prosecutor must be present when the questioning occurs. Prosecutors are normally not present at any point during the interrogation. First, a prosecutor is not trained to conduct interrogations. Second, if the prosecutor were present and the defendant made a statement that could be used at the trial, the prosecutor would now be a witness. As we have seen in other chapters, an attorney cannot be both a witness and an advocate in the same case. Because of these reasons, prosecutors do not participate in the questioning of suspects.

B. The Miranda Rights

When a police officer reads a suspect his rights, the officer normally follows some variation of the following:

- You have the right to remain silent.
- Anything you say can and will be used against you in a court of law.
- You have the right to talk to a lawyer and have him present with you when you are being questioned.

- If you cannot afford a lawyer, one will be appointed to represent you before any questioning.
- You can decide at any time to exercise these rights and not answer any questions. You can also decide not to make any statements.
- Do you understand these rights?

C. Exceptions to *Miranda*

Miranda rights must be read to a suspect who is taken into custody or arrested if he is going to be questioned. If the police do not intend to question him, then *Miranda* does not apply and the Miranda rights are not required. However, there is no requirement that Miranda rights be read to someone *before* he has been arrested. Police are free to question a suspicious person, obtain answers to questions, and use these statements at trial even when Miranda rights have not been given.

1. Voluntary Statements
When a suspect blurts out an incriminating statement, this statement may be used against him at trial even though he has not been "Mirandized."

2. Background or Routine Questioning
Miranda warnings also are not required when the police are asking background or information questions about name, age, date of birth, etc.

3. Emergency Situations
In emergency situations, officers are not required to give Miranda warnings to a suspect before asking such questions as "Where is the gun?" Officers have a duty to pacify a dangerous situation, and that duty may take precedence over the decision in *Miranda*.[3]

4. Traffic Stops
Routine traffic stops are not a situation requiring Miranda warnings because the motorist is not normally placed under arrest.[4] However, Miranda warnings do apply to all arrests, even when the offense is a minor misdemeanor, as long as the police intend to question the suspect.[5]

D. *Miranda* and Reinitiating Questioning

When the police have previously questioned a suspect and read him his Miranda rights at the first encounter, they are usually not required to re-read the Miranda rights on subsequent interviews.

Once the defendant has invoked his right to remain silent and has requested an attorney, the police are not allowed to ask him any more questions. In one case, *Edwards v. Arizona*,[6] a suspect (Edwards) was arrested on burglary and murder charges. During questioning, Edwards said that he wanted to consult with an attorney before making any further statements. The police officers stopped the interview and returned Edwards

■ BULLET POINT
There are several exceptions to the requirement that Miranda rights must be read to a suspect.

to his cell. At this point, the officers had acted in accordance with *Miranda*. However, the following day, two other police officers appeared at the jail and asked to see Edwards. He refused to speak with the officers but was told by a guard that he must. He was read his Miranda rights again and during this interrogation made incriminating statements that were later used against him at trial. The U.S. Supreme Court held that the use of his statement violated his right to have an attorney present during his questioning. Edwards, according to the Court, had made an unequivocal request for an attorney. His questioning the next day did not waive that right. A suspect must knowingly and intelligently relinquish his rights. The U.S. Supreme Court has placed the burden for showing compliance with its decisions squarely on the shoulders of the state. Therefore, the state must show that the defendant voluntarily waived his rights before the statement can be read to the jury.

E. When Questioning Must Cease

A criminal suspect has an absolute right to remain silent. When a defendant states that he has nothing to say, police are not permitted to force him to make incriminating statements. A statement obtained in a coercive way is not admissible at trial. When the suspect states that he does not want to say anything until he speaks with his attorney, questioning must also stop at that point. Police officers are not allowed to try and talk the suspect out of his need for an attorney or to continue questioning him until his attorney arrives. The U.S. Supreme Court has also ruled that a defendant must state that he or she wants to remain silent. If the suspect fails to do so, then the police may continue questioning the defendant.[7]

F. Voluntary Statements

Miranda does not apply to statements that the defendant makes voluntarily. However, law enforcement officers are not permitted to use subterfuge or trickery to overcome a suspect's desire not to answer questions. In one famous case, a murder suspect requested an attorney before he made any further statements. While he was being transported to another site, the two officers in the police car discussed the fact that the victim, whose body had not been recovered, hadn't even had a Christian burial. (See an excerpt from this case below.) Although the officers were not questioning the suspect, their conversation had the desired effect: The suspect made an incriminating statement—specifically that he knew where the victim's body could be found.

■ **THE ROLE OF THE PARALEGAL:**
Make sure that the government serves a copy of the defendant's signed Miranda waiver form so that you confirm with the client that the signature at the bottom actually is his and that he can read. The state must show a

■ **BULLET POINT**
The suspect cannot simply refuse to answer and have the police infer that he or she intends to remain silent.[8] A defendant must state that he or she wants to remain silent.

knowing and intelligent waiver, and when a defendant cannot read, the officer must read the form to him or her.

G. Use of Trickery or Deceit

It is not unconstitutional to trick the defendant. However, the trickery employed cannot overcome the defendant's constitutional rights. When law enforcement uses deceit to obtain a statement, such as telling the suspect that a co-conspirator has already confessed and implicated the suspect, this trickery will trigger close scrutiny by the court. Obviously, deceit cannot be used to trick a defendant into signing a waiver form or in fooling the defendant into thinking that his statements are off the record.[9]

Police may lie to a defendant so long as the lie is not designed to overcome any constitutional protections. Law enforcement might lie to a suspect and tell him or her that a witness saw the suspect or that they have evidence tying him to the scene when they actually do not. Trickery and deception are not commonplace during most interrogations because of the difficulties involved in maintaining the deception. The defendant might realize that the police are lying to him or at least exaggerating the amount of evidence. As a result, the trickery may have an unintended effect: The defendant may actually feel more emboldened and believe that the state's entire case is flimsy. For an example of the use of trickery in an interrogation, see this chapter's Case Excerpt.

H. When *Miranda* Is Violated

The penalty for violating *Miranda* or any of the subsequent Supreme Court decisions is very simple: The confession cannot be used at trial. The Court reasoned many years ago that by punishing the state this way, law enforcement would be more inclined to follow its rules because a violation could easily do away with a major lynch pin of the state's case. This so-called Exclusionary Rule was discussed in Chapter 4 and will be mentioned in later chapters. The Exclusionary Rule states that evidence or statements obtained in violation of the Constitution are inadmissible at trial.

BULLET POINT
Police are allowed to lie to a suspect, but not about any issue that would cause the suspect to waive his or her constitutional rights.

BULLET POINT
A statement obtained in violation of *Miranda* cannot be used at trial.

INSIDER'S VIEWPOINT

Bluffing the suspect

"I never bluff. The thing with bluffing is that you better know what you're doing. I won't tell someone, we know it was you, because we found your fingerprint on the gun. He's thinking: but I wore gloves. Then he knows that you're bluffing."

—Jack Burnette, Homicide Detective

III. The Art of Interrogation

interrogation
Questioning by police, especially of a person suspected or accused of a crime. A custodial interrogation involves a restraint of freedom, so it requires a Miranda warning.

Police officers are trained in the subtle art of **interrogation**. A good interrogator may take years to learn his craft. A careful questioner notes not only the verbal responses, but also the body language cues. Most people generally do not enjoy lying. Deceit causes stress, and this stress expresses itself in a variety of ways.

Body language can also provide clues to nontruthful statements. Some of the nonverbal responses that an interrogator looks for as an indication of lying include body movements and position changes, gestures, facial expressions, and failure to make eye contact. These nonverbal actions are caused by the subject's desire to reduce internal anxiety. On the other hand, immediate responses are a sign of truthfulness; a delay may indicate deception. When a person has to think about his answer, it is often because he is not telling the truth. People who tell the truth do not have to consider how various factors of their story fit together. However, a trained investigator also knows that sometimes the truthful person looks scared and nervous and sometimes the deceitful person is calm and quick with a response. The skill in interrogation comes when an officer can unravel the suspect's story and show how it is not the truth.

A. Psychological Profiling of a Suspect

One tool that law enforcement has turned to with greater frequency in recent years is the use of psychological profiling of a suspect before questioning him or her. Armed with background information about the suspect, a psychologist or psychiatrist can give the police a fairly accurate picture of how a suspect will respond to certain stresses. This information

Exhibit 5-3
Indicators of deceptions

- Evasive answers
- Repetition of the question
- Stalling for time to think up an answer
- Feigning memory failure when confronted with a probing question or to a direct accusation of lying
- Using statements such as "to be quite frank," "to be perfectly honest with you," "I swear to God," or "I swear on a stack of Bibles."

Exhibit 5-4
Indicators of truthfulness

- Reacts aggressively to a direct accusation of lying
- Usually answers immediately
- Often does not remember specific items because she hasn't been thinking over her story.

can be invaluable when a detective is deciding on a strategy to use to interrogate a suspect. Should the detective use a confrontational style or wait and let the suspect do the talking? A psychological profile of the suspect can answer the question. Psychological profiling is also used to determine basic features of serial rapists and murderers to help police narrow the field of suspects.

B. Custodial Interrogations: Not Free to Leave

The important consideration that triggers most of the protections the Supreme Court has created is whether the defendant is in custody. Custody does not mean confinement in jail. Custody means that the suspect is no longer free to go about his business. A suspect can be placed into custody while he is still inside his home. The test that the Supreme Court has established to determine if a suspect is in custody is whether the circumstances show that the defendant was not free to leave. This determination is based on the facts surrounding the defendant's questioning. In one case, the U.S. Supreme Court ruled that a suspect was in custody—and thus should have been informed of his Miranda rights—even though the entire interrogation took place in the suspect's bedroom.[10] If the suspect is free to leave, then the police do not have to read him his rights. This right to leave is not based on what the police officers say, but what the facts suggest. If the defendant believes that he is not free to leave and acts accordingly, the courts are more likely to consider the defendant to be in police custody and therefore protected by numerous constitutional safeguards. A suspect who is free to leave at any time does not need such protection.

C. "Picking Up" a Suspect for Questioning

In another landmark case, the U.S. Supreme court ruled that a suspect could not simply be "picked up" for questioning unless the police had probable cause to hold him. In *Dunaway New York,*[11] the police obtained a confession from a suspect who had been arrested without probable cause. The Court ruled that any confession obtained in this manner would be inadmissible at trial. Before a suspect can be arrested, or "picked up," probable cause must exist. If it does not, the suspect must be told that he is free to leave at any time and that he is not under arrest.

■ **BULLET POINT**
The test to determine if a suspect should have been read his or her Miranda rights is whether the suspect was free to leave the interrogation room and go home.

- ■ That they have the right to remain silent
- ■ That they have the right to seek the advice of a lawyer before making any statement
- ■ That they have the right to have a lawyer appointed to represent them if they cannot afford to hire one.

Exhibit 5-5
Defendants in custody must be told, before any questioning

■ **BULLET POINT**

When a suspect makes an unequivocal request to speak to a lawyer, all questioning about the case must stop.

confession
1. A voluntary statement by a person that he or she is guilty of a crime. 2. Any admission of wrongdoing.

Torture in America

Among the various methods of torture preferred in the early history of the American colonies, *pressing* was a favorite. A suspect was forced to lie on the ground and then was covered with a large piece of wood. Stones were added to the top of the wood until the defendant either confessed or was crushed. All such methods were abolished with the passage of the U.S. Constitution. However, after the events of September 11, 2001, so-called "enhanced interrogation" techniques were used against individuals captured outside the United States. It is still unconstitutional and illegal to use any of these techniques on criminal defendants.

D. What is a Suspect Required to Say to the Police?

Before a custodial suspect can be interrogated, even for the limited purpose of determining truthfulness or deception, he must be given his Miranda warnings. He also must knowingly and intelligently waive these rights and agree to speak with the police without a lawyer being present. However, these requirements do not exist when the person being interviewed is not in custody. In those situations, a suspect can limit his responses to identifying himself. He does not have to say anything else, except perhaps that he wants to speak with a lawyer.

E. When the Suspect Requests a Lawyer

Whenever the subject requests to speak with a lawyer, the rules are simple: Police must stop asking him questions. Officers cannot talk the defendant out of his desire for representation or use the intervening time waiting for the attorney to arrive to ask additional questions.

IV. Confessions

Before a **confession** may be admitted at trial, the state must show that the defendant gave it voluntarily. This rule has been a mainstay of Anglo-American law for centuries. A person cannot be compelled to give testimony against himself, especially through torture, which, unfortunately, was the preferred way of securing confessions in the Middle Ages and later. Confessions obtained through torture or other coercive means are notoriously unreliable. A suspect who is being tortured, guilty or not, will often confess to anything to stop the punishment. Physical pain is not usually an issue in confessions these days. However, police can bring other more insidious pressures to bear on a suspect. An unduly long or psychologically abusive interrogation can produce the same results as torture. Similarly, deprivation of the basic necessities of life: food, water, or sleep will also have the same effect. Because of this, the U.S. Supreme court requires that before a confession may be admitted at trial, the state must show that it was given voluntarily.

Following this line of reasoning, threats of physical harm will also result in a confession being ruled inadmissible. If harm or the threat of harm will result in a false confession, so too may promises of leniency. "Confess and go free" may be as coercive as threats of physical violence. All of these scenarios violate the U.S. Constitution. Before a confession can be admitted at trial, the circumstances of giving it are examined.

A. *Jackson v. Denno* Hearing

A so-called *Jackson v. Denno* hearing is a court proceeding that must take place before the defendant's confession can be admitted into evidence

At the hearing, a prosecutor will ask the officer:
- Was anyone else present during the interview?
- Did you advise the defendant of his Constitutional rights?
- Did the defendant appear to understand his rights as you read them to him?
- Did you promise the defendant anything in return for making a statement to you?
- Did you provide any hope of benefit in return for making a statement?
- Did you coerce the defendant into making a statement with fear of injury?
- To the best of your knowledge, was the defendant's statement freely and voluntarily given?

Exhibit 5-6
Questions in a Jackson v. Denno hearing

Copyright © 2015 Cengage Learning®

against him. Named after the U.S. Supreme Court case where it was first mentioned, a *Jackson v. Denno* hearing (sometimes called a Jackson-Denno hearing) is designed to prove that law enforcement did not violate a defendant's rights during interrogation. The state must show that the defendant was not coerced into giving his confession. In a *Jackson v. Denno* hearing, the burden is on the state. Until the state proves otherwise, the court must assume that the defendant was coerced either by threats or promises. A police officer's testimony at the hearing must establish that no irregularities occurred.[12]

1. Promises to the Suspect
Police officers are permitted to make certain limited promises to the suspect. For instance, they can tell the suspect that they will ask the judge for a reduced bond for the suspect or inform the judge of the suspect's cooperation. Police officers cross the line, however, when their promise goes beyond these issues. Police officers cannot promise, for example, that the suspect will not be charged with a crime or that the suspect will "only get probation." Such promises have been held to be unconstitutional. A confession obtained after such a promise would be inadmissible at trial.

2. Privileges
When interrogating suspects, police officers are also prohibited from violating recognized legal privileges such as attorney-client and pastor-penitent. For example, a police officer cannot pose as a priest to hear a suspect's confession. Police can, however, put another inmate in the suspect's cell and have him ask the defendant about the crime. Because no **privilege** is involved, the informer can report the suspect's statements to law enforcement.

BULLET POINT
The purpose of a *Jackson v. Denno* hearing is to determine that the defendant's statement was given freely and voluntarily without coercion, duress, or promises of leniency.

privilege
The right to prevent disclosure or the duty to refrain from disclosing information communicated within a specially recognized confidential relationship. (See Chapter 4.)

INSIDER'S VIEWPOINT

Interrogating a suspect

"I'll take the suspect by a fast food restaurant and get him a burger and some fries. I like to have the video running before I even go into the interview room. I don't tell them that they are being videotaped. We'll sit and talk for a while about whatever they want: cars, women, hunting, whatever. Then I'll say, 'you know you're under arrest for shooting that guy. Before we start, do you need to go to the bathroom? Do you need some more to drink?' I'll say, 'well you've probably seen this on TV a bunch, but I've got to do it.' Then I'll read them their rights one by one and ask them if they understand. They'll say 'yes, sir' to everyone. What that does, that just kills the Jackson-Denno before it even starts. Their lawyer can't get up there and say that I coerced them or did anything else if they see their guy sitting there [*sic*] with a mouthful of burger saying that he understands each of his rights."

—Jack Burnette, Homicide Investigator

3. Waiving Rights

A suspect must understand his rights and freely waive them before his statement can be used against him at trial. If he does not understand his rights, then he cannot knowingly and intelligently waive them and any statement obtained from him would be inadmissible at trial. This means that a suspect who speaks a foreign language must be told his rights in his native language. The best way to establish this **waiver** is through the defendant's signature or his videotaped statement where he clearly states he understands his rights and agrees to waive them and speak with police.

waiver
The voluntary giving up of a right.

ETHICAL CONSIDERATION: NATIONAL PARALEGAL ASSOCIATIONS

There are two major national paralegal associations, the National Federation of Paralegal Associations (NFPA) and the National Association of Legal Assistants. Practicing paralegals and paralegal students are eligible to join either or both of these organizations. Benefits of membership include newsletters, annual conventions, and a ready-made network of friendly professionals who often can assist a paralegal with difficult or unusual legal matters. Both organizations have created model rules of ethical behavior for paralegals. The web sites for both are provided in the section Web Sites of this chapter.

In addition to these national organizations, almost all states have some form of local paralegal association. These smaller chapters meet regularly to discuss important issues and practice concerns. You can often locate a local paralegal association by contacting the bar association or by asking practicing paralegals.

Case Excerpt. Examining Whether a Confession Was Coerced

STATE V. BROWN, 100 OHIO ST.3D 51, 66-65, 796 N.E.2D 506, 509 - 521 (2003) FRANCIS E. SWEENEY, SR., J.

On March 4, 1994, the Mahoning County Grand Jury indicted defendant-appellant, Mark A. Brown, for four counts of aggravated murder in the deaths of Isam Salman and Hayder Al Turk. Counts one and two alleged that appellant did purposely and with prior calculation and design cause the deaths of Salman and Al Turk. Each of these counts carried death penalty specifications alleging that the murders were committed as a course of conduct involving the purposeful killing or attempt to kill two or more persons and occurred while the offender was committing aggravated robbery. The counts also carried gun specifications. Counts 3 and 4 alleged that appellant committed aggravated murder while committing aggravated robbery, and contained the same death penalty and firearm specifications. Appellant was also indicted in count 5 for aggravated robbery and in count 6 for having a weapon under disability.

Facts

On the evening of January 28, 1994, appellant went with his friend, Allen Thomas, a.k.a. "Boonie," a juvenile, and Boonie's uncle, Gary Thomas, to a store to purchase beer and wine. Thomas then drove them to the home of Boonie's cousin, Kenny Dotson, to play cards. A group of juveniles was also at the house that evening. Appellant and Boonie drank wine mixed with a number of Valiums, and smoked marijuana in "blunts," which are cigars that have been cut open, emptied of tobacco, and filled with marijuana. Thomas stated that while playing cards, appellant pulled out a gun and put it back in his pants or coat pocket. Thomas further stated that appellant talked about the movie "Menace II Society" and said that he wanted to copy the scene in the movie where assailants robbed and killed two Oriental store clerks.

Later that night, Thomas drove appellant and Boonie to the Midway Market in Youngstown to buy more drinks. Thomas parked the car while appellant and Boonie entered the store together. A group of minors who had been at Dotson's house earlier were standing just outside the store. Two of the minors, Marcus Clark and Myzelle Arrington, saw appellant and Boonie leave the store. They then saw appellant reenter the store alone, wearing a mask or bandanna around his neck. They said that Boonie and Thomas were in the car. They then heard gunshots and ran back to the Dotson home.

Thomas verified the boys' account of what occurred, and added that before reentering the store, appellant said, "I forgot to do something." While appellant was in the store, Thomas heard gunshots. Thomas saw appellant casually walk away from the store and get back into his car. When Thomas asked appellant what went on in the store, appellant replied, "Oh, that wasn't nothing but some firecrackers." Thomas drove appellant and Boonie back to the Dotson home, where he observed appellant "messing with the gun." Thomas also noticed that there was blood on appellant's hand and clothing. Both Clark and Arrington saw appellant either wiping off or loading a 9–mm black gun. Arrington saw him counting money.

At approximately 9:55 that evening, Officer Timothy Morgan Jr. of the Youngstown Police Department received a call that a robbery was in progress at the Midway Market. He and his partner arrived on the scene and found two Arab males who had been shot and were apparently dead. One victim was found lying on the floor face up and the other was kneeling behind the register counter. A "blunt" and a packet of marijuana were on the floor nearby. The victims were later identified as storeowner Isam Salman and employee Hayder Al Turk. Dr. Anil Nalluri, Chief Deputy Coroner of Mahoning County, performed autopsies and determined that the victims died of hemorrhage and shock as a result of gunshot wounds to the head.

Lieutenant David McKnight interviewed several witnesses and, on January 31, 1994, secured a warrant for appellant's arrest. On February 3, 1994, appellant was arrested in Warren and transported back to Youngstown. After advising him of his Miranda rights, which he waived in writing, police began questioning him. During the questioning, appellant admitted being at the Midway Market but claimed that Boonie was the shooter. Although police knew that video cameras in the store were not operating during the murders, the lieutenant asked appellant whether he knew that there were video cameras in the store. Appellant said that he had not noticed. Police told him that there were two video cameras in the store. Appellant replied, "Well, I guess you know what happened there then." When the police answered, "yes," appellant stated, "Well, you've got me." He also said, "Then you know I did it." Appellant then admitted to shooting one of the victims, but stated that he did not recall shooting the second victim. Appellant claimed that he got the gun from Steven Dotson and had "just flipped out." Appellant expressed regret over what happened and explained, "It's the Valliums [sic]. They make you go off."

When appellant was apprehended, police retrieved a 9–mm Glock semiautomatic firearm under the couch cushion in the front room. The firearm was later identified by Steve Jones, who said that Brown had robbed him of his car at gunpoint on December 15, 1993; Jones's Glock was in the car's trunk at the time. Michael Roberts, a forensic scientist in the BCI firearms department, examined the Glock firearm, nine cartridge casings recovered from the crime scene, and four bullets retrieved from the victims. He concluded that all nine cartridges were fired from the Glock firearm. He further concluded that the bullets recovered from the victims indicated that they were fired from a Glock weapon; however, he could not confirm or eliminate the Glock retrieved from appellant as the weapon from which they were fired.

At trial, appellant took the stand in his own defense. Appellant admitted shooting one of the victims but not the other. He testified that Boonie was with him at the time of the shooting, and that Boonie took the gun from him after the first victim was shot. He stated that he did not steal any money from the store. Although he told police that he got the gun from Steven Dotson, he testified that he actually got it from a different friend, Mike Austin. Appellant further testified that he was "messed up" when police interviewed him, and that he requested an attorney two or three times, but that this request was denied.

The jury convicted appellant of two counts of aggravated murder committed with prior calculation and design. The jury also found him guilty of the firearm specifications attached to these counts and the death penalty specifications that the murders occurred in the course of killing two people, but acquitted him of

the specifications that the murders were committed while committing aggravated robbery. The jury returned not guilty verdicts as to counts three, four, and
five, which charged appellant with aggravated murder while committing aggravated robbery, and with the crime of aggravated robbery itself. The jury recommended that appellant receive the death penalty for the aggravated murder of
Salman and life imprisonment for the aggravated murder of Al Turk. The trial
court sentenced appellant to death and to life imprisonment with parole eligibil-
ity after 30 years, with the sentences to run consecutively, and to three years of
actual incarceration on the firearm specification for each of the two counts, to be
served consecutively.

Appellant appeals from the judgment to this court as a matter of right.

We have fully considered each argument advanced and have reviewed the
record in its entirety. We have also independently weighed the aggravating
circumstance against the mitigating factors and have reviewed the death penalty
for appropriateness and proportionality pursuant to R.C. 2929.05(A). Upon
review, and for the reasons that follow, we affirm appellant's convictions and sentence of death.

Pretrial Issue—Voluntariness of Confession

In proposition of law V, appellant argues that the confession he made to police on
February 4, 1994, was involuntary and that the trial court erred in refusing to suppress the confession.

In determining whether a pretrial statement is involuntary, a court "should
consider the totality of the circumstances, including the age, mentality, and prior
criminal experience of the accused; the length, intensity, and frequency of interrogation; the existence of physical deprivation or mistreatment; and the existence of
threat or inducement." Under the totality of the circumstances, and for the reasons that follow, we conclude that appellant made a knowing, voluntary, and intelligent waiver of his constitutional rights, and that his confession to police was
voluntarily made.

Appellant first argues that he was intoxicated and under the influence of
drugs when he made the statement; thus, he maintains that his signed waiver was
invalid because he did not fully understand his rights. The testimony of the detectives who interviewed appellant contradicts this claim. Detective McKnight
testified that appellant was cooperative and alert during the interview. He further
testified that he did not smell alcohol and did not observe anything that would
indicate that appellant was under the influence of drugs or alcohol. Furthermore,
at the suppression hearing, Detective Gerald Maietta, who also interviewed appellant, testified that he exhibited no signs of being intoxicated or on drugs, but was
"friendly, cognizant, appeared to understand what we were talking about." Neither
officer remembered appellant's telling them that he was under the influence of
drugs or alcohol.

It is well established that at a suppression hearing, "the evaluation of evidence and the credibility of witnesses are issues for the trier of fact." The trial
court was free to find the officers' testimony more credible than appellant's. We
therefore defer to the trial court's ruling regarding the weight and credibility of
witnesses.

Appellant also argues that because of his youth and lack of experience with
the criminal justice system, he was incapable of making a voluntary statement.

Appellant was 21 years old at the time of the offense, had finished tenth grade, and could read and write. He did not lack the intelligence to understand what was being asked of him. Moreover, appellant had been charged with and convicted of two prior felonies, at which times he was advised of his Miranda rights and was represented by counsel. He cannot legitimately argue that he was unfamiliar with the criminal justice system.

Appellant further asserts that he was coerced into signing the waiver and deceived into admitting to killing one of the victims. This argument lacks merit. Appellant conceded at the suppression hearing that he was not mistreated or deprived of sleep or food during questioning. The interview itself lasted for one hour and ten minutes and thus was not unduly long. Although the police misled appellant into thinking that his crime had been caught on video cameras, this fact alone was insufficient to render his confession involuntary, and appellant claims no further coercion.

Appellant next argues that the trial court should have suppressed his confession because police ignored his request to have an attorney present. Under the Fifth Amendment, if an accused requests counsel during questioning, the interrogation must cease until an attorney is present. For the interrogation to cease, however, the accused must clearly invoke his constitutional right to counsel. In order to do this, an accused "must articulate his desire to have counsel present sufficiently clearly that a reasonable police officer in the circumstances would understand the statement to be a request for an attorney." No cessation of questioning is required if the request is ambiguous.

In this case, Detective McKnight testified that he had no recollection that appellant requested a lawyer. However, even if we assume the truth of appellant's testimony, we would still find that he did not clearly invoke his constitutional right to counsel. At the suppression hearing, appellant testified as follows: "Before he asked me to understand my rights, he asked me do I have any questions, and I asked him, don't I supposed to have a lawyer present; and neither one of them answered." This statement is at best ambiguous. It is similar to the statement made in *State v. Henness* (1997), 79 Ohio St.3d 53, 62, 679 N.E.2d 686, where the defendant stated, "I think I need a lawyer." In *Henness*, we held that this remark was not an unequivocal assertion of the right to counsel. We likewise find that the alleged statement by appellant was not a clear invocation of his right to counsel.

Based on the foregoing, we find that the trial court did not err in failing to suppress appellant's confession. We overrule proposition of law V.

For the foregoing reasons, we affirm appellant's convictions and death sentence.

Judgment affirmed.

MOYER, C.J., RESNICK, PFEIFER, LUNDBERG STRATTON, O'CONNOR and O'DONNELL, JJ., concur.

CASE QUESTIONS

1. What crimes are alleged against the defendant?
2. What was the issue about the defendant's statement and the video cameras?
3. Was the defendant intoxicated at the time that he made his confession?
4. Was the defendant coerced into giving a confession?
5. How did the court rule on the defendant's purported request for an attorney?

✓ Paralegal To Do List

For the defense paralegal:

Confessions and interrogations

- Did the client give a statement?
- Was the statement put into writing?
- Did the client sign anything waiving his or her rights before giving a statement to police?
- Were any coercive tactics used, such as preventing the client from going to the bathroom, refusing drinks, food?
- How long did the interrogation last?
- From your observations, does the client make a believable witness? (Would it be a good idea to put the client on the stand, or would the jury react adversely?)

For the prosecution paralegal:

- Was the defendant promised anything before giving a statement?
- Did the defendant say anything in the statement that is beneficial to a codefendant? (Brady dictates that any beneficial information be turned over to the defense, whether they are otherwise entitled to it or not.)
- Was the statement videotaped or recorded? (This could help defeat a claim of coercion or threats.)
- If the defendant was not Mirandized before giving a statement, does it fall into one of the recognized exceptions to Miranda?

Chapter Summary

When a suspect is questioned by the police, he or she is protected by numerous U.S. Supreme Court decisions interpreting the Constitution. One of the most famous of these Supreme Court decisions is the *Miranda* case that states suspects must be read their constitutional rights before a custodial interrogation can proceed. Failure to read a suspect the Miranda rights can have dire consequences at trial. One such consequence is that whatever statement is given cannot be used. However, the Miranda rights do not apply to all situations. For instance, Miranda rights do not have to be read before the police question a person at a routine traffic stop or when there is an emergency situation. The government always has the burden of showing that any statement obtained from a criminal defendant was freely and voluntarily given. The government must show that the defendant's statement was not coerced or induced by promises or threats. Police officers are trained in interrogation techniques, but the most important part of their training is how to avoid violating a suspect's rights. The U.S. Supreme Court has been zealous in its protections of the suspect's rights.

WEB SITES

Arizona Judicial Branch
www.azcourts.gov

Delaware State Court System
www.courts.delaware.gov/index.stm

FBI – Public Exception to Miranda
www.fbi.gov/stats-services/publications/law-enforcement-bulletin
/february2011/legal_digest

Findlaw.com – enter phrase "Miranda rights"
Nolo.com – enter search string "Miranda rights"

Indiana State Court System
www.in.gov/judiciary/

National Association of Legal Assistants
www.Nala.org

National Federation of Paralegal Associations
www.paralegals.org/

New Mexico State Court System
www.nmcourts.com/index.php

Ohio Court System
www.supremecourt.ohio.gov/JudSystem/trialCourts

U.S. Courts – Miranda decision
www.uscourts.gov – enter phrase in search box: "fifth amendment
& Miranda"

REVIEW QUESTIONS

1. Normally, a defendant must be read his Miranda rights before being questioned. List and explain at least four exceptions to this rule.
2. Under what situations must a police officer stop questioning a suspect?
3. What is the significance of the "Christian Burial" case?
4. According to the U.S. Supreme Court, when is someone in custody?
5. What is the significance of being in custody in regards to the defendant's statements?
6. Why would psychological profiling of a suspect be helpful to police?
7. What is a *Jackson v. Denno* hearing?

QUESTIONS FOR REFLECTION

1. Are the Miranda rights really necessary? Why or why not?
2. When the police violate the Constitution in obtaining a confession, the confession is inadmissible at trial. Sometimes the rules about when the Constitution is violated are vague. Is there some penalty other than not permitting a confession to be used at trial that would serve the same purpose and still allow the confession to be used? Explain.

KEYWORDS AND PHRASES

Waiver
Miranda rights
Jackson v. Denno hearing
Interrogation
Voluntary statements
Background questions
Emergency situations
Right to remain silent

Edwards v. Arizona
"Christian Burial" case
Exclusionary Rule
Custodial interrogation
Psychological profiling
"Not free to leave"
Confessions

PRACTICAL APPLICATIONS

1. Is the U.S. Supreme Court overzealous in its protection of citizens charged with crimes? Create an argument in which you justify the Court's position.
2. Locate a recent newspaper article in which the suspect gave a statement or confession to the crime. Is the suspect's attorney planning on challenging the admissibility of the statement at trial? If so, on what grounds? If not, why not?
3. During Mr. Fortner's interrogation, Fortner states that he wants to speak with his lawyer. The police officer agrees, and then, while waiting for the attorney to show up, begins talking with his partner about how sad the defendant's family is going to be that he didn't "own up to his crime, like a man." The defendant then makes a statement incriminating himself. At trial, the defendant's attorney challenges the statement, saying that it was obtained in violation of the Constitution. Based on your understanding of this chapter, how is the judge likely to rule? Why? (For more information on the *Fortner* case, see the Appendix.)

NOTES

1. 384 U.S. 436, 86 S.Ct. 1602, 16 L.Ed.2d 694 (1966).
2. *Florida v. Powell*, 559. U.S. 722 (2010).

3. *New York v. Quarles*, 467 U.S. 649 (1984).
4. *Pennsylvania v. Bruder*, 488 U.S. 292 (1990).
5. *Berkemer v. McCarty*, 103 S.Ct. 3138 (1984).
6. 451 U.S. 477 (1981).
7. *Berghuis v. Thompkins*, 130 S.Ct. 2250 (2010).
8. *Berghuis v. Thompkins*, 130 S.Ct. 1499 (2010).
9. *Frazier v. Cupp*, 394 U.S. 731 (1969).
10. *Orozco v. Texas*, 89 S.Ct. 1095 (1969).
11. 442 U.S. 200 (1979).
12. *Jackson v. Denno*, 84 S.Ct. 1774 (1964).

Chapter 6

ARRAIGNMENT AND DISCOVERY

Chapter Objectives

At the completion of this chapter, you should be able to:

- Define what arraignment is and why it is so important
- Describe why plea bargaining it is so essential to criminal prosecutions
- Explain the procedure involved in a defendant's plea of guilty and the subsequent sentencing by a judge
- Describe the various aspects of criminal discovery, including what is and is not typically revealed by the state through discovery
- Explain the significance of the U.S. Supreme Court's *Brady* decision
- Provide an overview of how a motion to suppress is raised and what procedure is followed at such a motion

I. The Arraignment

When a defendant has been indicted by the grand jury in a felony case, the next important procedural step is the **arraignment**. The arraignment is normally scheduled several weeks after a true bill of indictment has been returned by the grand jury. At the arraignment, the defendant is told exactly what the charges are against him and is given an opportunity to plead either guilty or not guilty. If the defendant has hired an attorney, the attorney will respond for the defendant. Many defendants appear at the arraignment without an attorney and request that the judge appoint one for them.

arraignment
The proceeding where a defendant is brought before a judge to hear the charges and to enter a plea (e.g., guilty or not guilty)

The court is authorized to appoint an attorney when the defendant's financial status indicates that the defendant is not able to afford one. In a later chapter, we discuss the United States Supreme Court decisions that mandate such representation. The attorney who is hired by the court system to represent the defendant will defend the case as though the defendant was paying his fee. Such attorneys are called *appointed attorneys*, but their role in the process is no different than any other attorney.

A. Public Defenders

Many jurisdictions have a public defender's office. A public defender is a government-paid attorney whose sole responsibility is to represent defendants who cannot afford their own legal defense. The public defender acts in the same way as a privately hired attorney. They are, in fact, indistinguishable from a private attorney and will act in the case and are treated the same way as any other attorney.

B. Procedure at the Arraignment

The procedure followed at an arraignment is very simple. A list of cases (called a calendar or docket) is published. This list of cases contains the names of all the defendants who will be called on a particular day's arraignment schedule. The cases are normally announced according to their case file number. This case file number or docket number was assigned by the clerk's office after the grand jury returned a true bill of indictment.

On the day of arraignment, all of the defendants whose names appear on that calendar (or docket) must appear in court. The judge (or in some jurisdictions, the prosecutor) calls the calendar in the order of the case file numbers. "Calling" the calendar refers to the process of calling out the names of the defendants. Defendants are instructed that they must respond when their names are called. If a defendant fails to appear for the call of the calendar, the prosecutor may ask the judge to issue a bench warrant for the arrest of the defendant. (See "Bench Warrants" below). When the defendant's name is called, he usually stands, identifies himself, and then makes an announcement. If a defendant announces that he wishes to plead guilty, the prosecutor generally informs him that all guilty pleas and sentencing hearings will occur at the conclusion of the call of the arraignment calendar. If a defendant pleads not guilty, he will be given a new court date to return for his jury trial. If an attorney represents the defendant, the attorney will make all announcements for the defendant and the defendant will remain silent.

bench warrant
A paper issued directly by a judge to the police or other peace officers, ordering the arrest of a person.

C. Bench Warrants

When a defendant has been officially notified of his arraignment date and fails to appear, the judge is empowered to issue a bench warrant for his arrest.

Grand Jury witness:
S. Turlow, Prosecutor
	State of Placid
	Gannett Superior Court
	March Adjourned Term
	
	State of Placid
	    versus
	Richard Marbles
	    Offense (s):
	count 1: Burglary
	count 2-5: Aggravated Assault
	count 1: Burglary
	count 6-9: Kidnapping
	count10: Possession of a Firearm During the Commission of a Felony
	count11: Fleeing or Attempting to Elude a Police Officer
	count12: Aggravated Assault Upon a Police Officer
	count13: Reckless Driving
	_____Bill
	This_____day of_____, 200_.

	Seamus Kadirka Grand Jury foreperson
	Received in open court from the sworn Grand Jury bailiff and filed in office This_____day of_____, 200_.
	Deputy Clerk,
	Ronald Gauge District Attorney Gannett Judicial Circuit Special Presentation.
We the jury find the defendant _____ _____ _____ _____ _____	The defendant herein waives a copy of indictment, list of witness, formal arraignment and pleads _____ guilty. This_____day of_____, 200_.
	Defendant
	Attorney for the Defendant
Foreperson This_____day of_____, 200_.	Assistant District Attorney

Exhibit 6-1
Bill of Indictment

In the chapter on trials, we discuss the issuance of bench warrants, but a word about them here is also appropriate. When a defendant makes bond after his arrest, one of the notifications he receives is the date of his arraignment. The jail personnel usually give this notification to him. However, the prosecutor's office may also send him a certified letter informing him of his arraignment date, along with a letter informing him of the consequences should he fail to appear.

1. Revoking Bail Bond

There are two important consequences for the defendant when he or she fails to appear for arraignment. The first consequence is that the bail bond will be revoked, meaning that the bond will be forfeited to the state. In states that use bail bondsmen, the bondsman who put up the defendant's bail will now have to pay the full amount of the bond to the court. If someone has posted his or her real estate as a guarantee of the defendant's appearance, the house will now be subject to seizure by the state. This is a very serious matter. The bondsman, who was paid 10% of the bail amount by the defendant, has now lost the remaining 90%. Statutes in some states give the bail bondsman the authority to locate the defendant, bring him to the jail, and recover some of or the entire bond amount that he forfeited. This is what the so-called modern bounty hunters do for a living. The second consequence of failing to appear for arraignment is that the judge issues a bench warrant for the defendant's arrest.

A bench warrant is an arrest warrant issued by a judge that authorizes the local police or sheriff's deputies to arrest the defendant, once located, and incarcerate him. The defendant will generally remain in jail until the next arraignment calendar, which could be four to six weeks.

D. The Importance of the Arraignment

The arraignment is important for several reasons. At the arraignment, the defendant and his attorney are given a copy of the formal charges pending against the defendant. The formal charges in a felony case consist of the indictment. Traditionally, the indictment and the state's list of witnesses were the only items that the state was required to serve on the defendant at the arraignment. Historically, the state could serve other discovery materials at a later time. However, many states have changed their criminal discovery statutes and now require that the state serve its entire discovery on the defendant at the arraignment. Many of these new discovery statutes also require that the defense serve some discovery on the state at this same hearing. (See "Criminal Discovery" later.)

BULLET POINT
A bench warrant authorizes a police officer to pick up a defendant and the local jail to hold the defendant until the next scheduled court date.

Exhibit 6-2
Consequences when defendant fails to appear at court

- Bail bond is revoked.
- Bench warrant is issued for defendant's immediate arrest.
- Once arrested, defendant will often be held without bond until next court date.

INSIDER'S VIEWPOINT

How a paralegal helps an attorney prepare for court

"I try to run interference for the attorney by making a lot of phone calls. If a client calls, I return the call and talk with the client while the attorney is in court. I docket court dates and make sure that the clients are aware of when they're supposed to be in court. I contact them by phone and in writing. Then I schedule meetings between the attorneys and clients to get ready for trials or motions, whatever is upcoming."

—Jennifer DuBois, Paralegal

II. Plea Bargaining

A **plea bargain** is an offer by the prosecutor to recommend a lesser sentence in exchange for the defendant's plea of guilty to the charges against him. If a defendant accepts the state's offer, there will be no trial and the defendant will be sentenced. Prosecutors routinely make plea offers in almost all cases.

A. Most Cases End in the Defendant's Guilty Plea

Most criminal prosecutions end in the defendant's plea of guilty pursuant to a plea bargain. Although the prosecutor can make a recommendation to the judge about the defendant's sentence, the judge has the final say in the sentence that the defendant receives. The state may make a recommendation to the judge, and the judge may decide not to follow that recommendation. To give defendants some sense of security in the state's offer, the judge must tell the defendant when she has decided not to follow the state's recommendation. The defendant may then withdraw his guilty plea and renegotiate with the state.

B. Why Would a Prosecutor Plea Bargain a Case?

Why does a prosecutor give the defendant the chance to plead guilty to a lesser sentence or charge? The answer boils down to economics and efficiency. In large metropolitan areas, a prosecutor could easily have

■ **BULLET POINT**
Plea bargains are common in states courts. In a plea bargain, the state lowers its sentence recommendation in exchange for the defendant's guilty plea to the charges.

plea bargain
Negotiations between a prosecutor and a criminal defendant's lawyer attempting to resolve a criminal case without trial.

Federal Sentencing Guidelines and Plea Bargains

On the federal level, it is common for a prosecutor to dismiss one or more of the charges against the defendant to help persuade him to plead guilty. Federal prosecutors do this because under the federal sentencing guidelines, they have very little latitude in the kinds of recommended sentences they can give. On the state level, prosecutors have more autonomy—at least in states that have not followed the federal lead and enacted sentencing guidelines.

Exhibit 6-3
Discovery typically provided at arraignment

- Defendant given copy of formal charges (indictment)
- List of state's witnesses
- Police investigative report often provided
- Brady material provided

The Guilt of the Defendant

When a new case arrives on a prosecutor's desk, one of his or her first duties is to review the case with an eye toward a plea bargain. Unlike what is often portrayed on television, in the vast majority of cases, the evidence against the defendant is overwhelming. This could be explained by good police work or the poor quality of criminals or some combination of both. Because the facts against most criminals are obvious, taking the case to trial would seem to be a waste of time. The prosecutor will relay an offer to the defense attorney as a routine matter. Criminal defense attorneys often ask about the state's recommendation the first time they speak with the prosecutor. In courts where there are many cases, arraignment day sometimes resembles the floor of the New York Stock Exchange, with defense attorneys huddled around one harried prosecutor who is calling out recommendations on cases as fast as he or she can.

bench conference
A private meeting at the judge's bench between the judge, the lawyers for both sides of the case, and sometimes the parties. It is often called to discuss something out of the jury's hearing.

75 to 150 new cases on his arraignment calendar each month. Because most trials take one to three days, it would be impossible for every defendant to be tried. If they all got jury trials, the court system would immediately bog down.

C. The Rationale Behind Plea Bargaining: Trials are Expensive

The reason prosecutors focus so much on courtroom efficiency is that trials are expensive in terms of both real dollars and overall effort. In Chapter 12, we examine the many aspects of a trial, but a few words here should help. Trials are expensive. To bring a case to trial, the state must contact members of the community to serve as jurors. Courthouses are expensive to build. Transporting prisoners back and forth from the jail involves a great deal of man-hours and additional expense for security. The jurors will be paid a token amount for each day of jury service (often $25 or less). In addition to the costs associated with the actual trial, preparing a case for trial involves expenses in investigative time. All of these additional costs are unnecessary when a defendant pleads guilty.

D. Other Reasons to Plea Bargain: State's Case is Weak

The state may not be concerned just with expense. There are times when the state's case is weak because of witness or evidentiary problems. The prosecutor may believe that it will be best for all concerned if the defendant receives a lenient plea offer than risk taking a mediocre or poor case to trial.

E. The Defendant has the Final Say on the Plea Bargain

Once the prosecutor makes a plea offer in a case, the defense attorney's duty is to relay this offer to the defendant. The defense attorney cannot agree to the plea bargain without conferring with the defendant. The defendant has the final word on whether to agree with the offer. The defense attorney can recommend the offer to the defendant, but the defendant is not bound to accept it. The defendant can refuse any plea offer and proceed to trial. The defense attorney must accept the defendant's decision and represent him at trial.

F. Presenting the Plea Bargain: Bench Conferences

The attorney for the state and for the defendant will often meet privately with the judge at the bench for a **bench conference** to discuss the details of a proposed negotiated plea. Compared with prosecutors, judges have different pressures. Both the prosecutor and the judge would like to clear the docket. The judge would like to clear the docket because that means that she is making effective use of his time and his trial calendars will not continue to get backed up with more cases while the ones on the current calendar bog down. A prosecutor has a similar dilemma. A prosecutor would also like to "move" the cases off his docket. But a prosecutor often has a one or two cases that are very good for a trial or several that are very bad for trial. Obviously, the prosecutor would like to try the good case and make the bad cases go away. To get rid of a bad case, a prosecutor is likely to offer a good deal, hoping that the defendant will take it, plead guilty, and avoid the necessity of a trial. At this point, the concerns of the judge and prosecutor diverge.

The judge does not like to take plea bargains on cases that make it appear that the judge is being lenient on defendants. No judge likes to be thought of as soft on crime. A prosecutor wants the best resolution in the case, and sometimes that is accepting a negotiated plea of guilty instead of gambling on the outcome of a trial. The judge would like to clear his docket, but the judge is often an elected official, whereas the assistant district attorney is not. It is the judge's, not the prosecutor's, signature that will go on the defendant's official sentence. In the next election, a series of lenient sentences on cases might make it appear as though the judge is soft on crime or does not care about the community. Either situation is bad and makes a judge appear weak. A weak judge is more likely to face opposition in an election. A strong judge normally does not.

G. The Procedure Involved in Tendering a Guilty Plea

If the defense attorney, the defendant, and the state agree on the state's recommendation, the next step is to take it before a judge. The state is obligated to establish the factual basis of the charges against the defendant. Usually, the prosecutor does this by outlining the facts of the case for the judge. Once the facts have been relayed, the prosecutor will announce his recommendation as to sentencing, including a summary of the defendant's criminal history. The judge will often ask whether this is a negotiated plea. If the defense attorney responds that it is, the judge will then decide whether to go along with the recommendation. If the judge decides to do that, he will allow the state to proceed with the remainder of the sentencing phase. If not, the judge will state that he rejects the state's recommendation and will give the defendant the opportunity to withdraw his plea. The judge does not have to indicate what kind of sentence he believes is appropriate—although judges often do. The only statement the judge is obligated to make is to announce his refusal to follow the recommendation.

If the judge agrees with the recommendation, the prosecutor will normally ask the defendant a series of questions, orally or in writing, to ensure that the defendant is aware of all of his rights and is voluntarily surrendering them in this case. These questions and the defendant's response become part of the record, which means that the entire proceeding is being transcribed by a court reporter. The prosecutor will ask questions such as "Are you aware of the fact that the maximum sentence you may receive under these charges is...?" and "Are you voluntarily giving up your right to trial?" This litany of questions is often extensive. These questions are designed to verify that the defendant understands the proceedings. They are also designed to get the defendant's waiver of his rights and his desire to plead guilty on the record in case there should be a question at some later date.

1. The Defendant Must Voluntarily and Intelligently Surrender His or Her Rights

Numerous court decisions have held that for a valid guilty plea to be entered, the defendant must voluntarily and intelligently surrender his rights. To have a record of this waiver, a prosecutor will normally outline the state's case against the defendant by reciting the facts that lead to the arrest. Then either the prosecutor or the judge will ask the defendant if he understands the rights he is giving up by pleading guilty and whether he has had a chance to discuss his case with his lawyer. A defendant must answer yes to all of these questions before a judge is permitted to sentence a defendant.

Once the defendant has been asked all of the questions by the state (or filled out the appropriate paperwork), it is the judge's turn. The judge will ask about the defendant's criminal history. The judge will give both the defense attorney and the defendant the opportunity to address the court. Many defendants remain silent at this point, relying on their

Exhibit 6-4

Prosecutor's questions of each defendant during a guilty plea

After outlining the basic facts of the case to the judge, the prosecutor then questions the defendant on the record to verify that the defendant is pleading guilty voluntarily and intelligently. Here is a sample of the questions that will be asked:

- Do you understand that if you decide to plead not guilty that you have the right to a jury trial?
- Do you understand that by pleading guilty, you are giving up your right to a jury trial?
- Do you understand that the maximum sentence for this offense is _____?
- Have you had an opportunity to discuss this case with your attorney?
- Are you satisfied with the services your attorney has provided you in this case?
- Do you understand that the state's recommendation in this case is _____, but that the judge does not have to follow that recommendation and could give you any sentence authorized under the law?
- Do you understand all of these rights as I have read them to you?
- Understanding all of your rights, do you wish to enter a plea of guilty to the charges against you?

attorneys to make any important points for them. The defense attorney will almost always address the court. He will offer some evidence of mitigation or of the defendant's remorse and will request the judge follow the state's recommendation.

a. Is a Plea Agreement a Contract? A plea bargain resembles a contract in only superficial ways. What the state is agreeing to do is to make a recommendation to the judge in exchange for the defendant agreeing to plead guilty. However, because the judge has the option of deciding whether to accept the state's recommendation, a defendant cannot have a plea bargain enforced over the judge's objection.[1]

b. The Effect of Pleading Guilty When a defendant pleads guilty to the offenses against him, he effectively surrenders most of his constitutional protections, at least for that pending case. He waives his right to trial by jury, his right to be presumed innocent, and his right to an appeal. Once the defendant has knowingly and voluntarily entered his guilty plea, he also surrenders his right to appeal his sentence.

Once the judge has accepted the plea of guilty, sentence may be imposed. In most situations, the sentence will be entered immediately. In other situations, a sentencing hearing may be scheduled. This is especially true if the judge orders a **presentence investigation**, or PSI. A PSI is a report prepared by the defendant's new probation officer. This report details the defendant's circumstances, including the details of the crime, the defendant's upbringing and criminal history, and any other factors in mitigation or aggravation of sentence. Defense attorneys are given an opportunity to supplement the probation officer's materials with anything they believe is relevant. However, the judge still has the final decision on sentencing.

c. Pleading nolo contendere A plea of **nolo contendere** literally means "I will not contest it." A nolo plea carries the same consequences as a plea of guilty. All aspects of the defendant's sentence, probation, and punishment remains the same whether he pleads guilty or nolo contendere. That being the case, why would anyone bother to plead nolo contendere? A nolo plea is usually offered when there is a possibility of a civil case arising out of the defendant's actions. A plea of guilty may be used against the defendant in a civil case as an admission of liability. A plea of nolo contendere may not be used this way. In addition, for some traffic offenses where points may be assessed against a person's driver's license, a plea of nolo may prevent any new points from being added. Many states have passed laws limiting the defendant's right to use a plea of nolo contendere more than once. A defendant may plead nolo only with the judge's permission.

Special note: This plea is not available in all states or is strictly limited to specific offenses. In Illinois, for instance, this plea is available only to someone charged with a state income tax violation.

■ BULLET POINT
Before a judge will accept a defendant's plea of guilty to a charge, the judge must determine that the defendant's choice is freely, voluntarily, and knowledgeably made.

presentence investigation
An investigation by court-appoint social workers, probation officers, etc., into a criminal's background to determine the criminal's prospects for rehabilitation.

nolo contendere
(Latin) "I will not contest it." A defendant's plea of "no contest" in a criminal case. It means that he or she does not directly admit guilt, but submits to sentencing or other punishment.

d. The Alford plea The Alford plea allows a defendant an alternative to pleading guilty or not guilty. Under an Alford plea, a defendant can continue to maintain his innocence, but tender a guilty plea and be sentenced as though he had said he was guilty. A defendant might decide to use an Alford plea when the government's case against him seems strong and his possible defenses are weak. The Supreme Court first recognized the possibility of a defendant choosing to plead guilty while protesting his innocence in the case of *North Carolina v. Alford*, 91 S.Ct. 160 (1970), and it has since been referred to as an Alford plea.

H. Pleading Not Guilty at Arraignment

If the defendant pleads not guilty at the arraignment, he will be given a new trial date and instructed to return at that time for a jury trial. This date may be anywhere from two to ten weeks later. The turnaround time from arraignment to the actual trial varies considerably from county to county and often varies from judge to judge in the same county.

Another effect of pleading not guilty at the arraignment is that this plea triggers the criminal discovery statutes that the prosecutor (and sometimes the defense attorney) must obey.

III. Discovery

discovery
The formal and informal
exchange of information
between sides in a lawsuit.

Discovery refers to the process through which both sides in a case exchange information. In civil cases, the rules of discovery are quite liberal and the parties exchange a great deal of information. Both the civil plaintiff and defendant know the identities of each side's witnesses, the documents that will be relied upon, and the evidence that will be presented. In addition to this wealth of information, civil litigants can also depose witnesses. In a civil deposition, before the trial, the attorneys are allowed to question witnesses under oath and to have this testimony recorded or transcribed. Later, at the trial, the attorneys may rely on transcripts of these depositions when questioning the witness.

This extensive information exchange in civil cases is not found in criminal cases. In fact, until fairly recently, most states allowed very little discovery in a criminal case. The discovery that was required was one-way. The state had to produce certain items for the defendant, but there was no requirement on the defendant to produce anything. The result of this limited discovery was that a prosecutor often began a trial with no clear idea of what the defense would be, who the defense witnesses would be, what they would say, or what evidence the defense would seek to admit. The information that the state provided to the defense attorney was little better. The defense attorney would know the names of the state's witnesses, but would not know what these witnesses would say. He would receive crime lab and other forensic reports, but would rarely have access to the people who wrote the reports.

INSIDER'S VIEWPOINT

Preparing for motions

"When we receive notice that a motion has been set, I immediately call the client and notify them. I also send something in writing because I never know if the court has the correct address. Then, before the actual hearing, I try to prompt the attorney for five minutes. I tell them what case is coming up, the basic facts and then ask them who we need to issue subpoenas to or if we need to arrange for an expert witness to appear, that sort of thing."

—Jennifer DuBois, Paralegal

A. Use of Depositions in Criminal Cases

To **depose** a witness is to ask him questions under oath before a court reporter well in advance of trial. The deposition is then transcribed, and this transcript can be reviewed prior to trial. Depositions are used extensively in civil cases. Traditionally, depositions were not used in criminal cases. Because a criminal defendant has the right to confront the witnesses against him, a witness in a criminal case must appear in person to testify. A party in a civil case does not have this limitation. If a witness becomes unavailable in a civil case, the party may simply present the deposition of a witness instead of the witness himself. This generally is not true in criminal cases. The witness must appear, take the stand, and testify. Witnesses often do not understand this distinction, especially if they have some familiarity with civil trials. They often complain of missed time from work or other inconveniences in having to testify at trial and wonder why a deposition transcript or an affidavit is not being used instead.

However, some states have begun to allow the use of depositions in criminal trials. Under new discovery rules that are cropping up all over the country, some states permit both the state and the defendant to use depositions in limited circumstances.

Under the traditional system, where pre-trial discovery devices common to civil cases were not permitted in criminal trials, both the prosecutor and the defense attorney often began a trial with no clear idea of what the other side's witnesses would say. No doubt it made for an exciting trial, but it was not the most efficient use of court time. In many states, this traditional approach to discovery still exists.

depose
To give sworn testimony out of court.

■ **BULLET POINT**
In the past, discovery was limited in criminal cases. That has changed in most states.

Exhibit 6-5
Florida rules of criminal procedure, *rule 3.220. discovery*

(a) Notice of Discovery. After the filing of the charging document, a defendant may elect to participate in the discovery process provided by these rules, including the taking of discovery depositions, by filing with the court and serving on the prosecuting attorney a "Notice of Discovery."

© Cenhttp://www.floridabar.org/TFB/TFBResources.nsf/0/BDFE1551AD291A3F85256B29004BF892/$FILE/Criminal.pdf

THE ROLE OF THE PARALEGAL: ORGANIZING DISCOVERY

Sometimes the material provided by the state through discovery can be quite extensive. Organizing this material can be a daunting task, but one to which a paralegal should devote special care. Witness names and addresses should be noted. Incriminating statements by the defendant should be tagged for later review. Any possible exculpatory information should be culled out. Potential defense witnesses should also be noted. State crime lab reports contain a wealth of information if they are read closely.

B. Limited Discovery in Misdemeanor Cases

In criminal cases, there is a general rule: The more serious the offense, the more material the government generates. In misdemeanor cases such as shoplifting and driving under the influence of alcohol, the discovery materials could easily consist of just a few sheets of paper. In a capital murder case, on the other hand, the number of reports, witness statements, crime lab reports, and other items could easily fill several boxes.

C. Discovery not Automatic in All States

Although many states have modified their criminal discovery rules in recent years (see "Changes to Discovery Laws" below), this is not true in all states. In states that have not changed their discovery rules, a defendant must request discovery before he will receive most items from the prosecution. In such states, if the defendant fails to file discovery motions, then the prosecution is under no obligation to give him anything, except Brady material. (See later.)

D. Bill of Particulars

Another tool available to a criminal defendant is a Motion for a Bill of Particulars. A bill of particulars requests additional information about the counts of the indictment. For instance, a defendant might request "information concerning any oral statements of the defendant relied upon by the Government to support the charge in the indictment." Or the defendant's bill of particulars might request additional information about the evidence relied upon to support specific allegations in the indictment. In essence, the defendant is requesting that the government provide background information on specific charges to enable the defendant to better prepare his defense. However, a defendant might also file a bill of particulars simply to gather additional information, whether pertinent to the defense or not.

E. Changes to Discovery Laws

Many states have recognized the discrepancy between civil and criminal discovery and have made changes in their criminal discovery statutes. For instance, many states have amended their rules about what information a prosecutor must serve on a defendant. These statutes were amended to

Exhibit 6-6
Sample new discovery rules

Under the new discovery rules, a prosecutor must provide the following material to the defendant, at or before arraignment:

- Copy of indictment or accusation and list of witnesses
- The names, current locations, dates of birth, and telephone numbers of the state's witnesses (except for police witnesses)
- Statements of witnesses

In addition to the above, the new discovery rules also require that the defendant provide certain information to the state:

Alibi witnesses

The defendant must supply "a written notice of the defendant's intention to offer a defense of alibi. Such notice by the defendant shall state the specific place or places at which the defendant claims to have been at the time of the alleged offense and the names, addresses, dates of birth, and telephone numbers of the witnesses, if known to the defendant, upon whom the defendant intends to rely to establish such alibi unless previously supplied."

protect defendants from the consequences of unfair surprise at trial and to assist them in locating evidence that they could offer in their defense.

These new discovery statutes are designed to encourage voluntary disclosures of information like the information exchange that takes place in civil cases. These statutes also give the court the power to compel either side to disclose relevant facts to the other side. The judge may order such disclosure prior to trial. Many of these new changes require the state to turn over to the defendant far greater numbers of its prosecution and police files than were required before. This means that the state is now compelled to give the defendant copies of witness statements, police reports, and many other items traditionally withheld by the state.

Among the changes to the discovery rules is the requirement that the defense provide some information to the state. Traditionally, discovery in criminal cases was almost always one-way. In some very limited circumstances, discussed below, a criminal defendant might have to provide some minimal information to the state, but in most situations, the criminal defendant was not compelled to provide any discovery whatsoever. That rule changed under the new discovery statutes.

A criminal defendant does not have to produce the same amount of material(or to such an extent as the state does), but requiring the defendant to produce any information is a novelty in criminal law. Here is a sample of the kind of information a defendant must produce prior to trial:

- Specifics about alibi or other legal defenses
- List of defense witnesses and known addresses and telephone numbers

Exhibit 6-7
Federal rules of criminal
procedure, rule 16.
Discovery and inspection

A federal prosecutor must provide the following materials:
(A) Statement of Defendant
(B) Defendant's Prior Record
(C) Documents and Tangible Objects
(D) Reports of Examinations and Tests
(E) Expert Witnesses

http://www.justice.gov/dag/discovery-guidance.html

In redrafting their criminal discovery statutes, many states have followed the model set out in the federal rules of criminal procedure.

F. Types of Discovery Normally Produced by the State

When the defendant makes a discovery request under the new rules, the state
normally produces the following kinds of information:

- Statement of defendant (both written and oral)
- Statement of a codefendant
- Defendant's criminal record
- Documents and tangible objects (books; papers; documents; photographs;
  motion pictures; mechanical or electronic recordings; and locations of
  buildings, places, or any other crime scene)
- Reports of examinations and tests (physical or mental examinations or
  tests, measurements, or experiments made in connection with the case)
- Statements of witnesses

G. Types of Information Not Discoverable

The defendant is not allowed to use the discovery process as a fishing
expedition (i.e., as a means to go through all of the prosecution's files,
hoping to find something useful). The defendant can request specific
items or any exculpatory information (see "Brady Material" later) but is
not permitted to submit a general request for "all information."

1. Work-Product Not Discoverable

work product
The principle that a lawyer
need not show the other
side in a case any facts or
items gathered for the case
unless the other side can
convince the judge that it
would be unjust for the
items to remain hidden and
there is a special need for
them.

The prosecuting attorney's mental notes and strategy ideas about the case
are not discoverable. The prosecuting attorney's ideas and mental impressions
about a case are referred to as "**work product.**" As a general rule, work
product is not discoverable in either criminal or civil cases. This is based
on the premise that mental notes, ideas, and impressions form the very
core of the service provided by an attorney and that requiring the disclosure of such information would severely limit the attorney's effectiveness.
The general exception to this rule, however, comes when these notes focus
on witness testimony that may be exculpatory to the defendant. (See
"Brady Material" later.)

2. No Criminal Records of Witnesses

In many states, the criminal records of the witnesses, other than the defendant, are not made discoverable. This means that criminal records on all of the state's witnesses are not run and then handed over to the defendant. However, this rule can have several major exceptions, not the least of which comes when this information is potentially exculpatory to the defense. If, for instance, the defendant is on trial for armed robbery and the state's main witness against the defendant is a convicted armed robber, most interpretations of *Brady* (see later) would argue for turning over this information to the defense. This rule is not followed in states such as California. See Exhibit 6-8.

Why would the state volunteer this information to the jury at the beginning of the trial? The primary reason is because the jury is going to hear about it anyway. The defense attorney is going to hammer this point home at every opportunity. Why not steal his thunder and tell the jury about it first? Revealing this information to the jury in opening statements shows that the state is being forthcoming, and it gives the prosecutor an opportunity to shape the context of the testimony.

A prosecutor may even tell the jury that the state's main witness is not a nice person—that he is, in fact, a convicted felon who is ratting out his former friend. That may not make the witness a very likable person, but it doesn't make his testimony any less believable. Hearing it from the start

When the state's Witness Is a Convicted Felon

It is not unusual for the main witness against the defendant to be a codefendant. This person has often negotiated a deal with the state for a recommendation of a lesser sentence in return for taking the stand against the defendant. In such cases, the defense has the right to know the details of any deal the defendant made with the state. The defense will often file a motion requesting such information. The *Brady* decision might also require the handing over of any such information. But whether any Supreme Court cases require it, most prosecutors will let the defense as well as the jury know about this state witness's prior convictions. In fact, during opening statements, the prosecutor will tell the jury that the main witness against the defendant is a convicted felon and that this witness is testifying because he's worked out a deal with the state so that he will get a lighter recommendation on sentencing in exchange for his testimony.

§ 1054.1. Prosecuting attorney; disclosure of materials to defendant

The prosecuting attorney shall disclose to the defendant or his or her attorney all of the following materials and information, if it is in the possession of the prosecuting attorney or if the prosecuting attorney knows it to be in the possession of the investigating agencies:

(a) The names and addresses of persons the prosecutor intends to call as witnesses at trial.
(b) Statements of all defendants.
(c) All relevant real evidence seized or obtained as a part of the investigation of the offenses charged.
(d) The existence of a felony conviction of any material witness whose credibility is likely to be critical to the outcome of the trial.
(e) Any exculpatory evidence.
(f) Relevant written or recorded statements of witnesses or reports of the statements of witnesses whom the prosecutor intends to call at the trial, including any reports or statements of experts made in conjunction with the case, including the results of physical or mental examinations, scientific tests, experiments, or comparisons which the prosecutor intends to offer in evidence at the trial.[2]

http://www.leginfo.ca.gov/cgi-bin/displaycode?section=pen&group=01001-02000&file=1054-1054.10

Exhibit 6-8
California's criminal discovery statute

of the case prevents the defense from making a dramatic disclosure later in the trial when the defense attorney can shape the disclosure in a negative light.

H. Open File Policy

Many prosecutors maintain an open file policy. Under this policy, a defense attorney may review the entire state's file and copy anything useful or helpful. This policy short-circuits any claims that the defense has not been provided with all statutorily required information because the state is essentially giving the defense everything it has. Open file policies are not mandated by law, but are set up by individual district attorneys. Some prosecutors favor these policies; others do not. The fact that one district attorney's office operates under an open file policy cannot be used to force a district attorney in another county or state to open his files.[3]

I. Discovery Material Required by the U.S. Supreme Court: Brady Material

Regardless of whether a particular state has changed its discovery rules in criminal cases, the U.S. Supreme Court has mandated that certain kinds of information must be turned over to the defendant prior to trial in all criminal prosecutions. This is referred to as "**Brady material.**"

In the *Brady v. Maryland*[4] decision, the Court ruled that when the state has evidence or information tending to show that the defendant is not guilty of the crime (exculpatory information), the state must produce such evidence for the defendant whether or not the defendant has requested it. The Supreme Court reasoned that because the role of the prosecutor is not simply to convict a defendant but to seek justice, it is only proper that the state turn over such evidence to the defense so that the defendant can have a fair trial.

The *Brady* decision has been expanded over the years to include not only exculpatory information, but also any evidence or information that might mitigate the defendant's guilt. *Brady's* effect has been far-reaching. Most prosecutors now serve on the defendant a Brady notice detailing any evidence that has come to light during the state's investigation that might even arguably tend to mitigate the charges against the defendant.

1. How the Judge Handles Discovery Requests: In Camera Inspections

When a judge receives a request by a defense attorney under *Brady*, the judge must conduct an **in camera** inspection of the state's file. An in camera inspection is carried out by the judge in his or her chambers. The state provides the judge with its entire file, and the judge goes through all of the witness statements, police reports, and other material, looking for anything that might be construed under the *Brady* decision to be **exculpatory**. If the judge finds some material, he provides it to the defense. In this

---

Brady material
Information known to the prosecutor that is favorable to a criminal defendant's case. Brady material must be disclosed to the defense.

In camera
(Latin) "In chambers"; in a judge's private office.

exculpatory
Refers to providing an excuse or justification; showing that someone has not committed a crime or a wrongful act.

manner, the defense can be assured that an impartial party has reviewed the state's file and the defense attorney does not have to take the prosecutor's word that all exculpatory information has been provided. The judge must make appropriate findings of fact, detailing that he or she reviewed the state's file and found nothing that might be exculpatory to the defense that has not already been provided to the defendant.

Suppose the state has access to additional evidence that shows that the defendant is guilty of the crime. Is the failure to provide this information to the defense a violation of the Brady rule? Courts have answered this question with a no. Any evidence that shows more rather than less culpability is not required to be turned over to the defense.[5]

J. Changes to Discovery Rules: Duties of Defense Counsel

One of the more important changes to the discovery rules in recent years has been a duty imposed on defense attorneys to produce discovery for prosecutors. In the past, defense attorneys had very limited duties concerning defenses. In the vast majority of cases, defense attorneys produced no discovery whatsoever. For certain types of defenses, such as insanity and alibi, defense attorneys have been required to put the state on notice that the defense was intended, but as far as the identity of defense witnesses, their addresses, phone numbers, or other evidence, defense attorneys had no obligation to produce this material for the prosecutor. This often resulted in a trial where the defense attorney had a fairly solid grasp of the state's case, but where the prosecutor had no idea until the actual moment of the defense presentation what the defense would be or even if defense witnesses would testify. Many states have followed the example shown in Exhibit 6-9 where some reciprocal duties are imposed on defense attorneys.

■ **BULLET POINT**
New discovery rules require the state to produce more information than it had to in the past, but the statutes also impose duties on the defense to present evidence to the state.

(a) The defendant and his or her attorney shall disclose to the prosecuting attorney:
   (1) The names and addresses of persons, other than the defendant, he or she intends to call as witnesses at trial, together with any relevant written or recorded statements of those persons, or reports of the statements of those persons, including any reports or statements of experts made in connection with the case, and including the results of physical or mental examinations, scientific tests, experiments, or comparisons which the defendant intends to offer in evidence at the trial.
   (2) Any real evidence which the defendant intends to offer in evidence at the trial.[6]

http://www.leginfo.ca.gov/cgi-bin/displaycode?section=pen&group=01001-02000&file=1054-1054.10

Exhibit 6-9
§ 1054.3. Defense counsel; disclosure of information to prosecution

IV. Pre-Trial Motions

Defendants may raise a wide variety of motions before trial. These motions may involve evidentiary issues, but can also involve many other issues. Some defense attorneys will file dozens of motions before trial and insist that each motion be argued.

Some of these motions include motions to suppress and motions in limine.

A. Motion to Suppress

A motion to suppress requests the judge to rule that certain evidence is inadmissible at trial. The most common reason for this request is that the evidence was seized in violation of the defendant's constitutional rights. (See Chapter 2.) In situations where evidence has been seized illegally, the judge is authorized to rule the evidence inadmissible and therefore unusable at trial. Numerous Supreme Court decisions have established that when the state violates the defendant's rights while obtaining evidence, the best remedy is to prevent the state from using it. This is the famous Exclusionary Rule, already mentioned in several other chapters.

Defendants even file motions to suppress evidence in cases when there is no clear constitutional violation. Many defense attorneys believe that there is nothing to lose by filing such a motion. If the judge denies the motion, the defendant is in no worse a position than he was before the motion was filed. If the judge grants the motion, a crucial piece of evidence will be excluded from the trial. However, if the judge rules against the government on a motion to suppress, the government is permitted to appeal that decision. In Chapter 15, we will examine appeals in much greater detail.

■ **BULLET POINT**

A motion to suppress requests that the trial judge not allow specific evidence or testimony to be heard by the jury.

motion in limine

(Latin) "At the beginning"; preliminary. A motion in limine is a request that prejudicial information be excluded as trial evidence.

B. Motion in Limine

In addition to motions to suppress, a defendant will also file numerous motions in limine. A **motion in limine** is a motion requesting a ruling on the use of a particular piece of evidence or a limitation on the kind of testimony that a witness may give on the stand. For instance, if a defense attorney has reason to believe that a particular state's witness will refer to the defendant's criminal history during her testimony, the defense attorney may file a motion in limine requesting the judge to order the witness to make no such references. Because a defendant's prior criminal record is normally not admissible at trial, such a motion will usually be granted. The defense may file a motion in limine to restrict the use of other kinds of evidence or testimony. Each motion will be argued by the attorneys and may involve the testimony of a witness at a motion hearing prior to trial. These motion hearings are often days or weeks before the actual trial. Some motions may also be argued shortly before the trial begins. Still other motions may be raised during the course of the trial.

C. Other Motions

In addition to typical discovery motions and motions to suppress, a defense attorney may bring a variety of other motions. These are limited only by the creativity of the defense attorney. However, the judge always has the final say on whether the motions will be granted. Two of the more typical motions filed by defense attorneys are motions to reveal the deal and to sever offenses.

1. Motion to Reveal the Deal

When a defense attorney suspects that a prosecution witness has been offered a deal for his testimony at trial, he or she can file a motion requesting the details of the arrangement. When a defense attorney requests information about any arrangements between the prosecution and a witness, it is commonly referred to as a motion to reveal the deal. This is a motion asking that the state be ordered to reveal any deal entered into with any witness in which the state has offered immunity or some other benefit in exchange for testimony. It is fairly common for a state's witness to be granted some form of immunity or the promise of a light recommendation on sentencing in exchange for the witness's testimony against another codefendant. Defense attorneys rightly assume that such a promise could have an effect on the witness's performance on the stand. Although a prosecutor would probably think that any such promise would have to be revealed to the defense attorney because of the *Brady* decision (see above), a defense attorney might decide to cover his bases by filing a motion anyway.

2. Motion to Sever Offenses or Defendants

In some cases, the defendant may request a motion to **sever** offenses or parties. A motion for severance asks the court to try different counts of an indictment as a separate trial or different codefendants in separate trials. A defendant would request severance when he believed that by being tried with several other defendants, the jury would be more likely to assume that all of them were guilty, rather than focus on the merits of a particular defendant's case. In a similar vein, a motion to sever offenses requests a separate trial for offenses that may be unrelated from each other in time or action. The jury might not separate the proof of one offense from the other, but instead be more likely to assume that the defendant is guilty simply by the sheer number of offenses against him.

3. Motion for Change of Venue

A defendant who wants to move the location of the trial will request a change of venue. Generally, a defendant must show that his chances of receiving a fair trial in the original area have been diminished. Defendants will often present evidence of newspaper or other media reports that have focused on the case in a negative way. Because the potential jurors for the trial will be drawn from the same area, a motion for change of venue

sever
To cut off or separate into parts. For example, to sever the trial of a person from others who might otherwise be in the same trial is to try that person's case separately at another time. The process is often called severance.

alleges that the jury pool for this case has been influenced before they ever heard any testimony. If the judge grants a change of venue motion, it usually means that the trial will be moved to some other jurisdiction. The jury will be selected from the new area, but the prosecutor, judge, and defense attorney remain the same.

D. Motions Filed by the State

Although the state generally does not file many motions before trial, a prosecutor may consider a few. One such motion is a referred to as "similar transactions."

1. Evidence of Other Crimes or Similar Transactions

In many states, the prosecution is allowed to bring a similar transactions motion so that the jury can hear evidence of the defendant's prior crimes. Although the defendant's prior criminal record is normally inadmissible at trial, "similar transaction" laws do allow a limited use of such prior convictions. In situations where the current charge against the defendant is similar to a previous conviction, the state is permitted to present evidence of the prior conviction to show a common method, plan, or scheme by the defendant to carry out certain kinds of crimes. "If the defendant is proven to be the perpetrator of another…crime and the facts of that crime are sufficiently similar or connected to the facts of the crime charged, the separate crime will be admissible to prove identity, motive, plan, scheme, bent of mind, or course of conduct."[7]

However, before the state is allowed to present any such evidence to the jury, the court must rule on the evidence. A "similar transactions" hearing must be held in which the witnesses from the prior conviction testify and the state builds a case showing how the prior conviction has many of the same features as the current charge. If the judge rules that there is sufficient similarity between the two offenses to establish the defendant common motive, plan, or conduct, the evidence of the prior conviction can be used in the current case. The judge must give a limiting instruction to the jury, telling them that this evidence is only being admitted for the limited purpose of showing the defendant's common approach to similar crimes. Under this limitation, a prosecutor can only admit evidence of crimes substantially similar to the current charge. A "similar transactions" motion does not allow the prosecutor to put the defendant's entire criminal record into evidence.

E. Arguing Motions

Generally, when motions are filed, whether by the defense counsel or in far more limited fashion, the state, the motions must be argued prior to trial. Many courts set aside a particular day for the argument of all pending motions. These so-called "motions days" are set several days prior to trial so that arguing them will not slow down the jury trial. In some

Using Similar Transactions as a Negotiating Ploy

A prosecutor will often file a notice stating that he or she intends to use similar transactions in any case where they might apply. The practical effect of "similar transactions" testimony is to taint the defendant in the eyes of the jury. When a defense attorney learns that the prosecutor intends to use "similar transactions," even greater pressure is put on the defendant to plead guilty to the charge. The defense reasons that if the jury should learn that the defendant has been convicted of a similar crime. They will be far more likely to convict him or her of the present crime.

jurisdictions, motions are argued on the day of trial, but this arrangement is not satisfactory for many reasons. If extensive motions are to be argued in the case, addressing them just before the jury is set to come into the courtroom might delay the beginning of the trial for several hours. Judges are reluctant to inconvenience the jurors any more than they already have been. Arguing the motions on another day solves this problem.

The defense attorney and prosecutor are both notified as to the date that the motions will be argued. In death penalty cases, arguing motions could take several days. However, in most cases, motions can be disposed of in a few hours. In many cases, defense attorneys do not file motions other than routine discovery requests. The more serious the offense, the more likely numerous motions will be filed. In addition to motions to suppress specific evidence and motions in limine addressing such concerns as preventing a state's witness from mentioning prejudicial evidence, additional motions may address a variety of other issues, ranging from telling the defendant what clothes to wear at trial to allowing the jury to visit the scene of the crime to see it for themselves.

Arguing motions generally proceeds this way. The side bringing the motion has the burden of convincing the judge that he or she should grant it. The side bringing the motion may present the testimony of a witness or simply rely on researched case law to press his point about a particular issue. Once one side has presented its argument, the judge will allow the other side to argue against it. The other side may present testimony or other evidence in opposition to the motion and will almost certainly present case law and statutes to support its opposition. Because trials are adversarial in nature, when the defendant urges a motion, the state usually opposes it. Conversely, when the state brings a motion, the defense generally opposes it as well. Once the judge has heard argument from both sides and consulted relevant cases and/or statutes, he will make his ruling. A judge may *grant* the motion, meaning that he agrees with the request tendered in the motion. He may *deny* the motion. He also may take it under advisement. When a judge takes a motion under advisement, the judge is stating that he is reserving a ruling on the motion. A judge will do this when he believes that the motion is premature. For instance, if a defendant requests that a certain piece of evidence not be used at trial because it could unfairly prejudice the defendant at trial, the judge might take the matter under advisement because he does not know what evidence the state will offer. After all, the prosecutor might decide against using that particular evidence.

When the judge makes his decision, it is called an order of the court. This order is binding on all parties and witnesses in the action. Violation of the court's order could result in a contempt citation by the judge.

1. Drafting the Order

When a party wins a motion, the judge often requests the winning party to draft the order. State judges usually have small staffs, and by requesting that

Exhibit 6-10

Judge's possible rulings on a motion

Grant	Deny	Take under advisement
Judge agrees with theproposed motion and allows it.	Judge disagrees with the proposed motion and does not allow it.	Judge reserves ruling on the motion until a later time.

the winning attorney draft the order on the motion, the judge has saved his staff additional work. The judge also correctly assumes that the winning party has a vested interest in drafting the order and making it part of the record. Because it is to the party's advantage to get the ruling in writing, the judge leaves it to the winning party to write it up and present it to him for his signature.

THE ROLE OF THE PARALEGAL: PROPOSED ORDERS

In anticipation of an upcoming motion day, a paralegal might consider drafting a series of orders, stating that their side has won the motion. It looks impressive for an attorney, when asked to submit a written order to the court at a later time, to step forward and present the judge with such an order already drafted. One simple method for preparing such orders is to go through all pending motions and draft a series of court orders stating that the judge ruled favorably on the motion.

Case Excerpt. A Brady Violation?

TAYLOR V. STATE, 62 SO.3D 1101 (FLA., 2011) PER CURIAM.

Steven Richard Taylor appeals the denial of his amended motion for postconviction relief filed pursuant to Florida Rule of Criminal Procedure 3.850. Through his postconviction motion, Taylor challenges his capital murder conviction and sentence of death. Taylor has also filed a petition for writ of habeas corpus, through which he alleges ineffective assistance of appellate counsel due to counsel's failure to raise several issues on direct appeal. We have jurisdiction. See art. V, § 3(b)(1), (9), Fla. Const. For the reasons discussed below, we affirm the trial court's denial of his rule 3.850 motion and deny relief on his petition for writ of habeas corpus.

FACTS AND PROCEDURAL HISTORY

Taylor is an inmate under sentence of death. Through our prior opinion addressing Taylor's direct appeal, we have detailed the facts and procedural background surrounding the offense.

Brady Claim

Pursuant to *Brady v. Maryland*, 373 U.S. 83, 83 S.Ct. 1194, 10 L.Ed.2d 215 (1963), the State is required to disclose material information within its possession or control that is favorable to the defense. To demonstrate a Brady violation, a defendant has the burden to establish (1) that favorable evidence, either exculpatory or impeaching, (2) was willfully or inadvertently suppressed by the State, and (3) because the evidence was material, the defendant was prejudiced. This Court has explained that "there is no Brady violation where the information is equally accessible to the defense and the prosecution, or where the defense...had the information." Questions of whether evidence is exculpatory or impeaching and whether the State suppressed evidence are questions of fact, and the trial court's determinations of such questions will not be disturbed if they are supported by competent, substantial evidence. To satisfy the materiality prong of Brady, a defendant must prove that there is a "reasonable probability that, had the evidence been disclosed to the defense, the result of the proceeding would have been different. A 'reasonable probability' is a probability sufficient to undermine confidence in the outcome." In other words, the question is whether "the favorable evidence could reasonably be taken to put the whole case in such a different light as to undermine confidence in the verdict."

DNA Evidence

Taylor asserts that critical documents and witness names were either not provided to the defense or provided late. Those documents and names include: (1) FBI/FDLE protocols; (2) calculated fragment length reports, summaries, and bench notes; and (3) the name of Shirley Zeigler. For the reasons discussed below, we deny relief on each of these allegations.

FBI/FDLE Protocols

Taylor asserts that the FBI/FDLE protocols, allegedly not provided by the State until postconviction litigation, "established that Dr. Pollock either changed the protocol or violated the protocol in his conclusions." The only "violation" identified by Taylor, however, is the fact that the FBI protocols utilized five to eight probes, while Dr. Pollock only used four. This "violation," according to the defense's expert, undermined the reliability of the DNA evidence.

During the evidentiary hearing, Dr. Pollock acknowledged that he deviated from the FBI protocols. The only evidence presented by Taylor during the evidentiary hearing that directly challenged Dr. Pollock's ultimate findings, however, was the testimony of Dr. Libby, whom the postconviction court explicitly determined to be unreliable. Although the postconviction court did not examine this evidence in the context of a Brady or Giglio violation, it still assessed the credibility of Dr. Libby with regard to Dr. Pollock's ultimate findings. The postconviction court considered, and rejected, the relevance of the FBI/FDLE protocols in the ineffective assistance of counsel context.

This Court will defer to the factual findings of the postconviction court on this issue as this Court does not substitute its judgment for that of the postconviction court on questions of the credibility of witnesses and the appropriate weight to be given to the evidence. Even if we assume that the State inadvertently failed to disclose these protocols, in light of the trial court's findings of fact, the alleged violations cannot "reasonably be taken to put the whole case in such a different light as to undermine confidence in the verdict." *Smith*, 931 So.2d at 796 (quoting *Strickler*, 527 U.S. at 290, 119 S.Ct. 1936) (articulating the materiality prong of Brady). Further, there is no reasonable possibility that the allegedly false testimony could have affected the judgment of the jury.

Calculated Length Reports, Summaries, and Bench Notes

Taylor asserts that the calculated length reports are material because they establish critical differences in lengths of DNA strands calculated by Dr. Pollock compared to those calculated by Shirley Zeigler. In his initial brief to this Court, Taylor acknowledges that "it wasn't until three days before trial that the defense's DNA expert received the calculated fragment length reports/summaries and bench notes." Taylor further asserts that trial counsel "was essentially sandbagged into: (1) not calling the DNA expert to testify, (2) not having [the DNA expert] present during the trial, (3) withdrawing his Motion for Continuance, (4) being unable to discern what information Shirley Zeigler could supply, and (5) being unable to call her as a witness to impeach Dr. Pollock's trial testimony."

First, because Taylor ultimately asserts a discovery violation before trial, this claim should have been raised pursuant to *Richardson v. State*, 246 So.2d 771 (Fla.1971), during trial, not in a postconviction motion pursuant to Brady. "Where a defendant fails to timely object to a discovery violation or to request a Richardson hearing, the defendant does not preserve the point for appellate review."

Second, even if this were a cognizable Brady claim, the evidence is not material. As discussed above, the only evidence presented by Taylor during the evidentiary hearing that challenged the DNA evidence was the testimony of Dr. Libby and Shirley Zeigler. These two witnesses testified with regard to the potential discrepancies in the calculated fragment length reports. As previously articulated, however, Dr. Libby was found to be not credible by the trial court, and Zeigler did not disagree with the ultimate findings of Dr. Pollock. The alleged violations, therefore, cannot "reasonably be taken to put the whole case in such a different light as to undermine confidence in the verdict." Nor is there any reasonable possibility that the allegedly false testimony could have affected the judgment of the jury.

Name of Shirley Zeigler

Finally, Taylor asserts that the State suppressed the name of Shirley Zeigler, which was allegedly only revealed during the cross-examination of Dr. Pollock. Taylor asserts that Zeigler could have called into question Dr. Pollock's testimony, and had she been called at trial, the defense would have been able to impeach Dr. Pollock's testimony.

First, because Taylor ultimately asserts a discovery violation that was discovered and known during trial, this claim should have been raised pursuant to Richardson at trial, not in a Brady claim at the postconviction stage.

Second, this is not a valid Brady violation because the State did not suppress the evidence. Taylor admits in his brief that he possessed Zeigler's initials before trial as they were contained on the calculated fragment reports. Taylor simply accuses the State of failing to identify whom those initials represented. In fact, trial counsel was able to specifically identify those initials during the cross-examination of Dr. Pollock. Taylor thus fails to establish that the State suppressed Zeigler's name when it disclosed her initials through discovery.

Third, even if this were a cognizable Brady or Giglio claim, the evidence is not material. Zeigler testified that despite her disagreement with certain elements of Dr. Pollock's testing procedures, she did not ultimately disagree with his findings. Her testimony, therefore, is unlikely to undermine confidence in the outcome. Nor is there any reasonable possibility that the false testimony could have affected the judgment of the jury. Accordingly, relief is not warranted for this subclaim.

Newly Discovered Evidence

To obtain a new trial based upon newly discovered evidence, a defendant has the burden to establish two things: (1) the evidence was not known by the trial court, the party, or counsel at the time of trial and the defendant or defense counsel could not have known of it by the use of diligence; and (2) the newly discovered evidence is of such nature that it would probably produce an acquittal on retrial.

Here, Taylor asserts that the recanted testimony of Timothy Cowart, Taylor's former cellmate who testified against him during the initial trial, warrants a new trial. This Court has repeatedly held that recantations are "exceedingly unreliable" and that it is the duty of the court to deny a new trial where it is not satisfied that such testimony is true. Cowart's recanted testimony is therefore to be reviewed with extreme skepticism. Further, this Court will defer to the factual findings of the trial court on this issue as this Court does not substitute its judgment for that of the trial court on questions of the credibility of witnesses. Here, the trial court determined that the recanted testimony of Cowart was not credible. In light of the trial court's factual determination that Cowart's recanted testimony is not reliable, we deny relief on this claim.

CONCLUSION

For the foregoing reasons, we affirm the denial of the rule 3.850 motion by the postconviction court and deny relief on the petition for writ of habeas corpus.

It is so ordered.

CASE QUESTIONS

1. How does the Court define the prosecution's obligation under *Brady*?
2. What must a defendant do to establish a violation of *Brady*?
3. Was the DNA material provided by the state three days prior to trial a Brady violation? Explain.
4. Was there a Brady violation in failing to provide Zeigler's name to the defense? Why or why not?
5. Does the court offer an opinion about the reliability of recanted testimony? Explain.

ETHICAL CONSIDERATION: WHEN THE PROSECUTOR KNOWS SHE CANNOT PROVE HER CASE

What happens in a situation where a prosecutor knows that she cannot prove her case against the defendant? Suppose a key witness has changed his story or new evidence has surfaced exonerating the defendant? What should the prosecutor do? Options:

A. Offer a very good deal to a defendant on a plea bargain.

B. Go through with the trial anyway because you never know what a jury might do, and they could convict him.

C. Dismiss the case.

Answer: C. Dismiss the case. A prosecutor's ethical rules require her to seek *justice*, not convictions. Where evidence has surfaced that exonerates the defendant, the prosecutor must reveal that information to the defense and dismiss the case. It would be unethical for a prosecutor to try to force a guilty plea in a case where the evidence shows that the defendant was not the culpable party.

✓ Paralegal To Do List

For the defense paralegal:

- Confirm the arraignment date and make sure that the client knows where he/she should go.
- Has the prosecutor offered any kind of plea bargain? If so, pass it on to the attorney immediately.
- Is the judge assigned to this case notorious for being hard on this type of crime? For instance, some judges are known to be tough on drug dealers. Should the defense begin preparing the client for a rougher-than-usual court appearance?
- Is a plea of nolo contendere available in this case?
- Does the client have a prior criminal record?
- Should all routine motions be filed in this case, including motions for discovery, motions to suppress, etc.?
- Prepare drafts of orders granting all defense motions and put them in the file for later use.

For the prosecution paralegal:

- Has all statutorily required discovery been served on the defendant and/or attorney?
- Is there any Brady material that should be served?
- Work up the basic facts of the case so that the prosecutor can refer to this "factual snapshot" right before arguing any motions in the case.
- Has the defendant committed similar crimes in the past? If so, have you obtained certified copies of these prior convictions to use in similar transactions motions?
- Have you made sure that anything marked "work product" has been marked correctly so that it does NOT get served on the defendant with other discovery requests?

Chapter Summary

The arraignment is an extremely important step in any criminal prosecution. At the arraignment, the defendant is officially informed of the charges against him. He has the right to enter a plea of guilty or not guilty. If he pleads guilty, then he generally will be sentenced on the same day. When a defendant pleads guilty and the judge accepts that plea, the defendant is giving up his right to appeal any issues in the case. He can be sentenced to confinement, probation, or fines or all three. If the defendant pleads not guilty, he is informed of his trial date. The arraignment date is also important because it is at arraignment, in most states, where the defendant is served with discovery by the state.

Discovery refers to the sharing of information between the parties. In criminal cases, the state has a greater burden of producing information than does the defendant. In addition to producing lists of witnesses, scientific reports, and other items, the state is also compelled to produce any evidence that may show that the defendant is not guilty of a crime. This is referred to as Brady material, after the famous U.S. Supreme Court decision where this requirement was first imposed. Many states have modified their discovery rules in recent years, requiring the prosecution to deliver far more information to the defendant than in previous times. Whether or not a state has modified its discovery statutes, Brady material must be given to the defendant.

If the defendant has any pre-trial motions that he would like to bring, these are usually filed at the arraignment. Typical motions that a defendant might bring include a motion to suppress evidence, based on a claim that the defendant's constitutional rights were violated in obtaining the evidence. The defendant may also file a variety of other pre-trial motions. The state may also bring some limited motions, including a motion to introduce similar transactions (i.e., evidence of other crimes the defendant has committed that are substantially similar to the current charge against him).

WEB SITES

American Association for Paralegal Education
www.aafpe.org

Arraignment in the Court of Common Pleas – Delaware
www.courts.delaware.gov/help/proceedings/ccp_crarraignment.stm

Criminal Discovery for Federal Prosecutors
www.justice.gov/dag/discovery-guidance.html

Famous Trials—UMKC School of Law
www.law2.umkc.edu/faculty/projects/ftrials/ftrials.htm

HierosGamos—Legal Research Center
www.hg.org

Kansas State Court System
www.kscourts.org/

Legal Information Institute – Federal Arraignments
www.law.cornell.edu/rules/frcrmp/rule_10

Massachusetts State Court System
www.mass.gov/courts/index.html

Michigan Court System
www.courts.mi.gov/Courts/Pages/default.aspx

Puerto Rico State Court System
www.ramajudicial.pr/

REVIEW QUESTIONS

1. What happens at an arraignment?

2. What are bench warrants? When are they issued?

3. Explain how plea bargaining works. Why would the state offer to allow a defendant to plead guilty to a lighter sentence through a plea bargain?

4. Describe the process of entering a plea of guilty. What role does the judge play in the sentencing phase?

5. Criminal discovery has undergone drastic changes in recent years. What are some examples of these kinds of changes? Has your state modified its discovery statutes? If so, what information do prosecutors in your state now have to turn over to the defendant?

6. The Brady decision is extremely important in criminal discovery. What is the Brady decision, and why is it important?

7. Describe the process involved in bringing a motion to suppress.

QUESTIONS FOR REFLECTION

1. Although the general rule is that the jury in a case is never allowed to hear evidence of the defendant's past criminal record, there are several exceptions to this rule. Similar transactions is one such exception. Is it fair that the state can bring such a motion? Explain your answer.

2. New discovery statutes have imposed greater obligations on prosecutors to turn over more and more of their case files to the defense. These new statutes have also imposed some obligation on the defense to turn over information to the state. Should defendants have such obligations placed on them? If a defendant has the right to remain silent, should he not also enjoy the right not to deliver any information to the state?

KEYWORDS AND PHRASES

Arraignment	Brady material
Public defender	In camera
Plea bargaining	Exculpatory
Bench conferences	Motion to suppress
Nolo contendere	Motion in limine
Criminal discovery	Similar transactions
Depositions	Grant or deny motion
Work product	Take under advisement
Open file policy	

PRACTICAL APPLICATIONS

1. Contact your local court system and find out when the next arraignment is scheduled. Attend the arraignment and note the procedure it follows. If defendants announce that they want to plead guilty, are they sentenced immediately or given a date to return? Who calls the calendar—the judge or the prosecutor? What announcements do the defense attorneys make regarding discovery or motions?

2. Using the *Fortner* sample case as a model, draft a motion to suppress the photographic lineup used in that case.

3. Using the *Kline* case as a model, draft a motion in limine requesting that the police officers in that case be prevented from referring to Christine's prior arrest for sale of amphetamines.

4. Based on the facts in the *Marbles* case, will Annie be able to testify about Chad robbing the woman in Tennessee during the three days he held her hostage while they drove across Florida, Georgia, and Tennessee? Why or why not?

NOTES

1. *Mabry v. Johnson*, 467 U.S. 504, 104 S.Ct. 2543 (1984).
2. CA PENAL § 1054.10.
3. *State v. Moore*, 335 N.C. 567, 440 S.E.2d 797, cert. denied, 513 U.S. 898, 115 S. Ct. 253, 130 L. Ed. 2d 174 (1994).
4. *Brady v. Maryland*, 373 U.S. 83, 83 S. Ct. 1194, 10 L. Ed. 2d 215 (1963).
5. *U.S. v. Drake*, 543 F.3d 1080 (9th Cir. 2008).
6. CA PENAL § 1054.3.
7. *Hatcher v. State*, 224 Ga.App. 747, 752(3), 482 S.E.2d 443 (1997).

Chapter 7

PRINCIPALS, ACCESSORIES, AND ATTEMPT

Chapter Objectives

At the completion of this chapter, you should be able to:

- Explain how responsibility for a crime is divided among several codefendants
- Define the elements of conspiracy
- Define the difference between principal and accessory
- Describe how an accessory before the fact is different from an accessory after the fact
- Explain the difference between principals in the first degree and principals in the second degree
- Define *constructive presence at the scene of a crime*
- Explain Wharton's Rule
- Explain how and when the crime of attempt occurs

I. Introduction

This chapter focuses on how responsibility for a crime is apportioned when there is more than one defendant or when the crime is not actually carried out. When someone helps in the planning or carrying out of a crime but is not physically present when the crime occurs, should that person be considered equally as guilty as the person who was physically present? What about a person who has no knowledge of the crime prior to it occurring but who assists the defendant after it is over, with full

---

INSIDER'S VIEWPOINT

What the paralegal does on a day-to-day basis
"My involvement begins with the paper work, like filing discovery motions. I also help out from start to finish. Because the attorney is always in a trial somewhere, I do a lot of the hand holding, taking care of the clients, making sure that they get questions answered, making sure that no one is panicky. A lot of times the attorney can't return a call because he's in court. I ask him what would you like for me to say and then he'll tell me and I'll handle it from there. That's my biggest job, dealing with the clients and reassuring them."

—Mary Ann Davidson, Paralegal

---

knowledge she is helping someone avoid justice? As a natural extension, we will address the crime of conspiracy to commit a crime, when several defendants plan and execute a crime. We will also address the concept of solicitation of a crime, where one person persuades another person to commit a crime. In addition to these concepts, we will address the issue of how to assess guilt when the crime is not completed. We will answer this question: Under what circumstances is the attempt to commit a crime punishable as a crime?

II. Principals and Accessories

It is important to understand the difference between **principals** and **accessories** when assessing the culpability of the defendant. The principal is the person who actually commits the crime. An accessory is someone who helps in planning the crime or assists the principal in some way. The principal is someone who is actually present and commits the crime. An accessory (or accomplice) is normally not physically present when the crime occurs but may have given assistance to the principal before or after the crime occurred. The reason the distinction is important between principals and accessories is that they are punished differently. Principals, people who actually commit the crime, are normally punished more harshly than are accessories.

principal
A person directly involved with committing a crime, as opposed to an accessory.

accessory
A person who helps commit a crime without being present.

A. Principal in the First Degree

A principal in the first degree is the person who actually commits the crime. A principal in the second degree is someone who takes a less active role in the participation of the crime, such as the person who drives the getaway car during an armed robbery of a bank. This person is usually considered to be *constructively* present at the scene of the crime.

Constructive presence means that the person is actually helping the principal in the first degree commit the crime, but may not be in the immediate vicinity of the actual crime. However, they are normally close by. The further away the person is from the scene of the crime, the more likely she will be considered an accessory or accomplice than a principal. Waiting just outside the bank behind the wheel of the getaway car is an example of someone who is close enough to the main action of the crime to be considered a principal. The law will constructively place the person at the scene. The same may also be true for the lookout who is watching for police cars. Both of these people may be outside the bank when the crime is occurring, but will bear the same responsibility as though they were present inside the bank while the robbery took place. Principals in the first degree and principals in the second degree are normally punished just as severely. When it comes time to pass sentence, the courts generally do not make any distinction between principals in the first and second degree. See Exhibit 7-1 for a summary of homicides carried out by principals.

B. Principal in the Second Degree

When more than one person is involved in the perpetration of a crime and this person is not the main perpetrator of the crime, this person may be classified as a principal in the second degree. She might also be classified as an accessory before or after the fact (or in some states, an aider, abettor, or accomplice).

◼ **BULLET POINT**

A principal is a person who participates and is present when a crime occurs.

Exhibit 7-1

Homicides of children under age 5, by age of victim, 1980–2008

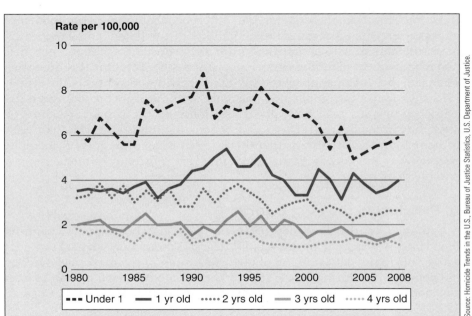

Source: Homicide Trends in the U.S., Bureau of Justice Statistics, U.S. Department of Justice.

INSIDER'S VIEWPOINT

Trigger man

"A lot of times, a suspect will tell me, 'I wasn't the trigger man. The other fellow, he was the one who pulled the trigger.' They don't realize that under the law, as long as they were both there and actively involved, it doesn't make any difference."

—Jack Burnette, Homicide Investigator

To be classified as a principal in the second degree, a person must be present, physically or constructively, when the crime is being committed and aid in the commission of the crime.[1]

C. Accessory Before the Fact

There are two types of accessories: accessories before the fact and accessories after the fact. An **accessory before the fact** is someone who helps the principal plan the crime. An accessory before the fact may be someone who provides resources, advice, or counseling to the principal.

An accessory before the fact is not physically or constructively present at the commission of the crime, however. If a person is present at the crime, he becomes the principal. An accessory before the fact helps organize the crime but is not actually present at the commission of the crime.

D. Accessory After the Fact

The other type of accessory, **accessory after the fact**, is someone who helps the defendant avoid prosecution or arrest after the crime has been committed. An accessory after the fact was not involved in planning or organizing the crime. An accessory after the fact simply aids or abets the defendant in avoiding prosecution or arrest. If a person is involved in the planning of a crime, that person becomes an accessory before the fact. The reason this distinction is so important is that of the two (accessory before the fact and accessory after the fact), accessories before the fact are punished more harshly than are accessories after the fact. A person can only be prosecuted as an accessory after the fact if he acted with knowledge that the person he assisted was in trouble with the law and he gave that person help or assistance to flee the jurisdiction or otherwise avoid arrest.

1. Codefendants

Whether classified as principals in the first or second degree or as accessories, codefendants are people charged with the same crime and who are often tried together. At trial, they are all lumped together under the single label "codefendant." The distinction between principals and accessories will only come during the trial and at sentencing, if the parties are convicted.

---

accessory before the fact
A person who, without being present, encourages, orders, or helps another person commit a crime.

accessory after the fact
A person who finds out that a crime has been committed and helps to conceal the crime or the criminal.

■ **BULLET POINT**
An accessory before the fact helps the principal plan the crime but is not present when it occurs.

■ **BULLET POINT**
An accessory after the fact helps a principal evade capture, knowing that the principal has committed a crime.

E. What if the Principal is Found not Guilty?

An interesting question arises when the principal is found not guilty at trial and the accessory is then brought to trial. Is it a proper defense for the accessory to state that the principal was acquitted? The answer is usually no. Most states that have addressed this question have held that the acquittal of the principal in a prosecution does not prohibit the conviction of an accessory before the fact.[2]

1. Abolishing the Category of Accessory

In some states, the old common law distinction between principals and accessories has been abolished by statute. In those states, a person may be charged as an accomplice to the crime committed by another person. Similar to an accessory, an **accomplice** must act in some way that aids, assists, or abets the crime.[3] To be considered an accomplice, a person does not have to plan the crime. He or she can be someone who helps the main culprit commit the crime.[4]

accomplice
A person who knowingly and voluntarily helps another person commit or conceal a crime.

III. Conspiracy

The crime of **conspiracy** is based on a fear of coordinated group-based behavior. When a group commits a crime, the participants bring more resources to the crime than a single individual would. Members of a conspiracy can set their sights on ambitious goals. They can commit greater and often more serious crimes because of the resources and talents of various members of the conspiracy. People feel safer in a group. Anyone having second thoughts about the crime will probably be discouraged from voicing them by other members of the conspiracy. As a result, a conspiracy may often continue with preparations to commit a crime where an individual might have abandoned the enterprise. As a result, the law takes a dim view of conspiracies and often provides enhanced punishment for people involved in them.

Because conspiracies have a greater potential for violating the law, statutes permit law enforcement to intercede in a conspiracy earlier in its development than in almost any other criminal enterprise.

Criminal conspirators are usually punished more severely than are individuals who commit crimes. Society wants to send a message to groups planning on committing crimes. Group action will result in stiffer sentences on conviction.

conspiracy
A crime that may be committed when two or more people agree to do something unlawful (or something lawful by unlawful means). The agreement can be inferred from the persons' actions. A person can be guilty of both conspiracy to commit a crime and the crime itself.

A. The Elements of a Conspiracy

A criminal conspiracy consists of the following elements:

1. The agreement between two or more persons
2. To work together to carry out an illegal act
3. An "overt act" in furtherance of the agreement

1. The Agreement

The most important element of a conspiracy is the agreement. The agreement has been called the essential ingredient of a conspiracy.[5] This is true whenever there is an agreement between two or more persons to commit an unlawful act, even when they have not worked out the actual details of the crime.[6] As we have already seen, the contemplated crime does not have to be completed before the parties can be charged with conspiracy.[7] In fact, as soon as the various members have reached an agreement and carried out some overt act (see below), they can be prosecuted for conspiracy.[8]

Obviously, to be prosecuted as a conspirator, a person must have knowledge of the conspiracy and of the illegal nature of the underlying crime. But more is required: The person must have agreed to participate in the conspiracy. The government must prove that each member of the group entered into an agreement to carry out the crime.[9]

No formal declaration is required for an agreement in a conspiracy. The agreement to engage in a crime can be very loose. In fact, a hallmark of conspiracies is secrecy. Therefore, the government can prosecute several individuals under a conspiracy theory even when the exact details of the agreement are not known or have never been made clear.[10]

As a result, no specific words must be spoken to create a conspiracy. Even if members speak in general terms or use code phrases, this can still be considered a valid agreement.[11] The interesting point about conspiracy is that an agreement to commit an offense by several people can still be criminal even if one of the members could have performed the act legally. Price fixing scams are an example. One individual is free to set the price for a particular item, but when he or she acts in concert with others to control the entire market, a legal action becomes an illegal conspiracy.[12]

This is not to suggest that each member of the conspiracy must have a complete picture of the criminal activity. A general understanding is enough to prosecute for conspiracy.[13]

2. Working Together to Carry Out an Illegal Act

Jurisdictions are split on the issue of the purpose of the conspiracy. Some states provide that people can be prosecuted for a conspiracy even when they are carrying out a legal act. In those states, the conspiracy charge arises because the conspirators are attempting to complete a legal action but are using illegal means. In some states, the object of the conspiracy must be the commission of a crime. In those jurisdictions, it is not a criminal conspiracy to carry out an act that is simply malicious.[14]

THE ROLE OF THE PARALEGAL: ESTABLISHING A GOOD RELATIONSHIP WITH THE PEOPLE AT THE LOCAL COURTHOUSE

Although it is seldom mentioned in textbooks, establishing a good relationship with people at the courthouse is essential to the working life of a paralegal. According to one paralegal, this relationship is extremely important.

overt act

An overt act in criminal law is more than mere preparation to something criminal; it is at least the first step of actually attempting the crime. The overt act need not be unlawful to be the first step in such crimes as treason and criminal conspiracy.

3. The Overt Act

In some states, an **overt act** is not a requirement of a conspiracy charge. The agreement alone is sufficient. However, in many other jurisdictions, some act carried out in furtherance of the conspiracy is required.[15] Overt acts are also a requirement of federal law.[16] This overt act does not have to be illegal; it can be any action that furthers the conspiracy. This means that lawful actions, when used to further a conspiracy, can be the basis of an overt act and justify a prosecution.[17] This action can be taken by any member of the conspiracy and will be applied against the entire group.[18]

An action by any member of the conspiracy is attributable to all of the other members. Simply put, if *one* member carries out an "overt act" in furtherance of the conspiracy, this act will be ascribed to *all* members.[19] The importance of the overt act in those jurisdictions where it is required is that this is a clear indication of the intent of the members to carry out a crime. The act does not have to be criminal in nature. Any act, even a legal one that furthers the aim of the criminal conspiracy, is enough to satisfy this element. This overt act helps the government prove that something was actually being planned and that the people involved were serious in carrying out the crime. The requirement of an overt act also helps to show that the conspirators were prepared to put their plan in effect.

■ **BULLET POINT**

A conspiracy consists of two or more people who agree to a criminal action and take some action to put it into motion.

B. Prosecuting and Defending a Conspiracy Case

Conspiracy prosecutions normally involve two different tacks: First, the prosecution focuses on the conspiracy to commit a particular crime. Second, there is the prosecution for the crime itself. There is no requirement that the conspiracy actually commit the crime. Essentially, preparation for a crime in a conspiracy is enough to justify prosecution.

Defense attorneys often focus on the linchpin of the prosecution's case: the agreement. Without an agreement, there can be no conspiracy. Because most conspiracies do not involve outright formalized agreements, defense attorneys often attempt to show that no real agreement existed and therefore no conspiracy could have existed.

One of the defenses often used in a criminal attempt case is **abandonment**. This is the claim that the defendant voluntarily discontinued the criminal act before it was completed. When the defendant can prove abandonment, it relieves the defendant of all guilt in the case. However, proving abandonment often is not as easy as it sounds. A defendant can make out a defense of abandonment when he or she voluntarily renounces the crime, ceases efforts to carry it out, or finds a way to stop the crime from occurring.[20] Voluntariness is the key component here. The defense must present some evidence showing that the defendant voluntarily decided not to carry out the crime. Getting caught by the police is not voluntarily abandoning the criminal enterprise. It also is not abandonment to run away from the scene when the defendant sees the police approaching.

The question with abandonment is, when is a person deemed to have abandoned the attempt? First, we can answer that question in the negative: It is not abandonment when a person has already injured someone or where some act of danger has already happened. It also is not abandonment when the defendant fails to complete the crime because of some unanticipated problem.[21] Once the substantial step has been taken, abandonment is no longer a defense.[22] See Exhibit 7-2 for a breakdown of homicides committed by various parties.

C. Conspirators: How are They Different from Accomplices or Accessories?

The important element distinguishing conspirators from accomplices or accessories is in the agreement between the various people involved. An accomplice or accessory can give aid without any agreement existing between the various participants. However, to have a conspiracy, there must be an agreement. This agreement denotes a concerted action among individuals to commit a crime. The members of a conspiracy know that they are attempting to commit a crime and are working toward that ultimate goal. An accomplice or accessory may not be aware of the details and certainly has not agreed to coordinate their efforts toward the fulfillment of the plan. It is this concerted action and agreement that makes conspiracy a more serious crime.[23] Putting it another way, in a prosecution for conspiracy, the focus is on the intent of the conspirators. In a prosecution against an accomplice or accessory, the focus is on how this person (or persons) aided the principals. No agreement is required between principals and accomplices. It is the agreement to commit a crime and the concerted group action to achieve the goal that creates a conspiracy and justifies a harsher sentence.[24]

D. An Exception to Conspiracy: Wharton's Rule

The so-called **Wharton's Rule** regarding conspiracies is relatively simple: When two people are needed to commit a crime (e.g., gambling and prostitution), there can be no charge of conspiracy where only two people are

---

abandonment
When a defendant voluntarily stops the criminal enterprise before it is completed.

■ **BULLET POINT**
If a defendant can convince the jury that he or she abandoned the act before it was completed, the jury is authorized to find the defendant not guilty.

Unknown Conspirators
Under conspiracy law, the conspirators can be guilty even if they do not know the identity of the other members of the conspiracy.[25]

Wharton's Rule
Also known as "Concert of Action Rule"; the rule that states that unless a statute specifies otherwise, it is not a conspiracy for two persons to agree to commit a crime if the definition of the crime requires the participation of two or more persons.

Exhibit 7-2

Homicide type, by age, 1980–2008

	Victims				Offenders			
	Total	Under 18	18–34	35–49	50 or older	Total	Under 18	18–34	35–49	50 or older
All homicides	100	10.0	53.2	22.8	14.0	100	11.0	65.5	17.1	6.5
Victim/offender										
relationship (in percent)										
Intimate	100	1.3	48.5	33.6	16.6	100	1.0	47.0	34.7	17.2
Family	100	19.3	32.8	26.0	21.9	100	6.1	50.5	27.5	15.9
Infants	100	100				100	7.4	81.2	10.2	1.1
Elders	100				100	100	9.4	47.8	20.7	22.1
Circumstances (in percent)										
Felony murder	100	7.5	48.2	22.2	22.1	100	14.6	72.7	10.7	2.0
Sex related	100	18.4	45.3	18.2	18.1	100	9.7	73.1	15.2	1.9
Drug related	100	5.4	70.9	20.2	3.6	100	10.8	76.4	11.5	1.3
Gang related	100	23.7	68.8	6.2	1.3	100	28.0	70.2	1.6	0.2
Argument	100	5.7	56.2	26.3	11.8	100	7.0	60.7	23.0	9.2
Workplace	100	0.5	26.7	33.5	39.3	100	2.8	53.6	28.0	15.6
Weapon (in percent)										
Gun homicide	100	8.1	59.7	22.0	10.3	100	12.2	65.9	15.1	6.9
Arson	100	27.9	26.4	20.4	25.2	100	10.6	57.0	24.9	7.5
Poison	100	28.6	20.8	16.8	33.8	100	3.5	48.8	29.8	17.8
Multiple victims or										
offenders (in percent)										
Multiple victims	100	17.9	47.0	19.3	15.8	100	9.5	66.3	18.3	5.9
Multiple offenders	100	10.4	58.4	19.2	12.0	100	17.9	73.1	7.7	1.3

Note: Detail may not sum to total due to rounding. The percentages of victim/offender relationships are based on the 63.1% of homicides from 1980 through 2008 for which the victim/offender relationships were known. The percentages of homicides involving multiple victims or offenders were known for 69.1% of incidents.

Source: Homicide Trends in the U.S. Bureau of Justice Statistics, U.S. Department of Justice.

involved. The reasoning behind this rule, which has been enacted in many states, is that conspiracies, by their very nature, bring together individuals with different resources and abilities. This group action is dangerous. However, where only two people are involved in a crime that requires two people to commit it, there is no concerted group action. To prosecute under gambling or prostitution as a conspiracy, most states require that more than two people be involved.

E. Organized crime

Although criminals have formed groups for thousands of years (pirates were a problem even for the Ancient Romans), the rise of sophisticated and organized crime groups began in the United States in the early part of the twentieth century. New immigrants to America often brought with them an old concept: organized criminal gangs. In New York, Chicago, Boston, and nearly every other major city in the United States, crime groups formed and carried out illegal activities. These loosely affiliated and often antagonistic groups underwent a dramatic change in the 1920s. With the ban on the sale of alcohol in the United States, criminal gangs soon realized the benefits of providing alcohol to a demanding public. They earned fantastic sums of money through bootlegging and consolidated their power through absorbing (or wiping out) rival gangs. This financial base allowed them to become more sophisticated and to expand their activities into other areas. Organized crime as a public threat was recognized in the late 1920s and early 1930s with the formation of special police squads to investigate organized crime activities. Law enforcement began targeting organized groups such as the Italian Mafia and their illegal activities that had branched out from illicit alcohol to gambling, narcotics, and prostitution. Police also requested—and received—greater authority and new laws to deal with organized crime. The result was the RICO statutes.

F. RICO

The Racketeering Influenced and Corrupt Organizations statute was a national response to widespread Mafia activity. RICO, as it is often called, allows law enforcement to prosecute individuals for organized crime activities if these activities meet certain basic requirements. See Exhibit 7-3.

If law enforcement can prove that a group's activities fall under RICO, the statute gives them considerable authority to seize the group's assets and enhance the sentences of those convicted for such violations. Although RICO prosecutions originally occurred on the federal level, many states have enacted their own versions of the RICO statute.

G. Gangs

A closely related phenomenon to organized crime is the rise of criminal street gangs. The typical gang has teenage members who engage in local drug dealing and extortion in much the same way the more traditional organized crime syndicates behave on a national level. Gangs often have

Different Kinds of Conspiracies

There are several different kinds of conspiracies. They have descriptive names. A wheel conspiracy, for instance, involves a central figure controlling the other participants. Those participants are the "spokes."

Chain conspiracies involve "links" from one individual to another. The person who sets the conspiracy in motion and the person who carries out the final act may be unknown to each other. However, all the "links" lead back to the first individual.[26]

- If an individual or an organization engages in two or more acts of murder, kidnapping, gambling, or extortion within a ten-year period
- And is involved in collecting unlawful debt or engages in a pattern of racketeering
- And the defendants are aware that they are engaged in racketeering activity
- Then the individuals involved can be charged both with the underlying offense (murder, kidnapping, etc.) and an additional offense with the resultant increase in the overall sentence received.

Exhibit 7-3
The elements required for a RICO prosecution

their own code of behavior for members, and to earn the privilege of becoming a gang member, initiates must often commit some crime to prove their fidelity to the gang. Most urban police forces have created specialized gang task forces to deal with the crimes associated with gang membership, including narcotics sales and drive-by shootings.

IV. Solicitation

solicitation
Asking for; enticing; strongly requesting. This may be a crime if the thing being urged is a crime.

The crime of **solicitation** involves an offer or a request by one person made to another person to commit a crime. The person making the offer can be prosecuted for soliciting a crime.[27] The point of a solicitation prosecution is criminalizing a serious effort by the defendant to induce another person to commit a crime.[28]

A. Comparing Solicitation to Conspiracy

Like conspiracy, there is no requirement that the crime actually occur before a person can be prosecuted for soliciting it.[29]

Conspiracy involves an agreement where solicitation involves a request or command by one person to another to commit a crime. Solicitation does not require any agreement to further a criminal design, but a conspiracy does.

■ **BULLET POINT**
Asking a person to commit a crime is also a crime.

V. Attempt: When the Crime is not Completed

attempt
1. An act that goes beyond preparation but is not completed. 2. An effort to commit a crime that goes beyond preparation and that proceeds far enough to make the person who did it guilty of an "attempt crime." For example, if a person fires a shot at another individual in a failed effort at murder, the person is guilty of attempted murder.

An **attempt** to commit a crime is by itself a crime. By its very nature, however, an attempted crime is a crime that has not been successfully carried out. When the crime has not been completed, some difficult questions arise. Just how far must a person go before she can be convicted of attempting to commit a crime? Suppose you daydream about committing a bank robbery? Have you committed a crime? What if you take the daydream one step further and actually go the bank to "case the joint"? Suppose you draw a map of the bank, placing the surveillance cameras and security guards in their correct positions? Obviously, just thinking about a crime is not attempting to commit a crime. But there must be some point at which a person crosses the line. Where is that line?

■ **THE ROLE OF THE PARALEGAL: RESEARCHING THE POSSIBLE PENALTY**
When dealing with attempt or other so-called "inchoate" crimes, it is important to know the penalties for various offenses. In many situations, the penalties for these offenses may be obscure. Suggestion: Create a separate file for sentencing and put a copy of the statute in that file.

A. Substantial Step

A person crosses the line between merely thinking about an offense and actually committing one when she takes some action to further the crime. Different jurisdictions refer to this stage as "substantial step" or "overt act"

1) An intent to engage in crime; and
2) Conduct that is a substantial step towards commission of the crime.[i]

[i]United States v. Figueroa, 976 F.2d 1446 (1st Cir. 1992).

Exhibit 7-4
Elements of attempt

- Preparing for a crime, unless the preparation constitutes a substantial step[i]
- A statement that a person plans on committing a crime[ii]

[i] People v. Reed, 53 Cal. App. 4th 389, 61 Cal. Rptr. 2d 658 (1996).
[ii] State v. Pooler, 696 So. 2d 22 (1997).

Exhibit 7-5
Activities that do not constitute an attempted crime

or "direct act." We will refer to this stage as *substantial step*. A substantial step that would authorize prosecution, given the example above, might be taking a handgun, driving to the bank, and parking outside. A substantial step does not necessarily have to be an act just short of committing a crime. However, a substantial step places the person dangerously close to actually committing the crime.[30] A crime novelist might spend all day thinking up different crimes and not be guilty of attempting any of them. But another person might suddenly decide to commit an action and take some action, even a small one, to carry out and be guilty of attempt. Given the fact that this definition is so hard pin down, each case must be considered on its merits.

BULLET POINT
The closer a defendant gets to actually committing a crime, the more likely he or she will be charged with attempt.

B. Prosecuting a Charge of Attempt

To prosecute someone for attempt, the government must show that the defendant acted with the intent to commit the crime and carried out some action that constituted a substantial step toward the commission of the crime.[32] The prosecution normally does this by showing the circumstances surrounding the defendant's actions. For instance, in a charge of attempted robbery, the prosecution might show that the defendant was short on money and spent a considerable amount of time preparing to commit the crime. This preparatory work would suggest that the idea of robbing a bank was no mere fancy, but a carefully laid out plan.

Action = Attempt?
A person is guilty of attempt to commit a crime when she takes some action that would have accomplished the crime had it not been for some intervening force.[31]

C. Defending a Charge of Attempt

One of the defenses to attempt is that the defendant voluntarily abandoned the criminal enterprise before carrying it out. Abandonment, when proved, will relieve the defendant of all culpability in the case. However, proving abandonment is often not as easy as it sounds. The defense must present some evidence showing that the defendant voluntarily decided not to carry out the crime. It is not a voluntary abandonment if the defendant changed her mind when she saw the police approaching.

Case Excerpt. Has the Crime of Attempt Been Established?

STATE V. DEVOID, 188 VT. 445, 8 A.3D 1076 (VT.,2010) DOOLEY, J.

1. Defendant Carl Devoid, Jr. appeals his jury conviction for attempted voyeurism, a crime that the State did not originally charge, but that the court instructed the jury could find was committed. Among other arguments, defendant contends that the evidence at trial does not support the conviction. We agree and reverse.

2. Complainant resides on the second floor of an apartment building located in a secluded area in Colchester, Vermont. There is a window in her bathroom shower that overlooks a parking lot used by residents of the building. The bottom of the window is at the level of complainant's mid-chest. When complainant moved in, her landlord suggested that she cover the window with a shower curtain to protect the window from water damage. Complainant, however, did not do so. She did not think anyone could see her through the window.

3. Defendant is complainant's neighbor who resides on the first floor. He can hear complainant's shower turn on and off from his apartment. On September 1, 2008, complainant saw defendant for a few moments while he stood in the parking lot looking at her bathroom window as she was showering. On September 15, 2008, complainant again saw defendant standing in the parking lot looking at her bathroom window while she was in the shower. This time, defendant stared at her window for three minutes with a hand on his crotch. Complainant left the shower, went into her bedroom and took a picture of defendant—still looking up with a hand on his crotch—with her cell phone.

4. Later that day, complainant asked her roommate—who is the same height as complainant—to stand in her shower. Meanwhile, complainant went to the parking lot and looked up at her bathroom window to determine whether anyone could see her from the ground. The parties disagree on what complainant saw when she looked up at her window and whether defendant could see any part of complainant's body that is protected by the voyeurism statute.

5. On September 16, 2008, complainant reported the incident, and the State charged defendant with voyeurism "by viewing complainant…through a window while she was showering in the privacy of her home" in violation of 13 V.S.A. § 2605(b)(1). The statute provides in relevant part that "no person shall intentionally view…the intimate areas of another person without that person's knowledge and consent while the person being viewed…is in a place where he or she would have a reasonable expectation of privacy." 13 V.S.A. § 2605(b)(1). The statute further defines "view" as "the intentional looking upon another person for more than a brief period of time, in other than a casual or cursory manner," and states that the term "intimate areas" includes a "female breast," which is defined as "any portion of the female breast below the top of the areola." Id. § 2605(a)(2), (4), (7).

6. The case went to trial, and defense counsel moved for judgment of acquittal, arguing that the evidence was insufficient to conclude either that defendant

intended to view the intimate areas of complainant's body or that defendant did view those areas. The court denied the motion and submitted the case to the jury. During deliberations, the jury sent a note to the judge that read: "If we think that he is guilty of trying; but was not able to see her nipples. What kind of verdict do we give? We have not proven that he saw anything. But we believe he was trying." In response, the judge, over defendant's objection, issued the following supplemental instruction on attempt:

> Under Vermont law, a person who attempts to commit an offense and does an act toward the commission thereof, but by reason of being interrupted or prevented in the execution of the same, may be found guilty of the offense charged if the jury finds, beyond a reasonable doubt, that the attempt to commit the offense was made.

7. The jury then asked the judge to clarify whether "by reason of being interrupted or prevented in the execution of the same" could mean a physical block, such as a windowsill, rather than an occurrence whereby someone physically prevented commission of the act. The judge did not give a direct answer, but instead cited a case that discusses the elements of attempt. The jury returned a verdict finding defendant guilty of attempted voyeurism. Defendant renewed his motion for judgment of acquittal, arguing that the evidence presented at trial was insufficient for a conviction of attempted voyeurism, and that the supplemental instructions were prejudicial to him. The court denied defendant's motion. The court held that the evidence that defendant looked up at complainant's window for three minutes while holding his crotch was sufficient to support a conviction for attempted voyeurism, and that the timing of the supplemental instructions was not prejudicial to defendant. This appeal followed.

8. On appeal, defendant argues that the trial court erred by giving supplemental instructions to the jury, by denying defendant's motion for acquittal, and by admitting evidence of a prior bad act—defendant's first alleged viewing of complainant. We first consider whether the evidence was sufficient to support the attempted voyeurism conviction. We hold that the evidence was insufficient and, therefore, reverse the conviction without reaching the other appeal issues.

9. When reviewing a denial of motion for judgment of acquittal, we view the evidence "in the light most favorable to the prosecution, . . . and determine whether the State's evidence sufficiently and fairly supports a finding of guilt beyond a reasonable doubt." Defendant claims he was entitled to judgment of acquittal because the State provided no evidence from which the jury could reasonably conclude that: (1) he intended to view complainant's intimate areas; (2) his actions constituted an overt act of attempt; (3) he was interrupted or prevented from committing the act, other than by physical impossibility; and (4) complainant had a reasonable expectation of privacy. Specifically, defendant argues that given the impossibility of his being able to see complainant's intimate areas from his vantage point on the ground, his act of merely looking at her window did not constitute an attempt. We agree that the evidence, taken in the light most favorable to the State, fails to support the charge of attempted voyeurism.

10. Vermont's attempt statute provides that "a person who attempts to commit an offense and does an act toward the commission thereof, but by reason of

being interrupted or prevented fails in the execution of the same, shall be punished as herein provided." 13 V.S.A. § 9(a). As we have previously held, two elements required for attempt are: (1) intent to commit a certain crime; and (2) "'an overt act designed to carry out that intent.'"

11. An overt act must advance beyond mere intent and "reach far enough toward accomplishing the desired result to amount to the commencement of the consummation." Preparation counts as an act if it "would be likely to end, if not extraneously interrupted, in the consummation of the crime intended." Once an actor commits an overt act, "the offense is complete, and abandonment of the enterprise does not negate guilt."

12. Here, the alleged overt act committed by defendant is standing on the ground, staring at complainant's second-floor bathroom window for three minutes with a hand on his crotch. The key point of disagreement is whether defendant was able to see complainant's intimate areas, as defined by the voyeurism statute, from his location on the ground. The State asserts that defendant could and did; defendant contends that he could not. Based on our review of the jury's conclusions and the evidence, we agree with defendant.

13. At trial, complainant agreed, in response to the prosecutor's question, that the bottom of the window was at her "mid-chest area," without specifying whether the intimate areas protected by the voyeurism statute were lower or higher than the windowsill. She also testified that she observed her roommate at the window from defendant's vantage point, but the prosecution did not ask whether she could see an intimate area of her roommate's body as defined by the voyeurism statute. Other evidence on this issue includes a picture taken from inside of complainant's bathroom that shows complainant standing in front of her bathroom window. This picture clearly demonstrates that intimate areas of complainant are lower than the windowsill. We must conclude from this evidence that the jury could not find that defendant could see intimate areas of complainant's body, as defined by the statute, particularly given that complainant's shower was located on the second floor and defendant was looking at her bathroom window from the ground. Obviously, the jury agreed. The jury's notes to the judge indicate that the jurors concluded that the State had failed to prove that defendant was able to see an intimate area of complainant's body from his vantage point. Thus, even when viewed most favorably to the State, the evidence reveals that the window was too high to allow defendant to see any intimate areas of complainant's body.

14. The critical question before us, then, is whether, given defendant's inability to see complainant's intimate areas, the jurors could still find him guilty of attempted voyeurism. We hold that they could not, as his actions did not constitute an overt act of attempted voyeurism and the State could not prove the requisite intent.

15. An overt act of attempted voyeurism requires an action that "would be likely to end" in acquiring a view of complainant's intimate areas. Here, because defendant was unable to see complainant's intimate areas from his position on the ground, his actions of standing and looking would not be likely to end "in the consummation of the crime intended." Had he attempted to elevate himself from the ground to a position from which he would be able to gain a view of complainant's intimate areas, this case would be different. The act of merely looking at complainant's window from a place where no view of her

intimate areas was possible, however, is insufficient for the jury to find defendant guilty of attempted voyeurism.

16. The State's theory in this case is that defendant's looking at the window is a sufficient overt act. There are significant difficulties with this theory. Under it, any looking in the direction of a person known to be naked is an overt act even if the person were fully behind a wall. Because defendant could not see the intimate areas of complainant's body and must have been aware of that circumstance, we cannot distinguish between desire to view those intimate areas and intent to do so. Thus, the alleged overt act is not corroborative of defendant's criminal purpose. See Model Penal Code § 5.01(2) (for conduct to be a "substantial step" to commission of the crime, the conduct must be "strongly corroborative of the actor's criminal purpose.").

17. For related reasons, we do not believe that the State has provided sufficient evidence of defendant's intent to view complainant's intimate areas as required for a criminal attempt. Defendant apparently obtains sexual gratification from watching the upper body of a woman he believes is naked, and we can infer from that fact that he would like to see her naked. We cannot infer from the facts in the record, however, that he had the intent to commit voyeurism or would have committed that crime. As Professor LaFave notes in discussing the interrelationship between impossibility and intent, "a defendant's declared intent to kill another person may be put in doubt if he only attacks with a small switch." 2 W. LaFave, Substantive Criminal Law § 11.5, at *2 (2009).

We hold that in this case the evidence presented did not "sufficiently and fairly" support a verdict of guilt of attempt to commit voyeurism. For that reason, the motion for judgment of acquittal should have been granted.

Reversed.

CASE QUESTIONS

1. With what is the defendant charged?
2. What is Vermont's definition of the crime of attempt?
3. What is an "overt act," and how does it apply to the crime of attempt?
4. What was the factual problem with proving that the defendant was attempting to view intimate areas of the complainant's body?
5. Why isn't the state's version—that simply looking at the window the defendant committed the offense—considered insufficient by the court?

ETHICAL CONSIDERATION: UNAUTHORIZED PRACTICE OF LAW

A paralegal must avoid the unauthorized practice of law (UPL). Traditionally, practicing law without a license involved carrying out any activity that an attorney usually carried out. However, these days, that description is not very helpful. For instance, paralegals routinely do legal research and draft pleadings (but should not sign them). They even are authorized to represent clients in some court proceedings (Social Security hearings, for example). All of these responsibilities were traditionally associated with lawyers, but are now legal for paralegals to do. In most jurisdictions, unauthorized practice of law is a crime, usually a misdemeanor. So a paralegal walks a fine line in daily practice. The question often arises,

At what point does a paralegal cross the line into unauthorized practice of law? The simple answer is that in almost all jurisdictions, a paralegal practices law when he or she gives legal *advice*.

There are other ways that a paralegal can cross the intangible line of UPL, but almost all jurisdictions recognize that legal advice is the very core of the service that an attorney provides. Paralegals give legal advice when they tell a client the best course of action for a legal problem. *Information* such as when a court date is scheduled or what a particular court hearing is about normally does not constitute UPL. However, to be on safe ground, a paralegal should inform clients that he or she is not giving legal advice. This usually helps protect a paralegal from a claim of UPL.

✓ Paralegal To Do List

For the defense paralegal:

- What is the statutory punishment for accessories charged with the client's crime? (In some states, it is only half what the principal would receive.)
- Have the codefendants given any statements to law enforcement?
- Are the codefendants' statements in conflict with our client's statement?
- Have the codefendants reached a deal with the prosecution?
- Are any of the codefendants on probation or parole? (This could mean that more pressure could be brought to bear on them.)

For the prosecution paralegal:

- Have the codefendants made any statements that favorable to the defendant? If so, they may have to be produced to the defense.
- Do the witnesses say that any one of the defendants in particular was more guilty or took a more active role than some of the others?
- Do any of the codefendants have a prior record? (That often gives an insight into the defense; the one without a criminal record will often blame the one with the record.)
- How extensive was the conspiracy? Are there actions that could be brought in other jurisdictions?
- Does RICO apply? If so, what kind of assets does the defendant have?

Chapter Summary

When more than one person commits a crime, it is often necessary to apportion the guilt among them. When a person is present at the commission of a crime, he or she is classified as a principal. Persons who act as lookouts or help someone commit a crime can be punished as principals even if they are not present at the exact moment that a crime occurs.

These individuals are classified as principals in the second degree. Someone who helps in the planning of a crime but is not present when the crime occurs is classified as an accessory before the fact. Someone who helps another conceal a crime or helps conceal the person who committed the crime is an accessory after the fact.

When two or more people enter into an agreement to commit a crime, they fall into the category of conspirators. They can be punished for committing the crime and for a separate crime of conspiracy to commit the crime. Conspiracies are punished so harshly because they are often more dangerous than the actions a single individual would take. In addition, individuals who ask or encourage others to commit a crime could themselves be guilty of solicitation.

Finally, the preparation to commit a crime is also actionable. Generally, the person charged must take some action to further the crime before the preparation is actionable.

WEB SITES

Federal Bureau of Investigation
www.fbi.gov

Idaho State Court System
www.isc.idaho.gov

Law Guru.com
www.lawguru.com

Legal Information Institute—Racketeer Influenced and Corrupt Organizations
www.law.cornell.edu/uscode/text/18/part-I/chapter-96

National Association of Legal Assistants
www.nala.org

Prosecuting Criminal Conspiracies—U.S. Department of Justice
www.justice.gov/usao/eousa/foia_reading_room/usab6104.pdf

Tennessee State Court System
www.tsc.state.tn.us

The Internet Lawyers
www.internetlawyer.com

REVIEW QUESTIONS

1. Explain the difference between a principal in the first degree and a principal in the second degree.
2. Explain the difference between an accessory before the fact and an accessory after the fact. Which is punished more severely?
3. Why was the classification of accomplice created?
4. What is the definition of *conspiracy*?

5. What qualifies as an overt act in conspiracy law?

6. The text suggests that members of a conspiracy don't have to know one another. On a practical level, how could such a conspiracy be organized? Explain.

7. Explain Wharton's Rule.

8. Explain solicitation.

QUESTIONS FOR REFLECTION

1. If someone asks another person to commit a crime, isn't it still the second person's decision to commit the crime? Why should such a request be deemed solicitation and be prosecuted?

2. Two friends are talking. John turns to Sue and says, "If it weren't for my wife, I'd be a happy man." The next day Sue kills John's wife. Should John be charged with solicitation? Why or why not?

3. Two friends are talking in a bar one evening. Ted says to Carl, "You know if we robbed this place, we could probably walk away with $5,000." For the next hour, they discuss exactly how they would go about robbing the bar. Could Ted and Carl be prosecuted for conspiracy? Explain.

4. (Same facts as the previous question) Carl purchases a handgun the next day (a legal act in his state). Could Carl be prosecuted for conspiracy to commit armed robbery? Could Ted? Explain.

5. (Same facts as question 3) Regardless of your answer for question 4, could Carl and Ted be prosecuted for attempted robbery? Could they be prosecuted after Carl purchases the handgun? Is that a sufficient substantial step? Explain your answer.

KEYWORDS AND PHRASES

Principal	Conspiracy
Accessories	Overt act
Principal in the first degree	Wharton's Rule
Principal in the second degree	Solicitation
Accessory before the fact	Attempt
Accessory after the fact	Substantial step
Accomplice	

PRACTICAL APPLICATIONS

1. While Sue is cashing a check at the bank, she notes the location of the various security cameras. She then notes that the bank has only one security guard, who is quite elderly. She hatches a plan to rob the bank. Has she committed attempted armed robbery? Why or why not?

2. (Same facts as the previous question) Sue goes home and draws a diagram of the bank, noting the location of the cameras and the security guard. Has she committed attempted armed robbery? Why or why not?

3. (Same facts as the previous question) Sue takes a revolver with her and drives to the parking lot of the bank. She sits in the car, studying her diagram and going over her plan to rob the bank. She is waiting there, with the gun in her hand, when a police officer stops and asks her what she is doing. Has she committed attempted armed robbery? Why or why not?

4. How far would Sue have to go before she could be charged with attempted armed robbery?

5. Review the facts in the *Marbles* case (Appendix). If Marbles had only climbed the back stairs of the movie theater and jimmied open the back door and was then caught before he actually entered, could he have been charged with any or all of the following: attempted burglary, attempted kidnapping, attempted assault? Explain your answer.

NOTES

1. 21 Am. Jur.2d, Criminal Law §§120 et seq.
2. *State v Massey*, 267 SC 432, 229 SE2d 332 (1976).
3. *State v Eyth*, 124 Kan 405, 260 P 976 (1927).
4. *Smith v State*, 229 Ind 546, 99 NE2d 417 (1951).
5. *U.S. v. Broce*, 488 U.S. 563, 109 S. Ct. 757, 102 L. Ed. 2d 927 (1989).
6. *U.S. v. Amiel*, 95 F.3d 135 (2d Cir. 1996).
7. *U.S. v. Pinckney*, 85 F.3d 4 (2d Cir. 1996).
8. *State v. Brewer*, 258 N.C. 533, 129 S.E.2d 262, 1 A.L.R.3d 1323 (1963), appeal dismissed, 375 U.S. 9, 84 S. Ct. 72, 11 L. Ed. 2d 40 (1963).
9. *U.S. v. Jensen*, 41 F.3d 946 (5th Cir. 1994).
10. *U. S. v. Varelli*, 407 F.2d 735 (7th Cir. 1969), affd, 452 F.2d 193 (7th Cir. 1971), cert. denied, 405 U.S. 1040, 92 S. Ct. 1311, 31 L. Ed. 2d 581 (1972).
11. *People v. Edwards*, 74 Ill. App. 2d 225, 219 N.E.2d 382 (1966).
12. *Gebardi v. U.S.*, 287 U.S. 112, 53 S. Ct. 35, 77 L. Ed. 206, 84 A.L.R. 370 (1932).
13. *U.S. v. Knowles*, 66 F.3d 1146 (11th Cir. 1995), cert. denied, 116 S. Ct. 1449, 134 L. Ed. 2d 568 (U.S. 1996).
14. *State v. Kaakimaka*, 84 Haw. 280, 933 P.2d 617 (1997), reconsideration denied, 84 Haw.496, 936 P.2d 191 (Haw. 1997).
15. *Williams v. State*, 665 So. 2d 955 (1994).
16. 18 USCA §371.

17. *State v. Ellis*, 657 So.2d 341 (La. Ct. App. 5th Cir. 1995); In Interest of P.A., 1997 ND 146, 566 N.W.2d 422 (1997).

18. *People v. Morante*, 56 Cal. App. 4th 163, 65 Cal. Rptr. 2d 287 (1997).

19. *Williams v. Aetna Fin. Co.*, 83 Ohio St. 3d 464, 700 N.E.2d 859 (1998).

20. *State v. Brown*, 999 A.2d 295 (N.H. 2010).

21. *State v. Mahoney*, 264 Mont. 89, 870 P.2d 65 (1994).

22. *State v. Devoid*, 2010 VT 86, 8 A.3d 1076 (Vt. 2010).

23. *U.S. v. Peterson*, 524 F.2d 167 (4th Cir. 1975), cert. denied, 423 U.S. 1088, 96 S. Ct. 881, 47 L. Ed. 2d 99 (1976).

24. *State v. Moretti*, 52 N.J. 182, 244 A.2d 499, 37 A.L.R.3d 364 (1968), cert. denied, 393 U.S. 952, 89 S. Ct. 376, 21 L. Ed. 2d 363 (1968).

25. *U.S. v. Monroe*, 73 F.3d 129 (7th Cir. 1995), affd, 124 F.3d 206 (7th Cir. 1997).

26. *U.S. v. Payne*, 99 F.3d 1273 (5th Cir. 1996).

27. *People v. Sanchez*, 60 Cal. App. 4th 1490, 71 Cal. Rptr. 2d 309 (1998).

28. *U.S. v. Holveck*, 867 F. Supp. 969 (D. Kan. 1994).

29. *People v. Hood*, 878 P.2d 89 (1994).

30. *People v. Johnson*, 186 A.D.2d 363, 588 N.Y.S.2d 162 (1992).

31. *People v. Carpenter*, 15 Cal. 4th 312, 63 Cal. Rptr. 2d 1, 935 P.2d 708 (1997), cert. denied, 118 S. Ct. 858, 139 L. Ed. 2d 757 (1998).

32. *People v. Harris*, 892 P.2d 378 (1994); *Moore v. State*, 673 N.E.2d 776 (1996).

Chapter 8

CRIMES AGAINST THE PERSON

Chapter Objectives

At the completion of this chapter, you should be able to:

- Explain the difference between murder in the first degree and other forms of murder
- Explain the felony-murder doctrine
- Define premeditation and explain how this term affects the analysis of murder
- Describe the differences between assault and battery
- Define the elements of various crimes against the person

I. Introduction

There are a wide variety of crimes against the person. They run the gamut from murder to assault. To master the subject of crimes against the person, it is necessary to pay close attention to the various elements of each crime. Many states divide murder into categories, or degrees. The degrees can have a profound impact on an individual case. For instance, the difference between murder in the first degree and murder in the second degree lies in the application of *one* element. But the difference for the person accused can be monumental. Murder in the first degree can be punishable by life in prison or by execution, whereas murder in the second degree is punished using more lenient sentences.

Exhibit 8-1

Sample case excerpt: the kline case

"…He started yelling and screaming, saying "Let me go, dammit!" Mark had him by his right arm, and his left wrist was handcuffed to the steering wheel. I had him in a headlock, and I kept telling him to quiet down, but he wouldn't listen. Mark turned to Christine and said, "Get something to shut him up." She climbed out of the car and went inside the house. She came back in a few minutes with a roll of duct tape. She put some of it over his mouth, and I let go of him. But then she kept on going, man. She just kept wrapping his face, unrolling more of that tape and looping it around his head. Doug was screaming and carrying on, but she wouldn't stop. I got out of the car and just stood there. I mean, I didn't know what to do. She covered his nose and his whole face, all the way up and over his eyebrows. You could see Doug trying to suck in his breath, but after just a few minutes, he slumped over. Mark let go of his arm then, and he and Christine got out of the car and stared at him. I reached up under Doug's shirt to feel for his heart, but there was nothing.

I turned to Christine then and said, "Hey, he's dead."

She just looked at me and said, "Good."

Excerpt from the statement of Ellis Sampson. For a complete overview of this case, see the Appendix.

II. Homicide

In any society, the most egregious crime a person can commit is the killing of another person. The term **homicide** is a broad term that simply means the killing of one human being by another. Not all forms of homicide are illegal. During war, a soldier may kill the enemy with no legal consequences at all. In fact, the soldier may even be praised for his actions. Police officers sometimes use deadly force when apprehending a suspect. As we will discuss in later chapters, if deadly force is authorized (e.g., if the suspect is firing a gun at an officer), then the officer's action in killing the suspect will not be a crime. Similarly, when we discuss defenses to criminal actions, a person is always justified to act in self-defense when presented with deadly force. In this instance, if self-defense is warranted, there will be no prosecution for the resulting death of the attacker. Because there are different levels of homicide ranging from the fully justified actions of a soldier in combat to the completely unjustified premeditated killing of another, our review of homicide must take all of these factors into account. We begin with the most serious form of homicide: premeditated **murder**.

A. Intent: Mens Rea and Actus Reus

In most criminal charges, the state must meet two essential requirements before a person can be convicted of a crime. These are **mens rea** and

homicide
Killing another person.

murder
The unlawful killing of another human being that is premeditated (planned in advance) or is with malice aforethought.

mens rea
Guilty mind; wrongful purpose; criminal intent.

actus reus. Mens rea is the mental element of a crime that must be present. The defendant must be aware of his actions and must have formed the mental state necessary to carry out the crime. This mental element is intent. In most prosecutions, this intent is simply a general purpose or plan aimed at achieving a result.

Now that we have established the basic formula found in most crimes, we must go further and develop additional concepts. Beyond simple guilty intent, or mens rea, crimes are divided into two subcategories, also based on intent. There are both **general intent** crimes and **specific intent** crimes. General intent refers to the simple intention on the part of the defendant to move his body or to take an action.[1]

Proving specific intent crimes is always more difficult than proving general intent crimes. In Chapter 14, we will also examine how insanity and other mental conditions can affect the prosecution of a specific intent crime.

Because a defendant can be prosecuted only for intentional crimes, when a person carries out some action unconsciously, there is no crime. For example, Bill is an insulin-dependent diabetic and suffers a seizure one day when his blood sugar gets out of control. During the seizure, Bill's hand strikes a friend's face. Because Bill had no voluntary control over his body, most people would agree that charging Bill with battery would not be appropriate. In any crime, the two basic elements must exist: guilty mind + guilty act. In almost all situations, the lack of guilty mind (intent) will negate a criminal prosecution. The equation works the other way, too. A guilty mind (intent) without a guilty act (actus reus) means that no crime occurred. In almost all situations, there can be no prosecution without both elements.

1. Exceptions to the Mens Rea Requirement

Although it is rare to have a crime that does not require a mens rea component, some do exist. They are often referred to as strict liability offenses. A strict liability offense makes an act illegal without regard to intent. For instance, in the crime of statutory rape, most states have removed the mens rea requirement. In statutory rape, an adult has sex with a child under the age of 14. (The age varies in some states.) The defendant's state of mind, or his intent (and many states are gender-specific with this crime), is not an element that the state must prove in the case. The fact that sexual intercourse occurred is enough, even if the other partner consented to the act. (We will discuss this crime in greater detail in Chapter 9.) Another example of a strict liability offense is the crime of Habitual Violator. In many states, when a person has committed a specified number of driving offenses (usually consecutive DUIs), the person is barred from driving an automobile for any purpose. If he or she is found to be driving after having been declared a Habitual Violator, that fact alone will justify a conviction. The reason the person was driving is irrelevant to the prosecution and to the defense.

actus reus
A "wrongful deed" (such as killing a person) which, if done with mens rea, is a crime.

general intent
Proof that the defendant acted knowingly and voluntarily.

specific intent
Proof that the defendant acted with a precise crime in mind.

■ **BULLET POINT**
Almost all crimes require two basic elements: mens rea and actus reus.

■ **BULLET POINT**
Most crimes fall into the category of general intent, but the most serious are recategorized as specific intent crimes.

2. Mens Rea and Specific Intent in Murder Cases

For a limited number of especially serious crimes, the state's burden of proof is higher. In cases such as murder, the state must prove specific intent. Specific intent does not mean that the defendant had a general scheme in mind, but that she actually intended to commit the specific crime. In a murder prosecution, the state must prove that the defendant intended to murder the victim. This specific intent is usually shown by the defendant's actions. Also, certain presumptions can aid the prosecution in proving specific intent. For instance, when the defendant assaults the victim with a deadly weapon and the victim dies, the law may presume specific intent to murder. Specific intent crimes are limited to only the most serious forms of felonies, such as murder and rape. The requirement of specific proof probably stems from the fact that in the past, the death penalty could be imposed for these crimes.

B. Premeditated Murder

Premeditated, or planned, murder is considered to be the most serious form of homicide. The deliberate destruction of another human being has been outlawed in one form or another since human beings formed societies. For thousands of years, no distinction was made between a homicide involving premeditation (or planning) and the act of killing another person with simple malice. Generally, both actions were punishable by death. European countries also imposed the death penalty for crimes such as murder, rape, and even armed robbery in some instances. The United States, which based its legal system on the laws of England, similarly imposed the death penalty for a wide variety of crimes, making no real distinction between premeditated murder and other forms of murder.

C. Classifying Murder by Degrees

After the colonies declared independence and established the United States of America, a movement began that sought to restrict the death penalty to only the most egregious crimes. This movement was primarily

Exhibit 8-2

Examples of general intent crimes

- Theft
- Assault and battery
- Robbery

Exhibit 8-3

Examples of specific intent crimes

- Murder
- Rape

Since the death of any human being is a serious matter, here is a ranking of the various types of homicide by severity of punishment:

Crime	Possible Punishment
Premeditated murder (First-degree murder)	Life in prison or death
Malice murder (Second-degree murder)	Life in prison
Felony murder	Life in prison or death
Manslaughter	Varies by state: twenty years or more
Involuntary manslaughter	Varies by state: one to ten years or more
Negligent homicide	Varies by state: often considered to be a misdemeanor (twelve month maximum sentence)
Vehicular homicide	Varies by state: often considered to be a misdemeanor (twelve month maximum sentence)
Justifiable or excusable homicide	No punishment

Exhibit 8-4
Ranking the various forms of homicide

responsible for making distinctions between various kinds of homicide. These distinctions, or degrees, were based on the facts of the individual case. Classifying murder by various degrees reflected the different levels of culpability for murders. It seemed obvious that a person who committed murder in cold blood had a different level of culpability than a person who lashed out in anger and caused a death. The various degrees would be punished differently to reflect this difference in guilt. First-degree murder would continue to be punished by execution, while lesser degrees would not. Pennsylvania was the first state to create degrees of homicide. In enacting this scheme, the legislature declared "several offenses, which are included under the general denomination of murder, differ…greatly from each other in the degree of their atrociousness." The Pennsylvania statute created a distinction between murder by means of poison, lying in wait, or premeditated killing (murder in the first degree) and other forms of murder, labeled murder in the second degree. The lesser degrees of murder were not punishable by death.[2] This concept of degrees of murder was eventually adopted, in one form or another, by all states. Although all states follow the scheme of classifying murder by the method in which it was carried out, not all states use the terms *first-degree* or *second-degree* to refer to these distinctions.

Exhibit 8-5
Elements of first degree murder

- The unlawful killing
- Of a human being by another
- With malice aforethought
- And with deliberation, specific purpose, or premeditation

Copyright © 2015 Cengage Learning®

■ **BULLET POINT**

Most states divide murder into various degrees, or types, all of which are punished in different ways.

1. Unlawful Killing

An unlawful killing is not legally justified or excused.[3] For example, a legally justified killing could be a homicide as a result of self-defense or a police officer's justified use of deadly force to apprehend a suspect. State executioners may legally kill someone condemned to death. When prosecuting a murder charge, the element of "unlawful killing" is normally one of the easiest to prove. The state simply has to show that the defendant was not acting in some legally permissible way when he killed the victim. Usually, the surrounding circumstances of the killing (e.g., committed during a robbery) are more than enough to establish this element.

2. Of a Human Being by Another

If a person intentionally kills himself, it is not murder, but suicide, which may also be illegal but is not prosecuted as homicide (see below). To convict someone of homicide, the state must show that the victim was a human being. In fact, studies show that it is far more likely that a victim will know his or her killer than for the murdered to be a stranger. See Exhibit 8-6. Although this would seem to be self-evident, it is not always so straightforward. For instance, in some cases, it could be difficult to prove this element. It is not murder to kill someone who was already dead or someone who is not considered to be a person, such as a newly formed fetus. In many states, a fetus is not considered to be a human being unless it can exist outside the mother's womb. In cases where a pregnant woman is assaulted and her fetus killed, the fact that her fetus is not developed to the point where it could exist outside her body would mean that the death of the fetus is not murder. Some states have addressed this particular problem in criminal law by enacting statutes that make it a crime to kill an unborn human being, no matter what stage of development the fetus may be.[4] Under these statutes, abortion would not qualify as murder because the U.S. Supreme Court has determined that an abortion during the first trimester of the fetal development is not a crime. The Court has held that the mother has a privacy interest that outweighs the common law definition of viable fetus.[5]

malice
Intentionally harming someone; having no moral or legal justification for harming someone.

3. With Malice Aforethought

Both murder in the first degree and murder in the second degree (below) involve malice. **Malice** is defined as an unlawful intent to kill. Malice is

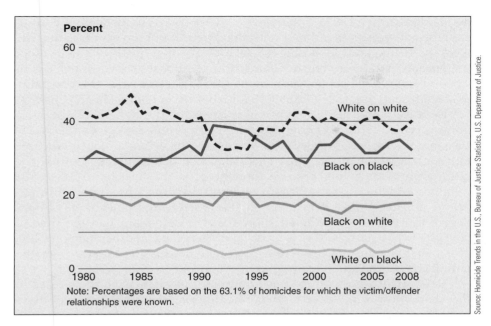

Percent

Note: Percentages are based on the 63.1% of homicides for which the victim/offender relationships were known.

Source: Homicide Trends in the U.S., Bureau of Justice Statistics, U.S. Department of Justice.

Exhibit 8-6
Stranger homicides, by race of offender and victim, 1980–2008

closely intertwined with the government's requirement of showing specific intent to kill. If the government fails to prove that the defendant acted with malice, the defendant cannot be charged with either first- or second-degree murder. Without the proof of malice, the crime must be **manslaughter** (see below) or some other lesser form of homicide. Malice is the unlawful, deliberate intention to kill a human being without excuse, justification, or mitigation. It is a state of mind and is a premeditated, deliberate intention, desire, and design to unlawfully kill another human being.[6]

Malice does not mean that the defendant had any particular animosity toward the victim, but instead refers to "an evil design in general, a wicked and corrupt motive, an intention to do evil, the event of which is fatal."[7] Malice has also been defined as "spiteful or malevolent design against another."[8]

4. With Deliberation, Specific Purpose, or Premeditation

To prove a first-degree murder case, the prosecution must not only prove the general intent of the defendant, but also go beyond that and prove **premeditation**. This is the only difference between first degree murder and second degree murder.

To premeditate is to think and consider what you are doing. When a person kills another with premeditation, he realizes that he is going to cause the death of another person, is conscious of the crime he is about to commit, and does it anyway. This moment to consider the consequences of the action, which is then followed by committing murder, is considered to

manslaughter
A crime, less severe than murder, involving the wrongful but nonmalicious killing of another person.

premeditation
Thinking about something before doing it; thinking in advance about how to commit a crime.

be the crucial point of a first-degree murder case. The defendant considered the consequences of the crime and carried it out anyway. It is this element of deliberately choosing to take a life that justifies the harsher sentence in first-degree murder conviction. In almost all states, such a conviction carries a life sentence. In many states, it also carries the possibility of a death sentence. (See Chapter 15 for a discussion of the death penalty.)

Because a murder prosecution must prove the defendant's state of mind, premeditation becomes the most important aspect of the state's case in a first-degree murder case. To convict the defendant of first-degree murder, the prosecution must show that the defendant committed the crime only after giving it some thought. It is this mental exercise, the weighing of what one is going to do, that gives the special edge to first-degree murder. Unlike manslaughter, discussed below, in a charge of first-degree murder, the state must show that the defendant had the time to consider what he was about to do and then took another person's life. This pause to consider his actions is crucial because it shows the "malignant heart" of the killer.

Defense attorneys often concentrate on this element in their cases. If they can show some doubt on premeditation, then the jury may have some hesitation as to whether the defendant meets the standards for first-degree murder. In that case, they could only convict of some lesser offense, such as second-degree murder or even manslaughter.

The first-degree murder statutes from any number of states are almost identical in defining exactly what premeditation is. All involve the element of the defendant's forethought, lying in wait (time to consider his actions), poison (which takes effect slowly and again shows a time element), or other aggravating feature. The premeditation does not need to exist for any specific period of time before the killing. It can be formed in an instant. The important aspect of premeditation is that the defendant did have the time to consider his actions and placed himself outside the law by deliberately committing a murder.

THE ROLE OF THE PARALEGAL: THE AUTOPSY REPORT
Although it is a gruesome task, a thorough reading of the autopsy report in a murder case is a good idea. This detailed report, prepared by the coroner or medical examiner, provides great detail about the injuries that the victim received. For instance, the wounds received may be inconsistent with the defendant's physical strength or the victim may have died from some intervening cause, such as medical malpractice at a hospital.

D. Motive

motive
The reason a person does something.

As you can see from reviewing the necessary elements of both first- and second-degree murder, there is no requirement that the government prove the defendant's **motive**. In fact, in a purely technical sense, motive is irrelevant to a prosecution. However, even though there is no legal requirement to prove motive, prosecutors often present evidence of the defendant's motive anyway. The reason for this is simple. Even though there may be no legal requirement to prove motive, the jury still wants to know why the defendant committed the crime. The more satisfactory an answer the prosecution can provide to that question, the more the jury will be convinced of the defendant's guilt. Attorneys often speak about motive during the closing argument. The defense often argues that the defendant did not have sufficient motive to kill the victim or that someone else had a greater motive, whereas the prosecutor often explores the evidence and demonstrates how the defendant's motive urged him to commit the crime. For a review of homicide victimization rates, see Exhibit 8-7.

E. Corpus Delicti

Corpus delicti refers to the proof that a crime has been committed. It is an ancient concept and although it sounds complicated, it is actually fairly straightforward. For a person to be convicted of a crime, there must be proof. Although this principle would seem to be self-evident, what about cases where the only evidence against a defendant is his confession? Because criminal prosecutions are based on the requirement of proof (*corpus delicti*), a confession standing by itself is not enough to convict anyone. *Corpus delicti* is often referred to in discussions of murder and manslaughter because the proof of a homicide is almost always the body of the victim. Because the victim's body is referred to as the corpse, these two terms have become intertwined. Actually, the victim's corpse and *corpus delicti* have very little to do with each other. A murder case can be proven against the defendant even when the victim's body is never

BULLET POINT

Motive is not required in a murder case, but prosecutors often present proof about why a defendant committed a murder. They realize that even though it is not technically required, the jury wants to know why the defendant committed the crime.

corpus delicti

"The body of the crime." The material substance upon which a crime has been committed—for example, a dead body (in the crime of murder) or a house destroyed by fire (in the crime of arson).

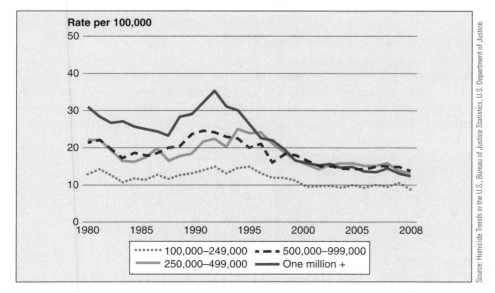

Source: Homicide Trends in the U.S., Bureau of Justice Statistics, U.S. Department of Justice.

Exhibit 8-7

Homicide victimization rates for cities with a population of 100,000 or more, 1980–2008

"No Body" Cases

In several states defendants have been successfully prosecuted for murder even when the body was never recovered. In one notable case, the evidence against the defendant consisted of the victim's blood soaked mattress. Because the body was not discovered—and to date still has not been found—the state took a novel approach to the case. Purchasing an identical mattress, they compared the weight of the new mattress with the blood-soaked mattress. The weight difference accounted for the amount of the victim's blood that had soaked into the mattress. Once they knew the weight, prosecutors asked the coroner to calculate how much blood the victim would have had to lose to account for the weight. The coroner then testified at trial that there is no way a person the size of the victim could have lost that much blood and still be alive. The defendant was convicted, and his life sentence has been upheld on appeal.

recovered. *Corpus delicti* simply refers to the proof that the government is required to present to prove that the defendant is guilty of the crime.

Almost all states have done away with the old common law rule that there must be a body to prosecute a defendant for murder. Given the wide variety of ways that clever defendants have used to dispose of bodies, it may be possible never to find a victim's body. Under the modern usage, *corpus delicti* no longer refers to the victim's body, but to the body of evidence against the defendant. When we talk about the *corpus delicti* in modern parlance, we are really talking about two separate phenomena: the fact that the victim is dead and that someone else caused the death.[9]

F. Felony-Murder Doctrine

When a suspect kills another person while he is committing another crime, such as robbery, the necessary elements of first-degree murder would seem to be lacking entirely. In such cases, it would be almost impossible to prove premeditation. Here, however, the courts have carved out a legal fiction, allowing a first-degree murder prosecution to be brought. In the felony-murder doctrine, the law supplies the specific intent to murder where it normally would not be present. The reason for such a rule is obvious. Without the felony-murder doctrine, a defendant in a robbery case who killed a security guard could not be charged with first-degree murder because the necessary elements of that crime are missing. However, most people would agree that the robber should not be given the benefit of this loophole, especially because the robber caused the security guard's death. There is also an important public policy component to the felony-murder doctrine. Knowing that he or she could be charged with first-degree murder for a killing during the commission of a felony might discourage someone from committing the felony in the first place.

G. Second-Degree Murder, or "Malice Murder"

Second-degree murder has the same elements of first-degree murder except for the element of premeditation. When the prosecution fails to prove that the defendant acted with premeditation, deliberate intent, or special purpose, a first-degree conviction cannot be sustained. The homicide must then be either second-degree murder or some lesser offense, such as manslaughter.

Exhibit 8-8

Crimes that will warrant the imposition of the felony-murder rule

- Sexual assault
- Arson
- Robbery
- Burglary
- Escape
- Resisting arrest
- Kidnapping

INSIDER'S VIEWPOINT

Working with psychics

"Have I ever worked with a psychic? No. Have I ever interviewed them, yes. My reasoning behind that is that if I'm sitting there in the office and we're working a murder case and somebody calls me up and wants to talk to me about it, then I'm going to talk to them. They may really be a psychic; they may not be. They may be somebody wanting to give me some information under the guise of being a psychic. You see what they're saying. 'I don't really want to get involved in this, but I know this information but I don't want them to think that I know it first hand, so I'm going to tell them about it, but I'm going to tell them I'm a psychic.' If you blow them off and laugh about them being a psychic and all, hell that might have been the information that was going to break the murder case. So you've got no other alternative. You never turn down anybody that wants to talk to you about anything about a murder case."

—Jack Burnette, Homicide Investigator

> ### ■ BULLET POINT
> When a person carries out a killing that might, under other circumstances qualify as second-degree murder, if the killing occurs during the commission of a felony, it is upgraded to first-degree murder.

H. Manslaughter

Just as there are degrees of murder, there are different kinds of manslaughter. Manslaughter is often divided into two different categories, and in some states, three.

- The unlawful killing
- Of a human being by another
- With malice aforethought

Copyright © 2015 Cengage Learning®

Exhibit 8-9

Elements of second degree murder

§ 18.2–32 First- and second-degree murder defined; punishment.

Murder, other than capital murder, by poison, lying in wait, imprisonment, starving, or by any willful, deliberate, and premeditated killing, or in the commission of, or attempt to commit, arson, rape, forcible sodomy, inanimate or animate object sexual penetration, robbery, burglary or abduction, except as provided in § 18.2–31, is murder of the first degree, punishable as a Class 2 felony.

All murder other than capital murder and murder in the first degree is murder of the second degree and is punishable by confinement in a state correctional facility for not less than five nor more than forty years.

Exhibit 8-10

First and second degree murder in Virginia

http://lis.virginia.gov/cgi-bin/legp604.exe?000+cod+TOC180200000040000C0000000

Exhibit 8-11
Elements of voluntary manslaughter

- The unlawful killing
- Of a human being by another
- Intentionally, but committed in the heat of passion or after provocation

Copyright © 2015 Cengage Learning®

1. Voluntary Manslaughter

Voluntary manslaughter is the intentional killing of a human being by another person without justification or legal excuse and committed under the influence of some overwhelming passion, often the result of provocation.

In voluntary manslaughter, the defendant has killed another person, but has done so without premeditation and/or after some provocation by the victim. The defendant may have acted on some irresistible impulse or been caught up in some intense emotion. The point, though, is that the defendant did not or could not form the specific intent necessary to charge him with murder in the first degree.

Voluntary manslaughter may be committed without malice, distinguishing it from murder. When malice is missing from a homicide, then the crime must be manslaughter or some lesser crime.

provocation
Words or conduct that incite anger or passion or that cloud judgment and the ability to reason.

a. Provocation　For a case to go from murder to manslaughter, the provocation must be great. Provocation involves some action that renders the defendant so overwrought with passion that he essentially loses control of his emotions. This is usually referred to as the "heat of passion." The theory is that the defendant has been so overcome with some emotion that he is unable to reason clearly and is therefore unable to form the specific intent necessary to commit premeditated murder. However, this "heat of passion" must be closely connected in time to the actual killing. There can be no "cooling off period" (i.e., some period of time in which the defendant could have calmed down). The jury usually decides the question of whether there was a sufficient cooling off period.

What is provocation? Provocation is something beyond simple apprehension or fear. The provocation must be some action by the victim that overwhelms the defendant's emotional control. Most courts view acts of provocation from an objective viewpoint. Appellate courts often ask the question, Would this have provoked a reasonable person? If the answer is yes, then the killing is manslaughter. If the answer is no, then the defendant was not so provoked to make the murder a "crime of passion" and he may be facing a first- or second-degree murder charge.

THE ROLE OF THE PARALEGAL: INVESTIGATING THE VICTIM

There are times when knowing the victim's past, especially his or her reputation for violence, is very helpful to the defense. If the defense is self-defense or provocation, some knowledge of the victim's background can help establish these facts.

- Sudden attack by the victim
- Physical injuries to the defendant
- Killing or assaulting of a family member

Exhibit 8-12
Actions that have been deemed to be sufficient legal provocation

Copyright © 2015 Cengage Learning®

b. How Long Does It Take to Cool Off? In trying to decide if certain facts constitute murder or manslaughter, the question for the jury often is, Did the defendant have enough time to cool off? If he did, then the subsequent killing was premeditated. If the defendant did not have sufficient time to calm down and consider what he was doing, the killing probably qualifies as manslaughter.

How long does it take to cool off? The answer is that it varies according to the case. In most states, any period of cooling off, no matter how brief, is enough. It is impossible to state a bright-line test for what always constitutes a cooling off period. Each case must be taken on its own merits. Therefore, it becomes a jury question as to whether the facts support the defendant's contention that he was acting under a sudden, overwhelming passion or the state's contention that the defendant had sufficient time to cool off and is therefore guilty of premeditated murder.

c. Provocation by Words Alone?
As we have already seen, when the victim does something to provoke the defendant, the killing may move from a murder charge to a manslaughter charge. On a practical level, this change in classification usually means substantially less prison time for the defendant. Faced with a charge of first- or second-degree murder, a defendant may often raise the issue of provocation. The defendant may present evidence of the victim's actions shortly before the killing to show that the defendant was provoked, that his mental equilibrium was overcome with anger, and that he was therefore unable to form premeditation.

Generally, statements or insults taken by themselves are not sufficient to come under the heading of "provocation." However, even this general rule has its exceptions. One such exception deals with adultery. In some states, it is sufficient provocation when the victim announces that he or she has just had sexual relations with the defendant's spouse. Many courts have ruled that such a statement clouds the defendant's emotions and creates a passion so great that it overwhelms the defendant's ability to think properly. In the grip of this passion, the defendant is incapable of cool reflection, lacks self-control, and thus is incapable of forming premeditation.

An Appellate Court Rules That the Defendant's Emotions Were Overwhelmed upon Finding His Wife in Bed with Another Man

"In our opinion the passions of any reasonable person would have been inflamed and intensely aroused by this sort of discovery."[10]

■ BULLET POINT
Provocation, when proven, can reduce a second- or first-degree murder charge to voluntary manslaughter. The jury must decide whether there is sufficient provocation.

2. Involuntary Manslaughter
When someone kills another person through recklessness or wanton disregard for safety, the charge is often involuntary manslaughter. When the facts do not suggest that there was any intent to do harm, let alone kill,

the necessary elements to support premeditated murder or manslaughter are missing. Some states label this crime as "negligent homicide." Here, the killing results through the defendant's reckless actions or negligence.

Involuntary manslaughter is sometimes called manslaughter in the second degree. When a killing occurs during the commission of some unlawful act, such as a misdemeanor traffic violation, the defendant may be charged with involuntary manslaughter. If the defendant had been committing some other felony at the time of the death, he or she would fall under the felony-murder doctrine and the charge would be first-degree murder. However, when the defendant is not committing some other felony and a person dies as a result of the defendant's negligence, then a charge of involuntary manslaughter is called for. It is essentially a catchall statute, including all forms of homicide that are not covered by the other statutes. If a killing does not fall under one of the homicide statutes, then it is either involuntary manslaughter or a justifiable killing. We discuss justifiable homicide (such as self-defense) in Chapter 14.

With regard to a discussion of involuntary manslaughter, the issue of intent, particularly special intent, disappears from the calculation. Essentially, involuntary manslaughter is the unintentional killing of another human being. It can be accomplished during the commission of some unlawful act (not a felony and not something that would normally endanger life—otherwise, that would fall under the felony-murder doctrine). It can also be caused by the actions on the part of the defendant that show a disregard for the health and safety of others, often referred to as the "wanton or reckless conduct" requirement. There is no malice requirement in the crime of involuntary manslaughter.[11] The element of "recklessness" or "wanton disregard" can be satisfied by showing that the defendant was aware of his or her actions but simply chose to disregard the risk he or she posed to others. To prove involuntary manslaughter, prosecutors are not required to show that a person intended to kill; it is enough to show the defendant acted with wanton negligence[12] Involuntary manslaughter convictions can also be had when the defendant suffers from some form of mental illness that prevents him from being able to form specific intent to kill.[13] Voluntary intoxication, however, does not qualify as a form of mental illness.

▇   **ROLE OF THE PARALEGAL: PROSECUTION PARALEGAL**

For a paralegal working with the prosecution, it is crucial to pinpoint the exact sequence of events that lead to the death of the victim. In particular,

Exhibit 8-13
Elements of involuntary manslaughter

- When a defendant
- Without malice, either express or implied
- Without intent to kill or inflict injury
- Causes the death of a human being

the time periods involved should be closely scrutinized. Any potential cooling off period for the defendant could be the difference between a manslaughter charge and a first-degree murder charge.

III. Suicide

Suicide is intentional self-destruction. It might seem odd to make killing oneself an illegal act. Under the common law, suicide (or attempted suicide) was a felony. Historically, suicide carried with it both a religious and ethical stigma. A person who committed suicide was not given proper burial and would often have his property surrendered to the state. In most states, suicide or attempted suicide is no longer considered to be a crime. It can, and often does, form the basis of a quasi-criminal action to declare a person a danger to himself and have him committed to a state mental institution. Although suicide has been essentially decriminalized in most states, the same is not true of assisted suicide.

A. Assisted Suicide

Many jurisdictions draw a distinction between assisting a person to commit suicide and withdrawing life-sustaining medical treatment. In fact, many states allow patients the option of selecting not to be revived should they slip into a coma or develop other medical problems that might facilitate their deaths. Medical personnel cannot be prosecuted for assisted suicide in such a scenario. Patients can also create living wills in which they specifically dictate that they do not want to be kept alive in a persistent vegetative state following some accident or the diagnosis of some disease. In these instances, the executor or the person with power of attorney for the patient has a clear directive to allow the patient to die naturally. Some states have ruled that advocating suicide is not a crime and is actually protected under the First Amendment to the United States Constitution.[14] In situations where a person requests another individual to kill him, the person who does the killing can be prosecuted for murder, not assisted suicide. The reason is that suicide is an action taken by the individual, while murder is carried out by another person.[15]

IV. Assault and Related Offenses

The terms *assault* and *battery* have become confused in modern usage. The statutes covering these particular offenses do not help with this confusion. Simple assault, as we will see later, involves no touching of any kind. Aggravated assault, however, involves great injury or the use of a weapon to severely injure the victim. Before detailing how these terms have become confused, we will first examine the law of assault and battery. See Exhibit 8-14 for a breakdown of violent crime in the United States.

■ BULLET POINT
Helping or assisting another person to commit suicide is a crime in most states.

Exhibit 8-14

Crimes and crime rates by type of offense: 1980–2009

[(13,408 represents 13,408,000). For year ending March 31. Data include offenses reported to law enforcement, offense estimations for nonreporting and partially reporting agencies within each state. Rates are based on Census Bureau estimated resident population as of July 1; 1980, 1990, and 2000, enumerated as of April 1. See source for details]

Item and year	All crimes	Violent crime					Property crimes			
		Total	Murder[1]	Forcible rape	Robbery	Aggravated assault	Total	Burglary	Larceny/ theft	Motor vehicle theft
Number of offenses (1,000):										
1980	13,408	1,345	23.0	83.0	566	673	12,064	3,795	7,137	1,132
1985	12,430	1,328	19.0	87.7	498	723	11,103	3,073	6,926	1,103
1990	14,476	1,820	23.4	102.6	639	1,055	12,655	3,074	7,946	1,636
1995	13,863	1,799	21.6	97.5	581	1,099	12,064	2,594	7,998	1,472
1996	13,494	1,689	19.6	96.3	536	1,037	11,805	2,506	7,905	1,394
1997	13,195	1,636	18.2	96.2	499	1,023	11,558	2,461	7,744	1,354
1998	12,486	1,534	17.0	93.1	447	977	10,952	2,333	7,376	1,243
1999	11,634	1,426	15.5	89.4	409	912	10,208	2,101	6,956	1,152
2000	11,608	1,425	15.6	90.2	408	912	10,183	2,051	6,972	1,160
2001[2]	11,877	1,439	16.0	90.9	424	909	10,437	2,117	7,092	1,228
2002	11,879	1,424	16.2	95.2	421	891	10,455	2,151	7,057	1,247
2003	11,827	1,384	16.5	93.9	414	859	10,443	2,155	7,027	1,261
2004	11,679	1,360	16.1	95.1	401	847	10,319	2,144	6,937	1,238
2005	11,565	1,391	16.7	94.3	417	862	10,175	2,155	6,783	1,236
2006	11,467	1,436	17.3	94.8	450	874	10,031	2,196	6,637	1,198
2007	11,295	1,422	17.2	91.9	447	866	9,873	2,187	6,587	1,098
2008	11,168	1,393	16.4	90.5	444	842	9,775	2,228	6,588	959
2009	10,639	1,318	15.2	88.1	408	807	9,321	2,199	6,327	795
Rate per 100,000 population:										
1980	5,950	597	10.2	36.8	251	299	5,353	1,684	3,167	502
1985	5,225	558	8.0	36.8	209	304	4,666	1,292	2,911	464
1990	5,803	730	9.4	41.1	256	423	5,073	1,232	3,185	656
1995	5,276	685	8.2	37.1	221	418	4,591	987	3,043	560
1996	5,087	637	7.4	36.3	202	391	4,451	945	2,980	526
1997	4,930	611	6.8	35.9	186	382	4,316	919	2,892	506
1998	4,619	568	6.3	34.5	166	361	4,053	863	2,730	460
1999	4,267	523	5.7	32.8	150	334	3,744	770	2,551	423
2000	4,125	507	5.5	32.0	145	324	3,618	729	2,477	412
2001[2]	4,163	505	5.6	31.8	149	319	3,658	742	2,486	431
2002	4,125	494	5.6	33.1	146	310	3,631	747	2,451	433
2003	4,067	476	5.7	32.3	143	295	3,591	741	2,417	434
2004	3,977	463	5.5	32.4	137	289	3,514	730	2,362	422
2005	3,899	469	5.6	31.8	141	291	3,432	727	2,288	417
2006	3,838	481	5.8	31.7	151	293	3,358	735	2,221	401
2007	3,749	472	5.7	30.5	148	287	3,277	726	2,186	365
2008	3,669	458	5.4	29.7	146	277	3,212	732	2,165	315
2009	3,466	429	5.0	28.7	133	263	3,036	716	2,061	259

[1] Includes nonnegligent manslaughter.
[2] The murder and nonnegligent homicides that occurred as a result of the events of September 11, 2001, were not included in this table.

Source: U.S. Census, Statistical Abstract of the United States, 2012.

> - Unlawfully placing another person
> - In fear or **apprehension**
> - Of a harmful or offensive contact

Exhibit 8-15
Elements of simple assault

A. Assault

Battery involves touching; assault is attempted touching. There is no physical contact in an assault. If someone swings a fist at another person and misses, it is an assault. These crimes are often prosecuted together. The reason is simple: A person charged with battery has usually committed an assault in the same event. A defendant may swing and miss the victim on one occasion and then swing and make contact on the second occasion.[16] In many states, assault is defined as the offer of violence, coupled with the contemporaneous apparent ability to carry through on the threat.[17]

1. Fear or Apprehension

In an assault, actual fear is not a requirement. The victim must simply be apprehensive of the contact. Because awareness is a requirement, a victim cannot be assaulted if he or she is unconscious. Unconscious people cannot be fearful or suffer from **apprehension**, so a simple assault cannot be committed against them.

    The defendant must have the apparent ability to carry through the threat of violence. If, for instance, a man is holding a baseball bat and screams at a woman passerby that I'm going to hit you with this bat, this may constitute an assault. If the man swings the bat and misses the woman, an assault has certainly occurred. However, if the man is standing on the other side of a tall fence with no way to get to the woman and he repeats the same threat, he now lacks the apparent ability to put the threat into action and no assault has occurred.

    The threat must be imminent and cannot be a future threat, such as "I'll hit you with this bat at three o'clock!"

2. Harmful or Offensive Contact

Assault involves the fear or apprehension of contact. However, the intended contact must be harmful or offensive. There is no requirement that the intended victim would be seriously injured had the contact occurred. Because different people have different standards about what they consider "offensive" touching, most states approach this issue from the hypothetical "reasonable person standard." The question becomes, Would a reasonable person have considered this attempted contact to be harmful or offensive? If the answer is yes, then an assault has occurred. The law does not take into account the subjective feelings of a particular victim. In many ways, assault is an attempted battery. We will discuss attempted and related offenses later in this text. If we view the crime of

apprehension
An expectation of an unwanted event.

Exhibit 8-16
Elements of simple battery

- The unlawful, intentional touching of another
- That is either offensive or harmful

assault as an attempted battery, how would we classify attempted assault? In some jurisdictions (e.g., Connecticut, Indiana, and Kansas), there is no such crime.[18]

BULLET POINT

Assault, under its strict legal definition, does not involve any touching.

B. Simple Battery

Simple battery involves the intentional touching of another person that is either harmful or offensive. Looked at another way, simple battery is a completed assault. Like assault, the actual touching does not have to rise to the level of severe injury for a simple battery to occur.

1. Unlawful vs. Lawful Touching

Not every touch is a battery. A touch may not be a battery because the defendant did not intend to touch. For instance, someone could stumble against you unintentionally, and that action would not constitute a battery. Other people have a protected privilege to touch you. A police officer has a lawful right to touch people he or she places under arrest. A medical doctor will touch an injured person brought into the hospital for treatment. Because these are "lawful" touches, they do not fall under the category of batteries.

In other situations, the victim can consent to the touching and therefore make it a lawful contact. When a victim consents to a battery, the first element of "unlawful touching" is removed. As we have seen in discussions about proving the elements of a crime, when any element is missing, the case cannot proceed.

2. Harmful or Offensive Touching

In construing what makes a touching a battery, the courts usually require that the touching be done in anger or in a rude or resentful manner. Accidental touching is not a battery because there is no intent. Obviously, if we could bring a charge of battery against everyone who touched us for any reason, the legal system would bog down immediately.

a. Using Objects to Touch While a battery can be committed by a defendant who reaches out and offensively touches a victim with his hands, it is also possible to use objects to touch. A battery could be committed with an object, a weapon, or even a projectile. Objects that are held or thrown by a defendant are considered to be extensions of the defendant's body and thus justify a charge of battery.

b. Degrees of Assault and Battery Just as we saw with murder, many states divide the crimes of assault and battery to various degrees. For

---

Assault requires

- Apprehension of harmful or offensive touching
- Victim must be conscious and aware of assault

Battery requires

- Harmful or intentional touching
- The victim can be unconscious

Exhibit 8-17
Summarizing the differences between assault and battery

---

example, Washington states divides up the crimes of assault and battery into four separate degrees. Other states take a different approach, simply referring to cases where there is little violence as 'simple battery' and those where the victim suffered severe injury—or where a weapon was used—as 'aggravated battery.'[19]

C. Aggravated Assault or Aggravated Battery

A battery or an assault can be classified as aggravated when a weapon is used, when the victim is severely injured, or when other circumstances are present. When an assault or battery is classified as "aggravated," the defendant can receive a more severe sentence. Simple battery or simple assault is normally a misdemeanor. Aggravated assault and aggravated battery are felonies, with a maximum sentence in many states of twenty years in prison.

The definition of aggravated assault (also referred to as aggravated battery) is the crime of a person who intentionally (or recklessly) causes great bodily harm to the victim.[20]

Any of the following can qualify as aggravated assault:

- Inflicting serious pain on the victim
- Causing serious physical injuries to the victim
- Bodily injury that is likely to cause death
- The victim suffers disfigurement[21]

■ BULLET POINT
Battery, under its strict legal definition, does not involve fear or apprehension, only harmful or offensive contact.

- A battery/assault committed while the defendant is engaged in the commission of another crime. Example: rape
- A battery/assault committed on specific groups of individuals. Example: police officers, senior citizens
- A battery/assault where the victim suffers serious bodily injury. Example: broken bones, brain damage
- A battery/assault committed with a dangerous or deadly weapon. Example: gun, knife, etc.

Exhibit 8-18
Situations where a battery or assault may be classified as aggravated

Exhibit 8-19
Types of implements that have been classified as deadly weapons

- Knives
- Handguns
- Hands
- Automobiles
- Brass knuckles

■ BULLET POINT

> Some states have revised the term *aggravated assault* to *aggravated battery* to bring it in line with the strict definition of the word *assault*.

deadly weapon
Any instrument likely to cause serious bodily harm under the circumstances of its actual use.

What separates simple battery from aggravated battery? The answer is that for a crime to be considered aggravated battery, the defendant must have caused serious bodily injury to the victim, disfigured the victim, or used a deadly weapon.[22]

1. Deadly Weapons

A battery or an assault can be reclassified as aggravated, and thus more severely punished, when a **deadly weapon** is used. The use of a deadly weapon in a simple assault is sufficient to increase the charge to aggravated assault even if the victim is uninjured.

2. Special Victims

A battery or an assault may also be classified as aggravated when the victim falls into a special category. For instance, many states classify any battery on a police officer as aggravated battery, justifying a more severe sentence. In many states, if the victim is over sixty-five years of age, a battery may be reclassified as aggravated even though it would be considered simple battery if the victim were younger. These statutes were enacted as a means to protect certain classes of individuals and to discourage people from committing batteries on them.

D. Domestic Violence

No discussion of crimes against the person would be complete without considering domestic violence. Unfortunately, domestic violence is a very common occurrence. In major cities, entire prosecutorial and law enforcement teams have been established just to deal with domestic violence cases.

Domestic violence consists of physical and verbal abuse, generally carried out by a man against a woman in a romantic relationship. This is not to say that domestic violence cannot occur in other relationships, but the most common form is an abusive boyfriend or husband. Abusive relationships normally go through cycles: Tension leads to abuse followed by remorse and regret followed by tension and so on.

It is oversimplistic to say of an abused woman, Why doesn't she simply leave that man? In many cases, the woman is financially dependent on the man. Also, children may be involved. The abuser sometimes threatens to kill the woman and her children if she leaves. In some cases, the abused woman also suffers from low self-esteem and believes that this relationship is what she deserves. Sometimes the woman believes that she can help the man work through his problems and stop the violence. In most situations, evidence shows that the violence continues to escalate over time until the woman is seriously injured or manages to get free of the relationship.

E. Child Abuse

All jurisdictions outlaw child abuse. At a minimum, child abuse is defined as any act (or failure to act) that puts a child in danger of serious physical and/or mental harm. Studies by the U.S. Department of Health and Human Services show a grim picture of child abuse. Recent statistics show the following:

- Girls are sexually abused three times more often than boys.
- Boys have a greater risk of emotional neglect and of serious injury than do girls.
- Children are generally vulnerable to sexual abuse beginning at age three.

Other statistics show a disturbing pattern:

- Children of single parents have a 77% greater risk of being physically harmed than do children living with both parents.
- Children from families with low annual incomes were 22 times more likely to receive some form of mistreatment.[23]

States and federal jurisdictions define child abuse in different ways. For instance, California's approach to child abuse is set out in Exhibit 8-20.

Child abuse prosecutions can be based on a single occurrence or a series of events. A person also can be charged for child abuse when he or she fails to act. For instance, if a parent or another caregiver fails to provide food, adequate shelter, or other necessities of life, this failure will justify an arrest as surely as physical abuse will.

(a) Any person who, under circumstances or conditions likely to produce great bodily harm or death, willfully causes or permits any child to suffer, or inflicts thereon unjustifiable physical pain or mental suffering, or having the care or custody of any child, willfully causes or permits the person or health of that child to be injured, or willfully causes or permits that child to be placed in a situation where his or her person or health is endangered, shall be punished by imprisonment in a county jail not exceeding one year, or in the state prison for two, four, or six years.

Exhibit 8-20
California penal code § 273. Willful harm or injury to child

http://www.leginfo.ca.gov/cgi-bin/displaycode?section=pen&group=00001-01000&file=270-273.75

> (1) "Child abuse" means:
>   (a) Intentional infliction of physical or mental injury upon a child;
>   (b) An intentional act that could reasonably be expected to result in physical or mental injury to a child; or
>   (c) Active encouragement of any person to commit an act that results or could reasonably be expected to result in physical or mental injury to a child.
> (2) "Aggravated child abuse" occurs when a person:
>   (a) Commits aggravated battery on a child;
>   (b) Willfully tortures, maliciously punishes, or willfully and unlawfully cages a child; or
>   (c) Knowingly or willfully abuses a child and in so doing causes great bodily harm, permanent disability, or permanent disfigurement to the child.

http://www.leg.state.fl.us/Statutes/index.cfm?App_mode=Display_Statute&Search_String=&URL=0800-0899/0827/Sections/0827.03.html

F. Elder Abuse

Some statistics claim that over 2 million elderly Americans are the victims of abuse every year. This abuse can come in the form of physical or psychological abuse or can arise out of simple neglect. Although at first blush the problem would seem to be limited to nursing homes, in fact, most cases of elder abuse occur within families where the victim often lives with relatives. This means that the abuser is a child, spouse, or caregiver. It is often brought about by the friction or stress of changes in the family dynamics, such as having to care for a physically frail or sick elderly person. The abuse can range from making verbal threats to punching, slapping, or even physically restraining and torturing the person. The problem with this crime is that it is chronically underreported. In many ways, an elderly person makes the perfect victim for a disturbed individual. The elderly person may be physically weak and easy to intimidate or may suffer from some form of mental disability that would make it difficult, if not impossible, for the person to report the crime. Finally, to make matters worse, because the person is already in poor health, he or she often does not survive until the time of trial. With no witness, there is generally no prosecution.

V. Mayhem

Originally, the term *mayhem* referred to injuring another person by depriving that person of the use of some part of his or her body. It was an offense because, under English law, it deprived the King of a warrior and was thus an offense against the monarch. Later, its meaning was modified

- Maliciously and intentionally
- Depriving another of the use of members of his body
- Making him less able to fight or defend himself

Exhibit 8-22
Elements of mayhem

to include any action that disfigured or caused a person to lose the use of a body part. A good example of mayhem would be cutting off or permanently crippling a person's fingers, arms, or legs. Eventually, it was expanded to include disfigurement. In most states, mayhem has been reclassified as a type of aggravated battery.

VI. Kidnapping

There is wide variation among states and federal statutes in the terms used in to define kidnapping. However, the basic idea is the same in any jurisdiction: The victim is restrained from moving about freely and is taken some distance away.

A. Unlawful Taking and Confinement

Kidnapping requires that the victim be restrained in some way. This does not necessarily mean that the victim be tied up. Confinement can be accomplished by threats, fraud, or deceit. When a defendant tricks a person into accompanying him, he has restrained his victim as much as if he had seized the victim.

B. Asportation

The term *asportation* refers to movement. In a kidnapping charge, the defendant must move the victim some distance. Some states construe asportation to mean a substantial distance, whereas other states define the "movement" requirement to be any slight, almost undetectable, distance. For instance, some states have said that when the defendant moves the victim, by force, only a foot, that is enough to satisfy this element. In some

- Unlawful
- Taking and confinement
- Asportation
- Of another person
- By use of force, threat, fraud or deception

Exhibit 8-23
Elements of kidnapping

states, this movement must be more than a few feet. Why would a jurisdiction have the requirement of asportation at all? Because kidnapping is a major felony that can be punished by life in prison, the crime of kidnapping requires that the defendant take an active role in moving the victim. When a defendant actively abducts a victim, he deprives the victim of a basic right and removes the victim from assistance. Where the statute does not specify what distance is required to satisfy asportation, the courts must determine it from the facts in a particular case. The element of asportation distinguishes the crime of kidnapping from the lesser offense of false imprisonment (see later).

Regardless of the distance the victim is moved, the main element of a kidnapping is forcibly detaining another against his or will and then moving that person some distance.

C. By Use of Force, Threat, Fraud, or Deception

Kidnapping can be accomplished not only by using force, but also by taking and detaining a person against his or her will by intimidation or fraud. A victim can be threatened into going with the defendant. The victim can also be tricked into accompanying the defendant. In either case, because the defendant overcame the victim's free will, it does not matter that the defendant used some tactic other than brute force to accomplish this end. As we have seen with the other crimes in this chapter, except homicide, consent can negate an essential element of the charge. When the victim consents to a kidnapping, the element of "unlawful taking" is removed and the case against the defendant fails.

When someone initially gives consent (e.g., someone agrees to go with the defendant on a trip but then is forced to remain in the car), consent no longer affects the prosecution. The moment the victim was restrained against her will, even if this should come several minutes or even hours into the trip on which she had initially consented, the "unlawful" element of the detention is triggered.

D. Aggravating Circumstances in Kidnapping

In many states, the punishment for kidnapping may be enhanced when the victim is injured during the kidnapping. Many states follow the pattern set out in the statute below.

E. Lawful Restraint

Police officers do not commit kidnapping when they arrest suspects. Of course, this is true only when police officers are acting in their official capacity. On duty, police officers cannot be charged with kidnapping for lawfully taking a suspect into custody. However, when police officers exceed their authority or engage in unlawful acts, the law no longer shields them.

Exhibit 8-24
Sample kidnapping statute

Kidnapping O.C.G.A. § 16-5-40	Any person who
	1. Without lawful authority
	2. Abducts or steals away another person, and
	3. Holds that person against her will.

- "Carrying away," or moving the victim, is an element of kidnapping. Courts use a 4-factor test to determine whether this element is met: (1) the duration of the movement; (2) whether the movement occurred during the commission of a separate offense; (3) whether the movement was an inherent part of that separate offense; and (4) whether the movement itself presented a significant danger to the victim independent of the danger posed by the separate offense.
- When the victim's movement is "merely incidental" to another offense, the carrying away requirement is not met.
- Force is not required, but the defendant must hold the victim against her will.
- There is no minimum amount of time that a victim must be held.
- Kidnapping with bodily injury requires only that an injury, no matter how slight, occur during the kidnapping incident, either during the abduction or afterward.

O.C.G.A. § 16-5-40   Penalty

- 10 to 20 years imprisonment, if the victim is age 14 or older.
- Imprisonment for life or a split sentence with at least 25 years in prison followed by life probation if the victim is younger than age 14.
- Life imprisonment if the kidnapping was for ransom or if bodily injury resulted.

http://children.georgia.gov/sites/children.georgia.gov/files/related_files/site_page/Addressing%20the%20Demand%20Side%20of%20CSEC.pdf

VII. False Imprisonment

False imprisonment is the intentional restraining of another person by the use of force or threats. In this context, "restraining" means that the defendant kept the victim from moving about freely. Usually, this restraint

- Intentionally and unlawfully
- Restraining another
- By the use of force or threats

is not physical. The person is often threatened, coerced, or tricked into restraint. Generally, any show of violence is usually sufficient to sustain a conviction for false imprisonment.

A. Lesser-Included Offenses

False imprisonment can be a confusing crime. Although it sounds as if the victim must be imprisoned in some way, this is misleading. False imprisonment is a lesser included offense of kidnapping. A lesser included offense is a crime that is similar to the greater offense (in this case, kidnapping), but is missing one or more of the elements of the greater offense. The sentence on a lesser included is always more lenient than the sentence would be on the greater offense.

VIII. Stalking

Although men and women have harassed each other throughout time, stalking as a crime is a relatively recent phenomenon. In most states, stalking statutes were enacted during the 1990s. Stalking generally consists of harassment such as making frequent telephone calls, sending threatening notes, and repeatedly following the victim.

Black's Law Dictionary defines stalking as "a course of conduct directed at a specific person that causes substantial emotional distress in such person and serves no legitimate purpose." Almost all jurisdictions have statutes that penalize stalking. Some even go so far as to specifically outlaw stalking via the Internet. (See "Cyberstalking," later.)

A. The Elements of Stalking

Most statutes define stalking as a course of conduct directed at a person that annoys or terrorizes her and causes substantial emotional distress. Because this definition is rather vague, most statutes also add a provision referred to as a "reasonable person" standard. The stalking activity must be something that would cause a reasonable person to suffer substantial emotional distress. In Exhibits 8-26 and 8-27, compare the approaches to stalking used by California and New York, respectively.

(a) Any person who willfully, maliciously, and repeatedly follows or harasses another person and who makes a credible threat with the intent to place that person in reasonable fear for his or her safety, or the safety of his or her immediate family, is guilty of the crime of stalking, punishable by imprisonment in a county jail for not more than one year or by a fine of not more than one thousand dollars ($1,000), or by both that fine and imprisonment, or by imprisonment in the state prison.

http://www.leginfo.ca.gov/cgi-bin/displaycode?section=pen&group=00001-01000&file=639-653.2

Exhibit 8-26
California Penal Code
§ 646.9. Stalking

A person is guilty of stalking in the fourth degree when he or she intentionally, and for no legitimate purpose, engages in a course of conduct directed at a specific person, and knows or reasonably should know that such conduct:

1. is likely to cause reasonable fear of material harm to the physical health, safety, or property of such person, a member of such person's immediate family, or a third party with whom such person is acquainted; or
2. causes material harm to the mental or emotional health of such person, where such conduct consists of following, telephoning, or initiating communication or contact with such person, a member of such person's immediate family, or a third party with whom such person is acquainted, and the actor was previously clearly informed to cease that conduct; or
3. is likely to cause such person to reasonably fear that his or her employment, business, or career is threatened, where such conduct consists of appearing, telephoning, or initiating communication or contact at such person's place of employment or business, and the actor was previously clearly informed to cease that conduct.

http://public.leginfo.state.ny.us/LAWSSEAF.cgi?QUERYTYPE=LAWS+&QUERYDATA=$$PEN120.45$$@TXPEN0120.45+&LIST=SEA5+&BROWSER=EXPLORER+&TOKEN=11950019+&TARGET=VIEW

Exhibit 8-27
New York Statute §
120.45. Stalking

Cyberstalking Techniques

- Posting someone's name, address, and telephone number on sex-related Internet sites
- Using the victim's e-mail address to send insulting e-mails to others
- Posting resignation notices to employers via e-mail
- "Mail-bombing" the victim's e-mail account with hundreds of nonsense e-mails with the express intention of shutting down the account
- Ordering magazines and other items using the victim's home address (and sometimes the victim's credit cards)

1. Cyberstalking

Some states, such as Michigan and Alaska, have expanded their stalking statutes to include a lesser known but rapidly growing phenomenon of cyberstalking.

In states that have enacted provisions outlawing Internet stalking, most have adopted language making it illegal to send threatening e-mail to another person. In one case, a male student posted fantasies about raping, torturing, and murdering a female student in his class. He was convicted of cyberstalking.

THE ROLE OF THE PARALEGAL: WHAT TO TELL A STALKING VICTIM

Here are some important things to tell a victim who believes he or she is being stalked or harassed:

1. Call the police. Make sure that law enforcement is aware of what is going on.
2. Do not give out any information about yourself over the telephone. No matter how eager a telemarketer is to give you a special "prize," do not give out your Social Security number, your credit card information, or any other identifying information.
3. Get caller ID.
4. Save any harassing telephone messages. If the person left the message, save the recording. If your answering machine is digital, replay the message and record it on a cassette player.
5. Keep track of every incident: Note the time, the day, what happened, who else witnessed it, and any other information. Then put this information in a safe place.
6. Get a cell phone so that you can make an emergency call from anywhere.

Case Excerpt. What Is the Difference Between Assisted Suicide and Murder?

STATE V. GOULDING, 799 N.W.2D 412 (2011) ZINTER, JUSTICE.

Allen Kissner wanted to die and had failed in an attempt to take his own life. Kissner subsequently asked Robert Goulding to take Kissner's life with a gun. Goulding agreed. He fatally shot Kissner and was convicted of first degree murder. Goulding now appeals his conviction arguing that the circuit court erred in precluding him from presenting a defense that the shooting constituted assisted suicide rather than murder. We affirm the conviction.

Facts and Procedural History

Kissner wanted to die because he was likely returning to prison, he was addicted to drugs, and he was in chronic, terminal pain. Kissner had failed in a recent attempt to take his own life, so he asked his friend, Goulding, to kill him with a gun. The two men drove to a remote location, and at Kissner's request, Goulding put a gun in Kissner's ear and pulled the trigger causing Kissner's instantaneous death. As he returned to his home, Goulding disposed of the gun and latex glove he used in the shooting. Kissner's body was found the next day by fishermen.

Goulding was charged with first degree murder. He wanted to present a defense that he did not commit murder because he was guilty of assisted suicide. The circuit court, however, precluded Goulding from mentioning the assisted suicide statute. The court also precluded Goulding from arguing that assisted suicide was the only crime Goulding could have committed. Over Goulding's objection, the court instructed the jury: "Suicide is the intentional taking of one's own life. As a matter of law, it is not suicide when another person actually performs the overt act resulting in the death of the decedent." Goulding was, however, permitted to establish that Kissner formulated the plan, took the preparatory steps, and requested Goulding to do the shooting. Goulding argued to the jury that under these facts, he was not guilty of murder. The jury found Goulding guilty of first degree murder.

Goulding advances three related arguments on appeal. He first contends that the court erred in instructing the jury that as a matter of law it was not suicide if a person other than the decedent performed the overt act resulting in the decedent's death. Goulding also contends that the court erred in refusing certain defense instructions that would have supported an alternative assisted suicide conviction by defining suicide, assisted suicide, and corpus delicti. Goulding finally contends that the court erred in prohibiting him from referring to the assisted suicide statute. We consider these contentions together because they are all predicated on Goulding's contention that the shooting constituted assisted suicide rather than first degree murder.

Decision

The question is whether the assisted suicide statute applies when, at the decedent's request, a person other than the decedent commits the overt act causing the death of the decedent. Statutory interpretation and application are questions of law that we review de novo.

Suicide is "the intentional taking of one's own life." SDCL 22–16–36. Assisted suicide occurs when a person "intentionally in any manner advises, encourages, abets, or assists another person in taking or in attempting to take his or her own life." SDCL 22–16–37. Goulding argues that because the assisted suicide statute refers to assistance "in any manner," the statute is broad enough to include an aider's overt act that directly causes the death of the decedent. We disagree.

The phrase "in any manner" modifies the phrase "advises, encourages, abets, or assists another person in taking or in attempting to take his or her own life." Therefore, the statute only applies when any manner of assistance is provided to another person in the other person's taking or attempting to take "his or her own life." But in this case, Kissner, the "other person," did not take his own life. Kissner's life was taken by Goulding when Goulding shot Kissner. Therefore, there was no suicide, and "without a suicide there can be no 'assisting a suicide.'" We conclude that the assistance "in any manner" language of SDCL 22–16–37 does not contemplate a third party's overt act that directly causes the death of another person.

"Other jurisdictions, interpreting similarly worded statutes, have reached the same conclusion. The difference between murder and aiding suicide generally hinges upon whether the defendant actively participates in the overt act directly causing death, or whether he merely provides the means of committing suicide.…This rule applies even where the victim has given his consent or requested the actual assistance provided." And even though Goulding points out that other state statutes do not contain the assistance "in any manner" language, the other statutes' "another" person language makes them indistinguishable. As the court in Gordon explained, the language "aiding another to commit suicide" evidences "a clear and unambiguous intent to penalize only persons who provide indirect types of aid or assistance to others who then go forward and kill themselves. It is well accepted that aiding, in the context of determining whether one is criminally liable for their involvement in the suicide of another, is intended to mean providing the means to commit suicide, not actively performing the act which results in death."

Cobb, 229 Kan. 522, 625 P.2d 1133, confirmed this consensus conclusion in a factually analogous case. Kathleen Cobb, at the request of the decedent, injected him with a fatal dose of cocaine and shot him in the head. Assisted suicide was defined as "intentionally advising, encouraging or assisting another in the taking of his own life." Id. at 525, 625 P.2d at 1135 (quoting Kan. Stat. Ann. § 21–3406). The Kansas court adopted the often-quoted language of the Oregon Supreme Court on this issue:

The statute does not contemplate active participation by one in the overt act directly causing death. It contemplates some participation in the events leading up to the commission of the final overt act, such as furnishing the means for bringing about death, the gun, the knife, the poison, or providing the water, for the use of the person who himself commits the act of self-murder. But where a person actually performs, or actively assists in performing, the overt act resulting in death, such as shooting or stabbing the victim, ... his act constitutes murder.

Kansas court concluded that there is no basis for an assisted suicide defense under this type of factual scenario: "It was Kathleen Cobb who picked up the pistol, found the decedent's temple and pulled the trigger." Id. "The decedent did not destroy himself. It is possible the decedent may have assisted Cobb in destroying himself, but the actual destruction was performed by Kathleen Cobb." Id. This same analysis applies to Goulding.

Goulding, however, argues that these authorities do not apply because they did not consider the language of SDCL 22–16–2, which defines corpus delicti. SDCL 22–16–2 provides: "No person may be convicted of murder or manslaughter, or of aiding suicide, unless the death of the person alleged to have been killed, and the fact of the killing by the accused are each established as independent facts beyond a reasonable doubt." Goulding contends that because the corpus delicti statute requires proof of the fact of a "killing by the accused" and he is the accused, his killing constituted assisted suicide. We disagree with this application of the corpus delicti statute.

A common element of suicide and assisted suicide is the requirement that the decedent take his or her own life. SDCL 22–16–36; SDCL 22–16–37. If the "killing by the accused" language in the corpus delicti statute were intended to change assisted suicide to require a killing by the accused instead of a killing by the decedent, the self-killing element of assisted suicide would be abrogated. That change would render SDCL 22–16–37 meaningless because assisted suicide would then apply to third-party killings but not to preparatory assistance provided by an accused in another person's self-killing. Moreover, if the corpus delicti statute were intended to alter the elements of the assisted suicide statute, the corpus delicti statute would also alter the elements of all other offenses referenced in SDCL 22–16–2; i.e., murder and manslaughter.*417 And, adding a "killing by the accused" element to murder and manslaughter offenses would in turn render felony murder (SDCL 22–16–15) and aiding and abetting murder and manslaughter (SDCL 22–3–3, 22–16–4, 22–16–7, 22–16–15, 22–16–20) meaningless because those offenses specifically contemplate that the direct act of the killing occur by the hand of someone other than the accused. The Legislature could not have intended such absurd results.

Goulding's argument presents a case of conflict between the corpus delicti and assisted suicide statutes. "Where conflicting statutes appear, it is the responsibility of the court to give reasonable construction to both, and to give effect, if possible, to all provisions under consideration, construing them together to make them harmonious and workable." Construing these statutes together to make them harmonious and workable, we conclude that the corpus delicti statute was not intended to redefine the statutory elements of the underlying offenses referenced in that statute. Instead, the concept of corpus delicti is intended to reduce the chance of punishing a defendant for a crime that was never in fact committed. 1 Wayne R. LaFave, Substantive Criminal Law § 1.4(b), at 29 (2d ed. 2003). It does so by requiring proof of a killing by "independent facts." SDCL 22–16–2.

"The corpus delicti rule was first developed more than three hundred years ago in England to prevent the conviction of those who confessed to non-existent crimes as a result of coercion or mental illness." David A. Moran, In Defense of the Corpus Delicti Rule, 64 Ohio St. L.J. 817, 817 (2003). The Supreme Court has confirmed this purpose of the rule:

Its purpose is to prevent 'errors in convictions based upon untrue confessions alone'. . .; its foundation lies in a long history of judicial experience with confessions and in the realization that sound law enforcement requires police investigations which extend beyond the words of the accused.

Thus, "in the United States, the prisoner's confession, when the corpus delicti is not otherwise proved, has been held insufficient for his conviction." 1 Simon Greenleaf, A Treatise on the Law of Evidence § 217, at 279 (14th ed. 1883).

South Dakota follows this view in applying SDCL 22–16–2. "Corpus delicti means the body or substance of the crime and may be defined in its primary sense as the fact that the crime charged has actually been committed by someone." The rule requires evidence corroborating an accused's admission through independent proof showing "(1) the fact of an injury or loss, and (2) the fact of someone's criminal responsibility for the injury or loss." *State v. Thompson*, 1997 S.D. 15, 560 N.W.2d 535, 543. "There must be 'such extrinsic corroborating or supplemental circumstances as will, when taken in connection with the accused's admissions, establish beyond a reasonable doubt that the crime was in fact committed by someone.'". . ."The evidence of corpus delicti, independent of the extrajudicial admissions of the accused, satisfies the rule requiring corroboration of an accused's admission if it is sufficient to convince the jury that the crime charged is real and not imaginary." Thus, the corpus delicti statute is an evidentiary requirement governing when a case may be submitted to a jury. It has also been used as an evidentiary prerequisite to introduction of a defendant's admissions.

We conclude that SDCL 22–16–2 was only intended as an evidentiary requirement to establish "independent facts," to warrant the introduction of extrajudicial statements of an accused or the submission of a case to a jury. It was not intended to add new substantive elements that supplant the statutory elements of the underlying offenses. Therefore, SDCL 22–16–2 does not incorporate into SDCL 22–16–37 a new element of a "killing by the accused" such that an accused third party can commit assisted suicide by an overt act that directly causes the death of another. Because a "killing by the accused" is not an element of assisted suicide, and because there is no dispute that Goulding committed the overt act that directly caused Kissner's death, Goulding could not have committed assisted suicide. The circuit court correctly precluded Goulding from presenting a defense that his shooting constituted assisted suicide rather than murder.

Affirmed.

CASE QUESTIONS

1. Why was the defendant prevented from presenting a defense concerning assisted suicide?
2. Does the statutory language about assisting a person to commit suicide "in any manner" assist the defendant's position? If so, how?
3. Would other states have allowed the defendant to present an assisted suicide defense? Why or why not?
4. Does the assisted suicide statute contemplate active or passive participation by the person who assists another to commit suicide? Explain.
5. What claim does the defendant make about *corpus delicti* in the case, and how does the court address this argument?

ETHICAL CONSIDERATION: LEGAL ASSISTANTS WHO CAN APPEAR IN COURT

As we have seen in previous chapters, a paralegal must avoid the unauthorized practice of law. This includes not only giving legal advice, but also appearing in court to represent a client. However, a paralegal can appear in court to represent clients in some hearings. For instance, there are proceedings involving Social Security benefits and other administrative hearings in which a paralegal can represent another person. However, there are no criminal proceedings, from initial appearance to trial, in which a paralegal is permitted to act as the representative for the client. A paralegal may accompany the attorney to court and may often act as an indispensable assistant to the attorney, but the paralegal is not allowed to conduct direct or cross-examination during the trial or to perform other duties normally associated with attorneys.

✓ Paralegal To Do List

For the defense paralegal:

- Was the defendant under the influence of alcohol or any other drug at the time of incident? (This may affect his/her ability to form specific intent.)
- Are there any factors that may mitigate the defendant's actions, such as provocation, emotional upset, etc.?
- Do the police allege that a weapon was used? If so, what does the client know about the weapon?
- In cases alleging Internet stalking, is there any evidence suggesting that the defendant's online title was used by someone else?

For the prosecution paralegal:

- Does the defendant have a violent history with the victim? Are there others who can testify to this violence?
- Carefully go through the autopsy report and pinpoint the exact cause of death. You may need a medical dictionary to understand some of the terms.

- Was there a "cooling off" period before the killing?
- Get photos of any bruises or other injuries as soon as possible. By the time an assault case comes to trial, the victim will usually be healed.
- If the case involves domestic violence, are there any independent witnesses?

Chapter Summary

Crimes of violence carry many consequences for both the victims and the perpetrators. To have a firm understanding of crimes against persons, it is necessary to learn the basic elements of each crime. Assault and battery are often mentioned in the same context and are often confused with each other, but they have distinct legal elements. This is true of the various categories of homicide as well. Nonlethal crimes against the person, such as kidnapping and false imprisonment, involve the restraint of the victim and an overpowering of the victim's will. Violent crimes often result in lengthy prison sentences and can be used to justify harsher sentences when carried out in conjunction with other crimes, such as sexual assault.

WEB SITES

American Academy of Forensic Sciences
www.aafs.org

Bureau of Justice Statistics
www.bjs.gov

Georgia Court System
http://www.georgiacourts.org/

Homicide Trends in the United States—U.S. Dept. of Justice
www.bjs.gov/index.cfm?ty=pbse&sid=31

Law Enforcement Jobs
www.policeemployment.com

Legal Information Institute—Felony-Murder Doctrine
www.law.cornell.edu/wex/felony_murder_doctrine

Louisiana State Court System
www.lasc.org/judicial_admin/default.asp

National Federation of Paralegal Associations
www.paralegals.org

New Jersey State Court System
www.judiciary.state.nj.us

Utah State Court System
www.utcourts.gov/index.html

U.S. Department of Justice
www.justice.gov

REVIEW QUESTIONS

1. Define premeditated murder.
2. What is the primary distinction between murder in the first degree and murder in the second degree?
3. How does specific intent factor into a consideration of homicide?
4. Explain motive.
5. Define *corpus delicti*.
6. Explain the felony-murder doctrine.
7. What is the difference between voluntary manslaughter and involuntary manslaughter?
8. What is the significance of the cooling off period in terms of prosecuting a murder charge?
9. Explain the difference between assault and battery.

QUESTIONS FOR REFLECTION

1. Why would a state specifically prohibit putting a mentally disabled or mentally ill person to death for first-degree murder?
2. Should suicide be legalized? Create an argument justifying legalization. How would you respond to this argument?

KEYWORDS AND PHRASES

Homicide	Motive
Murder	Provocation
Malice	*Corpus delicti*
Premeditation	Apprehension
Deadly weapon	Lesser included offense
Specific intent	Asportation

PRACTICAL APPLICATIONS

1. Locate your state statutes on homicide. Using the element analysis tools mentioned in the chapter, break down the homicide statute into its essential elements.
2. Locate a recent murder case in the local newspaper. Match the actions of the case to the elements of murder as set out in this chapter. What charge would be justified? Why?
3. Based on your review of the *Fortner*, *Marbles*, and *Kline* cases (Appendix), list the crimes against the person that each defendant committed.

NOTES

1. *State v. Contreras*, 142 N.M. 518, 167 P.3d 966 (Ct. App. 2007).

2. A History of American Law. Lawrence M. Friedman. 1973. Page 249.

3. *Holloway v. McElroy*, 632 F.2d 605 (5th Cir. 1980), cert. denied, 451 U.S. 1028, 101 S. Ct. 3019, 69 L. Ed. 2d 398 (1981).

4. *State v. Hampton*, 213 Ariz. 167, 140 P.3d 950 (2006), cert. denied, 127 S. Ct. 972, 166 L. Ed. 2d 738 (U.S. 2007).

5. *People v. Davis*, 7 Cal. 4th 797, 30 Cal. Rptr. 2d 50, 872 P.2d 591 (1994).

6. *Mason v. Balkcom*, 487 F. Supp. 554 (M.D. Ga. 1980), rev'd on other grounds, 669 F.2d 222 (5th Cir. 1982), cert. denied, 460 U.S. 1016, 103 S. Ct. 1260, 75 L. Ed. 2d 487 (1983).

7. *Roberts v. State*, 3 Ga. 310 (1847).

8. *Patterson v. State*, 85 Ga. 131, 11 S.E. 620 (1890).

9. *State v. Wilson*, 2011-NMSC-001, 248 P.3d 315 (N.M. 2010).

10. *State v. Thornton*, 730 S.W.2d 309 (1987).

11. *State v. Fritsch*, 351 N.C. 373, 526 S.E.2d 451 (2000).

12. *State v. Kaley*, 343 N.C. 107, 468 S.E.2d 44 (1996).

13. *People v. Rogers*, 39 Cal. 4th 826, 48 Cal. Rptr. 3d 1, 141 P.3d 135 (2006), cert. denied 127 S. Ct. 2129 (2007).

14. *Final Exit Network, Inc. v. State*, 290 Ga. 508, 722 S.E.2d 722 (2012).

15. *State v.Goulding*, 2011 SD 25, 799 N.W.2d 412 (2011).

16. *Saucier ex rel. Mallory v. McDonald's Restaurants of Mont., Inc.*, 2008 MT 63, 342 Mont. 29, 179 P.3d 481 (2008).

17. *In re T.Y.B.*, 288 Ga. App. 610, 654 S.E.2d 688 (2007).

18. *State v. Scheck*, 106 Conn. App. 81, 940 A.2d 871 (2008), certification denied, 286 Conn. 918,945 A.2d 979 (2008); *Ott v. State*, 648 N.E.2d 671 (Ind. Ct. App. 1995); *Spencer v. State*, 264 Kan. 4, 954 P.2d 1088 (1998).

19. West's RCWA 9A.36.041(1). *State v. Hahn*, 271 P.3d 892 (Wash. 2012).

20. *Com. v. Patrick*, 2007 PA Super 289, 933 A.2d 1043 (2007), appeal denied, 940 A.2d 364 (Pa. 2007).

21. *State v. Cunningham*, 1998 ME 167, 715 A.2d 156 (Me. 1998); *State v. Cepeda*, 588 N.W.2d 747 (Minn. Ct. App. 1999).

22. *State v. Smith*, 39 Kan. App. 2d 64, 176 P.3d 997 (2008), review denied, (July 3, 2008).

23. Executive summary of the third national incidence study of child abuse and neglect. By Andrea J. Sedlak, Ph.D. & Diane D. Broadhurst, M.L.A. U.S. Department of Health and Human Services, Administration for Children and Families, Administration on Children, Youth and Families National Center on Child Abuse and Neglect, September 1996.

Chapter 9

SEX-RELATED CRIMES

Chapter Objectives

At the completion of this chapter, you should be able to:

- Define rape and other forms of sexual assault
- Define the elements of rape
- Explain how evidence is gathered in a rape prosecution
- Explain rape shield statutes
- Contrast the common law elements of rape with the modern statutory elements of rape
- Describe how the attitude toward rape has changed over time
- Explain the significance of date rape and incest
- Define the elements of sodomy
- Define the elements of child molestation

I. Introduction

Unlike other crimes against the person, sexual assault is a crime fraught with emotional, psychological, and societal overtones. Because the physical contact inherent in rape is sexual in nature, it raises a whole host of issues that most people would rather not think about, let alone discuss. Sex-related offenses are usually grouped with other crimes against the person. However, the issues involved with sexual assault are so complex that they deserve treatment as a separate chapter. There are many

Training police to deal with rape

One of the first things we teach police to say to a victim is, "I'm sorry that this happened to you. I wish I could have prevented it." A lot of times officers don't think about that when they're caught up in investigating the case. But you have to consider the victim's feelings.

—Tom Garmon, Sexual Assault Investigator

differences between sex offenses and other kinds of assault cases. For one thing, the motivation of the offender is different. Rape is a crime of violence. The consequences and the emotional impact on the victim are certainly different from the impact on the victim of other crimes against the person. In addition to these differences, the way evidence is collected in a sexual offense case is dramatically different from what is typically seen in other assault cases. This area of law has undergone dramatic changes in the past few decades, unlike the other offenses categorized under crimes against person. Some sex-related crimes can be carried out between consenting adults and yet are still illegal.

II. Rape

Rape is a complex crime involving tremendous emotional impact on the victim. Many theories have been put forth about why men rape women. Some experts see rape as a crime more about control and domination than sexual urges. Regardless of the reason, forcing a woman (or a man) to have sex is a crime in all jurisdictions. Societal attitudes have changed a great deal about the topic of rape. In the past, the victim was often ostracized and often accused of having provoked the crime. Although those attitudes have not disappeared completely, there is a more informed view of this crime. In the past, the stigma attached to rape often destroyed the victim more assuredly than the attack had. Family and society often shunned a woman who survived a rape. Many people believed that a woman should have submitted to death rather than to succumb to rape. It was considered justifiable for a husband to abandon a wife who had been raped.

rape
The crime of a man imposing sexual intercourse on a woman by force or otherwise without legally valid consent.

- The unlawful carnal knowledge of a woman by a man
- Forcibly and against her will, or without her consent

Exhibit 9-1
The elements of rape

carnal knowledge
Sexual intercourse.

A. Unlawful Carnal Knowledge

The phrase *unlawful carnal knowledge* in its strictest sense refers to the penetration of the woman's vagina by the man's penis. Actual penetration is a requirement of rape, and penetration constitutes **carnal knowledge**, which is synonymous with sexual intercourse. The defendant does not have to ejaculate to complete the offense of rape. Although some penetration must be shown to convict the defendant, it does not have to be full penetration. In many states, slight penetration is sufficient. Most rape statutes use some variation on the following language: "any penetration of the female sex organ by the male sex organ."

How does the state prove penetration? There are a variety of ways in which the state can present evidence that the defendant penetrated the victim:

- The victim can testify that it happened.
- A witness can testify to seeing it happen (very rare).
- The state can present circumstantial evidence, the testimony of a medical doctor who examined the victim and offers expert testimony.

In almost all rape cases, a medical doctor or Sexual Assault Nurse Examiner will testify about the medical examination of the victim's body, specifically any injuries or tears to the vagina. In nonconsensual, or forced, sex, it is common for the vagina to undergo a great deal of trauma. A medical professional can offer a medical opinion about how these injuries occurred and whether the injuries are consistent with forced sex. However, the value of the testimony lies in the length of time between the assault and the medical examination. The longer the victim waits to report the crime, the more likely valuable evidence will disappear.

1. Why is Rape Such a Difficult Crime to Prosecute or Defend?

Rape cases are difficult for the victim, the police officers, and the attorneys involved. The difficulty arises in several ways. Victims are reluctant to report cases of rape, fearing that they will be publicly humiliated. Police officers are wary of rape claims because many have not been

Exhibit 9-2
Proof of penetration

- Victim's testimony
- Presence of sperm (although this is not essential to a prosecution for rape)
- Medical testimony detailing trauma to the victim's body
- Presence of male pubic hairs in or around the victim's vagina
- Traces of seminal fluid, tears, blood, sperm, pubic hair, and so forth on victim's clothing

trained sufficiently to deal with the emotional and psychological impact such a crime has on the victim. Attorneys find such cases difficult because any crime dealing with human sexuality raises uncomfortable issues. Prosecutors know that proving a rape charge can often be difficult because unlike almost any other crime against the person, sexual contact is something that people routinely seek out and find desirable. In some cases, the victim may have other reasons for prosecuting a charge other than the simple desire for justice against a violent attacker. Having said this, however, it is extremely rare for a woman to put herself through the process of a rape trial just to spite the defendant. Criminal defense attorneys do not like to defend rape cases because regardless of instructions to the contrary, jurors become upset when they hear the details of a rape charge and their emotions may sway them to a speedy guilty verdict before they have heard the entire story. In addition, for both attorneys, rarely are there other witnesses to the assault except the defendant and the victim, and the victim must testify about highly intimate and embarrassing events.

B. Forcibly and Against her Will—Without Consent

One of the most important and frequently contested elements of a rape charge has to do with the victim's **consent**. If the victim gave consent to the contact, then the crime is not rape. Because the issue of consent is so important, the courts have spent a great deal of time addressing this issue. First and foremost, a woman does not give consent when she refuses the sexual advances of a man, even if he secretly believes that "she wanted it." See Exhibit 9-3 for an overview of rape and other violent crimes.

consent
Voluntary and active agreement.

In addition to opposing the defendant's advances, the law makes certain presumptions about a woman's consent. For instance, when a woman is unconscious, and therefore unable to give consent, the law presumes no consent. The sexual assault of an unconscious woman qualifies as rape. The same situation applies to a woman who is incapable of giving consent for other reasons, such as mental incapacity. Females below a certain age are presumed not to be able to give consent to any sexual contact. In most states, the age of consent is 16, but it can be as low as 14.

The terms *forcibly* and *against her will* are actually two separate elements in rape cases. *Against her will* means without consent (see above). *Forcibly* means acts of physical violence or force, or threats of death or physical bodily harm. It can also mean mental coercion, such as intimidation. In most situations, this term will be satisfied by a threat of physical force or violence coupled with the defendant's ability to carry out the threat. When a deadly weapon is used, for instance, the force requirement is satisfied. Generally, courts have held that the element of force is satisfied when the defendant uses words or acts that would place a reasonable person in apprehension or fear of the consequences to her or others.

Exhibit 9-3

Rate of violent victimization and percent change, by type of violent crime, 2002, 2010, and 2011

Type of violent crime	Victimization rates[a]			Percent change, 2002–2011[b]	Percent change, 2010–2011[b]	Average annual change, 2002–2010[b]
	2002	2010	2011			
Violent crime[c]	32.1	19.3	22.5	−30%[†]	17%[†]	−6%
Rape/sexual assault	1.5	1.0	0.9	−37[†]	−10	−4
Robbery	2.7	2.2	2.2	−20[‡]	−3	−2
Assault	27.9	16.0	19.4	−30[†]	21[†]	−6
Aggravated assault	5.8	3.4	4.1	−29[†]	22[‡]	−6
Simple assault	22.1	12.7	15.3	−31[†]	21[†]	−6
Domestic violence[d]	5.6	4.4	5.3	−7	19	−3
Intimate partner violence[e]	4.0	3.0	3.3	−18[‡]	9	−3
Violent crime involving injury	8.2	5.0	5.6	−31[†]	12	−5
Serious violent crime[f]	10.0	6.6	7.2	−28%[†]	9%	−5%
Serious domestic violence[d]	1.9	1.5	1.4	−26[‡]	−4	−3
Serious intimate partner violence[e]	1.3	1.1	1.0	−21	−3	−2
Serious violent crime involving weapons	6.9	4.2	4.6	−33[†]	11	−6
Serious violent crime involving injury	3.3	2.6	2.7	−19	3	−3

Note: Total population age 12 or older was 231,589,260 in 2002; 255,961,940 in 2010; and 257,542,240 in 2011.
[†]Significant at 95%.
[‡]Significant at 90%.
[a]Per 1000 persons age 12 or older.
[b]Calculated based on unrounded estimates.
[c]Excludes homicide. The NCVS is based on interviews with victims and therefore cannot measure murder.
[d]Includes victimization committed by intimate partners (current of former spouses, boyfriends, or girlfriends) and family members.
[e]Includes victimization committed by current or former spouses, boyfriends, or girlfriends.
[f]Includes rape or sexual assault, robbery, and aggravated assault.

C. Gathering Evidence in a Rape Prosecution

When a victim reports that she has been raped, police will seek to gather as much evidence as possible. However, because of the sensitive nature of the crime, the only appropriate place to gather the evidence from the victim is a hospital or another medical facility. Some facilities have specially trained personnel on hand who know how to go about obtaining the evidence and

Exhibit 9-4

Sample rape statute

> (a) A person commits the offense of rape when he has carnal knowledge of a female forcibly and against her will;
> (b) A person convicted of the offense of rape shall be punished by death, by imprisonment for life without parole, by imprisonment for life, or by imprisonment for not less than ten nor more than twenty years.

- Pubic hair combings (trying to locate any left behind by the defendant)
- Pulled pubic hairs (to compare known samples of the victim's pubic hairs with those suspected of belonging to the defendant)
- Swabs of seminal or other fluid for later testing (including DNA testing)
- Collection of the victim's clothing (such as undergarments, etc.)

Exhibit 9-5
Evidence typically gathered in a sexual assault case

- Provide medical assistance to victim
- Protect the crime scene and evidence
- Establish an evidentiary link between the suspect and the victim

Exhibit 9-6
Steps in police investigation of a rape charge

preserving it for later testing. In some states, there are specially trained registered nurses called Sexual Assault Nurse Examiners (SANE). A SANE is trained not only in how to gather evidence, but also in how to present this evidence to a jury. A SANE often works in conjunction with counselors or a victim's advocate so that the victim will have help through the ordeal of reporting the crime and being examined for evidence.

D. Gender Bias in Rape Statutes?

So far, we have continually addressed the crime of rape with the assumption of a male attacker and a female victim. Traditionally, this is how many states phrased their sexual assault statutes. However, with the recognition that rape can involve male victims as well as male attackers,

■ **BULLET POINT**
Evidence must be gathered from the rape victim to prove rape.

INSIDER'S VIEWPOINT

Gathering evidence in rape cases

"I tell the victim that we have procedures in place to preserve and collect evidence. For instance, when we go across the hall to the exam room and the adjacent bathroom, I ask them to stand on a couple of floor drapes. The reason I do is because there may be evidence, trace or fiber, or something that is caught on their clothing that may fall off. That floor drape will catch that. I fold that up and that becomes part of the evidence, too."

—Ann Burdges, Director, Sexual Assault Center

numerous states have removed the gender-specific aspects of prior legislation. For instance, under the old statutes, it would not be rape when:

- A woman sexually assaults a man.
- A woman sexually assaults another woman.
- A man sexually assaults another man.

The changes in the legislation now make all of the above situations illegal under the broad category of rape. Under the new statutes, rape is more generally defined as follows: Penetration of the anus or female organ of another person by any means without the person's consent or penetration of the mouth of another person by the sexual organ of the actor without the person's consent. In recent years, there has been a push to redefine rape as any forced sexual act on another person, whether the victim is a woman or a man. However, states have been slow to pick up on this trend, and in many states, the definition continues to make gender-specific references.

E. Rape Under the Common Law

Common law required that the victim present evidence of resistance to her attacker; otherwise, it would be assumed that she consented. The victim had to show that she had used "maximum and reasonable resistance" in fighting off her attacker. States interpreted this phrase in different ways. While some states interpreted this phrase to mean any resistance to the assault, many states required the victim to put up a heroic effort before they would consider the victim to have properly resisted. This view slowly began to change in the 1960s and 1970s. Many state supreme courts began questioning the wisdom of state law requiring that the victim do more than passively resist or that the victim physically resist "with all her power and strength."[1]

1. Spousal Immunity

Under the common law, husbands could not be convicted of raping their wives. This was based on the theory that wives had consented to sexual contact by marrying their husbands and that they could not later revoke

BULLET POINT
There are some initiatives to redefine rape as including any forced sex between opposite-sex or same-sex individuals.

INSIDER'S VIEWPOINT

Interviewing rape victims

"What I tell victims is that what we want to do is to prevent this from happening to someone else. We can't turn back the hands of time, but we do want to utilize their resources and what happened to them to keep it from happening to somebody else."

—Tom Garmon, Sexual Assault Investigator

- The unlawful carnal knowledge of a woman
- By a man who was not her husband
- Forcibly and against her will, or without her consent

Exhibit 9-7
The elements of common
law rape

that consent. Fortunately, most states have changed these laws. Husbands can be charged with forcing sex on their wives; they no longer enjoy spousal **immunity**.

immunity
Freedom from prosecution.

2. Corroboration Required Under the Common Law

In the past, the victim's testimony about the assault would have to be **corroborated** by some independent evidence; otherwise, the charge could not stand. In most cases, that requirement has been removed or subsumed into the medical testimony offered at trial.[2]

corroborate
To add to the likely truth or importance of a fact; to back up what someone says.

F. Psychological Impact of the Sexual Assault

The psychological trauma suffered by the victim in a rape case is sometimes worse than the physical injuries. Victims of rape often feel shame and humiliation, and the criminal justice system often fails to alleviate those feelings. The victim must undergo a physical examination, and then, assuming that the attacker is caught, she will have to testify against him at trial. This means that she will have to recount the events of the rape in a courtroom filled with strangers and the person who attacked her. Inaccurate movie and television portrayals do not help to alleviate that anxiety. Victims on these shows are shown being cross-examined about their sex lives and accused of having loose morals. The fact that most of these portrayals are wrong, especially in regard to cross-examination about the victim's past sexual history, is never pointed out. For a more accurate picture of the arrest rate for rape and other offenses, see Exhibit 9-8.

Protecting the Identity of Rape Victims

Why is it still necessary to protect the identity of the rape victim? Because society's attitudes toward this crime have not changed as much as we would like to think. There is still some form of "unclean taint" affixed to a woman who has been raped. In modern society, no woman should be reluctant to come forward to report rape.

G. Rape Shield Statutes

Hollywood has made a great deal of money depicting rape trials. In the movies, scheming, immoral defense attorneys use cross-examination to verbally pounce on the defenseless rape victim, humiliating her with questions about all of her past sexual encounters. The defense attorney tries to paint the picture of the victim as a wayward woman, someone who was obviously "asking for it."

In the real world, questions about the victim's past sexual history are not permissible. All states have passed so-called **rape shield statutes**. These statutes prevent a defense attorney from asking the rape victim any questions about her other sexual encounters, unless they specifically involved the defendant. These statutes were enacted to alleviate some of

rape shield statute
A state law that prohibits use of most evidence of a rape victim's past sexual conduct or that protects the victim's identity.

Exhibit 9-8
Arrest in the United States by sex, age group, and race, 2010

Source: *Arrest in the U.S.*, Bureau of Justice Statistics, U.S. Department of Justice.

	Total	Sex		Age group		Race			
		Male	Female	Juvenile under age 18	Adult	White	Black	AIAN[a]	API[b]
Total	13,122,110	9,792,190	3,329,920	1,642,650	11,479,470	9,122,010	3,655,620	186,120	158,370
Violent									
Murder and non-negligent manslaughter	11,200	9,980	1,230	1,010	10,190	5,540	5,430	120	110
Forcible rape	20,090	19,860	230	2,870	17,220	13,210	6,300	290	280
Robbery	112,300	98,600	13,700	27,190	85,110	48,310	62,020	780	1,180
Aggravated assault	408,490	316,460	92,030	44,820	363,670	260,770	136,400	6,100	5,220
Simple assault	1,292,450	944,970	347,480	210,240	1,082,200	850,800	406,490	19,260	15,910
Property									
Burglary	289,770	245,770	44,000	65,200	224,570	195,780	88,740	2,500	2,750
Larceny-theft	1,271,410	717,770	553,640	281,060	990,350	875,620	359,080	18,130	18,570
Motor vehicle theft	71,490	58,980	12,500	15,760	55,730	45,340	24,200	890	1,060
Arson	11,300	9,350	1,950	4,560	6,740	8,520	2,520	130	130
Forgery and counterfeiting	78,100	48,780	29,320	1,690	76,410	51,860	24,890	440	900
Fraud	187,890	109,740	78,150	5,770	182,120	123,420	61,190	1,560	1,730
Embezzlement	16,620	8,230	8,390	440	16,170	11,020	5,160	110	330
Stolen property offenses	94,800	76,230	18,570	14,640	80,160	61,860	31,250	760	940
Vandalism	252,750	204,860	47,890	77,070	175,690	186,570	59,180	4,210	2,790
Drug									
Drug abuse violations	1,638,850	1,324,860	313,980	170,570	1,468,270	1,093,910	519,830	11,240	13,870
Drug sale/manufacturing	302,310	249,050	53,260	23,800	278,510	181,370	116,830	1,740	2,370
Drug possession/use	1,336,530	1,075,810	260,720	146,770	1,189,760	912,580	402,940	9,510	11,500
Other									
Weapon law violations	159,020	145,600	13,420	31,360	127,660	92,630	63,710	1,100	1,590
Prostitution and commercialized vice	62,670	19,480	43,190	1,040	61,630	33,990	26,590	430	1,650
Other sex offenses	72,630	67,020	5,610	12,970	59,660	53,490	17,130	950	1,050
Gambling	9,940	9,010	930	1,350	8,590	2,860	6,650	40	390
Offenses against family and children	111,060	83,250	27,810	3,780	107,280	74,270	34,030	2,000	760
Driving under the influence	1,412,220	1,078,070	334,150	12,030	1,400,200	1,209,990	162,160	18,310	21,760
Liquor laws	512,790	366,850	145,940	94,710	418,080	424,990	62,930	17,790	7,080
Drunkenness	560,720	463,240	97,480	12,700	548,020	461,340	84,920	10,820	3,650
Disorderly conduct	615,170	444,840	170,340	155,940	459,240	390,410	208,760	10,830	5,180
Vagrancy	32,030	25,680	6,350	2,140	29,900	17,900	13,190	720	210
Suspicion	1,170	890	280	130	1,030	740	410	10	10
Curfew and loitering law violations	94,800	66,690	28,110	94,800	0	56,190	36,300	1,010	1,300
Runaways	—	—	—	—	—	—	—	—	—
All other offenses except traffic	3,720,400	2,827,140	893,260	296,790	3,423,610	2,470,680	1,146,150	55,580	48,000
Violent Crime Index[c]	552,080	444,890	107,180	75,890	476,190	327,840	210,150	7,300	6,790
Property Crime Index[d]	1,643,960	1,031,870	612,100	366,590	1,277,370	1,125,260	474,550	21,650	22,510

Note: Counts may not sum to total due to rounding. The offense categories are based on the FBI's classification system. See the *Methodology* for details on UCR counting rules.

— Not collected. As of 2010, the UCR Program no longer collected arrests for runaways.

[a] American Indian or Alaska Native.
[b] Asian, Native Hawaiian, or other Pacific Islander.
[c] The Violent Crime Index is the sum of arrests for murder and non-negligent manslaughter, forcible rape, robbery, and aggravated assault.
[d] The Property Crime Index is the sum of arrests for burglary, larceny-theft, motor vehicle theft, and arson.

the anxiety that rape victims face when they testify. Screenplays generally overlook these protections because they take away from the drama of the story.

1. Cross-Examining the Rape Victim

Most defense attorneys are not the cruel, immoral creatures portrayed on television and in movies. Even if they are, it does not make sense to humiliate the victim. In the movies, the viewer feels sorry for the victim and begins to hate the defense attorney. Good defense attorneys know this and work very hard to keep that from happening in a real trial. Consequently, they rarely yell and scream at the victim. They do not ask insulting questions. Defense attorneys do not want the jury to hate them. They want the jury to like them. They want the jury to begin to doubt the victim's version of what happened, not to feel sorry for her. How do defense attorneys do this? They keep their voice at a moderate level and pick away at the details of the victim's testimony. If the defense is that the victim has not correctly identified her attacker, then the defense attorney will focus on those points. If the defense is that the victim consented to the contact, then the focus must be on the relationship—if any—between the defendant and the victim.

---

§ 60.42 Rules of evidence; admissibility of evidence of victim's sexual conduct in sex offense cases

Evidence of a victim's sexual conduct shall not be admissible in a prosecution for an offense or an attempt to commit an offense defined in article one hundred thirty of the penal law unless such evidence:

1. Proves or tends to prove specific instances of the victim's prior sexual conduct with the accused; or
2. Proves or tends to prove that the victim has been convicted of an offense under section 230.00 of the penal law within three years prior to the sex offense which is the subject of the prosecution; or
3. Rebuts evidence introduced by the people of the victim's failure to engage in sexual intercourse, deviate sexual intercourse, or sexual contact during a given period of time; or
4. Rebuts evidence introduced by the people which proves or tends to prove that the accused is the cause of pregnancy or disease of the victim, or the source of semen found in the victim; or
5. Is determined by the court after an offer of proof by the accused outside the hearing of the jury, or such hearing as the court may require, and a statement by the court of its findings of fact essential to its determination, to be relevant and admissible in the interests of justice.

http://public.leginfo.state.ny.us/menugetf.cgi?COMMONQUERY=LAWS

Exhibit 9-9
New York's Rape Shield Statute

H. Aggravated Sexual Assault

An assault may be classified as aggravated sexual assault when any of the following occurs:

- A deadly weapon is used.
- The victim is seriously injured.
- The victim was kidnapped.

Classifying a sexual assault as aggravated will justify a much harsher sentence for the defendant. In some circumstances, the defendant can be sentenced to life in prison for aggravated sexual assault.

I. Date Rape

Studies have shown that the majority of rape victims know their attackers. The rapist may be a friend, a coworker, an ex-boyfriend, or a date. Date rape has received more publicity in recent years as more victims have come forward to reveal that they have been assaulted on a first or second date. The fact that the rape occurs during a romantic date does not make the rape any less serious or the rapist any less culpable.

1. Date Rape Drugs

So-called "date rape drugs" have become widely available in recent years. These drugs, marketed under a variety of names, are generally clear, odorless, and tasteless liquids that would-be rapists put into victims' drinks. Once imbibed, the drug renders the victim unconscious. She is then raped. Following the rape, the attacker will attempt to arrange things so that it appears as though the victim simply passed out from drinking too much alcohol. Sometimes the victim does not even know she was raped. In one horrific case, the victim wasn't aware that she had been raped until she saw pictures of herself on the Internet being raped by two different men.

■ BULLET POINT
Date rape is still nonconsensual, forced sex.

IIII. Other Sexual Offenses

In the following section, we will examine other types of sexual offenses. Although some of these involve threats or violence, others do not. In fact, some statutes specifically provide that a defendant can be prosecuted even when the victim consents to the sexual contact. One such example is statutory rape.

A. Statutory Rape

statutory rape
The crime of a man having sexual intercourse with a girl under a certain state-set age (with or without the girl's consent).

Statutory rape is one of the few strict liability crimes. A strict liability crime does not require the two elements of any criminal offense: mens rea (intent) and actus reus (action). As we have seen in previous chapters, almost all crimes require intent and action before the defendant can be

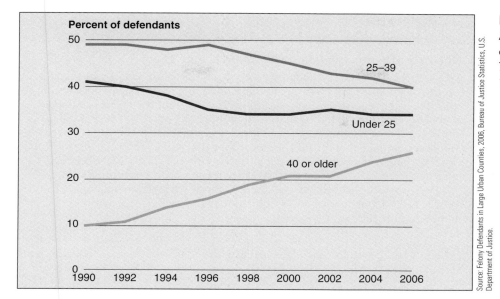

Percent of defendants

Source: Felony Defendants in Large Urban Counties, 2006, Bureau of Justice Statistics, U.S. Department of Justice.

Exhibit 9-10
Age at arrest of felony defendants in the 75 largest counties, 1990–2006

found guilty. This is not true of a strict liability crime. In a strict liability crime, just the act alone is sufficient. The defendant's intent is not relevant. The only requirement to be found guilty of statutory rape is that the defendant must have had sexual intercourse with an underage victim. The fact that the defendant may have believed that the victim was of proper age is not a defense to statutory rape. The fact that the victim consented to the action, which normally would eliminate any criminal charge, is also irrelevant. For additional information on age as it relates to violent crime, see Exhibit 9-10.

■ **BULLET POINT**
Statutory rape is one of the few strict liability crimes, meaning that the state does not have to prove the defendant's intent.

Exhibit 9-11
Statutory rape in North Carolina

> **§ 14-27.7A Statutory rape or sexual offense of person who is thirteen, fourteen, or fifteen years old.**
>
> (a) A defendant is guilty of a Class B1 felony if the defendant engages in vaginal intercourse or a sexual act with another person who is thirteen, fourteen, or fifteen years old and the defendant is at least six years older than the person, except when the defendant is lawfully married to the person.
>
> (b) A defendant is guilty of a Class C felony if the defendant engages in vaginal intercourse or a sexual act with another person who is thirteen, fourteen, or fifteen years old and the defendant is more than four but less than six years older than the person, except when the defendant is lawfully married to the person.

http://www.ncga.state.nc.us/EnactedLegislation/Statutes/HTML/BySection/Chapter_14/GS_14-27.7A.html

INSIDER'S VIEWPOINT

The role of the paralegal: background on the client

One important aspect of defending a criminal case is to have a good handle on the defendant's prior criminal record. Not all clients are as forthcoming with this information as they should be. The fact that the client has a prior conviction for rape could be extremely important. What should a paralegal do if a prior conviction is suspected but the client fails to bring it up? It's time for a paralegal to do a little background checking.

"We've got a computer at the Clerk of Court's office that will actually give us their entire criminal history. We can get a print out of their criminal history statewide. We can go over there and pull up anybody's name—it's all public record." Armed with this material, the defense team will be better prepared for trial.

—Linda McCurry, Paralegal

B. Fornication

In many states, it is still illegal for unmarried people to have consensual sex with each other. Although these statutes remain on the books, it is extremely rare for police to enforce them.

C. Adultery

Like fornication, adultery is also against the law in many states. However, prosecuting someone for adultery remains a low priority for most law enforcement.

D. Cohabitation

The crime of cohabitation is another crime that is rarely, if ever, enforced. Although these statutes remain current law in most states, law enforcement

Exhibit 9-12
Sample fornication statute

An unmarried person commits the offense of fornication when he voluntarily has sexual intercourse with another person and, upon conviction thereof, shall be punished as for a misdemeanor.

Exhibit 9-13
Sample adultery statute

If any man and woman, not being married to each other, but either of whom are married to another, shall lewdly and lasciviously associate, bed, and cohabit together, they shall be guilty of a misdemeanor.

§ 750.335. Lewd and lascivious cohabitation and gross lewdness

Any man or woman, not being married to each other, who shall lewdly and lasciviously associate and cohabit together, and any man or woman, married or unmarried, who shall be guilty of open and gross lewdness and lascivious behavior, shall be guilty of a misdemeanor, punishable by imprisonment in the county jail not more than one year, or by fine of not more than $500.00. No prosecution shall be commenced under this section after one year from the time of committing the offense.

http://www.legislature.mi.gov/(S(kvfkaw55hvmpkueppiceer2p))/mileg.aspx?page=GetObject&objectname=mcl-750-335

Exhibit 9-14
Michigan's statute on cohabitation

officers usually concentrate their efforts on crimes they consider to be more serious.

Some states have even taken the bold step of repealing these essentially unenforceable laws. One such state is Florida, which repealed the crime of cohabitation in 1983.

E. Sodomy

What constitutes **sodomy** varies depending on which state statute is being reviewed. Although generally held to involve "unnatural" sexual acts, sodomy can cover a broad range of activities involving both homosexual and heterosexual acts. The category of sodomy may also include a wide range of other offenses, including anal sex, fellatio, cunnilingus, bestiality, and necrophilia. Although often associated with homosexual acts, most state statutes do not make such a fine distinction. Consenting heterosexual couples may also be guilty of sodomy. Some states go so far as to outlaw these practices among married couples. Although law enforcement generally pays as much attention to sodomy laws as it does to fornication and cohabitation, there are times when individuals may be charged with sodomy. A distinction should be drawn here between consensual acts of sodomy and those involving force. Consensual acts are not punished as severely as forced acts of sodomy, which often fall under the category of rape.

However, that is not to say that consenting partners who commit sodomy are never prosecuted. Consider, for example, the case of *Lawrence v. Texas*.

■ **BULLET POINT**
Fornication, adultery, and cohabitation statutes are rarely enforced and have even been repealed in some states.

sodomy
A general word for an "unnatural" sex act or the crime committed by such act. While the definition varies, sodomy can include oral sex, anal sex, homosexual acts, or sex with animals.

■ **BULLET POINT**
As you can see in this chapter's Case Excerpt, the U.S. Supreme Court has overturned statutes that criminalize sexual activity between consenting adult homosexuals.

Case Excerpt. The U.S. Supreme Court Rules on Adult, Consensual Homosexual Acts

LAWRENCE V. TEXAS, 539 U.S. 558, 123 S.CT. 2472 (U.S., 2003).

Justice KENNEDY delivered the opinion of the Court.

Liberty protects the person from unwarranted government intrusions into a dwelling or other private places. In our tradition the State is not omnipresent in the home. And there are other spheres of our lives and existence, outside the home, where the State should not be a dominant presence. Freedom extends beyond spatial bounds. Liberty presumes an autonomy of self that includes freedom of thought, belief, expression, and certain intimate conduct. The instant case involves liberty of the person both in its spatial and in its more transcendent dimensions.

I

The question before the Court is the validity of a Texas statute making it a crime for two persons of the same sex to engage in certain intimate sexual conduct.

In Houston, Texas, officers of the Harris County Police Department were dispatched to a private residence in response to a reported weapons disturbance. They entered an apartment where one of the petitioners, John Geddes Lawrence, resided. The right of the police to enter does not seem to have been questioned. The officers observed Lawrence and another man, Tyron Garner, engaging in a sexual act. The two petitioners were arrested, held in custody overnight, and charged and convicted before a Justice of the Peace.

The complaints described their crime as "deviate sexual intercourse, namely anal sex, with a member of the same sex (man)." App. to Pet. for Cert. 127a, 139a. The applicable state law is Tex. Penal Code Ann. § 21.06(a) (2003). It provides: "A person commits an offense if he engages in deviate sexual intercourse with another individual of the same sex." The statute defines "deviate sexual intercourse" as follows:

(A) "any contact between any part of the genitals of one person and the mouth or anus of another person; or

(B) "the penetration of the genitals or the anus of another person with an object." § 21.01(1).

The petitioners exercised their right to a trial de novo in Harris County Criminal Court. They challenged the statute as a violation of the Equal Protection Clause of the Fourteenth Amendment and of a like provision of the Texas Constitution. Tex. Const., Art. 1, § 3a. Those contentions were rejected. The petitioners, having entered a plea of nolo contendere, were each fined $200 and assessed court costs of $141.25. App. to Pet. for Cert. 107a–110a.

We granted certiorari, 537 U.S. 1044, 123 S.Ct. 661, 154 L.Ed.2d 514 (2002), to consider three questions:

1. Whether petitioners' criminal convictions under the Texas 'Homosexual Conduct' law—which criminalizes sexual intimacy by same-sex couples, but not identical behavior by different-sex couples—violate the Fourteenth Amendment guarantee of equal protection of the laws.

2. Whether petitioners' criminal convictions for adult consensual sexual intimacy in the home violate their vital interests in liberty and privacy protected by the Due Process Clause of the Fourteenth Amendment.

3. Whether Bowers v. Hardwick, supra, should be overruled. See Pet. for Cert. i.

The petitioners were adults at the time of the alleged offense. Their conduct was in private and consensual.

II

We conclude the case should be resolved by determining whether the petitioners were free as adults to engage in the private conduct in the exercise of their liberty under the Due Process Clause of the Fourteenth Amendment to the Constitution. For this inquiry we deem it necessary to reconsider the Court's holding in Bowers.

There are broad statements of the substantive reach of liberty under the Due Process Clause in earlier cases, including *Pierce v. Society of Sisters*, 268 U.S. 510, 45 S.Ct. 571, 69 L.Ed. 1070 (1925), and *Meyer v. Nebraska*, 262 U.S. 390, 43 S.Ct. 625, 67 L.Ed. 1042 (1923); but the most pertinent beginning point is our decision in *Griswold v. Connecticut*, 381 U.S. 479, 85 S.Ct. 1678, 14 L.Ed.2d 510 (1965).

In *Griswold* the Court invalidated a state law prohibiting the use of drugs or devices of contraception and counseling or aiding and abetting the use of contraceptives. The Court described the protected interest as a right to privacy and placed emphasis on the marriage relation and the protected space of the marital bedroom. Id., at 485, 85 S.Ct. 1678.

After Griswold it was established that the right to make certain decisions regarding sexual conduct extends beyond the marital relationship. In *Eisenstadt v. Baird*, 405 U.S. 438, 92 S.Ct. 1029, 31 L.Ed.2d 349 (1972), the Court invalidated a law prohibiting the distribution of contraceptives to unmarried persons. The case was decided under the Equal Protection Clause, id., at 454, 92 S.Ct. 1029; but with respect to unmarried persons, the Court went on to state the fundamental proposition that the law impaired the exercise of their personal rights, ibid. It quoted from the statement of the Court of Appeals finding the law to be in conflict with fundamental human rights, and it followed with this statement of its own:

The opinions in *Griswold* and *Eisenstadt* were part of the background for the decision in *Roe v. Wade*, 410 U.S. 113, 93 S.Ct. 705, 35 L.Ed.2d 147 (1973). As is well known, the case involved a challenge to the Texas law prohibiting abortions, but the laws of other States were affected as well. Although the Court held the woman's rights were not absolute, her right to elect an abortion did have real and substantial protection as an exercise of her liberty under the Due Process Clause. The Court cited cases that protect spatial freedom and cases that go well beyond it. Roe recognized the right of a woman to make certain fundamental decisions affecting her destiny and confirmed once more that the protection of liberty under the Due Process Clause has a substantive dimension of fundamental significance in defining the rights of the person.

The facts in Bowers had some similarities to the instant case. A police officer, whose right to enter seems not to have been in question, observed Hardwick, in his own bedroom, engaging in intimate sexual conduct with another adult male. The conduct was in violation of a Georgia statute making it a criminal offense to engage in sodomy. One difference between the two cases is that the Georgia statute prohibited the conduct whether or not the participants were of the same sex, while the Texas statute, as we have seen, applies only to participants of the same sex. Hardwick was not prosecuted, but he brought an action in federal court to declare the state statute invalid. He alleged he was a practicing homosexual and that the criminal prohibition violated rights guaranteed to him by the Constitution. The Court, in an opinion by Justice White, sustained the Georgia law.

The Court began its substantive discussion in Bowers as follows: "The issue presented is whether the Federal Constitution confers a fundamental right upon homosexuals to engage in sodomy and hence invalidates the laws of the many States that still make such conduct illegal and have done so for a very long time." Id., at 190, 106 S.Ct. 2841. That statement, we now conclude, discloses the Court's own failure to appreciate the extent of the liberty at stake. To say that the issue in Bowers was simply the right to engage in certain sexual conduct demeans the claim the individual put forward, just as it would demean a married couple were it to be said marriage is simply about the right to have sexual intercourse. The laws involved in Bowers and here are, to be sure, statutes that purport to do no more than prohibit a particular sexual act. Their penalties and purposes, though, have more far-reaching consequences, touching upon the most private human conduct, sexual behavior, and in the most private of places, the home. The statutes do seek to control a personal relationship that, whether or not entitled to formal recognition in the law, is within the liberty of persons to choose without being punished as criminals.

This, as a general rule, should counsel against attempts by the State, or a court, to define the meaning of the relationship or to set its boundaries absent injury to a person or abuse of an institution the law protects. It suffices for us to acknowledge that adults may choose to enter upon this relationship in the confines of their homes and their own private lives and still retain their dignity as free persons. When sexuality finds overt expression in intimate conduct with another person, the conduct can be but one element in a personal bond that is more enduring. The liberty protected by the Constitution allows homosexual persons the right to make this choice.

It was not until the 1970's that any State singled out same-sex relations for criminal prosecution, and only nine States have done so. Post-Bowers even some of these States did not adhere to the policy of suppressing homosexual conduct. Over the course of the last decades, States with same-sex prohibitions have moved toward abolishing them.

It must be acknowledged, of course, that the Court in Bowers was making the broader point that for centuries there have been powerful voices to condemn homosexual conduct as immoral. The condemnation has been shaped by religious beliefs, conceptions of right and acceptable behavior, and respect for the traditional family. For many persons these are not trivial concerns but profound and deep convictions accepted as ethical and moral principles to which they aspire and which thus determine the course of their lives. These considerations do not answer the question before us, however. The issue is whether the majority may use the power of the State to enforce these views on the whole society through operation of the criminal law.

In Bowers the Court referred to the fact that before 1961 all 50 States had outlawed sodomy, and that at the time of the Court's decision 24 States and the District of Columbia had sodomy laws. 478 U.S., at 192–193, 106 S.Ct. 2841. Justice Powell pointed out that these prohibitions often were being ignored, however. Georgia, for instance, had not sought to enforce its law for decades. Id., at 197–198, n. 2, 106 S.Ct. 2841 ("The history of nonenforcement suggests the moribund character today of laws criminalizing this type of private, consensual conduct").

In our own constitutional system the deficiencies in Bowers became even more apparent in the years following its announcement. The 25 States with laws prohibiting the relevant conduct referenced in the Bowers decision are reduced now to 13, of which 4 enforce their laws only against homosexual conduct. In those States where sodomy is still proscribed, whether for same-sex or heterosexual conduct, there is a pattern of nonenforcement with respect to consenting adults acting in private. The State of Texas admitted in 1994 that as of that date it had not prosecuted anyone under those circumstances.

Equality of treatment and the due process right to demand respect for conduct protected by the substantive guarantee of liberty are linked in important respects, and a decision on the latter point advances both interests. If protected conduct is made criminal and the law which does so remains unexamined for its substantive validity, its stigma might remain even if it were not enforceable as drawn for equal protection reasons. When homosexual conduct is made criminal by the law of the State, that declaration in and of itself is an invitation to subject homosexual persons to discrimination both in the public and in the private spheres. The central holding of Bowers has been brought in question by this case, and it should be addressed. Its continuance as precedent demeans the lives of homosexual persons.

The stigma this criminal statute imposes, moreover, is not trivial. The offense, to be sure, is but a class C misdemeanor, a minor offense in the Texas legal system. Still, it remains a criminal offense with all that imports for the dignity of the persons charged. The petitioners will bear on their record the history of their criminal convictions. We are advised that if Texas convicted an adult for private, consensual homosexual conduct under the statute here in question the convicted person would come within the registration laws of at least four States were he or she to be subject to their jurisdiction. This underscores the consequential nature of the punishment and the state-sponsored condemnation attendant to the criminal prohibition. Furthermore, the Texas criminal conviction carries with it the other collateral consequences always following a conviction, such as notations on job application forms, to mention but one example.

The foundations of Bowers have sustained serious erosion from our recent decisions in Casey and Romer. When our precedent has been thus weakened, criticism from other sources is of greater significance. In the United States criticism of Bowers has been substantial and continuing, disapproving of its reasoning in all respects, not just as to its historical assumptions.

The doctrine of stare decisis is essential to the respect accorded to the judgments of the Court and to the stability of the law. It is not, however, an inexorable command. In *Casey* we noted that when a court is asked to overrule a precedent recognizing a constitutional liberty interest, individual or societal reliance on the existence of that liberty cautions with particular strength against reversing course. The holding in Bowers, however, has not induced detrimental reliance comparable to some instances where recognized individual rights are involved. Indeed, there has been no individual or societal reliance on Bowers of the sort that could counsel against overturning its holding once there are compelling reasons to do so. Bowers itself causes uncertainty, for the precedents before and after its issuance contradict its central holding.

The rationale of Bowers does not withstand careful analysis. In his dissenting opinion in Bowers Justice STEVENS came to these conclusions:

"Our prior cases make two propositions abundantly clear. First, the fact that the governing majority in a State has traditionally viewed a particular practice as immoral is not a sufficient reason for upholding a law prohibiting the practice; neither history nor tradition could save a law prohibiting miscegenation from constitutional attack. Second, individual decisions by married persons, concerning the intimacies of their physical relationship, even when not intended to produce offspring, are a form of 'liberty' protected by the Due Process Clause of the Fourteenth Amendment. Moreover, this protection extends to intimate choices by unmarried as well as married persons."

Justice STEVENS' analysis, in our view, should have been controlling in Bowers and should control here.

Bowers was not correct when it was decided, and it is not correct today. It ought not to remain binding precedent. *Bowers v. Hardwick* should be and now is overruled.

The judgment of the Court of Appeals for the Texas Fourteenth District is reversed, and the case is remanded for further proceedings not inconsistent with this opinion.

It is so ordered.

F. Indecent Exposure

A person commits the offense of indecent exposure when he exposes his or her sexual organs in public. In most of these prosecutions, the defendant is a man who exposed himself to others as a means of sexual gratification. Typically, indecent exposure is punished as a misdemeanor. In the past, these cases were treated lightly, but in recent years, prosecutors and others have noticed a disturbing trend among sexual offenders. There is a steady progression from these "minor" crimes to more serious crimes. In fact, a person who starts out committing the crime of indecent exposure rarely confines his activities to that crime. After a while, the defendant takes greater risks and engages in other crimes. For instance, a person who begins by committing the crime of indecent exposure might graduate to the crime of Peeping Tom. Then, interestingly, many defendants progress to the crime of burglary, which in some ways involves an invasion of privacy and an exercise of power and control of another. Eventually, some of these defendants who began their careers committing the misdemeanor of indecent exposure move up to the serious crime of rape. Because of this, prosecutors and probation officers now take a greater interest in these individuals.

G. Incest

incest
Sexual intercourse between a man and a woman who, according to state law, are too closely related by blood or adoption.

When family members have sex with one another, it is **incest**. Incest is a crime in all states. Obviously, when parents have sex with one of their children, it is incest. But how far apart does the family relationship have to be before the sexual contact is no longer incest? For instance, if cousins engage in sexual intercourse, is it incest? Usually, the rule is that if the family members can legally marry, they cannot be guilty of incest if they have sex. The opposite is also true: If they cannot legally marry, then they can be guilty of incest. This means that individuals who are first cousins or closer will be guilty of incest if they have sex with one another. In many states, this prohibition has also been applied to adopted children.

H. Voyeurism, or Peeping Tom, Statutes

A Peeping Tom is someone who spies on other people. This invasion of privacy is illegal in all states. Although it is defined in various ways, it essentially involves someone who goes on another person's premises for the purpose of observing that person. We include it here because it is almost invariably linked to some sexual purpose.

1(a) A person commits the offense of incest when he engages in sexual intercourse with a person to whom he knows he is related either by blood or by marriage as follows:
  (1) Father and daughter or stepdaughter;
  (2) Mother and son or stepson;
  (3) Brother and sister of the whole blood or of the half blood;
  (4) Grandparent and grandchild;
  (5) Aunt and nephew; or
  (6) Uncle and niece.
1(b) A person convicted of the offense of incest shall be punished by imprisonment for not less than one nor more than twenty years.

Exhibit 9-15
Sample incest statute

(a) It shall be unlawful for any person to be a "peeping Tom" on or about the premises of another or to go about or upon the premises of another for the purpose of becoming a "peeping Tom."
(b) "Peeping Tom" means a person who peeps through windows or doors, or other like places, on or about the premises of another for the purpose of spying upon or invading the privacy of the persons spied upon and the doing of any other acts of a similar nature which invade the privacy of such persons.

Exhibit 9-16
Sample peeping tom statute

I. Sexual Harassment

Sexual harassment is normally a civil action, not a criminal one. When a person is subjected to sexual harassment at work, he or she may file a civil suit. Only if the harassment takes a physical turn, such as touching or assault, does it become a potential criminal action.

J. Obscenity

We deal with **obscenity** in another chapter, but a few issues related to obscenity should be addressed in any chapter dealing with sex-related crimes. Although obscenity prosecutions often raise the issue of First Amendment protections (see Chapter 14), one issue in pornography has no such protections: child pornography. The mere possession of child pornography is a crime, usually both a federal and state offense. Transmitting child pornography through the mail or over the Internet is also a crime.

obscene
Lewd and offensive to accepted standards of decency.

IV. Child Molestation

Children fall into a class of people who deserve special protection under the law. This is especially true when the subject is sexual contact.

Little Tables
Prosecutors often put child witnesses at child-sized tables and chairs in the courtroom to make them more comfortable. Some prosecutors actually sit at the small table with the child while they ask questions.

BULLET POINT
Using a child for sexual gratification is child molestation.

entice
To try to persuade a child to come to a secluded place with the intent to commit an unlawful sexual act.

The laws against child molestation prohibit any sexual behavior with a child below a certain age. In many states, the age is 12. Most statutes prohibiting child molestation are very specific about the conduct that is forbidden. For instance, it is unlawful to touch or penetrate the sexual organ of a child with the mouth, anus, or sexual organ of another person or to contact or penetrate the mouth, anus, or sexual organ of a child with the anus or sexual organ of another person.

Although in most cases of sexual assault the issue of consent is of major importance, it has no application to sexual assaults on children. Adults can consent to sexual contact; children cannot (under any circumstances). The reason for making such a bright-line distinction between adults and children is that children lack the degree of emotional and physical development to understand the nature of the sexual act.

A. Enticing a Minor for Immoral Purposes

A variation on the charge of child molestation is the offense of **enticing** a child for immoral purposes. This is the crime of soliciting a child to come to the home of the molester in order to engage in sexual acts.

1. Internet Enticement of Children
In recent years, people intent on enticing children have turned to a new tool: the Internet. Using sites often visited by children, a potential molester makes contact with the child and uses various promises to entice

Exhibit 9-17
Nevada's child molestation statute

NRS 200.366 Sexual assault: Definition; penalties.

A person who commits a sexual assault against a child under the age of sixteen years is guilty of a category A felony and shall be punished:
    If the crime results in substantial bodily harm to the child, by imprisonment in the state prison for life without the possibility of parole.

http://www.leg.state.nv.us/NRS/NRS-200.html#NRS200Sec366

INSIDER'S VIEWPOINT

Interviewing child sexual assault victims

"We try to take a team approach. We find that you have to do a lot of listening more so than questioning. Patience is one of the things you need, especially when you're dealing with children. Although you don't want to interfere with their lives and you don't want to victimize them again by repeatedly talking with them, it may take a younger person, one, two, or three visits just to be comfortable being around you. We don't rush the issue with the kids. If they don't feel like talking that particular day, we'll reschedule. We try to be patient on that. We find that by exhibiting the willingness to do that, they do open up a little more readily."

—Tom Garmon, Sexual Assault Investigator

---

the child to a location. Sometimes the offer involves a free "modeling session." Many states have amended their statutes on enticing children to include the use of the Internet to make contact with the child.

CASE QUESTIONS

1. What is the main question before the U.S. Supreme Court in this case?
2. How does the Court compare the ruling in this case to the ruling in *Griswold v. Connecticut*?
3. How does the *Bowers* case compare to the present case, and what ruling did the Court reach in that case?
4. According to the Court, what was the principal error in the court's defining of the issue in *Bowers*?
5. What is the result in this case, and how does it apply to the *Bowers'* decision?

ETHICAL CONSIDERATION: CONFLICTS CHECK

An attorney is not permitted to have an interest in any legal matter that conflicts with that of her client. On a daily basis, this means that the attorney must constantly be on guard against accepting a case in which the interests of another client may be in conflict. Attorneys try to avoid this problem by conducting a "conflicts check." The attorney and the paralegal will closely scrutinize a new client's information to make sure that the new client's legal matter does not impinge on another client's case. Generally, conflicts checks are limited to civil cases, but there is an important point that should be raised in relation to criminal cases. It is very common for more than one person to be charged in a particular offense. In those instances, the codefendants often have antagonistic defenses. For instance, one defendant may accuse the other of actually committing the crime. In such situations, an attorney is asking for trouble in representing them both. However, because people charged with crimes do not always retain attorneys immediately, it is possible for both codefendants to seek out the same attorney without realizing it. The defense paralegal should be on the lookout for individuals who are charged with the same offense on the same day. This often means that they are codefendants.

✓ Paralegal To Do List

For the defense paralegal:

- Has the client had a prior relationship with the victim? Is there anyone besides the client who can testify about this relationship?
- Has the victim ever filed false accusations of sexual assault against anyone else?
- Who performed the examination? Was this person qualified?
- Was a DNA test performed?
- Would the client benefit from psychological counseling as a way to help mitigate his possible sentence?

For the prosecution paralegal:

- Copy off your state's rape shield statute and keep it handy in the file.
- Sexual assault victims are very anxious before trial. Arrange to have the victim come to the courthouse several days before the trial so that she can see the courtroom and where she will testify. This helps alleviate some anxiety.
- When working with victims, it helps to keep a sense of humor. A little humor sometimes helps break the ice and will often help you, too.
- If the victim is especially anxious, make sure that the prosecutor knows this before trial; it will affect how the prosecutor prepares the witness for direct examination.

Chapter Summary

This chapter, like the previous one, deals with crimes against the person. However, in this chapter, we discussed a significant subcategory: sexual assault. Rape and related offenses are both physically and psychologically damaging and are often charged with emotional as well as legal issues. Rape occurs when a man has forcible carnal knowledge of a woman against her will. Consent is a defense to rape, as it is to most sexual assaults. Society's approach to rape and to rape victims has changed substantially in the past few decades. Under the old common law elements of rape, the victim had to show violent and active resistance to prove that the rape was not consensual. However, this element is no longer required in states that have a more modern approach to this crime. As part of a discussion of rape, it is important to note that sexual assault victims are protected by statutes that prevent the defense from questioning them about their past sexual relations.

Among the other sex-related crimes are child molestation, sodomy, and date rape. Each of these offenses has separate elements of proof, and each presents both the prosecution and defense with unique challenges.

WEB SITES

American Psychological Association
www.apa.org

Bureau of Justice Statistics—Rape and Sexual Assault
www.bjs.gov/index.cfm?ty=tp&tid=317

Florida Sexual Offenders and Predators
http://offender.fdle.state.fl.us/offender

Maryland Court System
www.courts.state.md.us

Mississippi State Court System
http://courts.ms.gov/index.html

New Hampshire State Court System
www.courts.state.nh.us/index.htm

North Dakota State Court System
www.ndcourts.gov/court/news/annualreport2001/administrator.htm

Texas State Court System
www.courts.state.tx.us/oca

U.S. Department of Justice, Briefing on New Definition of Rape
www.justice.gov/opa/pr/2012/January/12-ag-018.html

U.S. Supreme Court
www.supremecourt.gov

REVIEW QUESTIONS

1. What are the elements of rape?
2. How are the modern elements of rape different from the common law elements of this crime?
3. Is it child molestation to touch a child in an inappropriate place? Explain.
4. What is the significance of the ruling by the U.S. Supreme Court in *Bowers v. Hardwick*?
5. Is it incest to have sexual relations with an adopted sibling? Explain.
6. What is date rape? What are date rape drugs?
7. Explain the elements of the crime of enticement of a child for immoral purposes.
8. What is a rape shield statute?

QUESTIONS FOR REFLECTION

1. In a rape prosecution, the identity of the victim is often protected. Is such protection still needed? Why or why not?

2. Should DNA evidence be required in all rape cases? If so, should the state always pay the several thousand dollars it costs to perform the test? Explain your answer.

3. Rape has sometimes been called a crime of violence, not of sex. Explain why you agree or disagree with the statement.

KEYWORDS AND PHRASES

Rape
Obscenity
Peeping Tom
Enticement
Incest
Sodomy
Statutory rape

Date rape
Rape shield statute
Corroboration
Immunity
Carnal knowledge
Consent
Circumstantial evidence

PRACTICAL APPLICATIONS

1. Is there a battered women's/sexual assault victim's shelter in your area? If so, under what circumstances are victims admitted to the shelter?

2. Some states do not call the crime rape when a man forces sex on another man. Usually, these states call such a crime aggravated sodomy or some other form of assault. Should the crime be called rape? Are there any reasons why it should not? Explain your answer.

3. Visit the web sites listed above and answer the following question: What are the current national statistics about sexual assault? Are these crimes on the rise, or are they declining? Explain the trend.

4. The victim in the *Marbles* case (see Appendix) told police that she was sexually assaulted during her four-day odyssey with the defendant. None of the assaults occurred in the state. Can the defendant be prosecuted for the out-of-state crimes in this state? Explain.

NOTES

1. *Curtis v. State*, 236 Ga. 362, 362, 223 S.E.2d 721 (1976).
2. *Baker v. State*, 245 Ga. 657, 266 S.E.2d 477 (1980).

Chapter 10

CRIMES AGAINST PROPERTY

Chapter Objectives

At the completion of this chapter, you should be able to:

- Identify the elements of proof for burglary and other property crimes
- Explain the elements of arson
- Describe the different elements of various theft crimes
- Explain the various kinds of crime involving fraud
- Discuss white-collar crime and computer-related crime
- Describe the activities of computer hackers

I. Introduction

Theft crimes cover a wide range of activity, from burglary to computer hacking to arson. Theft of property, including theft of services and armed robbery, is also a crime against property. Unlike other crimes, theft crimes are motivated primarily by greed. There are numerous theft crimes, ranging from larceny to robbery. Theft crimes, although similar in many ways, have distinct elements and should not be confused with one another. Theft by shoplifting has distinctly different elements than the crime of robbery. This chapter concludes with a discussion of computer hackers, who deal with the theft or destruction of information, another form of property. See Exhibit 10-1 for an overview of property crime arrests.

Exhibit 10-1
Arrests in the United States by property crime type, 2010

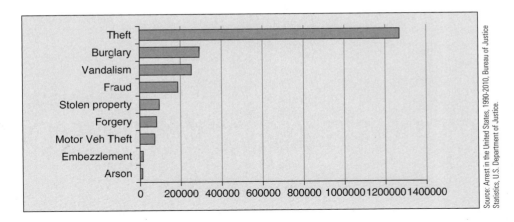

Source: Arrest in the United States, 1990-2010, Bureau of Justice Statistics, U.S. Department of Justice.

II. Burglary

Burglary is a relatively straightforward crime that often evokes strong feelings in victims. The laws criminalizing burglary are based on the obvious premise that having an intruder in a person's home is a potentially life-threatening situation. The burglar may harm or kill the occupants; the occupants may do the same to the burglar. At a minimum, the burglar may steal the occupants' personal belongings and disrupt their sense of security.

A. Breaking and entering

breaking
Using force or some kind of destruction of property (including actions that do not permanently destroy, such as picking a lock), to illegally get into a building by breaking and entering.

In some states, the **"breaking"** portion of breaking and entering has been eliminated from statutes, making burglary a crime. In those states, "entering" is enough. In fact, the slightest entry into the structure of any part of the defendant's property is sufficient to satisfy the element of "entering."[1]

However, not all states have disposed of the requirement of "breaking." In those states, the element of breaking continues to be an essential element of the crime of burglary. "Breaking" implies some use of force, even if it is slight. Actions that constitute breaking include opening a window, removing a window screen, or even turning the doorknob on an unlocked door. In some states, however, walking through an open door might not be considered "breaking" and would thus make prosecution difficult.[2] At law,

Exhibit 10-2
The elements of burglary

Burglary consists of:
1. (Breaking and) entering of a building or occupied structure
2. Without consent or permission
3. And with the intent to commit a theft or a felony

there are two kinds of breaking—actual and constructive. Actual breaking occurs when physical force is applied. Constructive breaking consists of obtaining entry through the use of fraud, trick, intimidation, or threat.

B. Building or Occupied Structure

The crime of burglary requires an unlawful entry into a building or another structure. In some states, the burglary statute specifically requires a "dwelling." Dwellings are places that are normally used by people for sleeping and general living. Apartments, mobile homes, and holiday cabins are all examples of dwellings.

1. Curtilage of a Dwelling
Another important consideration when dealing with burglary is the term *curtilage*. The curtilage of a dwelling is the area close to and surrounding the dwelling. This area is used for normal family functions and includes lawns, gardens, etc.[3] The reason curtilage is so important is that a person can be convicted of burglary when he or she enters the curtilage of the house. This means that a person can be guilty of burglary even if she does not actually enter the house.

C. Without Consent or Permission

One of the key elements of burglary is that the person who entered the dwelling did so without permission of the occupant. Where consent or permission exists, there is no burglary.[4] When a person remains in a structure without the occupant's knowledge, the law assumes that he did so without permission. This is not true in all states, however.[5]

D. With Intent to Commit a Theft or Felony

The final element of burglary is that the person must enter the structure with the intent to commit a theft or felony. A felony is any crime that carries a penalty greater than one year in custody. Examples of felonies are murder, rape, and robbery. When the defendant has entered the home to commit a theft, there is no minimum monetary value that the defendant must take before the crime becomes burglary. The actual value of the stolen items is not important: Any theft is enough to justify a prosecution for burglary. See Exhibit 10-3 for a breakdown of burglary arrests.

E. Common Law Burglary

In states where common law offenses are still alleged, burglary takes an interesting twist. In those states, the elements of burglary are

- Unlawful breaking and entering
- At night
- With the intent to commit a theft or felony once entry has been gained.

■ BULLET POINT
Burglary is the unlawful breaking and entering of a building with the intent to commit a theft or a felony.

curtilage
An area of household use immediately surrounding a home.

What is the Legal Definition of "Nightime"?

In those states where common law burglary is still a crime, one of the contested issues in the case can be whether it was nighttime. Here are some different definitions.

- Nighttime is when it so dark that a person's face cannot be identified except by artificial light or moonlight.[6] (North Carolina)
- Anytime from 30 minutes after sunset to 30 minutes before sunrise (common law definition)
- "If there be daylight... enough, begun or left, to discern a man's face withal, it is not burglary." (Sir William Blackstone)
- Neither moonlight nor artificial light turns night into day. (Tennessee)[7]
- Daytime is that time of day when there is light to be able to discern another person's features by natural sunlight. (Connecticut)[8]

Exhibit 10-3
Burglary arrest rates

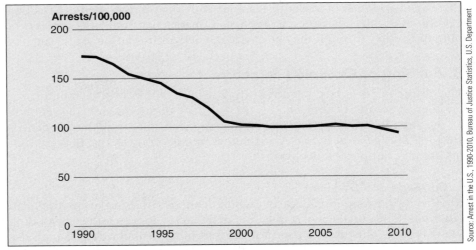

Source: Arrest in the U.S., 1990-2010, Bureau of Justice Statistics, U.S. Department of Justice.

> Burglaries occurred more commonly during the day, 53 percent, than at night (47 percent).
> —FBI Uniform Crime Report, 1999

One of the more obvious problems with the elements of a common law burglary is that if the burglary occurred during the day, there could be no prosecution. This flies in the face of statistics that show that most burglaries occur between 9 A.M. and 2 P.M.

Because common law burglary requires that the burglary occur at night, when the government fails to prove that the crime did occur at night, the charges against the defendant must be dismissed.

III. Arson

arson
The malicious and unlawful burning of a dwelling.

Arson is generally defined as:

- The malicious
- Burning of a
- Dwelling house or structure.

A. Malice Required

To prosecute someone for the crime of arson, it is necessary to show that the fire was started out of malice, not negligence. This means that the person who started the fire must have done so deliberately. Without this deliberate intent, the first element of arson is not met and the case against the defendant will fail. A person may be charged with some lesser crime for negligence in burning down a structure, but not with first-degree arson.[9]

B. New Statutory Approaches to Arson

Modern statutes have enlarged on the common law definition. There are some obvious problems with the common law definition, not the least of which is that under that definition, a person could not be prosecuted for burning down her own home.[10] Another obvious problem with the common law definition is that it applies only to "dwelling houses." Under this definition, businesses and other commercial enterprises, when burned, would not constitute arson. Modern statutes have addressed these problems, labeling it arson to burn either a home or a building whether owned by the perpetrator or not.

C. Using Arson to Defraud Insurance Companies

In modern times, the use of arson as a means to defraud insurance companies has increased dramatically. As a consequence, many states have expanded the definition of arson to include not only residences, but also businesses, warehouses, etc. Business owners facing financial loss might try to recoup their investments by burning the structure simply to collect the insurance proceeds.

D. Arson in the First Degree

Many states divide the crime of arson into various degrees, normally based on the seriousness of the offense or the danger to human life.

By dividing the crime of arson into various degrees, states can punish certain forms of arson more severely. In most states, first-degree arson involves causing threat of injury or death to another person.

IV. Theft

Theft of another person's property has always been against the rules of society. Every society has enacted laws against theft, and each society has had to deal with individuals who have broken those laws. In modern times, as society and personal interactions have become more complex, theft statutes have changed to reflect this complexity. In addition to statutes outlawing theft, robbery, theft by shoplifting, and theft by receiving

> **■ BULLET POINT**
> Under the modern, statutory definition of arson, it is a crime to deliberately burn your own home.

9A.48.020. Arson in the first degree

(1) A person is guilty of arson in the first degree if he knowingly and maliciously:
  (a) Causes a fire or explosion which is manifestly dangerous to any human life, including firemen; or
  (b) Causes a fire or explosion which damages a dwelling; or
  (c) Causes a fire or explosion in any building in which there shall be at the time a human being who is not a participant in the crime; or
  (d) Causes a fire or explosion on property valued at ten thousand dollars or more with intent to collect insurance proceeds.

http://apps.leg.wa.gov/rcw/default.aspx?cite=9A.48.020

Exhibit 10-4
Washington state arson statute

stolen property, many states have enacted laws dealing with theft of intellectual property, such as computer software. With the increasing level of sophistication among thieves, states have also been forced to modify their rules on embezzlement and fraud. The law of forgery for example, has recently had to grapple with the fact that an individual with a computer and a scanner can duplicate a person's signature and reproduce it on any number of checks. The signature is identical. We will be addressing these more complicated views of thievery later in this chapter. Now we begin with a more basic view of the law of theft.

A. Larceny

Larceny is a general term used to refer to any form of theft. For our purposes, the terms *theft* and *larceny* are interchangeable. In the next few pages, we will address many different forms of theft. At first, these crimes may seem complicated, but if you focus on the specific elements, you will see that the various kinds of offenses actually build on one another. The elements of theft are found in robbery. Robbery is, in fact, theft with violence. This is true of the apparently dissimilar crimes of grand larceny, robbery, and white-collar offenses. Each contains the basic elements of theft along with elements specific to each crime.

larceny
Stealing of any kind. Some types of larceny are specific crimes, such as larceny by trick or grand larceny.

Larceny is the wrongful taking and carrying away of personal property belonging to another person. To prove larceny, the state must prove that the defendant intended to permanently deprive the victim of the use of the property. The state proves this intent by showing what the defendant did with the property.

1. Larceny Applies Only to Personal Property
At common law, larceny could not be applied to real property (land). Larceny is a crime involving possession of property, not title to property.

INSIDER'S VIEWPOINT

Talking with witnesses
One of the things when I have the recruits in school that I tell is that all this stuff you see on TV with Joe Friday, 'Just the facts, ma'am' and all that, I say, 'Throw all that out the window.' All this stiff military personality stuff; throw all that out the window. The reason you're going to throw it out the window is that you want to learn something. You know I go around and talk to folks and whatever their interest is, is what my interest is, and it's not trickery but just trying to learn information. If people feel comfortable with talking to you, then they are going to tell you stuff that they might not normally tell you if you come on strong.

—Jack Burnette, Homicide Investigator

The elements of larceny are
1. The unlawful taking of property
2. With the intention to convert it to the taker's use
3. And to permanently deprive the victim of the property.

Exhibit 10-5
The elements of larceny

Personal property refers to movable things such as goods, cattle, and possessions. This rule has been modified in many states.

a. No Violence Required In larceny, there is no requirement that violence accompany the taking. In fact, if violence is used, this makes the crime robbery, and normally the perpetrator is sentenced to a much harsher sentence.

b. Converting the Property In larceny, the taker has no rights to the property itself, and this distinguishes it from the crime of embezzlement, which we will discuss below. The manner in which the taking occurs is also important. To be legally sufficient, the taker must exercise control, or dominion, over the property and convert the property to his use. **Converting** property refers to exercising this control over the property and removing it from the possession of the rightful owner. There can be no larceny if the perpetrator fails to gain possession of the property. Without possession, the taker cannot exercise dominion over the property. However, this dominion (or control) over the property does not have to be for a very long period of time. A few seconds may suffice to establish the taking requirement. Courts have interpreted this requirement, stating that the moment the possession of the owner is severed, a valid taking occurs, even if the taker is apprehended before he can get very far with the property.

c. Asportation As part of the element of conversion, the perpetrator must carry the property away. This is referred to as **asportation**. To constitute a valid asportation, the property must be moved from its original location. This does not mean it has to be moved very far. Numerous cases have held that if the property is moved just a few inches, it will satisfy the asportation requirement.

d. Permanently Depriving the Owner To constitute larceny, the thief does not need to know the identity of the owner of the property. The only requirement is that the thief knows that the property does not belong to him. The final element of larceny, proving that the defendant had the intention of permanently depriving the victim of his property, is sometimes rather difficult to prove. As in any situation where the state must prove what was in the defendant's mind at the time of the crime, the facts of the case play a major role. At common law, if the defendant could present a defense that he only intended to temporarily deprive the owner of the property, this was sufficient to warrant the dismissal of the case.

convert
To deprive an owner of property without that owner's permission and without just cause. For example, it is conversion to refuse to return a borrowed book.

asportation
An old word for the theft and removal of personal property.

Many states have modified the original language of common law larceny so that it now reads "with intent to steal" as opposed to with intent to permanently deprive the victim of the property. Intent to steal is far easier to prove at trial than is intent to permanently deprive.

B. Monetary Amounts

Many states place a monetary limit on the type of prosecution that can be had in a theft case. For instance, in many jurisdictions, theft of an article worth more than $500 is a felony. If the article taken is worth less than $500, the crime is a misdemeanor. This valuation of the property can have significant impact on the defendant. If the article taken is valued at $499, the most the defendant can receive in terms of punishment is twelve months in custody and a $1,000 fine (the maximum misdemeanor sentence in many states). However, if the value of the property is $500, the defendant is now a convicted felon and can face a maximum sentence of ten years or more. Because the valuation of the property can have such a significant impact on the case, it is important to discuss exactly how the state proves the value of the property taken.

1. Establishing Value

market value (fair market value)
The price to which a willing seller and a willing buyer would agree for an item in the ordinary course of trade.

Generally, the **fair market value** of the item determines its value. Fair market value does not mean that the particular item has a legal market for sale. Fair market value simply refers to what the article is worth on the open market. Proving the fair market value often involves expert testimony. This means that a person with extensive knowledge of the buying and selling or the valuation of property takes the stand and testifies as to what the value of this particular item is. In most situations, it is not enough for the state simply to present the price tag on the particular item. A used lawn mower, for example, will have a lower value than a brand new lawn mower. The value of the used lawn mower must be established by the state. Someone with extensive knowledge of used lawn mowers and the amount such a mower would fetch on the open market must testify as to its value. Although this testimony is crucial to the state's case, it generally makes for very dull testimony. Fair market value testimony is something you will never see portrayed in a movie.

■ BULLET POINT
The state must prove the value of the stolen item.

THE ROLE OF THE PARALEGAL: ESTABLISHING VALUE

Because the value of the item taken can be such a significant portion of a theft prosecution, paralegals are often called upon to seek out experts in the field to have them testify for the defense. It is quite common for two experts to disagree as to the value of a particular item. By presenting testimony from the defense side that the item's value was less than $500, the defense makes the issue of value a question for the jury. If the jurors agree with the defense expert, at worst, the client will only be convicted of a misdemeanor. Because the consequences of a felony conviction are so dramatic, it is often worth the extra effort to locate such an individual.

C. Theft by Shoplifting

In many jurisdictions, the crime of shoplifting has been codified independently of other theft crimes. Perpetrators can be guilty of shoplifting when they commit any of the following acts:

- Remove an item from the store premises
- Hide merchandise on their person
- Alter the price tag on goods
- Hide merchandise inside other merchandise and pay for only the larger item
- Interchange labels

Many states place monetary limits on shoplifting. For instance, many states make a distinction between articles worth more than $100 from those worth less. If the value of the items taken was less than $100, the defendant would be prosecuted for a misdemeanor. If the value was greater than $100, the defendant would be prosecuted for a felony.

D. Theft by Receiving Stolen Property

Coming into possession of stolen property is a separate offense from stealing the property in the first place. These statutes were created to punish people such as **fences**, who deal in stolen merchandise. Many statutes phrase the crime in such a way that a person can be prosecuted for this offense if he or she knew or *should have known* that the merchandise was stolen.

fence
A person in the business of intentionally buying stolen merchandise to resell it.

1. The accused purchased received goods.
2. The goods had been stolen by some other person.
3. The accused knew or should have known that the goods had been stolen.

Exhibit 10-6
Elements of theft by receiving stolen property

- Item purchased is well below fair market value
- Circumstances that would lead a prudent person to be suspicious
- Suspicious actions by the person offering the item for sale
- Inconsistent statements about ownership of the item

Exhibit 10-7
Indicators that would lead someone to believe that he or she was buying stolen merchandise

Exhibit 10-8
Elements of theft of services

1. The unlawful taking of services
2. With the intention to avoid payment for such services
3. Done knowingly and with intent

Exhibit 10-9
Examples of prosecution under theft of services

Obtaining any of the following without payment
- Electrical service
- Cable service
- Water and/or sewage service
- Other services, such as labor, computer services, maintenance, etc.

Exhibit 10-10
The elements of embezzlement

1. The unlawful taking of property
2. That the accused originally had legal possession of
3. With the intention to convert it to the taker's use
4. To permanently deprive the victim of the property.

E. Theft of Services

When someone obtains a service with the intent of avoiding payment (e.g., illegally breaking into a cable box to get free cable service), he or she has committed the crime of theft of services. In many cases, this is a misdemeanor crime. However, the number of services obtained might be enough to satisfy the threshold for felony prosecution.

embezzlement
The fraudulent and secret taking of money or property by a person who has been trusted with it.

F. Embezzlement

Embezzlement occurs when someone who has been entrusted with property decides to violate that trust and keep the property for his own use.[11] This crime is often carried out by employees, who routinely have access to cash or other items of value and exceed their authority by converting the property to their own use.

California Statute on Embezzlement

Embezzlement is the fraudulent appropriation of property by a person to whom it has been entrusted.
—California Penal Code § 503

G. Grand Larceny or Grand Theft

Grand larceny or grand theft statutes refer to theft of items above a certain value or theft of certain items. In many states, theft of an item worth more than $500 ($400 in some states) constitutes felony theft or grand larceny. In many states, the theft of an automobile, no matter what the car is actually worth, is considered to be grand larceny. The significance

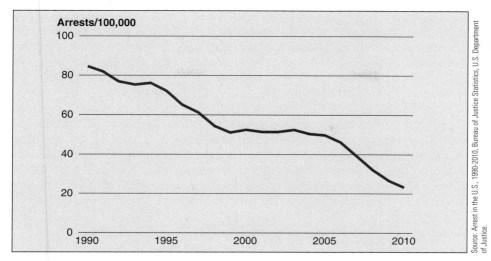

Arrests/100,000

Source: Arrest in the U.S., 1990-2010, Bureau of Justice Statistics, U.S. Department of Justice.

Exhibit 10-11
Motor vehicle theft arrest rates

1. The unlawful taking
2. Of property of another
3. From the person of the victim and against the victim's consent
4. With the intent to convert it to the taker's use
5. Carrying away (asportation)
6. Through the use of force, threat, or intimidation.

http://www.leg.state.fl.us/statutes/

Exhibit 10-12
Elements of robbery

of these statutes is that the value of the items taken makes the crime a felony instead of a misdemeanor.

V. Robbery

Robbery is an aggravated form of larceny. In Figure 10-12, you can see many of the basic elements of theft contained in the elements of robbery. Robbery is, in fact, theft with violence. In robbery, there is also the additional requirement that the property be taken from the person or the immediate presence of the victim. Because the core elements of robbery are the same as theft, we will address only the elements of robbery that are different from other forms of theft.

robbery
The illegal taking of property from the person of another using force or threat of force.

A. From the Person of the Victim, Without the Victim's Consent

No matter what form robbery takes, the element of "taking" is always present. In a robbery, the defendant must actually take possession of someone else's property. *Taking* means that the defendant reduces the property to his possession. That means that the defendant must have complete control over the property. If the defendant has not acquired complete control over the item, then no taking has occurred and a robbery charge cannot be sustained against the defendant. A defendant acquires complete control over an item by removing it from the victim and placing it in his own possession.

One of the unique elements of robbery is the requirement of taking the property from the person of the victim. This element, really an aggravating circumstance in a theft case, justifies the more severe penalties found in robbery cases than in almost all other forms of theft. Because robbery also involves the threat of violence or actual violence, as well as the fact that the property was taken from the immediate presence or person of the victim, robbery is one of the more dangerous felonies. As such, robbery is often punished by terms in prison of 20 years or more. In fact, as we will see, armed robbery is often punished very severely.

B. Asportation

We have already addressed the element of asportation in regard to larceny. To sustain a conviction for robbery, the state must show not only that the defendant acquired the property, but also that he moved it. This movement does not have to be very far. In fact, the movement of property only a few inches may satisfy the element of asportation. The reason asportation is so important is that by moving the item of property, the defendant is showing his intent to deprive the owner of possession and satisfies the requirement of the defendant's control over the property.

C. Through Force, Threat, or Intimidation

Another unique element to a robbery prosecution is the element of violence, threat, or intimidation. Robbery is theft with force or the threat of force. Because this force or threat of force is usually brought about by the use of a weapon, armed robbery is the most severely punished of all of the theft statutes.

D. Armed Robbery

Armed robbery is robbery carried out with a weapon. A person charged with armed robbery may receive an enhanced sentence when he or she uses a weapon to threaten or injure the victim in order to steal. A robbery may also be classified as "aggravated" when certain conditions are met. For example, a defendant may receive a harsher sentence if he commits any of the following during a robbery:

- Causes serious bodily injury to another person
- Uses a deadly weapon (e.g., gun or knife)
- Threatens or injures someone who is 65 years of age or older or a disabled person

Is a Pickpocket a Robber?

The answer to this question is almost always no. A pickpocket, by very definition, takes money or belongings from the victim's immediate presence without the victim's knowledge. Because one of the requirements of robbery is that force or a threat of force or intimidation is used to accomplish the theft, the very fact that the victim is unaware that his belongings are being taken negates this element.

VI. Fraud and False Pretenses

The crime of false pretenses is another form of larceny. Although originally a distinct crime at common law, it has been codified in most states under the general theft or larceny statutes.

To defraud someone is to trick him out of his money. To do this, con men often invent elaborate schemes. Con men are often charged with the crime of false pretenses. The crime of false pretenses involves a misrepresentation of a **material fact**. This fact is crucial to the parties' understanding of the transaction. For instance, defendants commit false pretenses when they represent that they own the car they are trying to sell to an innocent third party when in fact they do not. The ownership of the car is a material fact for the buyer. Many statutes phrase misrepresentation in terms of a "material past or present fact." This simply refers to the kind of misrepresentation made. It is not false pretenses to claim that this car is the "best car in the world." Salesmanship, puffing, and other exaggerations are par for the course in a transaction, and most buyers do not take such claims seriously. However, a claim that the car had "never been in an accident" could be a material misrepresentation and make the person liable to prosecution if the person knows that the statement is false at the time the statement is made.

A. Forgery

No discussion of theft crimes would be complete without addressing the topic of forgery. At common law, forgery consisted of writing someone else's signature on a document and passing it off as authentic. Forgery is a specific intent crime, meaning that to convict, the prosecution must prove that the defendant specifically intended to commit the crime of forgery. Forgery can be committed by any of the following:

- Using someone's signature without authorization
- Transferring a genuine signature to a bogus document
- Using scanners and technology to print another's name on a document

1. Degrees of Forgery

Many states categorize forgery by the actions taken. In some jurisdictions, forgery is divided into different degrees, with first-degree forgery being punished more severely than second-degree.

a. Discussing the Elements of Forgery *Intent to defraud:* One of the important elements of forgery is that the defendant intended to defraud another by use of the altered or fictitious signature. If there is no intent to defraud, then there is no forgery. For instance, if a husband signs his wife's name on a check and then deposits the check in their account, it is not forgery. Because the husband is not attempting to defraud anyone, the essential element is not present.

Bank Robbers

Armed robbery of a banking institution often falls under federal law. Federal laws are very harsh when it comes to dealing with bank robbers. Federal statutes often mandate sentences of 20 or more years for the armed robbery of a banking institution. Statistics show that most armed robberies of banks only net $4,000 or less. These facts probably explain why so few banks are robbed.

material fact
A fact that is central to winning or deciding a case.

Ponzi Schemes

In a Ponzi, or pyramid, scheme, a promoter approaches investors with a "can't miss" investment opportunity. The first few investors see amazing returns on their money. This return on the investment is considered proof of the credibility of the scheme and brings in more investors. Unfortunately, the amazing returns seen by the first investors are actually paid out of the money invested by the later investors. Later investors end up losing all of the money they invested, and the original promoter disappears with most of the money. The Internet is becoming the newest medium for these schemes.

Exhibit 10-13
The elements of forgery in the first degree

- The defendant did, with the intent to defraud
- Knowingly made, altered, or possessed any writing
- In a fictitious name or in such manner that the writing appeared to have been made by another person
- Who did not give authority for his or her name to be used
- And the defendant uttered or delivered the writing to another

Copyright © 2015 Cengage Learning®

Exhibit 10-14
The elements of forgery in the second degree

- The defendant did, with the intent to defraud
- Knowingly made, altered, or possessed any writing
- In a fictitious name or in such manner that the writing appeared to have been made by another person
- Who did not give authority for his or her name to be used

Copyright © 2015 Cengage Learning®

Forgeries

Forgeries do not involve only personal and business checks. Sophisticated forgers now produce phony birth certificates, professionally laminated driver's licenses, and motor vehicle titles.

utter

Put into circulation; issue or put out a check.

Making or altering a signature: Forgery applies to written documents. It is distinct from the crime of printing fake money (counterfeiting—see below) or passing off a fake painting as genuine (fraud). The term *writing* is generally held to mean any handwritten, typewritten, computer-generated, printed, or engraved document.

Authority to sign: If a person gives permission to another individual to sign his name, then no forgery has occurred.

b. Uttering The important element that distinguishes first-degree forgery from lesser offenses of forgery is uttering. To **utter** a forged document means to pass it off to someone else or make use of it as though it was a valid document. Most jurisdictions punish the presenting or passing off of a document more seriously than simply possessing a forged document. The reasoning behind this is simple. In the first example, the defendant has actually defrauded someone. In the second example (possessing), he has not yet carried out the fraud. Most states that make a distinction between first- and second-degree forgery place the dividing line at uttering and simply possessing a forged document.

B. Bad Check

Although "bad check" is thought of as closely related to forgery, it is actually another form of false pretenses. Many people have written a check on an account and had it bounce. This does not, in itself, constitute a crime. The crime of bad check occurs when a person writes a check on an account *knowing* that there are insufficient funds in the bank to cover the check. By some estimates, as many as 1.3 million bad checks exchange hands in the United States every day. The law on bad checks is an interesting mixture of

http://www.leginfo.ca.gov/cgi-bin/displaycode?section=pen&group=00001-01000&file=470-483.5

> (a) Every person who, with the intent to defraud, knowing that he or she has no authority to do so, signs the name of another person or of a fictitious person to any of the items listed in subdivision (d) is guilty of forgery.
> (b) Every person who, with the intent to defraud, counterfeits or forges the seal or handwriting of another is guilty of forgery.
> (c) Every person who, with the intent to defraud, alters, corrupts, or falsifies any record of any will, codicil, conveyance, or other instrument, the record of which is by law evidence, or any record of any judgment of a court or the return of any officer to any process of any court, is guilty of forgery.
> (d) Every person who, with the intent to defraud, falsely makes, alters, forges, or counterfeits, utters, publishes, passes or attempts or offers to pass, as true and genuine, any of the following items, knowing the same to be false, altered, forged, or counterfeited, is guilty of forgery: any check, bond, bank bill, or note, cashier's check, traveler's check, money order.
>
> *CA Section 470. Forgery; signatures or seals; corruption of records*

Exhibit 10-15
California's statute on forgery

both civil and criminal remedies. Merchants are often reluctant to prosecute bad check cases because of the additional costs involved to bring the charge, generally resorting to civil remedies first. Many states have made the offense of bad checks into something closer to a civil suit, rather than clogging the criminal courts with these prosecutions.

C. Credit Card Theft and Fraud

The use of credit cards to make purchases has become so prevalent in our society that a consumer can charge a fast-food meal. Crimes involving credit cards have skyrocketed in the past few decades. The federal government recognized the growing problem of credit card fraud when it passed Title 18, Section 514 of the United States Code. This statute was specifically designed to address the increasing amount of fraud through the use of credit cards and other fraudulent financial instruments. The Secret Service was given jurisdiction to investigate and prosecute credit card cases. Interestingly, the U.S. Secret Service also has jurisdiction over counterfeit currency cases (see later).

Each year, businesses lose billions of dollars to credit card and other fraud. The Secret Service has numerous task forces devoted to various organized gangs and foreign Mafias that use credit card theft and fraud to earn millions of dollars.

In a typical scheme, a criminal finds out a person's name and credit card number and expiration date and uses this information to order

One of the easiest ways for a credit card thief to get access to a person's credit card number and other information is from the person himself. The thief will call the person with a bogus offer of "free" merchandise and request the credit card information for "shipping charges." Of course, the free prize never arrives, but now that the thief has the credit card information, he can charge items to the card. He does not even need the physical card; all he really needs is the information.

The average credit card scam involves losses of more than $2,000.
—U.S. Secret Service study

white-collar crimes
Commercial crimes such as embezzlement and price fixing.

thousands of dollars of goods. The goods are delivered to an abandoned house or another area under control of the criminal; then he or she resells the goods or returns them for a cash refund.

1. "Skimming"

Another method of getting credit card information involves a process called "skimming." Through the use of a small machine that can easily be concealed on a person's body, a waiter, for example, can swipe a customer's card through a "skimmer," which records the card information in electronic format. Later, the information can be downloaded to a computer. In some cases, individuals acquired hundreds of credit card numbers and sold them to credit card thieves who then used the information to bill thousands of dollars on the customers' credit cards.

D. Counterfeiting

The U.S. Secret Service is also responsible for investigating and prosecuting cases involving counterfeit U.S. currency. In recent years, the Secret Service has noted an alarming trend: criminals printing U.S. currency on home-based color printers. Using a sophisticated scanner, a counterfeiter could scan a $20 bill and then re-create as many copies of it as he chose. Before the advent of this technology, it was far more common for counterfeiters to be members of a large, organized group, one with the resources necessary to process the color plates and buy the other equipment necessary to reproduce fake currency. It was partly out of the concern that small-time crooks could reproduce their own currency that all major denominations of U.S. bills were redesigned, adding features that would be difficult if not impossible to reproduce using a typical scanner and home color printer.

E. White-Collar Crime

White-collar crime refers to any crime in which technology or nonviolent or indirect methods are used. Examples of white-collar crime include embezzlement, computer hacking, and fraud. The term was first coined in the 1930s to describe crime carried out by the rich and powerful.

Exhibit 10-16
Types of white-collar crime

- Illegal corporate business practices
- Governmental irregularities and "kickbacks"
- Employee theft and embezzlement
- Conspiracies to defraud the government, investors, etc.
- Entry into restricted computer databases and/or destruction of computer information

White-collar crimes often cause headaches for governmental agencies when they involve several different jurisdictions and present crimes never before seen.

1. Identity Theft

The crime of identity theft is a relatively recent phenomenon. A criminal will gain access to a surprisingly small amount of someone's personal information (full name, date of birth, Social Security number) and use this information to obtain credit cards, personal loans, and car financing. Once the criminal has fleeced all of the companies, he disappears, leaving the innocent party holding the financial bag. The victim may find it very hard to convince the credit card companies and others that the person who racked up all of the charges was someone else. The effects on the victim's credit history can be devastating. It often takes years and a large amount of the victim's own money to clear up the mess left by the criminal.

2. Computer-Related Offenses: Hacking

Bringing a prosecution against a computer hacker often involves complicated evidentiary issues. In one case, a young man deliberately sabotaged the telephone system for the school district in which he was a student. He gained access to the system by dialing in using a modem. Once he had gained access to the system, he sabotaged it by changing the passwords and many of the hardware configurations so that no one else could use the system. The loss of the telephone system for the school district amounted to over $80,000.

Telephone companies and other information-based companies take a dim view of computer hacking. In this case, the local telephone company provided major assistance to law enforcement. Investigators for the telephone company had become suspicious about a number of dial-outs from a certain telephone number in which the school system's telephone bridge had apparently been targeted. Using a PIN detector, the telephone

How Do Criminals Get Sensitive Financial Information?

A person can easily obtain information about another person in a variety of ways:

- Look over the victim's shoulder while he punches in his credit card number for a long-distance telephone call.
- Go through the victim's trash—people through away an amazing amount of sensitive data in their trash; if the trash has been placed on the street for collection, it isn't a crime to go through it.
- Make a telephone call—a criminal calls the victim and tells him that he has won a prize in a contest and that the only thing keeping the prize from being sent is to "process" the information. The information includes, of course, the victim's full name, date of birth, and Social Security number.

INSIDER'S VIEWPOINT

White-collar crime and computers

"Computers are becoming a big thing. Typical computer cases include disgruntled employees destroying the computer systems as a final act of revenge. We're seeing computers come up a lot in more traditional crimes. People are just storing information on it. Particularly true of identify fraud cases, which are becoming pretty big. People are essentially manufacturing either completely fictitious identities with the help of the computer or compromising real people's identifying information."

—George Hutchinson, Assistant District Attorney

Many states have passed statutes making it illegal to enter restricted databases or to destroy or make inaccessible the data stored in computer systems.

company was able to keep track of every telephone number that was dialed from the computer hacker's system. This helped the prosecution prove that the hacker had targeted the school system's telephone and had dialed it up on numerous occasions until he had finally gained access and had been able to sabotage it.

The investigators for the telephone company, however, were so nervous about the computer hacker's ability that they took numerous precautions to protect their own safety. They were not concerned about physical threats from the computer hacker. Instead, they were concerned about the hacker's attacks to their credit standing or job status. A computer hacker may be able to access any of the national credit reporting agencies and change an individual's credit rating. This can have as devastating an effect on a person's life as a physical assault.

THE ROLE OF THE PARALEGAL: USING THE INTERNET
Many paralegals know that the Internet is rapidly becoming an excellent place to do legal research, but few realize that the Internet can be useful in other ways as well. "On the Internet, there are sites that give you a virtual tour of certain automobiles," said Tom Garmon, a sexual assault investigator. "If you can find the same style car that you're talking about, you can take the victim to the virtual tour and have her show you where things happened in the car."

Such sites are important whether you are working with the prosecution or the defense.

a. The Hacker's World Computer hackers often use pseudonyms, or handles, in their contact with other computer hackers. These nicknames are often quite exotic. For instance, "dark angel" might post a message in a chat room or bulletin board service on the Internet advertising the fact that he has been able to access sensitive information at a local corporation. This information can then be used by other hackers to gain access to that system or to attack other computer systems. Many computer hackers have never met in person. When police officers catch a computer hacker, they often use this person against other members of the community. In many situations, the computer hacker will not be prosecuted in exchange for his cooperation in locating and arresting other computer hackers. Because the computer hacker's knowledge and ability are so technically complicated, often the only way law enforcement can locate and track down other hackers is to use one of them against the others. In the past, corporations who had been targeted by a specific hacker would hire the hacker to work for them instead of prosecuting him or her for the crime. However, in recent years, that trend has slowly disappeared and has been replaced with more successful prosecutions against computer hackers.

b. Denial of Service Attacks Other ways that computer hackers may attack a system involve denial of service attacks (DSAs). A DSA involves the use of many computers to send junk information to an Internet service provider or a company located on the Internet. The computer hackers use other people's machines without their knowledge to send a barrage of useless information to the computer server. This information inundates the system and prevents other legitimate users from logging on. Doubtless, computer hackers will come up with even more innovative ways of sabotaging computer systems.

c. Social Engineering Computer hackers also often use a technique they refer to as "social engineering" to gain more information about a particular topic. When they need to learn more information about, for instance, the Southern Bell telephone system, they call an operator and pretend to be an employee of Southern Bell. Social engineering refers to the process of learning information about a particular company from the company itself. The person working for the company believes that she is talking to a fellow employee, so she is very forthright with certain kinds of information. Many companies have instituted new training policies and other guidelines to avoid giving away sensitive information to computer hackers. Many of these guidelines involve having the employee identify himself or use a certain code phrase before information will be released over the phone. As you can see, companies and governmental organizations remain vigilant for attacks by computer hackers.

Case Excerpt. What Makes an "Occupied Structure" in a Burglary Case?

STATE V. CALDERWOOD, 194 OHIO APP.3D 438, 956 N.E.2D 892 (2011)
PATRICIA ANN BLACKMON, PRESIDING JUDGE.

Appellant, William Calderwood, appeals his burglary conviction and assigns the following three errors:

I. The trial court erred in denying appellant's motion for acquittal pursuant to Ohio Criminal Rule 29 where there was insufficient evidence that appellant trespassed by force, stealth, or deception, in an occupied structure.

II. Appellant's conviction for burglary was against the manifest weight of the evidence.

III. The trial court erred by allowing a police detective to testify that he spoke with the owner of the property who advised him that appellant did not have permission to be inside the structure.

Having reviewed the record and relevant law, we affirm Calderwood's conviction. The apposite facts follow.

Facts

The Cuyahoga County Grand Jury indicted Calderwood on one count of burglary and 72 counts of arson arising out of a burglary of a house, which subsequently exploded, damaging several houses on West 83rd Street. The state presented 67 witnesses to testify at trial. The jury acquitted Calderwood of the arson counts but found him guilty of the burglary count; therefore, we will focus on the evidence surrounding the burglary.

While investigating the explosion, detectives learned that neighbors had seen Calderwood removing items such as appliances and pipes from the house. Calderwood lived next door to the home and also owned rental property down the street. Neighbors observed Calderwood use a dolly to transport the items to his rental property. Calderwood admitted to the arson investigators that he had taken the property. He also admitted to his cellmate and to his wife during a phone call from jail that he had taken the copper and appliances from the house. Thus, it was undisputed that Calderwood took the items. The disputed issues are whether the house was occupied and whether Calderwood had permission to be inside the house.

Daniel Garman testified that he had lived in the house for 15 years. In late 2008, the home was in the process of being sold but was not abandoned. In fact, Garman periodically checked on the house, paid to have the lawn cut, and paid the utility bills. The home was eventually sold to EZ Access Funding, which is a real estate holding company located in California. In February 2009, EZ hired Marty Rickelman as a property manager to prepare the home for rental or sale.

Rickelman assessed the property as needing minor repairs in order to be ready for sale or rental. On one of his visits to the property, Rickelman was approached by Calderwood. Rickelman explained that he worked for the owner of the home and was preparing the house for sale or rental. Calderwood offered to help clean out the house, but Rickelman told him that it was the contractor's job. Rickelman did not give Calderwood permission to enter the house and did not give him a key. Rickelman ceased working for EZ in May 2009.

In June 2009, EZ hired Rajsunhip Sandhu as Rickelman's replacement. When Sandhu visited the property in the fall of 2009, the side door was open and the lights were on. He took photos of the home and then rekeyed and locked the side door. At that time, the appliances were still there.

When he returned to the property on January 12, 2010, there was a sign in the window saying "No copper. Stolen by Travis Hopp." Also, the door that he had previously rekeyed appeared to have been kicked open and was braced with a two by four so that it could not be reopened with his key. Sandhu was about to leave when Calderwood approached him. Calderwood produced a key that opened the front door. He told Sandhu that the prior property manager, Rickelman, had given him the key. Calderwood admitted that he put the sign in the front window and that he had called the police regarding the stolen copper. Sandhu's inspection of the property indicated that all the appliances and copper pipes were missing. Sandhu noted that the copper pipes were removed with precision and not simply yanked out, indicating that the vandal took his time.

At a Weed and Seed meeting conducted after the explosion, Calderwood admitted taking the appliances and copper but stated that he had the owner's permission and that he had capped the pipes. He also told the leader of the program, Brian Kazy, and Lieutenant Stevens from the Cleveland Arson Investigation Unit that he had obtained the key by breaking into the lock box on the door. The jury found Calderwood guilty of burglary; the trial court sentenced him to three years in prison.

Insufficient Evidence

In his first assigned error, Calderwood argues that there was insufficient evidence to support his conviction for burglary.

Crim.R. 29 mandates that the trial court issue a judgment of acquittal when the state's evidence is insufficient to sustain a conviction for the offense. Crim.R. 29(A) and sufficiency-of-evidence review require the same analysis. *State v. Tenace*, 109 Ohio St.3d 255, 2006-Ohio-2417, 847 N.E.2d 386.

In analyzing the sufficiency issue, the reviewing court must view the evidence "in the light most favorable to the prosecution" and ask whether "any rational trier of fact could have found the essential elements of the crime proven beyond a reasonable doubt." *Jackson v. Virginia* (1979), 443 U.S. 307, 319, 99 S.Ct. 2781, 61 L.Ed.2d 560.

A conviction for burglary pursuant to R.C. 2911.12(A)(3) requires the state to prove that Calderwood, by force, stealth, or deception, and with the intent to commit any criminal offense, entered an occupied structure with the purpose to commit in the structure a criminal offense. Calderwood contends that the evidence failed to show that the house was an occupied structure, because no one had lived in it for two years.

R.C. 2909.01(C) defines an "occupied structure" as "any house, building, out-building, watercraft, aircraft, railroad car, truck, trailer, tent, or other structure, vehicle, or shelter, or any portion thereof, to which any of the following applies: (1) It is maintained as a permanent or temporary dwelling, even though it is temporarily unoccupied and whether or not any person is actually present."

While Calderwood contends that the house was not occupied because no one lived there, the relevant inquiry in determining whether a structure is occupied concerns the residential purpose of the dwelling, rather than the presence or absence of an occupant. *State v. Green* (1984), 18 Ohio App.3d 69, 18 OBR 234, 480 N.E.2d 1128 (home left vacant after the owners moved to another residence was still an occupied structure because it was being maintained as a dwelling); *State v. Williams*, Cuyahoga App. No. 92668, 2009-Ohio-6826, 2009 WL 4986108 (fact that no one lived in the house for four months is irrelevant in determining whether it was an occupied structure); *State v. Charley*, Cuyahoga App. No. 82944, 2004-Ohio-3463, 2004 WL 1472745 (structure is still occupied despite the fact that the owner was in a nursing home and the daughter was having the house restored); *State v. Sharp*, Cuyahoga App. No. 86827, 2006-Ohio-3158, 2006 WL 1704529 (structure's status as an occupied structure depends on the residential purpose of the dwelling rather than the presence or absence of an occupant); *State v. Tornstrom* (Nov. 19, 1998), Cuyahoga App. No. 72898, 1998 WL 811314 (a home uninhabitable while undergoing major renovations was found to be an occupied structure).

Here, although no one had been living in the house, the house was not abandoned. The evidence showed that the house maintained its residential purpose even though it was vacant. The owners of the property had hired property managers to supervise the property until renovations were completed and the house was sold or rented. In fact, until the burglary, the house was fully equipped with appliances and a furnace. Given these facts, we conclude that the house was an "occupied structure" within the meaning of R.C. 2909.01(C)(1). Accordingly, Calderwood's first assigned error is overruled.

Manifest Weight of the Evidence

In his second assigned error, Calderwood argues that his burglary conviction was against the manifest weight of the evidence. He argues that the evidence showed that he had permission to be on the premises because he had a key to the house and helped take care of the property by turning the lights on to make the house look occupied.

In *State v. Wilson*, 113 Ohio St.3d 382, 2007-Ohio-2202, 865 N.E.2d 1264, ¶ 25, the Ohio Supreme Court addressed the standard of review for a criminal manifest-weight challenge, as follows:

The criminal manifest-weight-of-the-evidence standard was explained in *State v. Thompkins* [(1997)] , 78 Ohio St.3d 380, 678 N.E.2d 541. In *Thompkins*, the court distinguished between sufficiency of the evidence and manifest weight of the evidence, finding that these concepts differ both qualitatively and quantitatively. The court held that sufficiency of the evidence is a test of adequacy as to whether the evidence is legally sufficient to support a verdict as a matter of law, but weight of the evidence addresses the evidence's effect of inducing belief. In other words, a reviewing court asks whose evidence is more persuasive—the state's or the defendant's? We went on to hold that although there may be sufficient evidence to support a judgment, it could nevertheless be against the manifest weight of the evidence. "When a court of appeals reverses a judgment of a trial court on the basis that the verdict is against the weight of the evidence, the appellate court sits as a 'thirteenth juror' and disagrees with the factfinder's resolution of the conflicting testimony."

Calderwood contends that the evidence did not support the state's contention that he obtained the key by breaking into the lock box on the door. Both of EZ's property managers testified that Calderwood was not given permission to go into the homes and that they did not provide Calderwood with a key to the home. Moreover, the Weed and Seed program director, Brian Kazy, and Lieutenant Stevens testified that Calderwood had told them that he obtained the key to the house by breaking into the lock box.

Calderwood argues that it would have been impossible for him to have a key from the lock box because Sandhu testified that he had removed the lock box and rekeyed the door. However, the door that Sandhu rekeyed was the side door, not the front door. Calderwood had a key to the front door. While Sandhu testified that Calderwood told him that the prior property manager, Rickelman, gave him the key, Rickelman stated that he did not give Calderwood a key nor did he give him permission to be inside the house. Given this evidence, we conclude that the jury did not lose its way and create a manifest miscarriage of justice by finding that Calderwood did not have permission to be inside the home. Accordingly, Calderwood's second assigned error is overruled.

Judgment affirmed.

JONES and CONWAY COONEY, JJ., concur.

CASE QUESTIONS

1. What was Calderwood's connection to the neighborhood?
2. Did Calderwood have permission to enter the house?
3. Was there ever a question as to whether Calderwood took the appliances and the copper from the house? Explain.
4. What was Calderwood's contention about whether the house was an occupied structure, and was he right?
5. Did the fact that the defendant had a key to the house support his argument that he had permission to be on the premises? Explain.

ETHICAL CONSIDERATION: CONTACT WITH WITNESSES—WHAT YOU SHOULD (AND SHOULD NOT) TELL THEM

Whether working for defense or prosecution, a paralegal should never tell witnesses that they are forbidden to speak with the opposing side. There are two reasons for this rule. First, a paralegal could be accused of the crime of tampering with witnesses. This crime is a misdemeanor in most states and provides that a person can be charged for preventing a witness from testifying or in some way impeding justice. The second reason is more practical: As a general rule, it is always better that both sides know as much about the case prior to trial as possible. When paralegals tell "their" witnesses not to speak with the other side, they shouldn't be surprised to learn that the other side has given the same advice to its witnesses. Finally, neither a paralegal nor an attorney has the authority to prevent a person from speaking with the opposition. Should it come out at trial that one side attempted to keep its witnesses from speaking with investigators for the other side, the jury will almost always draw a negative conclusion. The jurors will often ask themselves "What is the other side trying to hide?"

✓ Paralegal To Do List

For the defense paralegal:

- Unless the client was caught inside the house, the only evidence against him that he committed burglary is his/her possession of stolen items. Perhaps the prosecutor would be open to a lesser charge of theft by receiving stolen property?
- What physical evidence actually links the defendant to the break-in?
- In arson cases, are there any other people who would benefit from burning the structure down?
- You can often find other experts who will give a different fair market value for a stolen item than the state's witness.
- In fraud cases, has the victim actually been defrauded or just made a bad bargain?

For the prosecution paralegal:

- After a burglary, the defendant often pawns the stolen items. Contact local pawn shops and see if they record information or even take photos of the people who pawn items. (Many do.)
- Stores often keep videotapes of thefts on the premises, but they don't always mention them to the prosecution. Contact the victims to see if any videotapes exist.
- Scanners can be used to duplicate a person's signature perfectly—with one flaw: A person applies different pressures when writing his/her signature.

A scanner won't duplicate those pressure points. Turn a suspected fraudulent signature over and see if the paper is creased by the pen marks or whether a printer was used to duplicate the signature.

- In white-collar crimes, consider a subpoena directed at the defendant's ISP (Internet Service Provider). The defendant's email will often be stored on the server, even if it has been erased from the defendant's hard drive.

Chapter Summary

Crimes against property involve a wide-ranging assortment of infractions. Burglary, arson, theft, and computer hacking are all crimes against property. The various elements of these offenses should be reviewed carefully because many of these crimes are similar in description but very different in the ultimate outcome. Theft by shoplifting, for instance, is punished much less severely than is armed robbery, for obvious reasons.

WEB SITES

CNN Justice
www.cnn.com/JUSTICE

FBI
www.fbi.gov

Hawaii State Court System
www.courts.state.hi.us

Iowa State Court System
www.iowacourts.gov

National White Collar Crime Center
www.iir.com/nwccc

Office of Victims of Crime
www.ojp.usdoj.gov/ovc North Carolina State Court System
www.nccourts.org/default.asp

Thomson Learning
www.thomsonlearning.com

United States Secret Service (SS)
www.secretservice.gov

REVIEW QUESTIONS

1. What are the elements of burglary? How are the modern statutory elements of burglary different from the common law definition of this crime?

2. Define *breaking and entering.*

3. What is the curtilage?

4. Can a person be guilty of arson if she burns down her own home? Why or why not?

5. Explain conversion of property.

6. Is white-collar crime a major problem in the United States? Explain your answer.

QUESTIONS FOR REFLECTION

1. Sam is caught just as he has broken into a home. He claims that he was entering the home to "scare" the occupants, not to commit a theft or a felony. Under your reading of the material, can Sam be prosecuted for burglary? Why or why not?

2. Sam takes Carl's car without Carl's permission. The next day, when the police pull Sam over for a traffic stop, Sam claims that he did not intend to deprive Carl of the car permanently. Sam claims that he was only borrowing the car for a short period of time—then he planned on returning the car. Can Sam be prosecuted for theft? Why or why not?

3. Sam works for a local retailer. While he is at work, he sees a pair of binoculars that he likes. He removes a pair from the display case and hides them in the warehouse. Later, after the store is closed, Sam returns and unlocks the back door to retrieve the binoculars. However, the police arrive at the scene before Sam can get to the binoculars. Can Sam be charged with theft by shoplifting? Can Sam be charged with theft? Why or why not?

KEYWORDS AND PHRASES

Breaking

Curtilage arson

Burglary

Breaking and entering

Intent to commit a felony

Larceny

Conversion

Asportation

Market value (fair market value)

Fence

Embezzlement

Robbery

Material fact

White-collar crimes

PRACTICAL APPLICATIONS

1. Sam is at a bus stop one afternoon waiting for a ride downtown. A man approaches Sam and shows him a camera. The camera is obviously new and looks very expensive. The man offers the camera to Sam for $10. Sam asks the man if the camera is stolen, and the man

places his hand over his heart and swears that it is not. Just as Sam is paying the $10 and taking possession of the camera, the police arrive and arrest both Sam and the man selling the camera. Has Sam committed a crime? If so, what crime? Explain. If not, why not?

2. One day while Sam is at the airport waiting for a friend to arrive, he sees a passenger who has fallen asleep in a nearby chair. The sleeping man does not realize that two $20 bills have fallen out of his pocket. Sam moves closer, picks up the bills, and puts them in his pocket. Unfortunately for Sam, someone sees him and reports him to the police. Has Sam committed a crime? If so, which one? If not, why not?

3. An employee is fired. Shortly before leaving the office, he hits a few keys on his computer that causes the entire computer system to crash. Has he committed a crime? Explain your answer.

4. Review the facts in the *Marbles* case (see Appendix). What crimes against property, if any, did the defendant commit?

NOTES

1. *State v. Whitaker*, 275 S.W.2d 316 (1955).
2. *State v. Styles*, 93 N.C. App. 596, 379 S.E.2d 255 (1989).
3. *United States v. Potts*, 297 F2d 68.(C.A.Tenn. 1961).
4. *Nickell v. State*, 722 So. 2d 924 (Fla. Dist. Ct. App. 2d Dist. 1998).
5. *Smith v. State*, 362 P.2d 1071 (1961).
6. *State v. Rick*, 342 N.C. 91, 463 S.E.2d 182 (1995).
7. *State v. Hammonds*, 616 S.W.2d 890 (1981).
8. *State v. Briggs*, 161 Conn. 283, 287 A.2d 369 (1971).
9. *Kellenbeck v. State*, 10 Md 431 (1857); *People v. Fanshawe*, 137 NY 68, 32 NE 1102 (1893).
10. *Commonwealth v. Bruno*, 316 Pa 394, 175 A 518 (1934).
11. *People v. Talbot*, 220 Cal. 3, 28 P.2d 1057 (1934).

Chapter 11

CRIMES AGAINST PUBLIC ORDER, MORALITY, AND HEALTH

Chapter Objectives

At the completion of this chapter, you should be able to:

- Identify the specific elements of crime against public order, health, and morality
- Explain the impact of the First Amendment on certain crimes, such as obscenity
- Describe the various types of drug possession
- Explain the elements of crimes against public justice, such as perjury and bribery
- Describe how a person can commit various federal and state tax offenses

I. Crimes Against Public Health and Morality

This chapter covers a wide array of crimes—from prostitution to tax offenses. What these crimes have in common is that there is no specific victim. Society as a whole is injured when these crimes occur, but it is difficult or impossible to single out a specific person who has been injured by the crime.

A. Prostitution

Prostitution has probably existed throughout human history. Some of the earliest known laws mention it. It is denounced in the Bible. The selling of

prostitution
A person offering her (in most state, his or her) body for sexual purposes in exchange for money. A crime in most states.

Exhibit 11-1
The elements of
prostitution

> 1. Performing a sexual act
> 2. In exchange for money.

sex services has been considered a moral and legal violation in many societies, yet the crime has persisted. In recent years, many states have made changes in their statutes outlawing prostitution. Gender-specific language has been removed to reflect the fact that both and women can commit the crime of prostitution.

1. Prosecuting Johns

Recently, many states have enacted legislation specifically targeted at prostitutes' clients (sometimes called "johns"). In these states, it is a crime to solicit sex from a prostitute. These new crimes have resulted in cleaning up certain areas that had traditionally been known as "red-light districts." Despite these legislative changes, prostitution is generally a low priority for law enforcement.

■ **BULLET POINT**
These days, both prostitutes and their clients are prosecuted.

B. Indecent Exposure

Unlike the previously mentioned crimes, indecent exposure is rigorously enforced. This crime is often characterized as a sex crime (see Chapter 9). The elements of indecent exposure are

1. Exposure
2. Of one's sexual organs
3. In public

People who engage in such acts often act under a compulsion to do so. In many situations, the perpetrators are suffering from some form of mental disorder. This crime is normally punished as a misdemeanor.

First Amendment

"Congress shall make no law respecting an establishment of religion, or prohibiting the free exercise thereof; or abridging the freedom of speech, or of the press; or the right of the people peaceably to assemble, and to petition the Government for a redress of grievances."

II. Constitutional Limits on Certain Crimes

Before beginning a discussion of the individual crimes against public order, it is important to note that many of these crimes carry constitutional limits on their enforcement. Many of these crimes, such as regulations on public assembly, carry First Amendment considerations. The First Amendment to the United States Constitution guarantees the right of freedom of speech for all citizens. The difficulty in analyzing crimes against public order is to know when a particular statute or police action has crossed the line between enforcement and a constitutional right. One example of a crime carrying enormous First Amendment concerns is the area of obscenity law.

A. Pornography and Obscenity

Obscenity law has triggered a vast number of court decisions. Drawing a line between what is and is not obscene and what is **pornography** is sometimes difficult to do. One person's obscenity can easily be another person's art.

1. What Can Be Regulated?

Obscenity laws have been passed that regulate pictures, photographs, movies, television, and the Internet. However, many of these statutes have been invalidated by decisions in the U.S. Supreme Court.

a. The Miller Test The United States Supreme Court has wrestled with the legal standard of obscenity for decades. In *Miller v. California*,[1] the court announced some guiding principles to help others know when something is or is not **obscene**. The *Miller* test has three basic components:

1. Whether the average person, applying "contemporary community standards" would find that the work, taken as a whole, appeals to prurient interest.
2. Whether the work displays or describes, in a patently offense way, sexual contact specifically defined by a state statute.
3. Whether the work, again taken as a whole, lacks serious literary, artistic, political or scientific value.

According to the U.S. Supreme Court, "obscenity" only refers to works involving sexual activity.

b. Possession of Obscene Material One of the more unusual aspects of obscenity law is that simply possessing obscene materials in one's home (in most situations) is not a crime. Sending it by mail, selling it, and even giving it away may all be violations of state and/or federal obscenity laws, but simply possessing it is not a violation. One could easily argue that the only way to get obscene materials is to acquire them from some other source, but simple possession is constitutionally protected. This exemption does not apply to child pornography (see below).

THE ROLE OF THE PARALEGAL: OBSCENITY LAW
The area of obscenity law is constantly changing. If you have a case involving this topic, the safest course of action is to review the most recent U.S. Supreme Court decisions. There is almost always a recent case that has made a slight alteration or refinement to this controversial area.

B. Child Pornography

The constitutional protections on obscenity disappear when the subject matter concerns child pornography. The U.S. Supreme Court has recognized that states have a compelling interest in the protection of children.

pornographic
Depicting sexual behavior to cause sexual excitement. Nonobscene pornography is protected by the First Amendment, but child pornography is not.

obscene
Lewd and offensive to accepted standards of decency.

■ **BULLET POINT**
To prosecute someone for obscenity, the prosecution must establish that the defendant's actions satisfy all three prongs of the *Miller* test.

States are given greater latitude when dealing with child pornography as opposed to pornography involving consenting adults. States can pass statutes limiting children's access to obscene material and can completely ban material depicting children as sexual objects. Statutes may also criminalize the possession of child pornography, unlike adult pornography. The *Miller* test does not apply to child pornography. The government does not have to show that the material involving children appeals to the prurient interest. All the state must show is that the material displays a lewd exhibition of the child's sexual organs and that the defendant knew that the material contained such exhibitions. All states have enacted statutes outlawing child pornography.

C. Other Crimes Against Public Morality: Gambling

■ **BULLET POINT**
The *Miller* test does not apply to child pornography.

Under the common law, gambling itself was usually not illegal. However, gambling was often seen as part of a symptom of greater moral decline. Gambling statutes were enacted because of the breaches of the peace and other crimes that often went hand in hand with gambling. Because gamblers have money, they often attracted other professions to help them dispose of it. It is no accident that Las Vegas, the gambling capital of the world, is also one of the few places in the United States where prostitution is legal.

In some jurisdictions, it is a crime to be present at an illegal gambling event. In many states, gambling at a private house where the general public is not allowed is exempted under the statute. This means that a local Friday night poker party is probably not subject to prosecution, at least in these jurisdictions.

III. Drug Crimes

■ **BULLET POINT**
Gambling can be, but often is not, prosecuted.

A drug is any substance used for medicinal purposes. The use of many types of drugs does not involve criminal culpability. However, when a drug is classified as a "controlled substance," various statutes control its use, sale, and distribution.

A. Controlled Substances

Controlled Substances Acts
Federal and state laws to control or ban the manufacture, sale, and use of dangerous drugs (such as certain narcotics, stimulants, depressants, and hallucinogens).

A **controlled substance** is what most people consider an illegal drug. Examples of controlled substances include cocaine, hashish, and marijuana. These are drugs that normally affect a person's mental equilibrium or mood. Some of these drugs cause hallucinations. However, not all drugs that affect a person's mood are considered to be controlled substances. Alcohol, tobacco, and caffeine are not controlled substances. The significance of classifying a drug as a controlled substance is that simply possessing it is a crime. See Exhibit 11-2 for an overview of drug possession and arrest rates.

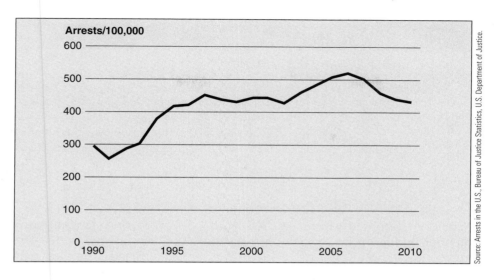

Arrests/100,000

Source: Arrests in the U.S. Bureau of Justice Statistics, U.S. Department of Justice.

Exhibit 11-2
Drug possession/use arrest rates

B. Narcotics

A narcotic is a drug that induces sleep, affects the senses, or induces hallucinations. The government is authorized to regulate such drugs under the police powers granted to it under the federal and state constitutions.[2]

C. Schedules

Narcotics are classified into various schedules. Sentences vary with the type of schedule, of which there are five. Generally, the first and second schedules contain the hard drugs, whereas later schedules contain lesser known and less powerful drugs.

- Opium and its derivatives like morphine
- Heroin, which is a derivative of morphine
- Coca and its derivatives such as cocaine, crack, etc.

Exhibit 11-3
Drugs that have been categorized as narcotics

Schedule I—opium, heroin, morphine, marijuana, mescaline, etc.
Schedule II—coca leaves, cocaine, crack, methadone
Schedule III—amphetamines, barbiturates, LSD, anabolic steroids
Schedule IV—barbital, chloral hydrate
Schedule V—codeine and related substances

Exhibit 11-4
Examples of drugs in various schedules

INSIDER'S VIEWPOINT

Crack and heroin

"Crack use kind of depends on the neighborhoods. Some neighborhoods you only find powdered cocaine, some it's crack only. There's some heroin coming back, too. It's making a big comeback."

—Robert Riffe, Narcotics Investigator

What is Crack?

Crack is a slang term for a specific form of cocaine. Powdered cocaine is "processed" by being combined with other substances and "cooked." The final form is a waxlike substance that can be smoked for a more intense high.

BULLET POINT

To prove that a substance is a narcotic, it must be tested by government experts.

actual possession
Direct possession of narcotics.

constructive possession
Possession of narcotics in some object under the dominion, custody, or control of the defendant.

D. Sale of Controlled Substances

Sale of a controlled substance carries different levels of sentencing, usually depending on how much is being sold. The general rule is that the greater the amount, the more severe the sentence. Besides proving that the substance falls into one of the schedules listed above, the state also must prove the exact amount.

E. Proving the Substance is a Narcotic

The government is required to prove that the item recovered from the defendant's possession was actually a narcotic. Therefore, the suspected drug must be tested. A state crime lab or another agency normally conducts these tests. Experts in drug identification perform several chemical tests on the suspected narcotic. Later, the expert takes the stand at trial, testifies about performing these tests, and states her opinion that the substance is, in fact, a narcotic.

F. Possession

Possessing a controlled substance is a violation of law, whether it is being used or intended to be sold to another. When the drug is in a person's hand, there are no real issues about whether she possessed it. However, the question becomes a little more complicated when the drug is found in her purse, luggage, or car. With regard to the law, there are two kinds of possession: actual and constructive.

Actual possession refers to the simple act of having a drug in your immediate possession. Holding a drug in your hand or having stuffed it in your shirt pocket would constitute actual possession. It is also possession to have the narcotic in your inner or outer clothing or in a container, such as a book bag or purse. When the possession is more removed, the law of constructive possession is triggered.

Constructive possession refers to the defendant's custody and control over an item where drugs are found. If the accused happens to be standing by a trash can at the local mall where drugs are recovered, it could hardly be said that she had exclusive custody and control over the trash can. After all, any member of the public could have put an item in that trash can without the suspect knowing it. For the government to charge a person with possession of items not found on the person of the accused, the government must show that the item was in the exclusive custody and control of the accused.

1. Proving Constructive Possession

To prove the accused guilty of constructive possession of drugs, the government must prove that (1) the accused had knowledge of the presence of the drugs and (2) the accused exercised custody, control, or dominion over the item. Proving number 2 can be as simple as showing that the defendant had exclusive contact with the item or that she owned the item and no one else was permitted to use it. Defendants have been prosecuted for drugs found in luggage, cars, and other items, all under the theory of constructive possession.

a. Constructive Possession and Cars A driver is pulled over on a routine traffic stop, and the police ask for permission to search the car for drugs. The driver gives permission, and narcotics are found. Is this an open-and-shut case? Not really. The mere fact that the accused was driving a car in which narcotics were found is usually not enough to justify a conviction. The government must prove that the accused had exclusive access to the car or that the car was her property. Showing that the car belonged to the accused raises a presumption that the accused owned the drugs, but not in all jurisdictions. To deal with this situation or where several people are in the car when it is pulled over, courts have developed various tests to justify the driver's conviction for possession. The court will often ask, "Were the narcotics in 'plain view?'" Were the drugs found in the defendant's personal effects? Were the drugs found in close proximity to the defendant? Is the accused the owner of the car? Did the defendant act in a suspicious manner? If the answer to all of these questions is yes, then the defendant can be convicted of possession.[3]

2. Possession with Intent to Sell

Most jurisdictions provide enhanced sentences for individuals who possess items with the clear intent of reselling them. Possession with intent to

■ **BULLET POINT**
There are two types of possession: actual and constructive.

INSIDER'S VIEWPOINT

What drugs are currently in fashion?

"We get a lot of cases involving meth (methamphetamine). Ecstasy is also making a comeback. They sell it for $30 a pop. We seized a load of thirty thousand a couple weeks ago. That's $900,000 worth."

—Robert Riffe, Narcotics Investigator

Exhibit 11-5

Example of narcotics sentence

"If the quantity of the cocaine or the mixture involved is 400 grams or more, the person shall be sentenced to a mandatory minimum term of imprisonment of twenty-five years and shall pay a fine of $1 million."

Copyright © 2015 Cengage Learning®

Exhibit 11-6

California enhanced sentencing for drug amounts

CA HLTH & S § 11370.4

Where a person is convicted of sale or possession with intent to distribute heroin or cocaine (and derivatives):
(1) Where the substance exceeds one kilogram by weight, the person shall receive an additional term of three years....
(6) Where the substance exceeds eighty kilograms by weight, the person shall receive an additional term of twenty-five years.

http://www.leginfo.ca.gov/pub/97-98/bill/asm/ab_2351-2400/ab_2369_bill_19980908_chaptered.pdf

Exhibit 11-7

Other actions that justify a greater sentence in narcotics cases

- Selling drugs to persons under a specific age (eighteen in many jurisdictions)
- Selling drugs within 1000 feet of a school or playground.

Copyright © 2015 Cengage Learning®

sell can be shown by the amount of the drug in the defendant's possession. For instance, if the defendant has numerous small packages in her possession, this may indicate that the accused is in the business of selling drugs. Other indicators that the defendant possessed with intent to sell are that she had a large number of small bills on her person and that the amount in her possession was more than a person would have for personal use.[4]

THE ROLE OF THE PARALEGAL: DESIGNER DRUGS

Advances in biochemistry have made it possible for people to create new designer drugs that are often not listed in any of the schedules for illegal narcotics. Some jurisdictions have addressed this problem by making the substances that go into these new drugs illegal. Either way, a close review of your jurisdiction's drug laws, especially in regard to new drugs, would be time well spent.

IV. Driving Under the Influence

All states have laws that criminalize driving a car under the influence of alcohol or other drugs. Some states refer to this crime as DUI (Driving Under the Influence) or DWI (Driving While Intoxicated).

In previous decades, drunk driving was not seen as a very serious crime, and in many jurisdictions, a person charged would get off with a relatively light sentence. In some jurisdictions, the crime was routinely reduced to a minor traffic offense. Much of this changed in the 1980s with the formation of national groups such as Mothers Against Drunk Driving. These groups began putting pressure on state legislatures and courts to increase penalties for drunk driving and to enforce the laws already on the books. The initiatives resulted in a new outlook on drunk driving. Among the changes were mandatory jail terms for repeat offenders, community service requirements for all offenders, a lowering of the "legal limit" from 0.12 gram/percent to 0.10 (and in many states to 0.08), and even provisions for publishing the pictures of convicted drunk drivers in local newspapers.

A. Prosecuting Drunk Driving

Under the drunk driving statutes, a defendant can be prosecuted for driving with greater than a specified blood/alcohol level in his system. A defendant can also be prosecuted for driving in an unsafe manner with any amount of alcohol and/or drug in his system. In many situations, a defendant is charged with both offenses, but can only be sentenced for one.

B. Proving Drunk Driving

One of the problems police have when pulling an individual over for suspected drunken driving is establishing that the person is, in fact, intoxicated. Erratic driving could be the product of alcohol, but it could also be the product of fatigue or other problems. Roadside sobriety tests help the officer establish whether the person is operating under the influence of alcohol or some other drug.

1. Roadside Sobriety Tests

If a police officer suspects that a driver is operating under the influence, she can request that the driver submit to roadside field sobriety tests. These are the well-known "walk-a-straight-line" and "touch-finger-to-nose" assessments that help law enforcement determine whether the defendant is intoxicated. The fact that the defendant fails any of these tests is not conclusive of intoxication, but is certainly suggestive.

2. Implied Consent

Almost all states have passed implied consent statutes. These statutes declare that a driver has already given consent for a blood or breath test simply by getting a license. When a driver is pulled over and the officer suspects that the driver may be operating under the influence, the officer can request that the driver submit to a test. If the driver refuses, his driver's license can be revoked under the provisions of the implied consent law.

■ **BULLET POINT**
Roadside sobriety tests allow law enforcement officers to evaluate a driver to see if he or she is operating under the influence.

3. Blood and Breath Tests

A police officer can request either a blood or breath test. In most cases, when an officer suspects that the driver has been drinking, a breath test will be requested. A breath test machine (e.g., an Intoximeter 3000) has a mouthpiece that connects to a unit about the size of a portable typewriter. When a suspect expels a breath inside the tube, the machine compares this breath sample with known samples and gives an accurate assessment of the suspect's blood alcohol content. In jurisdictions where driving with greater than 0.08 gram/percent of alcohol is a crime, if a defendant's breath test registers 0.08 or greater, she can be charged with DUI. In other instances, a police officer can request a blood test. In these cases, the suspect is normally taken to a local hospital where trained personnel take a blood sample and then send it to the state crime lab or other testing facility.

V. Crimes Against Administration of Justice

Crimes against the administration of justice are acts that go to the very heart of what is supposed to be a fair—an unbiased criminal justice system.

A. Bribery

Bribery is the illegal offering of money to a public servant to receive an action helpful to the person making the offer. Public servants can be police officers, municipal employees, or building inspectors, among others. Many states divide the crime of bribery into two offenses: bribery of public servants and commercial bribery. See Exhibit 11-8.

B. Commercial Bribery

Commercial bribery consists of offering a bribe to an employee to get the employee to do something improper. These bribes might concern awards of lucrative business contracts or the release of confidential information. In either case, offering the bribe or accepting it would be a crime. However, not all jurisdictions make commercial bribery a crime.

bribery
The offering, giving, receiving, or soliciting of anything of value to influence the actions of a public official.

■ **BULLET POINT**
It is a crime to offer a government official compensation to do something or to refrain from doing something that benefits a person.

Exhibit 11-8
New York statute on bribery

NY PENAL § 200.00

"A person is guilty of bribery in the third degree when he confers, or offers or agrees to confer, any benefit upon a public servant upon an agreement or understanding that such public servant's vote, opinion, judgment, action, decision, or exercise of discretion as a public servant will thereby be influenced. Bribery in the third degree is a class D felony."

http://ypdcrime.com/penal.law/article200.htm#p200.00

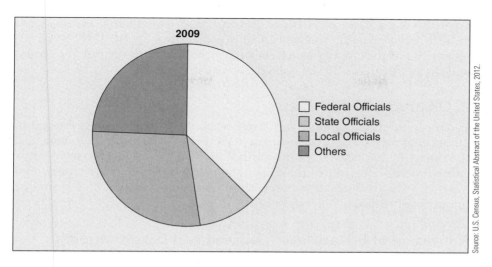

2009

Source: U.S. Census, Statistical Abstract of the United States, 2012.

☐ Federal Officials
◻ State Officials
▨ Local Officials
■ Others

Exhibit 11-9
Federal bribery
prosecutions, 2009

1. A false statement
2. Made under oath
3. With knowledge that the statement is false
4. About a material fact

Exhibit 11-10
Perjury is defined as

C. Perjury

People can commit **perjury** by giving false testimony before a grand jury or during a trial. In one notable case, a sitting U.S. President was accused of perjury when he testified about his alleged sexual affair with a White House intern. Prosecutions for perjury are relatively rare for the simple reason that, opposed to outright lying, most people shade their meaning when they testify. Because perjury charges generally involve proof of a false statement about a material fact, incidental falsehoods often do not rise to the level of perjury. As we have seen in previous chapters, a material fact is crucial to a case and generally involves the main aspects of a case. A material fact focuses on who, what, when, or where. False testimony about these matters could result in a perjury prosecution. However, opinions, feelings, and other speculations, even if false, are usually not actionable.

perjury
Lying while under oath, especially in a court proceeding.

D. Resisting Arrest

When a person violently opposes being taken into custody, she may be charged with resisting arrest. This charge would be in addition to whatever crime she was originally charged with. Generally speaking, resisting

■ **BULLET POINT**
Although a prosecutor suspects that a witness is lying in many instances, actually proving perjury is difficult.

arrest involves some physical resistance. Mere statements, insults, even mild threats, generally do not constitute resisting arrest. Only when an officer has a reasonable belief that the person may carry out the threat will the suspect's actions be considered resisting arrest.

E. Obstruction of Justice

Persons who shield others from arrest or actively interfere in the arrest of others may be charged with obstruction of justice. Obstruction can take the form of actively helping another person to escape, delaying law enforcement's efforts to take that person into custody. This charge can also be brought against someone who conceals evidence of a crime or intentionally misleads investigators.

F. Invasion of Privacy: Wire Tapping and Eavesdropping

Law enforcement officials are authorized to listen in on telephone conversations or private conversations only after they have obtained a warrant to do so. Private individuals are barred from listening in on telephone conversations to which they are not a party. It is also illegal to listen in on other people's private conversations, often called a "**wiretap**." In some states, it is a felony to place recording instruments on private individuals' telephones to listen in on their conversations. With the advent of the Internet, whole new areas of invasion of privacy concerns have arisen. For instance, is e-mail a private communication?

wiretap
An electronic or other intercept of the contents of a communication. Government wiretaps must be authorized by a judge for probable cause, and private wiretaps must have the consent of one participant (in some states, all participants).

1. E-mail

Case law on e-mail is still developing, but most courts have ruled that e-mail is not a protected form of communication. These rulings fly in the face of what most people believe. Millions of e-mails are sent every day, and the people sending them usually think that an e-mail is just as protected as regular mail. If law enforcement wants to read a suspect's letters, they must obtain a warrant to do so. The same is true for telephone conversations. However, e-mail is often the exception to this rule. For instance, many people have e-mail accounts through their jobs. Many would be surprised to learn that their supervisors have the right (and often take advantage of that right) to review their employees' e-mail. Can law enforcement pull up a listing of a person's received and sent e-mail? The simple answer may be yes. However, many law enforcement agencies have policies in place that dictate that a warrant must be sought for these communications. Because the law on this issue is still evolving, police often opt for the safer course: When in doubt, get a warrant.

G. Jury Tampering

embracery
An old word for attempting to bribe a jury.

Jury tampering (or **embracery**) is a crime in almost all jurisdictions. Influencing or attempting to influence a juror's decision in a case strikes at the very heart of the administration of justice, tainting the group who is supposed to remain fair and reach an unbiased decision. This influence might come in the form of bribes paid to jurors or threats to jurors if they do not vote a certain way. In either case, a crime has occurred.

H. Witness Tampering

In a similar vein, attempting to influence a witness's testimony is also a crime in most jurisdictions. Similar to jury tampering, threatening or bribing a witness is also a crime. It is viewed as a serious crime and is often classified as a felony.

VI. Crimes Against Public Order

Statutes creating crimes against public order are based on the belief that when large groups of people act in concert, they can do far more damage than an individual acting alone. Large, destructive groups are dangerous to lives and property, and this threat has been addressed in all jurisdictions. See Exhibit 11-11 for a breakdown of arrests for crimes against public order.

Al Capone's Jury

In the 1920s, when Al Capone was being tried for federal tax evasion (for failing to pay income taxes on his illegal activities), evidence came to light that Capone's men had bribed the entire jury panel. Just before the trial began, the judge in the case switched Capone's jury with a jury across the hall that had been called in to sit on a divorce case. The judge neatly solved the problem of what to do with an entire jury who been "tampered with." The jury found Capone guilty, and he received the longest sentence (11 years) that had ever been given for tax evasion.

Exhibit 11-11
Total arrests: other

Other									
Weapon law violations	159,020	145,600	13,420	31,360	127,660	92,630	63,710	1,100	1,590
Prostitution and commercialized vice	62,670	19,480	43,190	1,040	61,630	33,990	26,590	430	1,650
Other sex offenses	72,630	67,020	5,610	12,970	59,660	53,490	17,130	950	1,050
Gambling	9,940	9,010	930	1,350	8,590	2,860	6,650	40	390
Offenses against family and children	111,060	83,250	27,810	3,780	107,280	74,270	34,030	2,000	760
Driving under the influence	1,412,220	1,078,070	334,150	12,030	1,400,200	1,209,990	162,160	18,310	21,760
Liquor laws	512,790	366,850	145,940	94,710	418,080	424,990	62,930	17,790	7,080
Drunkenness	560,720	463,240	97,480	12,700	548,020	461,340	84,920	10,820	3,650
Disorderly conduct	615,170	444,840	170,340	155,940	459,240	390,410	208,760	10,830	5,180
Vagrancy	32,030	25,680	6,350	2,140	29,900	17,900	13,190	720	210
Suspicion	1,170	890	280	130	1,030	740	410	10	10
Curfew and loitering law violations	94,800	66,690	28,110	94,800	0	56,190	36,300	1,010	1,300
Runaways	—	—	—	—	—	—	—	—	—
All other offenses except traffic	3,720,400	2,827,140	893,260	296,790	3,423,610	2,470,680	1,146,150	55,580	48,000
Violent Crime Index[c]	552,080	444,890	107,180	75,890	476,190	327,840	210,150	7,300	6,790
Property Crime Index[d]	1,643,960	1,031,870	612,100	366,590	1,277,370	1,125,260	474,550	21,650	27,510

Note: Counts may not sum to total due to rounding. The offense categories are based on the FBI's classification system. See the *Methodology* for details on UCR counting rules.
—Not collected. As of 2010, the UCR Program no longer collected arrests for runaways.
[a]American Indian or Alaska Native.
[b]Asian, Native Hawaiian, or other Pacific Islander.
[c]The Violent Crime Index is the sum of arrests for murder and non-negligent manslaughter, forcible rape, robbery, and aggravated assault.
[d]The Property Crime Index is the sum of arrests for burglary, larceny-theft, motor vehicle theft, and arson.

Source: Arrests in the U.S. 1990-2010, Bureau of Justice Statistics, U.S. Department of Justice.

A. Carrying Concealed Weapons

A person commits the offense of carrying a concealed weapon by:

- Knowingly carrying on his or her person (unless in an open manner, fully exposed to view) any of the following outside his or her home:
  - Brass knuckles
  - Firearm
  - Knife designed for offense or defense
  - Martial arts weapons

Generally, a conviction for this offense is a misdemeanor. However, when the person carrying the concealed weapon is a convicted felon or has been convicted of this offense before, many jurisdictions make this a felony. See Exhibit 11-12.

Possessing a weapon during other crimes can also enhance the sentence. For instance, when a gun or knife is used to commit robbery, the offense then becomes armed robbery and is punished more severely.

1. Handgun Permits

In all jurisdictions, a person is allowed to apply for a handgun permit or license. This permit allows a person to conceal the pistol in a holster or purse and provides a statutory exception to the rule that a person must always display a weapon in his or her possession. However, simply because a person can apply for a handgun permit does not necessarily mean that a person will get one. The U.S. Supreme Court has given states wide discretion in denying handgun permit applications.

a. Exceptions to the Handgun Permit Requirement There are several exceptions to the rule that a person carrying a concealed handgun must have a permit to do so. For instance:

Exhibit 11-12
Weapon law violation arrest rates

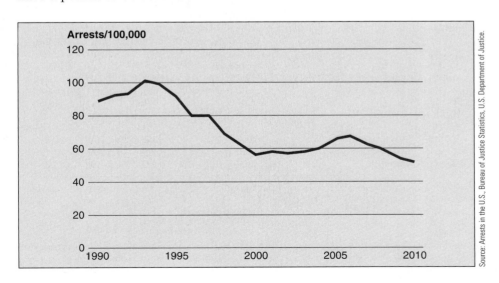

Source: Arrests in the U.S., Bureau of Justice Statistics, U.S. Department of Justice.

- **Permits from other states.** Under the "full faith and credit" provision of the United States Constitution that requires one state to recognize a legal decision from another state, states recognize the legality of handgun permits issued in other states. In fact, many states have statutes that specifically recognize the legality of out-of-state permits. This benefit is normally limited to people passing through the state; persons who plan on relocating to another state must obtain a handgun permit from that state.
- **Glove compartment.** Many states also allow a person to have a handgun in the car's glove compartment without requiring a permit.
- **Off-duty police officers.** Many off-duty police officers are authorized to carry handguns even when they are not in uniform. However, this provision only applies to police officers who are legally authorized to make arrests. Honorary deputies and others do not benefit from this exception and must have a valid handgun permit.

B. Public Fighting, or Affray

In addition to other offenses against public peace, most jurisdictions outlaw public fighting, or affray. An affray is an old common law offense based on the laudable goal of preventing public fighting in which others can easily be hurt. For an affray to take place, three distinct elements must be met:

1. Fighting
2. Between two or more individuals
3. In a public place

It is not affray where one person is acting in self-defense, attempting to ward off blows delivered by another person. The attacker can be charged with assault and battery, but neither person can be charged with affray.

C. Terrorism

Since the destruction of the World Trade Center on September 11, 2001, the issue of terrorism has been in the forefront of the national consciousness. Although we have yet to undergo a similar attack, there have been numerous attempts to re-create a similar event that would kill and maim hundreds if not thousands. The United States has also dealt with local terrorism carried out by extreme domestic groups. In most situations,

Exhibit 11-13
Georgia's statute on affray

O.C.G.A. Section 16-11-32

(a) An affray is the fighting by two or more persons in some public place to the disturbance of the public tranquility.
(b) A person who commits the offense of affray is guilty of a misdemeanor.

http://www.legis.ga.gov/en-US/default.aspx

Exhibit 11-14

Federal statute
on terrorism

> **8 USCA § 37. Violence at international airports**
>
> (a) Offense.—A person who unlawfully and intentionally, using any device, substance, or weapon—
>
>   (1) performs an act of violence against a person at an airport serving international civil aviation that causes or is likely to cause serious bodily injury (as defined in section 1365 of this title) or death; or
>
>   (2) destroys or seriously damages the facilities of an airport serving international civil aviation or a civil aircraft not in service located thereon or disrupts the services of the airport, if such an act endangers or is likely to endanger safety at that airport, or attempts or conspires to do such an act, shall be fined under this title, imprisoned not more than twenty years, or both; and if the death of any person results from conduct prohibited by this subsection, shall be punished by death or imprisoned for any term of years or for life.

http://uscode.house.gov/

terrorism prosecutions occur at the federal level and can be punished with the death sentence. As shown in Exhibit 11-14, the penalty for killing innocent people in a terrorist attack is death.

D. Riot

A riot is defined as a public disturbance involving a group of three or more people who engage in destruction of personal property or who injure people. A full-blown riot is an ugly affair, often involving extensive property damage and great loss of life. In recent years, citywide riots have broken out because of verdicts in high profile criminal cases.

1. Riot and Unlawful Assembly

The two offenses of riot and unlawful assembly carry many First Amendment concerns. In the United States, citizens are allowed to gather together to express their views even when these views are unpopular. The First Amendment guarantees the right of freedom of speech. However,

Exhibit 11-15

Elements of **riot**

> 1. A public disturbance
> 2. Involving a group or assemblage of three or more people
> 3. Who engage in disorderly or violent conduct
> 4. Resulting in injury or damage or presenting a clear and present danger of injury or damage to persons or property

citizens cross the line when they begin to advocate violent conduct. A **riot** is full-blown public fighting and destruction of property.

a. Inciting a Riot **Inciting** a riot is often a separate offense from rioting itself. A person may be charged with inciting a riot when he or she encourages others to riot. This offense goes to the heart of disturbing the peace.

b. Unlawful Assembly Closely related to rioting is unlawful assembly. Here, a group of people gathers together, often spontaneously. As police are well aware, an unlawful assembly can lead to full-blown riot. The problem for law enforcement is to recognize the difference.

E. Disorderly Conduct or Disturbing the Peace

There was no common law offense known as "**disorderly conduct**." Individual states have enacted legislation creating a crime referred to as disorderly conduct. However, this particular offense varies considerably from state to state. The United State Supreme Court has declared many disorderly conduct statutes unconstitutional. As a result, many states have redrafted their disorderly conduct statutes to bring them in line with the strict limitations imposed by the Supreme Court.

To determine what constitutes disorderly conduct in any particular state, it is necessary to refer to the statute. Most states define disorderly conduct as words or acts that tend to disturb the peace or actions that endanger the morals, safety, or health of the community. A closely related offense of disturbing the peace is often defined in similar terms. By their very nature, both disorderly conduct and disturbing the peace are difficult to define. Because the actions of individuals can vary considerably, police have wide latitude in determining when someone has disturbed the peace or committed disorderly conduct. It is that vagueness of definition that often gets these statutes into trouble with the constitutional interpretation by the Supreme Court. For instance, a statute that defined disorderly conduct as acts that "annoy, disturb, interfere with or obstruct, or are offensive to others" was declared unconstitutional by the U.S. Supreme Court, specifically because it was too broad in its terms and definitions of what constituted disorderly conduct. Disorderly conduct involves words or actions that would tend to breach the peace of the community.

F. Threats

Is it a crime to threaten to punch someone in the nose? Surprisingly enough, many times the answer is no. Generally, a threat does not become

riot
A vague word for a public disturbance, especially a violent one created by three or more persons acting together.

incite
To urge, provoke, strongly encourage, or stir up.

disorderly conduct
A vague term for actions that disturb the peace or shock public morality. The prohibited conduct must be precisely defined by state criminal laws, and the conduct must not be protected by the Constitution; otherwise, the laws are unconstitutional under the due process clause of the Fourteenth Amendment.

1. A gathering of persons, usually three or more,
2. Who have a common intent to do an unlawful act.

Exhibit 11-16
The elements of unlawful assembly

Identifying the Caller

In the days before the prevalence of caller ID, identifying the harassing caller was often difficult. Running a trace on a phone call was a time-consuming process, and unless the case involved some risk of injury, the procedure was rarely used. However, there are a variety of ways of identifying harassing phone calls these days. Caller ID is one way. However, some telephone harassers place caller ID blocks on their phones so that their numbers will not be displayed. New devices now allow the recipient to unblock the block. Other services include blocking all calls to the home where the dialer's phone number is not revealed. This also works to block out telemarketers. (For a discussion of Internet harassment and cyberstalking, see Chapter 8.)

vagrancy
Hanging around in public with no purpose and no honest means of support.

a crime unless it is coupled with some other action. If, for instance, the person making the threat is holding a weapon, the threat may now be an assault. (See Chapter 8). Usually, the person making a threat must have the apparent ability to carry it out. However, there are times when a simple threat may be actionable. For instance, federal statutes prohibit threats made against witnesses or court officials to influence the outcome of a case.

G. Harassment

The crime of harassment encompasses a wide range of activities. Some statutes specifically bar telephone harassment of individuals. Other types of harassment may include stalking an individual. In recent years, many states have enacted new and tougher stalking statutes in response to a growing trend among abusive ex-husbands and boyfriends who stalk their victims and occasionally kill them.

1. Telephone Harassment
Almost all states have statutes that make it a crime to telephone another person and engage in harassing, annoying, or threatening activities. Most statutes make this crime a misdemeanor.

a. Obscene Phone Calls A person who calls another and uses lewd, obscene, or profane language may be prosecuted as well. The First Amendment does not shield such speech.

H. Vagrancy and Loitering

Most of the early **vagrancy** and loitering statutes have been declared unconstitutional. In many instances, the United States Supreme Court or the state supreme courts ruled that the vagrancy statutes were overbroad, encompassing a range of activities far in excess of what was needed. Most state legislatures have changed their statutes to more narrowly define what constitutes a vagrant.

The problem with vagrancy and loitering is that it remains hard to define. Different states use different definitions for these crimes, which causes confusion. In *Papachristou v. City of Jacksonville*,[5] the United States Supreme Court struck down a vagrancy statute that defined vagrants as "rogues and vagabonds, or dissolute persons who go about begging, common gamblers . . . able to work but habitually living upon the earnings of their wives or minor children." The Court ruled that such a definition was too broad.

I. Public Drunkenness

In England, public drunkenness was not an offense against the common law. Instead, it was an offense against church doctrine. In the United States, public drunkenness is outlawed in all fifty states. However, the same problem that is seen with vagrancy and loitering also confronts the definition of public drunkenness (i.e., how to interpret the statute in conjunction with the U.S. Constitution).

J. Begging or Panhandling

In many states, begging or panhandling is illegal but often difficult to enforce. Some statutes give the local cities and towns the authority to pass ordinances outlawing begging.

K. Tax Crimes

Unlike most of the other crimes we have discussed, prosecution for tax crimes often occurs in federal courts, and this book focuses primarily on state law violations. However, because this crime is fairly common and is prosecuted on the state level, we will spend some time discussing it. A citizen's obligation to pay taxes arises under the federal and state constitutions. When a taxpayer resorts to fraud or other means to conceal his income, he has committed a tax crime.

Tax crimes can be committed in a variety of ways. **Tax evasion** is illegally paying less tax than is owed. It is also illegal to fail to file a tax return if the taxpayer has taxable income. There is also **tax fraud** where the taxpayer creates a fake financial picture to avoid paying taxes.

L. Cruelty to Animals

Another crime that does not necessarily fall into the category of crimes against public health or administration of justice but can be construed as a crime against public morality is cruelty to animals. All states have legislation criminalizing the unnecessary suffering of animals or that specifically prohibit people from torturing animals for pleasure.

In the past, animals were seen as the property of their owners and the owners could essentially do with them as they saw fit. However, all states have passed laws banning animal cruelty, and a person who engages in practices such as torturing animals or neglecting them can be prosecuted, often as a misdemeanor.

Case Excerpt. Tax Evasion in Hollywood

U.S. v. Snipes, 611 F.3d 855, 859-873 (C.A.11 (Fla.),2010) Marcus, Circuit Judge.

Defendant Wesley Trent Snipes appeals from his criminal convictions, after a jury trial, on three counts of willful failure to file individual federal income tax returns for calendar years 1999, 2000, and 2001, in violation of 26 U.S.C. § 7203. Snipes alleges that the trial court committed reversible error in sentencing, jury instructions, and on issues of venue. After thorough review, we affirm the rulings and judgment of the district court in all respects.

How is a Tax Case Investigated?

The IRS has its own set of investigators who work cases involving tax evasion or tax fraud. The Internal Revenue Service Criminal Investigation Division is staffed by federal agents who are trained as both law enforcement officers and accountants. In fact, many of these investigators are also accredited accountants, carrying their CPA card along with their badge. These investigators launch an investigation once they have targeted a suspect. The result can be a recommendation that the taxpayer be prosecuted. Prosecutors at the United States Department of Justice Tax Division review this recommendation. If these prosecutors give the go-ahead, the case is forwarded to the U.S. Attorney's office closest to the residence of the accused. From there, it is prosecuted like any other federal case.

tax evasion
Paying less tax than was owed.

tax fraud
The deliberate nonpayment or underpayment of taxes that are legally due. Tax fraud can be civil or criminal, with criminal fraud (tax evasion) having higher fines and the possibility of a prison sentence.

Militia Movements: "Taxes are Unconstitutional"

Many so-called "militia movements" are organized around the central theme that paying taxes is unconstitutional. The members refuse to pay their federal or state taxes and do not use their Social Security numbers on any documents, believing that by doing so, they are placing themselves outside the enforcement of the tax laws. These groups are sometimes lulled into a false sense of security when failure to pay taxes for several years brings no obvious consequences. The IRS moves slowly but resolutely. When the agency finally turns its attention on tax defrauders, it generally does a very thorough job, seizing property, bank accounts, and all other assets. The tax defrauder often ends up in a minimum to medium security federal facility for a few years, paying his debt to society.

"Only poor people pay taxes."
—Leona Helmsley, Convicted of tax evasion in the 1990s

I

The essential facts adduced at trial and the procedural history are these: Wesley Trent Snipes is a movie actor and owner of film production companies, including Amen RA Films and Kymberlyte Productions. Sometime around the year 2000, Snipes became involved in co-defendant Eddie Ray Kahn's organization, American Rights Litigators ("ARL"), that purported to assist customers in resisting the Internal Revenue Service ("IRS"). ARL employees, including co-defendant Douglas Rosile, and ARL members sent voluminous letters to the IRS, challenging the agency's authority to collect taxes. The centerpiece of this resistance was the "861 argument" that the domestic earnings of individual Americans do not qualify as "income" under 26 U.S.C. § 861, because the earnings do not come from a listed "source."

The ARL message appeared to have found a welcome audience in Snipes. Although Snipes earned more than thirty-seven million dollars in gross income from 1999 to 2004, he did not file individual federal income tax returns for any of those years. These were not, however, silent years. After meeting with ARL, Snipes began a long conversation with the IRS. He sent treatises describing theories about why the IRS was powerless to collect income taxes from him and several altered tax forms demanding money for taxes he had rendered in earlier years. Thus, for example, in April 2001, Snipes sent an altered form 1040X, styled as an Amended United States Individual Income Tax Return, in which he demanded a refund of over seven million dollars for taxes paid for the calendar year 1997, allegedly paid in error.

Snipes's correspondence with the IRS advanced several arguments justifying his failure to file his personal tax returns, including that he was a "non-resident alien to the United States," that earned income must come from "sources wholly outside the United States," that "a taxpayer is defined by law as one who operates a distilled spirit Plant," and that the Internal Revenue Code's taxing authority "is limited to the District of Columbia and insular possessions of the United States, exclusive of the 50 States of the Union." Snipes also claimed that as a "fiduciary of God, who is a 'nontaxpayer,'" he was a "'foreign diplomat'" who was not obliged to pay taxes. When Snipes consulted his long-time tax attorneys about his resistance to paying federal income taxes, they advised him that his position was contrary to the law and that he was required to file tax returns. The firm terminated Snipes as a client when Snipes refused to file his tax returns.

Snipes's resistance to the IRS did not stop at his personal filings. Snipes integrated the ALR tax "teachings" into the accounting methodology of his film production companies. After June 2000, his companies stopped deducting payroll and income taxes from employees' salary checks. Snipes began to proselytize this theory of tax resistance. He invited several employees to an "861" educational seminar at his home. When accounts-payable employee Carmen Baker attended the seminar and questioned the "861" theory, Snipes ordered her to leave his house, later telling her that he was "disappointed" in her and that if she was "not going to play along with the game plan," she should find another job.

The IRS launched a criminal investigation of Wesley Snipes after the agency received the April 2001 altered form 1040X for the year 1997, demanding refund of over seven million dollars based upon the "861" argument. On October 12, 2006, a grand jury sitting in the United States District Court for the Middle District of Florida returned a superseding indictment, charging Snipes and his two co-defendants, Eddie Ray Kahn and Douglas Rosile, with various crimes relating to a fraudulent tax scheme. Count One charged Snipes, Kahn, and Rosile with conspiracy to defraud the United States by impeding the IRS in its collection of income taxes, in violation of 18 U.S.C. § 371. Count Two charged all three defendants with filing a false claim for a refund of Snipes's taxes, in violation of 18 U.S.C. §§ 2 and 287. Counts Three through Eight charged Snipes alone with six counts of willfully failing to file his individual federal income tax returns for calendar years 1999 through 2004, in violation of 26 U.S.C. § 7203. Each defendant pled not guilty. Snipes surrendered voluntarily and was arraigned on December 8, 2006.

At the time of arraignment, a magistrate judge set a deadline for pretrial motions for January 12, 2007. On January 12, Snipes moved for an extension of time to file motions, due to the complexity of the case and the need to analyze discovery. The magistrate judge granted the extension, resetting the motions deadline to June 4, 2007, and the trial date to October 2007. On June 4, 2007, Snipes filed several motions, including a motion to transfer venue to the Southern District of New York, under both 18 U.S.C. § 3237(b) and Federal Rule of Criminal Procedure 21(b).

The district court denied Snipes's motion for elective transfer under 18 U.S.C. § 3237(b) as untimely, because it had been filed more than five months past the twenty-day elective transfer period defined by § 3237(b). The district court also denied Snipes's motion to transfer venue under Federal Rule of Criminal Procedure 21(b), determining that Snipes's claim that his wife and children lived in his home in California was insufficient to overcome the hardship a transfer of venue would place on his significantly poorer co-defendants and on many Florida-based witnesses. On Snipes's motion for reconsideration of the venue issue, the court again denied the motion to transfer venue.

In early October 2007, Snipes moved for a continuance after he had fired his counsel for claimed incompetence and hired new lawyers. After the district court granted the continuance, Snipes's new lawyers challenged venue still again, alleging that the government had chosen Ocala County, Florida, for trial for racially discriminatory reasons. Snipes again attempted to make a 18 U.S.C. § 3237(b) statutory transfer election, claiming that the district court could disregard the statutory twenty-day deadline because the ineffective assistance of his prior counsel constituted "good cause." The trial court denied both venue motions.

The case proceeded to a fourteen-day trial in January 2008. At trial, an IRS witness testified that although Snipes had regularly filed individual federal income tax returns for the years 1993 through 1998, he had not filed any returns for calendar years 1999 through 2004.

IRS Special Agent Cameron Lalli testified extensively about the investigation of the alleged tax conspiracy. Agent Lalli described a telephone conversation with Snipes and his lawyer in May 2002, during which Agent Lalli had informed Snipes that Snipes was under investigation for tax crimes. When he read Snipes his non-custodial rights, which included the right to remain silent, Snipes replied, "very interesting." In the course of the investigation, the grand jury served subpoenas on the office staff of Amen RA films. Former accounts-payable employee Carmen Baker testified at trial that when she received the grand jury subpoena, Snipes ordered her "not to respond, not to talk to anybody or to disclose any information on the company." When Baker asked Snipes why she should not respond, Snipes replied, "It doesn't matter. I have a confidentiality agreement with your signature on it.... If you do contact them, you will have to pay the consequences." According to Baker, Snipes's warning made her feel "very upset," "uneasy," and "scared."

Snipes also sought jury instructions on both general good faith and good faith reliance upon the advice of counsel to supplement the standard willfulness instructions. The district court granted these requests, too, and instructed the jury that "good faith is a complete defense to the charges in the indictment since good faith on the part of the Defendant is inconsistent with intent to defraud or willfulness which is an essential part of the charges." The judge reminded the jury that the government was obliged to prove willfulness beyond a reasonable doubt and that the defendant had no burden to prove good faith. The court also gave Snipes's good faith instruction on intent, telling the jury that "one who expresses an honestly held opinion or an honestly formed belief is not chargeable with fraudulent intent, even though the opinion is erroneous or the belief is mistaken." As for good faith reliance upon counsel, the trial court instructed that willfulness could not be found if Snipes had consulted in good faith with an attorney and strictly complied with the attorney's advice.

On February 1, 2008, the jury convicted co-defendants Kahn and Rosile on Counts One and Two (the conspiracy and false claim charges), but acquitted Snipes on the same charges. The jury convicted Snipes, however, on Counts Three, Four, and Five, for the willful failure to file individual federal income tax returns for calendar years 1999, 2000, and 2001. The jury acquitted Snipes on Counts Six, Seven, and Eight, the failure-to-file charges for 2002, 2003, and 2004.

The probation office's presentence investigation report ("PSI") recommended that Snipes be assigned a base offense level of 28 under U.S.S.G. §§ 2T1.1(a) and 2T4.1. The PSI measured Snipes's intended tax loss at $41,038,051, and assigned a two-level increase under U.S.S.G. § 2T1.1(b)(2), determining that Snipes had used sophisticated means to hide assets from taxation by using foreign accounts. The PSI also recommended a two-level increase pursuant to U.S.S.G. § 3C1.1, because Snipes had obstructed justice by directing Carmen Baker to conceal evidence from a federal grand jury investigation. Finally, the PSI recommended a guidelines sentence of thirty-six months' imprisonment. Snipes objected to the PSI's sentencing recommendations and challenged the PSI's reliance on any extra-verdict facts for enhancing his sentence. Snipes also objected that the obstruction of justice adjustment was unsupported, because Baker's testimony was unreliable.

The district court sentenced Snipes on April 24, 2008. The court sentenced Snipes to a total term of thirty-six months' imprisonment, comprised of three one-year terms for the failure-to-file convictions, to be served consecutively, followed by one year of supervised release and a $75 special assessment fee.

As for sentencing errors, Snipes first claims that the district court erred in sentencing him pursuant to U.S.S.G. § 2T1.1. According to Snipes, Section 2T1.1 is invalid because it (1) violates Title 28 U.S.C. § 994(j)'s prescription that a misdemeanor be treated as a less serious offense; (2) creates unwarranted disparity in contravention of 28 U.S.C. § 991(b)(1)(B); and (3) is not the product of careful empirical evidence.

Section 2T1.1 (the Sentencing Guideline for willful failure to file returns) directs the district court to calculate the offense level for the advisory guideline range with the use of the Tax Table (§ 2T4.1) that measures the tax loss and an assessment of specific offense characteristics. Section 2T1.1 embodies a change from pre-guidelines sentencing practice. Although under "under pre-guidelines practice, roughly half of all tax evaders were sentenced to probation without imprisonment,...§ 2T1.1 is intended to reduce disparity in sentencing for tax offenses and to somewhat increase average sentence length." U.S.S.G. § 2T1.1.

This graduated penalty structure reflects the Sentencing Commission's assessment that a "greater tax loss is obviously more harmful to the treasury and more serious than a smaller one with otherwise similar characteristics." U.S.S.G. § 2T1.1. Thus, the Commission complied fully with § 994(j) by ensuring that the tax offense "guidelines reflect the general appropriateness of imposing a sentence other than imprisonment" for first time offenders who have committed less serious crimes. 28 U.S.C. § 994(j). If the defendant's crime were not "serious" because the tax loss was minor and if his criminal history so warranted, the guidelines would advise a sentence of probation. In contrast, if the tax loss were high and thus more "serious" and "harmful to the treasury," as it was in this case, the guidelines would advise a longer sentence. Snipes merely disputes Congress's and the Commission's assessment of major tax losses as serious. We are unpersuaded.

Snipes's challenge to Section 2T1.1 on disparity grounds is also unsuccessful. Snipes claims that "by treating misdemeanors the same as felonies, the tax guidelines violate" 28 U.S.C. § 991(b)(1)(B). Yet Congress was concerned about the disparity of sentences "among defendants with similar records who have been found guilty of similar criminal conduct," not between misdemeanants and felons. Id. The district court noted that misdemeanants who, like Snipes, had willfully failed to file their personal income tax returns had engaged in similar behavior to the felons who had received similar sentences. The guideline does not create disparity of the kind that would violate 28 U.S.C. § 991(b)(1)(B).

The district court did not err in applying U.S.S.G § 2T1.1 to Snipes's crimes.

Snipes says next that the district court erred in imposing a two-level enhancement under U.S.S.G. § 3C1.1 for obstruction of justice. The enhancement was based on Snipes's instruction to Amen RA employee Carmen Baker not to respond to a grand jury subpoena. Snipes warned her that she would have to "pay the consequences" if she cooperated with the federal tax investigation. Snipes argues that because the subpoena was never entered into evidence, the government did not prove that the subpoena actually related to the charges in the indictment. Snipes also benignly characterizes the phrase "pay the consequences" as a reference to potential legal action that Baker might face for breach of a confidentiality agreement.

The district court did not clearly err in finding the evidence was sufficient to establish that the subpoena was related to the charged tax offenses. Although the grand jury subpoena was never placed into evidence, it is undisputed that the subpoena was delivered by the investigating IRS agent to a former employee of Snipes's film company, Amen RA, in an attempt to obtain records about Amen RA. And Baker testified that Snipes "told her not to respond, not to talk to anybody or to disclose any information on the company." The context of the subpoena's delivery, Baker's response, and Snipes's comments were sufficient to allow the trial court to determine that the subpoena was related to the tax investigation.

The district court also did not err in finding that Snipes's instruction to Baker to refuse to comply with the subpoena and his threat that "if you do contact them, you will have to pay the consequences" constituted obstruction of justice. We have long held that encouraging another person to avoid complying with a grand jury subpoena may be considered to be obstruction. The commentary to the Guidelines describes this kind of conduct as amounting to obstruction: "(a) threatening, intimidating, or otherwise unlawfully influencing a...witness,...directly or indirectly, or attempting to do so"; and (d) "directing or procuring another person to destroy or conceal evidence that is material to an official investigation." U.S.S.G. § 3C1.1 comment. (n.4(a) and (d)). The application of this Guideline was not legal error.

Finally, we address whether Snipes's thirty-six month prison sentence was unreasonable because the district court allegedly placed undue reliance on general deterrence as a sentencing factor under 18 U.S.C. § 3553(a). Snipes insists that the only reasonable sentence for his failure to file convictions would have been a period of probation.

In reviewing reasonableness, we begin by examining the procedural reasonableness of a sentence, ensuring "that the district court committed no significant procedural error, such as failing to calculate (or improperly calculating) the Guidelines range, treating the Guidelines as mandatory, failing to consider the § 3553(a) factors, selecting a sentence based on clearly erroneous facts, or failing to adequately explain the chosen sentence." The sentencing judge must "consider all of the § 3553(a) factors to determine whether they support the sentence requested by a party. A district court's unjustified reliance on any one Section 3553(a) factor may be a symptom of an unreasonable sentence," *Pugh*, 515 F.3d at 1191, although attaching great weight to any one factor does "not necessarily make a sentence unreasonable." Id. at 1192.

Here, the district court carefully complied with the sentencing procedures. The judge conducted an extensive sentencing hearing and listened to Snipes's allocution, several character witnesses, and argument about sentencing. The court correctly calculated the guideline range and, again, noted that the guidelines were advisory. The sentencing transcript reveals that the judge weighed each factor embodied in the Section 3553(a) calculus before pronouncing the sentence, which was within the recommended guideline range. The sentence was not procedurally unreasonable.

Next, we "consider the substantive reasonableness of the sentence imposed under an abuse-of-discretion standard. We will not second guess the weight (or lack thereof) that the judge accorded to a given factor…under § 3553(a), as long as the sentence ultimately imposed is reasonable in light of all the circumstances presented." The party challenging a sentence has the burden of establishing that it was unreasonable.

The district court gave ample consideration to each of the relevant considerations found in 3553(a). Although the discussion about general deterrence was somewhat longer than the discussion of the other factors, its length corresponds with the emphasis the Sentencing Guidelines placed on deterrence in the criminal tax context. The introductory commentary to the Tax section of the Sentencing Guidelines explains that because of the limited number of criminal tax prosecutions relative to the estimated incidence of such violations, deterring others from violating the tax laws is a primary consideration underlying these guidelines. Recognition that the sentence for a criminal tax case will be commensurate with the gravity of the offense should act as a deterrent to would-be violators.

Moreover, "when the district court imposes a sentence within the advisory Guidelines range, we ordinarily will expect that choice to be a reasonable one." Although Snipes argues that there were mitigating factors that the judge did not specifically mention at sentencing, these facts—his college education, his family, and his charitable activities—do not compel the conclusion that the sentence crafted in accordance with the 18 U.S.C. § 3553(a) factors was substantively unreasonable. The district court acted well within its considerable discretion in sentencing Snipes to thirty-six months in prison.

AFFIRMED.

CASE QUESTIONS

1. On what charges was the actor Wesley Snipes convicted?
2. How much money did Snipes earn in 1999 through 2004, and how much did he pay in taxes?
3. What were some of Snipes's claims about why he should be compelled to pay income tax?
4. What was the basis of the obstruction of justice claim that enhanced his sentence?
5. What was the court's reasoning in sentencing Snipes to 36 months?

ETHICAL CONSIDERATION: FREELANCE PARALEGALS

In recent years, some paralegals have realized the benefits of working as independent contractors with attorneys. The attraction of this arrangement is obvious: Because the paralegal is not a permanent employee of the attorney, the paralegal is free to pursue arrangements with other attorneys; for the attorney, the advantage is that the paralegal is neither a permanent employee who must be paid an annual salary nor someone to whom the attorney must provide insurance and other benefits. Having said that, however, the freelance paralegal is still in a gray area sometimes. Many states define a paralegal as a legal assistant who works under the direct supervision of an attorney. By their nature, independent paralegals work more or less without supervision of the attorney. In some states, the freelance paralegal has come under considerable pressure from judges and other legal authorities claiming that freelancers are practicing law without a license. In states such as California, however, the independent paralegal has gained a stronghold and is recognized for providing greater flexibility for attorneys.

✓ Paralegal To Do List

For the defense paralegal:

- Does the defendant have a valid defense to the claim of indecent exposure? Can it be argued that he was exercising his constitutional right to freedom of expression?
- In drug cases it is often helpful to show that the quantity the client had in his/her possession was for "personal use." Is that the situation in this case?
- DUI/DWI cases: Does the defendant have a medical condition that could account for slurred speech, unbalanced walk, and so forth?
- In resisting arrest cases, are there facts to suggest that the police overreacted?

For the prosecution paralegal:

- DUI/DWI cases: Check with the person who administered the test. Did he/she keep any notes about the defendant?
- The book-in photo in DUI/DWI cases is often helpful to the prosecution.

- Many police cars are equipped with video recorders. Is there a video of this arrest?
- In drug cases, how was the narcotic packaged? Lots of small packages may indicate a dealer.
- Child pornography: Can anyone identify the child? Look at the details in the background of any photographs. There may be a clue to the child's location.

Chapter Summary

This chapter deals with a wide assortment of crimes against public health, morality, and justice. Morality-based crimes, such as the laws outlawing prostitution and gambling, are often holdovers from earlier times in our country when more statutes were seeking to impose a certain morality on the populace. However, crimes dealing with narcotics and other drugs are usually based more on protecting public health than on public morality. In recent years, however, some have begun to question the benefits of statutes outlawing drug offenses. Some have even called for the wholesale legalization of these crimes. No such movement is anticipated for crimes against public justice. Perjury, bribery, and resisting arrest are firmly established infractions. All are based on the premise that justice must be untainted and free from the influence of money, threats, or other inducements.

WEB SITES

Bureau of Alcohol, Tobacco, Firearms and Explosives
www.atf.gov/

Connecticut State Court System
www.jud.ct.gov

Drug Enforcement Agency (DEA)
www.dea.gov

Indiana Court System
www.in.gov/judiciary

Kentucky State Court System
http://courts.ky.gov/pages/default.aspx

Ohio State Court System
www.sconet.state.oh.us

Oklahoma State Court System
www.oscn.net/applications/oscn/start.asp?viewType=COURTS

Securities and Exchange Commission (SEC)
www.sec.gov

Tennessee State Courts
www.tncourts.gov

United States Code
http://uscode.house.gov
United States Department of the Treasury
www.treasury.gov/pages/default.aspx

REVIEW QUESTIONS

1. Is there a difference between obscenity and pornography? Explain.

2. Are there situations in which child pornography is legal? Explain.

3. What is the *Miller* test?

4. What is the difference between actual possession and constructive possession?

5. What are narcotics schedules, and what effect do they have on a defendant's sentence?

6. Why do most states punish drug dealers who possess or sell large quantities more severely than those who handle smaller amounts?

7. What is the significance in a DUI/DWI case of a suspect having failed a roadside sobriety test?

8. What is implied consent, and what does it have to do with a driver's right to refuse a blood or breath test?

9. What are the elements of bribery?

10. What are the elements of perjury?

11. What is commercial bribery?

12. What is a material fact in the context of a perjury prosecution?

13. What is the standard for determining when a person has resisted arrest?

14. What is the legal definition of *riot*?

15. How does unlawful assembly differ from a riot?

QUESTIONS FOR REFLECTION

1. Many states have now created state-run lotteries. People who play these lotteries essentially bet one or two dollars for the chance to win several million. What is the difference, if any, between a lottery and general gambling? Can you justify a legalized lottery over criminal gambling? Why or why not? Can you build an argument that there is no moral difference between the two? Explain.

2. Prostitution and gambling are often referred to as "victimless crimes." As such, many critics claim that these crimes should be legalized. Are they in fact victimless crimes? Depending on your answer, should these crimes be legalized? Explain.

3. Why does the law take jury and witness tampering so seriously?
4. Explain the difference between tax evasion and tax fraud.

KEYWORDS AND PHRASES

Perjury	Protected expression
Material fact	Pornography
Riot	Obscenity
Incite	Child pornography
Disorderly conduct	*Miller* test
Vagrancy	Gambling
Tax evasion	Possession of narcotics
Tax fraud	Actual possession
Cruelty to animals	Constructive possession
DWI/DUI	Controlled substance
Sobriety tests	Bribery
Prostitution	

PRACTICAL APPLICATIONS

1. Many people, including some conservative leaders, have called for the legalization of narcotics such as marijuana and cocaine. Create an argument both for and against this stance.
2. If Sam listens in on Carl's telephone conversation without Carl's knowledge, has Sam committed the offense of illegal eavesdropping? Does the relationship between these two make a difference to your determination? For instance, what if Sam is Carl's father? What if Sam is Carl's roommate? What if Sam is a guest in Carl's house?
3. Review the *Fortner* case (Appendix) and then answer the following question: When the police arrive at the Fortner home to question him, his wife claims that he is not home and tells them to leave. In fact, Mr. Fortner is hiding in the basement. According to this chapter, has she committed a crime? Explain.

NOTES

1. 413 US 15, 93 S Ct 2607, 37 L Ed 2d 419 (1973).
2. *Employment Div., Dep't of Human Resources v. Smith*, 485 US 660, 99 L Ed 2d 753, 108 S Ct 1444 (1988).
3. *United States v. Shabazz* 993 F2d 431 (C.A.5 (Tex.),1993).
4. *U.S. v. Andrade*, 94 F.3d 9 (1st Cir. 1996).
5. 405 US 156, 31 L Ed 2d 110, 92 S Ct 839 (1972).

Chapter 12

RIGHTS ASSOCIATED WITH THE TRIAL

Chapter Objectives

At the completion of this chapter, you should be able to:

- Describe the various rights associated with the trial of a criminal defendant
- Identify when the right to a jury trial attaches in a criminal prosecution
- Explain under what circumstances an accused criminal is not entitled to a jury trial
- Balance the right of the press under the First Amendment with the defendant's right to a fair trial under the Sixth Amendment
- Explain the circumstances under which a trial may be closed to the public
- Describe the right of confrontation under the Sixth Amendment
- Explain the right of cross-examination
- Describe the presumption of innocence
- Explain the state's burden in a criminal prosecution
- Explain the defendant's right to an attorney and when and how this right attaches

I. Introduction

In this chapter, we discuss the various rights associated with the trial of a criminal defendant. The rights associated with trial are numerous and complex, but most arise from a few limited sources. The most important source of the rights of an accused under our system is the United States Constitution.

II. The Sixth Amendment and the Right to Attorney

Before beginning a discussion of the rights of a defendant during and after the trial, an important question must be answered: At what point do suspects have the right to have an attorney represent them? Much of the case law about this question focuses on a discussion of whether a particular stage is "critical." If the stage of the prosecution is critical, then the defendant should have an attorney representing his or her interests. But what is a "critical" stage? In most situations, this refers to some form of adversarial hearing against the suspect. For instance, the defendant has the right to attorney at the preliminary hearing because this is a court proceeding. Does the defendant have the right to attorney before then? Yes. As we already saw in Chapter 5, a suspect has the right to request an attorney before or during an interrogation by law enforcement.

The general rule is that a defendant has the right to an attorney whenever his or her legal rights are in jeopardy or during any adversarial hearing. In some jurisdictions, the right to counsel attaches when the investigation focuses on a specific defendant.[1]

III. The Sixth Amendment and the Right to Trial by Jury

The Sixth Amendment to the U.S. Constitution provides several of the basic rights associated with the defendant's trial. It is the Sixth Amendment that assures a defendant a trial by an impartial jury. This same amendment mandates that a criminal defendant be given the opportunity to confront the witnesses against him. This same amendment allows a criminal defendant to cross-examine these witnesses.

A. Does a Defendant Always Have the Right to a Trial by Jury?

The simple answer to this question is no. There are numerous types of charges and prosecutions where a defendant does not have a right to a jury trial. Traffic citations are a common example of the kind of criminal charge where the defendant is not provided a jury. Different states have different rules, of course, but for many routine offenses involving only a small fine, trials are not provided.

1. No Jury Trials for Juveniles or Other Offenses

There are no **jury trials** in juvenile court. Instead, a juvenile court judge hears all evidence and reaches a decision in the case. The U.S. Supreme Court has agreed that jury trials are not appropriate in juvenile court.[2] Others who do not have the right to a jury trial include members of the

---

■ **BULLET POINT**

A criminal defendant charged with a felony has the right to an attorney to represent him or her.

Amendment VI. Jury Trials for Crimes and Procedural Rights

"In all criminal prosecutions, the accused shall enjoy the right to a speedy and public trial, by an impartial jury of the State and district wherein the crime shall have been committed, which district shall have been previously ascertained by law, and to be informed of the nature and cause of the accusation; to be confronted with the witnesses against him; to have compulsory process for obtaining witnesses in his favor, and to have the Assistance of Counsel for his defense."

---

jury trial
A trial with a judge and jury, not just a judge. This is a constitutional right in criminal cases and in many civil cases.

military (for many but not all infractions) and those charged with a minor or petty offense.

2. Trials for Offenses Involving More than a Six-Month Sentence

Trials are not permitted for petty offenses. According to the United States Supreme Court, jury trials are only required for "serious offenses."[3] The Court defined a "serious" offense as one in which the potential sentence after conviction is more than *six months* in custody. If the potential punishment for an offense is less than six months, a state does not have to provide a jury trial for the defendant.[4] This is true even when the defendant is charged with more than one crime and the aggregate amount of each sentence would exceed six months.

Despite the fact that they are not required to do so, many states provide jury trials for people charged with minor offenses. In some states, the defendant is tried first without a jury and only if he is convicted does he then have the right to a jury trial.

3. Legislature Determines the Maximum Sentence

To determine the maximum sentence for a particular offense, the criminal sentencing statute should be reviewed. The state legislature sets the maximum sentence for an offense. The legislature generally includes the nature of the punishment in the statute making a certain action illegal. Where the maximum sentence is set at six months or greater, a jury trial is required. Sometimes, however, the legislature does not specify the sentence for a particular offense. In those situations, courts use the severity of the penalty actually imposed to determine whether a defendant should have received a jury trial.[5] For instance, if a defendant is charged with a relatively minor offense but is sentenced to twelve months in custody, the court would most likely rule that the defendant should have received a jury trial. In such situations, when the defendant appeals his conviction, the appellate courts will generally insist that the defendant be retried, this time with a jury.

4. Felonies vs. Misdemeanors

We have already seen that a felony refers to any crime for which the punishment exceeds one year in custody. Whenever a person is charged with

---

■ BULLET POINT

A criminal defendant has the right to a public trial.

■ BULLET POINT

There are some crimes for which there is no jury trial.

Trial *De Novo* in North Carolina

In North Carolina, a person charged with a misdemeanor first receives a bench trial (trial without a jury) in state District court. If he is found guilty by the judge, he may appeal to the superior court, where he will receive a jury trial, referred to as a trial *de novo*. G.S. Const. Art. 1, § 24

de novo
New. For example, a trial de novo is a new trial.

Exhibit 12-1
A summary of when a jury is authorized

No Jury Trial Authorized:	Jury Trial Authorized:
Petty offenses: where the punishment is less than six months in custody	Serious offenses: greater than six months in custody
Juvenile is charged	Adult is charged
Members of military	Civilians

a felony, that person must have a jury trial. Although we generally associate the term *felony* with major crimes such as robbery, rape, arson, and murder, many felonies do not carry the severe potential penalties of those crimes and yet are still classified as felonies. Trials are also authorized for many types of misdemeanor offenses. A misdemeanor offense is punishable by less than a year in custody or by no more than a $1,000 fine (in most cases). Given the definition of "serious" offense set out above, many misdemeanors also fall into the category of offenses for which a jury trial must be provided. See Exhibit 12-2 for a breakdown of arrests.

B. The Right to a Public Trial

"In all criminal prosecutions, the accused shall enjoy the right to a speedy and public trial, by an impartial jury...."

—Sixth Amendment

The Sixth Amendment also provides that a trial must be conducted in public. The Supreme Court has stated that the right to a public trial is one of the most important guaranteed to a criminal defendant. "Without the freedom to attend such trials, which people have exercised for centuries, important aspects of freedom of speech and of the press could be eviscerated."[6]

Anyone may attend a trial, and many people often do. The only hearings that are closed to the public are juvenile hearings, to safeguard the identity of the child. It is very rare to close other trials to the public, even for short periods of time. A judge is permitted to briefly close a trial only under extraordinary circumstances (see later). Even though a trial is open to the public, the trial judge may bar specific people from attending if they prove to be disruptive or dangerous to the proceedings.[7]

1. Closing a Criminal Trial to the Public

Closing a trial to the public is allowed only under limited circumstances. A trial can only be closed for a "compelling interest."[8] To close a trial, the state must show that some overriding interest is at stake. Reasons to close a trial are listed in Exhibit 12-2. Even in these situations, the court is not authorized to close the entire trial to the public, just those parts that could involve sensitive or vulnerable witnesses.

Whether a trial should be closed to the public is something that requires a case-by-case review. For instance, Massachusetts once passed a statute that required a trial to be closed whenever a minor sexual assault victim testified. The U.S. Supreme Court ruled the statute unconstitutional. No one factor will always justify the closing of a trial. The judge must try to make some accommodation short of closing the trial if at all possible.

2. Cannot Close Jury Selection to the Public

The rule prohibiting the closing of a trial also applies to the process of selecting a jury. Generally, the courtroom must be open during jury

Source: Arrest in the United States, 1990–2010, Bureau of Justice Statistics, U.S. Department of Justice.

Exhibit 12-2

Arrest in the United States by sex, age group, and race, 2010

	Total	Sex		Age group		Race			
		Male	Female	Juvenile under age 18	Adult	White	Black	AIAN[a]	API[b]
Total	13,122,110	9,792,190	3,329,920	1,642,650	11,479,470	9,122,010	3,655,620	186,120	158,370
Violent									
Murder and non-negligent manslaughter	11,200	9,980	1,230	1,010	10,190	5,540	5,430	120	110
Forcible rape	20,090	19,860	230	2,870	17,220	13,210	6,300	290	280
Robbery	112,300	98,600	13,700	27,190	85,110	48,310	62,020	780	1,180
Aggravated assault	408,490	316,460	92,030	44,820	363,670	260,770	136,400	6,100	5,220
Simple assault	1,292,450	944,970	347,480	210,240	1,082,200	850,800	406,490	19,260	15,910
Property									
Burglary	289,770	245,770	44,000	65,200	224,570	195,780	88,740	2,500	2,750
Larceny-theft	1,271,410	717,770	553,640	281,060	990,350	875,620	359,080	18,130	18,570
Motor vehicle theft	71,490	58,980	12,500	15,760	55,730	45,340	24,200	890	1,060
Arson	11,300	9,350	1,950	4,560	6,740	8,520	2,520	130	130
Forgery and counterfeiting	78,100	48,780	29,320	1,690	76,410	51,860	24,890	440	900
Fraud	187,890	109,740	78,150	5,770	182,120	123,420	61,190	1,560	1,730
Embezzlement	16,620	8,230	8,390	440	16,170	11,020	5,160	110	330
Stolen property offenses	94,800	76,230	18,570	14,640	80,160	61,860	31,250	760	940
Vandalism	252,750	204,860	47,890	77,070	175,690	186,570	59,180	4,210	2,790
Drug									
Drug abuse violations	1,638,850	1,324,860	313,980	170,570	1,468,270	1,093,910	519,830	11,240	13,870
Drug sale/manufacturing	302,310	249,050	53,260	23,800	278,510	181,370	116,830	1,740	2,370
Drug possession/use	1,336,530	1,075,810	260,720	146,770	1,189,760	912,580	402,940	9,510	11,500
Other									
Weapon law violations	159,020	145,600	13,420	31,360	127,660	92,630	63,710	1,100	1,590
Prostitution and commercialized vice	62,670	19,480	43,190	1,040	61,630	33,990	26,590	430	1,650
Other sex offenses	72,630	67,020	5,610	12,970	59,660	53,490	17,130	950	1,050
Gambling	9,940	9,010	930	1,350	8,590	2,860	6,650	40	390
Offenses against family and children	111,060	83,250	27,810	3,780	107,280	74,270	34,030	2,000	760
Driving under the influence	1,412,220	1,078,070	334,150	12,030	1,400,200	1,209,990	162,160	18,310	21,760
Liquor laws	512,790	366,850	145,940	94,710	418,080	424,990	62,930	17,790	7,080
Drunkenness	560,720	463,240	97,480	12,700	548,020	461,340	84,920	10,820	3,650
Disorderly conduct	615,170	444,840	170,340	155,940	459,240	390,410	208,760	10,830	5,180
Vagrancy	32,030	25,680	6,350	2,140	29,900	17,900	13,190	720	210
Suspicion	1,170	890	280	130	1,030	740	410	10	10
Curfew and loitering law violations	94,800	66,690	28,110	94,800	0	56,190	36,300	1,010	1,300
All other offenses except traffic	3,720,400	2,827,140	893,260	296,790	3,423,610	2,470,680	1,146,150	55,580	48,000
Violent Crime Index[c]	552,080	444,890	107,180	75,890	476,190	327,840	210,150	7,300	6,790
Property Crime Index[d]	1,643,960	1,031,870	612,100	366,590	1,277,370	1,125,260	474,550	21,650	22,510

Note: Counts may not sum to total due to rounding. The offense categories are based on the FBI's classification system. See the *Methodology* for details on UCR counting rules.

—Not collected. As of 2010, the UCR Program no longer collected arrests for runaways.

[a]American Indian or Alaska Native.

[b]Asian, Native Hawaiian, or other Pacific Islander.

[c]The Violent Crime Index is the sum of arrests for murder and non-negligent manslaughter, forcible rape, robbery, and aggravated assault.

[d]The Property Crime Index is the sum of arrests for burglary, larceny-theft, motor vehicle theft, and arson.

- Undercover police officer testifying
- Child-victim in sexual assault case testifying
- Victim testifying about particularly gruesome or sexually-related activities.

selection as well.[9] If jury selection involves some sensitive issues, the jurors can be questioned in the judge's chambers.

3. Cannot Close Preliminary Hearings to the Public

The rule against closing trials to the public has also been extended to the preliminary hearing. The United States Supreme Court has stated that a preliminary hearing can be closed to the public only when there is a substantial probability that the defendant's right to a fair trial will be infringed.[10]

> **BULLET POINT**
> A jury trial can be closed only for certain, specific points.

> *"Congress shall make no law abridging the freedom of speech, or of the press."*
> —First Amendment.

C. Public Trials and the Right of the Press

Because a criminal trial is to be conducted in public, the press has the right to attend, just like any other member of the public. However, there are special considerations when the press attends the trial. Press coverage of the trial may make it more difficult for the defendant to get a fair trial. Here, we see a conflict between two competing constitutional rights. A defendant's right to a fair trial must be balanced against the guarantees of the First Amendment, which bars any laws restricting the freedom of the press. Nowhere is the conflict between the First and Sixth Amendments more pronounced than in a criminal trial. Resolving this dispute is often tricky.

When a trial involves a great deal of publicity, a trial judge cannot simply issue a gag order on all parties and the press to prevent any coverage. Such an order would be unconstitutional under the First Amendment.[11] Judges must find a balance between these two conflicting rights.[12] There is also no magic formula for apportioning the weight to be given one amendment over another. The right to a fair trial, for instance, does not necessarily outweigh the freedom of the press. These various rights must be safeguarded by the trial judge, who is often faced—in highly publicized trials—with an avalanche of media coverage that the Founding Fathers would never have foreseen.

The United States Supreme Court confirmed the right of the press and public the right to attend criminal trials in *Richmond Newspapers Inc. v. Virginia*.[13]

1. The Press Has No Access to Jurors During the Trial

During the trial, the press has no access to the jury. The jurors are not allowed to discuss the case with each other, and they are certainly barred from discussing the case with the press. When jurors are away from the courtroom, they usually wear some form of badge identifying them as jurors in a case. Anyone attempting to communicate with them about the case—or worse, trying to sway them to a particular viewpoint while they are out of the courtroom—may be guilty of the crime of **jury tampering**. Attorneys generally make every effort to avoid even the appearance of impropriety when dealing with jurors. For instance, if an attorney sees a member of the jury in the hallway on a break, the attorney will often not even exchange pleasantries with the juror. We will discuss more aspects of the jury in the next chapter.

THE ROLE OF THE PARALEGAL: INSTRUCTIONS TO WITNESSES

Attorneys often instruct their own witnesses to stay clear of any jurors they may encounter. The paralegal, whether working with the defense attorney or the prosecutor, should emphasize these instructions to witnesses. Witnesses should be told not to speak with members of the jury. They should not ride in the courthouse elevator with the jury. They should not eat in the same restaurant as the jury. If they encounter members of the jury in the hallways or other places, they should simply smile and move on without speaking. Witnesses may not understand just how vitally important this is. Witnesses often look upon a chance encounter with a juror as an opportunity to discuss the case. The paralegal should explain to the witnesses just how dire the consequences of such communication is. Judges take a dim view of any attempt to tamper with a jury and may hold the witness in contempt of court. In addition to being held in contempt, which may involve a fine and a brief stay in the county jail, the prosecuting attorney may decide that the action warrants prosecution. Witnesses should be informed that jury tampering is a crime and, in many states, a felony. Because "tampering" with a jury is such a vague term, the witnesses should be told not to speak with the jurors for any reason. That is the safest course.

2. The Number of Jurors Used in a Trial

Almost everyone knows that the jury is composed of twelve persons. However, the U.S. Constitution does not mandate any particular number of jurors. There is no requirement for twelve people on a jury. The U.S. Supreme Court has stated that "the 12-person requirement...is not an indispensable component of the right to trial by jury."[14] Many states allow six-person juries to hear misdemeanor cases. Despite the fact that twelve-person juries are not a constitutional requirement, most states have opted for that number and require twelve people to sit as the jury in felony cases. Having twelve jurors has been such a tradition, at least in felony cases, that changing the number is unlikely.

a. Why Twelve Jurors?
Although twelve is the number usually associated with trials (at least all felony trials), why was twelve the number originally

jury tampering
Illegally influencing a juror or jurors (often through bribery) to influence the outcome of a trial.

Dealing with the Press

Sometimes the most taxing part of trial preparation for an attorney has nothing to do with the actual case. Trying to handle the press coverage of a big case can be exhausting. In most cases, though, there is no press coverage of any kind. However, for those cases that do receive press coverage, there are a variety of ways to try to short-circuit jury overexposure before the trial begins. One way of dealing with the problem is to bring the jury panel in earlier than normal. Most press coverage about a big trial comes to a head the weekend before the trial starts. Because most jury selection begins on the Monday morning of the trial week, some judges bring the panel in on Thursday or Friday of the preceding week. The judge will then instruct the panel not to read any newspapers or watch any television broadcasts about the case. By doing so, fewer members of the panel are likely to be prejudiced by the coverage before the jury has even been chosen in the case. (See "Jury Selection," Chapter 13.)

Exhibit 12-4

Sample statute for jury panels in misdemeanor trials

> For the trial of misdemeanors in all courts, each party may demand a full panel of twelve competent and impartial jurors from which to select a jury. When one or more of the regular panel of trial jurors is absent or for any reason disqualified, the judge, at the request of counsel for either party, shall cause the panel to be filled by additional competent and impartial jurors to the number of twelve before requiring the parties or their counsel to strike a jury. From this panel, the accused shall have the right to challenge four peremptorily, and the state two. The remaining six shall constitute the jury.

chosen? The simple answer to the question of why the American court system has twelve jurors is that twelve is the number used in England. The American court system is modeled closely on the English system, and when we adopted its laws, we also adopted its tradition of twelve jurors serving on a jury. But that really begs the question, Why are there twelve jurors in the English system? That question does not have an easy answer.

In 1164, Henry II decreed that a jury of twelve men should decide certain cases involving claims between the Church and state.[15] Twelve has always been a number of special significance. There are twelve months in the year. Roman law, which forms an important foundation of our own legal system, was first promulgated in the Twelve Tables.[16] Beyond that, law is a very conservative profession, and a custom, once adopted, is seldom abandoned unless there is a very good reason. Because twelve person juries have been the custom for almost a millennium, it is likely to remain so for the next thousand years.

b. Nonunanimous Verdicts in Jury Trials Even more surprising than the fact that twelve-person juries are not required by the Constitution is the Supreme Court's decision that unanimous verdicts are not required. There has long been an assumption that the jury in a criminal case must agree unanimously to the verdict in the case. If all twelve jurors do not reach a unanimous verdict on a case, the jury is labeled a "**hung jury**" and the case is declared to be a **mistrial**. However, some states have challenged the perceived requirement of unanimous verdicts by passing statutes stating that a jury could convict a defendant on a vote of 11–1 or even 10–2. In reviewing these statutes, the U.S. Supreme Court held that nothing in the Sixth Amendment requires unanimous verdicts and allowed these statutes to stand.[17] However, as in the twelve-person requirement, most state statutes require that a defendant be convicted by unanimous verdict of the jury.

c. Unanimous Verdicts Required in Six-Person Juries The Supreme Court's view on nonunanimous verdicts changes when dealing with six-person juries. In *Burch v. Louisiana*,[18] the Court held that nonunanimous verdicts

hung jury

A jury that cannot reach a verdict because of disagreement among jurors.

mistrial

A trial that the judge ends and declares will have no legal effect because of a major defect in procedure or because of the death of a juror, a deadlocked jury, or another major problem.

by six-person criminal juries do pose a threat to constitutional principles and will not be allowed.

THE ROLE OF THE PARALEGAL: INVESTIGATING THE JURY

Before trial, it is sometimes possible to obtain a list of people who have been called in to serve on jury trials. In high-profile cases, attorneys often hire private investigators to prepare background material on all of these people. However, in most cases, the economics involved do not make this feasible. How can a paralegal do—at least in a limited way—the job that a private investigator would have done? For one thing, a few hours at the local courthouse can help build a basic picture of almost anyone. Where does the prospective juror live? Has he or she ever been sued or prosecuted? Has the opposing attorney ever represented the prospective juror? All of this information is available at the courthouse and can be invaluable background material when it comes to selecting a jury.

IV. Other Rights Guaranteed in a Trial

"In all criminal prosecutions, the accused shall enjoy the right to... be confronted with the witnesses against him."

—*United States Constitution, Sixth Amendment*

A. Confrontation

In addition to creating the right to trial by jury, the Sixth Amendment states that the criminal defendant has the right to confront the witnesses against him. Confrontation means not only being able to see the witnesses, but also to question them on cross-examination.

The reason the Constitution gives the defendant the right to confront the witnesses against him is to ensure the reliability of their evidence. When the witnesses appear in court, the defendant's attorney can cross-examine each witness and the jurors can evaluate the credibility of each witness for themselves. The U.S. Supreme Court has stated on many occasions that the face-to-face confrontation is generally the only way to enhance the accuracy of the fact-finding process. It also ensures that the witness identifies the right person as the wrongdoer.[19] When a witness takes the stand, he is first sworn to tell the truth. This impresses on the witness the solemnity of the proceedings. The witness is also in the physical presence of the defendant and the jury. Both attorneys will then question him, and both the judge and the jury will observe his demeanor. The jurors are permitted to believe or disbelieve a witness based on their own observations.

1. Exceptions to the Face-to-Face Requirement

Victims who have been physically abused by the defendant are often very anxious about testifying in court only a few feet away from their attacker.

BULLET POINT
Some states allow juries to reach nonunanimous verdicts.

Even knowing that the defendant is in custody and that the defendant is under tight security does not help many witnesses feel better about facing him in court. Added to this, the witness must recount the entire episode from a witness stand in front of a microphone to a room full of strangers. This can be an intimidating event, and many witnesses freeze up when the time comes to testify. Recognizing this, many states have passed statutes and many courts have made special accommodations to ensure that the experience of testifying is a little less traumatic. For instance, a child witness in a sexual abuse case may testify by closed-circuit television.[20] Some witnesses can testify behind a screen or simply not look at the defendant during the testimony. In the next chapter, we explore many of the devices and techniques used in direct and cross-examination.

B. Right of Cross-Examination

Cross-examination is "beyond any doubt the greatest legal engine ever invented for the discovery of truth."[21]

The Founding Fathers of our country had had enough experience with trials in which no right of cross-examination existed to make sure that such a device was an important part of trials in America. Cross-examination has been called the greatest tool for the discovery of truth ever invented. Of the many gross inaccuracies portrayed in nightly television shows, cross-examination is perhaps the most blatantly incorrect. On TV, defense attorneys are practically crawling into the witness box to yell at some hapless victim. The victims are abused verbally and are never given the opportunity to explain their answers. The attorneys scream, "Yes or no! Yes or no! What is your answer?" In the next chapter, we will address the reality of the right of cross-examination. See this chapter's Case Excerpt for a discussion of the importance of cross-examination.

C. Other Rights: Defendant Has the Right to be Present at the Trial

BULLET POINT
The right of cross-examination is one of the most important rights given to a criminal defendant.

In almost all situations, the defendant must be present for his trial. Although this would seem obvious, what happens when a defendant is so unruly that his presence disrupts the trial? In that situation, the trial

INSIDER'S VIEWPOINT

Cross-Examination
"I don't think that all good trial attorneys are necessarily great cross-examiners. I think the key to being a good trial attorney is preparation. I may or may not do well cross-examining a particular witness, but I try to be more prepared for the trial than anyone else. It's that extra work that pays off in the end."

—Christine Koehler, Defense Attorney

judge is authorized to remove the defendant from the courtroom and keep him nearby. The defendant can be informed about the various stages of the trial by his attorney or can listen (or watch) the trial through a closed-circuit system. This is a better alternative to gagging or binding the defendant to prevent him from acting out in court.

1. Waiving Presence at Trial
In some cases, a defendant can actually waive his presence at trial. This is usually allowed only in misdemeanor cases. Most states provide that a defendant can waive his presence for certain minor offenses. A defendant can never waive his presence at trial in a capital case (where the death penalty can be imposed) or when he is charged with a felony. Some states, however, do occasionally allow a defendant to waive his presence at some stages of a felony prosecution.

a. Removing a Defendant from the Courtroom
A defendant may be removed from the courtroom and the trial continued without him when his conduct disrupts the proceedings. Although the courts have a strong preference for having the defendant present throughout, it is not unconstitutional to remove a defendant who misbehaves during the trial. In addition to removing the defendant from the courtroom and continuing the trial without him, the judge is also authorized to have the defendant bound and gagged to keep him from disrupting the trial.[22]

b. Defendant Absconds During the Trial
What happens when the defendant is present at the beginning of the trial and then absconds during the trial? Many defendants are out on bail and are therefore free to come and go during the course of the trial. In such a situation, if the case is a misdemeanor, the judge may decide to continue the trial without the defendant. This is called "trying the defendant in absentia." Trials in absentia are not permissible in death penalty cases or in most felony trials. Even in misdemeanor prosecutions, where a judge could technically proceed without the defendant, most judges opt for declaring a mistrial and issuing a bench warrant for the defendant's arrest. This bench warrant authorizes the immediate arrest of the defendant and often contains a "no bond" provision. A "no bond" provision means that when the defendant is arrested, he will be placed in jail and not be allowed to post bond for his release. This procedure ensures that the defendant will be present for his retrial.

D. Putting the Defendant on Trial in Prison Clothes
The U.S. Supreme Court has declared that it is improper to try a defendant in prison clothes. These clothes, normally the bright orange or blue jumpsuits issued by prisons or local jails, are usually emblazoned on the back with the word *County Jail* or "*Prisoner*. These clothes could prejudice a jury against the defendant and therefore should not be worn during a jury trial.[23]

INSIDER'S VIEWPOINT

When the defendant refuses to wear prison clothes

In one case, a defendant refused to wear any clothes at all. He had been arrested stark naked near a shopping mall and taken to jail. He had been given a mental evaluation and found to be legally competent to stand trial. However, he constantly removed his jumpsuit at the local jail, stating that by wearing such clothing, he was subjecting himself to the jurisdiction of the United States, which he had patently refused to do. He had declared himself to be his own sovereign. When it came time for trial, he appeared wrapped in a sheet that his wife had provided him. He refused a public defender and sat through the entire trial, wrapped in his makeshift toga, facing in the opposite direction. He was convicted.

—Prosecutor who preferred to remain anonymous

To avoid this, judges will order that the defendant be provided with the clothes that he had with him when he was arrested. If these are not available, a defense attorney may provide the defendant with a new suit of clothes so that he can create a more positive impression with the jury.

V. Other Rights: The Presumption of Innocence, etc.

In any prosecution, there is a presumption that a defendant is innocent until proven guilty. This is a very powerful presumption. What this means is that barring any evidence showing the defendant's guilt, the jury must acquit the defendant. This presumption follows the defendant throughout the trial. Judges inform the members of the jury about this presumption, telling them that they must find the defendant not guilty unless the state proves its case beyond a reasonable doubt. The presumption of innocence can only be overcome by evidence produced against the defendant.

In a trial, the state always presents its case first. This is because the state has the burden of proof and must prove the defendant guilty. A defendant does not have to produce a single witness, a scrap of evidence, or even a defense. A defendant is authorized, under the Constitution, to stand mute throughout a trial, never saying a word, and the jury must still presume that he is innocent.

A. Inferences and Presumptions

presumption
A presumption of fact is a conclusion that because one fact exists, another fact exists.

We have said that a criminal defendant is always presumed innocent. A **presumption** is a conclusion that a judge or jury must make in certain situations. For instance, when a defendant is charged with a crime, the jury has no choice in the matter: They must presume that the defendant is not guilty. If during jury selection a potential juror states that he or she cannot make this presumption, that person will be dismissed from the panel.

An **inference** is an assumption that *may* be made from the facts. If it snows during the night and you glance out your window in the morning and see footprints in the snow, you can infer that a person walked by your house. Even though a criminal defendant is protected by numerous presumptions, these presumptions can be overcome by the state's case. The jurors are told that they can make inferences based on the facts presented. But they are also told that they are never to presume that the defendant is guilty until the state proves it.

Once the state has presented its case, the defense has the opportunity to proceed. In many trials, no defense is presented. Instead, the defendant simply attacks the state's case. We will explore the aspects of presenting a criminal defense in the next chapter.

inference
A fact that is probably true. For example, if the first four books in a set of five have green covers, it is a reasonable inference that the fifth book has a green cover.

B. Prosecutor Cannot Comment on the Defendant's Silence

The right to be presumed innocent in a criminal trial is such a fundamental right and so closely guarded that a prosecutor is not even permitted to refer to the defendant's silence. A prosecutor is not allowed to stand before the jury; point to the defendant; and say, "If our case isn't true, why hasn't the defendant denied it?" Such a statement would be grounds for a mistrial.

C. State Must Prove That the Defendant is Guilty Beyond a Reasonable Doubt

The state, in the person of the prosecutor, has the burden of proving the defendant's guilt. There is no burden on the defendant to prove his innocence. The standard the prosecutor must meet is proof beyond a reasonable doubt. *Reasonable doubt* is a difficult term to quantify. In civil cases, where the burden on the plaintiff is "preponderance of the evidence," quantifying that level of proof is simple. In a civil case, preponderance of the evidence simply means "more likely than not." This is not the standard in criminal cases. Beyond a reasonable doubt is a much higher standard than preponderance of the evidence. Proving a case beyond a reasonable doubt does not mean that the state must prove the case beyond all doubt or beyond a shadow of a doubt. Reasonable doubt means a doubt based on a commonsense reason, not some capricious or ill-advised opinion. If at the end of the trial a juror is still unsettled in his mind or has qualms about the proof, this is a reasonable doubt. The judge's instruction to the jury leaves little doubt about what should happen if a juror has a reasonable doubt. In any situation where a reasonable doubt exists, the juror must vote to acquit the defendant.

The practical effect of such a high standard is that a jury might reach a conclusion that the defendant is guilty but that the state has failed to prove that guilt and would therefore vote not guilty.

1. The Burden of Proof is Always on the State

In a criminal trial, the burden of proof is always on the state to prove the defendant guilty beyond a reasonable doubt. This burden never shifts to the defendant. For instance, at the conclusion of the state's case, the burden does not shift to the defendant to prove his innocence. If a defendant presents a defense, such as an alibi or insanity, it continues to be the state's obligation to disprove the defense. The burden in a criminal case never rests on the defendant to prove that he is not guilty. In cases where the defense is insanity, for instance, the state must present rebuttal evidence establishing that the defendant was legally sane at the time of the crime. (See the Chapter 14.)

2. When the Defendant Decides to Present a Defense

The defendant has the same right to present evidence and witnesses as the state. The defendant is under no obligation to present a perfect defense. A defendant may raise several different defenses to an action and have all of them considered by the jury.

D. The Right to a Speedy Trial

"…the accused shall enjoy the right to a speedy and public trial…"

—*United States Constitution, Sixth Amendment*

The right of an accused to a speedy trial has a long history. Originally mentioned in the Magna Carta in 1215, the defendant's right to a speedy trial was considered to be an important, if often ignored, right. The right to a speedy trial was embodied in the Virginia Declaration of Rights of 1776, then incorporated into the later United States Constitution, and then included in all state constitutions.

In *Klopfer v. North Carolina*,[24] the Supreme Court declared that the right to a speedy trial was as important as any other right guaranteed in the Sixth Amendment, calling it "one of the most basic rights preserved by our Constitution."

All states have laws that are commonly referred to as "speedy trial statutes." Speedy trial statutes seek to enforce the Sixth Amendment guarantee of a speedy trial. These statutes allow a defendant to serve on the state a demand that the defendant be tried in this or the next **term of court**.

term of court
The time period in which the court may hear cases.

1. Dismissing a Case for Failure to Receive a Speedy Trial

If the defendant serves a speedy trial demand and is not tried in the specified time, then the charges against the defendant must be dismissed and the defendant released from confinement. Serving a "speedy" on a prosecutor often has a galvanizing effect on the state. Because a prosecutor knows that if the defendant is not tried he must be released, the practical effect of serving a speedy trial demand usually is that the defendant's case is moved up to the number one trial in the next trial week.

While this right is considered one of the fundamental rights guaranteed in the Constitution, defining exactly what constitutes a "speedy" trial has been difficult to quantify. The U.S. Supreme Court has grappled with this issue in many cases.

2. How Long Must a Defendant Wait to Receive a Trial?

The Supreme Court has held that a delay of eight years between indictment and trial is too long[25]; five years may also be too long[26]. The problem is that each case must be considered on its own facts. The Supreme Court has been reluctant to state a maximum period that will always mean a violation of the Sixth Amendment. Despite the Court's reluctance to name a specific period of time in which a defendant must be tried, the Court has been specific about the sanction imposed for failing to try a defendant. Where the defendant's right to a speedy trial has been violated, only one sanction is allowed: dismissal of the state's case. This drastic remedy was authorized in *Strunk v. United States.*[27]

3. Circumstances When the Defendant May Not Want a Speedy Trial

Although each state has a statute authorizing the filing of a speedy trial demand to enforce the Sixth Amendment guarantee, a speedy trial may actually work against the defendant. Often, a delay in bringing the case to trial will help the defendant. Memories fade over time. Evidence may be lost. In fact, taking a case to trial sooner rather than later may only be helpful to the defendant when the prosecution is not prepared. Otherwise, a quick trial may actually work against the defendant. The defense team should evaluate these potential difficulties before filing a statutory speedy trial demand.

4. When Does the Right to a Speedy Trial Attach?

The right to receive a speedy trial is triggered when an indictment has been lodged against the defendant.[28] The right to a speedy trial also attaches when a defendant has been *accused*—that is, when he is charged with a misdemeanor.

Even when the defendant is in prison serving a sentence on an unrelated offense, he is still entitled to receive a speedy trial on another charge.[29]

VI. The Right to be Represented by an Attorney at Trial

> *"In all criminal prosecutions, the accused shall enjoy the right…to have the Assistance of Counsel for his defense."*
>
> —Sixth Amendment

For decades, the Sixth Amendment guarantee of right to assistance of counsel at trial was interpreted to mean that a defendant could have any attorney he could afford. If he could not afford an attorney, then he had to represent himself. It was not until a famous series of cases that these rules were changed. The most famous of these was *Gideon v. Wainwright*.

A. *Gideon v. Wainwright*

Clarence Earl Gideon was charged with breaking and entering a poolroom. This was a felony level offense in Florida. Mr. Gideon appeared in the case without an attorney, stating to the court that he could not afford to hire one. Under Florida law, the only time that a person was entitled to have a court-appointed attorney was when he was charged with a capital offense (i.e., punishable by death). Gideon was then put on trial and represented himself, giving an opening statement to the jury and cross-examining witnesses. He was found guilty and sentenced to serve five years in state prison.

Gideon appealed his case to the U.S. Supreme Court. In one of its most popular decisions, the Court sided with Gideon. The Court stated that "assistance of counsel is one of the safeguards of the Sixth Amendment deemed necessary to insure fundamental human rights of life and liberty.... The Sixth Amendment stands as a constant admonition that if the constitutional safeguards it provides be lost, justice will not...be done." The Court ruled that Gideon should be retried and that this time he should have an attorney to represent him—one appointed by the Florida court. Gideon was subsequently retried and found not guilty.

Since the *Gideon* decision, the Supreme Court has continued to expand the requirement of appointed counsel for defendants who cannot afford to hire their own attorneys. The law now requires that a defendant be appointed an attorney when he cannot afford one whether the offense is categorized as a misdemeanor or felony, serious or petty and the punishment involves a potential sentence of more than six months in custody.

B. Court-Appointed Attorney vs. Public Defender

This emphasis on court-appointed attorneys focuses on states or counties within states that do not possess public defender's offices. We discussed public defenders in the chapter dealing with the various court personnel, but a brief word about them may be helpful here as well. Public defenders are government employees—often paid by the county—whose sole duty is to represent persons who have been charged with a crime and cannot afford to hire their own attorney. Where public defenders exist, there is no need for court-appointed attorneys. In counties that have no public defender's office, the county contracts with local private attorneys and pays them a flat fee to take cases for people who cannot afford to have an attorney represent them. Court-appointed attorneys are often young lawyers who recently have been admitted to the bar. However, seasoned attorneys are often on the court-appointed list as well. The younger attorneys get on the appointed list to gain much-needed courtroom experience. However, do not make the mistake of believing that a court-appointed lawyer is inferior to a highly paid defense attorney. Some of the finest criminal defense attorneys in the county may be on the court-appointed list.

C. When the Defendant Cannot Afford an Attorney

Before a judge will appoint an attorney to represent a defendant, he must inquire about the defendant's finances. The state has specific financial guidelines that a person must meet before an attorney will be appointed to represent him. Generally, if the defendant is in custody and cannot afford to make bail/bond, an attorney will be appointed to represent him. Defendants who are not in custody must often complete a questionnaire, providing details about how much money they make. Different states have different guidelines that a defendant must meet. If the defendant does not meet the financial criteria (i.e., because he makes too much money), then he may not qualify for a court-appointed attorney or a public defender. A great many people with well-paying jobs but huge debt loads cannot raise the up-front retainer of a skilled criminal defense attorney. They find themselves in a classic catch-22 situation: They do not have enough money to pay an attorney, but they make too much money to have an attorney appointed for them.

D. Right of a Defendant to Represent Himself

Whether a defendant can afford an attorney or whether the state will provide a court-appointed attorney, a defendant has the right to defend himself. This is called **pro se**. A pro se defendant acts as his own attorney. The defendant gives an opening statement, questions the state's witnesses on cross-examination and gives a closing argument.

pro se
For himself or herself; in his or her own behalf.

Unfortunately, the old saying about a lawyer representing himself having a fool for a client is even truer for a nonlawyer representing himself. Attorneys attend law school for three years to learn their craft, often followed by an intensive, informal apprenticeship the first few years out of law school. The rules of evidence at trial are complex, as are the legal issues. Conducting legal research into particular issues is also difficult. When the outcome could be a prison sentence, it makes sense for a defendant to hire a professional to safeguard his rights.

1. Prosecuting a Pro Se Defendant

Judges often appoint an attorney to sit with a pro se defendant even when the defendant has expressed a desire to represent himself. The attorney is there to advise the defendant should he need any information about the court procedures.

VII. Other Rights: The Right to Present Evidence and Witnesses

In addition to the many other rights granted to a criminal defendant, the defendant also has the right to present evidence during the trial. Although this would seem obvious, criminal defendants have not always had this right. The ability to present evidence and witnesses subjects the defendant

U.S. Supreme Court on the Right of Representation

"Even the intelligent and educated layman has small and sometimes no skill in the science of law. If charged with crime, he is incapable, generally, of determining for himself whether the indictment is good or bad. He is unfamiliar with the rules of evidence. Left without the aid of counsel he may be put on trial without a proper charge, and convicted upon incompetent evidence, or evidence irrelevant to the issue or otherwise inadmissible. He lacks both the skill and knowledge adequately to prepare his defense, even though he have a perfect one. He requires the guiding hand of counsel at every step in the proceedings against him. Without it, though he be not guilty, he faces the danger of conviction because he does not know how to establish his innocence."
—*Powell v. Alabama*, 287 U.S. 45, 53 S.Ct. 55, 77 L.Ed. 158 (1932)

to the same rules of evidence as the prosecutor. Although a defendant can present evidence, he is under no obligation to do so. As stated previously, a defendant does not have to do anything during the course of his trial. He does not have to refute any of the evidence presented by the prosecution. He does not have to take the stand and protest his innocence, and the state cannot make any negative inference from his failure to do so.

Case Excerpt. Com. v. Avalos, *454 Mass. 1, 906 N.E.2d 987 (Mass.,2009)*

CORDY, J.

After a jury trial, the defendant, Salvatore Avalos, was convicted on three indictments charging rape of a child in violation of G.L. c. 265, § 23, and three counts of indecent assault and battery on a child under fourteen, in violation of G.L. c. 265, § 13B. On appeal, Avalos claims that the trial judge erroneously restricted defense counsel's cross-examinations of Commonwealth witnesses, preventing Avalos from exposing their bias, prejudice, and motives to lie. We transferred the case from the Appeals Court on our own motion. We affirm the convictions.

Background. The victim in this case is Natasha, the stepgranddaughter of Avalos. The criminal investigation preceding the defendant's indictment originated after Natasha's mother, Diane, discovered **989 and read a "diary" FN2 belonging to Natasha. Natasha received the diary, and wrote in it, when she was in the eighth grade. Diane found the diary in 2004, when Natasha was in the ninth grade, while unpacking from a move they made.

In the diary, Natasha answered several questions posed by the book; after one question, "Have you ever been sexually abused?" she wrote, "Yes." On other pages, Natasha had written "unflattering" descriptions of Diane. Natasha also wrote that she would "flirt" with boys; that she wanted a boy friend; that she "cuddled" with a boy; that she "needed to forgive herself for keeping so many secrets, and lying"; that she had forged her mother's name, causing Diane to beat her; and that she could tell her grandmother "everything."

After discovering the diary, Diane confronted Natasha, angered primarily by what Natasha had written about her rather than by what she had written about being sexually abused. Natasha appeared nervous and upset, and later became ill. The two went to the Chelsea police station where Natasha filed a report of sexual abuse.

Before trial, the Commonwealth filed a motion in limine to exclude the contents of the diary. At the hearing on the motion, defense counsel stated that he intended to use the diary in his defense of the case. In particular, he intended to ask Natasha whether she had ever "characterized herself or thought of herself as a flirt," and, if she answered, "No," to introduce a portion of the diary in which she described herself as "flirtatious." He also stated that he intended to introduce statements in the diary showing Natasha's "wanting to have a boyfriend" in support of his theory that some of the abuse that she blamed on Avalos had actually occurred, consensually, with a boy friend. He further intended to introduce the portion of the diary describing Diane as, in his words, "a big pain in the ass." Finally, he argued that Natasha's writings in the diary were "directly relevant to her credibility and her lifestyle," especially the writings describing herself as a flirt, as a liar, and as someone who wished she had a boy friend.

The judge ruled that in opening statements, the attorneys could mention only the question and answer from the diary regarding sexual abuse. She reasoned that "whether Natasha thinks of herself as a flirt or as a liar or what she wants with respect to her boyfriend and her position with respect to her mother that it's in the diary is not germane to any issue before the jury." The judge reserved ruling on the Commonwealth's motion in limine beyond the opening statements, asking each attorney to "approach the sidebar before he seeks to offer any of that during trial."

The Commonwealth's first witness was Natasha, who was sixteen at the time of trial. She testified that Avalos sexually molested her over the course of several years, beginning when she was six or seven years old, and ending when she was about twelve. She testified that on different dates, Avalos indecently touched her, and made her engage in specific sexual acts with him. Natasha also testified that her first oral report of the abuse occurred in a conversation with a classmate, when Natasha was in the ninth grade. The report occurred at the high school she was attending before Natasha and Diane moved, and before Diane discovered the diary.

On cross-examination, defense counsel spent much of his time highlighting inconsistencies in Natasha's account. He asked how she could remember so many details from events that occurred years earlier, why she did not "call out" for her grandmother when Avalos touched her at his house, and why she chose, in the ninth grade, to tell the classmate about incidents that occurred much earlier. He also elicited testimony from Natasha that her mother was angry with her after reading the diary, and that at the time Natasha was writing in the diary, she did not consider herself to be a completely truthful person.

Defense counsel also asked if the diary contained a question about people Natasha felt she could "tell anything at all to." The judge sustained an objection by the Commonwealth, ruling that defense counsel could ask about the content of the diary only if Natasha testified in a manner that was inconsistent with those writings. Defense counsel proceeded accordingly, and Natasha testified that she felt she could tell her grandmother "anything," but had not told her grandmother about the sexual abuse. The judge later sustained objections when defense counsel asked whether Natasha had trouble with lying during that period; whether she had ever forged her mother's signature; and whether her mother had ever struck her.

The Commonwealth then called Diane to the stand. She explained that she met Avalos when she was about thirteen, and that Avalos later married her mother, Lucilla. She also testified that Avalos was alone with Natasha on several occasions over many years. Finally, she described finding Natasha's diary, reading it, becoming upset and angry, and taking Natasha to the police station.

On cross-examination, defense counsel asked Diane about a period around 2001 when Avalos moved to Florida for a few months, and Lucilla later joined him. He asked whether Avalos moved without Lucilla because "they weren't getting along." Diane testified that to her knowledge, that was not the reason, and that she was "under the impression that he was going to buy a house and they were going to move in there." On further questioning about the marriage between Lucilla and Avalos during that period, Diane testified that it was doing both fine and not fine "on occasion." She also denied that Avalos chose to move to Florida because Diane prevented his daughter from a prior marriage from visiting him.

The judge sustained objections to a series of questions posed to Diane about statements written by Natasha in her diary: whether Natasha had described herself as a liar; whether Natasha had described Diane as "rude and crude"; and what Diane read that caused her to be angry.

On the third day of trial, Avalos took the stand. He denied touching Natasha inappropriately in any way. He also testified that at one time, a boy friend of Diane lived with Diane and Natasha. Avalos then testified that he eventually moved to Florida to "put an end to" problems he was having with Diane. The problems arose, he said, when Diane attempted to prevent his daughter from staying with him for a week.

Defense counsel asked if Avalos was also having marital difficulties with Lucilla at the time, and the Commonwealth objected on relevance grounds. At sidebar, defense counsel argued that he wished to show that Lucilla believed Avalos was seeing another woman, that Lucilla may have told Natasha the same, and that Natasha may have then become biased against Avalos. The judge sustained the objection, saying, "You need something that's a little bit more concrete and not totally speculative." Defense counsel did not pursue this line of inquiry further, but later elicited testimony from Avalos that Diane had told him (in 2001) that, "I was going to be sorry I left her mother in the future."

In closing, defense counsel argued that Natasha and Diane were not credible witnesses, noting that they cried during direct testimony but not during cross-examination. He attacked details of Natasha's testimony; for example, he argued that it would make little sense for Avalos to commit a sexual assault while his wife (Lucilla) was somewhere in the house. He also gave his broader theory of the case, arguing that when Diane angrily confronted Natasha about the contents of the diary, Natasha blamed Avalos for a sexual assault to appease Diane.

The jury returned a verdict of guilty on all the indictments.

Discussion. Avalos argues that the judge impermissibly restricted his ability to cross-examine Commonwealth witnesses to demonstrate bias, prejudice, and a motive to lie. He contends that at several junctures, the judge prevented him from exploring Avalos's marital problems with Diane's mother, Lucilla; Natasha's and Diane's knowledge of these marital problems; Natasha's relationship with Diane; the details of the confrontation between Diane and Natasha about the diary; Diane's relationships with men; Natasha's truthfulness; and Natasha's "dreams... of having a relationship."

If he had been allowed to explore those avenues, Avalos argues, he would have been able to prove his theory of the case: that when Diane angrily confronted Natasha about the diary, Natasha blamed Avalos for a sexual assault to diffuse Diane's anger. Blaming Avalos would have effectively shifted Diane's attention, he contends, because Diane was angry at Avalos for causing problems in his marriage to Lucilla (Diane's mother). Avalos also argues that he could have undermined Natasha's credibility by introducing portions of the diary where Natasha called herself a "liar," and might even have shown that the entire assault was the figment of Natasha's imagination, rooted in a desire to have a boy friend.

"Cross-examination of a prosecution witness to show the witness's bias or prejudice is a matter of right under the Sixth Amendment to the Constitution of the United States and art. 12 of the Declaration of Rights of the Commonwealth." *Commonwealth v. Allison*, 434 Mass. 670, 681, 751 N.E.2d 868 (2001). "If 'on the facts, there is a possibility of bias, even a remote one, the judge has no discretion to bar all inquiry into the subject'"

Nonetheless, "determining whether the evidence demonstrates bias...falls within the discretion of the trial judge." We also have held that "a judge does have discretion to limit cross-examination concerning possible bias when further questioning would be redundant," where there has been such "extensive inquiry" that the bias issue "has been sufficiently aired...The burden of showing an abuse of that discretion, an abuse that must be shown on the trial record, rests on the party claiming it, in this case Avalos."

For the reasons that follow, we conclude that the judge did not impermissibly restrict Avalos's ability to cross-examine witnesses and present his defense.

Second, Avalos argues that he was prevented from cross-examining Natasha and Diane to establish that they knew about the marital problems between Avalos and Lucilla. There was no abuse of discretion because the issue was "sufficiently aired." Defense counsel was permitted to ask Natasha four questions on this subject; she denied any knowledge of the reasons for the separation between Avalos and Lucilla. The judge sustained only two objections, preventing defense counsel from asking, "She Lucilla was pretty mad at your grandfather for leaving her, wasn't she?" and "Did she ever discuss with you any feelings that she had about the fact that your grandfather had left her?" Natasha had already denied knowledge of their marital problems in nearly identical questions; further questioning on the subject was therefore unnecessary.

Third, Avalos argues that he was prevented from probing the relationship between Natasha and Diane. The trial record reflects otherwise. Defense counsel was able to explore the relationship sufficiently. As Avalos concedes, Natasha testified that her relationship with Diane "wasn't perfect." She also agreed that she sometimes "thought Diane was rude and crude and negative," and conceded that sometimes she "wanted to be free as a bird, and not have Diane around her." Defense counsel was also permitted to ask Diane whether, in the diary, Natasha called Diane "rude," "crude," and "hateful."

Finally, Avalos argues that the judge erred in preventing defense counsel from establishing that boy friends of Diane might have had the opportunity to commit the crimes. He is incorrect. At the hearing on the motion in limine, the judge never excluded evidence of Diane's boy friends. During trial, the judge repeatedly allowed testimony that a boy friend of Diane lived with her and Natasha. Objections were sustained only when Avalos testified that Diane and Natasha later lived "with another boyfriend," and when defense counsel asked, "Was that the same person who had been living with Diane previously or a different person?" This was not an abuse of discretion.

In sum, Avalos had ample opportunity to cross-examine Natasha and Diane for the purpose of laying the groundwork for his argument that Diane was angry, and that Natasha named Avalos to diffuse that anger. Defense counsel was prevented from asking only whether Diane ever struck Natasha and which other diary writings had angered Diane. Each of these questions would have created a trial-within-a-trial on collateral issues. Excluding those lines of inquiry was not an abuse of the judge's discretion.

Conclusion. Avalos was granted adequate license to cross-examine Commonwealth witnesses as to their bias and to present evidence supporting his defense. The judge's rulings were well within her discretion and did not infringe on Avalos's rights under the Sixth Amendment and art. 12. We affirm the convictions.

So ordered.

CASE QUESTIONS

1. What is the crime charged in this case?
2. How does the defendant claim that his right to cross-examination was unfairly limited?

3. Did the court rule that the defendant's right to cross-examination was unfairly restricted? Explain.
4. What does the court mean when it says that the issues concerning the defendant's marital problems were "sufficiently aired"?
5. Did the trial judge unfairly restrict the defendant's cross-examination of Natasha and her relationship with her mother? Explain.

ETHICAL CONSIDERATION: SHOULD YOU ASK THE DEFENDANT IF HE COMMITTED THE CRIME?

Many paralegals are surprised to learn that defense attorneys normally do not ask their clients if they committed the offense. There are several reasons they do not ask, and a defense paralegal should be aware of them. Suppose the attorney asks if the client committed the crime with which he was charged? In conference, the client admits that he did commit the crime. Later, however, the client informs the attorney that he wants to take the stand and testify that he did not commit the crime. The attorney is now in a very awkward ethical situation: If she allows the client to testify, she knows that he will be committing perjury. The attorney has taken a sworn oath not to permit any perjury or other fraud on the court. On the other hand, the attorney also has a sworn oath to protect the interests of her client. If she tells the judge that the client is committing perjury, she will open her client to additional charges. Attorneys attempt to avoid this dilemma by not asking the client if he committed the crime. It is safer for all concerned if the attorney does not know. The defense paralegal must behave in a similar way. Besides the potential ethical problem, the paralegal might make herself a witness in a perjury case if the defendant says one thing to her then contradicts it on the stand.

✔ Paralegal To Do List

For the defense paralegal:

- Does the juror administrator release information about the jury panel prior to selection? If so, get as much information about the panel as possible. See if the client knows any of the people on the panel.
- Does the juror administrator give out a questionnaire to the panel members? Get a copy of the blank questionnaire to see what questions are asked.
- Research what the maximum sentence is for each charge against the defendant and keep it in the client's file. The client will want to know, and it may come in handy during sentencing.

For the prosecution paralegal:

- Has all discovery been served in the case, including any new information that has come to light through pretrial investigation?
- Is the defendant represented by an attorney? If so, find out what you can about him/her. What are the attorney's strengths and weaknesses?

- If the defendant is pro se, alert the attorney. This could mean that the defendant may hire an attorney at the last moment or worse, that the defendant will conduct the trial alone.

- Have all basic fact sheets been prepared for each case? The prosecutor may end up presenting a lot of guilty pleas on calendar call day and a basic factual overview for each case will be very helpful.

Chapter Summary

The accused in a criminal prosecution is protected by numerous rights set out in the United States Constitution. The Sixth Amendment to the Constitution creates many of these rights, including the right to trial by jury, the right to a public trial, and the right to be represented by an attorney. However, the Constitution is silent on many of the practical aspects of these rights. The Constitution does not say how many jurors should be seated in a trial, nor does it state whether the jurors should reach unanimous verdicts. For these details, one must turn to the United States Supreme Court. In its many decisions applying the Sixth Amendment as well as other Amendments, the Court has interpreted the Constitution as requiring a jury trial whenever the defendant is facing a potential sentence of six months or more in custody. The actual number of jurors seated on a case can range from six to twelve. In a trial with twelve jurors, unanimous verdicts are not required. The U.S. Supreme Court has also interpreted the Constitution as requiring unanimous verdicts only when there are six jurors. When the defendant cannot afford an attorney and he is charged with a felony, an attorney must be appointed to represent him. Courts can provide legal services in the form of public defenders or private attorneys on a court-appointed list. In addition to these rights, the defendant has the right to confront the witnesses against him. On a practical level, this means that the defendant or his attorney is permitted to cross-examine the state's witnesses. The defense also has the right, but not the obligation, to present evidence and witnesses on its own behalf.

WEB SITES

Administrative Office of the Federal Courts
www.uscourts.gov

Arizona State Court System
www.azcourts.gov

Legacy of Gideon v. Wainwright—U.S. Department of Justice
www.justice.gov/atj/gideon

Legal Information Institute—Right to Counsel
www.law.cornell.edu/wex/right_to_counsel

Maryland State Court System
www.courts.state.md.us

Michigan State Appellate Defender Office and Criminal Defense Resource Center
www.sado.org

Missouri Court System
www.courts.mo.gov

Pennsylvania State Court System
www.pacourts.us

Sixth Amendment Right to Counsel—U.S. Printing Office
www.gpo.gov/fdsys/pkg/GPO-CONAN-1992/pdf/GPO-CONAN-1992-10-7.pdf

The American Bar Association
www.americanbar.org/aba.html

West Virginia State Court System
www.courtswv.gov/court-administration/administrative-office.html

Wisconsin Court System
www.wicourts.gov

REVIEW QUESTIONS

1. The U.S. Supreme court has interpreted the Sixth Amendment to require jury trials only when the defendant is facing a term of six months or more. Fashion an argument supporting this conclusion. Why six months? Why not one month or twelve months?

2. Although states do not have to provide twelve-person jurors or require that the jurors be unanimous in their verdicts, most states do so. Why?

3. Does the press have a greater right to attend a trial than the average citizen? Frame an argument in support of the right of the press. Frame an argument against the right of the press.

4. The U.S. Supreme Court has rules that a defendant cannot be tried before a jury while he is wearing prison clothes. These are clothes, usually brightly colored jumpsuits, that declare that the defendant is in custody. Might a jury make a negative assumption against a defendant simply because he is wearing such clothes? Explain your answer.

5. In cases where a defendant is violent during his trial, he is often restrained or removed from the courtroom. How lenient should the court be before removing the defendant? Isn't it just as damaging to handcuff or gag the defendant as it is to remove him from the courtroom?

6. You have read that cross-examination has been called one of the great tools for the discovery of the truth. Why? What is it about cross-examination that assists or detracts from the search for truth? Does cross-examination allow an attorney to put words in the mouth of a witness, or does it allow the attorney to probe for bias and lies? Explain your answer.

7. During the course of a trial, the prosecutor is barred from even mentioning that the defendant has not refuted a single allegation made against him. Why? Why do the courts extend the right of the defendant to remain silent to cover any comments made by the prosecutor or state's witnesses?

8. In a prosecution, the state must prove the defendant's guilt beyond a reasonable doubt. Should there be a sliding scale for different situations? For instance, in cases where the defendant has confessed to the crime, does it make sense to have the same standard of proving the defendant's guilt as in cases where the evidence against him is less? Explain.

QUESTIONS FOR REFLECTION

1. Why doesn't the Constitution do a better job of spelling out the details? Why didn't the Founding Fathers give some direction about how many jurors should be required in a trial or whether unanimous verdicts were mandatory? James Madison tried to get some very specific rights included in the Bill of Rights. His original draft contained more than twenty amendments. However, a majority whittled them down to ten and made them less specific. Is there an advantage to being vague about some of these rights? Explain.

2. Why is it so important that no one communicate with the jurors during the case? What if a juror overhears something about the case while he is having lunch? Should he communicate that information to the other jurors? What if this information is something the jurors would like to know (e.g., that the defendant confessed to the crime) but the confession was obtained unconstitutionally and cannot be used in the trial? Shouldn't the jurors know this fact? Wouldn't it affect their verdict? Explain your answer.

3. When jurors cannot reach a verdict, they are referred to as a hung jury. Sometimes, before a judge declares a mistrial and dismisses the jury, he will deliver a speech to the jury called the "dynamite charge." This charge to the jury tells them that they are there to do a job (i.e., to reach a verdict) and that they better resolve their differences and come up with one. Is this an appropriate charge to give to a deadlocked jury? Should the judge simply let them go and put the defendant and the state through another trial? Or should the judge make the jurors stay until they reach a verdict, no matter how long it takes? What if a member of the jury goes into the jury room and before deliberations declares that no matter what the rest of them decide, she will not vote guilty for any reason because she has religious objections to judging her fellow man? Should that juror's vote be discounted and the defendant convicted on the votes of the remaining jurors? Is this a situation that we, as a society, must simply accept because of the very nature of jury trials? Explain your answer.

4. In cases where the defendant is facing trial and has only prison clothes to wear, what should be done? Why not try the defendant in prison clothes? Couldn't the judge simply give the jury an instruction to disregard what the defendant is wearing and instead focus on the facts of the case? If the state is obligated not to try the defendant in prison clothes, why isn't the state required to buy him a brand new suit for his jury trial?

5. In the trial of Charles Manson, at one point, Manson leaped from the defense table and tried to climb the judge's bench. He was forcibly restrained and removed from the courtroom. He then listened to the trial in his holding cell. In cases where the defendant is charged with a violent crime, wouldn't it make more sense to have him watch the proceedings by closed-circuit television? Is there some reason why the U.S. Supreme Court is so concerned about having the defendant present? Why does the Constitution insist that the defendant be allowed to confront the witnesses against him?

6. In some countries a defendant is presumed guilty until proven innocent. Should the United States adopt this standard? Why or why not?

7. When the defendant raises a defense, he does not have to prove it beyond a reasonable doubt. He simply has to present enough evidence to make it an issue; then the state must disprove it beyond a reasonable doubt. Does this make sense? Should there be a point when the burden should shift to the defendant to prove his part of the case? Why or why not?

8. In what other situations do you believe a criminal trial should be closed to the public? What about rape cases?

9. Are there times when the trial is too public? The Supreme Court has said that public attendance ensures fairness, yet many of the people who closely followed that particular case came away with a much lower opinion of the criminal justice system. Why? Does television coverage help or hurt the trial? Does it matter if you approach the argument from the defendant's perspective or the state's perspective?

KEYWORDS AND PHRASES

Jury trial	Speedy trial demand
Felony	*Gideon v. Wainwright*
Misdemeanor	Public defender
Jury tampering	Court-appointed attorney
Hung jury	Pro se defendant
Mistrial	Trial de novo
Cross-examination	Serious offense
Term of court	

PRACTICAL APPLICATIONS

1. Does your state allow six-person juries? Locate the statute that provides the answer. If your state does allow six-person juries, for what kinds of cases may that number be seated?

2. Does your state allow jurors to reach nonunanimous verdicts? Locate the statutes that provide the answer. If your state does allow nonunanimous verdicts, how many people can dissent from the majority before the jury is considered a hung jury? For example, can the jury return a verdict of 11–1, 10–2, or 9–3?

3. Does your county or state provide public defenders for an accused, or does it rely on an appointed list. Contact your local superior court clerk's office (or similarly named office) for the answer.

4. Contact the local clerk's office and find out when the next criminal trial is scheduled. Attend the trial and take notes about what happens.

5. Contact the local prosecutor's office and ask if it ever petitions the court to close a trial (or some portion of it) to the public. If it has, under what circumstances does it make such a request?

6. Talk to a local newspaper reporter about what guidelines, if any, he or she uses to report on big cases. Do reporters ever ask the prosecutors or judges about information those individuals think should not go into the story? Do they normally do a big article about the case the week or weekend before jury selection begins?

7. Contact a local criminal defense firm and see if they use paralegals in their criminal defense work. Talk to a paralegal and find out what he or she does in such cases. Does the paralegal assist in the investigation? Does he or she interact with the client? Does he or she draft motions? Does the paralegal ever speak with defense witnesses? If so, what procedures does he or she follow when speaking with them?

8. Review the facts in the *Kline* case (Appendix). Scenario: The police request to meet with Christine after Doug's body is found. She has already spoken with them on at least two occasions. This time, the police ask her to come to headquarters. Christine says that she will come only if her attorney comes with her. Does she have the right to make such a precondition? According to your reading of the chapter, can the attorney accompany her into the interrogation room?

NOTES

1. *State v. Armfield*, 214 Mont. 229, 693 P.2d 1226 (1984).
2. *McKeiver v. Pennsylvania*, 403 U.S. 528, 91 S.Ct. (1976).
3. *Lewis v. U.S.*, 518 U.S. 322, 116 S.Ct. 2163, 35 L.Ed.2d 590 (1996).
4. *Baldwin v. New York*, 399 U.S. 66 (1970).

5. *Codispoti v. Pennsylvania*, 418 U.S. 506, 94 S.Ct. 2707 (1974).

6. *Richmond Newspapers, Inc. v. Virginia*, 100 S.Ct. 2814 (1980).

7. *Estes v. Texas*, 381 U.S. 532 (1965).

8. *Globe Newspaper Co. v. Superior Court*, 457 U.S. 596, 102 S.Ct. 2613 (1982).

9. *Press Enterprise Co. v. Superior Court (Press Enterprise I)*, 464 U.S. 501 (1984).

10. *Press Enterprise Co. v. Superior Court (Press Enterprise II)*, 478 U.S. 1 (1986).

11. *Nebraska Press Assn. v. Stuart*, 427 U.S. 539 (1976).

12. *Bridges v. California*, 314 U.S. 252 (1941).

13. 448 U.S. 555 (1980).

14. *Williams v. Florida*, 399 U.S. 78, 90 S.Ct. 1893, 26 L.Ed.2d 446 (1970).

15. *Foundations of Modern Jurisprudence*, William Seal Carpenter, 1958, page 114.

16. *The Grandeur That Was Rome*, J.C. Stobart, 4th Edition. 1961.

17. *Apodaca v. Oregon*, 406 U.S. 404, 92 S.Ct. 1628, 32 L.Ed.2d 184 (1972).

18. 441 U.S. 130, 139, 99 S.Ct. 1623, 60 L.Ed.2d 96 (1979).

19. *Maryland v. Craig*, 497 U.S. 836, 110 S.Ct. 3157 (1990).

20. *Maryland v. Craig*, 497 U.S. 836, 110 S.Ct. 3157 (1990).

21. 5 J. Wigmore, Evidence § 1367, p. 32 (J. Chadbourn rev.1974).

22. *Illinois v. Allen*, 397 U.S. 337, 90 S.Ct. 1057, 25 L.Ed.2d 353 (1970).

23. *Estelle v. Williams*, 425 U.S. 501 (1976).

24. 386 U.S. 213, 87 S.Ct. 988, 18 L.Ed.2d 1 (1967).

25. *Doggett v. United States*, 5 U.S. 647, 112 S.Ct. 2686, 120 L.Ed.2d 520 (1992).

26. *Barker v. Wingo*, 407 U.S. 514, 92 S.Ct. 2182, 33 L.Ed.2d 101 (1972).

27. 412 U.S. 434 (1973).

28. *Unites States v. Marion*, 404 U.S. 307 (1971).

29. *Smith v. Hooey*, 393 U.S. 374, 89 S.Ct. 575, 21 L.Ed.2d 607 (1969).

Chapter 13

THE TRIAL

Chapter Objectives

At the completion of this chapter, you should be able to:

- Explain the basic layout of a jury trial courtroom
- Describe the steps in a jury trial from jury selection through closing arguments and jury charges
- Explain how jury selection proceeds
- Describe the basic steps used to admit evidence
- Compare and contrast direct examination with cross-examination
- Explain how a jury deliberates and reaches a verdict

I. Introduction

In law, few moments are more dramatic than the return of the jury with a verdict. In this chapter, we examine the various phases of the trial, beginning with the layout of the courtroom and concluding with the verdict.

II. The Layout of the Courtroom

All courtrooms where jurors hear a case share the same components. No matter how different a courtroom may appear at first, each courtroom has these elements in common.

Exhibit 13-1
Diagram of the courtroom

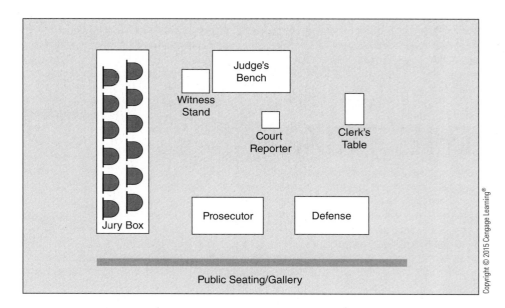

A. The Jury Box

The jury box is where the jurors who have been selected to hear the case sit. Previous chapter have already discussed how most juries are composed of twelve people, although in many states, juries of six are permitted on certain kinds of cases. The jury box often contains more than twelve chairs. Extra chairs are usually added to accommodate alternate jurors. (See "Jury Selection" below.) The jury box is usually set off from the rest of the courtroom by a low partition or a railing, something to indicate that this space is reserved for the jury. No one else is allowed to enter the jury box. The same applies for the jury room.

B. The Jury Room

The jury room is usually a small room off the courtroom where the jury retires to deliberate in the case. This room is often small and frequently windowless. The sparse accommodations encourage the jurors to make up their minds quickly. No televisions, radios, or newspapers are permitted in the jury room. There are no particular rules about how this room should look. The only requirement is that it be private. No one other than members of the jury are allowed in the room while the jury is deliberating. The court bailiff is allowed to bring in the evidence for the jury to review during deliberations. The bailiff also brings refreshments. When the bailiff is present, all discussions about the case cease. They resume once the jurors are alone.

C. The Witness Stand

The witness stand is located next to the judge's bench. The witness stand is a small, enclosed area, where the witness sits while testifying. In modern courtrooms, it is common to have a microphone positioned there so that the witness's testimony can be heard throughout the courtroom. The witness stand is located next to the jury box so that the jurors have a clear view of the witness. The jurors, after all, will be evaluating the witness.

D. The Judge's Bench

The judge sits on an elevated platform called the bench. It is the highest point in the courtroom, emphasizing the judge's authority. The bench is positioned so that the judge has a clear view of the jury box, the witness, and the attorneys. Many modern courtrooms have laptop computers at the bench, allowing the judge to pull up legal references from a CD or to view the transcript of the case in real time through a link to the court reporter's machine. When the judge calls the attorneys up for a midtrial discussion, it is called a "bench conference." See Exhibit 13-2 for an overview of judicial positions across the United States.

E. Clerk's and Court-Reporter's Tables

Spaces for the court reporter and the **clerk** of court are usually located in front of or on the far side of the bench. The court reporter occupies a central position in the courtroom because he or she must take down every word spoken in the courtroom. A table or other space is usually set aside for the clerk of court. This space is usually empty during a trial. The clerk is normally present only for calendar calls or sentencing hearings, when the details of a case must be recorded in the pertinent file.

clerk
A court official who keeps court records, official files, etc.

F. Attorneys' Tables

Two tables are set aside for the attorneys. One is reserved for the prosecution; the other, for the defense. Tradition has it that the table closest to the jury is for the prosecution. The one farthest from the jury box is for the

BULLET POINT
Courtrooms in which jury trials are held have many of the same elements.

Exhibit 13-2

Percent change in total number of judges, 1987–2004

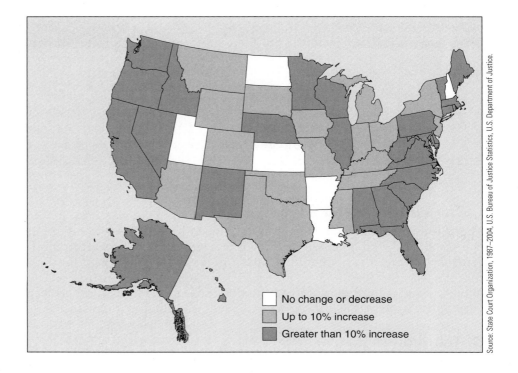

Source: State Court Organization, 1987–2004, U.S. Bureau of Justice Statistics, U.S. Department of Justice.

☐ No change or decrease

☐ Up to 10% increase

■ Greater than 10% increase

defense. There are no rules specifying this arrangement, and occasionally, a defense attorney will get to court early and take the prosecutor's table, just to rattle him. These kinds of mind games and strategies occur at every phase of a trial.

Modern courtrooms have computer hook-ups at these tables, similar to the arrangements at the bench. The attorneys, like the judge, can connect their computers directly to the court reporter's terminal and see a live transcript of the trial as it is generated. This can be very useful for reviewing testimony.

G. The Bar

The courtroom is the area consisting of the jury box, witness stand, bench, and attorneys' tables. This is separated from public seating by some form of partition. This area is commonly referred to as the **bar**, and it sets off the public section of the courtroom—the gallery—from the area reserved for the parties. In some states, the area where the trial actually occurs is still called the "arena," recalling the days of trial by combat.

A courtroom's layout is meant to emphasize the solemnity of the proceedings. In older courthouses, these rooms are elegant, formal settings and can be quite beautiful. They have seen thousands of trials and

bar

The part of some courtrooms where prisoners stand.

INSIDER'S VIEWPOINT

When the defendant is in restraints or chains

"You certainly are trying to get him to not call attention to it. In death penalty cases, they always start off with them wearing the (Tazer) belt [a device that shocks the wearer into unconsciousness when a deputy pushes the trigger]. Then we have to beg to get it off. In each instance, I've always stressed to my client, if he continues to show some good faith and good behavior in front of the judge, the judge is going to think that the Sheriff is unreasonable for putting that on him. Then, if it's going to be on him no matter what we do, you try to get your client not to call attention to it. In terms of argument, I think it's hard, if the jury's going to see it, it's hard to argue that it means anything other than what it means, that the judge is saying that he's unruly."

—W. Keith Davidson, Criminal Defense Attorney

hundreds of lawyers. Their empty seats are mute witness to closing arguments that brought tears to the eyes of jurors and the solemn occasions when a judge sentenced a defendant to death or a lengthy prison term. They have also seen the jubilance of a defendant who was found not guilty and all of the many dramatic moments that make up a criminal trial.

III. Beginning the Trial

Before the trial begins, the state and the defendant must **join issue**. This involves the defendant entering his plea of "not guilty" on the indictment. Joining issue signifies that the parties are still in conflict, which will be resolved by the trial. Once the defendant has officially entered his plea, the selection of the jury begins.

join issue
When a lawsuit gets past the preliminary stages and issues are clearly laid out.

A. Voir Dire, or Jury Selection

Jury selection is also known as **voir dire**. This is a French term meaning "look-speak," which is what happens during jury selection. Members of the community are brought into a courtroom and asked questions. Their responses determine whether they will serve on the jury. For the sake of clarity, we will refer to this group of citizens as the "panel." The term *venire* also is often used, but *panel* will serve just as well. The attorneys listen to the responses and take this opportunity to look over the panel members. See Exhibit 13-3 for a summary of jury duty.

voir dire
(French) "To see, to say"; "to state the truth." The preliminary in-court questioning of a prospective juror to determine competency.

Exhibit 13-3
Fewer persons exempted from jury duty

Jury Duty exemptions have historically been allowed for professions, such as doctor, lawyer, elected official, clergymen, and active military personnel. Exemptions were also given for medical or child care reasons. To expand the jury pool, 12 states eliminated exemptions from 1987 to 2004. By 2004, less than half of the states acknowledge any grounds for jury duty exemption.

General jurisdiction trial court felony and civil jury trial regulations, 1987-2004

| | Number of states | | | |
Jury requirement and case type	1987	1993	1998	2004
General jurisdiction trial court 12-person jury requirement*				
All felony cases	45	45	45	45
All civil cases	26	28	26	25
General jurisdiction trial court unanimous jury requirement*				
All felony cases	49	49	49	49
All civil cases	20	20	20	20
Exemptions from jury duty allowed	35	27	27	23

Note: Data collected from all 50 states.
*States that use a 12-member, unanimous jury typically allow for a smaller, non-unanimous jury with the consent of both parties.

Source: State Court Organization, 1987–2004, U.S. Bureau of Justice Statistics, U.S. Department of Justice.

BULLET POINT
The first step in a jury trial is jury selection, or voir dire.

INSIDER'S VIEWPOINT

Investigating the jury pool

"Not all counties will give out a list of the people called in for jury duty, but some will. The next thing I do is sit down with the attorney and figure out what type of jury we want. If the defendant is elderly, for example, you want people on your jury who are going to realize that if this man gets convicted, he is going to spend the last years of his life in prison. You want jurors who can appreciate that.

"When I get a juror list, I start my digging. Sometimes, you can go to the Census records; they'll let you have some information. There's also a place on the web where you can type in their social security number and find out the last five places that they've lived. You can go to the Clerk's office and find out if they've ever been sued or charged with a crime or had a bad child custody case. If you know what you're doing, you can find out a lot about people."

—Ben Smith, Private Investigator.

1. Qualifying for Jury Service

For many years, the only people who could serve on juries in this country were men who owned real property in the county where the trial occurred. This system changed over time, gradually admitting women, then non-propertied individuals, and then minorities. Today, there are few restrictions on jury service, except those set out in Exhibit 13-4.

Jury administrators use a variety of means to locate panel members. They do not simply rely on the list of registered voters in the county, although this still forms an important source of names. In addition to the list of registered voters, jury administrators also obtain names from tax and motor vehicle records.

The manner in which a jury is selected to serve on a criminal case can vary considerably from state to state, even from county to county within the same state. No matter what method is used, the basic process remains the same: the panel is asked *general questions* and *individual questions*.

2. General Questions

During the general questions phase of selection, all of the panel members are asked a series of broad-based questions to make sure that all members are qualified to serve on the panel. These questions may come from the judge or the attorneys or both.

The questions in Exhibit 13-5 are designed to make sure that all members of the panel are legally authorized to sit on a jury and meet the minimum requirements.

In some states, attorneys question the potential jurors; in other states and in federal court, the judge asks all of the questions. When the attorneys ask the general questions, they may begin with a few preliminary comments to the panel. The prosecutor, who usually goes first, may explain what jury selection is all about.

- Must be a citizen of the United States
- Must be a resident of the county where the trial is to take place
- Must not be a convicted felon

Exhibit 13-4
Modern requirements to serve on a jury

- Are all members of the panel citizens of the United States?
- Are all panel members residents of this county?
- Has anyone here ever been convicted of a felony?

Exhibit 13-5
Common general questions of the panel

"Ladies and Gentlemen, my name is John Doe, and I am an assistant district attorney. I'm going to ask you some questions this morning, and if you have a positive response to a question, just raise your hand and I'll jot down your juror number. Later on, we'll have a chance to ask some individual questions, and at that time, I may follow up on the question you raised your hand about. I'd like to tell you that the purpose of these questions isn't to embarrass or humiliate anybody. These questions are designed to make sure that we get a fair and impartial jury. My first question for the panel—and remember that if this applies to you, just raise your hand—my first question is Does anyone here know the defendant personally?"

Once the prosecutor has finished with his or her general questions, the defense attorney has the opportunity of addressing the panel and asking general questions. The attorneys have very different general questions for the panel. For instance, if the case involves the sale or possession of narcotics, the prosecutor may ask the general question "Does anyone here believe in the legalization of cocaine?" The defense attorney in that case, however, may ask the question "Is there anyone here who would always believe a police officer over any other kind of witness?"

a. Juror Questionnaire Many of these general questions are answered by the panel members in juror questionnaires that are filled out prior to arriving for jury duty. This greatly speeds up the process of qualifying the panel members for service. If a panel member responds on the questionnaire that he has moved to a different county, this fact can often be caught prior to his arrival in the courtroom and save some of the valuable time it would take to remove him and send him home. These questionnaires often ask for more information than just the statutorily required questions. One such question will be whether the panel member has ever been the victim of a crime (because this question is almost always asked during jury selection). The panel member's responses to these questions are provided to the attorneys shortly before jury selection. This basic information greatly speeds up the process of jury selection because the attorneys can simply review the responses instead of asking every panel member the same series of questions.

b. General Questions and Jury Education During general questioning, the attorneys may also take the opportunity to subtly educate the jury about the law in the state. They do this through the way that they phrase certain questions. In a case involving the carrying of a concealed weapon, the prosecutor might ask, "Do any of you have a statutorily required concealed handgun permit?" The prosecutor is not concerned about the panel members' answers; he just wants the jury to start thinking about the fact that there is a statute requiring a permit for carrying a handgun. In the same case, the defense attorney might ask the panel, "Does anyone here have a handgun at home for self-defense?" Again, the fact that a panel member does or does not own a gun is not really the issue. Twelve of these people will sit on the jury in this case, and the defense attorney wants to get them thinking about self-defense and handguns.

3. Individual Questions

Following general questions, the attorneys are allowed to ask questions of the individual members of the panel. The prosecutor again goes first, followed by the defense attorney. Here, the attorneys may follow up on any issues raised during general questions or ask questions about a response on the jury questionnaire. In addition to gathering more information, attorneys see this as an opportunity to establish a personal rapport with the panel members, which may carry over to the trial for those panel members who end up as jurors on the case. Attorneys also want to see how interested the panel members are, whether they make eye contact, and the myriad other body language clues that people give off. Jury selection often boils down to a gut instinct appraisal of a person. It is often more art than science. Barring any openly hostile panel member, whom the attorney will eliminate, in the end, the attorney removes people often based on nothing more than a negative feeling.

B. Jury Selection

Jury "selection" is really a misnomer. Jurors are not selected. Instead, from a panel of potential jurors, panel members are eliminated until twelve jurors remain. This process of removing panel members is called "striking a jury." When a panel member is struck, this person will not serve on the jury. In a typical example, forty-two panel members are brought into a courtroom and questioned. Thirty panel members are removed, or struck, leaving twelve. These are the jurors who will sit on the case.

Members of the jury panel can be removed in one of two ways. A panel member can be removed by a *peremptory challenge* or can be *challenged for cause*.

1. Peremptory Challenges

A **peremptory challenge** is the right of a party to strike a panel member for almost any reason. One of the attorneys may not like the way that the person answers a question, or the attorney just has a gut feeling about the panel member. Except in certain instances (set out below), peremptory strikes do not have to be justified. Both sides are given a specific number of peremptory strikes. When they have used up their strikes, they are not permitted to remove any more panel members. In many jurisdictions, the defense generally has twice as many peremptory strikes as the state.

In the example set out above, where forty-two panel members are brought to the courtroom and questioned, the defendant would often have the right to remove twenty; the state, ten. After these thirty people are removed, twelve jurors are left.

peremptory challenge
A challenge to a potential juror that is the automatic elimination of that person from the jury by one side before trial without needing to state the reason for the elimination.

challenge for cause

A formal objection to the qualifications of a prospective juror.

a. **The Batson Case** In the last two decades, the unlimited power of peremptory strikes has been curtailed. In a landmark decision by the United States Supreme Court, *Batson v. Kentucky*, 476 U.S. 79 (1986), the Court ruled that peremptory strikes could not be used by a prosecutor to remove all African American panel members simply because of their race. The Court reasoned that because the court system is a function of the government funded by the government, it could not be used to further discriminatory practices.

The *Batson* decision has been extended to other types of discriminatory peremptory strikes. For instance, *Batson*-type decisions have forbidden striking panel members on the basis of any racial affiliation, as well as gender-based discrimination. Many commentators have predicted that the peremptory strike may become a thing of the past.

2. Challenge for Cause

A member of the panel may also be removed or challenged for "cause." A **challenge for cause** is the process of removing a panel member because the person demonstrated some prejudice to one of the parties or indicated that he or she will not follow the judge's instructions.

When either the state or the defense uncovers any of these attitudes, that party normally moves to have the panel member dismissed for cause. A dismissal for cause does not count against a side's number of peremptory strikes.

C. Striking the Jury

Once all of the questioning has been completed, striking the jury begins. Different courts handle this process in different ways, but two generally accepted procedures are used to strike a jury. In the first scenario, the clerk of court reads the panel member's name and he or she stands. The prosecutor either strikes this juror (using one of his peremptory strikes) or accepts the juror. This is done aloud. The prosecutor may say, "The state strikes this juror" or, a little more politely, "The state excuses this juror." This eliminates the panel member from serving on the jury. If the state accepts, the defendant has the right to strike the panel member. If the

Exhibit 13-6

Common reasons that a panel member may be dismissed for cause

> - Cannot, for religious or other reasons, render a verdict in a criminal case;
> - Announces that he cannot be fair to the defendant or to the state;
> - Has an opinion about the guilt of the defendant that will not change no matter what he hears during the course of the trial;
> - Knows the defendant personally and would be unable to put those feelings aside as a juror in the case;
> - States that he will not follow the judge's instructions.

defendant accepts, this person becomes a member of the trial jury. Each panel member's name is called until twelve jurors have been selected. If either the prosecutor or the defendant uses all of his allotted peremptory strikes, he has lost the right to strike any more panel members.

THE ROLE OF THE PARALEGAL: HELPING TO STRIKE THE JURY

The reactions of the various members of the panel are extremely important during jury selection. While the attorney may be focused on one individual, another person several rows back may make a face, cross his arms, or do something to indicate his strong views on a subject. A good attorney knows that he cannot see everything that goes on in jury selection, so he often brings a paralegal with him. The paralegal is instructed to take notes on the reactions of any of the panel members to questions. Did someone react very strongly to a question, even if the question was not directed at him? Later, when the attorney begins to strike the jury, he will compare his own impressions with the notes of the paralegal.

Paralegals should look for body language cues during jury selection. When people think that they are not being observed, their body language can be very telling. Look for strong reactions, especially among members of the panel who are not being asked any questions at the time. Do they cross their arms or turn away? Do they scoff or look impatient? Such a person is sending a signal that he or she is not sympathetic to the attorney asking questions and should be a serious candidate for removal.

1. Silent Strikes

Some courts prefer a system referred to as "silent strikes." Under this system, the attorneys do not announce their acceptance or rejection of the panel member aloud. Instead, they simply mark the panel list with their strikes. The list is handed back and forth between each attorney until twelve jurors have been selected. Many judges prefer the silent strike because it moves the jury selection along at a faster pace and causes less inconvenience for the panel members.

2. Alternate Jurors

In some trials, alternate jurors are selected. Alternates are used when the trial is going to be lengthy. Having backup jurors helps when one of the main jurors becomes ill and can no longer continue. In most cases, alternates are not necessary because jury trials usually last only a day or two. However, in complex cases that may drag on for weeks, selecting alternates is a good idea. Alternate jurors sit in the jury box during the trial but do not retire with the jury at the end to deliberate. Only the twelve main jurors are allowed to deliberate. Alternate jurors are normally released at this point.

a. Selecting Alternate Jurors The process of selecting alternate jurors is just like the process for selecting the twelve main jurors. Once the twelfth

BULLET POINT
In most cases, alternate jurors are not selected.

juror has been selected, the judge announces that selection will continue for one or two alternates. The prosecutor and the defendant have the right to use peremptory strikes to eliminate panel members, just as they did when selecting the main jury. Once accepted, these alternate jurors join the main group in the jury box. Jury selection has now concluded.

D. Preliminary Instructions to the Jury

Once a jury has been selected and seated in the jury box, the rest of the panel is excused. The people who were not selected to serve on the jury return to the jury administration area where they may be released from any further jury duty or be called to sit on another panel in a different case.

> **When Do Jurors Make Up Their Minds?**
>
> Jurors are allowed to discuss the case with each other only when deliberations begin at the end of the trial. They are specifically instructed not to make up their minds about the case until the end of the trial. Whether most jurors actually abide by these rigid constraints is another matter. Study after study has shown that jurors tend to start making up their minds at the beginning, not the end, of the trial. Often, they decide who should win sometime during the opening statements (discussed below).

The jurors who have been selected to sit on the trial are now given badges identifying them as jurors in an on-going trial. They are given pads and pencils to use in taking notes. The judge also gives them some preliminary instructions, such as informing them about their duties in the trial. One of the most important instructions that a judge gives the jurors is that they must wait until the end of the case before they reach a decision about the defendant's guilt or innocence. The judge tells them that they will hear from witnesses and will consider physical and other evidence. They are not permitted to discuss the case with anyone, including each other, until the case is over. This prohibition about discussing the case helps to ensure that the only information the jury receives about the case comes from the courtroom, not from other sources. To that end, jurors are instructed to avoid reading newspaper accounts of the trial or watching television coverage about the case, if there should be any.

In addition to these instructions, the judge also tells the jury that neither the attorneys nor the witnesses in the case are allowed to speak with them outside the courtroom. Most attorneys take this instruction so seriously that they will not even greet a juror if they see one in the hallway during a break in the trial. Jury tampering is a serious offense, and because most attorneys are ethical people, they try to avoid even the appearance of impropriety. On lunch breaks from the trial, attorneys often avoid a restaurant where jurors from the case are eating. Jurors are told that if anyone attempts to approach them and discuss the case, they should report this fact to the judge immediately.

THE ROLE OF THE PARALEGAL: WARNING WITNESSES

The paralegal should make sure that the witnesses in the case understand just how important it is that the jurors are left alone. The witnesses should be told that the case is not to be discussed anywhere within ear-shot of a juror. Judges take a dim view of any attempts to communicate with a juror, no matter how well-meaning or subtle such influences might be. In addition to bringing down the wrath of the judge, jury tampering is a felony in most states.

E. Jury Sequestration

In some trials where the publicity is intense, jurors may be sequestered. **Sequestering** a jury means that the jurors are effectively cut off from outside information. At the end of the day, they are not allowed to go home. Instead, they stay at a local hotel. They are not permitted to watch television or to read newspapers. Jury sequestration is expensive, and most cases do not require such extreme measures to ensure the defendant's right to a fair and impartial jury.

sequester
To keep a jury from having any contacts with the outside world during a trial.

■ **BULLET POINT**
It is rare to sequester a jury for the entire length of the trial.

F. Opening Statements

Once jury selection has been completed, the twelve jurors (and any alternates) are seated in the jury box. The jurors are then sworn in by the judge. The oath they are given has them swear to try the case fairly. After being sworn, the judge turns to the prosecutor and asks the fateful question, "Mr. Prosecutor, are you ready to proceed?" At this point, the prosecutor stands before the jury to give an opening statement.

An opening statement is the attorney's outline of the trial. In an opening statement, an attorney tells the jurors what they can expect to happen during the trial. The attorney explains how the trial will proceed, what witnesses will take the stand, and what evidence will be presented. Unlike what often happens on television, an opening statement is not a persuasive argument. It is intended only as a vehicle for the attorneys to explain what the jury will see. The attorney shows how this testimony and evidence establishes a certain conclusion. For the prosecutor, this conclusion is always the guilt of the defendant. Once the prosecutor has completed his opening statement, the judge asks the defense attorney if he wants to make an opening statement. Although attorneys can waive opening statements, a good attorney never does. Attorneys know that the jurors begin to make up their minds during the opening statements. A good opening statement may sway the jury to their side. The defense attorney often explains what the defendant's version of the case is or what the defense will be or simply asks the jury to keep an open mind until the defense gets an opportunity to present its case.

■ **BULLET POINT**
The opening statement is used by both the prosecutor and the defense attorney to explain what their view of their case is and what the jury members can expect to see in the trial.

IV. The Case-in-Chief

Once opening statements are concluded, the government then presents its case. This is often referred to as the government's **case-in-chief**. This is where the prosecution presents its entire case, attempting to prove the defendant guilty beyond a reasonable doubt. The prosecutor accomplishes this proof through witnesses and evidence. Witnesses will testify about what occurred. Evidence to support the state's case is introduced while the state's witnesses are testifying. This questioning is referred to as "direct examination."

case-in-chief
The main evidence offered by one side in a lawsuit.

direct examination
The first questioning in a trial of a witness by the side that called that witness.

A. Direct Examination

At the beginning of the trial, the prosecutors call a witness to the stand and question this person. This is referred to as **direct examination**. The first witness for the state is important. If this witness does well, the state's case will start out on the right footing, building a momentum that may carry the case all the way through to jury deliberations. A witness who does poorly at this point may have the opposite effect.

The witness is called to the stand and sworn in. In some states, the prosecutor swears in the witness by asking the witness to raise his/her right hand and repeat the oath "Do you solemnly swear or affirm that the testimony you are about to give will be the truth, the whole truth, and nothing but the truth?" In other states, the judge, the court clerk, or the bailiff swears in the witness. The days of the witness swearing by placing her hand on the Bible are long gone in most jurisdictions. When the witness answers yes to the oath, the witness takes a seat in the witness stand and the questioning begins.

The attorney usually asks the witness some preliminary questions: name, address, and other identifying information. The purpose of these questions is to introduce the witness to the jury, but these questions also serve another important function: They get the witness accustomed to talking. Most people are terrified of speaking in public, and most witnesses share that apprehension. Asking easy questions first usually helps the witness overcome some initial nervousness and allows him to settle down and concentrate. Now the serious questioning can begin.

On direct examination, the attorney builds his case. By asking questions and receiving answers, the attorney brings out the facts for the jury. Facts can be developed only through witnesses or evidence. Unlike TV lawyers who often stop in the middle of the trial to address the jury, real lawyers can develop their cases only through direct examination of their witnesses. This makes the role of the witnesses crucial to the presentation of the case.

1. What Order to Call the Witnesses?

When numerous witnesses will testify during the trial, how does the prosecutor decide which one to call first? The usual method is to call a witness who can testify about the facts in chronological order. Following this method means putting up the witness who can explain the events in the case as they happened. Chronological order is usually a good idea but not always possible or practical. The state also wants to start out with a strong witness, one who will make a positive impression on the jury and help to build momentum. Momentum is rarely discussed in textbooks, but is a very real factor in a trial. The state's first witness must be someone who can clearly present the facts of the case and someone whom the jury will like. When the prosecutor has a witness that he knows will make a bad impression with the jury, he will not use this witness first, unless he has no other choice. Such witnesses are usually sandwiched between other stronger witnesses to minimize their impact. The order in which the prosecutor calls his witnesses depends a great deal on who the witnesses are. Jurors tend to dislike codefendants who are testifying against each other because they have negotiated a "deal" with the state. Such a witness would not be used first in a trial. Instead, the prosecutor might call the investigating officer or detective first.

▪ THE ROLE OF THE PARALEGAL: PREPARING WITNESSES FOR TRIAL

A paralegal often helps the attorney prepare the witness for trial. Preparation is not the same thing as coaching. To coach a witness is to tell the witness what to say. This is unethical and may be illegal, especially if the testimony is perjury. Preparing a witness focuses on the presentation of the case instead. Before trial, witnesses are often given a run-through of what testifying will be like and are asked the same questions that they will later be asked during the trial. The paralegal should go through the direct examination questions with the witness several times so that the witness becomes more comfortable with the issues.

The paralegal should also tell the witnesses to look at the jury when they are testifying. Attorneys often help a witness make eye contact by standing close to the jury box on direct examination. People have a tendency to look at the person asking questions. By standing close to the jury box, the attorney is attempting to force the witness to look in the jury's general direction. Later, we will see how the attorney's tactics will change dramatically on cross-examination of witnesses.

The witnesses who testify on direct are generally considered to be friendly to that side. State's witnesses often include police officers, coroners, and victims. Because these witnesses are friendly to the side calling them, attorneys are not allowed to ask leading questions on direct examination. The witness must testify in his own words. A leading question suggests an answer. Compare the two questions in Exhibit 13-7.

2. Introduction of Evidence During Direct Examination

In a previous chapter, we discussed the crucial role that evidence plays in the trial. Here, we will discuss the role of evidence as it is introduced during witness testimony. Physical evidence is introduced at the trial through witnesses. Whenever an attorney wants to have the jury consider any evidence, it must first be admitted at trial. **Admission of evidence** follows a set pattern. Here, we will show how a murder weapon is introduced at trial. The procedure involved is the same for most kinds of physical evidence, whether it is a murder weapon or a handkerchief.

Admission of evidence
A decision by a judge to allow evidence to be used by the jury.

Exhibit 13-7
Leading v. nonleading questions

- Did you then go down the hallway? (Leading)
- Where did you go? (Not leading).

---

a. Laying the Foundation Before any evidence may be considered at trial, it must be shown to have some relevance to the issues in the case. Asking *foundation questions* shows this relevancy. A foundation question is designed to show how the evidence is relevant and legally admissible at trial. The attorney asks these foundation questions of a witness. As the witness answers the questions, the relevancy of the evidence is established.

b. Admitting Evidence Once the foundation questions have been asked, the attorney then asks the judge that the evidence be admitted. Admitting evidence is very important. Until evidence has been admitted at trial, it cannot be used, shown to the jury, or referred to. The judge is the only person qualified to admit evidence in a trial. Before deciding to admit the evidence, the judge will ask the opposing attorney if he has any objections. An attorney cannot object to evidence simply because he does not like it. He must have some legal ground for his objection. The most common objection to any evidence is "improper foundation." This means that the opposing attorney is objecting to the evidence because the proper series of questions were not asked or that some legally significant connection between the evidence and the case has not been established.

Attorneys often do extensive research on foundation questions to make sure that they ask the correct questions to get certain kinds of evidence admitted. The foundation questions to get a written contract admitted into evidence are different from the questions that must be asked to admit a kilo of cocaine.

The opposing attorney may also object to the evidence on grounds other than improper foundation. Evidence may be relevant to the issues at trial and yet still be excluded. The opposing attorney may object to the evidence because it is unfairly prejudicial to his client. Autopsy photographs of murder victims, for example, although relevant to the issues in a murder case, may be excluded because they are unduly gruesome and may prejudice the jury against the defendant.

Exhibit 13-8

Laying the foundation for the admission of a murder weapon

ATTORNEY: Mr. Witness, I'm handing you what has been marked as State's Exhibit Number One. Can you identify it?
WITNESS: Yes, this is the handgun that I retrieved from the scene.
ATTORNEY: Does it have any identifying marks?
WITNESS: Yes, when I picked it up, I put an evidence tag through the trigger guard, and then placed it inside a plastic evidence bag.
ATTORNEY: Has this gun been altered or tampered with in any way since the time that you first recovered it?
WITNESS: No, it looks exactly the same.
ATTORNEY: Your Honor, at this time, I move to admit State's Exhibit Number One into evidence.

Once the opposing attorney has entered his objection to the evidence, the judge makes a ruling. If the judge rules that the evidence is admissible, then the attorney can refer to it in open court. Admitting evidence has another important aspect. All admitted evidence will go with the jury during its deliberations, meaning that the jury will have an opportunity to examine it closely in the jury room. If the judge rules that the evidence is inadmissible, then the evidence cannot be used at trial, nor can the attorney refer it to.

B. Cross-Examination

Once the direct examination has been completed, the attorney asking questions sits down. Now the opposing attorney has the opportunity to question the witness. The right to **cross-examine** witnesses arises under the Sixth Amendment. The Constitution guarantees the defendant's right to question the state's witnesses. Later, we will see that this right also applies to the prosecutor, who may cross-examine the defendant's witnesses.

cross-examine
To question an opposing witness during a trial or hearing.

Cross-examination is very different from what just occurred on direct examination. When the defense attorney cross-examines the state's witnesses, he often attempts to discredit the witness's testimony or attempts to use it to develop points favorable to the defense. When the prosecutor cross-examines the defendant's witnesses, his main goal is to discredit the witness, show a bias, or develop points helpful to the state. Cross-examination is both an art and a skill. Attorneys spend many years developing good cross-examination skills. On television, cross-examination is usually shown because it is more dramatic than direct examination. A good cross-examination is like playing a game of chess. The attorney springs traps on the unsuspecting witness, making the witness commit to increasingly exaggerated versions of his story until the entire testimony cracks or making the witness look foolish. However, not all attorneys are good at cross-examination. A bad cross-examination can just as easily make the attorney look foolish.

The ground rules of cross-examination are very simple. Unlike direct examination where the witness is the star of the show and where the questioning attorney wants the witness to appear calm, to make eye contact with the jury, and to make a good overall impression, the attorney on cross has an entirely different goal in mind. The opposing attorney wants the witness to appear less credible. Instead of standing quietly at the podium, gently asking questions of a witness, on cross-examination, the attorney takes center stage. Attorneys often move around the courtroom during cross-examination. Being asked questions by someone who is moving around is a little unnerving. When the attorney moves around, the jurors naturally watch her, not the witness. But this is not the only tactic used by an attorney on cross. During direct examination, the attorney asking questions faced many restraints. That is not true of cross-examination. The first rule of cross-examination is that leading questions not only are permitted, but also are an excellent idea.

> **Bad cross-examination question:**
>
> "So, are you pretty sure the light was red?"
> Answer: "I've never been surer of anything in my life."
>
> **Good cross-examination question:**
>
> "So, you aren't really sure what color the light was, are you?"
> Answer: "Uh…no."

Another ground rule of cross-examination is that the attorney will try to limit the witness to yes or no answers. The attorney does this by the way he or she phrases the question, unlike television, where the slathering defense attorney is practically standing in the witness box as he screams, "Yes or no, yes or no! What is your answer?" In the real world, once witnesses answer the question, they have the right to explain it. Good witnesses, like seasoned police officers and expert witnesses, for example, know this and use it to their advantage. A good cross-examiner does not keep the witness from explaining an answer. Instead, a good cross-examiner asks questions that do not require any explanation and yet still make the witness look less than credible.

1. Cross-Examining the Sensitive Witness

In Hollywood movies, the defense attorney subjects the anxious victim, already at the end of her emotional tether, to a savage cross-examination. He screams; he yells; he pounds the table. We watch the victim struggling on the stand and cannot help but think that for the victim, the cross-examination is like being victimized all over again. In reality, the screaming and yelling would never be allowed. Most good defense attorneys do not yell and scream at victims, not the least because the judge would not allow it. For another reason, the prosecutor would object to such treatment of the victim, and finally, perhaps most important, it does not make sense. On cross-examination, the defense attorney does not want to do anything that will make the witness more sympathetic to the jury. The defense attorney may be trying to show how this particular victim's story does not stand up to scrutiny or that the witness is not believable for some other reason. The one thing that the defense attorney does not want to do is to make the jury feel sorry for the victim. When we watch such episodes on television, we hate the defense attorney badgering the poor witness. Defense attorneys do not want the jury to hate them. They want the jury on their side. This is not to say that it never happens. Occasionally, an inexperienced defense attorney might try yelling and screaming to rattle a witness. But most judges do not put up with such shenanigans in their courtrooms.

Attorneys often use cross-examination as a way of developing a particular theme of the trial. The defense attorney may emphasize the fact that there is some question about the eyewitness identification of the defendant, for example, or establish some evidence of alibi. In many cases, the defense will not put up any witnesses; so the only way to develop these issues is by cross-examination of the state's witnesses.

a. Cross-Examination of Child Sexual Assault Victims

The defendant's Sixth Amendment right to confront the witnesses against him is not absolute. The witness does not always have to testify on the witness stand directly in front of the defendant. Witnesses may testify behind screens or over closed-circuit television or from somewhere else in the courtroom. No matter what technique is used, however, the defendant or his attorney always has the right to see and to cross-examine the witness.

For instance, in a child abuse case, the child-witness can be allowed to testify by closed-circuit, one-way television. The child can be in another room and testify there, avoiding having to take the stand in a courtroom in front of the defendant and many other people.[1] In many states, the child victim may testify at a small table set up in the courtroom, one more proportional to the child's size. Seated at this table, while playing with a doll or coloring a picture, the child answers questions posed by the prosecutor. Cross-examination of such a witness is often difficult for a defense attorney. Generally, the judge gives the defense attorney strict guidelines about the kinds of tactics to be used on the child, and the judge does not permit the same kind of intense cross-examination as he might permit with an adult witness.

In other situations, the Supreme Court has ruled that the child may not have to testify at all if the child's statements about abuse fall into one of the clearly established exceptions to the use of hearsay.[2]

2. Cross-Examination and Hearsay Evidence

Generally, the Supreme Court has held that **hearsay** statements may not be admitted at trial in place of a live witness's testimony. As we have already seen in the chapter on evidence, *hearsay* refers to an out-of-court statement offered to prove a particular point in the trial. It usually occurs in the following way: A witness testifying on the stand says, "Well, I turned around and there was Bill. Bill told me that the defendant was the one who had done it."

In recent decisions by the Supreme Court dealing with similar scenarios, the Court has consistently assumed that all hearsay statements are "witnesses against" a defendant within the meaning of the Sixth Amendment.[3] As such, hearsay statements are not permitted, and the person who made the statement ("Bill" in our example) would have to take the stand and testify. His statement about the defendant could not be relayed through another witness because the defense attorney would want to cross-examine Bill about his statement, not the person relaying what Bill said.

hearsay
A statement about what someone else said or wrote or otherwise communicated.

■ **BULLET POINT**
Hearsay is generally not admissible during a trial, but there are exceptions.

THE ROLE OF THE PARALEGAL: RELUCTANT WITNESSES

Many witnesses do not want to testify at the trial. Often, they will ask the paralegal if they can simply write out an affidavit or testify by deposition instead. The answer to these questions is almost always no. The defendant has the right to confront the witnesses against him. That means that the witnesses must testify at trial. Depositions, affidavits, and other devices are not permitted—in most situations—in a criminal trial.

C. Re-direct Examination

Once the defense attorney has finished questioning the state's witness on cross-examination, the prosecutor has the opportunity to question the witness again on re-direct examination. This questioning is usually limited to points raised on cross-examination and is not designed to allow the state's attorney to go through the entire direct examination again. The attorney will ask questions to help clear up any apparent contradictions the witness may have made during the cross-examination.

THE ROLE OF THE PARALEGAL: RE-DIRECT EXAMINATION

Most witnesses do not know about re-direct examination. Witnesses should be informed that if something is brought up on cross-examination that is not favorable or they have made a statement that is confusing, the attorney will be permitted to ask further questions on re-direct examination to clear up this matter. All witnesses have seen courtroom dramas where a witness has been badgered into giving a yes or no answer and not given the opportunity to explain the contradiction. The paralegal should inform the witness that the attorney who originally questioned her on direct will have a chance to question her after she has been cross-examined. The attorney will make sure that these points are cleared up. Telling a witness about re-direct will make her feel less anxious and may prevent her from volunteering information during cross-examination that she believes will help the case but may, in fact, cause serious problems.

D. Resting the Government's Case

Once the prosecution has presented all of its witnesses and evidence, the state rests its case. This means that the state has no more evidence to present and is ready to submit the case to the jury. This has several practical consequences. Resting the case means that the state is now opening up the case to the defense. It also means that if the state has left out some important evidence or failed to prove the defendant's guilt, the state cannot present any more evidence on the point. The state's case is over and must rest on what has been presented, unless an opportunity for rebuttal arises. (See "Rebuttal" later.)

Often, before prosecutors rest their case, they review the essential elements of the charge, confirm the evidence that has been admitted in the case, and double-check that all witnesses who could have testified have actually done so. After confirming these details, the prosecutor makes the announcement, "Your Honor, the prosecution rests."

E. Motion for Directed Verdict

When the state rests, the defense attorney almost always makes a motion for a **directed verdict**. A motion for directed verdict requests the court to enter a verdict of not guilty on some or all of the charges against the defendant. Normally, the court grants such a motion only when there is no evidence to support the charge.

There are many reasons why the court may grant a motion for directed verdict. The state's witnesses may have failed to identify the defendant as the person who committed the crime. A witness may have changed his testimony on the stand. Because each trial is different and there are many reasons why a court might grant such a motion, most defense attorneys believe that they have nothing to lose by asking for a directed verdict. If the judge fails to grant the motion, the defense is no worse off. The case will still go to the jury for a verdict. However, if the judge grants the motion for directed verdict, the case will not go to the jury and a verdict of not guilty will be entered for the defendant. Some defense attorneys argue any possible reason why a directed verdict should be entered. The judge applies the following legal standard in determining whether to grant the motion: Has sufficient evidence been presented by the state to justify leaving the case in the jury's hands? If so, then the judge must deny the motion for directed verdict. In most prosecutions, motions for directed verdict are unsuccessful.

Following the denial of the motion for directed verdict, the defense then has the opportunity to present its case.

F. Defense Case-in-Chief

The defense is under no obligation to present any evidence or testimony. In fact, there are very good reasons for the defense to stand mute. The defendant may not make a very good witness. Other defense witnesses also may not make a good impression on the jury.

Despite the judge's instructions to the jurors that they may not make any negative inference against the defendant for failing to testify, it is human nature to want to hear the defendant proclaim his innocence. However, in most situations, putting the defendant on the stand is not a good idea. If the defendant takes the stand, he will then be subject to cross-examination. The defense attorney must decide whether the defendant will make a good witness on cross-examination. If the prosecutor is a particularly good cross-examiner, putting the defendant up on the stand could prove to be a disaster.

There is another reason for the defense attorney's reluctance in putting the defendant on the stand. In many jurisdictions and in federal

directed verdict
A verdict in which the judge takes the decision out of the jury's hands.

■ **BULLET POINT**
When a defendant brings a motion for a directed verdict, he or she is saying that the state has failed to present sufficient evidence to meet its burden.

court, when the defendant takes the stand, he places his character in evidence.

1. Defendant's Character in Evidence

Placing the defendant's *character in evidence* means that one of the questions that a prosecutor may ask the defendant involves his criminal record. Up to this point, no mention of the defendant's prior criminal record has been allowed. In fact, had the prosecution even alluded to the defendant's prior criminal record, an immediate mistrial would have been declared. However, this limitation disappears when the defendant takes the stand and puts his character into evidence. The prosecutor can ask the defendant about his prior convictions in front of the jury, with the obvious devastating consequences. Although the defendant's prior record is usually not relevant to the proceedings, the prosecutor would like the jury to hear that the defendant has prior convictions.

In some states, the defendant can be asked about his criminal record only when he has said something on the stand that puts his character into evidence. Prosecutors are always watchful for this opening. In states where it is harder to put the defendant's character into evidence, the prosecutor must wait for the defendant to give him an opening. When a defendant makes a statement such as "I've never been in trouble with the law" or "I've never been convicted," the prosecutor can bring up the defendant's prior criminal record.

The defense attorney must weigh all of these factors before deciding to put the defendant on the stand. If the defendant has an unpleasant personality or could easily be lead astray on cross-examination, the best course is not to put the defendant on the stand. (See "What If the Defendant Insists on Testifying?" below).

2. Other Defense Witnesses

The same factors that militate against putting the defendant on the stand may apply to a lesser extent with other defense witnesses. Character witnesses are another example of a double-edged sword for the defense. In the first instance, it may be difficult to locate character witnesses for some defendants. In the second instance, character witnesses are very limited as to what they may say on the stand. Other witnesses may be just as difficult to locate. There may not be any witnesses to the event other than the defendant and the police officer who arrested him.

3. What If the Defendant Insists on Testifying?

As you can see, the defense attorney has a great deal to think about in preparing a defense. He or she must evaluate many factors before deciding what is the best course. In addition to all of these problems, if the defendant insists on taking the stand, then the attorney has no choice in the matter. The attorney can strongly encourage a defendant to stand mute, but the attorney works for the defendant. If the defendant insists on taking the stand, the attorney may note for the record his strongest possible disagreement; however, the decision is ultimately the defendant's.

4. Presentation of the Defense

If the defense decides to put up witnesses and admit testimony, the defense attorney must follow the same rules as the prosecutor. Witnesses must be sworn in. Foundation questions for evidence must be asked of witnesses. The attorney must restrict his questions on direct examination in the same way that the prosecutor did. Once he has finished with the witness on direct examination, he must allow the prosecutor to cross-examine.

What follows is a mirror image of the prosecution's case, with witnesses testifying and evidence being admitted. Here, the defense attempts to show through its witnesses whatever its theory of the case may be. If the theory is that the police have arrested the wrong person, the identification of the defendant as the perpetrator will be attacked. If the defense is alibi, the defense will present witnesses to testify that the defendant was somewhere else at the time of the crime. As the defense attorney attempts to build his case, the prosecutor will try just as hard to tear it down on cross-examination.

THE ROLE OF THE PARALEGAL: GOING TO THE SCENE

Most attorneys visit the physical scene of the crime to get it fixed in their minds. Knowing what the scene looks like is often helpful when questioning witnesses, either on direct or on cross-examination. It is a good idea for you to visit the scene, too. If the defendant was charged with driving under the influence of alcohol and the police gave him roadside sobriety tests, it may be helpful to see where these tests were carried out. Visiting the scene may be as simple as driving by the place where the defendant was pulled over by the police. If the police made the defendant walk a straight line on the steep side of the road shoulder, that fact may prove to be important at trial. Many attorneys will request that you not only visit the scene, but also take photographs. When the scene is a public area, taking photographs is usually not a problem. The best method is just to start taking pictures. Most people do not question a professionally dressed person with a camera. If the scene is a private residence or another private place, you should politely ask permission before taking any photographs.

G. Resting the Defense Case

When the defense attorney is finished presenting his case, he will announce that he rests his case. Here, we have an important distinction in the rules governing the state and the defense. At the conclusion of the state's case, you will recall that the defense attorney made a motion for a directed verdict of acquittal. Now that the defense case has rested, the prosecutor is not permitted to make a similar motion. There is no such thing as a motion for directed verdict of guilty. Instead, the prosecutor is given the opportunity of rebuttal.

H. Rebuttal

rebuttal
The act of disputing, defeating, or taking away the effect of acts or arguments.

At the conclusion of the defense case, the prosecution may be given the opportunity to dispute any of the claims raised by the defense. The state does this by calling witnesses in **rebuttal**. The rules for rebuttal are the same as those for the state's case-in-chief. The prosecutor may call witnesses to the stand and present evidence. However, rebuttal is usually limited to the issues raised by the defense. The prosecutor is not allowed to retry his entire case. In some cases, rebuttal is required, as, for instance, when the defendant raises the defense of insanity. (See Chapter 14.) However, when rebuttal is not required, many prosecutors waive it so that the trial can conclude.

I. Closing the Evidence

Once the state and defense have rested their cases, the judge announces that all evidence in the case has been closed. This means that no more witnesses will testify and no more evidence will be admitted for either side. The trial is almost over. Now only the closing argument and jury charge are left. However, before the jury can be instructed about what they are to do during deliberations, a charge conference is normally called.

J. Charge Conference

A charge conference is called at the conclusion of the evidentiary phase of the trial and before closing arguments. Attorneys for both sides of the case and the judge meet in private and discuss which instructions the judge will read to the jury. Jury instructions or jury charges are very important, at least for appeal purposes. Many defendants will base their appeals on the grounds that the judge gave an improper instruction to the jury. Judges like to limit such claims on appeal as much as possible, and one of the best ways to do that is to sit down with the state and the defense and review exactly which instructions the judge will read to the jury. Both attorneys are also given the opportunity to submit jury instructions that they would like the judge to read to the jury. The judge reviews the requested charges, researches the issues involved, and then decides whether to read the proposed charge.

The charge conference often lasts several hours while all the parties attempt to work out differences and objections to particular instructions. While this is going on, the jurors are usually waiting in the jury room, wondering about the delay. When the issues are finally resolved, the attorneys and the judge return to the courtroom and the judge asks the attorneys to give closing argument.

K. Closing Arguments

On television, the prosecutor gives an emotional, gripping closing argument to the jury. She is forceful and persuasive; her argument stirs the souls of the jury with its emotional impact. At the same time, her remorseless logic leaves no other conclusion than the guilt of the defendant. The closing argument is also short enough to fit between commercial breaks. However, the real world of closing arguments is a little different.

The purpose of a closing argument is to summarize the evidence and to help the jury reach a decision—a verdict. In a closing argument, the attorney is allowed to argue, to make deductions, to offer emotional appeals, and to reach unlikely or even unreasonable conclusions. There are very few restrictions on what can be done during a closing argument. An attorney is not allowed to refer to inadmissible evidence or to misstate the evidence that was admitted at trial. The attorney cannot offer her personal opinion about the case, but short of that, the attorney is given broad freedom to say just about anything. Some attorneys use closing argument like a grand finale performance, pulling out all the stops to convince the jury to rule their way. In past decades, some closing arguments would last for days. In the early part of the twentieth century, some attorneys would actually receive applause when they finished their arguments.

The length of a closing argument can vary considerably, but they are not as long as the arguments of decades ago. In general, the more evidence and witnesses in a case, the longer the closing argument. However, many courts impose a one-hour limit on the closing argument. A party can request additional time if the case is complex. Unlike television closings that last about three minutes, real closing arguments must encompass a great deal of information. The attorneys summarize the case, pointing out the evidence that was favorable to their side and explaining away or ignoring the evidence that was detrimental. Attorneys often appeal to the jurors' emotions, asking them to send a message to the community with their verdict.

The prosecutor will ask the jury to return a verdict of guilty. The defense attorney will ask them for a not guilty verdict. Despite this difference, the closing arguments are similar. Both closings rely heavily on the evidence. Both refer to the instructions that the judge is about to give the jury. Both ask the jurors to uphold the oath that they took, (i.e., to reach a fair verdict based on the facts of the case). Once the attorneys have completed their closing arguments, the judge gives instructions to the jury.

L. Jury Instructions

The judge's charge to the jurors instruct them on what they are supposed to do in the jury room and what law they are to apply. This is undoubtedly the most boring part of a jury trial. The instructions usually begin, "Ladies and gentlemen of the jury, I charge you that the law in this state is that a person is presumed innocent until proven guilty. . . ." The charge then proceeds with the judge reading various points of law to the jury. This is how jury charges have been done for centuries. Some jury charges will last an entire day—or longer. The jurors, in most states, even in this modern era, are not given a written copy of their instructions. Instead, the judge simply reads to them. Because a jury charge frequently lasts several hours, this monotonous recitation soon becomes excruciatingly dull. The jury charge is a very important phase of the trial, however. The instructions tell the jurors what their purpose is and what they can and cannot do. Most **jury instructions** tell the jurors that they are to retire to the jury room and consider their verdict. They are to weigh the evidence that they have heard and come to a decision. Their decision about the guilt of the defendant must be beyond a reasonable doubt (i.e., a doubt based on reason).

The defense attorney pays close attention to the instructions that are read to the jury because they often form a key part of the defendant's appeal. The prosecutor also listens to make sure that the correct law is being stated so that the defendant will not be able to raise that ground on appeal.

When the judge has completed the charge, he or she instructs the bailiff to escort the jurors out of the courtroom and into the jury room. They are usually instructed not to begin their deliberations until the evidence has been brought to them. Normally, the judge reviews all of the evidence that has been admitted at trial before allowing it to go to the jury room. Once satisfied, the judge has the bailiff take all evidence to the jury room and has the bailiff tell the jurors that they may begin their deliberations. The jurors also are given the original indictment. The judge has instructed them that once they reach a verdict, they must write it down. They may write it on the indictment or on a verdict form provided for that purpose. Now that they are alone, the jurors begin to discuss the case for the first time, exchanging opinions and ideas.

jury instructions
Written explanations of the law normally read to the jurors just prior to them being given the responsibility of considering the case and reaching a verdict.

THE ROLE OF THE PARALEGAL: KEEPING TRACK OF THE JURY INSTRUCTIONS

During the jury charge, one of the things that a paralegal can do to assist the attorney is to keep track of which closing instructions were given and make sure that the judge gave the instructions he said he would give. In the charge conference, the judge clearly stated which instructions these would be, and listing all of the charges and checking them off can be a tremendous help to the attorney.

M. Jury Deliberations

The jurors now have the case. One of the first things they do is to elect one of the members to act as the foreperson. This person generally keeps things organized and acts as the jury's spokesperson when dealing with the judge. The jury may take as much or as little time in the jury room as necessary. Normally, the judge allows the jurors considerable time to reach their decision before he calls them out and makes an inquiry as to how things are going. In most jurisdictions, the verdict must be unanimous—agreed to by all. If even one member of the panel refuses to go along with the majority and they are unable to convince him to change his mind, then the jury foreperson must announce that they are a hung jury. When faced with a hung jury, the judge has no option but to declare a mistrial.

N. Mistrial

Many events can cause a **mistrial**. Declaring a case to be a mistrial means that the judge has determined that the case cannot go on because the jury cannot reach a decision or because something occurred in the case that is prejudicial to the defendant. An order of mistrial simply means that all of the parties act as though the trial never occurred. The state is free to try the case again. This means that all of the witnesses must testify and all evidence must be admitted—everything, in fact, must be repeated as though it never happened.

O. Verdict

While the jury has been deliberating, time has dragged on slowly for both parties. Because the prosecutor's office is usually in the courthouse, she may have returned there to await the **verdict**. The defense attorney and defendant may be waiting in the hallway or break room. If the defendant is in custody, he will wait for the jury in his holding cell, and the defense attorney lingers somewhere nearby. The attorneys go over the case in their minds, thinking they could have done some things differently. They wonder what the jury is doing and why it's taking so long. Conventional wisdom is that the longer the jury is out, the better it is for the defendant. However, no one can predict what a jury is going to do. In the final analysis, many attorneys believe that the jury's verdict is like rolling dice: You never know what you're going to get.

If the jurors reach a unanimous verdict, they write it down and then tell the bailiff they have reached a decision. They do not tell the bailiff what their decision is. Instead, they come back to the courtroom for the announcement. See Exhibit 13-10 for a review of states that continue to require twelve-person unanimous verdicts.

When the bailiff learns that the jury has reached a verdict, he immediately informs the judge. The judge tells the parties to gather in the courtroom and waits until they are all assembled before bringing in the jury from the jury room. Once the jury has filed in, the judge asks the foreperson if the jury has reached a verdict. When the foreperson announces that they have, the judge asks the foreperson for the document showing what verdict they have reached (and to make sure that it is in the correct form). After reviewing the indictment and verdict to make sure that it is legally

---

■ **BULLET POINT**
During jury deliberations, no one is allowed inside the jury room except the jurors.

mistrial
A trial that a judge ends and declares will have no legal effect.

■ **BULLET POINT**
If the jurors are unable to reach a verdict, then the court is forced to declare a mistrial.

verdict
The jury's decision.

Exhibit 13-10

> In the 1970s, the U. S. Supreme Court ruled in two separate cases that a jury could be comprised of as few as six jurors without violating a defendant's right to a fair and impartial jury*. The majority of states permit less than a twelve-member jury for misdemeanor cases†. However, the number of states adhering to a twelve-person jury requirement for all felony cases in general jurisdiction trial courts remained unchanged at forty-five (table 9). Nearly all states from 1987 to 2004 required a unanimous jury decision in felony cases.
>
> *Williams v. Florida, 399 U. S. 78 (1970); Colgrove v. Battin, 413 U. S. 149(1973).
> †Bureau of Justice Statistics, *State Court Organization, 2004* <http://www. ojp .usdoj.gov/bjs/pub/pdfsco04.pdf>.

Source: State Court Organization, 1987–2004, U.S. Bureau of Justice Statistics, U.S. Department of Justice.

sufficient, the judge may read the verdict himself, have the clerk read it, or (in many jurisdictions) ask the prosecutor to read it in open court.

The verdict is then read. This is the most dramatic moment of a trial. "In case of *State v. John Doe*, we the jury find the defendant. . . ." If the defendant is found not guilty, the jury is dismissed, and assuming that the defendant has no other charges pending against him, he is released immediately. If the verdict is guilty, then the trial moves into the final phase—sentencing.

1. Polling the Jury

When the jury reaches a verdict of guilty, the defense attorney has the right to ask that the jurors be polled. Polling means that each juror will be asked if this verdict is his or her personal decision in the case. This means that the judge will ask each juror the following series of questions: "Mr. Juror/Ms. Juror, was this your verdict in the jury room? Is this your verdict now?" Assuming that everyone answers yes to that question, the judge will excuse the jury from any further attendance in the case.

2. Excusing the Jury

Once the verdict has been returned, the jury is told that they are free to discuss the case with anyone. The prohibitions about talking about the case are lifted. The attorneys who tried the case will, in many instances, talk to the jury so that they can learn what the jury thought was important in the case. This is a great way for young attorneys to learn how to improve their performance in the courtroom, assuming that they get forthright answers from the jury.

P. Sentencing and Appeal

In Chapter 15, we will discuss the sentencing and subsequent appeal in a criminal case.

Case Excerpt. Batson Challenges Against the Defendant

STATE V. MCMILLAN, 734 S.E.2D 171 (S.C.APP.,2012) SHORT, J.

Jeremy McMillan appeals his convictions for two counts of murder and possession of a weapon during the commission of a violent crime, arguing the court erred in (1) finding his reason for striking jurors was pretextual; (2) not following this court's order requiring it to hold a hearing to address his motion for remand to reconstruct the record; and (3) not making an evidentiary ruling regarding the State's introduction of prior bad acts because it inflamed the jury. We reverse and remand for a new trial.

Facts

In the early morning of April 29, 2006, McMillan and Toby Fulmore, III, went to a club in Lee County named Mr. C's. Before arriving at the club, Fulmore drove McMillan to his house, where McMillan retrieved a rifle and put it in Fulmore's truck. Fulmore later testified McMillan also had two pistols with him at the time. After the two arrived at the club, a fight broke out, and McMillan shot Patrick Hood and Joshua Lee, killing them both. During the shooting, McMillan also shot and injured nine others. McMillan was indicted for two counts of murder, nine counts of assault and battery with intent to kill, and possession of a weapon during crimes of violence.

A trial was held December 8–11, 2008. At the beginning of trial, the State announced it was only proceeding on two counts of murder (counts one and two) and possession of a weapon during a violent crime (count twelve). At the close of the State's case, McMillan made a motion for directed verdict, which the court denied. A jury found McMillan guilty, and the court sentenced him to life without parole for murder and five years' imprisonment for possession of a weapon during the commission of a violent crime. McMillan's motion to set aside the verdict was denied by the court. This appeal followed.

Standard of review

In criminal cases, the appellate court sits to review errors of law only and is bound by the trial court's factual findings unless they are clearly erroneous. Thus, on review, the appellate court is limited to determining whether the trial judge abused his discretion. An abuse of discretion occurs when the court's decision is unsupported by the evidence or controlled by an error of law.

Law/Aanalysis

McMillan argues the trial court erred in finding his reason for striking juror 34 was pretextual. We agree.

In *Batson v. Kentucky*, 476 U.S. 79, 89, 106 S.Ct. 1712, 90 L.Ed.2d 69 (1986), the Supreme Court of the United States held the Equal Protection Clause of the Fourteenth Amendment to the Constitution of the United States forbids a prosecutor from challenging "potential jurors solely on account of their race or on the assumption that black jurors as a group will be unable impartially to consider the State's case against a black defendant." In *Georgia v. McCollum*, 505 U.S. 42, 59, 112 S.Ct. 2348, 120 L.Ed.2d 33 (1992), the Supreme Court held the Constitution also prohibits a criminal defendant from engaging in purposeful racial discrimination in the exercise of peremptory challenges. Additionally, the Equal

Protection Clause prohibits the striking of a venire person on the basis of gender. When one party strikes a member of a cognizable racial group or gender, the trial court must hold a Batson hearing if the opposing party requests one.

In *State v. Evins*, our supreme court explained the proper procedure for a Batson hearing:

> After a party objects to a jury strike, the proponent of the strike must offer a facially race-neutral explanation. Once the proponent states a reason that is race-neutral, the burden is on the party challenging the strike to show the explanation is mere pretext, either by showing similarly situated members of another race were seated on the jury or that the reason given for the strike is so fundamentally implausible as to constitute mere pretext despite a lack of disparate treatment.

The proponent's reason for striking a juror does not have to be clear, reasonably specific, or legitimate—the reason need only be race neutral. "The burden of persuading the court that a Batson violation has occurred remains at all times on the opponent of the strike." The opponent of the strike must show the race or gender-neutral explanation was mere pretext, which generally is established by showing the party did not strike a similarly-situated member of another race or gender.

"Whether a Batson violation has occurred must be determined by examining the totality of the facts and circumstances in the record." Under some circumstances, the explanation given by the proponent may be so fundamentally implausible the trial judge can find the explanation was mere pretext, even without a showing of disparate treatment. "The trial judge's findings of purposeful discrimination rest largely on his evaluation of demeanor and credibility. Often the demeanor of the challenged attorney will be the best and only evidence of discrimination, and an 'evaluation of the attorney's state of mind based on demeanor and credibility lies peculiarly within a trial judge's province.'" The judge's findings regarding purposeful discrimination are given great deference and will not be set aside by this court unless clearly erroneous. "This standard of review, however, is premised on the trial court following the mandated procedure for a Batson hearing....Where the assignment of error is the failure to follow the Batson hearing procedure, we must answer a question of law. When a question of law is presented, our standard of review is plenary."

During jury selection, McMillan struck five jurors: 27, 34, 72, 138, and 174. The State requested a Batson hearing, asserting "there were twenty-three jurors drawn and the Defendant struck five white . . . males from the jury." Although the court ultimately found McMillan's reasons for striking jurors 27, 34, and 138 were pretextual, McMillan only appeals as to jurors 27 and 34. During the second jury selection, juror 34 was seated on the jury, and juror 27 was seated as an alternate. We find we need not discuss juror 27 because he was never required to serve as a juror; therefore, we only discuss the Batson issue as it relates to juror 34.

In response to the State's Batson motion, McMillan explained he struck juror 34 because someone told him juror 34 "displayed attitudes that he believed to be not consistent with being a good and unfair and unbiased juror in this matter." McMillan also asserted he seated one white male on the jury in response to the State's challenge that he struck five white males from the jury. Responding to McMillan's explanation, the State questioned McMillan's stated reason for dismissing juror 34, arguing:

Unless he can articulate some reason, other than somebody told me he wouldn't be a good juror. I don't see where that would be per-textual [sic] or an excuse. I mean somebody told me he wouldn't be a good juror, well a lot of people tell me if people will be a good juror, but I need to know something about that person. He should have said why would he [sic] be a good juror. What has he said about this case or what's he said about the Defendant or whatever.

Judge Howard King found McMillan's reason for striking juror 34 was pretextual, and therefore, his strike was improper. Following the trial court's quashing of the first jury, McMillan was not allowed to strike juror 34 from the second jury, and juror 34 was impaneled for McMillan's trial.

On appeal, McMillan argues "the State was not required to meet its burden of establishing purposeful discrimination because the trial court effectively placed the burden of disproving pretext on the appellant." He maintains the court failed to follow the Batson requirements set out in *Purkett v. Elem*, 514 U.S. 765, 115 S.Ct. 1769, 131 L.Ed.2d 834 (1995), and *State v. Adams*, 322 S.C. 114, 470 S.E.2d 366 (1996), and the "State simply argued that the defendant had not met his burden of giving a racially neutral reason for the strike."

In *Purkett*, the Supreme Court stated the opponent of a peremptory challenge must first make out a prima facie case of racial discrimination (step one). 514 U.S. at 767, 115 S.Ct. 1769; see also *Adams*, 322 S.C. at 124, 470 S.E.2d at 372 (adopting the standard delineated in *Purkett*). Then, the burden of production shifts to the proponent of the strike to come forward with a race-neutral explanation (step two), and if a race-neutral explanation is tendered, the trial court must then decide whether the opponent of the strike has proved purposeful racial discrimination (step three). *Purkett*, 514 U.S. at 767, 115 S.Ct. 1769. " 'Unless a discriminatory intent is inherent' in the explanation provided by the proponent of the strike in step two, 'the reason offered will be deemed race neutral' and the trial court must proceed to the third step of the Batson process." The Purkett court found the Eighth Circuit Court of Appeals had "erred by combining Batson's second and third steps into one, requiring that the justification tendered at the second step by the proponent be not just neutral but also at least minimally persuasive, i.e., a 'plausible' basis for believing that 'the person's ability to perform his or her duties as a juror' will be affected." 514 U.S. at 768, 115 S.Ct. 1769. The court explained the persuasiveness of the justification does not become relevant until the third step when the trial court determines whether the opponent of the strike has carried his burden of proving purposeful discrimination. Id. "At that third stage, implausible or fantastic justifications may (and probably will) be found to be pretexts for purposeful discrimination." Id. The court found the prosecutor's proffered explanation—that he struck the juror because he had long, unkempt hair, a mustache, and a beard—was race-neutral and satisfied the prosecution's step two burden of articulating a nondiscriminatory reason for the strike because the wearing of beards and the growing of long, unkempt hair, are not characteristics peculiar to any race. Also, in Adams, our supreme court found the explanations given by defense counsel—that one juror was a court reporter and looked "too intelligent," and that another juror knew the judge—were racially-neutral, legitimate reasons for exercising peremptory strikes.

Here, McMillan's stated reason for striking juror 34 was that he had reason to believe the juror would not be unbiased based on his counsel's conversation with members of the Lee County Bar. We find this reason, although questionable, is race neutral. We also find the State, as the opponent of the strike, failed to prove

McMillan's strike was purposeful racial discrimination. Furthermore, the fact that McMillan "used most of his challenges to strike white jurors is not sufficient, in itself, to establish purposeful discrimination." Therefore, we find the trial court erred in ruling McMillan's stated reason for striking juror 34 was not race neutral and in granting the State's Batson motion.

Further, because juror 34 was seated on the second jury, we remand the case for a new trial.

Because we reverse and remand the case for a new trial based on this issue, we need not address the remaining issues.

Reversed and Remanded.

KONDUROS and LOCKEMY, JJ., concur.

CASE QUESTIONS

1. What standard does the appellate court follow in reviewing the actions of the trial court?
2. What is the significance of *Georgia v. McCollum*?
3. What is the proper procedure for a *Batson* hearing?
4. Will the appellate courts second guess the trial judge's findings? Why or why not?
5. Was McMillan's strike of juror 34 racially neutral, and what result did this have on the case?

ETHICAL CONSIDERATION: LICENSING AND CERTIFICATION OF PARALEGALS

In recent years, momentum has been growing across the country to license or certify paralegals in much the same way that accountants, nurses, and attorneys are licensed. A certified paralegal would voluntary submit to the specifications of a particular organization, such as NALA's Certified Legal Assistant program. On the other hand, a governmental body would oversee licensing of paralegals. In states that required it, paralegals would have to obtain a license from the state before they could call themselves "paralegal" or "legal assistant." At the present time, no jurisdiction certifies or requires licensing of paralegals, but that may change in the next few years. For more information on NALA's certification program, visit their web site at www.nala.org.

✔ Paralegal To Do List

For the defense paralegal:

- If you are unfamiliar with the courtroom, visit it before the trial. Does it have:
  - Electric outlets for overhead projectors, laptops, etc.?
  - White boards or easels for charts or diagrams?
  - A screen for computer projections?
- In addition to this, make sure that you know where the bathrooms are. (Everyone will need to know about this.)

- Does this jurisdiction require "pre-labeling" of defense exhibits? Find out from the judge's secretary, and get the right labels.
- Will the attorneys have to prepare a verdict form, or does the judge have one?

For the prosecution paralegal:

- Prepare a chart with the names of all panel members and enough space to make notes under each name as voir dire proceeds.
- Sit with the prosecutor during jury selection and make notes about the panel members during questioning. Watch the people who aren't being questioned. How do they react to certain questions? Note any strong reactions on your chart. Do any of the panel members seem to dislike either attorney?

Note that information prominently.

- Many prosecutors are beginning to see the benefits of using a PowerPoint™ presentation during their closing argument. Prepare a basic PowerPoint™ template that the prosecutor can use during the trial.
- Meet with the witnesses and go over the testimony. Tell the witness what he/she can expect on cross-examination.

Chapter Summary

All courtrooms are designed along the same lines with many of the same features. These features include the bench, the witness stand, the attorneys' tables, and the jury box. All of these features serve specific functions during a trial. The trial itself follows a predictable pattern, beginning with jury selection and ending with the jury's verdict. Regardless of where the trial occurs, the same general rules apply. Although the settings are different, the basic structure of the trial remains the same pattern it has for decades.

WEB SITES

Alaska State Court System
www.courts.alaska.gov/index.html

All Law
www.alllaw.com

Colorado State Judicial Branch
www.courts.state.co.us

Cross-Examination for Prosecutors—National Highway Traffic Safety Administration
www.nhtsa.gov/staticfiles/nti/pdf/811671.pdf

Minnesota Judicial Branch
www.mncourts.gov

Missouri State Court System
www.courts.mo.gov
New York State Court System
www.nycourts.gov/index.shtml
Vermont State Court System
www.vermontjudiciary.org/default.aspx

REVIEW QUESTIONS

1. How many jurors serve on juries in your state? Twelve? Six? Does it depend on the nature of the crime? For instance, in many states, there are only six-person juries on misdemeanors, but twelve on felony cases. Is that true in your state?

2. Why is the state prohibited from calling the defendant to the stand? The state can call any other witness and ask him or her questions. Why not the defendant?

3. Explain jury selection in fifty words or less.

4. Have you ever been called for jury duty? If not, talk to a friend or family member who has. Describe the experience. Were you or your friend/family member selected to sit on a criminal case? If so, what was the crime?

5. Should the juror's instructions be provided in written form to the jury? Can you come up with a reason as to why they should not be provided in writing?

6. What is the significance of the *Batson* decision? Should the reasoning in *Batson* be extended to all kinds of peremptory challenges? Why or why not?

7. Should all forms of peremptory challenges be removed? Why or why not?

8. Explain the different limitations on an attorney depending on whether she is asking questions on direct examination or cross-examination.

9. What is the significance of jury instructions?

10. A verdict means that by their decision, the jury members speak the truth. What does *verdict* mean in regard to the jury's decision in a criminal case? What "truth" are they speaking with their verdict?

QUESTIONS FOR REFLECTION

1. Periodically, cries go out to modify the "system" because the criminal justice system is too lenient or too harsh on criminals. Which particular rules would you change if you had the power to make the change? What effect would your change have on the rest of the criminal justice system?

2. Cross-examination has been called the greatest engine for discovery of the truth ever invented? Do you agree with that assessment? Why or why not?

3. Our criminal justice system is built on the principle of equally matched adversaries pitted against each other. Some argue that having two sides present opposing viewpoints and perspectives on the same evidence is the best chance to get at the truth. Do you agree? Is there a better way to get at the truth? Explain your answer.

KEYWORDS AND PHRASES

Jury box
Jury room
Witness stand
Judge's bench
Bench trial
Joining issue
Voir dire
Venire
Jury selection
Peremptory challenges
Challenge for cause
Striking the jury
Jury sequestration
Opening statements
Case-in-chief
Direct examination

Leading questions
Admissible evidence
Laying the foundation
Cross-examination
Re-direct examination
Motion for directed verdict
Venue
Rebuttal
Charge conference
Closing arguments
Jury instructions
Jury deliberations
Mistrial
Verdict
Polling the jury

PRACTICAL APPLICATIONS

1. Locate your state statute regarding juries. Are unanimous juries the only types permitted in criminal cases, or does your state authorize 11-1, or even 10-2 decision in criminal cases?

2. Contact your local courthouse and see when the next jury trial is scheduled. It does not matter if the trial is a civil or criminal trial because once a trial has begun it is often difficult to tell them apart. Keep in mind that many trials settle or plea-bargain before they begin. You may have to go several times before you actually get to see a trial. How is it different than what you expected? Did you have some preconceived ideas about trials that proved to be incorrect? What were they? Where do you suppose those preconceived ideas came from?

3. Review the *Marvel* case (Appendix) and consider the following jury selection problem. The jury panel has been brought in, and the attorneys have begun asking general questions. The defense attorney asks,

"Has anyone read any accounts of this case in newspapers or seen any coverage on television?" Over half of the members of the panel raise their hands. This is far more people than the defense attorney thought would have some knowledge about the case. He asks a few more general questions, each one designed to discover if any panel members have formed an opinion about the case based on the coverage. Not a single person responds that he or she has formed an opinion about the case, but the defense attorney is unconvinced. He announces that he has a motion and asks that the panel members be removed from the courtroom so that he can bring his motion. Although the judge is reluctant, he consents. Once the panel members have been sent back to the juror administration area, the attorney says, "Your Honor, I renew my motion for a change of venue. The jurors in this case have all stated that they have either read or heard about this case. My client cannot get a fair trial under these circumstances."

How does the judge rule? How does the prosecutor respond?

4. Review the *Kline* case and consider the following jury selection problem.

The panel has been brought into the courtroom to begin selecting the jury in the *Kline* case. The attorneys have rearranged their chairs, reversing them so that they face into the gallery. That way they can see the entire panel and ask general and specific questions of the panel members. There is a lull while everyone waits for the judge to take the bench. A couple of panel members seem a little uncomfortable in the silence. A woman in the first row, directly across from Christine Kline, suddenly asks, "Are you the defendant?" Christine Kline answers yes. The woman then says, "Well, you sure don't look guilty to me."

There is an embarrassed silence while all the panel members look at one another and the attorneys consider what just occurred. Then the bailiff announces that the judge is entering the courtroom.

"All rise," he says.

The judge takes the bench and asks if the attorneys are ready to proceed.

"No, your honor," Paul Prosecutor says. "The state would like to approach."

Both attorneys approach the bench, and the prosecutor informs the judge about what just occurred.

What does the judge do?

NOTES

1. *Maryland v. Craig*, 497 U.S. 836, 110 S.Ct. 3157 (1990).
2. *White v. Illinois*, 502 U.S. 346 (1992).
3. *Idaho v. Wright*, 497 U.S. 805, 110 S.Ct. 3139, 111 L.Ed.2d 638 (1990).

Chapter 14

DEFENSES

Chapter Objectives

At the completion of this chapter, you should be able to:

- Identify the various defenses available to an accused
- Discuss the elements of defenses
- Describe how and under what circumstances certain defenses may be raised
- Identify and discuss affirmative defenses
- Discuss various procedural defenses, such as statute of limitations

I. Defenses

One of the most common misconceptions about criminal law has to do with defenses. When a defendant is charged with a crime, he has no obligation to say anything during the course of his trial. The defendant cannot be compelled to take the stand in his trial. A prosecutor cannot put the defendant on the stand and cross-examine him about what happened when the crime occurred. In fact, a prosecutor cannot even refer to the fact that the defendant has failed to deny the charge.

As anyone who watches police dramas on television knows, when a defendant is arrested, he is advised of his Miranda rights. One of those rights is the right to remain silent. This right to remain silent stays with the defendant throughout the entire prosecution, from arrest to conviction. The defendant is also protected by other rights. These rights are triggered in every criminal case without the defendant having to take any action to obtain them. These rights are automatic. Among them are the right to remain silent, the right to be presumed innocent, and the burden on the state to prove the crime against the defendant.

In other cases, however, the defendant has an obligation of presenting some evidence if he wants to raise certain defenses. These defenses, which require some affirmative action on the defendant's part, are referred to as "affirmative defenses." Among the many affirmative defenses are self-defense, alibi, consent, and insanity.

Finally, a defendant has certain constitutional and statutory defenses. These defenses must be raised during the trial. These defenses include statute of limitations and U.S. constitutional defenses such as equal protection and due process.

A. Presumption of Innocence

The government must prove every element of an offense beyond a reasonable doubt, and that burden of proof never shifts to the defendant to prove his innocence.[1]

A defendant enters a criminal trial protected by the presumption of innocence. The jury is instructed that unless and until the state presents enough evidence to overcome this presumption, the jury has no other choice but to find the defendant not guilty. This is a powerful safeguard in criminal cases and one of the important hallmarks of the American judicial system. Because of this presumption, a defendant does not have to produce a single witness in his defense, nor does he have to take the stand and dispute the evidence against him. The defendant does not have to prove that he is innocent of the charge; the burden always remains on the state to prove that he is guilty.

1. State's Burden of Proof

In criminal cases, the burden that the state must meet is guilt beyond a reasonable doubt. Reasonable doubt has been interpreted and quoted thousands of times. Trying to quantify exactly what reasonable doubt is is often easier if we approach it from what it is not. Reasonable doubt is not proof beyond all doubt. It is not proof beyond a shadow of a doubt. If the state were required to prove a case beyond all doubt or beyond a shadow of a doubt, very few criminals would be convicted. Instead, the state's burden is proof beyond a reasonable doubt. This is, essentially, a doubt based on a specific reason. It is not a doubt based on philosophy, but on fact. If a juror believes that the state failed to prove an essential element of the case (e.g., that the defendant may not have been the person who shot the victim), then that would be a reasonable doubt.

a. Guilty but Not Proven Jurors are instructed that even if they suspect that the defendant is guilty but the state has failed to prove the case against the defendant, they have no choice but to reach a verdict of not guilty. This principle underlies every phase of a criminal trial. This is not to say, however, that the jury is prevented from making commonsense

---

■ **BULLET POINT**
A defendant always has the right to present a defense; in some cases, the defense is automatic.

■ **BULLET POINT**
Every criminal defendant enters a trial presumed to be innocent unless and until the government proves that he or she is guilty.

■ **BULLET POINT**
The burden of proof never shifts from the state to the defendant in a criminal case; the state must always prove that the defendant committed the offense beyond a reasonable doublt. The defendant does not have to prove that he or she is innocent.

conclusions about the evidence produced at a trial. If, for instance, a witness takes the stand and identifies the defendant as the perpetrator of the crime, the jury is allowed to infer that the witness is telling the truth.

II. Affirmative Defenses

A defendant enters a criminal trial with certain defenses already in place. He or she is not required to raise them at the trial. These are the legal or constitutional defenses that all defendants have. However, there are other defenses that the defendant must raise. The so-called **affirmative defenses** are defenses that the defendant must bring up during the course of his trial to take advantage of them. If the defendant wants to raise the defense of insanity, for example, then she must put up evidence and raise this issue with the jury. This does not necessarily mean that the defendant must take the stand, but the defense will have to present some evidence and witnesses to raise the affirmative defense. Affirmative defenses attempt to explain, refute, or excuse criminal conduct. If the jurors believe the affirmative defense, then they would be authorized to find the defendant not guilty.

For instance, if the defendant raises the defense of insanity and the jury believes this defense, the jury would be authorized to find the defendant not guilty by reason of insanity. Insanity is just one of the many affirmative defenses available to a defendant in a criminal action.

Generally, when a defendant raises an affirmative defense, he admits that he actually committed the offense. For instance, in raising the claim of self-defense, a defendant is admitting that he took violent action against another person. However, the defendant is attempting to show that the violence was unavoidable.

We have already seen that the state has the burden of proving a defendant guilty beyond a reasonable doubt. This remains true when the defendant raises an affirmative defense. The burden never changes and never shifts during the course of the trial, even when the defendant raises an affirmative defense. For instance, when a defendant raises the defense of insanity, the defendant is not under the obligation to prove that he is innocent. It is up to the state to disprove his affirmative defense. When a

affirmative defense
A defense that goes beyond mere denial and alleges facts that if true, would mitigate the defendant's sentence or even require a not guilty verdict.

BULLET POINT
Affirmative defenses go beyond mere denial; a defendant must present some evidence to support an affirmative defense.

- Insanity
- Alibi
- Self-defense
- Infancy
- Intoxication
- Mistake
- Entrapment

Exhibit 14-1
Common affirmative defenses

Copyright © 2015 Cengage Learning®

defendant presents evidence of insanity, the state must prove that the defendant was sane beyond a reasonable doubt. All affirmative defenses work this way. Once the defendant raises some evidence of alibi or entrapment or mistake, it is up to the state to disprove that affirmative defense.

A. The Jury's Function

Remember that it is always up to the fact finder, the jury, or the judge to decide whether to believe an affirmative defense. If the defendant presents evidence of insanity or self-defense, the jury still has the responsibility of deciding whether the facts warrant a not guilty verdict based on that affirmative defense.

B. How Much Evidence Does the Defendant Have to Produce?

preponderance of evidence
The greater weight of evidence, not as to quantity, but quality.

In most states, the defendant's burden is preponderance of evidence. The defendant is never obligated to prove his or her affirmative defense beyond a reasonable doubt. **Preponderance of evidence** means "more likely than not." In some jurisdictions, the defendant simply has to produce "some" evidence or "any evidence" to support the affirmative defense.

INSIDER'S VIEWPOINT

Preparing for defenses

"When you're dealing with defenses, you have to put yourself in the defendant's (or defendant's attorney's) shoes. You have to see the case the way they see it, both the good and the bad. That way you can build a better case for the prosecution."

—R. Keith Miles, Prosecutor

INSIDER'S VIEWPOINT

First meeting with the client

"When I first meet with the client, I usually want to know what it is that the government is alleging (about the crime), not the client's version. What is the government saying about the crime? Then I concentrate on getting the details: the police report, getting a feel for a client, for who they are, other than talking about the offense. When I ask questions, it's more of 'what is it that the police are saying? Did you talk to the police? Did they take anything? Was there any sort of search?' Sometimes, I stay away from the client's version until I've heard what the government has to say."

—B.J. Bernstein, Criminal Defense Attorney

Can a defendant raise inconsistent defenses? For instance, can a defendant raise the affirmative defenses of alibi and self-defense? These two defenses contradict each other. The defendant is essentially saying, "I wasn't there, but if I was there, I was justified in using force." Despite the fact that the defenses may be inconsistent, many jurisdictions allow a defendant to use as many defenses as he or she wants, even if they are inconsistent. However, many defense attorneys realize that using inconsistent defenses takes away from the case and may confuse the jury.

C. Notice Requirements

In many jurisdictions, the defendant is required to put the government on notice if he intends to use certain affirmative defenses. Alibi and insanity are two common examples. At some point prior to trial (usually a minimum of ten days), the defendant must serve a notice on the government detailing the specific affirmative defense planned. This allows the government time to gather evidence because the prosecution has the responsibility of rebutting the evidence offered by the defendant.

THE ROLE OF THE PARALEGAL: AFFIRMATIVE DEFENSES

When offering any affirmative defense, the paralegal must have as firm a grasp on the notice and other requirements as the attorney. The reason for this is simple: When raising some affirmative defenses, the defendant must serve notice on the prosecutor a specified number of days prior to the trial. Knowing exactly what this time period is can be very helpful in making sure that notice is served in time.

D. The Prosecution's Responsibility to Rebut Affirmative Defense

In almost all jurisdictions, the government is required to present evidence rebutting the affirmative defense. If the prosecution fails to rebut the evidence, then the defendant is entitled to a directed verdict in his favor. Rebuttal comes at the end of the defense. Once the defense has presented all of its evidence and rested, the state again comes forward to present evidence and testimony attempting to disprove the affirmative defense.

E. Specific Affirmative Defenses

In the following sections, we will discuss specific affirmative defenses. Each of these defenses has basic components that must be proven to the jury's satisfaction. Failure to prove the elements of an affirmative defense often results in the jury voting a guilty verdict.

1. Alibi

Alibi is one of the few affirmative defenses that does not require the defendant to admit to the crime, then seek to justify or excuse it. When

---

Simple Defenses vs. Affirmative Defenses

A simple defense is a mere denial.
An affirmative defense involves presentation of evidence or testimony.
A simple defense rises automatically.
An affirmative defense must be raised by the defendant.

■ **BULLET POINT**

The defendant's burden of proof in presenting an affirmative defense is usually preponderance of evidence, although some states require "clear and convincing" evidence.

■ **BULLET POINT**

If a defendant fails to put the government on notice of a specific affirmative defense, then the defendant will be prevented from presenting the defense.

defendants raise an alibi defense, they are claiming that they were not present when the crime occurred. Because the defense of alibi would be a complete defense to the charge, the state must *disprove* the defendant's alibi. Defendants normally raise this defense through the testimony of witnesses who claim that the defendant was somewhere else when the crime occurred. An alibi is a complete defense to a crime. A **complete defense** exonerates the defendant and, if believed, leaves the jury with no choice but to reach a verdict of not guilty.

2. Self-Defense

Perhaps the most misunderstood affirmative defense is self-defense. A person always has the right to defend himself against a physical threat. However, there are severe limitations on this affirmative defense. In most situations, the response of the person raising the claim of self-defense must be comparable to the threat. This means that when someone is threatening the defendant with bare fists, the defendant is not permitted to retaliate with a weapon.

A claim of self-defense seeks to excuse the violence used by the defendant. To use self-defense, the defendant must admit that he used force, but only for protection.

a. Use of Deadly Force Generally, people must meet a threat with a similar level of violence. A defendant cannot claim self-defense if he uses "excessive force." This would be an action far in excess of the threat. There are times when even deadly force can be excused under the law. A person threatened with deadly force may respond with deadly force.

b. What Constitutes Deadly Force? In most states, when a person is threatened with a deadly weapon, he can assume that deadly force is being offered. Deadly weapons include guns, knives, and other weapons that could inflict serious or deadly injury.

c. Limitations on Self-Defense No Self-Defense Claim for Aggressor A defendant cannot use the defense of self-defense, however, when the defendant was the person who began the assault. When the defendant started a fight, he cannot claim that he was defending himself when he carried the fight through.

d. The State's Burden When Self-Defense Is Raised Like all affirmative defenses, the state has the burden of disproving one or more of the elements of the self-defense beyond a reasonable doubt. To do this, the state must present evidence in rebuttal showing that the defendant's actions were not justified because the defendant used excessive force or because the defendant was the aggressor or because of some other reason.

e. How the Jury Evaluates the Defendant's Actions When self-defense is raised, most jurisdictions require the jury to make a determination as to whether the defendant acted reasonably when he used force. If the jury

---

complete defense
A defense that if proven to the jury's satisfaction, would require a verdict of not guilty.

■ **BULLET POINT**
The defense of alibi claims that the defendant could not have committed the offense because he or she was somewhere else when the crime occurred.

■ **BULLET POINT**
In a claim of self-defense, a person can respond with deadly force only when he or she has been presented with deadly force.

finds that the defendant did not act reasonably, the jury could refuse to take self-defense into account.[2]

f. Victim's Reputation for Violence What if the victim had a reputation for being a violent and aggressive person? Could the defendant present such evidence to prove that the defendant acted reasonably? The answer is maybe. In most jurisdictions, if the defendant was aware of the victim's violent history, it may be admissible. However, if the defendant did not know the victim's history, it probably would not be admissible. The reason for this discrepancy is simple: Self-defense has a great deal to do with what was in the defendant's mind at the time of the attack. If the defendant did not know that the victim was a violent person, then he could not have based his actions on that fact.

g. Defendants with Special Abilities: Black Belts, Etc. At times, a claim of self-defense is not available to a suspect, even when he used only his bare hands. Martial artists, professional boxers, and others are at a tremendous advantage in a fight with an untrained individual. These professionals have hands that are "deadly weapons," and when they use them aggressively, they may no longer have the protection of self-defense. Usually, it is the jury's role to decide if the defendant's abilities were so great that a claim of self-defense against an untrained opponent is not warranted.

h. Police Officers and Use of Force An officer is authorized to use force to make an arrest. However, a police officer is restricted to reasonable force to do so. A police officer is not permitted to use excessive force. A police officer may use deadly force only when confronted with deadly force or when deadly force is the only way to keep others from being injured or killed by the aggressor.

i. Defense of Others Under the common law, a person could only defend another person with whom he had a close, legally recognized relationship. Parents could defend children; husbands could defend wives. But at common law, a stranger could not use force to defend another stranger. That rule is no longer followed in most jurisdictions. Like self-defense, however, the other person must be faced with the immediate threat of bodily injury before the stranger acts to defend him. The threat must be one that a reasonable person would perceive as a threat.

j. Deadly Force Cannnot Be Used to Defend Property It is important at this point to draw a distinction between the legal term *property* and the way this term is used in everyday language. In law, there are two forms of property: real and personal. Real property refers to land, houses, and things permanently attached to land. The other category is personal property. This refers to nonland, usually movable items: cars, pencils, and computers, for example.

When we say that deadly force cannot be used to defend property, we are referring to personal property. Force can be used to defend property, but only when it is reasonable to do so. If a thief is stealing the victim's car, the victim does not have the right to shoot the thief. When defending property, force is never the first remedy; it is the last. If a nonviolent alternative is available, the person must use it.

However, the situation changes when a person is defending real property, or more specifically, her home. If a burglar is breaking into someone's house, many jurisdictions permit the homeowner to use deadly force to protect the residents. In many states, for example, courts have decreed that homeowners are permitted to use deadly force to stop someone from breaking in and harming the occupants.

k. "Stand Your Ground" Laws Some states have amended the rules on self-defense to include so-called "stand your ground" laws. Traditionally, most states followed the retreat doctrine. Under this doctrine, a person who is presented with violence, even deadly force, must retreat if he or she can reasonably do so. The reasons for the retreat doctrine are easy to understand: If a person can avoid being injured by a simple action, then he or she should do so. However, the doctrine has never required a person to retreat in all circumstances—only when it was reasonable to do so. If a person would put himself in greater jeopardy retreating, then the doctrine did not apply. However, in recent years, some states have decided to repeal the retreat doctrine and replace it with "stand your ground" laws. Under these new laws, a person who is presented with violence, including deadly force, is not obligated to retreat, even when it is reasonable to do so. In these states, if a judge makes a determination that the person was under a threat and the person responds with deadly force to a perceived deadly force attack, the person is protected under the laws of self-defense.

3. Consent

Another affirmative defense is consent. When a defendant raises the defense of consent, he is, in effect, saying that the victim agreed to the crime and therefore it is not a crime. The consent defense is used most frequently in prosecutions for crimes against the person: battery, assault, rape, etc.

a. Who Can Give Consent? Not all persons are able to give consent. Children, for example, are limited in the kind of consent they may give. Because they lack the level of maturity and experience that adults have, statutes prohibit them from giving legal consent to many actions. For instance, a child below the age of twelve (in almost all jurisdictions) cannot not give consent, under any circumstances, to sexual activity with an adult.

Consent carries with it the concept that the person understands what he or she is consenting to and has knowingly agreed to take on the possibility of injury, whether financial, physical, or emotional. Because this is the rule, it becomes clear why other individuals are legally incapable of consenting to certain activities. People who are mentally handicapped, for instance, are protected under the law in most states by statutes that limit the kind of consent that they can give.

b. *Consent Is Not a Defense to All Crimes* For many crimes, consent is not an issue. In a murder prosecution, for example, consent is not a defense. A person cannot consent to being murdered. Consent also is not a defense in a crime such as statutory rape, where one partner is legally incapable of giving consent. Third parties cannot consent for others. A husband cannot give consent to another man to have sex with his wife. In other situations, the law recognizes that people are not given authority to allow another person to commit a crime. For example, upon entering a convenience store, Lou turns to the assembled customers and asks if it is okay if he robs the owner. The customers nod. When Lou is later arrested, he does not have the legal defense of consent because the customers were not legally able to consent for the owner.

4. Mutual Combat

The affirmative defense of mutual combat arises when the defendant and the victim agree to fight each other. Similar to consent, when the victim agrees to enter a fight, he often gives up his right to charge the defendant with battery. However, mutual combat has some strict limitations. If the defendant exceeds the understanding of what weapons will be used in the fight or uses excessive force, mutual combat as a defense may not be available.

For example, two men push and shove and then punch each other. One man then attacks the other with a deadly weapon, severely injuring him. In such a case, the jury would not be instructed about the affirmative defense of mutual combat.[3]

5. Duress, Necessity, Compulsion, and Coercion

The affirmative defenses of duress, necessity, compulsion, and coercion are similar in that the defendant claims that he committed a crime because he was forced to.

For instance, in the defense of duress, a defendant admits that he committed the crime, but did so only because his personal safety was in jeopardy.

a. *Necessity* The affirmative defense of necessity is similar to duress. When a defendant claims necessity, he admits that he committed the

> ■ **BULLET POINT**
> There are some crimes where consent is not available as a defense. A child cannot consent to sexual activity; a person cannot consent to being murdered.

Exhibit 14-2
Elements of duress

In order to prove duress, the defendant must show:
1. That he or she was threatened and
2. Because of that threat he or she committed a crime as the only way to avoid being either injured or killed.

---

crime, but in this case, he did so to avoid some catastrophe or force of nature. A common example of necessity is when someone breaks into a cabin to wait out a blizzard. Normally, he would be guilty of breaking and entering. However, the offense is excused by his need to stay alive. In this case, burglary would be the lesser of two evils and the defense of necessity would apply.

Balancing Act in Necessity Defenses Many courts have held that the danger to the defendant must outweigh the damage he does in committing the crime. A defendant could not use the defense of necessity in attempting to excuse a murder, for example, because all jurisdictions have held that no danger outweighs the value of another person's life.

b. Duress, Compulsion, and Coercion Duress is the undue influence of one person over another. This influence can come about through threats, intimidation, or other means. Whatever form it takes, the duress must be something that reasonable people agree would cause someone to feel that she must commit a crime. It is not duress if the defendant "felt like" someone was pressuring him. Duress is viewed from an objective viewpoint. The same holds true for compulsion and coercion. If a person claims that he was compelled to commit a crime, the compulsion must be something that reasonable people agree would be an action that compels someone to commit a crime. To succeed with a defense of duress, the defendant must show that he committed a crime to avoid immediate death or serious bodily injury.[4]

6. Intoxication as a Defense: Voluntary Intoxication

Voluntary intoxication is not a defense to most crimes. Permitting a defendant to avoid responsibility for a crime by getting drunk would not serve society's interests. However, there are times when voluntary intoxication does affect criminal liability. For instance, voluntary intoxication may affect the analysis when the crime involves specific intent. As we have seen in other chapters, specific intent crimes such as murder and rape call for the defendant to intend to commit the actual crime. Intoxication that affects the person's judgment and reasoning might render him incapable of forming specific intent. In this case, the crime might be reduced in severity from premeditated murder to some lesser crime such as manslaughter. However, except for specific intent crimes, a defendant's claim of voluntary intoxication does not excuse his crime or lessen his sentence.

A man breaks into the home of a wealthy jeweler and threatens to kill the jeweler's wife unless the jeweler breaks into the store where he works and steals expensive diamonds for the burglar. When the jeweler is later arrested for burglary, his claim of duress or coercion would probably find a sympathetic ear with the jury.

Exhibit 14-3

A sample statute on the affirmative defense of coercion

A person is not guilty of a crime, except murder, if the act upon which the supposed criminal liability is based is performed under such coercion that the person reasonably believes that performing the act is the only way to prevent his imminent death or great bodily injury.

a. Involuntary Intoxication as a Defense Voluntary intoxication is not a defense to crime, but involuntary intoxication may be. Involuntary intoxication results when a person is overcome by fumes or chemicals to such an extent that he is no longer capable of rational thought. When the defendant is overcome with these substances and has not voluntary induced this state, he may not be criminally liable. Situations that bring about involuntary intoxication are rare.

7. Other Defenses: Mistake

"Ignorance of the law is no excuse." We have all heard this statement, but is it true? If a person commits a crime without realizing that his or her actions are a crime, has a crime occurred? In a previous chapter, we discussed that for almost all crimes, two basic elements are required: mens rea (intent) and actus reus (act). Intent does not mean the intent to commit a crime. Instead, it means the natural consequences of actions. If a person believes that he is committing a legal action and is mistaken about the interpretation of the law, has a crime occurred? Usually, the answer is yes.

a. Mistake Not a Defense to Certain Crimes Mistake is not a defense to a crime such as statutory rape. In that crime, the defendant is charged with having sexual relations with a female who is under a certain age. Even if he had good reason to believe that the female was over eighteen years of age, he will not be permitted to present the defense of mistake. Mistake also is not available to a defendant who sets out to injure or kill a specific person and kills another person instead. In this case, "mistake" does not mitigate or excuse his actions.

8. Other Defenses: Age

In many jurisdictions, children below a certain age are presumed to be incapable of committing a crime. The reason for this assumption is based on the two basic elements required for almost all crimes: mens rea and actus reus (guilty mind + guilty act). A child of six, for example, could take a handgun to school and use it to shoot a classmate, but the child would not be prosecuted for murder. In many states, a child below the age of seven is presumed to be incapable of forming the intent necessary to commit a crime. Between the ages of seven and fourteen, this is a rebuttable presumption. For children fourteen or older (this age may be more or less in different states), a child is presumed to be capable of forming

> ■ **BULLET POINT**
> Voluntary intoxication is a not a legally recognized defense, but involuntary intoxication is.

> In most situations, mistake can be a defense where it negates the defendant's intent.

In order for a defendant to succeed on the affirmative defense of mistake, the defendant must show:
1. A misapprehension of a fact
2. Which, if true, would have justified the act or omission.

Exhibit 14-4
The elements of mistake

criminal intent. Children who commit crimes are normally prosecuted in juvenile court.

9. Other Defenses: Entrapment

The defense of entrapment is used when a defendant claims that law enforcement tricked or bullied him into committing a crime. Entrapment exists when the idea for the crime originates with the government. When a defendant claims that he or she has been entrapped, the defendant is saying that both the idea and the means for committing the crime originated with the government. Because the government should not be in the business of creating crime, jurors are authorized to punish the government for doing so by finding the defendant not guilty.

However, entrapment does not exist when the government simply provides the defendant with an opportunity to commit a crime he was already predisposed to commit. If the defendant wanted to sell narcotics, for example, and an undercover police officer offered to purchase them, there is no entrapment. In this scenario, if the government induced the defendant to sell narcotics and then provided him with the drugs, entrapment would probably exist.

a. A Simple Test for Entrapment
One way of determining whether entrapment exists is to answer this question: Did both the idea for the crime and the means to carry it through originate with the government? If the answer is yes, then there is a solid case for entrapment. If the answer is no, then the judge may not instruct the jury about the defense of entrapment or the jury may not find entrapment as a valid defense.

As is true with all affirmative defenses, the government must show that the defendant was not entrapped. Usually, the government rebuts the defense of entrapment by showing that the defendant was predisposed to commit the crime. When a defendant is predisposed, it means that he is ready to commit a crime and the government simply provided him with an opportunity. In some states, the government is required to prove that law enforcement did not overcome the defendant's free will.[5]

10. Other Defenses: Battered Woman Syndrome

Battered woman syndrome (BWS) was developed by the courts as a way of addressing the complexities of an abusive relationship. Women who

Exhibit 14-5
Elements of entrapment

> To prove entrapment, the defendant must show:
> 1. A government agent sought out the defendant—or initiated the contact with the defendant—or the government agent was the person who first proposed the illegal act and
> 2. The government agent induced or suggested that the defendant commit the crime.

are battered by their male lovers or husbands often are not in a situation where they can adequately defend themselves. In some cases, women retaliate at times when they are not being beaten. Some women, for example, retaliate against men when the men are sleeping. Ordinarily, such actions do not constitute self-defense. As we have already seen, the doctrine of self-defense excuses violence only when the person who is defending herself is under immediate threat of bodily injury. By waiting until the attacker is somehow incapacitated, a woman who retaliates against her attacker often finds herself deprived of a claim of self-defense. BWS developed as a direct response to these situations.

In BWS, a woman can seek to have her attack mitigated or excused by presenting evidence that she has been the victim of repeated domestic violence at the hand of the man.

11. Unusual Defenses

At various points, defendants have come up with a variety of novel and interesting defenses. Among the more unusual and generally ineffective defenses are claims that anti-depressant drugs caused the defendant to black out and commit murders.[6] Other defenses have attempted to show that the defendant was overcome by being addicted to carbohydrates, watching too much violent television programming, being addicted to sugar, and suffering from premenstrual syndrome, among others. These novel defenses have rarely been successful.

III. The Insanity Defense

Insanity is perhaps the most complicated of all the affirmative defenses. To be found not guilty by reason of insanity in a criminal case, a defendant must show that he did not know the difference between right and wrong when he committed the crime. To show this, a defendant must present expert testimony from a psychiatrist or a psychologist who will testify that at the time the defendant committed the crime, he was not aware of the legal difference between right and wrong. Defendants can be suffering from a wide range of mental disabilities and still not be considered legally insane. Someone suffering from schizophrenia, for example, may still be legally sane because the standard is not whether the defendant was suffering from mental illness, but whether the defendant knew the difference between right and wrong.

A. Misconceptions About the Insanity Defense

There are many misconceptions about the defense of insanity. One common misconception is that people who have a mental illness are automatically considered not guilty by reason of insanity. That is not true. People with multiple personalities, people who hear voices, and people who have hallucinations have all been held to be legally sane. Another common

Exhibit 14-6
The M'Naghten test

Defendant could be considered not guilty by reason of insanity if he or she:
1. Suffered from disease or defect of the mind.
2. Did not know the nature and quality of the act or did not know that the act was wrong.

misconception about the defense of insanity is that if the defense is raised successfully and a verdict of not guilty by reason of insanity is entered, the defendant is released. That also is not true. If a defendant has been found not guilty by reason of insanity, she is usually placed in a mental hospital for the criminally insane.

B. How Insanity Affects the Mens Rea Analysis

One of the interesting points raised by the insanity defense is why such a defense is permitted at all. Under the law, a legally insane person is not responsible for his or her actions in the same way children are not legally responsible for theirs. As we have already seen, to commit a crime, a person must have intent and take action based on that intent. If a person is incapable of forming mens rea, then he or she cannot be guilty of a crime.

C. A Brief History of the Insanity Defense

Courts have been wrestling with the insanity defense for centuries. As time has passed, different standards for insanity have come into vogue and then disappeared. One of the earliest was the **M'Naghten test**.

Since M'Naghten, there have been many modifications to the insanity defense. Various states have sought their own standards, and the Model Penal Code also has weighed in on the issue.

1. The Modern Definition of Insanity

In most states, the modern definition of insanity is some variant on the definition shown in Exhibit 14-7.

M'Naghten test
An early attempt (1843) to establish a workable scheme to determine who was and was not legally insane.

Exhibit 14-7
Durham test for insanity

A defendant is considered to be legally insane when:
■ He or she cannot distinguish between right or wrong.
■ He or she suffers from an irresistible impulse that precludes him or her from choosing between right and wrong.
■ His or her lawful act is the product of a mental disease or defect (Durham test).

D. Insanity at the Time of the Crime vs. Insanity at the Time of the Trial

There are two different insanity pleas. A defendant may plead insanity by providing proof by a preponderance of evidence that at the time of the crime, he was legally insane. A defendant may also raise what in many states is referred to as a "special plea" of insanity and claim that he cannot stand trial because he is insane. Although these two defenses sound similar, in practice, they are quite different. When defendants raise the defense of insanity at the time of the crime, they are saying that they could not form mens rea to commit a crime and therefore are not guilty of the crime. When defendants raise a "special plea" of insanity, they are stating that they are unable to participate in their own trial because of mental illness. Defendants who claim that they are insane at the time of trial do not get the benefit of the insanity defense. The jury is not authorized to find them not guilty by reason of insanity because they are not alleging that they were insane at the time the crime was committed. A defendant who is not competent to stand trial may be remanded into a state facility until such time that he or she is able to stand trial. In many cases, a defendant may claim both forms: insanity at the time of the crime and insanity at the time of the trial.

E. New Approaches to the Insanity Defense

A growing dissatisfaction with the plea of not guilty by reason of insanity brought about legislative initiatives in many jurisdictions that modified this defense. For example, in many states, a new verdict was created: guilty but mentally ill. This verdict means that a defendant will be incarcerated in a prison facility that provides some form of mental counseling. The jurors (in many states) make the determination as to whether the defendant is mentally ill.

Before this modification, when the defense of insanity was raised, the jury had three verdict choices:

- Guilty
- Not guilty
- Not guilty by reason of insanity

In states that have revised their insanity defense laws, the verdict choices look like this:

- Guilty
- Not guilty
- Not guilty by reason of insanity
- *Guilty but mentally ill*

In almost all situations, the defendant has the final say about what defense is used. If he or she does not want to use the insanity defense, it will not be used.

■ BULLET POINT

Although the insanity defense receives a great deal of attention, it is used in less than 1% of all criminal cases, and even when it is used, the defense is rarely successful.

F. The Procedure Used to Raise the Defense of Insanity

The defendant who wants to use the defense of insanity must serve notice on the state prior to trial that he plans to do so. This notice allows the state to hire its own expert to evaluate the defendant to reach a decision as to whether the state's expert believes the defendant was legally insane at the time of the crime. Insanity trials often boil down to a battle of the experts. The jury is presented with testimony of an expert who states that the defendant was legally insane at the time of the crime. Then the state's expert testifies that the defendant was legally sane at the time of the crime. When the jury returns to the jury room, they must decide which of the experts to believe and reach a decision as to whether the defendant was legally sane or insane at the time the crime was committed.

Defendants in criminal actions rarely use the defense of insanity. In those few instances where the defense is raised, it usually is not successful.

THE ROLE OF THE PARALEGAL: LOCATING A HELPFUL EXPERT

If your client is intent on using an insanity defense, how do you locate an expert who is sympathetic? In the old days, the process was hit and miss. But in these days of advanced technology and a new openness among the professions, the best place to find an expert is in the classified ads. Look in the back of any legal publication and you will often see dozens of experts listed along with their specialties. Do you need an expert who will testify that excessive sugar intake causes blackouts? You will probably find one in the legal classifieds. Experts realized years ago that being in the business of testifying is lucrative. Many experts also advertise on the Internet.

G. The Defendant's Burden in an Insanity Defense

As is true with many other affirmative defenses, the defendant who raises the defense of insanity must present enough evidence to establish by a preponderance of evidence that he or she is legally insane. In some jurisdictions, the standard the defendant must meet is "clear and convincing" evidence of legal insanity. Once the defendant has presented this evidence, the prosecution must rebut the defendant's evidence. The government must show that the defendant was legally sane at the time of the crime.

H. Disposition of the Criminally Insane

Depending on the law of the jurisdiction where the defendant is charged and the facts of the defendant's case, a person who has been found not guilty by reason of insanity faces several possible dispositions. See Exhibit 14-8.

I. Other Insanity Defenses: Diminished Capacity

The defense of diminished capacity is a form of insanity defense. Although it is not recognized in all jurisdictions, the defense of diminished capacity

- Immediate discharge and release (rare in most jurisdictions)
- Released on condition that he or she receive psychiatric or psychological treatment
- Involuntarily commitment to a state mental institution (common in both state and federal prosecutions)[1]

[1]See 18 USCA §4243(a).

http://www.gpo.gov/fdsys/granule/USCODE-2010-title18/USCODE-2010-title18-partIII-chap313-sec4243/content-detail.html

Exhibit 14-8
Possible dispositions for a defendant found not guilty by reason of insanity

allows a defendant to offer testimony and evidence about his or her mental condition. This evidence is intended to mitigate or excuse the defendant's guilt in the crime. Often, diminished capacity defenses focus on the mens rea element of a crime. A defendant presents evidence of lower-than-normal IQ or slow mental development as a way to show the jury that he lacked the ability to form mens rea. In specific intent cases, such as murder, diminished capacity may be used as a defense to show that the defendant lacked the ability to form specific intent and therefore could not be guilty of first-degree murder.[7] The problem with diminished capacity defenses is defining exactly what a "diminished capacity" is. For instance, courts have held that a defendant does not fall under the category of diminished capacity if he suffers from mood swings, feelings of insecurity, an overwhelming fear of disease, or an inability to care about others.[8]

IV. Constitutional and Statutory Defenses

As we have seen before, the Fifth Amendment to the U.S. Constitution provides numerous protections to a person accused of a crime. However, because this Amendment is part of the United States Constitution, a question that lingered in the Republic for decades after the foundation of our country was whether this Amendment applied to the states. The Civil War helped to answer that question. The Fourteenth Amendment, voted into existence as a direct result of the Civil War, decreed that the United States Constitution—and the Bill of Rights in particular—would apply to all states.

A. Equal Protection

The Fifth and Fourteenth Amendments require that all citizens be treated fairly. As far as criminal law is concerned, this means that people falling into different socioeconomic, religious, or racial categories cannot be treated differently under the law. Any law that contains classifications based on these factors is immediately suspect and may be found unconstitutional.

The Fourteenth Amendment

"No State shall make or enforce any law which shall abridge the privileges or immunities of citizens of the United States; nor shall any State deprive any person of life, liberty, or property, without due process of law; nor deny to any person within its jurisdiction the equal protection of the laws."

B. Due Process

The Due Process clause requires that the same procedures be used in all criminal cases. The rules do not change when someone is *obviously* guilty as opposed to someone who *may* be guilty.

For example, Ron Roe has been sentenced to life in prison for murder. After serving two years, he escapes from the maximum-security facility where he has been serving his life sentence. Escape is a felony carrying a ten-year maximum sentence. Can this ten years automatically be added to Roe's sentence, thereby affecting his possible parole review date? No. Roe must be charged with escape, and if he should plead not guilty, he will be tried. The Due Process Clause requires that the same procedures be followed in every case. The state is not allowed shortcuts in cases such as Roe's.

C. Double Jeopardy

> "...*Nor shall any person be subject for the same offense to be twice put in jeopardy of life or limb....*"
>
> —*Fifth Amendment*

In elegantly brief words, the Fifth Amendment to the United States Constitution creates a plethora of rights for the criminal defendant. The protection of double jeopardy is straightforward: No person who has been found not guilty of an offense may be tried again. If a jury has decided that the defendant is not guilty of the charge and the state later discovers additional evidence of his guilt, the defendant will not be charged again. The law on this point has been refined over many decades. One of the key points in analyzing double jeopardy is answering this question: When does it apply? Clearly, a defendant cannot be retried if the jury finds him not guilty. However, what if the jury cannot reach a verdict and a mistrial is declared? In the case of a mistrial, the parties are put back into a posture as though the trial never occurred. Obviously, it is very important to a criminal defendant when this right of double jeopardy "attaches."

1. When Double Jeopardy Attaches

Various states have approached the problem of when the protection of double jeopardy attaches. For instance, what if a prosecutor, realizing that his case is not going very well, deliberately causes a mistrial? Should he be free to try the defendant again? The general rule is that double jeopardy "attaches" when the jury is sworn and enters the jury box. A clever defendant, knowing this, might try to cause a mistrial. Many states have addressed this issue by declaring that if the prosecution deliberately causes a mistrial, the case cannot be retried, but if the defendant deliberately causes a mistrial, the case can be retried.

2. Double Jeopardy and Cases on Appeal

When a higher court orders a new trial because of some procedural or other error, is this a violation of double jeopardy? The answer is no. This new trial acts in much the same way as a trial that ended in mistrial. The court assumes that the first trial never occurred, and the case must be retried without reference to it. This means that the same witnesses will be called and the same evidence introduced. If several years have passed since the first trial (which is common), it may be difficult or impossible for the state to retry the defendant.

D. Vagueness and Overbreadth

The same constitutional protections that we have seen above also apply to claims that a particular statute is vague or overbroad. A defendant may challenge the statute under which he or she has been charged by claiming that the statute is worded in such a vague manner that people of common intelligence would have to guess at its meaning. The underlying principle in criminal law is that people must be able to figure out what is and is not illegal. When a statute fails to make this notice clear, a court may declare it unconstitutional.

In a similar vein, a court may strike down a statute if it is overbroad. A statute that is overbroad makes constitutionally protected and *unprotected* activities equally illegal. For example, a statute that criminalizes the homeless when they carry out inoffensive conduct is considered overbroad.[9]

E. Bills of Attainder and Ex Post Facto Laws

"No Bill of Attainder or ex post facto Law shall be passed."

—*Article I, Section 9, U.S. Constitution*

A bill of attainder is a legislative action attempting to short-circuit a criminal trial and declare an individual guilty of a crime (usually treason). Bills of attainder are not permitted in the United States. Challenges to a law based on a claim that it is a bill of attainder are extremely rare. Instead, it is far more common to base a claim on ex post facto laws.

For example, a statute that enhanced criminal penalties for members of religious sects who committed crimes would violate the prohibition on bills of attainder.

1. Ex Post Facto

An ex post facto law criminalizes behavior or increases punishment for an action *after* it has occurred. In many cases, a person may carry out an activity that is not technically illegal. For instance, when the crime of computer hacking first began, most states had no statute on the books that made this illegal. The prohibition against ex post facto laws prevents the legislature from making that action illegal, after the fact, just to punish that individual. The legislature can, and often does, address the situation by enacting laws, but these laws only apply to people who commit the crime *after* the statute has been enacted.

Ex post facto defenses also apply to sentences. A person's sentence must reflect the law at the time he committed the action. The legislature cannot, in a fit of outrage, seek to enhance the punishment for a particularly gruesome crime. The legislature can only enhance the sentence for others who commit it. The constitutional limit of ex post facto means that these new statutes cannot be applied to a defendant who committed the crime before the new law was created.

F. Other Constitutional Defenses: First Amendment

In previous chapters, we discussed the impact of the First Amendment on other offenses. A defendant is permitted to challenge the constitutionality of a statute accusing him of a crime. The First Amendment to the U.S. Constitution guarantees freedom of speech for all citizens. When a statute seeks to impose limitations on someone's expressive conduct, the First Amendment is often used as a defense.

G. Statutes of Limitation

A statute of limitations provides a time limit for how long the state has to prosecute a person for committing a crime. Different crimes have different time limits. The idea behind a statute of limitations is to provide some sense of finality to a criminal prosecution. If a defendant is not prosecuted during the statutorily mandated time period, he can never be prosecuted. Generally speaking, the less serious the crime, the shorter the time period for the statute of limitation. Some crimes, such as murder, have no statute of limitation. A murder suspect can be prosecuted decades after committing the crime.

1. "Tolling" the Statute

There are times when the running of the statute stops, or is tolled. For instance, if the defendant jumps bail and flees the jurisdiction after his arrest, the statute will stop running and will not begin running until the defendant returns to the jurisdiction. This prevents people who have been charged with crimes from fleeing the state long enough for the statute to run and then returning, knowing that they cannot be prosecuted.

THE ROLE OF THE PARALEGAL: STATUTES OF LIMITATION

Always check the statute to see what the statute of limitations is on a particular crime. For some crimes, such as assault, it may be surprisingly short, such as two years or less. Make a copy of the applicable statute and keep it handy in the file. You never know when this may become an issue.

H. State Defenses in Addition to U.S. Constitutional Defenses

The U.S. Constitution is clear on the point that the states cannot take any action that denies or reduces the rights guaranteed on the federal level. However, there is nothing preventing the states from giving its citizens *more* rights than those guaranteed in the United States Constitution. Some states have responded by giving criminal defendants additional protections and recognizing other rights not specifically referred to in the U.S. Constitution. One such right is the right to privacy. Oddly enough, the U.S. Constitution does not mention this right, at least explicitly. The U.S. Constitution makes several references to the right of citizens to be free from unlawful searches and seizures and to be secure in their homes and possessions, but does not refer to a right of privacy. Some states have filled this gap by specifically guaranteeing their citizens the right of privacy. These rights, when guaranteed by the state constitution, have an important impact on the prosecution of a defendant. The individual state constitution should be reviewed to verify what, if any, rights in addition to federal constitutional rights a criminal defendant may have.

I. Technical Deficiencies in Indictments

The terms **allegata** and **probata** refer to the Latin terms for allegations and proof, respectively. Essentially, this defense is based on what the state has alleged is the crime and what the state has proven at trial. At times, the proof does not match the allegations. A motion for directed verdict is often based on the simple premise that the crime charged against the defendant does not match the evidence produced against him or her at trial. In such a situation, the defendant might claim that although the state has produced evidence that he or she committed a crime, it was not the crime originally alleged in the indictment. In most cases, such claims are not successful. It is rare for the state to bring charges against a defendant and then seek to prove some other crime instead.

allegata
(Latin) The allegations contained in a charging document.

probata
(Latin) The proof elicited in a trial.

Case Excerpt. Are There Times When the Defendant is Presumed to Be Insane?

Durrence v. State, 287 Ga. 213, 695 S.E.2d 227 (2010) Thompson, Justice.

Appellant Stacy Durrence was found guilty of malice murder but mentally ill in connection with the shooting death of Lee Woodcock and sentenced to life in prison under OCGA § 17-7-131. He appeals from the denial of his motions for new trial. For the reasons that follow, we affirm.

The evidence was uncontroverted that on the morning of March 31, 2002, appellant went to the victim's home where he hid in the bushes and waited. When the victim stepped outside, appellant fatally shot him three times with a 20 gauge shotgun. Appellant obtained the gun and shells the previous day from his father, claiming he needed the gun for his own protection.

Appellant asserted an insanity defense at trial. Evidence showed he had a history of mental illness dating from August 2001 and had been admitted and released from Georgia Regional Hospital on two occasions. The first, a ten-day voluntary commitment to Georgia Regional Hospital in August 2001, resulted in a diagnosis of Bipolar Type II and the development of a treatment plan. Appellant was involuntarily re-admitted to Georgia Regional Hospital in November 2001 after he made threats against his father. The affidavit and forms supporting the involuntary commitment were not admitted at trial, but the Durrence family attorney testified the commitment was based on a determination that appellant posed a risk of harm to himself or others, not that he was unable to determine right from wrong. See OCGA § 37–3–42 (emergency admission for person believed to be mentally ill). After a hearing before the Chatham County Probate Court, appellant was discharged to home in December 2001, again with a diagnosis of Bipolar Disorder Type II, after it was determined he was no longer a threat to himself or others and his judgment was not impaired. See OCGA § 37–3–1(12.1). Because the court determined appellant was still a mentally ill person requiring involuntary treatment as an outpatient, however, the court ordered continued involuntary outpatient treatment through a Tattnall County mental health center where his medications could be monitored and he could receive professional counseling. See OCGA § 37–3–1(12) (defining "mentally ill person requiring involuntary treatment"); OCGA § 37–3–81.1(a)(2) (disposition of patient as outpatient); OCGA § 37–3–93 (court-ordered outpatient treatment).

The victim was shot on March 31, 2002. Appellant's father testified that on the day before the crime appellant was behaving in a normal manner and he noticed nothing unusual that would have caused him not to give appellant the gun and ammunition. Both appellant's father and sister testified that appellant came to his parents' home shortly after the crime and that although appellant was walking or pacing in circles, he frequently would do so and otherwise appeared fine. A psychologist who first examined appellant a year after the crime testified that based on her review of his mental health history and interviews with appellant and other sources, she believed that at the time of the crime he was experiencing a manic episode and did not know right from wrong.

Appellant challenges the sufficiency of the State's evidence and in a related enumeration of error contends the trial court erred by placing on him the burden of proving the affirmative defense of insanity. We consider these issues seriatim.

Under Georgia law, a person is insane, and shall not be guilty of a crime, if at the time of the act, omission, or negligence constituting the crime, the person did not have mental capacity to distinguish between right and wrong in relation to the criminal act or acted because of a delusional compulsion which overmastered his will to resist committing the crime. OCGA §§ 16–3–2, 16–3–3 A defendant claiming insanity has the burden of proving the defense by a preponderance of the evidence. Because Georgia law presumes every person is of sound mind and discretion, criminal trials begin with the rebuttable presumption that the defendant is sane and this presumption is evidence. OCGA § 16–2–3; *Gilbert v. State*, 235 Ga. 501, 501–502, 220 S.E.2d 262 (1975).

It is also true, however, that our law presumes the continued existence of a mental state once it is proved to exist. OCGA § 24–4–21 It is for this reason that where a defendant previously has been adjudicated insane, introduction into evidence of the insanity order raises a counter-presumption. *Durham v. State*, 239 Ga. 697(1), 238 S.E.2d 334 (1977). In such cases, the burden shifts to the State to prove the defendant was sane at the time of the crimes. Id. The counter-presumption does not survive once the defendant is properly released from the hospital or institution, but instead the presumption of sanity is restored.

Here, appellant contends the burden to prove his insanity at the time the crime was committed was improperly placed upon him because his prior involuntary commitment to Georgia Regional Hospital and subsequent discharge with an involuntary treatment order raised a presumption of insanity under OCGA § 24–4–21, thereby shifting the burden to the State to prove he was not insane at the time of the crime. The record, however, is devoid of any evidence of a prior adjudication of insanity. Appellant was admitted to Georgia Regional Hospital on two occasions. Both times he was diagnosed with Bipolar Disorder and released, the first time without conditions and the second as an involuntary outpatient with treatment conditions. Bipolar Disorder is a mental illness or mental abnormality but is not the equivalent of legal insanity. Our statutes and case law make a clear distinction between being insane at the time of the crime and being mentally ill or mentally retarded, each requiring different forms of proof. Appellant's status as an involuntary outpatient after his second release from Georgia Regional Hospital does not change the fact that there was no prior adjudication of insanity.

Because there was no prior adjudication of insanity giving rise to a presumption of insanity, the trial court correctly placed upon appellant the burden of proving by a preponderance of the evidence that he was insane at the time of the crime.

The burden of proof having properly been placed upon appellant, we find the jury's rejection of his insanity defense is supported by sufficient evidence. The trial began with the presumption of sanity, and while appellant presented lay and expert testimony to rebut the presumption, presumptions of sanity do not dissipate on the presentation of contrary evidence. OCGA § 16–2–3; *Durham*, supra, 239 Ga. at 699, 238 S.E.2d 334. In Georgia, jurors are free to reject the testimony of witnesses as to the sanity of the accused, and to instead rely on the presumption of sanity. The evidence in this case thus authorized the finding that appellant knew right from wrong at the time of the crime, and appellant's mental illness, which was not the equivalent of legal insanity, did not require a verdict of not guilty by reason of insanity.

Construing the evidence in a light most favorable to the verdict, we also find that a rational trier of fact could have found appellant guilty but mentally ill beyond a reasonable doubt. *Jackson v. Virginia*, 443 U.S. 307, 99 S.Ct. 2781, 61 L. Ed.2d 560 (1979). Accordingly, the evidence in this case was sufficient to support the verdicts beyond a reasonable doubt, and the trial court did not err by failing to grant the motion for directed verdict.

Judgment affirmed.

All the Justices concur.

CASE QUESTIONS

1. How does the law in this state define insanity?
2. What presumption does the law make in regard to a person's sanity?
3. Why does the defendant claim that the burden of proving his insanity was unfairly shifted to him?

4.   Did the appellate court agree that the defendant had had a prior adjudication of insanity? Explain.
5.   What role does the jury play in a case involving the insanity defense?

ETHICAL CONSIDERATION: FINDING HIRED GUNS

There are experts who can and will testify to almost any kind of defense. The problem with expert witnesses usually isn't finding one; the problem is finding one who is credible and reliable. Some experts in the legal field are commonly referred to as "hired guns." These are fringe experts who will testify to the most outrageous claims. To avoid a potential fraud on the court—and serious loss of credibility for the client—a paralegal should request a resume or curriculum vitae from an expert and verify any claims made. Hired guns often charge considerably less than other experts, but it is often true that you get what you pay for. An expert who makes outlandish and baseless claims not only cheapens the legal profession, but also hurts the client's chances with the jury.

✔ Paralegal To Do List

For the defense paralegal:

- Has the client ever received any psychiatric counseling or treatment?
- Has the client ever been in a mental hospital or institution? If so, what is the name and address?
- Has the client ever received any serious injuries, especially to the head?
- Is the client suffering from any physical disabilities?
- Does the client have any medical condition that could account for mood swings or depression?
- Has the client ever used prescription drugs?
- Was the client under the influence of any drug (including alcohol) at the time of the offense?
- (In an insanity defense) How much time did the state's expert spend with the client? Detail each meeting and the time spent. If the time period is very short, prepare a chart showing how little time the expert actually spent with the client and compare it with the time your expert spent with the client.

For the prosecution paralegal:

- If the defense is insanity, the defense will have to present an expert. Who is this person? Dig into this person's background: Has he/she ever been published? What kind of degree does this person have? Has he/she ever practiced psychiatry or psychology? What other jobs has this person had?
- Did the defendant say anything during arrest or afterwards that could signal the kind of defense to be used? For instance, did the defendant claim that he/she was with others at the time of offense? If so, find these people and interview them.

- How much time has passed between the incident and prosecution? Is there a statute of limitations problem?

- Does the defense attorney have a regular expert he/she uses in cases where this defense is being used? If so, contact other prosecutors who have gone against this attorney and ask for information about experts and the attorney's skill.

- Go through all pending motions and double-check that the issues have been disposed of. Are there any clues in the pre-trial motions about unusual facts or circumstances that will come up during the trial? How can you help prepare for these facts?

- In an insanity case the prosecution must present an expert to rebut the defense. Talk to this witness. Is he/she likable? Will the expert make a good witness? Can he/she explain technical terms in a way that the jury will understand? If not, it may be time to think about getting an additions expert.

Chapter Summary

A person charged with a criminal offense has a litany of defenses available to him or her. It is important to understand the different levels of defenses. Some defenses require very little of the defense, while others require the presentation of witnesses and evidence. Some defenses are mere denials; others are affirmative defenses. An affirmative defense requires the defendant to present some evidence to support his or her contention. Although affirmative defenses do not require the defendant to take the stand at trial, they often require the defense to present testimony from witnesses.

WEB SITES

Affirmative Defenses—California
www.courts.ca.gov/partners/documents/PLEADING-AffDeflist.doc

Kentucky Court of Justice
http://courts.ky.gov/pages/default.aspx

Nebraska State Court System
www.supremecourt.ne.gov

Nevada State Court System
www.nevadajudiciary.us/index.php/administrativeofficesofthecourt

Oklahoma State Courts Network
www.oscn.net/applications/oscn/start.asp

Oregon Judicial System
http://courts.oregon.gov/OJD/courts/Pages/index.aspx

South Dakota State Court System
http://ujs.sd.gov

Stand Your Ground Laws—Huffington Post
www.huffingtonpost.com/news/stand-your-ground-laws

Virginia State Court System
www.courts.state.va.us/main.htm

REVIEW QUESTIONS

1. Steve is the star quarterback for the local high school football team. One Friday night in a game against the cross-town rivals, he is tackled and breaks his neck, leaving him permanently disabled. Can Steve seek criminal charges against the players who tackled him? Do the players have a legal defense? Explain.

2. Same facts as in question 1. This time, however, the play ends without Steve being injured. As Steve is getting up, a member of the opposing team rushes up to him and kicks him in the neck. Steve's neck is broken. Can Steve seek criminal charges against the player? Does the player have a legal defense? Explain.

3. A man goes out to his car and discovers that his key does not fit in the lock. He tries the key several times, then seeing that the back window of the car is open, he reaches inside and unlocks the back door. When he climbs into the backseat, he realizes that he is not in his own car. His car, which looks exactly like the car he is in, is actually two spaces down. Has he committed breaking and entering of an automobile? Why or why not?

QUESTION FOR REFLECTION

1. What happens if the defense attorney believes that her client is insane, the defendant's psychologist believes that the defendant is legally insane, but the defendant does not want to raise the insanity defense?

KEYWORDS AND PHRASES

Mistrial	Self-defense
Affirmative defense	Deadly force
Simple defense	Defense of others
Presumption of innocence	Consent
Inferences	Mutual combat
Presumptions	Duress
Preponderance of the evidence	Necessity
Rebuttal	Compulsion
Alibi	Coercion
Complete defense	Mistake

Entrapment

Insanity

M'Naghten test

Guilty but mentally ill

Diminished capacity

Battered woman syndrome

Equal protection

Due process

Double jeopardy

Vagueness

Overbreadth

Bills of attainder

Ex post facto laws

Statute of limitation

PRACTICAL APPLICATIONS

1. You see a man pointing a gun at a stranger, and you shoot the man to stop what you believe will be a homicide. Should you be entitled to use the defense of self-defense? Does it matter that the stranger's gun was empty or was a water pistol? Why or why not?

2. Do you have a legal defense when you shoot a person who is about to shoot your dog? Explain.

3. One day you are pulled over for speeding. The officer informs you that you were driving 60 mph in a 35 mph work zone. When you drove through the day before, the speed limit was 60 mph. The officer points to a small sign, which states the new speed limit. Do you have a valid defense of mistake? Why or why not?

4. In the *Marbles* case, the defendant claims that because he had been diagnosed with bipolar disorder (manic-depressive disorder), he was legally insane at the time of his crimes. Is this a valid insanity defense? Why or why not? (For a complete overview of the *Marbles* case, see the Appendix.)

NOTES

1. *Patterson v. New York*, 432 U.S. 197, 97 S. Ct. 2319, 53 L. Ed. 2d 281 (1977).

2. *State v. Adams*, 52 Conn. App. 643, 727 A.2d 780 (1999).

3. *Martin v. State*, 258 Ga. 300, 368 S.E.2d 515 (1988).

4. *State v. Getsy*, 84 Ohio St. 3d 180, 702 N.E.2d 866 (1998).

5. *Quick v. State*, 660 N.E.2d 598 (1996).

6. *State v. Clemons*, 82 Ohio St. 3d 438, 696 N.E.2d 1009 (1998).

7. *State v. Warden*, 133 Wash. 2d 559 (1997).

8. *State v. Wilburn*, 249 Kan. 678, 822 P.2d 609 (1991).

9. *Pottinger v. Miami*, 810 F Supp. 1551 (S.D.Fla.,1992).

Chapter 15

SENTENCING AND APPEAL

Chapter Objectives
At the completion of this chapter, you should be able to:
- Explain how a defendant is sentenced
- Describe sentencing hearings
- Describe the importance of the Eighth Amendment in sentencing
- Explain the importance of sentencing guidelines
- Explain the circumstances that must be present to impose the death penalty
- Describe the various kinds of prisons
- Explain the procedures involved in probation and parole
- Describe how an appeal proceeds through the various appellate courts

I. Sentencing

sentence
The punishment, such as time in jail, given to a person convicted of a crime.

The judge **sentences** defendants who are found guilty at trial. Because there are no further proceedings in cases where defendants are found not guilty, we will concentrate on the sentencing and appeals phase of criminal prosecutions in this chapter. In most jurisdictions, the judge has specific restrictions on the ultimate sentence that he or she can impose on the defendant. For instance, all crimes carry maximum sentences. In some states, for example, a conviction for armed robbery carries a maximum sentence of twenty years. Following a conviction for this crime, the judge

Exhibit 15-1

HIGHLIGHTS

- Adult correctional authorities supervised about 6,977,700 offenders at year-end 2011, a decrease of 1.4% during the year.

- The decline of 98,900 offenders during 2011 marked the third consecutive year of decrease in the correctional population, which includes probationers, parolees, local jail inmates, and prisoners in the custody of state and federal facilities.

- About 2.9% of adults in the United States (or 1 in every 34 adults) were under some form of correctional supervision at year-end 2011, a rate comparable to 1998(1 in every 34).

- At year-end 2011, about 1 in every 50 adults in the United States was supervised in the community on probation or parole, while about 1 in every 107 adults was incarcerated in prison or jail.

- The community supervision population (including probationers and parolees, down 1.5%) and the incarcerated population (including local jail inmates and federal and state prisoners, down 1.3%) decreased at about the same rate in 2011.

- The majority (83%) of the decline in the correctional population during the year was attributed to the decrease in the probation population (down 81,800 offenders).

Source: Capital Punishment, 2010, U.S. Bureau of Justice Statistics, U.S. Department of Justice.

cannot sentence a defendant to more than twenty years. See Exhibit 15-1 for an overview of sentencing in the United States.

A. Cruel and Unusual Punishment

"Excessive bail shall not be required, nor excessive fines imposed, nor cruel and unusual punishments inflicted."

—Amendment VIII, U.S. Constitution

One of the other important restrictions placed on the kind of sentence that can be imposed is set out in the Eighth Amendment to the United States Constitution. In very few words, that Amendment prohibits any punishment deemed "cruel and unusual." This Amendment was made applicable to the states through the Fourteenth Amendment. Many state constitutions also have similar provisions. Because the Amendment does not define exactly what constitutes cruel and unusual punishment, the U.S. Supreme Court has been called on to interpret it. The Court's decisions have established that a sentence cannot involve torture and that the sentence must be "proportional" to the crime.

■ **BULLET POINT**
Only defendants who have been found guilty or pled guilty are sentenced.

1. Proportionality

The U.S. Supreme Court has mandated that a sentence must be proportional to the crime to satisfy the Eighth Amendment. For instance, without some other aggravating circumstance, a life sentence for a petty infraction would be out of proportion and would be a violation of the Eighth Amendment.[1]

2. "Three Strikes and You're Out"

The so-called "three strikes" statutes generally require a lengthy prison sentence (sometimes even life in prison) for a third felony conviction. These statutes have been deemed constitutional by the Supreme Court because they place conditions on imposing such a severe sentence (namely, two prior felony convictions before the statute is triggered). In practice, this means that a defendant's third felony conviction could be for a relatively minor felony yet still satisfy the minimum requirements of the statute and trigger a mandatory life sentence.

▨ THE ROLE OF THE PARALEGAL: SENTENCING LAWS

It is important to know the sentencing laws in your state. Whether working with the prosecution or the defense, creating a sentencing folder is a good idea. This folder should contain the statute governing sentencing for a particular crime as well as any case law about mitigating or enhancing the sentence.

parole

A release from prison before a sentence is finished that depends on the person's "keeping clean" and doing what he or she is supposed to do after being released.

3. Life Sentence Without Parole

The U.S. Supreme Court also has held that sentences of life without **parole** do not violate the Eighth Amendment for certain offenses, including murder, kidnapping, bank robbery, narcotic offenses, and aggravated rape. Except for murder, life sentences without parole are only authorized when the other listed crimes (kidnapping, rape, etc.) involve violence or repeated convictions. See Exhibit 15-2.

4. Innovative Sentences

Many jurisdictions have passed statutes that call for the registration of known sex offenders or the photos of convicted drunk drivers to be posted in the local newspaper. In most situations, these statutes have been held to be constitutional.

B. Sentencing Guidelines

Many states and the federal government have imposed sentencing guidelines for individuals convicted of crimes. These guidelines have been imposed in many situations as a way of reaching more uniform results in sentencing. Essentially, these statutes take away some of the judge's discretion in imposing a sentence and require specific sentences for specific crimes.

Exhibit 15-2

Most severe sentence received by convicted offenders, by most serious conviction offense, 2006

Most serious conviction offense	Number of offenders	Total	Percent of convicted offenders sentenced to—					
			Incarceration			Non-incarceration		
			Total	Prison	Jail	Total	Probation	Other
All offenses	33,025	100%	70%	35	36	30%	25	5
Felonies	27,810	100%	73%	40	32	27%	25	2
Violent offenses	4,713	100%	80%	55	26	20%	18	1
Murder	147	100%	100%	98	2	0%	0	0
Rape	146	100%	80%	67	12	21%	21	0
Robbery	1,515	100%	86%	72	14	14%	13	1
Assault	1,893	100%	76%	43	33	24%	23	1
Other violent	1,014	100%	76%	42	34	24%	20	4
Property offenses	8,573	100%	75%	38	37	25%	23	2
Burglary	2,307	100%	82%	47	35	18%	16	1
Larceny/theft	2,685	100%	71%	32	39	29%	27	2
Motor vehicle theft	997	100%	87%	50	37	13%	12	1
Forgery	662	100%	72%	38	34	28%	27	1
Fraud	964	100%	55%	24	31	45%	40	5
Other property	957	100%	78%	34	43	22%	20	2
Drug offenses	10,710	100%	67%	36	32	33%	31	2
Trafficking	3,370	100%	77%	47	30	23%	22	1
Other drug	7,339	100%	63%	30	32	37%	35	3
Public-order offenses	3,749	100%	73%	41	32	27%	25	2
Weapons	1,100	100%	80%	53	27	20%	19	1
Driving-related	1,197	100%	65%	35	30	35%	31	4
Other public-order	1,451	100%	74%	37	37	26%	24	2
Misdemeanors	5,212	100%	57%	3	54	43%	22	21

Note: Data on type of sentence were available for 94% of convicted defendants. Sentences to incarceration that were wholly suspended are included under probation. Nine percent of prison sentences and 68% of jail sentences included a probation term. Sentences to incarceration or probation may have included a fine, restitution, community service, treatment, or other court-ordered conditions. Other sentences may include fines, community service, restitution, and treatment. Total for all felonies includes cases that could not be classified into one of the four major offense categories.

Details may not sum to totals because of rounding.

Source: Felony Defendants in Large Urban Counties, 2006, U.S. Bureau of Justice Statistics, U.S. Department of Justice.

The rationale for sentencing guidelines is that they provide more consistent sentences. When a judge has wide discretion in the sentence to be meted out, he or she may give a sentence that is considerably less or considerably more than the sentences other individuals have received for the same offense. This gives the criminal justice system the appearance of being arbitrary and capricious. Under sentencing guidelines, or "structured sentencing" as it is sometimes called, judges have far less discretion in the sentence they can impose on the defendant. When the judge is confronted with a defendant convicted of a crime, the judge must refer to a schedule that determines the sentence based on the kind of infraction and the defendant's prior criminal record. In many cases, the guidelines were

Exhibit 15-3

Correctional populations	Population, 12/31/2011	Percent of total	Population change, 2011	
			Number	Percent of total decline
Total*	6,977,700	100	−98,900	100
Probation[†]	3,971,319	56.9	−81,796	82.7
Parole[‡]	853,852	12.2	13,254	−13.4
Prison[§]	1,504,150	21.6	−17,264	17.5
Local jail[¶]	735,601	10.5	−13,127	13.3
Multiple correctional status[**]	87,200	:	:	:

Note: Estimates were rounded to the nearest 100. Details may not sum to totals due to rounding.
:Not calculated.
*Equals the sum of each correctional population and excludes the number of offenders with multiple correctional statuses. Change equals the sum of the change for each correctional population. See *Methodology*.
[†]Change equals the difference between the January 1 and December 31,2011, populations.
[‡]Custody prison population as of December 31. See the text box on page 2 for a discussion of the difference between the custody and jurisdiction prison populations. Change equals the difference between the December 31 custody prison populations for 2010 and 2011.
[§]Population is as of the last weekday in June. Change equals the difference between the populations on the last weekday in June 2010 and 2011.
[**]Some probationers and parolees on December 31,2011, were held in a prison or jail but still remained under the jurisdiction of a probation or parole agency and were excluded from the total correctional population to avoid double counting. See table 4 and *Methodology*.

Source: Correctional Populations in the U.S. 2011, U.S. Bureau of Justice Statistics, U.S. Department of Justice.

imposed by legislatures eager to show a "get tough on crime" stance.[2] See Exhibit 15-3.

■ **BULLET POINT**

Sentencing guidelines have been passed in many states and in the federal system.

1. Judge's Discretion

Sentencing guidelines were imposed as a way of curbing a judge's discretion. In jurisdictions where sentencing guidelines do not exist, just how much discretion does a judge have? The answer is that that the judge has broad discretion. The judge can take into account a wide range of factors when fashioning a sentence.

2. Sentencing Hearings

At the conclusion of a trial or as part of the defendant's guilty plea, the judge may hold a sentencing hearing to determine what sentence the defendant should receive. A sentencing hearing allows the prosecution to

Exhibit 15-4

Factors thar a judge may consider in sentencing

- Facts of the offense
- Aggravating or mitigating factors of the crime
- Aggravating or mitigating factors in the defendant's personal background
- Impact of the crime on the victim and community
- The defendant's remorse (or lack thereof)
- The defendant's criminal history

present evidence to justify a harsher sentence. The defense also has the opportunity of presenting any evidence that might mitigate the sentence. This hearing is like a mini-trial. Witnesses may testify and both sides may introduce evidence to support their positions.

a. Pre-sentence Investigation At the conclusion of a trial where a defendant has been found guilty or after a defendant has entered a guilty plea, a judge may delay sentencing until some future date to allow the probate/parole office to conduct a **pre-sentence investigation** (PSI). The purpose of a pre-sentence investigation is for the authorities to prepare a report that examines the defendant's circumstances prior to the commission of the crime (including the details of the crime), the defendant's upbringing, and his or her criminal history. The PSI will also examine any other factors that go toward mitigation or aggravation of the defendant's sentence. Defense attorneys are given an opportunity to supplement the probation officer's materials with anything they believe relevant. However, the judge has the final decision on sentencing.

3. Presentation of Evidence in Aggravation of Sentence

During a sentencing hearing, the prosecutor may seek to introduce a wide range of evidence to justify a harsher sentence for the defendant. For example, the prosecution might show that:

- The defendant has prior criminal convictions.
- The defendant's actions have had an adverse impact on the victim or the victim's family.
- The defendant poses a significant threat to the community or is likely to commit more crimes in the future.

If the state plans on presenting evidence to support its request for a tougher sentence, then the state must produce this evidence during the trial. In that way, the aggravating factors are proven beyond a reasonable doubt and the judge is then allowed to consider them during sentencing.[3]

4. Presentation of Evidence in Mitigation of Sentence

The defense may also present evidence in mitigation of the defendant's sentence. For instance, the defense may show that the defendant has a poor education or had a bad childhood to help explain why the defendant resorted to crime. In addition to family life and education, the defense might introduce evidence of the defendant's mental stability or intelligence. In addition, the defendant may take the stand and testify about the circumstances of his life as a way to explain why he committed the crime.

II. Victim-Witness Programs

Many prosecutors' offices have established victim-witness coordinators to assist victims and others in recovering from the effects of a crime. These offices normally operate under the supervision of the district attorney or

pre-sentence Investigation
An investigation by court-appoint social workers, probation officers, etc., into a criminal's background to determine the criminal's prospects for rehabilitation.

■ **BULLET POINT**
When the state requests that the defendant serve the maximum sentence, it often presents evidence in aggravation of sentence to justify the sentence.

■ **BULLET POINT**
A defendant is permitted to present evidence that might lower his or her total sentence, such as evidence of mistreatment as a child, extreme financial problems that caused his or her actions, or some other factor that might lessen the defendant's culpability in the eyes of the court.

State's attorney. Victim-witness coordinators help ensure that victims and witnesses know where to go to testify and help them prepare for trial. These offices often provide separate facilities for particularly vulnerable people, such as child molestation and sexual assault victims. Some coordinators also arrange counseling and other programs to help victims after the trial has concluded. In addition, these individuals often work closely with the prosecution team, advising them on the best way to approach a witness and acting as a guide and helpmate to the victim throughout the ordeal of the trial.

A. Victims' Rights

Many states have enacted statutes that allow victims of specific kinds of crime to recover money from state or federal funds. These funds are designed to help defray some of the costs associated with obtaining replacement goods (or to meet insurance deductibles when insurance coverage exists).

1. Victim Impact Statement

victim impact statement
An oral or written statement by the victim of the crime that explains how the defendant's crime has changed the victim's life and can include a victim's request for a specific type of sentence.

Another victims' right initiative includes statutes that allow a victim to have some personal input at the defendant's sentencing hearing. A victim is permitted and often encouraged to file such a statement that can be read at the hearing and is made a part of the defendant's file. A **victim impact statement** allows the victim to tell the judge what effect the defendant's crime has had on the victim's life. Victim impact statements are often an important part of the healing process that occurs in the aftermath of a crime, especially a violent crime.

III. The Death Penalty

Originally, the prohibition of cruel and unusual punishment was enacted to prohibit torture. The Founding Fathers had seen enough of such practices. The Eighth Amendment does not forbid a sentence of death; it simply means that the sentence must be carried out with as little pain as possible. Most "innovations" in the mechanisms of executing a human being have been based on making the death as painless as possible. In the early part of the twentieth century, Thomas Edison advocated the newly invented electric chair as a "painless" form of execution.

A. Procedures in Death Penalty Cases

■ **BULLET POINT**
Many prosecution offices across the United States now have full-time victim/witness coordinators.

Issues surrounding the imposition of the death penalty could fill an entire volume. Sentencing a person to execution at the hands of the state has always been considered the most extreme sanction in law. As such, death penalty cases, or capital murder cases, have different safeguards and procedures than are seen in other charges. As we have seen, a death sentence

- ■ Death by hanging
- ■ Death by firing squad
- ■ Death by electrocution
- ■ Death by gas
- ■ Death by lethal injection

Exhibit 15-5
Methods of execution not deemed cruel and unusual

is not necessarily cruel and unusual punishment, but the manner in which it is carried out may be. Many jurisdictions limit the methods of execution to those that are proven.

B. Sentencing in Death Penalty Cases

Sentencing in death penalty cases raises a whole host of crucial issues. Death penalty trials are always **bifurcated**, meaning that there are two trials. When a defendant is charged with capital murder and the government announces its intention to seek the death penalty, special rules are triggered to protect the defendant. The bifurcated trial consists of the guilt phase, where the jury decides whether the defendant is guilty of the crime, and the sentencing phase, where the judge or jury is called upon to decide if the defendant's actions warrant a death sentence. After recent U.S. Supreme Court rulings, the only crime that warrants a death sentence is murder. Although in the past it was possible to be sentenced to death for crimes such as rape, all jurisdictions limit a death sentence to cases involving homicide. In some states, only a jury can decide to impose a death sentence. In other jurisdictions, the judge decides to impose death. In either situation, the fact finder must not only decide that the defendant is guilty of the crime, but also decide that the defendant's actions warrant a death sentence. The only way to reach this conclusion is to find that certain aggravating factors were present. Simply killing another person is not enough to warrant a death sentence. For a person to be sentenced to death, the murder must have been committed during the commission of another crime (such as rape) or in a particularly gruesome way. See Exhibit 15-7 for the number of persons executed in the United States.

To put a convicted murderer to death, it is not enough that the defendant simply have committed a murder. For the death sentence to be justified, the defendant must have committed the murder under special—or

bifurcated
Refers to separate hearings for different issues in the same case (e.g., for guilt and sanity or guilt and punishment in a criminal case).

- ■ Torture
- ■ Act committed in an outrageously or wantonly vile, inhuman way
- ■ Committed during another crime, such as rape
- ■ Involved depravity of mind

Exhibit 15-6
Aggravating factors that would justify a death sentence

Exhibit 15-7
Number of Executions in
State System, 1930–2009

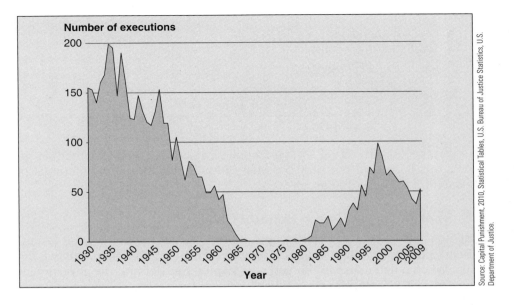

Source: Capital Punishment, 2010, Statistical Tables, U.S. Bureau of Justice Statistics, U.S. Department of Justice.

BULLET POINT

Only after a defendant has been found guilty of first-degree murder and the jury has reached a conclusion that the death penalty is warranted because of aggravating factors in the case will the defendant be sentenced to death.

"aggravating"—factors. Only when the factors are present in a case is the death penalty authorized. Among the most common aggravating factors are that the murder was:

- Committed during the course of a felony, such as rape or kidnapping.
- Done for money.
- Done in a particularly heinous, cruel, or depraved manner, including torture.
- Committed by a defendant who killed two or more people.
- Carried out while the defendant was escaping from legal confinement.
- Committed against a child.
- Committed during an act of terrorism.
- Carried out by a defendant who had a prior conviction for first-degree murder.
- Committed against an elected official or a police officer.

C. Eliminating Death Penalty Sentences

In recent years, states such as Connecticut have eliminated the option of the death penalty. Although the majority of states still use the death penalty, it is interesting to note that many European countries have bans on its use.

D. Bills Barring Execution of Mentally Retarded

Several states have passed legislation barring the execution of the mentally retarded. Some states, such as Georgia, have prohibited executing the mentally handicapped for decades. In 2001, Governor Jeb Bush signed such a law into effect for Florida. States such as Texas have consistently failed to enact such a provision.

IV. Non-capital Sentencing

When the judge sentences a defendant to a term in prison, the judge may order that the sentence be served consecutively to other prison terms or concurrently with other terms. A **consecutive** prison term is added to a current prison term. If a defendant has been sentenced to a five-year prison term on one offense, then his new sentence will begin when the first prison term has ended. On the other hand, a **concurrent** sentence is served at the same time as another prison term. Obviously, a defendant would prefer to be sentenced to a concurrent sentence instead of a consecutive sentence. Judges often sentence defendants to consecutive sentences to increase the overall time that a defendant will serve in custody.

A. Types of Prisons

There are different types of prisons. Depending on the nature of the offense and the defendant's prior record, time may be served in a maximum, medium, or minimum security facility. The differences in these institutions are profound. A maximum security facility houses some of the worst offenders: rapists, murderers, etc., whereas a minimum security facility is home to nonviolent offenders. Maximum security facilities often have double rows of razor wire-topped fencing and guard towers manned by armed security guards who are authorized to shoot anyone attempting to escape. Minimum security facilities, on the other hand, often look more like dormitories, have less security, and rarely see escape attempts.

B. Private Prisons

In some states, private companies have gotten in the business of running prisons. Claiming that they can run a prison more efficiently, these companies house, feed, and secure prisoners in privately constructed facilities. Private prisons can be lucrative.

V. Probation and Parole

When a defendant is released from prison, he will often continue to serve the balance of his sentence on **probation** or parole. Probation officers ensure that the defendant follows the conditions of his sentence. For instance, if the defendant has been ordered to pay fines or restitution, the probation officer is the person who monitors these payments. In addition, the probation officer also makes sure that the probationer obtains employment, refrains from drug use, etc. If the probationer commits another

---

consecutive sentencing
A sentencing of a defendant that requires multiple sentences to be served one after another.

concurrent sentencing
A ruling by the judge that the defendant's multiple sentences may be served at the same time.

■ **BULLET POINT**
Whether a defendant serves a sentence concurrently or consecutively can have a big impact on the total amount of time he or she serves in prison.

probation
The action of allowing a person convicted of a criminal offense to avoid serving a jail sentence so long as he or she abides by certain conditions (usually including being supervised by a probation officer).

crime while serving probation, the probation officer can seek to have the original probation revoked and the defendant returned to prison.

A. Comparing Probation to Parole

Probation is usually given in place of a prison sentence. When a convict is placed on probation, it means that he will monitored to see that he does not commit any new crimes, does not engage in the use of drugs or other harmful practices, and is gainfully employed. **Parole**, on the other hand, is the term used when a person is released from prison before serving his full sentence. The balance of his sentence will be served on parole. While he is on parole, he is subject to many of the same conditions that the probationer faced: supervision, employment requirements, etc.

B. Probation Revocation Hearings

When a probationer violates one or more conditions of his probation, the probation officer is authorized to file a petition with the original sentencing judge, asking that the probation be revoked. In many states, prosecutors can also file such petitions. Probation revocation hearings are similar to trials. The state presents evidence to justify revoking the defendant's probation, and the defense is permitted to present evidence to show that the defendant should be allowed to continue on probation.

C. Private companies and probation

Private industry has also gotten in the business of monitoring probationers. In some states, private companies monitor all people sentenced on misdemeanor cases and state probation officers monitor convicted felons.

D. Fines

The Eighth Amendment to the U.S. Constitution not only forbids cruel and unusual punishment, but also prohibits excessive fines. Many states have enacted minimum fines that a convicted defendant must pay as part of his sentence. For instance, some states require a minimum fine of $1000 on a third conviction for driving under the influence of alcohol in a five-year period. Other offenses, such as trafficking in narcotics, carry much stiffer fines. Fines for some narcotics offenses are as high as $250,000 in some

---

Probation? Parole? What's the Difference?

Probation and parole are both confinement sentences. For example, a person receives a five-year sentence. If he is released from prison early because of good behavior, he will serve the balance of his sentence on parole. Probation is usually given to people who are not sentenced to confinement.

parole
A sentence served under supervision after a defendant is released from prison.

■ **BULLET POINT**
If a defendant commits another offense while out on probation, his or her original probationary sentence can be revoked and the defendant can be returned to prison where he or she will await trial on the new case.

Exhibit 15-8
Infractions that would justify revocation of probation or parole

---

- Committing a new offense
- Failure to pay fines and/or restitution
- Failure to abide by the terms of probation: drug use, etc.
- Absconding from supervision (e.g., leaving the state without permission)

INSIDER'S VIEWPOINT

Technology and Probation

"We have an electronic kiosk in our front office where probationers can check in. They are issued a card that they use in it and they have to put their thumb on the screen, for a positive identification. They can pay their fines there and do some basic checking in."

—Mike Burgamy, Probation Officer

---

states. However, the fine must still be proportional to the nature of the offense. A minor offense should not be assessed a huge fine.

Once a defendant is sentenced and begins serving his sentence on probation, he must make regular payments to the probation office on his fine. When a probationer fails to make payments on his outstanding fine, his probation can be revoked and he can be returned to incarceration. A person serving time in custody does not have to make any payments on fines, court costs, or restitution.

E. Community Service

For misdemeanors and some types of minor felonies, a court may sentence a defendant to **community service**. A sentence served on community service usually puts the defendant to work picking up trash on roads around the county, working in local government offices, or carrying out light labor such as collecting trash or processing materials at a state-run recycling plant. Community service is frequently required in cases involving driving under the influence and for some first-time offenders.

community service
A provision in a defendant's sentence that requires him or her to perform some basic functions for the local government, such as picking up trash or assisting at a recycling center.

F. Suspended Sentence

A defendant may also be sentenced to a suspended sentence. A suspended sentence is essentially no sentence at all. A defendant sentenced to a suspended sentence is still technically convicted of a crime, but does not serve any time in prison and will probably not pay a fine.

G. Pardons and Commutations

State governors and the President are authorized to issue **pardons** for people convicted of crimes. A pardon rescinds the conviction. Usually, a pardon is issued only when there is some question about the defendant's guilt or there are other concerns about justice in the case. The power to issue pardons is considered to be an executive privilege and cannot be rescinded by the other branches of government. In recent years, a few questionable pardon cases on the national level brought this fairly low-key

pardon
A President's or governor's release of a person from punishment for a crime.

commute
To change a criminal punishment to one that is less severe.

executive privilege into the limelight. The president or state governors are also empowered to reduce an overall sentence. For example, to **commute** a death sentence would be to reduce it to life in prison.

H. Early Release

Most jurisdictions have provisions that allow a prisoner to be released prior to serving his full sentence. For instance, in many states, there is a provision called "day for a day." If the prisoner abides by the rules and has "good behavior," the state will take away one day of his sentence for every day that he has been a model prisoner. In those jurisdictions, a prisoner serving a six-year sentence could be released in three years. If the prisoner becomes a trustee at the facility or gets a job with a certain amount of responsibility, he might get more than a day for a day. In jurisdictions that have imposed sentencing guidelines, however, these programs have often been eliminated. On the federal level, for example, a sentence of six years means that the prisoner will serve six years.

VI. Civil Remedies in Criminal Cases

restitution
Programs in some states that make a convicted criminal repay the crime victim in money or work.

forfeiture
Loss of the right to something due to neglect of a duty due to an offense. For example, if a criminal defendant fails to show up for trial, the judge may order a forfeiture of the defendant's bail bond.

In addition to fines, a defendant may also be ordered to compensate the victim for damages or items taken. **Restitution** is like damages in civil cases, where the defendant pays money to compensate the victim for injuries. The restitution amount must normally be proven during the sentencing hearing unless the defendant agrees to pay the restitution as part of a plea agreement. As the defendant makes payments to his probation officer on his fines and fees, the probation department also collects restitution for the victim. In many cases, the victim receives the final restitution amount as a lump payment.

A. Forfeiture

Other criminal remedies also resemble civil remedies. In some cases when a defendant commits certain types of crimes, he may face **forfeiture** of personal property. For instance, a defendant who uses a car to help distribute narcotics may not only be arrested and charged for sale of narcotics, but also have his car forfeited to the state. Forfeiture proceedings are more civil than criminal in nature. If the state can show that the defendant's car was used to further criminal activity, the judge may order that the seized car be given to the state or, more specifically, to the local police department to use for official business.

■ **BULLET POINT**
   Although civil remedies are available for most types of criminal actions, the civil plaintiff faces a practical issue: If the defendant is in prison, it will be virtually impossible to force him or her to pay damages.

B. Suing the Defendant in Civil Court

Crime victims also have the right to file civil suits against perpetrators regardless of the outcome of the criminal case. In fact, a victim can file a civil suit against a perpetrator even before the criminal case is disposed of.

VII. Alternative Punishment

In some situations, a judge may consider an alternative form of punishment. For instance, in appropriate cases, a judge may order that a defendant be held under house arrest. Several private companies specialize in monitoring services, some of which use advanced technology such as electronic ankle bracelets and computer terminals to confirm that a defendant remains within the confines of the home.

A. Boot Camps

Other alternative forms of punishment include boot camps and shock incarceration. Someone who has been sentenced to a boot camp is normally sent there for a maximum period of 90 days. The conditions are stricter than what is seen in most prisons. Modeled on military boot camps, prisoners of such facilities must abide by a strict code of conduct. The advantage for a prisoner is that with successful completion of the program, he is released sooner than he would have been normally. Of course, if the defendant cannot abide by the limitations of the boot camp, his sentence will convert to a more conventional prison sentence.

B. Prisoner Rights

Several federal and Supreme Court decisions have stated that prisons must maintain an adequate law library. Because a criminal defendant incarcerated in the prison system has a great deal of time on his hands, the defendant often learns a great deal about the law during his incarceration. Some inmates become experts at the appellate process and are often referred to as "jailhouse lawyers." These individuals have developed an expertise in the area of appellate law and often assist other inmates with their knowledge. Most attorneys are reluctant to take cases on appeal, primarily because they often do not get paid. Because of this, many convicted prisoners end up representing themselves on appeal.

VIII. Appealing a Criminal Case

A defendant who has been found guilty has the right to **appeal** the conviction. How this appeal is raised and to whom it is presented vary from jurisdiction to jurisdiction, however. For the sake of clarity, we will assume that a defendant has been found guilty of a major felony (sexual assault, for example) in a state court because there is more uniformity from state to state in such cases than in other types of charges.

The appellate process begins by the defendant filing of a motion for new trial.

A. Motion for New Trial

The appeal process begins shortly after the trial ends. In many jurisdictions, the defendant has ten days after being sentenced to file a motion

---

Using a Computer to Monitor People on Probation

Computers have now been added to the arsenal of monitoring devices for people serving sentences on probation. In some cases, judges sentence people to house arrest as an alternative to placing them in jail. A computer randomly calls the person to make sure he or she is at home. Some units have cameras and breathalyzers so that a probation officer can see the person as well as obtain a random breath sample (for instance, when the defendant is known to abuse alcohol).

"At least 80% of all criminal jury trials worldwide take place in the United States."[4]

appeal
To ask a higher court to review the actions of a lower court to correct mistakes or injustice.

Exhibit 15-9
Typical appellate court
structure on the state and
federal level

Trial court → Court of Appeals → Supreme Court

for a new trial. A motion for new trial states specific irregularities that occurred in the trial that justify a new trial for the defendant. In most jurisdictions, the judge who heard the trial also hears the motion for new trial. If the judge grants the request, then a new trial is ordered and the process over as though the first trial never occurred. If the judge denies the request, then the defendant's appellate rights are triggered. In most situations, the motion for new trial is denied. Because we are assuming that this is a state prosecution, the defendant may now seek to have his conviction appealed in the state appellate court. In many states, this appellate court is called the court of appeals, and we will use that name for the rest of the discussion.

■ **BULLET POINT**
The appeal of a criminal case can only begin after the defendant has been found guilty, has been sentenced, and has filed a motion for new trial.

B. Notice of Appeal

Once the motion for new trial has been denied, a defendant files a notice of appeal. This places the state on notice that the defendant intends to appeal his conviction to the court of appeals. The filing of a notice of appeal with the court of appeals triggers the deadlines that both the state and the defense must follow to have a legal appeal. The time limits vary from state to state, but most states have a specific time period from the time of a notice of appeal has been filed until the time the appeal must be docketed with the court of appeals. Once the defendant files his brief, the state has a set period of time in which to respond to that filing.

brief
A written statement prepared by one side in a lawsuit to explain its case to the judge.

C. The Brief

Cases are appealed by the filing of a written **brief** in a case. A brief is often dozens of pages long in which the legal issues and the research accompanying those issues are documented for the court of appeals. A brief for the defendant lists the actions that occurred at the trial, the reasons these are errors under the law, and a request that the court of appeals reverse the conviction.

Here is an example of a typical enumeration of error in a trial brief:

The trial court committed reversible error by allowing into evidence autopsy photographs of the victim.

reversible error
A mistake made by a judge in the procedures used at trial or in making legal rulings during the trial.

Following this enumeration of error, the defendant would then explain to the court of appeals why allowing such evidence into the trial was **reversible error**. Not all errors in a case justify the reversal of a defendant's conviction. Reversible error could have affected the outcome of the case. The defense would base its claim of reversible error on both the events of the trial and legal research. A brief contains a blending of facts and research to support a particular claim. The defense would rely on previous cases in which similar events occurred that were considered to be error.

▊ THE ROLE OF THE PARALEGAL: CREATING A BRIEF BANK

Many subjects recur in criminal appellate briefs. One way to keep from "reinventing the wheel" is to create a brief bank. A brief bank is a folder or computer file where previously drafted briefs are stored. When a new brief calls for material that was thoroughly researched in a previous brief, an enterprising paralegal can simply pull the old brief out of the file or pull it up on the computer screen and save hours of work.

1. The Prosecution Brief

The brief filed by the prosecution refutes the claims of the defense. The prosecution argues that the trial was proper and that a new trial is not justified.

D. What Appellate Courts Can and Cannot Do

Appellate courts can only review the **record** of the case on appeal. No witnesses testify before the court of appeals or Supreme Court. An appeal is not a new trial. It is a review of the record balanced with previous case law. No new evidence will be produced in an appellate court. In fact, appellate courts are limited in what they can do with the case on appeal. An appellate court can **affirm**, **reverse**, or **remand** a case.

When an appellate court affirms a decision, it agrees with the lower court's decision in the case. If the decision is reversed, it means that the appellate court is changing the decision of the lower court. A reversal at the first appellate court means that the defendant's conviction is invalidated and the defendant must be retried. To justify a reversal, the appellate court must point to some irregularity or legal violation that occurred in the trial. In cases where an appeal results in a reversal, the prosecution must decide whether to continue to appeal to a higher court or to retry the defendant. In most cases where the appeal results in a decision of reversal, the state decides to appeal them to the next higher court. A decision of remand, which is a relatively rare decision, simply means that the court does not have sufficient information to make a decision and is therefore sending the case back to a trial court for a further hearing on some specific issue. Once this hearing is held, the case is sent back to the appellate court for further review.

E. The Supreme Court

Whenever a party loses before the court of appeals, that party has a right to continue with the appellate process. However, appealing to the supreme court is a good deal harder than appealing to the court of appeals. All states have some form of supreme court. This is the highest state level

record
The actual evidence (testimony, physical objects, etc.) as well as the evidence that was refused admission by the judge.

affirm
To validate. For example, when a higher court declares that a lower court's action was valid and right, it affirms the decision.

reverse
To set aside. For example, when a higher court reverses a lower court on appeal, it sides aside the judgment of the lower court.

remand
To send back. For example, a higher court may remand a case to a lower court, directing the lower court to take some action.

certiorari

(Latin) "To make sure."
A request for certiorari (cert)
is like an appeal, but one
that the higher court is not
required to take for
decision.

appellate court. Unlike an appeal to the court of appeals, appeals to the supreme court of the state involve different procedural requirements. For one thing, almost all state supreme courts have the power of **certiorari**, or *cert*.

1. Cert

State supreme courts, like the U.S. Supreme Court, have the power of cert. This means that they do not have to accept all cases that are appealed to them. When a court has the power of cert, it can decide which cases it will and will not hear. If a court grants cert, this simply means that the court has decided to hear the appeal. It does not mean that either party has won; it means that the appeal can proceed. If a state supreme court denies cert, this means that the court has decided that it will not hear the appeal, and barring some further development, the appeal is over. A denial of cert effectively ends the appeal process unless the person appealing can get a higher court to review the case. In an appeal where the original defendant has been denied cert in the state supreme court, he may decide to appeal his case to the U.S. Supreme Court. This court, like the state supreme court, also has the power of cert.

In cases where the state Supreme Court grants cert, the appeal will be heard in that court. Here, the procedure on appeal is similar to the procedure used in the state Court of appeals. Both parties submit briefs, and both have the right to argue their case orally before the court. There is no requirement of an oral argument before the state supreme court, and in most appeals, oral argument is waived. However, there are times when the issues are of such importance that the parties may decide to make an oral argument to press home the seriousness of the issues involved in the case.

2. Oral Argument

An oral argument before the state supreme court consists of presenting the case before the assembled state supreme court justices. Oral arguments are usually scheduled for a specific day of the week in which all parties who have requested oral argument are scheduled to appear. During the course of one side's oral argument, any of the supreme court justices may interrupt with questions about procedural or legal issues. The justices expect prompt and accurate answers to their questions. There is old saying among lawyers that oral argument will never win a case, but can often lose it. The effect of a well-written and well-presented brief may be diminished by a poor performance during oral argument phase.

Exhibit 15-10
Cert

Trial court → Court of Appeals → Supreme Court

3. Opinions

The court publishes its decision in an **opinion**. An opinion contains the legal reasoning and ultimately the court's justification for its decision in the case. Opinions can be somewhat lengthy documents in which the court spends a great deal of time justifying its decision on both the facts and the law of the state. The decision of the court will be set out at the end of the opinion in which the court lists that it affirms the decision of the lower court or reverses the decision of the lower court. Because the decision of the supreme court or court of appeals is so important—not only for the parties involved, but also for other legal researchers—these opinions are gathered and published. A set of published opinions is referred to as a case reporter. Reporters simply lump together all of a court's published decisions during a specific term. The cases are bound and put in chronological order. Each year a hardcover edition of these cases is put out, and most attorneys then place this book in their library.

opinion
A judge's statement about the conclusions in an appeal.

F. The Appellate Process: Why Does It Take So Long?

It is not unusual for appeals in criminal cases to go on for years. The process discussed above sounds relatively straightforward, but in practice, it normally takes considerable time. It can easily take six to eighteen months to complete an appeal to the court of appeals. These courts hear all appeals in criminal and civil cases and usually have a substantial backlog of cases. Whoever loses in the court of appeals will probably want to appeal to the supreme court. An appeal there can easily take another one to three years. Sometimes, these appeals can last considerably longer. It is not unusual, therefore, for a defendant's first appeal to last anywhere from two to three years. This is just the *first* appeal. Once a defendant has exhausted her first round of appeals, it is common for her to bring another appeal. This new round of appeals may involve the federal court system.

G. Habeas Corpus

A habeas corpus action is an appeal using the federal court system. **Habeas corpus** is based on U.S. constitutional amendments requiring that a criminal defendant must be held for reasonable grounds. Although it was not originally designed to give a criminal defendant a second round of appeals, habeas corpus is now used to appeal many criminal convictions. In a habeas corpus action, a criminal defendant is requesting the federal court system to remove the defendant from a state prison system based on some alleged unconstitutional action that occurred in the trial. Because a habeas corpus action is brought in federal court, it follows the federal appellate court system perhaps all the way up to the U.S. Supreme Court. Appeals through the federal court systems sometimes take five to ten years.

Habeas corpus
(Latin) "You have the body." A judicial order to someone holding a person to bring that person to court. It is most often used to get a person out of unlawful imprisonment by forcing the captor and the person being held to come to court for a decision on the legality of the imprisonment.

H. Appeals in Death Penalty Cases

In death penalty cases, appeals often take years. In some states, the highest court has no power of cert in such cases. This means that the state supreme court cannot refuse to hear such an appeal. This is one reason appeals in death penalty cases take so long to be heard. Normally, a person sentenced to death will try every possible avenue of appeal. Defendants routinely appeal death sentences all the way to the U.S. Supreme Court. After losing there, a death row inmate oftens turn to the federal courts on a habeas action. This appeal often winds up in the U.S. Supreme Court again. This is why death penalty appeals often go on for ten to fifteen years.

Case Excerpt. Ted Bundy's Death Sentence

BUNDY V. STATE, 538 SO.2D 445 (FLA.,1989) PER CURIAM.

Theodore Robert Bundy, a prisoner under sentence of death and execution warrant, appeals the trial court's denial of his Florida Rule of Criminal Procedure 3.850 motion for postconviction relief and his application for stay of execution. We have jurisdiction under article V, section 3(b)(1), of the Florida Constitution.

Bundy was convicted of the first-degree murder of twelve-year-old Kimberly Leach and sentenced to death. The conviction and sentence were affirmed by this Court in *Bundy v. State*, 471 So.2d 9 (Fla.1985), cert. denied, 479 U.S. 894, 107 S.Ct. 295, 93 L.Ed.2d 269 (1986). After the governor signed a death warrant, Bundy filed a motion for postconviction relief under Florida Rule of Criminal Procedure 3.850, which was denied. This Court affirmed and at the same time denied a petition for writ of habeas corpus. *Bundy v. State*, 497 So.2d 1209 (Fla.1986). Bundy then filed a petition for habeas corpus in federal district court, which was also denied. However, the court of appeals stayed Bundy's execution pending appeal from the denial of his petition for habeas corpus. *Bundy v. Wainwright*, 805 F.2d 948 (11th Cir.1986). That court later directed the district court to hold an evidentiary hearing on Bundy's claim that he was incompetent to stand trial. *Bundy v. Dugger*, 816 F.2d 564 (11th Cir.), cert. denied, 484 U.S. 870, 108 S.Ct. 198, 98 L.Ed.2d 149 (1987). After holding such a hearing, the district court ruled that Bundy "was at all times competent to stand trial for the murder of Kimberly Diane Leach." *Bundy v. Dugger*, 675 F.Supp. 622, 635 (M.D.Fla.1987). This order was affirmed by the court of appeals in *Bundy v. Dugger*, 850 F.2d 1402 (11th Cir.1988). The U.S. Supreme Court denied Bundy's petition for writ of certiorari. *Bundy v. Dugger*, 488 U.S. 1034, 109 S.Ct. 849, 102 L.Ed.2d 980 (1989). On January 17, 1989, the governor signed a second death warrant and scheduled Bundy's execution for January 24, 1989.

On January 17, 1989, Bundy filed his new motion in the trial court, together with an application for stay of execution. Because he was the judge at Bundy's trial, Circuit Judge Wallace Jopling, now retired, was assigned to hear the motions. However, Bundy filed a motion to recuse Judge Jopling, which was granted. Thus, Circuit Judge John W. Peach heard Bundy's motions. After a review of the pleadings and listening to the argument of counsel, the trial court granted the state's motion to dismiss and denied Bundy's motion for an evidentiary hearing and application for stay of execution.

All of Bundy's claims are related to his convictions for the Chi Omega killings which were affirmed by this Court in *Bundy v. State*, 455 So.2d 330 (Fla.1984), cert. denied, 476 U.S. 1109, 106 S.Ct. 1958, 90 L.Ed.2d 366 (1986). The trial on the Chi Omega case took place several months before the Kimberly Leach trial. While those convictions and sentence of death remain intact, the court of appeals has also directed the federal district court to conduct an evidentiary hearing on Bundy's claim that he was incompetent during the Chi Omega trial. See *Bundy v. Dugger*, 816 F.2d at 568.

Bundy's first claim is that the trial court should have held a hearing concerning Bundy's competency, particularly in view of Bundy's rejection of a proposed plea agreement which would have spared his life. Notwithstanding the fact that after an evidentiary hearing the federal courts have concluded that Bundy was competent, he argues that the testimony of Judge Jopling given at the federal court hearing that there was no need for a competency hearing was flawed because it was based in part upon his knowledge that Bundy had been found competent in a full hearing in the Chi Omega case, and the validity of this finding remains in question in federal district court.

Bundy's claim is procedurally barred because he failed to raise the issue on direct appeal. Furthermore, Bundy did raise the issue of his mental competence in his earlier unsuccessful motion for postconviction relief. Thus, the reassertion of this claim constitutes an abuse of process. *Booker v. State*, 503 So.2d 888 (Fla.1987).

This claim is also barred by the provisions of rule 3.850 which require motions for postconviction relief to be filed within two years after the judgment and sentence become final (1) unless the facts upon which the claim is predicated are unknown and could not have been reasonably ascertained, or (2) the fundamental constitutional right asserted was not established within the applicable time period and has been held to apply retroactively. Bundy's conviction and sentence became final when the United States Supreme Court denied his petition for certiorari on October 14, 1986. Hence, this claim should have been raised by October 14, 1988, providing it was known. Judge Jopling testified at the federal court competency hearing in December of 1987. Therefore, Bundy had at least ten months before the expiration of the two-year period within which to raise the claim but failed to do so.

Bundy's second claim relates to the validity of the Chi Omega convictions which were used in part as a basis for the finding of the aggravated circumstance that Bundy had committed prior violent felonies. He says that the Chi Omega convictions may be set aside in the pending federal court proceedings. Under such circumstances, he argues that he would be entitled to resentencing pursuant to the rationale of *Johnson v. Mississippi*, 486 U.S. 578, 108 S.Ct. 1981, 100 L.Ed.2d 575 (1988).

This claim is procedurally barred for failure to raise it on direct appeal or in the first motion for postconviction relief. It is also barred by the two-year provision of rule 3.850. At Bundy's trial, his attorney asserted that the Utah conviction could not be used to support any aggravating factors because they were not proven. In his first rule 3.850 motion, Bundy attacked the competence of his trial attorney for failing to challenge the constitutionality of both his Utah and Florida convictions so as to eliminate aggravating factors. Citing *United States v. Tucker*, 404 U.S. 443, 447, 92 S.Ct. 589, 591, 30 L.Ed.2d 592 (1972), Bundy argued that the reliance upon his prior convictions meant that his death sentence was predicated upon "misinformation of constitutional magnitude." Therefore, Bundy has long been aware that he could challenge his death sentence by challenging the validity of his prior convictions, even though Johnson v. Mississippi had not yet been decided.

In any event, and in the alternative, *Johnson v. Mississippi* provides no basis for relief in this case. In *Johnson v. Mississippi*, the defendant's death sentence was set aside because his New York assault conviction, which was the entire predicate for the aggravating circumstance of a prior violent felony, had been reversed. Here, the validity of Bundy's Utah conviction of aggravated kidnapping, which was also considered as a basis for the finding of a prior violent felony, has not been challenged. Moreover, there were two other valid aggravating circumstances which were unaffected by the Chi Omega convictions and a complete absence of mitigating circumstances. Finally, it must be remembered that his Chi Omega convictions have been final for several years and have not been set aside. The fact that these convictions are being attacked in collateral proceedings does not entitle Bundy to relief.

Finally, Bundy argues that his right to a fair sentencing pursuant to *Gardner v. Florida*, 430 U.S. 349, 97 S.Ct. 1197, 51 L.Ed.2d 393 (1977), was violated because during his trial Judge Jopling and the prosecutors had ex parte communications about the Chi Omega competency hearing and Bundy's mental condition. He asserts that this first came to light in the federal court evidentiary hearing concerning Bundy's competency to stand trial for the Leach killing. Once again, Bundy has failed to timely raise his claim under rule 3.850 because he knew of Judge Jopling's testimony ten months before the expiration of the time in which he was required to file his motion for postconviction relief.

Even if there were no procedural bar, the pertinent portions of the record belie Bundy's contentions. The predicate for Bundy's assertion comes from Judge Jopling's testimony that at the trial he may have heard about some of the details of the Chi Omega competency hearing from the state attorney, though he was uncertain of this. There was a specific reference to a medical report of Dr. Tanay which was part of that proceeding. However, it is clear from the record of the original trial that Judge Jopling received Dr. Tanay's report from Bundy's counsel. Moreover, at sentencing Judge Jopling specifically announced that he had "considered no evidence or factors in imposing the penalty herein and has no information not disclosed to the Appellant or his counsel which the Appellant has not had an opportunity to deny or explain." The remaining assertions that Judge Jopling improperly received ex parte communications concerning the Chi Omega competency hearings consist of nothing more than conclusory statements drawn from generalized responses made by the judge at the federal court hearing which took place eight years after the trial.

We affirm the order denying Bundy's motion for postconviction relief and Bundy's application for stay of execution. We also deny his application for stay of execution filed in this Court. No petition for rehearing shall be permitted.

It is so ordered.

CASE QUESTIONS

1. From the court's description, how many different appeals did Bundy bring in this case alone?
2. What was Bundy's claim about competency in this case?
3. How does this court deal with Bundy's claim?

4. Bundy also raised an issue concerning the aggravating factors in this case that resulted in his death sentence and that were based on his murders in another case at the Chi Omega sorority house. What were those issues?

5. How did the court deal with the Chi Omega murder convictions as aggravating factors?

ETHICAL CONSIDERATIONS: PARALEGALS AND CLAIMS OF "INEFFECTIVE COUNSEL"

Criminal defendants who have been convicted often raise ineffectiveness of counsel claims against their trial attorneys. This claim asserts that the trial attorney failed to carry out basic requirements or failed to safeguard the defendant's rights. Because many defense attorneys use paralegals to prepare for trial, both the trial attorney and paralegal often testify in a hearing for a new trial. The defense paralegal should make notes during the course of the trial about strategy and other issues so that he/she can recall why specific discussions occurred and why specific actions were taken during the trial.

Paralegals have also been named as defendants in legal malpractice actions filed by disgruntled clients. A paralegal can be liable for actions done on behalf of the attorney. These are all good reasons why a paralegal should document the client's file so that if a claim comes up several year's later, the paralegal can recall the specifics of the case.

✓ Paralegal To Do List

For the defense paralegal:

■ Review the sentencing guidelines (if any) for your jurisdiction. What is the client's likely sentence?

■ If a presentence investigation has been ordered, make sure that the probation officer conducting the investigation has every piece of favorable information possible. Send it to the officer by registered mail so there cannot be any claim of not receiving it.

■ Has a motion for new trial been filed after the conviction? If not, do so immediately.

■ Are there any facts that may mitigate the defendant's sentence? If possible, find someone who will testify during sentencing about what a nice person the client is.

■ Carefully note any appellate deadlines and make sure that they are met.

For the prosecution paralegal:

■ Are there any victim impact statements in the file that should be presented to the court during sentencing? Mark them prominently for the attorney.

- Have any of the victims expressed a desire to be present at sentencing? Make sure that they are notified of the correct day and time. A follow-up letter explaining what sentence the defendant received is a nice touch.

- Many defense attorneys file similar briefs on appeal. Has the attorney already filed a similar brief with this or some other office? If so, maybe another paralegal has already researched these issues. Ask around; you may save yourself a lot of work.

- Have any new appellate cases come out recently on the issues raised in the defendant's appeal. You might want to consider keeping an up-to-date file on recent important cases.

- Once the defendant has filed an appeal, it is the state's turn. Note the deadline for the state's appeal and then subtract two or three days. This will be the in-office deadline, just to make sure that everything gets done in time.

- Does the appellate court have particular rules about the color, size, and binding of briefs? (Most do.) Find out what these rules are or talk to other paralegals who have submitted briefs. Keep a sample brief in your file along with the appellate rules to make it easier on you the next time you handle an appellate brief.

Chapter Summary

When a jury has found a defendant guilty, a new phase of criminal procedure is triggered. In most cases, the judge has the responsibility of sentencing a defendant. The ultimate sentence depends on many factors, including the facts of the case, the seriousness of the charge, and the defendant's prior history, to name just a few. A convicted defendant may be sentenced to prison, followed by some period on probation or parole. While on probation, a convicted defendant must abide by the restrictions imposed by probation officers, including an obvious prohibition against committing additional crimes.

Following sentencing, a convicted defendant has the right to appeal his or her sentence. Appeals follow a standard format, with the defendant filing a brief on the prosecution, listing reasons why he or she is entitled to another trial, including the improprieties that the defendant claims occurred at the trial. Appeals are heard in higher courts. These courts do not retry the case. Instead, they review the record of the case and the written briefs of the parties to determine whether the trial judge committed reversible error at trial. Higher appellate courts have the power of certiorari, which is the right to refuse to hear any appeal.

WEB SITES

Capital Punishment in Arizona
www.azag.gov (Search for *capital punishment.*)

Federal Bureau of Prisons
www.bop.gov

Florida State Court System
www.flcourts.org/index.shtml

Montana State Court System
http://courts.mt.gov/cao/default.mcpx

Michigan Public Sex Offender Registry
www.mipsor.state.mi.us

Oregon State Court System
http://courts.oregon.gov/ojd/pages/index.aspx

Rhode Island State Court System
www.courts.ri.gov/default.aspx

United States Sentencing Commission
www.ussc.gov

United States Supreme Court
www.supremecourt.gov/default.aspx

REVIEW QUESTIONS

1. Is it a violation of the Eighth Amendment prohibition against cruel and unusual punishment to order a defendant to be spanked in front of the courthouse? Explain.

2. Does a jury in a death penalty case have to be told that the defendant faces life without parole? Explain.

3. What role do private companies play in probation and prison facilities?

4. What are sentencing guidelines, and why were they created?

5. List and explain at least four factors that a judge may take into account when entering a sentence.

6. What function do victim-witness programs serve?

7. Can the death penalty be imposed in any murder case? Why or why not?

8. Who is generally responsible for sentencing a person in a death penalty case?

9. What is a pardon?

10. What kinds of civil remedies are available to victims of crime?

11. What is cert?

12. What are the three actions that an appellate court can take on an appeal? Is an appeal a retrial of the case? Why or why not?

13. What is habeas corpus?

QUESTIONS FOR REFLECTION

1. Should the judge take into account the victim's desires before entering a sentence? Why or why not?
2. If corporal punishment (e.g., whipping) is considered cruel and unusual punishment under the Constitution, why isn't execution?
3. Explain how an appeal proceeds from the moment that the defendant is sentenced.

KEYWORDS AND PHRASES

Sentence	Commutation
Parole	Restitution
Probate	Forfeiture
Probation revocation hearing	Appeal
Sentencing guidelines	Briefs
Proportionality	Reversible error
Cruel and unusual punishment	Record
Eighth Amendment	Affirm
Concurrent sentence	Reverse
Consecutive sentence (cumulative)	Remand
Victim-impact statement	Certiorari
Fines	Opinion
Pardon	Habeas corpus

PRACTICAL APPLICATIONS

1. Review a recent U.S. Supreme Court case dealing with criminal law and determine if the Court reversed, affirmed, or remanded (or some combination of all three) in the case. What reasons does the Court give for its decision?
2. Contact your local probation office and ask about felony vs. misdemeanor probation. Does it have private companies that are involved in either? Does it use any special technology to monitor probationers (computer house arrest or random telephone calls, for instance)? Ask the probation officer what the most common reason is for people to violate probation.
3. Contact the clerk of the court of appeals or supreme court (your state may have different names for these courts) and ask how long it normally takes for the justices to report a decision on a particular case. Ask about the delay. What causes it? Do these courts have a high volume of cases?
4. What sentence do you believe would be appropriate for the defendants in each of the sample cases (*Kline*, *Marbles*, and *Fortner*) if each were convicted?

NOTES

1. *Solem v. Helm*, 463 U.S. 277, 103 S. Ct. 3001, 77 L. Ed. 2d 637 (1983).

2. Fear of Judging: Sentencing Guidelines in the Federal Courts, Kate Stith and Jose A. Cabranes. Chicago: The University of Chicago Press, 1998.

3. *Southern Union Co. v. U.S.*, 132 S. Ct. 2344 (2012).

4. *Beyond A Reasonable Doubt*: Inside the American Jury System. By Melvin Bernard Zerman, Thomas Y. Crawl Publishers, New York, Copyright, 1981.

Appendix A

THE KLINE CASE

Christine Kline has been charged with the first degree murder of her ex-husband, Doug Clark.

The prosecution alleges that Ms. Kline's former husband, Doug Clark, who was living with Ms. Kline, left for a party on November 17 of last year, at approximately 7 P.M. from her home at 133 Rockford Road, Anytown. Mr. Clark had fallen on tough times and Ms. Kline had allowed him to move in with her for a few months so that he could be close to the daughter they had had together. The daughter's name is Vickie. Ms. Kline's current boyfriend, Mark Layton, also lived in the home. Mr. Clark worked as a house painter and sub-contractor, and he often worked alongside his ex-wife and her boyfriend as they installed air-conditioning and heating units in new buildings. On the night in question, Mr. Clark, while visiting with his daughter, began talking to a friend, who was also visiting at the Kline/Layton house. This friend, a man named Ellis Sampson, often worked with Doug Clark. They had purchased a paint-spraying machine together and often worked as a two-person team on house painting jobs. Sampson suggested that Clark accompany him to a party that Sampson had heard about earlier that day. Clark agreed, and they both left together.

After Clark and Sampson left, Ms. Kline and her boyfriend, Mark Layton, sat in the back yard near a bonfire and drank a large amount of alcohol, ingested some cocaine, and talked.

Shortly after midnight, Ms. Kline and Mark Layton were still out in the back yard, when Clark and Sampson returned. Sampson was driving. Clark, because he had had too much to drink, had passed out in the passenger seat of Sampson's car. Sampson left Clark, still asleep, in the car and walked around to the back yard, where he found Ms. Kline and Mark Layton, still sitting by the fire. Kline and Layton invited Sampson to have a drink with them, which he did.

At this point, the stories of all defendants begin to diverge. Sampson, who later testified for the state, says that while sitting around the fire, he told Ms. Kline and Layton about a conversation he heard Clark engage in earlier that evening at the party. According to Sampson, Clark had bragged that he would soon be getting full custody of his daughter, Vickie, by taking her away from Ms. Kline. Clark stated that he would be able to do this because Ms. Kline and Layton had recently been arrested for selling drugs out of their home at 133 Rockford Road. Clark also stated to several people at the party that he was the person who had reported them to the police. He said that he had even told the police where Christine hid her drugs in the house.

After hearing this information, according to the state's witness, Ms. Kline became enraged and stormed into the house. After a few minutes, according to Sampson, they heard Clark yelling from the front yard. Sampson and Layton got up to see what was going on. When they came around the corner of the house, they could clearly see that Clark's left hand was handcuffed to the steering wheel of Sampson's car and Ms. Kline was slapping Clark across the face. Clark was attempting to restrain her with his right hand. As Sampson got closer to the car, he distinctly heard Christine say, "You son of a bitch, you're never going to get Vickie!"

Clark began yelling and thrashing about in the car. Mark Layton joined Ms. Kline in attempting to subdue Clark. Kline told Clark to admit that he had "ratted them out" to the police. Clark denied reporting Kline to the police. Kline turned to Sampson and had Sampson repeat what Clark had said at the party. Clark again denied making the statement. Sampson climbed into the back seat of his own car, reached over the front seat, and put Clark into a headlock. Layton seized Clark's right arm and pinned it down. Christine was seated on the driver's side of the car, and while Layton and Sampson held Clark, she continued to accuse him of trying to take away her daughter. Sampson told Clark that he should "own up" to what he had said, but Clark continued to yell and deny making any such statement.

Because Clark was making so much noise, Layton told Christine to go into the house and get something to "shut him up." Ms. Kline went into the house and returned in a few seconds with a role of silver duct tape, approximately two inches wide. She re-entered the car from the driver's seat and wrapped some tape over Clark's mouth. At this point, Sampson says that he let go of Clark and climbed out of the back seat. He says that he thought the incident was over and they had all taught Clark "a lesson." However, as Sampson watched, Ms. Kline continued to wrap Clark's entire face and head with the tape. Sampson says that he was frozen to the spot while he watched Clark struggle and could hear him trying to scream through the tape. Clark struggled for a few moments more, then slumped over. The entire episode took less than a minute. Christine and Layton stepped away from the car and stood staring at Clark.

Sampson went to the front passenger side and put his hand on Clark's chest. He couldn't feel a heartbeat. He stepped back from the car and said to Christine, "I think he's dead."

Christine said, "Good." Then she turned to Sampson and said, "You're in on this, too, you know. You're as guilty as we are. If we go to the chair, you go with us."

They argued about this for several minutes, before Christine said that they had to get rid of the body. Christine went into the house to find the keys to the handcuffs, but came out again in a few minutes and said that she couldn't find them. Sampson rummaged through the toolbox in his trunk and found some pliers. He pried the handcuff chains apart, leaving one manacle on the steering wheel and the other manacle on Clark's left wrist. Sampson and Layton lifted Clark's body out of the front seat and put it into the trunk of Sampson's car.

Christine suggested that they take the body to a construction site and dump it "somewhere that it won't be found." She said that she would remain behind and clean things up. Sampson and Layton then drove around for approximately an hour. They couldn't find any construction sites, and as they were getting back onto the interstate highway, Layton suggested that they just dump the body right here. Sampson said that he believes it was the Porter Mill Road exit, on the northbound entrance ramp. They stopped the car on the shoulder of the entrance ramp, looked around to make sure that there were no other cars around, and then lifted Clark's body out of the trunk. They carried his body several feet into the high grass and bushes that run alongside the entrance ramp and placed the body near the base of a tree. They left the area quickly and returned to the house on Rockford Road. Sampson estimates that it was about 3:30 A.M. when they returned to the house.

According to Sampson, he was threatened by both Kline and Layton to keep his mouth shut, "or else." Several days after the incident, Sampson left the state and didn't tell the authorities about the killing. Three months later, Sampson was arrested in the next state on an aggravated assault charge and was being held in the local jail, when he was approached by Detective Able. At that time, Able informed him that the badly decomposed body of Clark had been found beside the interstate. Sampson then told the detective the version of events outlined above.

There is no dispute about the fact that on November 18 of last year, Christine Kline called the police saying that she wanted to file a missing person's report on her ex-husband. Detective Baker, of the Missing Person's Division, went to the house on Rockford Road and met with Ms. Kline on November 19. Detective Baker asked Christine how long her ex-husband had been missing. Christine told Detective Baker that her ex-husband had been gone "about a week." She said that the last time she'd seen her ex-husband was when he'd come over to her house to see Vickie and then had left with another man to go to a party. She said that she didn't know the other man's name, but thought it was something like Dennis Barber or Dennis Baker. He had never returned from the party, and she hadn't seen him since. She said that she had never known him to be gone so long and said that he was very devoted to their daughter, Vickie. She said that Vickie had been crying a lot, and Christine had told her that the police would find her father and bring him home. Christine provided a photograph of Doug Clark, along with a physical description that included a tattoo on his upper right arm. That tattoo was of a red rose with a knife through the bud. She said that the tattoo was very distinctive.

Detective Baker filed the report and spent several days trying to locate Mr. Clark. He found that Clark had not returned to the house-painting job he had only half-finished and had left an expensive paint-spraying machine at the site. Although Detective Baker considered this to be suspicious, he had no further leads and eventually marked the case "Open, Pending Further Information."

On January 17 of this year, there was a bad snowstorm. Many cars were having trouble moving down the interstate. One motorist, Terry Larson, skidded off the road and couldn't get his car to start. He began walking south down the interstate towards the nearest exit, which was the Porter Mill Road intersection. As he walked, he tried to stay off the icy road and walked through the grass. He reports that he almost stepped on what he at first thought was a pile of clothes. When he looked again, however, he saw a human skull and realized that he was looking at a body. He ran to a gas station and called the police.

When the police arrived, they found that the body was so badly decomposed that a visual identification would be impossible. Given the fact that a handcuff manacle was attached to the left wrist, police assumed foul play and contacted the homicide division. The body was also frozen and would have to be thawed out before an autopsy could be performed. Detective Able was assigned to the case and as the body was being removed, he noted that the right arm had been lying under the body and therefore had not decomposed as much as the other arm. He saw that a tattoo was clearly visible on the right forearm and made a rough sketch of it. He noted that the tattoo appeared to be some kind of flower with a knife blade cutting through the bud.

Detective Able went to the Missing Person's Division and searched for any reports of a person with such a tattoo. He located the report filed by Christine Kline and noted that the tattoo mentioned in the report appeared to be identical to the one found on the body. Based on this preliminary identification, he asked the evidence technician, Kathy Singleton, to try and lift fingerprints from the right hand. She was able to get prints from the right forefinger, and this print was compared with the finger-prints taken of Doug Clark when he was arrested three years ago on a driving under the influence charge. The prints were identical.

After the autopsy revealed an exact match of the dental records of Doug Clark with those of the body, Detective Able went to the home of Christine Kline and told her that her ex-husband was dead. According to Detective Able, Ms. Kline was very shocked by the news and began crying. She kept repeating aloud that she didn't know how she was going to tell her daughter, Vickie. Detective Able asked for more information about the person that Doug Clark had gone to the party with, but Ms. Kline said that she didn't know anything more than she'd already stated on the missing person's report.

Detective Able attempted to locate a "Dennis Baker" or "Dennis Barber" but with no success. While speaking with other people who had known Doug Clark, Detective Able was informed about Ellis Sampson, who had worked very closely with Clark until a few months ago, when he had abruptly left the state. Detective Able contacted the police in Sampson's hometown, hoping that they would know where to find him. They did. Local police informed Detective Able that Sampson was currently in their jail, awaiting trial on an aggravated assault charge. Detective Able requested additional information on the charge and discovered that Sampson was alleged to have stabbed another man in a bar fight. Detective Able then went to meet Sampson and obtained his statement.

When Detective Able returned to the state, he confronted Christine with Sampson's statement. Kline then said that she wanted to tell the truth and gave the following statement:

On the night that Sampson and Clark left for the party, she had been sitting at a small fire in the back yard with her live-in boyfriend, Mark Layton. Around midnight, Sampson returned and joined them at the fire. She stated that Sampson seemed nervous, jumpy, and irritable. They asked him what was wrong, and Sampson stated that he and Clark had gotten into a fight, and that Clark had had too much to drink, as usual, and had passed out in the front seat on the way home.

According to Kline, Sampson continued to talk, and continued to seem more and more angry. After a few minutes, he got back up and without saying a word went around to the front of the house. Ms. Kline got curious, went to the front yard to see what was going on, and clearly saw Sampson stab Clark in the throat with a knife. She stated that Clark slumped forward in the seat immediately and appeared to be dead.

She agrees that she did help conceal Clark's body, but did it out of fear of Sampson, whom she says threatened to kill her, Layton, and her daughter Vickie. Several days later, Sampson came by their house again, threatened them again, and told them that he was leaving town and to keep their mouths shut. After he left town, she filed a bogus missing person's report, because she wanted someone to start looking for Clark, and was hoping that someone would find his body, so that she wouldn't have to put her life in jeopardy by reporting the killing herself.

Following her statement, Ms. Kline was placed under arrest for murder. Her boyfriend, Mark Layton, was also arrested and charged with murder. He refused to give any statements to the police. Ellis Sampson was also charged with murder.

Mr. Sampson has agreed to testify for the state in exchange for a recommended sentence of five years in custody on a charge of concealing the death of another. Ms. Kline faces a charge of first-degree murder, with a possible sentence of life in prison. The state has not elected to seek the death penalty in her case.

Statement of Ellis Sampson

I had been a friend of Doug Clark for several years. Doug picked me up one day while I was hitchhiking from Alabama. He put me up in his house, and I started working with him as a house painter. We worked together on a lot of different jobs. I eventually moved out of the trailer. I heard that Doug had gone to live with his ex-wife, Christine Kline.

On November 17 of last year, I went by Kline's house to pick up Doug Clark so that we could both go to a party. While I was there, I saw that Christine and her boyfriend, Mark Layton, were sitting in the back yard around a small fire. Me and Doug went to the party, and Doug got real drunk.

While we were at the party, Doug told me that he had been the one to "turn in" Christine. I asked Doug what he meant. Doug told me that Christine and Mark had been arrested two weeks ago on possession of amphetamine charges and that it had been Doug who had contacted the police and informed on them. I hadn't heard about the arrests. Doug said that Christine and Mark were out on bail. Doug said that he'd been living at the house for a couple of months and had seen just how heavily they were into drugs. He said that he hoped that Christine would get convicted and then he could have custody of their daughter, Vickie.

Doug got real drunk at the party and passed out in the passenger seat of my car on the trip home. When we got to Christine's house, I left Doug asleep in the front seat. I could see that the fire was still burning in the back yard, and I walked around to see who was out there. I found Christine and Mark Layton sitting around the fire and talking. I sat down and shared a few beers with them.

Christine began talking about how she got arrested two weeks before and wondered how the cops had known exactly where to look for her "stash." I felt bad for her, and I told her that it was Doug who'd told the cops. I told her that he was trying to get custody of Vickie. At first, Christine didn't believe it. But then she started getting more and more angry. She said she wanted to talk to Doug. I told her that he was asleep in the front seat of my car. Christine got up from the fire and walked around to the front of the house.

After a little bit, I heard yelling and what sounded like a fight out front. Me and Mark got up and walked around the house into the front yard. When I walked up the car, I saw that Doug had his left wrist handcuffed to the steering wheel. He was struggling with Christine. She was slapping him, and he was trying to push her away with his right arm.

Christine called us over. She told me to repeat what I'd told them just a minute before about the drug bust. Doug said I was a liar. That got me angry. I got into the back seat of the car, and put Doug into a headlock. I said, "Tell the truth, Doug. Tell 'em what you told me at the party. Don't call me no liar."

But Doug kept saying that I was a liar. He started yelling even louder. Mark got angry, opened the front passenger door, and climbed in on Doug.

He grabbed Doug's right arm and then told Christine to get something to "shut him up." Christine went into the house and came back with a roll of that silver duct tape. You know, the kind they use to run air conditioning conduit. She climbed in the driver's side and while Mark held Doug down and while I had him in a headlock, she tore some off and put it over his mouth. I let go then, thinking it was all over. But once I'd gotten out of the car, I looked in and saw that Christine was wrapping Doug's whole face with the tape. Doug was still struggling and trying to yell. Mark still had him pinned down. Christine wrapped Doug's whole face and his head above his eyes. In what seemed like a few seconds, he sort of fell forward and stopped moving. I mean, I couldn't believe how fast he smothered to death.

Mark and Christine got out of the car and just stood there, looking at him. I felt Doug's chest, but I didn't feel any heartbeat. I didn't know what to do. Right then, Christine turned to me and said that I was just as much involved as they were, and that we would all "fry." She told me to take the handcuffs off Doug's wrist and to "get rid of the body." I asked where was the key to the handcuffs? Christine went inside for a few minutes, then came out, and said that she couldn't find the key. I got a pair of pliers and snipped the small chain that held the two handcuffs together. Mark Layton found some scissors and cut the duct tape off Doug's face. I felt real bad and couldn't look at Doug's face.

Mark and me dragged Doug out of the front seat and put him in the trunk. We drove around for a while, trying to find a place to bury the body. By then it was almost four o'clock, and we were afraid that the sun would be coming up soon. We pulled over on the onramp of the interstate and lifted Doug's body out of the trunk. We kind of half-carried, half-dragged him a few feet into the woods and left him there.

We got back to Christine's house, and I told them I was leaving. Before I left both Mark and Christine threatened me. They told me that I should keep my mouth shut "or else." I knew what they meant. Christine was basically saying that if I talked to the cops, she or Mark would kill me.

A few days after all this, I decided to leave town. I went back to Alabama and I've been here every since.

Signed: *Ellis Sampson*

Supplemental Report: Detective Able

On Monday, January 17 of this year, a motorist was walking down the ramp of the northbound interstate at Porter Mill Road. Mr. Larson, the motorist, observed what he at first took to be a pile of clothes, lying a few feet off the shoulder of the road in some trees. As he approached, he realized that it was a dead body. He went up to the gas station at the intersection and called the police.

I was called to the scene within an hour of the discovery of the body. The weather conditions were very bad, with ice coating the roads and sleet coming down. After allowing crime scene identification technicians to mark the body and take photographs, I approached the scene. The body appeared to be that of a white male, lying partially on his back with his feet near the state right-of-way fence and his head facing towards the interstate. His hips and legs were twisted so that the right leg was lying over the left leg. His right arm stretched backwards, and his left arm was lying horizontally. There was one handcuff locked on his left wrist. The victim had on a pair of blue jeans and a purple sweater. There was a small piece of silver tape, with human hair attached, lying three feet from the victim's body. The tape appeared to be duct tape. ID Tech Singleton retrieved this tape and placed it an evidence bag.

I could not locate any other evidence and instructed the coroner's investigators to remove the body. The body was placed inside a plastic body bag and placed inside Investigator Jack's vehicle.

After processing the scene for any further evidence and failing to find any, I proceeded to the county morgue where I met with Coroner Joe White. The coroner informed me that the body was frozen and would have to be thawed out before a complete autopsy could be performed.

I returned to my office and sent out a teletype to all police agencies advising of the discovery of a body and requesting any information on missing persons matching the description of the body.

The following day I attended the autopsy of the victim. His clothes had been processed, and no identifying information had been found on him. Coroner White stated that the only identifying mark on the victim was a tattoo of a rose on the upper right arm and a surgical mark on the abdominal area.

I met with Detective Baker, the current head detective for Missing Persons. Together we reviewed missing person's reports attempting to match the tattoo with any reported missing persons for the past year. We located a report for a Douglas Clark.

On November 18 of last year, a report was filed by Clark's ex-wife, Christine Kline. Among the identifying marks listed for Mr. Clark was a tattoo on the right forearm. The tattoo was listed as being a rose with a knife through the top.

After obtaining the missing person's report on Doug Clark, I used the information to run a criminal history on Mr. Clark. I discovered that Clark had been charged with DWI three years ago. I went to the Fingerprint Section and requested a copy of Clark's fingerprint card from the DWI arrest. I also requested ID Tech Singleton to take a fingerprint sample from the corpse—now tentatively identified as Doug Clark—at the morgue. After some difficulty, ID Tech Singleton was able to obtain a partial set of fingerprints from the deceased's right hand. These fingerprints were compared with the known fingerprints of Doug Clark. They were a perfect match.

I contacted Mr. Clark's parents in Ohio and informed them that their son was deceased. Next, I contacted Christine Kline and also informed her. Later that day, I traveled to Ms. Kline's residence and met with her.

Ms. Kline stated to me that she didn't know how she was going to explain Mr. Clark's death to his daughter, Vickie. Ms. Kline stated that she met Doug in Ohio in 1982 and that they have a daughter (Vickie) together. Doug had been living in the home since July 1 of last year. She stated that on the night of November 17 of last year, Doug and Dennis Baker had gone to a party together. They left in Baker's tan colored Oldsmobile Omega around 10 P.M. They were both very drunk.

Around 2 A.M., Dennis returned alone. She was sitting out in the back yard with her boyfriend, Mark Layton. They were sitting around a fire. Dennis stated that Doug had left the party with a guy in a dark colored pickup truck. Christine and the two other men chatted for a while, and then everyone went inside the house to go to sleep. When Christine woke up the next day, Dennis was gone and she hasn't seen him since. She never saw Doug Clark again since the night he left for the party. She had no idea how he could have ended up dead beside the interstate with a handcuff on his wrist.

After meeting with Ms. Kline, I made repeated attempts to locate Dennis Baker. I could not locate anyone by that name. However, several witnesses stated that an "Ellis Sampson" was known to be a close friend of Doug Clark. Mr. Sampson's description seemed very close to the person Ms. Kline had identified as "Dennis Baker." I began looking for Ellis Sampson. Several sources indicated that he had moved back to the state of Alabama. I learned that his hometown was Brunswick, Alabama. I contacted the sheriff of Brunswick and asked him about Mr. Sampson. He said that he knew exactly where to find Ellis. He said that Ellis was currently sitting in cell three of his jail, having been arrested for assault at a local bar the night before. Upon learning this information, I drove to Brunswick, Alabama, and met with Ellis Sampson.

After informing Mr. Sampson of his rights, I obtained a waiver and permission to speak with him. I asked him about Doug Clark. "So, y'all finally found his body," Sampson said. I had not told him that Doug was dead, or that his body had been recovered.

Without any further prompting, Sampson informed me that he had known that Doug was dead for about three months. He said that he had been there when Doug had been murdered. He said that Christine and Mark Layton had murdered Doug Clark, then insisted that Sampson help conceal the body. Sampson said that he had been feeling "real bad" about the whole thing and was glad to talk about it.

Mr. Sampson informed me that on the night of November 17 of last year, he and Doug Clark had gone to a party together. While they were at the party, Doug had revealed to him that he had been the one to "turn in" Christine. Sampson asked Doug what he meant. Doug told him that Christine and Mark had been arrested two weeks ago on possession of amphetamine charges and that it had been Doug who had contacted the police and informed on them. (See Sampson's statement for a complete account of the killing.) After talking with Sampson, I returned to this state

---

GANNETT POLICE DEPARTMENT
SUPPLEMENTAL REPORT

CASE #: 94-01930
VICTIM:
SCENE ADDRESS: Interstate at Porter Mill Road, North Bound entrance
INCIDENT DATE: 01-17
REPORT DATE: 01-27

ASSIGNED INVESTIGATOR: Detective Able
SUPPLEMENT BY: Tech. II K. Singleton

DISPATCHED. . . . .   1035 hours
ARRIVED. . . . .   1215 hours
IN-SERVICE. . . . .   1505 hours

On the above date and time, Tech.II K. Singleton was requested to be enroute to the above location to process the scene of a person dead. Upon arriving on the scene Tech Singleton observed a white male laying on the ground with his head near a tree his feet next to a barbed wire fence. There was tape laying on the ground beside the white male with hair attached to the tape. The white male had blue jean pulled down off his hips and down to his knees. The white male's neck and face were decomposed beyond the point of recognition. There was a maroon sweater laying on the other side of the barbed wire fence. Singleton photographed and video taped the scene.

OBJECT BEING MEASURED	THE 17TH POST ON THE GUARD RAIL COUNTING FROM PORTER MILL RD. FACING S.E.	LAND SURVEY STUB ON THE OTHER SIDE OF THE BARBED WIRE FENCE.
The head of the white male	66 FEET	8 FEET 3 INCHES OR
The heel of the left foot	71 FEET 4 INCHES	3 FEET 10 INCHES
The toe of the right foot	71 FEET 9 1/2 INCHES	4 FEET 1 INCH
The fence	70 FEET 8 INCHES	
Tree near head		9 FEET 1 1/2 INCHES
The sweater on the ground across the fence	74 FEET 5 INCHES	

The tape was 1 foot 2 inches from the tree near the head and 1 foot and 2 inches from head.

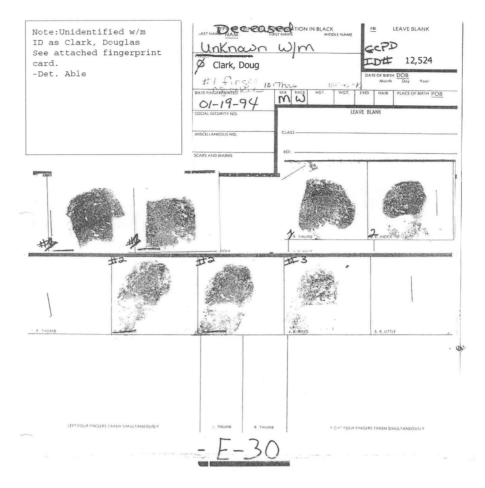

to interview Christine Kline. I told her about my meeting with Mr. Sampson and his version of events, she called Sampson a liar. I read Ms. Kline her *Miranda* rights and asked her if she wished to make a statement. She told me that Ellis had killed Doug with a knife and had threatened to kill her and her daughter if anyone told the police. When I asked for more details, she requested to speak with an attorney. I placed Ms. Kline under arrest and transported her to the county jail. Charges of first-degree murder are pending against Ellis Sampson, Christine Kline, and Mark Layton. At present, we have been unable to locate Mr. Layton to place him under arrest.

I have attached some exhibits to this narrative. They consist of I.D. Tech Singleton's supplemental report from the scene where the body was recovered and the fingerprint card showing a positive match between the book-in prints of Doug Clark and the body found on 17 January.

THE MARBLES CASE

The defendant, Richard Marbles, is charged with numerous offenses, including kidnapping, stalking, aggravated assault, aggravated assault on a police officer, reckless endangerment, and so forth.

Marbles worked at a movie theater in Anytown. One of his coworkers was a young lady named Paula Burke. Ms. Burke is very pretty, and Marbles was attracted to her and asked her out. They went out on one date, but things didn't work out, and Ms. Burke refused to go out with Marbles again. Marbles began calling Ms. Burke at her home and pestering her at work. Ms. Burke's father warned Marbles to stop calling and then had the telephone number changed when he continued to call. In these telephone calls, some of which were taped, Marbles proclaimed his undying love for Ms. Burke and told her that she was being unfair to him. At work, the movie theater manager, Tom Smith, warned Marbles that he must leave Ms. Burke alone or he would be fired. When Marbles continued to try and speak with Ms. Burke, he was terminated. His termination was April 4.

April 6 is Marbles's birthday. Sometime after being fired on April 4 and the evening of April 6, Marbles acquired a .22 caliber handgun. In the late afternoon on April 6, Marbles called the movie theater and asked to speak with Ms. Burke. When this request was refused, he became verbally abusive to the manager, Tom Smith, saying that they would regret treating him so badly.

Around 10 P.M. on April 6, Marbles went to the movie theater's back entrance. He was familiar with the routine at the movie theater and knew that only two members of the staff remained on the premises. These two staff members were the manager, Tom Smith, and Paula Burke. Paula remained at the concession stand until 10:30, when it was closed down. The last movie ended at 10:45 P.M. The moviegoers would then exit the front of the building, and the movie theater would be empty. Marbles pried open the locked back door of the theater with a small crowbar that he had brought with him for that purpose. He entered the back of the building and worked his way around to the theater offices. The normal routine was that Tom Smith would leave after securing the refreshment area, while the closing employee, in this case Paula, would remain on the premises long enough to make sure that the building was empty and to put the evening's receipts in the safe. However, Tom Smith was concerned about the phone call that he had received from Marbles and decided to remain on the premises while Paula finished her duties. They were both seated in the office when Marbles walked in with the gun in his hand.

He told them not to move. He said that he thought that Paula would be alone. His purpose in breaking in, he said, was so that he could commit suicide in front of her. However, Tom's presence had spoiled everything. He sat down across from them and began a long monologue detailing his love for Paula and how she had treated him badly. He said that he didn't know what else to do. Without her, he said, he didn't have a reason to live. For a few moments, he discussed the merits of killing Paula and Tom instead of himself, but then changed his mind. Paula tried to talk him out of what he was doing, but found that she couldn't get through to him. After an hour of holding them both hostage, Marbles made a decision.

"Get on your hands and knees," he told them both and made them crawl out of the office. There are windows in the hallway that look out on the rest of the refreshments area. These windows are not floor to ceiling, however. They start about waist high. By keeping the victims on their hands and knees, no one who happened to be looking in the front area would be able to see them. He made them crawl into another area of the offices and had Tom crawl into a supply closet. Marbles then locked the supply closet from the outside and forced Paula to leave the theater. They got into her car and drove away. Tom was able to force open the door in about twenty minutes, and he called the police.

Marbles made Paula drive. He told her to head north. He said that he had always wanted to kill himself in the "woods." He told her to head to the forest, where he would kill himself to prove how much he loved her. They drove for several hours, but Marbles didn't like the look of the country and told her to turn around. She was hoping that they were going back to Anytown, but he suddenly told her to pull over. Placing the gun against her head, he tried to sexually assault her, but she kept fending him off. When a car approached, he stopped his attempt and told her to drive.

They headed east and crossed the state line. By then it was daylight and Paula told Marbles that she was tired and hungry and needed to go to the bathroom. He ordered her to pull over at a motel and with the gun concealed, they registered for a room under a fake name. He paid cash and Paula saw that once he had paid for the room, he had very little cash left.

They went into the room, and Marbles put the gun to her head and told her to strip for him. She refused, and he became enraged. He told her that he would "blow her brains out," but she still refused. He grabbed a towel from the bathroom and wrapped it around her throat and began strangling her with it. She began to lose consciousness, and Marbles stopped choking her. He splashed water on her face to revive her and then helped her to bed. He tied her hands and feet and fell asleep beside her. When she woke up, he was watching television. There was a news story about her abduction, including photographs of both Marbles and Paula. Marbles became very agitated, worrying aloud that the clerk at the motel might have recognized him. He laughed, however, when the reporter described Marbles as "armed and very dangerous."

He allowed Paula to use the bathroom, and then they got back into the car and began driving towards Anytown. Once they were across the state line, Marbles began to get nervous. He forced Paula to stop at an ATM and remove some money from her account. She didn't have a large balance, and he became more upset when he saw how little money she had. He considered shooting the ATM camera, but when Paula pointed out that that would certainly set off alarms, he relented. They returned to the car, and Paula began driving towards Anytown again, but Marbles told her to change direction and head south. They pulled into a small town and parked outside a grocery store. Marbles waited until he saw a woman coming out of the store and told Paula to grab her purse or he would shoot the woman and then shoot her.

As Marbles drove by the woman, Paula reached out and grabbed her purse and they sped off. However, the woman had only twenty dollars in her purse, and Marbles became angry. "Why do you need more money?" Paula asked. "So I can get away," he replied.

She pleaded with him to take her home, and he finally relented. As they reached the outskirts of the city, however, a police car spotted them and began following them. Marbles banged the steering wheel with his fists and said that they should have changed cars. The police obviously had a description of her car and her license plate. As they drove, more police cars fell in line behind them and Marbles panicked. He began driving at high speed, and the police moved in. He rammed several police cars, driving one off the road and injuring an officer. However, in one of these attempts, he misjudged his speed and flipped the car over. It tumbled several times and came to rest upside down on the roadway. The police swarmed in and quickly removed Paula. They placed Marbles under arrest and transported him to the hospital.

Appendix C

THE FORTNER CASE

On Wednesday, May 15, it was Jessica Rivers's birthday, and her father presented her with a new car. She was very excited and wanted to show off her new car to a friend who worked as a cashier at a local grocery store. She drove up to the store, spent a few minutes with her friend, and then returned to her car. She saw immediately that the right front tire was flat. A man approached her and asked her if she needed any help changing the tire. She said that she needed to call her father. She went inside the grocery store and called her father. She told her father that a man had offered to help. Her father asked her if the man looked "okay," and she said that he seemed very nice. Her father said that it would take him at least thirty minutes to get to the store, so if the man was willing to help, to let him change the tire and then she should call her father back and say that everything was all right.

Jessica went back out to the parking lot and thanked the man for his offer. He changed her tire in just a few minutes. She noticed that he was wearing a blue sport shirt with some kind of logo on the front. He was also wearing a baseball cap and was carrying a baseball glove with him. After he changed the tire, he mentioned that his ride hadn't shown up to take him to a softball game. He was already late. He asked her if she wouldn't mind dropping him off at the softball field. She felt grateful to the man and said, "Sure, I'll drop you off."

He gave her directions, and after they had been driving a few minutes, she noticed that he didn't seem to have a firm idea about where he was going. He told her to pull into a cemetery, and she followed his directions. They drove towards the back of the cemetery, and she mentioned that she didn't see any baseball field. He took a knife out of his pocket and held it to her throat. He told her to turn off the engine. He told her that they were going to get out of the car and go into the woods. He said that if she tried to run or called out, he would stab her in the throat. While they were in the car, he had her remove her shirt. He told her that he was going to rape her. They both began to slide out the driver's side door and in the instant that she was standing and he was still climbing out, she tore out of his grip and started running. She had seen a church in the distance when they had first pulled in, and she ran as fast she could towards it. She could hear him behind her, cursing and yelling obscenities, but she didn't stop running.

She saw a side door to the church and burst through the door. A regular Wednesday evening service was going on, and the church was packed. Everyone froze in surprise when a half-naked young woman came screaming into the hall. As soon as they had heard her explanation, she was wrapped in someone's coat jacket and several men went out looking for the attacker. They found no one, but one church member did recover the glove. He wrapped it in a handkerchief and brought it back to the church. The glove had a name stitched into the side: "Jimmy." The police arrived in a few minutes, and Jessica explained what had happened.

That evening the local television news broadcast the story, complete with a composite sketch of the man. Detective Decker, who was assigned to the case, asked that if anyone had any information about the case they should call the police. To Detective Decker's surprise, he received five calls that evening from women who shopped at the same grocery store. Each claimed that a man fitting the suspect's description had approached them, made lewd comments, or stalked them. Most of them had filed police reports. When the local media learned of other cases, they dubbed the suspect the "Store Stalker," since all of his encounters seemed to focus on grocery stores.

Detective Decker located the other reports and was struck by a recurring pattern. Six months previous to the attack on Jessica, a woman had reported that a man wearing a blue "Pal's Pizza" T-shirt had accosted her in the parking lot of the same store. The man had propositioned her and had left only when she went inside the store to complain to the manager. Three months ago, another woman reported that a man matching the suspect's description had helped her change a flat tire and then had requested oral sex from her. She had jumped into her car and locked the doors and sped away from the store. She had not returned to that particular store since. Other reports contained the same elements: a man of similar description accosting women in the parking lot, trying to touch their legs, or helping them to change tires that had gone flat while the women were inside shopping.

Decker decided to go to the store and view the scene. He noticed that there was a Pal's Pizza delivery just a few doors down from the grocery store. He presented his credentials to the manager and asked if he had anyone on the staff who matched the description the women had provided. The manager said he had a large staff of part-time drivers and that there were several who could match such a description. Detective Decker asked if any of them played softball. The manager said, "Yes, Mark does." The manager identified Mark Fortner as one of his part-time evening pizza delivery men. He said that Fortner didn't work every night and that he had a full time job at Wilson Electronics Warehouse.

Based on the information provided by the restaurant manager, Detective Decker ran a criminal background check on the defendant, but found that he had no prior record. Next, he obtained Fortner's driver's license photograph and created a photographic lineup, using that picture and five pictures of other men similar in appearance to Fortner. Jessica Rivers positively identified Fortner as the man who had attacked her. Based on this information, Detective Decker sought and obtained an arrest warrant for Mark Fortner. He served the warrant himself, arresting Fortner at his day job at Wilson Electronics. After taking Fortner into custody, he read Fortner his *Miranda* warnings and then explained the allegations made by Jessica Rivers. Fortner said that he wished to give a statement.

Fortner said that he had worked part time as a pizza delivery man in the evenings to help make ends meet at home. He admitted that he had talked with some of the women in the parking lot of the grocery store when he was on break. He also admitted that he had had an affair with at least one of the women that he had met. However, he adamantly denied having any contact with Jessica Rivers, including asking her to drive him anywhere and forcefully denied trying to rape her. He said that on May 15, he was at home with his wife and son. He said that he had injured his back at work the day before and had taken the fifteenth off to rest and recover. He said that his wife was home with him all day. His son, James, saw him when James got home from school.

After talking with Fortner, Detective Decker met with some of the other women who had reported incidents at the store. All together, he located seven different women. Five agreed to speak with the police. Two recanted their earlier reports and said that they didn't wish to have anything to do with the investigation. Of the five, four identified Fortner as the man who had approached them in the store or had offered to fix the flat tires on their cars. One woman reported that when she'd taken the tire in to have it patched, the mechanic had told her that it looked as though the sidewall of the tire had been slashed with a knife. One woman reported that the man who had been identified as Fortner had asked for a ride to a softball game after fixing her tire, but she had refused. She said that the man had given her the "heebie-jeebies."

Once Detective Decker arranged all of the reports, he began to see an interesting pattern: In the most recent incidents, the suspect had gotten bolder and more daring. It was only the most recent incidents where the man had actually tried to touch women. In the older incidents, he had been more cautious. Decker also noticed that the age of the victims had steadily decreased. The most recent incidents all involved women aged twenty or younger.

Fortner was charged with kidnapping, attempted rape in the Jessica Rivers incident, as well as additional charges based on the incidents with the other women.

GLOSSARY

Abandonment   When a defendant voluntarily stops the criminal enterprise before it is completed.

Accessory   A person who helps commit a crime without being present.

Accessory after the fact   A person who finds out that a crime has been committed and helps to conceal the crime or the criminal.

Accessory before the fact   A person who, without being present, encourages, orders, or helps another person commit a crime.

Accomplice   A person who knowingly and voluntarily helps another person commit or conceal a crime.

Accusation, information, complaint   A formal charge made to a court that a person is guilty of a crime.

Actual possession   Direct possession of narcotics.

Actus reus   A "wrongful deed" (such as killing a person) which, if done with mens rea, is a crime.

Admissible   Proper to be used in reaching a decision; describes evidence that should be "let in" or introduced in court, or evidence that the jury may use.

Admission of evidence   A decision by a judge to allow evidence to be used by the jury.

Admission   Refers to a decision by a judge to allow evidence to be used by the jury (or if no jury, by the judge).

Affidavit   A written statement in which a person swears an oath that the facts are true.

Affirmative defense   A defense that goes beyond mere denial and alleges facts that if true, would mitigate the defendant's sentence or even require a not guilty verdict.

Affirm   To validate. For example, when a higher court declares that a lower court's action was valid and right, it affirms the decision.

Allegata   (Latin) The allegations contained in a charging document.

Answer   The defendant's written response to the complaint, usually containing denials of the defendant's responsibility for the plaintiff's injuries.

Anticipatory Warrant   A warrant issued for contraband or evidence that has not yet arrived at its final destination.

Appeal   To ask a higher court to review the actions of a lower court to correct mistakes or injustice.

Apprehension   An expectation of an unwanted event.

Arraignment   The proceeding where a defendant is brought before a judge to hear the charges and to enter a plea (e.g., guilty or not guilty).

Arrest   The official taking of a person to answer criminal charges. This involves at least temporarily depriving the person of liberty and may involve the use of force.

Arson   The malicious and unlawful burning of a dwelling.

Asportation   An old word for the theft and removal of personal property.

Attempt   (1) An act that goes beyond preparation but is not completed. (2) An effort to commit a crime that goes beyond preparation and that proceeds far enough to make the person who did it guilty of an "attempt crime." For example, if a person fires a shot at another individual in a failed effort at murder, the person is guilty of attempted murder.

Bail or bond   A written statement of debt that is put up by an arrested person or others who back it. It promises that the arrested person will show up in court or risk losing the amount of the bond.

Bar   The part of some courtrooms where prisoners stand.

Bench conference   A private meeting at the judge's bench between the judge, the lawyers for both sides of the case, and sometimes the parties. It is often called to discuss something out of the jury's hearing.

Bench warrant   A paper issued directly by a judge to the police or other peace officers, ordering the arrest of a person.

Bifurcated   Refers to separate hearings for different issues in the same case (e.g., for guilt and sanity or guilt and punishment in a criminal case).

Brady material   Information known to the prosecutor that is favorable to a criminal defendant's case. Brady material must be disclosed to the defense.

Breaking   Using force or some kind of destruction of property (including actions that do not permanently destroy, such as picking a lock), to illegally get into a building by breaking and entering.

Bribery   The offering, giving, receiving, or soliciting of anything of value to influence the actions of a public official.

Brief   A written statement prepared by one side in a lawsuit to explain its case to the judge.

burden of proof   The burden that a party must meet in order to establish the minimum facts of a case.

Calendar   The day-by-day schedule of trials in a given court.

Carnal knowledge   Sexual intercourse.

Case-in-chief   The main evidence offered by one side in a lawsuit.

Certiorari   (Latin) "To make sure." A request for certiorari (cert) is like an appeal, but one that the higher court is not required to take for decision.

Chain of custody   The chronological list of those in continuous possession of a specific physical object. A person who presents evidence (such as a gun used in a crime) at a trial must account for its possession from time of receipt to time of trial for evidence to be admitted by the judge.

Challenge for cause A formal objection to the qualifications of a prospective juror.

Chromosome The site inside the cell where the genes are located.

Circumstantial evidence Facts that indirectly prove a main fact in question.

Citizen's Arrest An arrest by a private person, rather than by a police or other law enforcement officer. A person usually may arrest another for any crime committed in his or her presence or for a felony committed elsewhere.

Clerk (of Court) A court official who maintains records of dispositions in both civil and criminal cases.

Clerk A court official who keeps court records, official files, etc.

Code A collection of laws.

Common Law Either (1) all case law or the case law that is made by judges in the absence of relevant statutes or (2) the legal system that originated in England and is composed of case law and statutes that grow and change.

Community service A provision in a defendant's sentence that requires him or her to perform some basic functions for the local government, such as picking up trash or assisting at a recycling center.

Commute To change a criminal punishment to one that is less severe.

Complaint The document filed by the plaintiff and served on the defendant that sets out the plaintiff's factual allegations that show the defendant is responsible for the plaintiff's injuries.

Complete defense A defense that if proven to the jury's satisfaction, would require a verdict of not guilty.

Concurrent sentencing A ruling by the judge that the defendant's multiple sentences may be served at the same time.

Conference A fact that is probably true. For example, if the first four books in a set of five have green covers, it is a reasonable inference that the fifth book has a green cover.

Confession (1) A voluntary statement by a person that he or she is guilty of a crime. (2) Any admission of wrongdoing.

Consecutive sentencing A sentencing of a defendant that requires multiple sentences to be served one after another.

Consent Voluntary and active agreement.

Consent Voluntary and active agreement.

Conspiracy A crime that may be committed when two or more people agree to do something unlawful (or something lawful by unlawful means). The agreement can be inferred from the persons' actions. A person can be guilty of both conspiracy to commit a crime and the crime itself.

Constructive possession Possession of narcotics in some object under the dominion, custody, or control of the defendant.

Contraband Things that are illegal to import, export, transport, or possess.

Controlled Substances Acts Federal and state laws to control or ban the manufacture, sale, and use of dangerous drugs (such as certain narcotics, stimulants, depressants, and hallucinogens).

Convert To deprive an owner of property without that owner's permission and without just cause. For example, it is conversion to refuse to return a borrowed book.

Corpus delicti   "The body of the crime." The material substance upon which a crime has been committed—for example, a dead body (in the crime of murder) or a house destroyed by fire (in the crime of arson).

Corroborate   To add to the likely truth or importance of a fact; to back up what someone says.

Cross-examine   To question an opposing witness during a trial or hearing.

Curtilage   An area of household use immediately surrounding a home.

Damages   Money that a court orders to be paid to a person who has suffered damages by the person who caused the injury.

De novo   New. For example, a trial de novo is a new trial.

Deadly weapon   Any instrument likely to cause serious bodily harm under the circumstances of its actual use.

Defendant   The person charged with the commission of a crime.

Defense Attorney   A member of the bar who represents individuals who have been charged with or are suspected of committing a crime.

Demonstrative evidence   Charts, diagrams, or other displays designed to persuade the jury to a particular viewpoint.

Depose   To give sworn testimony out of court.

Direct evidence   Proof of a fact without the need for other facts leading up to it. For example, direct evidence that dodos are not extinct would be a live dodo.

Direct examination   The first questioning in a trial of a witness by the side that called that witness.

Directed verdict   A verdict in which the judge takes the decision out of the jury's hands.

Discovery   The formal and informal exchange of information between sides in a lawsuit.

DNA   Material in living organisms used to compare body issue samples (such as blood, skin, hair, or semen) to see if the genetic materials match. It is used to identify criminals by comparing their DNA with that found at a crime scene and is used to identify a child's parents.

Docket   A list of cases, usually with file numbers, scheduled for trial in a court.

Document   Something with a message on it(e.g., a contract, a map, a photograph, or a message on wood.

Documentary evidence   Evidence supported by writings and all other documents.

Embezzlement   The fraudulent and secret taking of money or property by a person who has been trusted with it.

Embracery   An old word for attempting to bribe a jury.

Entice   To try to persuade a child to come to a secluded place with the intent to commit an unlawful sexual act.

Evidence   All types of information (observations, recollections, documents, concrete objects, etc.) presented at trial or another hearing. Statements made by judges and lawyers, however, are not evidence.

Exclusionary Rule   The Supreme Court ruling that states that illegally obtained evidence may not be used in a criminal trial.

Exculpatory   Refers to providing an excuse or justification; showing that someone has not committed a crime or a wrongful act.

Exigent Circumstance   Circumstances that permit law enforcement officers to conduct a search or arrest a person without a warrant, but only when there is a legitimate threat to persons or evidence.

Expectation of Privacy   A constitutional standard that a court must determine before issuing a search warrant. In situations where a suspect has a high expectation of privacy, such as in the suspect's home, a warrant will be required; if low or nonexistent, no warrant is required.

Felony   A crime with a sentence of one year or more to be served in prison or on probation; often includes mandatory minimum fines.

Fence   A person in the business of intentionally buying stolen merchandise to resell it.

Flight   When a suspect flees the police after being told to stop.

Forfeiture   Loss of the right to something due to neglect of a duty due to an offense. For example, if a criminal defendant fails to show up for trial, the judge may order a forfeiture of the defendant's bail bond.

Fresh Pursuit Doctrine   A court-created doctrine that allows police officers to arrest suspects without warrants and to cross territorial boundaries while they are still pursuing the suspect.

Fruit of the poisonous tree doctrine   The rule that evidence gathered as a result of evidence gained in an illegal search or questioning cannot be used against the person searched or questioned even if later evidence was gathered lawfully.

General intent   Proof that the defendant acted knowingly and voluntarily.

Good Faith Exception   An exception to the rule that a valid search warrant must be issued; under this doctrine, if the officer has a reasonable belief that a search warrant is properly executed, any evidence seized, even though the warrant is defective, will not be excluded.

Guilty   A finding by a criminal court that a defendant is guilty beyond a reasonable doubt.

Habeas corpus   (Latin) "You have the body." A judicial order to someone holding a person to bring that person to court. It is most often used to get a person out of unlawful imprisonment by forcing the captor and the person being held to come to court for a decision on the legality of the imprisonment.

Hearsay   A statement about what someone else said or wrote or otherwise communicated.

Homicide   Killing another person.

Hung jury   A jury that cannot reach a verdict because of disagreement among jurors.

Immunity   Freedom from prosecution.

In camera   (Latin) "In chambers"; in a judge's private office.

Incest   Sexual intercourse between a man and a woman who, according to state law, are too closely related by blood or adoption.

Incite   To urge, provoke, strongly encourage, or stir up.

Indictment   A document that charges a defendant with a felony.

Initial appearance   A court proceeding held shortly after the suspect's arrest in which he or she is apprised of specific constitutional rights.

Interrogation   Questioning by police, especially of a person suspected or accused of a crime. A custodial interrogation involves a restraint of freedom, so it requires a Miranda warning.

Join issue   When a lawsuit gets past the preliminary stages and issues are clearly laid out.

Judge   The legal authority in the courtroom; a person empowered to make and enforce rulings and to keep the peace during court proceedings.

Jurisdiction   The persons about whom and the subject matters about which a court has the right and power to make decisions that are legally binding.

Jury instructions   Written explanations of the law normally read to the jurors just prior to them being given the responsibility of considering the case and reaching a verdict.

Jury tampering   Illegally influencing a juror or jurors (often through bribery) to influence the outcome of a trial.

Jury trial   A trial with a judge and jury, not just a judge. This is a constitutional right in criminal cases and in many civil cases.

Larceny   Stealing of any kind. Some types of larceny are specific crimes, such as larceny by trick or grand larceny.

Liable   A finding in a civil action that one party must pay money or take some other action in favor of the opposing side.

Lineup   A group of persons, placed side by side in a line, shown to a witness of a crime to see if the witness will identify the person suspected of a committing the crime. A lineup should not be staged so that it is suggestive of one person.

M'Naghten test   An early attempt (1843) to establish a workable scheme to determine who was and was not legally insane.

Malice   Intentionally harming someone; having no moral or legal justification for harming someone.

Manslaughter   A crime, less severe than murder, involving the wrongful but nonmalicious killing of another person.

Market value (fair market value)   The price to which a willing seller and a willing buyer would agree for an item in the ordinary course of trade.

Material fact   A fact that is central to winning or deciding a case.

Mens rea   Guilty mind; wrongful purpose; criminal intent.

Misdemeanor   A criminal offense that is punishable by 12 twelve months or less in custody or on probation.

Mistrial   A trial that a judge ends and declares will have no legal effect.

Mistrial   A trial that the judge ends and declares will have no legal effect because of a major defect in procedure or because of the death of a juror, a deadlocked jury, or another major problem.

Motion in limine   (Latin) "At the beginning"; preliminary. A motion in limine is a request that prejudicial information be excluded as trial evidence.

Motive   The reason a person does something.

Murder   The unlawful killing of another human being that is premeditated (planned in advance) or is with malice aforethought.

Nolo contendere (Latin) "I will not contest it." A defendant's plea of "no con-test" in a criminal case. It means that he or she does not directly admit guilt, but submits to sentencing or other punishment.

Obscene Lewd and offensive to accepted standards of decency.

Obscene Lewd and offensive to accepted standards of decency.

Open Fields Doctrine A court principle that allows police to search without a warrant when the evidence is located in a public setting such as farmland or beside a road.

Opinion A judge's statement about the conclusions in an appeal.

Ordinance A law passed by a local government, such as a town council or city government, that regulates matters dealing with peace, noise levels, or nuisances such as trash burning.

Overt act An overt act in criminal law is more than mere preparation to something criminal; it is at least the first step of actually attempting the crime. The overt act need not be unlawful to be the first step in such crimes as treason and criminal conspiracy.

Paralegal A legal assistant who provides services and support to an attorney.

Pardon A President's or governor's release of a person from punishment for a crime.

Parole A release from prison before a sentence is finished that depends on the person's "keeping clean" and doing what he or she is supposed to do after being released.

Parole A sentence served under supervision after a defendant is released from prison.

Peremptory challenge A challenge to a potential juror that is the automatic elimination of that person from the jury by one side before trial without needing to state the reason for the elimination.

Perjury Lying while under oath, especially in a court proceeding.

Plain View Doctrine A court doctrine that allows police to search without a warrant when they see evidence of a crime in an unconcealed manner.

Plaintiff The common name for the party who brings a civil suit against another; also known as a petitioner.

Plea bargain Negotiations between a prosecutor and a criminal defendant's lawyer attempting to resolve a criminal case without trial.

Pleadings (1) In a civil case, the pleadings set out the wrong suffered by the parties against one another. (2) In a criminal case, the pleadings are often referred to as indictments (in felony cases) and accusations/informations (in misdemeanor cases) where the state sets out an infraction by the defendant who violates the law.

Police Officer A law enforcement officer who is empowered to make arrests within a specific jurisdiction.

Pornographic Depicting sexual behavior to cause sexual excitement. Nonob-scene pornography is protected by the First Amendment, but child pornography is not.

Preliminary hearing The first court proceeding on a criminal charge in fed-eral courts and many state courts by a magistrate or a judge to decide whether there is enough evidence for the government to continue with the case and to require the defendant to post bail or be held for trial.

Premeditation Thinking about something before doing it; thinking in advance about how to commit a crime.

Preponderance (of the Evidence) A showing by one side in a suit that its version of the facts is more likely to be true than not.

Preponderance of evidence The greater weight of evidence not as to quantity, but as to quality.

Preponderance of evidence The greater weight of evidence, not as to quantity, but quality.

Pre-sentence Investigation An investigation by courtappoint social workers, probation officers, etc., into a criminal's background to determine the criminal's prospects for rehabilitation.

Presentence investigation An investigation by courtappoint social workers, probation officers, etc., into a criminal's background to determine the criminal's prospects for rehabilitation.

Presumption A presumption of fact is a conclusion that because one fact exists, another fact exists.

Pretextual stop The detention or arrest of a person for a minor offense, usually a traffic violation, when the officer suspects that the defendant has committed a more serious crime.

Prima facie (Latin) At first sight; on the face of it, presumably. Describes something that will be considered to be true unless disproved by contrary evidence.

Principal A person directly involved with committing a crime, as opposed to an accessory.

Privilege The right to prevent disclosure, or the duty to refrain from disclosing, information communicated within a specially confidential relationship.

Pro se For himself or herself; in his or her own behalf.

Probable Cause The U.S. constitutional requirement that law enforcement officers present sufficient facts to convince a judge to issue a search warrant or an arrest warrant.

Probata (Latin) The proof elicited in a trial.

Probation (Parole) Officer Allowing a person convicted of a criminal offense to avoid serving a jail sentence imposed on the person so long as he or she abides by certain conditions (usually including being supervised by a probation officer).

Probation The action of allowing a person convicted of a criminal offense to avoid serving a jail sentence so long as he or she abides by certain conditions (usually including being supervised by a probation officer).

Prosecutor A representative of the local, state, or federal government whose duty is to bring charges against defendants and to prove those charges at trial beyond a reasonable doubt.

Prostitution A person offering her (in most state, his or her) body for sexual purposes in exchange for money. A crime in most states.

Provocation Words or conduct that incite anger or passion or that cloud judgment and the ability to reason.

Quash Overthrow, annul, completely do away with.

Rape shield statute A state law that prohibits use of most evidence of a rape victim's past sexual conduct or that protects the victim's identity.

Rape   The crime of a man imposing sexual intercourse on a woman by force or otherwise without legally valid consent.

Reasonable Doubt   The standard of proof that the prosecution must meet in order to prove that a defendant committed a crime.

Rebuttal   The act of disputing, defeating, or taking away the effect of acts or arguments.

Record   The actual evidence (testimony, physical objects, etc.) as well as the evidence that was refused admission by the judge.

Remand   To send back. For example, a higher court may remand a case to a lower court, directing the lower court to take some action.

Restitution   Programs in some states that make a convicted criminal repay the crime victim in money or work.

Reverse   To set aside. For example, when a higher court reverses a lower court on appeal, it sides aside the judgment of the lower court.

Reversible error   A mistake made by a judge in the procedures used at trial or in making legal rulings during the trial

Riot   A vague word for a public disturbance, especially a violent one created by three or more persons acting together.

Robbery   The illegal taking of property from the person of another using force or threat of force.

Search Warrant   A warrant that authorizes the police to enter and conduct a search and to seize items that are evidence of a crime.

Sentence   The punishment, such as time in jail, given to a person convicted of a crime.

Sequester   To keep a jury from having any contacts with the outside world during a trial.

Sever   To cut off or separate into parts. For example, to sever the trial of a person from others who might otherwise be in the same trial is to try that person's case separately at another time. The process is often called severance.

Showup   A pretrial identification procedure in which only one suspect and a witness are brought together.

Sodomy   A general word for an "unnatural" sex act or the crime committed by such act. While the definition varies, sodomy can include oral sex, anal sex, homosexual acts, or sex with animals.

Solicitation   Asking for; enticing; strongly requesting. This may be a crime if the thing being urged is a crime.

Specific intent   Proof that the defendant acted with a precise crime in mind.

Stale   When too much time has passed between the application and issuance of a warrant and the search that it authorizes.

Statute   A law that is voted on by the Legislature branch and enacted by the Executive branch.

Statutory rape   The crime of a man having sexual intercourse with a girl under a certain state-set age (with or without the girl's consent).

Style   The title or heading listing the parties to the case; caption.

Subpoena   A court's order to a person that he or she appear in court to testify (give evidence) in a case.

Supremacy Clause   The provision in Article VI of the United States Constitution that the Constitution, laws, and treaties take precedence over conflicting state constitutions or laws.

442 *Glossary*

Supreme Court The name for the highest court of the United States courts and the name used by the highest court of most, but not all, of the states. In some states, the highest state court is referred to by another name. In New York, for example, this court is called the superior court.

Suspect A person who has been implicated in a crime but has yet to be charged with a crime.

Tax evasion Paying less tax than was owed.

Tax fraud The deliberate nonpayment or underpayment of taxes that are legally due. Tax fraud can be civil or criminal, with criminal fraud (tax evasion) having higher fines and the possibility of a prison sentence.

Term of court The time period in which the court may hear cases.

Testimony Evidence given by a witness under oath. This evidence is "testimonial" and is different from demonstrative evidence.

Utter Put into circulation; issue or put out a check.

Vagrancy Hanging around in public with no purpose and no honest means of support.

Vague A warrant that fails to meet the specificity requirements of the Fourth Amendment.

Verdict The jury's decision.

Verdict The jury's finding in a trial.

Victim impact statement An oral or written statement by the victim of the crime that explains how the defendant's crime has changed the victim's life and can include a victim's request for a specific type of sentence.

Voir dire (French) "To see, to say"; "to state the truth." The preliminary in-court questioning of a prospective juror to determine competency.

Waiver The voluntary giving up of a right.

Warrant Written permission given by a judge to a police officer to arrest a person, conduct a search, seize an item, etc.

Wharton's Rule Also known as "Concert of Action Rule"; the rule that states that unless a statute specifies otherwise, it is not a conspiracy for two persons to agree to commit a crime if the definition of the crime requires the participation of two or more persons.

White-collar crimes Commercial crimes such as embezzlement and price fixing.

Wiretap An electronic or other intercept of the contents of a communication. Government wiretaps must be authorized by a judge for probable cause, and private wiretaps must have the consent of one participant (in some states, all participants).

Work product The principle that a lawyer need not show the other side in a case any facts or items gathered for the case unless the other side can convince the judge that it would be unjust for the items to remain hidden and there is a special need for them.

INDEX